FEMA
Disaster Operations
Legal Reference

Verison 2
June 1, 2013

edited by
Brian Greul

The Second Edition of the Disaster Operations Legal Reference (DOLR 2.0) describes the legal authorities for FEMA's readiness, response, and recovery activities. It supersedes DOLR 1.0 issued in November 2011. Because this reference is not exhaustive, the legal authorities are subject to modification and change, and the specific facts surrounding an issue may change the legal analysis, use of the information contained here should be verified with the FEMA Office of Chief Counsel before becoming the basis for a final decision by the Agency.

Should you have suggestions or feedback on ways to improve this book please send email to Books@Ocotillo-Press.com

Edited 2021 Ocotillo Press
ISBN 978-1-954285-39-2

Ocotillo Press
Houston, TX 77017
Books@OcotilloPress.com

Disaster Operations Legal Reference

Version 2.0

June 1, 2013

FEMA

June 2013

The Second Edition of the Disaster Operations Legal Reference (DOLR 2.0) describes the legal authorities for FEMA's readiness, response, and recovery activities. It supersedes DOLR 1.0 issued in November 2011. Because this reference is not exhaustive, the legal authorities are subject to modification and change, and the specific facts surrounding an issue may change the legal analysis, use of the information contained here should be verified with the FEMA Office of Chief Counsel before becoming the basis for a final decision by the Agency.

Table of Contents

CHAPTER 3: Declarations

CHAPTER 4: Response

CHAPTER 5: Public Assistance

Part One: Public Assistance Eligibility

Part Two: Public Assistance and Grants Management Process

CHAPTER 6: Individual Assistance

Chapter 7: Hazard Mitigation

CHAPTER 8: Environmental and Historic Preservation Laws

CHAPTER 9: Information Management

CHAPTER 10: Human Capital

CHAPTER 11: ETHICS

Appendix A: Advice In Crisis: Towards Best Practices for Providing Legal Advice under Disaster Conditions

Appendix B: Disaster Operations Legal Analysis Checklist

Appendix C: Key to Significant Stafford Act and Regulatory Provisions

Appendix D: Electric Power Restoration Primer

Acknowledgements

We are pleased to issue this Second Edition of the Disaster Operations Legal Resource (DOLR 2.0). This text collects, in a single volume, a coherent narrative that both describes and explains the essential elements of the Robert T. Stafford Disaster Relief and Emergency Assistance Act (Stafford Act) and related legal authorities underpinning FEMA's disaster operations.

When we began our respective tenures at FEMA, we encountered a host of FEMA "urban myths"—Agency folklore consisting of "stories" about the application of FEMA that authorities usually believed by their tellers to be true. As we delved deeper into these beliefs, we often learned they were persistent but based on erroneous or needlessly inflexible interpretations of the Stafford Act. It became clear that these urban myths propagated because FEMA had not preserved acquired legal knowledge—the kind of knowledge that accelerates learning as personnel rotate in and out of Joint Field Offices, ensures consistency of advice across time and location, and promotes solution oriented lawyering.

To dispel the urban myths, we commissioned the DOLR to provide a "place"—both paper and virtual—where FEMA attorneys and their client-partners can identify, create, represent, distribute, and enable adoption of insights and experiences relevant to the practical application of FEMA's authorities in disaster operations. With the DOLR, we have begun to capture legal "lessons learned" in an organized system connected to existing statutes, regulations, and policies so that users can easily locate and retrieve useful information, particularly in the field, and so that we can continuously update our evolving interpretations of the Stafford Act.

We expect the DOLR to:

- Sustain FEMA's disaster-related legal knowledge across Stafford Act events and over time by identifying, capturing, and validating relevant legal information and analysis that exists throughout the Agency;

- Help FEMA attorneys and their client-partners find, organize, and share the knowledge of disaster legal operations we already have; and

- Increase consistency, collaboration, and the creation and sharing of knowledge and innovative, flexible legal solutions for response and recovery.

We dedicate the DOLR to Alfred O. Bragg, III (1947-2005), the former legal advisor to the Florida Division of Emergency Management and a grand master of providing "Advice in Crisis."

W. Craig Fugate
Administrator
Federal Emergency Management
Agency

Brad J. Kieserman
Chief Counsel
Federal Emergency Management
Agency

The Disaster Operations Legal Reference (DOLR), a product of the Office of Chief Counsel (OCC) for the Federal Emergency Management Agency (FEMA), is a legal resource that provides a detailed description of the authorities under which FEMA operates when the President declares a major disaster or emergency under the Robert T. Stafford Disaster Relief and Emergency Assistance Act (Stafford Act).[1] The DOLR is intended to provide FEMA, as well as our state, tribal, local government, and non-governmental partners, with detailed legal information that explains how and when the Stafford Act applies and how it relates to the Homeland Security Act (HSA) and other relevant authorities and policies.

This Preface traces the history of federal emergency assistance from its beginning in a bill of relief passed by Congress after a single fire over 200 years ago, to FEMA's creation as an independent agency by Executive Order in 1979, and FEMA's evolution into the federal agency charged with comprehensive all-hazards emergency management for the nation.

FEMA was first created by Presidential directive but it is now a creature of federal law and its mission is defined by the HSA:

> The primary mission of the Agency is to reduce the loss of life and property and protect the Nation from all hazards, including natural disasters, acts of terrorism, and other man-made disasters, by leading and supporting the Nation in a risk-based, comprehensive emergency management system of preparedness, protection, response, recovery, and mitigation.[2]

Disaster strikes anytime, anywhere, and in many forms – a hurricane, an earthquake, a tornado, a flood, a fire, or a hazardous spill, an act of nature or an act of terrorism. It may build over days or weeks, or strike suddenly without warning. Every year, millions of Americans face the devastating consequences of disasters and emergencies. The individual states and local governments have the primary legal authority and responsibility to protect

---

[1] 42 U.S.C. sections [hereinafter §§] 5121-5207.
[2] 6 U.S.C. § 313.

their citizens and respond to disasters and emergencies. It is the local police, fire, and emergency medical technicians, as first responders, who do the "heavy lifting" in the first few days after a disaster or emergency strikes. It is the mission of voluntary agencies like the American Red Cross and The Salvation Army to provide aid and support to disaster survivors, be they victims of a single house fire or a statewide event. Additional assistance from the federal government may be required, however, when state and local governments and nonprofit agencies cannot adequately respond to a disaster or emergency. FEMA's statutory authorities, implementing regulations and policies authorize and facilitate the provision of this federal assistance and reflect that a whole community approach is imperative if disaster response and recovery is to be timely and effective, and survivors are to be quickly set on the path toward self-sufficiency.

I. History of Federal Emergency Assistance[3]

The federal government can trace its first involvement in emergency management to the Congressional Act of 1803 which authorized federal assistance to a New Hampshire town following an extensive fire,[4] generally considered the first piece of federal disaster legislation. Congress passed additional event specific disaster legislation more than 100 times in the next century. By the 1930s, Congress granted the Reconstruction Finance Corporation[5] authority to lend money to banks and to dispense federal dollars in the wake of disasters to repair and reconstruct certain public facilities.

The U. S. Army Corps of Engineers,[6] as well as other agencies, continued to provide piecemeal disaster response and Congress continued to fund

---

[3] *See* CONGRESSIONAL RESEARCH SERVICES: REPORT FOR CONGRESS, *Federal Emergency Management and Homeland Security Organizations: Historical Development and Legislative Options*, Order Code RL 33369 (updated June 2006).
[4] "An Act for the Relief of the sufferers by fire, in the town of Portsmouth", ch. 6, 2 Stat. 201 (1803).
[5] Reconstruction Finance Corporation, 47 Stat. 5.
[6] Numerous laws since 1932 are referred to as "Flood Control Acts"; however, it is the Flood Control Act of 1944, Pub. L. No. 78-534, that granted authority to the Corps for the design and construction of flood control projects. That legislation had a significant impact on emergency management.

---

disaster relief on a case-by-case basis until enactment of the Federal Disaster Relief Act of 1950. That Act empowered the President to utilize, coordinate, and direct all federal agencies to respond to major disasters without independent approval of Congress but with a budget, modest even for 1950, of only $5 million.[7] After this initial framework of federal-to-state disaster relief assistance was established, additional laws increasing the scope of federal assistance further shaped the process for administering disaster relief.

II. How and Why FEMA Came Into Being

During the 1960s and 1970s, massive disasters requiring major federal participation in response and recovery efforts served to focus attention on the issue of natural disaster response. These included Hurricane Carla in 1961, the Alaska Earthquake of 1964, and Hurricane Betsy in 1965. Following these events, Congress enacted the Disaster Relief Act of 1966,[8] which, among other things, authorized a 50% federal cost share to repair, restore, or reconstruct public facilities damaged or destroyed as a result of a major disaster. Following Hurricane Camille in 1969 Congress passed the Disaster Relief Act of 1969[9] (effective for only 15 months), directing, among other things, that the President appoint a "Federal coordinating officer" responsible for coordinating federal assistance in a major disaster area and establishing field offices; and authorizing temporary dwelling accommodations for individuals and families displaced by a major disaster. The Disaster Relief Act of 1970,[10] incorporated additional disaster support provisions including emergency support teams, emergency shelter, emergency communication, emergency transportation, and disaster legal services. It also authorized a federal cost share of up to 100% for the repair, restoration, and reconstruction of damaged or destroyed public facilities. Following the San Fernando Earthquake in 1971 and Hurricane Agnes in 1972, Congress enacted the Disaster Relief Act of 1974,[11] which established the process of Presidential disaster declarations, created the first program to provide direct assistance to

---

[7] Pub. L. No. 81-875 (1950).
[8] Pub. L. No. 89-769 (1966).
[9] Pub. L. No. 91-79 (1969).
[10] Pub. L. No. 91-606 (1970).
[11] Pub. L. No. 93-288 (1974).

---

individuals and households, and authorized efforts to mitigate disasters, as opposed to merely responding to them.

Other disasters, including the contamination of Love Canal, the Cuban refugee crisis, and the nuclear accident at Three Mile Island, emphasized the growing complexity of emergency management. By 1979, more than 100 federal agencies were involved in some aspect of disasters, hazards, and emergencies. Parallel programs and policies existed at the state and local levels. To address this fragmentation at the federal level, President Jimmy Carter issued Executive Order 12,127[12] of March 31, 1979 transferring many of the separate disaster-related responsibilities from other federal agencies (OFAs) to FEMA. President Carter's Reorganization Plan # 3 of 1978,[13] which became effective on April 1, 1979, created the "Federal Emergency Management Agency" as an independent agency. Pursuant to that Plan, among others, FEMA absorbed the Federal Insurance Administration, the National Fire Prevention and Control Administration, the National Weather Service Community Preparedness Program, the Federal Preparedness Agency of the General Services Administration, and the Federal Disaster Assistance Administration activities from the Department of Housing and Urban Development. Civil defense responsibilities were also transferred to the new agency from the Defense Department's Defense Civil Preparedness Agency.[14]

FEMA relied for nearly a decade on the Disaster Relief Act, as amended, as its primary statutory authority to respond to disasters. In 1988, Congress amended the Disaster Relief Act of 1974 by enacting the Stafford Act.[15] The 1988 Stafford Act created a new category of "emergency" declarations for those incidents that do not rise to the level of, or are different in nature from, a major disaster.[16] It also confirmed the importance of individual assistance and emphasized mitigation of future hazards. With the Loma Prieta Earthquake in 1989 and Hurricane Andrew in 1992, national attention focused on FEMA revealed, however, the need for improvements. Between 1993 and 1995 FEMA initiated reforms that

---

[12] The provisions of EXEC. ORDER 12,127 appear at 44 Fed. Reg. 19,367, 3 C.F.R., 1979 Comp., at 376.

[13] 43 Fed. Reg. 41,943 (1978).

[14] See also EXEC. ORDERS 12,148 (1979) and 12,656.

[15] Pub. L. No. 100-707 (1988).

[16] See Appendix C for a summary table of Stafford Act provisions.

streamlined disaster relief and recovery operations, partly as a result of settling two lawsuits. These reforms included a new emphasis on preparedness and mitigation, and focusing agency efforts on customer service, including the ability to serve non-English speaking customers, providing detailed program information for disaster survivors, and broadening outreach to community based organizations.[17]

The FEMA OCC[18] hired several attorneys in the aftermath of Loma Prieta and Hurricane Andrew and the Northridge Earthquake in 1994 to specifically work on disaster related issues for these events. FEMA OCC also established a field attorney cadre to deploy attorneys to field offices and provide legal counsel to Federal Coordinating Officers and program leads. This focus on providing legal advice on-site and in real-time to decision-makers continues today and has contributed to the evolving body of emergency management law and the growing emergency management legal practice.

III. FEMA's Changing Role to Include All Hazards

Executive Order 12,148, which President Carter issued on July 20, 1979, assigned FEMA responsibility for anti-terrorism programs. Numerous other orders and White House policies confirmed FEMA's role in anti-terrorism,[19] FEMA's focus, however, ultimately was largely on natural disasters until the terrorist attacks of September 11, 2001. Congress reacted to 9/11 with the passage of the HSA[20] in 2003 and FEMA joined 22 OFAs, programs, and offices in becoming part of the new Department of Homeland Security (DHS). The HSA transferred the "functions, personnel, assets and liabilities" of FEMA to DHS, including the functions of the FEMA Director to the DHS Secretary. The Secretary thereafter

---

[17] Memorandum from Director, Human Services Division, to Regional Human Services Officers and HQ Human Services Division, *Implementation of commitments resulting from settled lawsuits* (July 7, 1995).

[18] The FEMA Office of Chief Counsel was then known as the Office of General Counsel. It became the Office of Chief Counsel following FEMA's inclusion into the DHS and the establishment of the DHS Office of General Counsel.

[19] For a detailed chronology of FEMA's role in terrorism attacks, *see* <http://www.fas.org/irp/agency/dhs/fema>.

[20] Homeland Security Act of 2002, Pub. L. No. 107-296, 116 Stat. 2135, 6 U.S.C. § 101-557.

delegated the authority for activities under the Stafford Act to the now-defunct Under Secretary of Emergency Preparedness and Response.[21] DHS has worked to bring a coordinated approach to national security from emergencies and disasters – both natural and man-made. In addition, Homeland Security Presidential Directive (HSPD) -5 and HSPD-8 implemented many of the mandates of the HSA.

Once again, however, a natural disaster resulted in significant legislative change. As a result of the issues that arose during the federal government's response to Hurricane Katrina in 2005, Congress passed the Post-Katrina Emergency Management Reform Act (PKEMRA)[22] in 2006 which amended both the HSA and the Stafford Act and provided substantial new authorities to FEMA. Title V of the HSA, as amended by PKEMRA, designates the head of FEMA as the "Administrator" and for the first time statutorily mandates the Administrator have a specific level of emergency management and leadership experience and provides the Administrator with specified authority and responsibilities.[23] In particular, "the Administrator shall lead the Nation's efforts to prepare for, protect against, respond to, recover from, and mitigate against the risk of natural disasters, acts of terrorism, and other man-made disasters, including catastrophic incidents," and he is "the principal advisor to the President, the Homeland Security Council, and the Secretary [of Homeland Security] for all matters relating to emergency management in the United States."[24] In addition, the HSA, as amended by PKEMRA mandates that FEMA be maintained as a distinct entity within DHS.[25]

In practice, FEMA works within the DHS structure to assure coordination in the field (i.e., at or near the location of an incident), as well as with federal departments and agencies, nonprofit organizations, and the private sector to assist states, localities, and tribal organizations most effectively and efficiently with their recovery needs. The National Response

---

[21] DHS Delegation 9001.1 (Dec. 10, 2010).
[22] PKEMRA, Pub. L. No. 109-295 (Oct. 4, 2006).
[23] See 6 U.S.C. §§ 313(c)(2) & 314.
[24] See 6 U.S.C. §§ 313(b)(2)(A) & 313(c)(4)(A).
[25] 6 U.S.C. § 316(a). The DHS Secretary may not change the responsibilities or functions of the agency, nor direct any assets, function, or mission to another entity within DHS. The Secretary's authority to reprogram or transfer funds is also limited. See 6 U.S.C. §§ 316 (c) and (d).

Framework, dated January 2008,[26] provides a comprehensive, national, all-hazards approach to domestic incident response, while the National Disaster Recovery Framework provides a structure to manage and promote effective long-term recovery by enabling disaster recovery managers to operate in a unified and collaborative manner.[27]

IV. Disaster Response and Recovery Legal Framework

In utilizing the DOLR, it is important to understand that the Stafford Act and the HSA are two statutes amongst a myriad of statutes and authorities under which FEMA operates. The following provides a brief outline and broad overview of the framework of the legal authorities applicable to the delivery of FEMA's mission.

1.   The Constitution of the United States of America

The Supremacy Clause of the Constitution affirms that it is the supreme law of the United States.[28] It is the framework for the organization of the U.S. government and for the relationship of the federal government with the states and citizens. The Constitution creates three branches of the federal government: a legislature, the bicameral Congress; an executive branch led by the President; and a judicial branch headed by the Supreme Court. The Constitution specifies the powers and duties of each branch and reserves all unremunerated powers to the respective states and all the people within the United States.[29] In addition, the Constitution and its amendments establish that no person shall be deprived equal protection of the laws or deprived of life, liberty, or property without due process. When disasters occur, FEMA must be mindful that the federal government does not have a general police power, the states do, and federal assistance, even though discretionary, must be delivered in a manner that is not arbitrary or capricious.

---

[26] The Homeland Security Act, at 6 U.S.C. § 314(a)(13), requires the Administrator to administer and implement a "National Response Plan" which is now know as the National Response Framework. *See* <http://www.fema.gov/emergency/nrf/>.

[27] <http://www.fema.gov/recoveryframework/>.

[28] U.S. CONST., art. VI, § 2.

[29] U.S. CONST., amend. X.

2.   Federal Statutes

The United States Congress is the sole legislative body within the federal government.[30] The Government Printing Office codifies and publishes most federal statutes in the United States Code (U.S.C.). Federal statutes applicable to FEMA include authorizing statutes, appropriations acts and statutes imposing responsibilities on the federal government in carrying out its authorities. Authorizing statutes can be found in volumes of the U.S.C. For example, the Stafford Act can be found in Volume 42, U.S.C., Sections 5121 through 5207. Congress passes appropriations acts each fiscal year (October 1st to September 30th) to provide funds to operate each federal department, among other things. FEMA's actions must conform with the requirements set forth in numerous other statutes; only Congress may waive or make exceptions to requirements in federal statutes.

3.   Presidential Executive Orders

The President has the power to issue Executive Orders, directives, and other forms of direction to the executive branch. Executive Orders and other directives of the President govern actions by federal officials and agencies. Only the Constitution and federal statutes limit the President's authority over the executive branch. Executive Order 13,286 (February 28, 2003) is an example of an Executive Order; it transfers certain agencies and agency components to the DHS.[31] Examples of other forms of directives include HSPDs and Presidential Policy Directives.

4.   Federal Regulations (sometimes called Rules)

Departments and agencies in the Executive Branch, based on either general authority assigned to them under the law or directions Congress mandates in a specific piece of legislation, draft regulations to implement their authorizing legislation. A properly promulgated regulation has the full force and effect of law. Regulations therefore bind agency officials who

---

[30] U.S. CONST., art. I, § 1.
[31] *See* 3 United States Code (U.S.C.), § 301, that provides the general authority of the President to transfer authority to various departments within the federal government.

do not have discretion to violate them. Agencies may implement and change regulations through rulemaking procedures set forth in the Administrative Procedure Act,[32] which includes giving notice to the public through publication in the Federal Register. The Government Printing Office codifies and publishes the rules in the Code of Federal Regulations (CFR). FEMA's rules are published in 44 CFR Parts 1-362.

5. Department of Homeland Security Directives

FEMA is a federal agency and a component of the DHS. The DHS Directives System is an official means of communicating to all DHS components and employees the policies, delegations of authority, and procedures necessary for DHS to comply with pertinent Executive Orders, statutes, regulations, and policies. Policy statements address the overarching objectives of major departmental or governmental initiatives or programs. Policy Statements may trigger the issuance of a directive. Directives articulate and build on DHS policy statements, missions, programs, activities, or business practices of a continuing nature. Instructions implement or supplement DHS Directives, Executive Orders, regulations, and Federal Register notices, by providing uniform procedure and/or prescribing the manner or plan of action for carrying out the policy, operating a program or activity, and assigning responsibilities. Certain implementing documents that provide more detailed information include manuals, guides, handbooks, reference books, standard operating procedures, and other similar documents. *See, e.g.,* DHS Directive Number 112-01, issued 04/10/2008.

6. FEMA Directives, Publications, Guidance, Policy statements

In addition to rules and regulations, which have the full force and effect of law, FEMA publishes information to assist and inform employees and the public, including Administrator directives, policy statements, policy guides and manuals.

---

[32] 5 U.S.C. § 553.

The Administrator's directives are internal documents that provide policy and program guidance to FEMA employees. Directives publish policies, delegate authority, establish programs, and assign responsibilities. An example of an Administrator's directive is number 112.5, dated September 21, 2008, entitled *"Obtaining Legal Review and Assistance."* This directive sets forth issues that require legal review, issues where such review is advisable, and establishes procedures for seeking review or advice. The Administrator also issues policy statements of special interest that expire after 90 days.

FEMA publishes procedures, policies, and guidance for employees and the public. These publications are indexed and available on FEMA's website. An example is the 9500 Series of Public Assistance (PA) Policy and Guidance that includes the PA Policy Digest (FEMA 321), the PA Guide (FEMA 322), the Applicant Handbook (FEMA 323), and the Debris Management Guide (FEMA 325). Agency policy and guidance sets out "rules of the game" to ensure: 1) that the agency implements its actions and programs in a consistent, non-arbitrary manner; and 2) that all recipients of FEMA assistance receive fair and equitable treatment by being aware of and subject to the same procedures and requirements.

7. Judicial Opinions or "Case Law"

The federal and state court systems consist of two levels of courts: trial courts and appellate courts. The federal courts have jurisdiction over cases involving federal statutes and other "federal questions." They also have jurisdiction over cases in which the parties reside in different states. State courts have jurisdiction over most other types of cases.

Statutes or executive office action are the basis upon which most courts settle disputes and make decisions in cases; however, another body of law exists based on prior decisions of courts. This "common law" system gives precedential weight to past decisions of the courts.[33] If a similar

---

[33] BRITANNIA CONCISE ENCYCLOPEDIA, describes "common law" as the "Body of law based on custom and general principles and that, embodied in case law, serves as precedent or is applied to situations not covered by statute. Under the common-law system, when a court decides and reports its decision concerning a particular case, the case becomes part of the body of law and can be used in later cases involving similar matters. This use of

dispute has been resolved, the court is bound to follow the reasoning used in the prior decision if the case is in the same jurisdiction. Judicial decisions for a relevant court represent law that the agency must follow.

Interactions between constitutional law, statutory law, common law, and regulatory law give rise to considerable complexity.

8. State Constitutions and Statutes

State legislatures can pass laws on matters for which they share jurisdiction with Congress and on matters in which the Constitution does not grant jurisdiction to the federal government. For example, the Constitution by not assuming the authority for police power, leaves the police power to the individual states.[34] State constitutions and statutes are the supreme law within the state, but federal legislation and the Constitution can preempt state and local rules. State agencies may adopt regulations to carry out state laws. The individual states have the primary role in emergency management; state and local officials are the true first responders to emergencies and disasters within their state borders, just as tribal officials are on tribal lands.

9. Municipal Charters, Ordinances, Rules and Regulations

These mechanisms of local governance apply only to local issues. State and federal rules typically preempt these local rules if there is conflict.

---

precedents is known as *stare decisis*. Common law has been administered in the courts of England since the Middle Ages; it is also found in the U.S. and in most of the British Commonwealth. It is distinguished from civil law."

[34] Courts have broadly defined the police power as the inherent authority never surrendered by the states to the federal government to control matters within their territories relating to the public health, safety, and welfare. *New Orleans Gas Co. v. Louisiana Light Co.*, 115 U.S. 650, 1885 U.S. LEXIS 1879 (1885).

V. The Future

The DOLR intends to describe and interpret for lawyers as well as emergency management professionals the many authorities that pertain to FEMA's emergency and disaster response and recovery authorities. It will always be a work in progress as future versions endeavor to add depth and nuance amidst a dynamic and ever-changing emergency management environment. For suggestions and feedback, please utilize the DOLR Team at DOLR@fema.dhs.gov.

CHAPTER 1
Emergency Management Operational Life Cycle
Table of Contents

Emergency Management Operational Life Cycle

I. Introduction

Practicing operational law in the federal emergency management environment is dynamic and exciting with issues coming at rapid speed depending on the phase or stage of disaster relief operations. The successful emergency management operations law practitioner has the ability to create order out of the seeming chaos by quickly gathering the relevant facts and intended purpose, framing the legal issues, and identifying the relevant authorities necessary to provide timely, legally sufficient, and responsive advice for decision-makers

II. All-Hazards Operational Life Cycle

Disaster relief operations, which operate with a constantly changing scenario, can be described as following a life cycle with the following phases:

All-Hazards Operational Life Cycle

- General Readiness or Steady State

- Threat Identification

- Event Imminent/Event Occurs

- Federal Declaration Issued

- Response

- Recovery

- Closeout

Each phase has its unique challenges, time frames, responsible and interested parties, and authorities. A mastery of these phases enables experienced operations law practitioners to quickly identify relevant issues, associated authorities, and attendant risks. Learning to recognize these phases is one of the first crucial steps for the beginning operations law practitioner to understanding the emergency management environment.

A. The **General Readiness or Steady State Phase** is comprised of nationwide and regional monitoring, planning, training, and preparation. The primary federal components involved include FEMA headquarters, the regional offices, and the Emergency Support Function Leaders Group. This phase includes drafting and revising policies, standard operating procedures, memoranda of understanding, and "pre-scripted" mission assignments both in reaction to lessons learned from past events and in anticipation of future events. It also entails working with other federal agencies (OFAs) on delineating areas of responsibility and authority with respect to OFA authorities when gaps and seams exist between Stafford Act assistance and those OFA authorities. Preparation includes the execution of in-place contracts for evacuation transport support and for perishable commodities, as well as the purchase, storage, and maintenance of other commodities and equipment. This phase is described in detail in Chapter 2 Readiness and Pre-Declaration Activities.

B. The **Threat Identification Phase** is a trigger point in disaster relief operations for notice events, such as hurricanes or severe storms and flooding, for increased and focused monitoring, including limited activation of the National Response Coordination Center (NRCC), Regional Response Coordination Centers (RRCCs), and the Emergency Support Functions (ESFs); and the forward movement of personnel including Incident Management Assistance Teams (IMATs) and commodities and equipment. Additional staff and ESFs may be placed on alert, and staging areas may be identified and established. Close coordination with state emergency management officials is crucial in order to gauge likely response needs and to plan accordingly for potential evacuations and sheltering, and other emergency response measures as indicated by the nature of the threat. This phase is described in Chapter 2 Readiness and Pre-Declaration Activities.

C. The **Event Imminent/Event Occurs Phase** is another critical trigger point along the disaster life cycle leading to mobilization of federal assets in a targeted manner, and it involves constant communication and coordination with state officials through deployed IMATs and state liaisons often co-located with the state officials at the state Emergency Operations Center (EOC). This phase will rapidly involve necessary assessments to support issuance of a federal declaration. A notice event, such as an approaching hurricane, may trigger an emergency declaration if there is an imminent threat in order to support emergency protective measures under the Public Assistance (PA) program. A no-notice event, such as an earthquake, will cause an abrupt transition from General Readiness, creating a very fluid and time-compressed operational environment. Prior to a declaration being issued, the thrust of federal activity is to pre-position assets for rapid deployment. Ongoing state and local response activity may be reimbursed if a declaration is issued, including for evacuations and sheltering and other emergency protective measures. Temporary federal facilities, such as an Initial Operating Facility, may be identified and secured. This phase moves the Disaster Life Cycle from Readiness to Federal Declaration to Response, and further information can be found in Chapter 2 Readiness and Pre-Declaration Activities, Chapter 3 Declarations, and Chapter 4 Response.

D. The **Federal Declaration Issued Phase** is the turning point in the Life Cycle because a federal declaration authorizes implementation of Titles IV or V of the Stafford Act for disaster relief assistance and the appointment of a Federal Coordinating Officer who is responsible for coordinating disaster relief. Until and unless a declaration is issued, financial and other assistance under these titles is not authorized. Full mobilization of federal assets and assistance may be triggered depending on the type of declaration (major disaster or emergency) and its scope (programs and designated areas). The declaration sets out the specific parameters for the Stafford Act assistance to be provided in response to the event. The ability to tailor the framework of assistance (designated programs and eligible areas) to meet the needs of the affected community is one of the great strengths of the Stafford Act disaster relief statutory scheme. This requires close coordination between the state, FEMA, and the President of the United States, as this is not a "one size fits all" program of assistance. This phase is described in Chapter 3 Declarations.

E. The **Response Phase** primarily deals with life-saving and sustaining measures and the protection of public health and safety with little or no time to spare. This is a very fluid phase requiring a proactive (two steps ahead) not reactive (one step behind) approach in order to be successful, which is why this phase is fraught with risk. Action may be taken with little or no review of costs or discussion of exit strategies. Large scale operations may be commenced without a clear understanding of actual need because of limited windows of opportunity to act, changing circumstances, and lack of adequate information. A failure or perceived failure of leadership at this critical juncture may not only potentially endanger lives and property, but may also lead to a lack of public trust in government.

This phase includes the transition of operations from the NRCC and RRCC to the Joint Field Office (JFO) and the establishment of Disaster Recovery Centers and congregate shelters, responder support camps, and planning for Direct Housing Operation Programs (DHOPs) under the FEMA Individuals and Households Program (IHP) under the Individual Assistance (IA) Program. Although IHP is considered a Recovery Program, the DHOP may need to be immediately initiated when there is widespread devastation of housing stock. A dedicated surge staff of FEMA disaster assistance employees, in addition to regional and national office subject matter expert employees, will be activated to respond. Search and rescue teams and medical assistance teams may also be activated. FEMA works closely with the state and FEMA's ESF partners, who may be providing assistance under their own authorities and funding, or via mission assignment (MA) taskings under Stafford Act authority.

The primary focus during the response phase is on Emergency Work including debris removal (Category A) and emergency protective measures (Category B) under the PA Program. PA work conducted as direct assistance is handled by the Logistic Directorate of the FEMA Office of Response and Recovery (ORR) for in-house direct assistance and the Response Directorate of ORR for MAs within the ORR. Reimbursement of PA work conducted by PA applicants under Project Worksheet (PW) grant assistance is handled by the Public Assistance Branch in the Recovery Directorate of ORR. DHOP activity may include direct assistance activity for the establishment of group sites via contract or MA and may involve the Logistics and Response Directorates and the IA Branch of the Recovery Directorate. Please see Chapter 4 Response for direct assistance, Chapter 5 Public Assistance for PWs, and Chapter 6 Individual Assistance for DHOP activity for in-depth information.

F. The **Recovery Phase** signals an affected community's shift in focus from response to moving forward in the aftermath of a disaster. Rather than just an attempt to dial back to conditions as they existed pre-event, a successful recovery phase will result in a more resilient community, both in infrastructure and in attitude. Very large scale events may require a transition from a JFO setting to a longer term Recovery Office setting with a longer term workforce, including locally hired staff and Cadre of On-call Response and Recovery Employee (CORE) positions.

This phase includes the repair/replacement of infrastructure (PA Permanent Repair work), residences (IHP) and personal property (Other Needs Assistance, or ONA), temporary housing (IHP), and hazard mitigation measures. Issues arise regarding program-wide implementation and case specific eligibility determinations. The IA and PA recovery programs are implemented by the Recovery Directorate. Hazard Mitigation measures may be funded under PA permanent repair or under the Hazard Mitigation Grants Program (HMGP), which is under the auspices of the FEMA Federal Insurance and Mitigation Administration.

There is an inherent tension between applying the broad statutory authorities of these recovery programs in a predictable manner from disaster to disaster and state to state and in taking unique, disaster specific circumstances into account in providing assistance and support in a meaningful way in order to maximize a speedy and comprehensive recovery.

This phase is generally not affected by a lack of information but rather by an excess of information, which can lead to a paralysis of action when attempting to implement programs while trying to anticipate every possible variance in fact patterns. It is the trap of allowing the perfect to be the enemy of the good.

Vulnerabilities in this phase may include class action lawsuits regarding eligibility determinations and termination of IA temporary housing

---

assistance programs, and responses to information requests including case specific media and congressional inquiries subject to Privacy Act protections. Program specific information for Recovery activity can be found in Chapter 5 Public Assistance for PWs, Chapter 6 Individual Assistance, and Chapter 7 Hazard Mitigation.

G. The **Closeout Phase** is a winding down of operations and transition from a JFO or Recovery Office to the Regional Office. This includes making final eligibility determinations, including resolving appeals, and terminating DHOP activities, which may require legal enforcement action. It also involves reassessment of the assistance provided both on a program-wide and case specific basis, which may include DHS Office of Inspector General audits or investigations. Program-wide, there will be lessons learned that may identify gaps and vulnerabilities that may lead to changes in policies. Case specific activity may include the recoupment (IA) or deobligation (PA or HMGP) of assistance already provided. Some events are so catastrophic or extraordinary (e.g., 2001 World Trade Center and Pentagon attacks and 2005 Hurricane Katrina) or the type of event so pervasive (1993 Midwest flooding) that, in their aftermath, they trigger major federal legislation, causing a retooling or even a paradigm shift in how the federal government will respond in the future to such events.

III. Conclusion

The all-hazards operational cycle emanates from more than 200 years of emergency management history and practice, and congressional reaction, particularly since 1950, to numerous significant disaster events. It reflects a present day statutory scheme that provides a flexible and dynamic construct for the federal government to respond to all hazards whenever state and local governments are overwhelmed. The following chapters of the Disaster Operations Legal Reference provide a much greater level of detail with respect to the legal parameters FEMA must operate within to execute its responsibilities within this life cycle. In addition, the appendices include practical tools for the emergency management practitioner to navigate the law and authorities applicable to the life cycle, including a paper on best practices for providing legal advice under disaster conditions and a checklist for the provision of legal analysis in the emergency and disaster context.

CHAPTER 2
Readiness and Pre-Declaration Activities
Table of Contents

Readiness and Pre-Declaration Activities

I. Introduction

Under the Stafford Act, the President's declaration of a major disaster or an emergency triggers FEMA's authority to respond to the declared incident.[1] Readiness and pre-declaration activities, however, are critical in ensuring an effective disaster or emergency response and recovery, and they generally include three categories of activity:

- Non-disaster specific activities that are necessary to maintain FEMA's readiness to respond to threats as they arise;

- Disaster-specific activities that occur when there is an identified threat and a declaration is anticipated, such as pre-positioning and staging commodities and response personnel; and

- The provision of equipment or commodities to a state, local, or tribal government, by sale, loan, or lease to respond to a hazard in the absence of a Stafford Act declaration.[2]

It is imperative that FEMA have personnel, contracts, and resources immediately available in anticipation of deployment so that it can tactically pre-position assets as necessary in a proactive posture for a seamless transition to response if a declaration is issued.

This chapter provides an overview of FEMA's pre-declaration authorities and activities.

---

[1] Stafford Act §§ 401 and 501, 42 U.S.C. §§ 5170 and 5191.

[2] *See* Memorandum from Brad Kieserman, Chief Counsel to William Carwile L. III, Associate Administrator for Response and Recovery: Providing Non-monetary Federal Assistance to State and Local Governments in the Absence of a Stafford Act Declaration - Part I, Dated November 27, 2012. The provision of personal property by these methods will be governed by a FEMA Directive, currently being drafted.

II. Funding Pre-Declaration Activities

Congress appropriates funds to carry out activities under the Stafford Act to an account known as the Disaster Relief Fund (DRF).[3] The budget justification that DHS submits to Congress describes FEMA's use of the DRF for major disaster declarations, emergency declarations, fire management assistance, pre-declaration "surge," and disaster readiness and support costs (critical readiness initiatives and administrative functions supporting disaster response and recovery that are not disaster-specific or in support of a pre-declaration).[4] Therefore, with a declaration from the President, FEMA may expend funds from the DRF to provide assistance to eligible individuals and entities (including grants and direct assistance) that the Stafford Act authorizes under Title IV, Major Disaster Assistance Programs, and Title V, Emergency Assistance Programs.

FEMA may also use the DRF prior to a declaration for its own Disaster Readiness and Support (DRS) costs that are necessary to support the agency's primary response and recovery mission, and for pre-declaration surge expenses it incurs to prepare for an identified threat, such as an approaching hurricane. Although these activities are not specified in the Stafford Act, FEMA may use the DRF to fund them because they are necessary expenses under the "necessary expense doctrine,"[5] which requires, among other things, that the expense materially contribute to an agency's ability to carry out an object of the appropriation funding the activity.

DRS activities materially contribute to FEMA's ability to carry out its response and recovery activities under Titles IV and V of the Stafford Act.

---

[3] For example, the Department of Defense and Full-Year Continuing Appropriations Act, 2011 [hereinafter Department of Homeland Security, Congressional Budget Justification FY 2011] Title VI, Pub. L. No. 112-10, Sec. 1634, at 3093, appropriated $2,650,000,000 for Disaster Relief. In support of its budget request each year, FEMA and the Department submit a budget justification for the "Disaster Relief Fund."

[4] *See* Department of Homeland Security, Congressional Budget Justification FY 2012, at 2592. *See also* FEMA Directive 125-2, *Disaster Relief Fund (DRF)-Pre-Disaster Declarations (Surge) Funding* [hereinafter *Surge Directive 125-2*](2011), available at: http://on.fema.net/employee_tools/forms/Pages/Directives.aspx.

[5] *See* Government Accountability Office (GAO), Principles of Federal Appropriations Law [hereinafter the Red Book], Vol. I, at 4-21 and 4-22. (3rd ed.) *See also, Surge Directive 125-2*, at Section III. C.

Consequently, the DRS activities may be sourced by the DRF, as they are a necessary expense of carrying out activities under the Stafford Act.

A. Disaster Readiness and Support (DRS) Costs

The $273 million Disaster Readiness and Support FY 2011 Expenditure Plan[6] that FEMA submitted to Congress includes a broad range of non-disaster specific FEMA organizational elements and activities that are critical to support FEMA's response and recovery mission.

Examples include:

- A Housing Inspection Services readiness contract covering inspections of disaster damaged homes and personal property to determine applicant eligibility;[7]

- The Individual Assistance (IA) and Public Assistance (PA) technical assistance contracts[8] (TACs) to support the delivery of program services;

- The funding of standing Interagency Agreements (IAAs)[9] to ensure readiness of Stafford Act programs and services, such as Crisis Counseling[10] through the U.S. Department of Health and Human Services, Disaster Unemployment Assistance[11] through the U.S. Department of Labor, and Disaster Legal Services[12] through the Young Lawyers Section of the American Bar Association; surge staffing for disaster survivor tele-registration intake by the Internal

---

[6] Department of Homeland Security, *Disaster Readiness and Support FY 2011 Expenditure Plan and Quarterly Obligations, Fiscal Year 2011 Report to Congress* (June 20, 2011) [hereinafter DRS FY 2011 Report].

[7] Id. item 6, at 4.

[8] Id. items 10 and 11 at 5-6.

[9] Id. item 14, at 7.

[10] Stafford Act, § 416, 42 U.S.C. § 5183.

[11] Id. § 410, 42 U.S.C. § 5177.

[12] Id. § 415, 42 U.S.C. § 5182.

Revenue Service;[13] and the purchase of commodities through the General Services Administration;[14]

- Funding of FEMA's Logistics Supply Chain Management System to manage critical disaster assets and commodities;[15]

- FEMA Logistics Directorate logistics maintenance of national sites for Temporary Housing Units (THUs)[16] and Distribution Centers[17] for pre-positioned disaster commodities and assets;

- Response operations emergency evacuation contracts[18] (air, rail, bus, and ambulance);

- Maintenance and operator training for fleet of Mobile Communications Office Vehicles (MCOVs), mobile registration intake centers, and mobile rest and recovery vehicles;[19] Logistics Distribution Management Branch supervises FEMA's Distribution Centers where FEMA pre-positions disaster assets and, at a disaster or emergency, Logistics Operations moves these assets to needed locations through the use of contractors, full-time personnel and temporary personnel;[20] and

- Non-disaster specific two-year CORE (Cadre of On-Call Response Employees) positions.[21]

Many of these costs are for advance contracts, discussed at V.

---

[13] *DRS FY 2011 Report*, item 17, at 9.
[14] *Id.* item 31, at 16.
[15] *Id.* item 25, at 12.
[16] *Id.* item 26, at 13.
[17] *Id.* items 35-36H, at 18-21.
[18] *Id.* item 27, at 14.
[19] *Id.* item 30, at 15.
[20] *See id.* item 25, at 12.
[21] *Id.* item 1, at 2.b

B. Disaster Relief Fund (DRF) Surge Accounts

The FEMA Office of the Chief Financial Officer (OCFO) established the "surge account" within the DRF, which FEMA utilizes for pre-declaration activities. FEMA may use the DRF surge account to fund certain costs prior to a declaration as a necessary expense when an identified threat could reasonably be expected to result in a declaration by the President.[22] Surge costs are pre-declaration mobilization and readiness expenditures of time, money, and labor to mobilize or prepare to mobilize support when a major disaster or emergency is imminent, but not yet declared, and the disaster or emergency will clearly require federal resources and assets.[23] The DRF pays the cost of surge activities, including:[24]

- Pre-positioning assets and commodities;

- Mission assignments for federal operational support for pre-event deployment (but not operational assistance to states or local governments until a declaration issued);

- Certain surge-related personnel costs; and

- Supply costs directly associated with the initial response to events not yet declared.

---

[22] Surge Directive 125-2.
[23] Id.
[24] Id.

C. Budget Control Act of 2011 and Disaster Funding

The Budget Control Act of 2011 (BCA)[25] imposes a new budgetary restraint on "disaster funding" [26] by placing a cap on the upward adjustment of spending[27] on major disaster response activities based upon the average funding for disaster relief over the previous 10 years, excluding the highest and lowest years within that 10-year period. The purpose of this action was to move "disaster funding" out of "emergency" spending,[28] which has a potentially unlimited upward cap adjustment.

Implementing the BCA's disaster relief spending construct, Congress appropriated funds for the DRF in fiscal year 2012 through two separate appropriations reflecting the BCA's distinction between "disaster relief,"[29] which refers to major disaster declaration activity, and any other necessary expenses of activities authorized under the Stafford Act, which includes emergency declaration activities.

The Consolidated Appropriations Act, 2012 provides "for necessary expenses in carrying out the Robert T. Stafford Disaster Relief and Emergency Assistance Act . . . , $700,000,000, to remain available until expended."[30] The Disaster Relief Appropriations Act, 2012 provides "[f]or an additional amount for the 'Disaster Relief Fund' for major disasters declared pursuant to the Robert T. Stafford Disaster Relief and

---

[25] Pub. L. No. 112-25, 2 U.S.C. § 900 et *seq.*
[26] 2 U.S.C. § 901(b)(2)(D). Disaster funding is defined as discretionary accounts Congress designates as being for "disaster relief" in statute. Id. § 901(b)(2)(D)(i) "'Disaster relief' is defined activities carried out pursuant to a determination under section 102(2) of the Robert T. Stafford Disaster Relief and Emergency Assistance Act (42 U.S.C. 5122(2))." Id. § 901(b)(2)(D)(iii). Section 102(2) of Stafford Act, 42 U.S.C. § 5122(2), provides a definition for the term "major disaster." Consequently, the BCA defines "disaster funding" as appropriations that Congress designates in statute as being for activities carried out pursuant to a presidential determination of a "major disaster."
[27] This "upward adjustment" is represented by supplemental funding beyond the annual base appropriation to the Disaster Relief Fund. See, e.g. Disaster Relief Appropriations Act, 2012, Pub. L. No. 112-77.
[28] Id. § 901(b)(2)(D)(iv)).
[29] "'Disaster relief' is defined as activities carried out pursuant to a determination under section 102(2) of the Robert T. Stafford Disaster Relief and Emergency Assistance Act (42 U.S.C. 5122(2))." 2 U.S.C. § 901(b)(2)(D)(iii). Section 102(2) of Stafford Act, 42 U.S.C. § 5122(2), provides a definition for the term "major disaster."
[30] Pub. L. No. 112-74.

Emergency Assistance Act . . . , $6,400,000,000, to remain available until expended.[31]"

Previous supplemental appropriations to the Disaster Relief Fund did not limit the purpose of those funds to "major disasters." Instead, prior supplemental appropriations mirrored the purpose of the annual appropriations and provided FEMA with the flexibility to expend those funds for any disaster relief activity.[32] FEMA must now account for emergency declaration activity out of the lesser necessary expenses fund, which may lead to budget allocation determinations between funding emergency declaration activity and standing necessary expenses line items not attributable to specific major disasters.

III. Pre-positioned Equipment Program (PEP)

The PEP program[33] has been discontinued as of July 2012.

IV. Initial Response Resources (IRR)

FEMA maintains pre-positioned critical disaster relief assets and supplies, called IRR,[34] in strategically located distribution centers within and outside the continental United States.[35] These IRR were initially created as a result of leftover commodities purchased through the DRF for disasters, and the DRF funds their periodic replenishment. The IRR contains two tiers of equipment.

Tier I life-saving and life-sustaining resources include water, tarps, meals, cots, blue roofing sheeting, blankets, hygiene kits, and generators

---

[31] Id.

[32] Pub. L. No. 112-77.

[33] The Prepositioned Equipment Program was authorized by the Post-Katrina Emergency Management Reform Act (hereinafter PKEMRA), Pub. L. 109-295, 637, 6 U.S.C. § 725 (2006)

[34] See Joint Explanatory Statement for PKEMRA, Cong. Rec. H7813 at H7828 (2006).

[35] Logistics Management Directorate Fact Sheet (2011) [hereinafter Log Fact Sheet]. http://on.fema.net/components/orr/lmd/Documents/Forms/AllItems.aspx?RootFolder=%2fcomponents%2forr%2flmd%2fDocuments%2fLM%20Fact%20Sheet&FolderCTID=&View=%7b65AD2A63%2dCE5F%2d4126%2d9B29%2dBBAF016CEEFE%7d.

intended to sustain lives and prevent further property damage during an emergency or disaster. Primary distribution centers for pre-positioned IRR are located in Atlanta, GA; Fort Worth, TX; Cumberland, MD; Frederick, MD; Moffett Field, CA; Puerto Rico; Hawaii; and Guam. During catastrophic events, IRR may be distributed to as many as 60 forward sites for distribution. During complex disaster scenarios, IRR flows through specifically designed FEMA Incident Support Bases and Joint Field Office (JFO) Staging Areas, to Resource Staging Areas or points of distribution that state and local governments operate.

Tier II key operational support resources include JFO kits consisting of tables, chairs, computer support equipment, and cables for 100- to 250-person offices; temporary housing units (THUs); and mobile communications office vehicles (MCOVs), formerly called Mobile Disaster Recovery Centers (MDRCs).[36] THUs and MCOVs are discussed in more detail later in this chapter.

Based on lessons learned from prior hurricane response operations, as well as enhanced relationships with logistics partners at all levels of government, FEMA announced in 2007 that it would no longer purchase, distribute, or store ice as one of the basic response commodities. FEMA will reimburse eligible applicants for the eligible costs of purchasing and distributing ice as an emergency protective measure, or use other agreements with entities to augment local supplies.[37]

V. Advance Contracting

The Post-Katrina Emergency Management Reform Act (PKEMRA)[38] directed FEMA to identify and contract for recurring disaster response

---

[36] See Standard Operating Procedure for Mobile Communications Office Vehicle Deployments (2011) [hereinafter SOP for MVOCs], http://on.fema.net/components/orr/lmd/lmd_divisions/lod/Documents/CONOPS%20and%20SOPs/MCOV%20Deployment%20SOP.pdf
[37] Purchase and Distribution of Ice Number: FP 203-075-1 http://www.fema.gov/9500-series-policy-publications/purchase-and-distribution-ice.
[38] See PKEMRA. Department of Homeland Security Appropriations Act, 2007, Title VI, Post-Katrina Emergency Management Reform Act [hereinafter PKEMRA], Pub. L. No. 109-295, § 637, 6 U.S.C. § 725.

requirements.[39] FEMA currently has over 60 advance contracts[40] with private companies, non-profit organizations, and other federal agencies that may be activated following a declaration to supply essential disaster-related supplies and services. Many of these contracts are listed in the discussion of Disaster Readiness and Support costs at Section II(A). In awarding contracts, by law, FEMA must give preference "to the extent feasible and practicable" to local firms and individuals.[41] This provision applies not only to FEMA contracts but to all expenditures of federal funds for "debris clearance, distribution of supplies, reconstruction, and other major disaster or emergency assistance activities,"[42] including, for example, contracts that the U.S. Army Corps of Engineers awards for debris removal, the Blue Roof program,[43] and other disaster-related work.

Since advance contracting cannot anticipate the location of an event in order to meet the required local preference, FEMA has arranged for national contracts to meet early expected demands for supplies and equipment. Unless FEMA determines that it is not feasible or practicable, however, FEMA must transition work performed under these national contracts for response, relief, and reconstruction that are in effect on the date of a declaration to entities residing in or doing business primarily in the affected area.[44] A principal purpose of this requirement is to assist the economic recovery of communities affected by disasters. FEMA Administrator Fugate reiterated FEMA's commitment to comply with the letter and the spirit of the local preference provision in a Memorandum

---

[39] Id. § 691; 6 U.S.C. § 791.

[40] Master Pre-positioned Contract List, Acquisition Operations Division, FEMA Office of Chief Procurement Officer (2010).

[41] Stafford Act, § 307(a)(1); 42 U.S.C. § 5150(a)(1); 44 C.F.R. § 206.10; Federal Acquisition Regulations [hereinafter FAR] 48 C.F.R. § 26.202.

[42] Stafford Act, § 307(a)(1); 42 U.S.C. § 5150(a)(1).

[43] See Chapter 4, Response, for more detail on the Blue Roof program.

[44] Stafford Act § 307(b)(2), 42 U.S.C. § 5150 (b)(2); FAR, § 6.203(b). The Local Community Recovery Act of 2006, Public L. No. 109-218 (2006), amended the Stafford Act to authorize set-asides for major disaster or emergency assistance acquisitions to businesses that reside or primarily do business in the geographic area affected by the disaster or emergency. The DHS Appropriations Act of 2007, No. 109-295 (2007), § 694, enacted requirements for transitioning work under existing contracts. An interim rule implementing this amendment to § 307 of the Stafford Act, 42 U.S.C. § 5150, is available at 71 Fed. Reg. 44,546 (2006). A second interim rule was necessary because of a later statutory amendment to this section. 72 Fed. Reg. 63,084 (2007).

called *Promoting the Use of Local Vendors in a Disaster*.[45] FEMA established a Local Business Transition Team within the OCFO and gained experience transitioning national contracts to local vendors following Hurricane Ike in 2008.

VI. Advance Contracts for Temporary Housing Units (THUs)

The Stafford Act authorizes housing assistance for eligible applicants after a major disaster or emergency.[46] When financial assistance is inadequate due to a lack of available housing resources, FEMA may provide direct housing assistance,[47] usually in the form of temporary housing units (THUs). To meet critical housing needs in the immediate aftermath of a disaster, FEMA is currently planning to maintain a baseline inventory of approximately 2,000 one-bedroom, two- bedroom, or three-bedroom THUs, all of which meet the standards of the Department of Housing and Urban Development. *See* Chapter 6, *Individual Assistance*, for a more detailed discussion of FEMA's direct housing mission.

The THUs are stored and maintained at temporary housing staging sites located in Selma, AL and Cumberland, MD.[48] FEMA may acquire additional units as needed through multiple advance contracts with THU manufacturers; most contracts require the contractor to reach production capacity of between 125 and 150 units per week within four weeks of FEMA's order. The contracts cover a mix of differently sized units, some of which must comply with the UFAS.[49]

---

[45] Memorandum from the Administrator: *Promoting the Use of Local Vendors in a Disaster* (2010), http://on.fema.net/regions/regional_operations/Documents/Forms/DispForm.aspx?ID=131.

[46] Stafford Act, §§ 408 and 502 (a)(6), 42 U.S.C. §§ 5174 and 5192 (a)(6).

[47] Id. at § 408(c)(1)(b), 42 U.S.C. § 5174(c)(1)(b).

[48] *See* DRS FY 2011 *Report*, which refers to two "enduring sites" and "3 disposal sites," item 35-36H, at 18-21.

[49] Architectural Barriers Act, Pub. L. No. 90-480 (1968) (codified as amended at 42 U.S.C. §§ 4151- 4157); 36 C.F.R. Part 1190. *See* 49 Fed. Reg. 31, 528 (1984).

VII. Mobile Communications Operation Vehicles (MCOVs)

FEMA maintains a fleet of 60 MCOVs[50] strategically located in Atlanta, GA; Cumberland, MD; Fort Worth, TX; Moffett Field, CA; Denver, CO; Bothell, WA; and Holliston, MA. The MCOV provides a rapidly deployable, self-contained mobile office and communications platform.[51] Depending upon a vehicle's primary mission, FEMA may equip it with a satellite voice/data system, computers, phones, and workstations. When used in the response and recovery phases, the MCOV is capable of providing a flexible office space to ensure individuals and families have timely access to FEMA's Individual Assistance programs and can provide communications and registration capability to support Disaster Recovery Centers. When an MCOV supports the National Processing Service Centers, it may become a Mobile Registration Intake Center (MRIC). These MRICs can provide Internet and phone service for disaster survivors in areas where the disaster has interrupted the normal telecommunications infrastructure. FEMA internally transferred the MCOV program to the Response Disaster Emergency Communications Branch on October 1, 2011.

VIII. Pre-scripted Mission Assignments (PSMAs)

A mission assignment is a work order issued by FEMA to another federal agency, with or without reimbursement, directing the agency to complete a specific task.[52] Congress directed FEMA in the Post-Katrina Emergency Management Reform Act (PKEMRA)[53] to develop Pre-scripted Mission Assignments (PSMAs) with federal agencies having responsibilities under the National Response Framework in areas that include logistics, communications, mass care, health services, and public safety.

---

[50] *See* SOP for MVOCs, (January 3, 2011)
http://on.fema.net/components/orr/lmd/lmd_divisions/lod/Documents/CONOPS%20a nd%20SOPs/MCOV%20Deployment%20SOP.pdf
[51] Response MCOV Fact Sheet, (November 8, 2012)
http://on.fema.net/components/orr/response/Pages/MCOV%20Support.aspx
[52] 44 C.F.R. § 206.2(18).
[53] PKEMRA, a§ 653, 6 U.S.C. § 753.

Key examples of the over 250 PSMAs FEMA has issued include agreements with these agencies:

- Department of Health and Human Services, including the National Disaster Medical System (NDMS), for medical care and support;
- U.S. Army Corps of Engineers for debris removal, logistics, and water;
- Department of Defense for aero-medical patient evacuation;
- U.S. Coast Guard for search and rescue support.

See Chapter 4, *Response*, for a detailed discussion of mission assignments.

IX. Pre-positioned Personnel

Depending on the nature and scope of an incident, FEMA may pre-position Incident Management Assistance Teams (IMATs), Urban Search and Rescue (US&R) teams and Mobile Emergency Response Support (MERS) personnel in anticipation of a declaration of a major disaster or emergency. In certain circumstances, Nuclear Incident Response Team (NIRT) assets may be deployed from the Department of Energy. *See* Chapter 4, *Response*, for a more detailed discussion of these teams. Pre-positioning is funded from the Surge Account of the Disaster Relief Fund, as discussed above in Section II(B).

FEMA also deploys a broad range of specialized staff, including damage assessment teams, who may be full-time employees or Reservists[54] from Headquarters and regional cadres, depending on the nature of the incident. For example, the Logistics Management Directorate maintains a national Logistics Fly-Away Team of fully trained logistics personnel ready to deploy during the first 7–10 days of a major disaster if a FEMA region so requests.

---

[54] A special type of federal employee allowed under the Stafford Act, § 306(b)(1), 42 U.S.C. § 5149. *See* Chapter on *Human Capital* for a more detailed discussion of Reservists.

X. Provision of Commodities or Equipment

FEMA may provide commodities or equipment to a state (territory or possession) in the absence of a Presidential declaration immediately before, during, and after a hazardous event.[55]

FEMA may sell expendable property (e.g., MREs, water, tarps) and may lease or loan non-expendable property (e.g. generators).[56] When requesting such assistance, a state or local government must indicate they cannot meet the need themselves and the property is necessary to save lives or protect property. Confirming such assistance is necessary for a hazardous event, FEMA must also determine the state cannot meet the need from another source and that FEMA possesses the capability in its current inventory to meet the requirement without negatively impacting other operational needs.

A revocable license must be completed for loans and a personal property lease for property rented for a fee. A license must be revocable at the will of the federal government at any time.[57] Loaned or leased assets must be returned to FEMA in the same or similar condition, and the state must agree to repair or replace any damaged or missing property.

Loan of Equipment

In preparation for an approaching hurricane, a state requests that FEMA provide generators to shelters and other facilities. FEMA may loan generators to the state prior to a declaration, provided it determines that the loan would be beneficial to the federal government.

When providing commodities or equipment in the absence of declaration, employees should consult with the Office of Chief Counsel, because of the possibility of violating the prohibition against FEMA providing assistance

---

[55] FD 075-2, Provision of Personal Property (Commodities and Equipment) in the Absence of a Presidential Emergency or Major Disaster Declaration (2013); Stafford Act Title VI.
[56] See for loans: 47 Comp. Gen 387 (1968) and 44 Comp. Gen 824 (1965).
[57] 47 Comp. Gen 387 (1968) and 44 Comp. Gen. 824 (1965).

prior to a declaration and a signed FEMA-State Agreement.[58] Moreover, if a FEMA employee makes an unauthorized commitment, that commitment does not bind the agency and may result in disciplinary action towards, and personal liability of, the employee.[59]

XI. Mission Assignments for Federal Operations Support

In addition to the pre-scripted mission assignments discussed earlier, to facilitate pre-positioning, FEMA may issue 'federal operations support' mission assignments that are 100% federally funded and essential for FEMA to be ready for an imminent federal emergency or disaster declaration. A mission assignment FEMA issues in anticipation of a declaration that is essential for FEMA to be ready for an anticipated declaration is authorized under the "necessary expense" doctrine, discussed earlier.[60] *See* Chapter 4, *Response*, for a detailed discussion of mission assignments.

Readiness Activities

While FEMA may not mission-assign the U.S. Army Corps of Engineers (USACE) to set up and use the generators in advance of a declaration, FEMA did permit the USACE to move generators to Puerto Rico in preparation for a disaster in 2008 but did not actually "employ" or use them until the President made a declaration. Pre-positioning the generators was a necessary expense in order to be able to mount an effective response if the approaching hurricane resulted in a declaration.[61]

---

[58] 44 C.F.R. § 206.44(a).
[59] FAR, 48 C.F.R. § 1.602-3.
[60] *See* GAO Red Book, Vol. I, at 4-21 and 4-22 (3rd ed. 2004).
[61] *See* discussion of the "necessary expense" doctrine in the GAO Red Book, Vol. I, at. 4-21 and 4-22 (3rd ed. 2004).

XII. Memoranda of Agreement (MOA), Memoranda of Understanding (MOU), and Interagency Agreements (IAA)

FEMA coordinates with numerous federal agencies and with non-profit organizations in advance of disaster or emergency activity, often to establish a clear understanding, pre-declaration, of each agency's roles and responsibilities. To memorialize these understandings, FEMA may execute with another agency or a non-profit a Memorandum of Agreement (MOA) or Memorandum of Understanding (MOU). MOAs and MOUs are agreements between government agencies or non-profits that state mutual goals, actions, and responsibilities. These pre-declaration arrangements can improve relations substantially between agencies and non-profits in field operations because these roles and responsibilities are resolved ahead of time. Often conflicts at an earlier event allow agencies and non-profits to realize that these MOUs and MOAs can be of enormous assistance in assuring that response and recovery activities proceed smoothly. Since they involve no exchange of government funds, they do not need a contracting officer's review, but relevant program specialists in FEMA's Office of Chief Counsel (OCC) should review them. A DHS management directive addresses the format, contents, and procedural requirements for MOAs and MOUs.[62]

In the event that an agreement with another federal agency requires a transfer of funds, an Interagency Agreement (IAA)[63] will be required. An IAA is a written agreement between government agencies to acquire supplies or services as authorized by statute.[64] Because IAAs involve the payment of government funds, OCC attorneys must review them, and a contracting officer must sign them. An IAA is distinct from a mission assignment. A mission assignment is utilized for short-term taskings (generally less than 60 days) provided to another agency, whereas an IAA is utilized for longer term projects.

---

[62] DHS Management Directive No. 0450.1, Memoranda of Understanding (MOU) and Memoranda of Agreement (MOA) (2003), <http://dhsconnect.dhs.gov/policies/Instructions/Forms/Management%20Directives%20by%20Number.aspx>.
[63] DHS Management Directive No. 125-02, Interagency Agreements (2008).
[64] Id. at IV. C.

MOA and IAA with the American Red Cross

The American Red Cross (ARC) is a non-profit, humanitarian organization chartered by Congress as a federal instrumentality and is required to carry out responsibilities as the nation's primary provider of disaster preparedness and response services.

FEMA has executed an MOA with the American Red Cross to clarify the roles of FEMA and the American Red Cross in field operations in providing mass care through sheltering and feeding disaster survivors as co-leads for mass care under ESF 6 – Mass Care, Emergency Assistance, Housing and Human Services. FEMA and ARC have agreed to assist states in training, coordination, development of mass care exercises and reporting tools, facilitating development of mass care plans in states and communities. As is true of MOAs, this has no fiscal obligations and is specifically not enforceable in a court of law.

Because the ARC is a federal instrumentality, FEMA and ARC have also signed an IAA so that FEMA may request ARC assistance with response support goods and services during presidentially declared emergencies or disasters.[65] The IAA addresses services for which FEMA can reimburse ARC and which are outside the scope of ARC's normal activities. Only those services that are requested by FEMA and agreed to by ARC, in writing, are reimbursable.

XIII. Incident Support Bases (ISBs)

An ISB is a designated site where uncommitted resources are temporarily received, pre-positioned, and held[66] until the Unified Command Group at

---

[65] Interagency Agreement between the American Red Cross and the Federal Emergency Management Agency dated 10/22/2010.
https://nmcs.communityos.org/cms/files/os114/p75/FEMA%20American%20Red%20Cross%20MOA%20October%202010.pdf. Stafford Act §§ 304, 309, 402, 403, 502; 42 §§ 5147, 5152, 5170(a), 5170(b) and 5192.

[66] FEMA Logistics Management Directorate, Incident Support Base Concept of Operations [hereinafter ISB Con Ops], at 1-1 (March 2010),
http://on.fema.net/components/orr/lmd/lmd_divisions/lod/Documents/CONOPS%20and%20SOPs/FEMA%20Interim%20ISB%20CONOPS%20Mar%202010.pdf.

the Joint Field Office orders their use.[67] These may be set up either before or after the President makes a Stafford Act declaration. FEMA locates ISBs as close to the impacted area as practicable. ISBs may receive resources from FEMA Distribution Centers, commercial vendors, other federal agencies, and non-governmental organizations. While FEMA's distribution strategy is to direct ship resources to the requestor's site to the extent possible, early in the response phase, the strategy may require intermediate stops until FEMA staff receives specific requirements and ultimate destinations. For this reason, FEMA may establish ISBs as pre-positioning sites to expedite immediate delivery of resources once the states request them.[68]

XIV. Staging

FEMA sends equipment, commodities, and personnel committed to an incident to staging areas convenient to the impacted area awaiting tactical assignment. The region or Joint Field Office Operations Section manages staging areas.[69] FEMA consults with the affected state(s) and local governments to select convenient locations for state access to disaster relief supplies for distribution to the local population. In the past, FEMA has used military bases, athletic stadiums, and similar types of facilities near an impacted area as staging areas. The mobilization for Hurricane Earl illustrates the breadth of resources that FEMA and its partners can mobilize prior to a declaration to prepare for a major disaster or emergency.[70]

---

[67] The Unified Command Group leads the Joint Field Office (JFO) and consists of the Federal Coordinating Officer, the State Coordinating Officer and, as appropriate, senior officials from other federal, state, tribal, and local governments with primary jurisdictional or operational responsibility for an aspect of the incident. National Response Framework at 64 (Jan. 2008), http://www.fema.gov/emergency/nrf/; Incident Management Handbook, FEMA B-761, Interim Change at 3.2 to 3.4.

[68] ISB Con Ops, at 1-1.

[69] Id. Appendix A, at A-6.

[70] FEMA Press Release Number HQ-10-169; FEMA Weekly, Sept. 2, 2010, Vol. 3, No. 32. See also National Situation Updates, Aug. 30 to Sept. 3, 2010.

Case Study: Preparations for Hurricane Earl, August 2010

Hurricane Earl was a Category 4 storm of considerable size and intensity that skirted the U.S. Virgin Islands and Puerto Rico and appeared headed toward major cities on the U.S. East Coast in late August and early September, 2010. FEMA coordinated across the federal government to ensure that state, commonwealth, and territorial officials had the necessary support. Nearly every FEMA region provided support. The Hurricane Liaison Team[71] flew to Miami and set up its offices inside the National Oceanographic and Atmospheric Administration's National Hurricane Center. FEMA activated the National Response Coordination Center and four Regional Response Coordination Centers located in Boston, New York, Philadelphia, and Atlanta. Incident Management Assistance Team staff from Regions V, IX, and X flew to Regions I, III, and IV, as teams were deployed to North Carolina, Virginia, Maryland, Connecticut, Massachusetts, New Hampshire, Rhode Island, Vermont, and Maine.

FEMA Urban Search and Rescue teams were staged in Region I, and Mobile Emergency Response Support teams from different locations mobilized to assist various regions. Logistics personnel from Regions X, VIII, VI, I, and IV moved 400,000 liters of water, 300,000 meals, and 54 generators to an Incident Support Base (ISB) in Ft. Bragg, N.C., and over 210,000 meals, 160,000 liters of water, 41 generators, and 12,500 tarps to an ISB in Westover, MA.

Additional support included:

- **Department of Health and Human Services (HHS)** transported and pre-positioned caches of medical equipment and supplies in the Northeast, and pre-positioned seven National Disaster Medical Teams. Hundreds of U.S. Public Health Service Commissioned Corps officers were placed on alert.
- **Department of Defense (DOD)** positioned a Defense Coordinating Element in the FEMA Regional Response Coordination Center in New York. DOD also had Defense
- Coordinating Officers in St. Thomas, U.S. Virgin Islands, Massachusetts, and Georgia.
- **U.S. NORTHCOM's** Hurricane Hunters conducted weather reconnaissance flyovers.
- **U.S. Coast Guard's** First Coast Guard District Units prepared for search and rescue capability and closed ports in North Carolina.
- **American Red Cross** deployed more than 350 trained disaster workers to North Carolina, Massachusetts, and Rhode Island, along with more than 60 emergency vehicles. Red Cross shelters were prepared in North Carolina, New York, Massachusetts, and Rhode Island, with emergency planning continuing in 10 other states along the coast

---

[71] *See* Chapter 4, *Response*, for a more detailed discussion of this and other response teams.

CHAPTER 3

Declarations

Table of Contents

Declarations

I. Introduction

A Presidential major disaster[1] or emergency[2] declaration under the Stafford Act initially triggers FEMA's broad statutory authorities[3] to provide financial assistance and Direct Federal Assistance (DFA)[4] from the Disaster Relief Fund (DRF)[5] to affected state, tribal, and local governments for immediate aid and emergency services, and to provide assistance to individuals and households.[6] In addition, in the case of a major disaster declaration, FEMA may provide assistance to repair, restore, or replace disaster damaged public facilities and eligible private non-profit facilities;[7] mitigate the risk from future hazard events;[8] and provide, among other programs, crisis counseling,[9] disaster unemployment,[10] and disaster case management[11] to those who need more help recovering.

No state or territory has escaped the need for a major disaster or emergency declaration; on average, at least 34 major disaster declarations have been issued annually since 1953.[12] The President authorizes an

---

[1] Stafford Act § 401, 42 U.S.C. § 5170.

[2] Id. § 501, 42 U.S.C. § 5191.

[3] Id. §§ 402, 403, 502, and 503, 42 U.S.C. §§ 5170a, 5170b, 5192, and 5193.

[4] Id. § 402, 403, 407, and 502, 42 U.S.C. § 5170a, 5170b, 5173, and 5192; 44 C.F.R. § 206.208. FEMA may provide DFA through its own personnel, outside contractors, and/or through mission assignments to OFAs. *See* Chapter 4, *Response*, for a more detailed discussion of mission assignments.

[5] The DRF is the FEMA appropriation that funds Major Disaster and Emergency Declarations, Fire Management Grants, the Disaster Readiness and Support (DRS) account and the Surge accounts. *See* Chapter 2, *Readiness and Pre-Declaration Activities*, for a discussion of the DRS and Surge accounts.

[6] Stafford Act § 408, 42 U.S.C. § 5174.

[7] Id. § 406, 42 U.S.C. § 5172.

[8] Id. § 404, 42 U.S.C. § 5170c.

[9] Id. § 416, 42 U.S.C. § 5183.

[10] Id. § 410, 42 U.S.C. § 5177.

[11] Id. § 426, 42 U.S.C. § 5189d.

[12] *See* http://www.fema.gov/news/disaster_totals_annual.fema. The annual number of major disasters for the last 15 years has been much greater.

extraordinary array of direct and financial assistance in support of an impacted state or federally- recognized tribe whenever he makes a major disaster or emergency declaration.[13] Please note that the Sandy Recovery Improvement Act of 2013 (SRIA) which was signed into law on January 29, 2013, amended the Stafford Act to allow federally-recognized tribes to seek Stafford Act assistance from the President directly in the event of an emergency or major disaster.[14] Please refer to the discussion in Section XIII of this Chapter regarding this recent legislative change. The Stafford Act has broad authorities that allow the President to tailor the declaration (declaration type, incident type, programs designated, areas covered and forms of assistance) to meet the disaster or emergency related needs of those affected.[15]

The statutory definitions of "major disaster" and "emergency" define not only the type of event or circumstances that the President may consider, but also the scale of the disaster-related needs that the Stafford Act authorizes FEMA to address.

A major disaster is any natural catastrophe (including any hurricane, tornado, storm, high water, wind-driven water, tidal wave, tsunami, earthquake, volcanic eruption, landslide, mudslide, snowstorm, or drought), or, regardless of cause, any fire, flood, or explosion, in any part of the United States, which in the determination of the President causes damage of sufficient severity and magnitude to warrant major disaster assistance under [the Stafford] Act to supplement the efforts and available resources of States, local governments, and disaster relief organizations in alleviating the damage, loss, hardship, or suffering caused thereby.[16]

An emergency is any occasion or instance for which, in the determination of the President, Federal assistance is needed to supplement State and local efforts and capabilities to save lives and protect property and public health and safety, or to lessen or avert the threat of a catastrophe in any part of the United States.[17]

The emergency definition is broader than that for a major disaster. However, the assistance available for an emergency is narrower than for a

---

[13] Stafford Act § 401 and 501, 42 U.S.C. § 5170 and 5191.

[14] Sandy Recovery Improvement Act of 2013, Pub. L. No. 113-2, § 1110, Tribal Requests for a Major Disaster or Emergency Declaration under the Stafford Act (2013).

[15] Id. § 101, 42 U.S.C. § 5121.

[16] Stafford Act § 102(2), 42 U.S.C. § 5122(2); 44 C.F.R. § 206.2(a)(17).

[17] Id. § 102(1), 42 U.S.C. § 5122(1); 44 C.F.R. § 206.2(a)(9).

major disaster. Please see Table 2, *Summary of Federal Activities and Programs: Emergency v. Major Disaster Declaration* later in this chapter.

The President has sole authority to issue major disaster and emergency declarations.[18] FEMA provides the President with a recommendation to grant or deny the declaration request. In order to determine whether it is appropriate to recommend a declaration to the President, FEMA considers a variety of factors discussed in this chapter. These include the nature and scale of the impact of the incident; whether the need for assistance under the Stafford Act is present and not met by state, local, or tribal resources; and whether the response and recovery fall within the authorities or responsibilities of another federal department or agency.[19]

II. Requesting a Declaration

A. Requirements for Governor's Request

The governor[20] (or acting governor) of a state[21] or the chief executive of an Indian Tribal Government[22] must request a Presidential declaration of a major disaster or emergency, except in the case of an emergency declaration involving primary federal responsibility, which is discussed in section D. The request must be based on a finding that the major disaster or emergency is of such severity and magnitude that an effective response

---

[18] No executive order has delegated Stafford Act §§ 401 and 501, 42 U.S.C. §§ 5170 and 5191(a), which are the declaration sections, from the President to any agency or department.

[19] 44 C.F.R. §§ 206.35, 206.37 and 206.48.

[20] Defined as the chief executive of any state, which would include the Mayor for the District of Columbia. Stafford Act § 102(4) and (5), 42 U.S.C. § 5122(4) and (5).

[21] Defined as any U.S. state, the District of Columbia, Puerto Rico, the Virgin Islands, Guam, American Samoa, and the Commonwealth of the Northern Mariana Islands. Stafford Act § 102(4), 42 U.S.C. § 5122(4).

[22] *See* Stafford Act §§ 102(6) and (12), 401(b) and 501(c), 42 U.S.C. §§ 5122(6) and (12), 5170(b) and 5191(c). For purposes of this Chapter, please consider any references to "governor" as including "chief executive" and references to "state" and including "Indian Tribal Government" as it relates to requests for a major disaster or emergency declaration. *See also* Stafford Act §§ 103, 42 U.S.C. § 5123.

---

is beyond the capabilities of the state and local governments and that federal assistance is necessary.[23]

The governor submits a request and supporting documentation to the appropriate FEMA Regional Administrator (RA), who analyzes the state's request and makes a recommendation to the Deputy Associate Administrator, Response and Recovery,[24] who forwards it to the FEMA Administrator for submittal to the President.

Beginning with events occurring on July 16, 2012, and thereafter, the governor's request must include OMB No. 1660-0009/ FEMA Form 010-0-13: Request for Presidential Disaster Declaration, Major Disaster, or Emergency.[25] The form includes the minimum necessary information and certifications legally required by the Stafford Act for a declaration request and must be signed by the governor. Omission of the form may result in failure to meet those requirements and may delay the processing of the declaration request. A cover letter in support of the governor's request typically accompanies the form. FEMA has created a sample request package that includes a template governor's cover letter.[26]

1. Request Deadline

A request for an emergency declaration should be submitted within five days after need becomes apparent but no longer than 30 days after the incident.[27] A filing extension may be granted by FEMA if the governor submits a request for an extension within the 30-day period providing the reason for the delay.[28]

---

[23] Stafford Act §§ 401 and 501(a), 42 U.S.C. §§ 5170 and 5191(a).
[24] Note that 44 C.F.R. § 206.37 states that the Regional Administrator submits the recommendation to the Assistant Administrator for the Disaster Assistance Directorate, which, as a result of organizational realignment, no longer exists.
[25] The Request form and accompanying template cover letter is available at http://on.fema.net/programs/orr_programs/declarations/Pages/default.aspx. This site also includes a webinar on use of the new form.
[26] Id.
[27] 44 C.F.R. § 206.35(a).
[28] Id.

A request for a major disaster declaration must be submitted within 30 days of the incident unless the governor submits, and FEMA approves, a request for an extension within the 30-day period, providing the reason for the delay.[29]

2. Severity of Situation Finding

The governor's request for an emergency declaration must include a finding that the situation is of such severity and magnitude that effective response is beyond the capability of state and affected local governments, and that the state requires supplementary federal emergency assistance to save lives and to protect property, public health, and safety, or to lessen or avert the threat of a disaster.[30]

The governor's request for a major disaster declaration must include a finding that the situation is of such severity and magnitude that effective response is beyond the capability of state and affected local governments, and that federal assistance is necessary to supplement resources of states, local governments, disaster relief organizations, and available insurance.[31]

3. Required Governor's Actions

The request for emergency or major disaster declarations must include confirmation that the governor has taken appropriate action under state law and directed the execution of the state emergency plan.[32] Additional information should include the date on which the action was taken and the areas covered.[33] The state emergency plan is defined as that state plan which is designated specifically for state level response to emergencies or major disasters and which sets forth actions to be taken by the state and

---

[29] 44 C.F.R. § 206.36(a).
[30] Stafford Act § 501, 42 U.S.C. § 5191; 44 C.F.R. § 206.35(b).
[31] Stafford Act § 401, 42 U.S.C. § 5170; 44 C.F.R. § 206.36(b).
[32] 44 C.F.R. §§ 206.35(c) and 206.36(c).
[33] This may include whether and when a state of emergency has been issued and its coverage.

---

local governments, including those for implementing federal disaster assistance.[34]

The request must include information describing state and local resources committed to disaster relief.[35] This may include actions pending or taken by the state legislature and governing bodies.

4. Specification of Incident Type

The request must indicate the type of incident (e.g., severe storms, flooding, hurricane) and specific dates and time period establishing the basis for a declaration of an emergency or a major disaster. [36]

5. Nature of Assistance Required

In a major disaster request, the governor must provide information indicating the types and amount of federal assistance required.[37] In an emergency declaration request, the governor should include preliminary estimates of the types and amount of emergency assistance needed under the Stafford Act, and information concerning emergency assistance from other federal agencies under other statutory authorities. [38]

In general, a statement that a joint federal, state, and local survey of the damaged areas was requested, a description of the types of facilities and damage, and the adverse effect the damage has on the public and private sectors is required for a major disaster declaration.[39] This will include preliminary estimates of types and amount of supplementary federal assistance needed under the Stafford Act, including the results of the joint preliminary damage assessments.

The request should include the specific FEMA programs requested and the counties for which each program is requested, for example, Individual

---

[34] 44 C.F.R. §§ 206.2 (24) and 206.4.
[35] 44 C.F.R. §§ 206.35(c)(2) and 206.36(c)(3).
[36] *See* 44 C.F.R. §§ 206.32(e) and (f), 206.35 and 206.36.
[37] 44 C.F.R. §§ 206.36(c)(4).
[38] 44 C.F.R. § 206.35.
[39] 44 C.F.R. §§ 206.33 and 206.36. *See* discussion of damage assessment.

Assistance (including the Individual and Households Program, Disaster Unemployment Assistance, Crisis Counseling); Public Assistance; Small Business Administration (SBA) disaster loans; and Hazard Mitigation (HM). Note that the Hazard Mitigation Grants Program (HMGP) targets risks to the state unrelated to the damage caused by the event and may be requested for specific counties or statewide.

a.) Debris Removal

If debris removal is requested or anticipated, the state must agree to indemnify the United States from any claims arising from the removal of debris or wreckage, and the state must agree that debris removal from public and private property will not occur until the landowner signs an unconditional authorization for the removal of debris. [40]

b.) Direct Federal Assistance (DFA)

If DFA is requested, the following information and certifications must be provided before DFA can be provided:[41]

i). The specific type of work requested;

ii). The reasons the state and local government cannot perform or contract for performance of the work;

iii). That the state will provide, without cost to the United States, all lands, easements and rights of way necessary to accomplish the approved work;

iv). That the state agrees to indemnify the United States from damages and claims arising from the requested work;

v). That the state will provide reimbursement for the non-federal share of the cost of work pursuant to the terms of the FEMA-State Agreement (FSA); and

---

[40] Stafford Act § 407(b) and 502(a)(5), 42 U.S.C. §§ 5173(b) and 5192(a)(5).
[41] 44 C.F.R. §§ 206.208

vi). That the state will assist the performing federal agency in all support and local jurisdictional matters.

6. Compliance with Non-Federal Cost Share Requirements

A governor's certification that the state will comply with Stafford Act cost sharing requirements is specifically required for major disaster declaration requests.[42] FEMA requires a certification for emergency declaration requests also to ensure timely provision of assistance. Cost share commitments are included in the FSA for both emergencies and major disasters[43] and are required for the provision of DFA.

7. Designation of Primary State Officials

Generally, there will be a designation of a State Coordinating Officer (SCO) in the governor's request.[44] Please see discussion in Section VII of this chapter.

B. Pre-Disaster Emergency Declarations

The Stafford Act requires FEMA to establish guidelines to assist governors in requesting an emergency declaration in advance of a natural or man-made event that may be declared a disaster.[45] In policy, FEMA has set forth the circumstances under which a state may request a pre-disaster emergency declaration.[46] The policy limits recommendations for assistance under a pre-disaster emergency declaration to Emergency

---

[42] Stafford Act § 401, 42 U.S.C. 4170; 44 C.F.R. § 206.35(c)(5).
[43] 44 C.F.R. §§ 206.44(b) and 206.208(b)(1)(iii).
[44] 44 C.F.R. § 206.41(c), See description in Section VII of this chapter.
[45] Stafford Act § 502(c), 42 U.S.C. § 5192(c). The Post Katrina Emergency Management Reform Act of 2006 [hereinafter PKEMRA], Title VI of the Department of Homeland Security Appropriations Act, 2007, § 681, Pub. L. No. 109-295 (2006) added this requirement.
[46] Office of Response and Recovery Policy FP010-4, Pre-Disaster Emergency Declaration Requests (May 18, 2012) [hereinafter FP010-4]. ..

Protective Measures,[47] including DFA.[48] Assistance may be limited to DFA.[49]

If a state is immediately threatened with impact from an existing hurricane or typhoon, or by any other natural or man-made incident, FEMA's policies set forth that the state must meet the following criteria to be considered for a pre-disaster emergency declaration:

1. Hurricanes/Typhoons

- Comply with the regulation regarding requests for emergency declarations;

- Have at least a portion of the state be under a National Weather Service or Joint Typhoon Warning Center hurricane or typhoon watch or warning as a result of a major hurricane or typhoon (equivalent of a category 3, 4, or 5 on the Saffir-Simpson scale;[50]

- The governor has directed execution of the state's emergency plan;

- Have issued mandatory evacuation of three or more counties (or geographical area with population exceeding 100,000), or a declaration is necessary to provide DFA to meet critical emergency protection needs.

---

[47] Emergency Protective Measures are measures taken immediately to save lives and protect property and public health and safety, or lessen or avert the threat of a major disaster, called "Category B" measures. 44 C.F.R. §§ 206.201(b) and 206.225; PUBLIC ASSISTANCE POLICY DIGEST, FEMA 321, at 46 (Jan. 2008) [hereinafter PA DIGEST]. *See also* Chapter 4, *Response*, and Chapter 5, *Public Assistance*.

[48] 44 C.F.R. § 206.208; PA DIGEST, at 36. DFA is emergency work that a state requests that a federal agency directly carry out. As we discuss later in this publication,, FEMA may use OFAs to perform the work or to contract to have the work performed. *See* Chapter 4, *Response*.

[49] *See* FP010-4, at 3.

[50] The intent of FP010-4 is that only major hurricanes would be considered for a pre-landfall declaration, and the strong presumption is that a request for a minor hurricane would not be favorably considered. However, FEMA will consider a pre-landfall declaration request based on a minor hurricane if the state is able to clearly articulate that the event meets the other criteria in section VI.B of the policy (particularly that DFA is needed or that the specified mandatory evacuations orders have been issued).

---

2. Any Other Natural or Man-Made Disaster

- Comply with the regulation regarding requests for emergency declarations;[51]

- Be under a qualified federal agency determination that catastrophic incident is imminent;

- The governor has directed execution of the state emergency plan; and

- The state has issued mandatory evacuation of three or more counties (or geographical area with population exceeding 100,000), or FEMA determines that the scope of the potential incident could constitute a catastrophe, and the declaration is necessary to provide DFA to meet critical emergency protection needs.

C. Expedited Request for Major Disaster

The state's governor may send an abbreviated written request for a major disaster declaration for catastrophes of such unusual severity and magnitude that field damage assessments are not necessary to determine the need for supplementary federal assistance.[52] All declaration requests, including expedited requests, must comply with minimum information and certification requirements set forth in regulations.[53] FEMA has set out its procedures for processing an expedited major disaster declaration request in a separate policy.[54]

The purpose of such an expedited request is generally to obtain emergency work as quickly as possible. Depending upon the specific request of the governor, under this policy, FEMA may recommend emergency work, Category A (Debris Removal), and/or Category B (Emergency Protective Measures), which will generally be limited to DFA.[55] This policy also includes the possibility that FEMA may

---

[51] See FP010-4.
[52] Id. § 206.36(d).
[53] Id. §§ 206.35 and 206.36; Interim DAP 1004, Procedures for Processing Requests for Emergency or Expedited Major Disaster Declarations (2007) [hereinafter Interim DAP 1004], http://www.fema.gov/pdf/hazard/major_disaster_requests.pdf
[54] Interim DAP 1004.
[55] See Chapter 5, Public Assistance, for a more detailed discussion of these and other Categories.

recommend to the President that an emergency declaration is more appropriate for the particular event than an expedited major disaster declaration.[56]

Generally, FEMA will withhold a recommendation regarding any concurrent request for Individual Assistance (IA), other categories of Public Assistance (PA), and Hazard Mitigation Grant Program (HMGP) assistance until the results of Preliminary Damage Assessments (PDAs) are available. (This reference book discusses PA, IA, and Hazard Mitigation in chapters 5, 6, and 7, respectively.) Exceptions to this policy may occur:

- In the event of a catastrophic or high impact event when damage is empirically overwhelming, FEMA may, without PDAs,[57] recommend limited IA and HMGP assistance, in addition to PA (Categories A and/or B only); or

- In accordance with FEMA's policy[58] on pre-disaster declarations, FEMA may recommend Category B financial assistance, if the state submits an emergency declaration with such a request.

These limited exceptions notwithstanding, in the absence of PDAs, when a state makes an expedited request for a major disaster declaration, FEMA will only initially recommend limited assistance.

D. Emergency Involving Primary Federal Responsibility

The President may declare an emergency in the absence of a state's request for declaration for an event for which the United States exercises exclusive or preeminent responsibility under the Constitution or laws of the United States.[59] The President exercised this authority following the Alfred P. Murrah Federal Building bombing in Oklahoma City (1995), the September 11 Pentagon bombing (2001), and the Space Shuttle Columbia

---

[56] Interim DAP 1004.
[57] This chapter discusses PDAs, at III.
[58] Interim DAP 1001 which is the predecessor to FP 010-4, and is referenced in Interim DAP 1004.
[59] Stafford Act § 501(b), 42 U.S.C. § 5191(b).

---

disaster for both Texas and Louisiana (2003).[60] In each case, the federal government had primary responsibility because a fire and explosion was limited to federally-owned property. Before exercising this authority, the Stafford Act requires the President to consult with the governor of the affected state, if practicable.[61] This consultation is particularly important because of the potential involvement of state and local officials, such as local responders, and the implications for the state and local jurisdictions where the event is occurring, such as associated state/local impacts, costs, and associated cost share, if applicable. The four declarations that have been issued under this authority did not require a state cost share.

III. Preliminary Damage Assessment (PDA)

The PDA is a tool to quantify the magnitude of damage that an incident caused and the resulting unmet needs of individuals, businesses, the public sector, and the community. The state requests PDAs and teams consisting of federal, state, local, and tribal officials to conduct them. PDAs form the basis of a governor's request for declaration and are usually submitted with the governor's request for declaration.[62]

The state uses the information collected as its basis for its declaration request, and FEMA uses the data to document its recommendation to the President. FEMA has found that a combined state and federal or "joint" PDA, before the governor's request, is usually the most efficient use of resources.

When an incident occurs or is imminent, the state should determine whether its initial information is sufficient to request a joint PDA. Not every incident requires federal assistance. When the state official responsible for disaster operations determines the incident is beyond the state and local government capabilities to respond, however, the state

---

[60] Although the statutory authority was somewhat different, President Carter declared an emergency at Love Canal in New York State on August 7, 1978, and May 22, 1980. See STATE OF NEW YORK, DEPARTMENT OF HEALTH, LOVE CANAL, EMERGENCY DECLARATION AREA, DECISION ON HABITABILITY 3 and 5 (1988),
http://www.health.state.ny.us/environmental/investigations/love_canal/lcdec88.pdf.
[61] Stafford Act § 501(b), 42 U.S.C. § 5191(b).
[62] 44 C.F.R. § 206.33 describes the PDA process.

typically requests the appropriate FEMA RA to perform a joint FEMA-State PDA.[63]

Damage assessment teams, composed of at least one representative of the federal government and one representative of the particular state involved, carry out PDAs. The state should also include, if possible, a local government representative on its team who is familiar with the specific extent and location of damage. The state and FEMA may also ask other governmental representatives and voluntary relief organizations to participate in the PDA process, if needed. The state is responsible for coordinating state and local participation in the PDA and ensuring that the participants receive timely notification concerning the schedule. A FEMA official will brief team members on damage criteria, the kind of information to be collected for the particular incident, and reporting requirements.[64] When the PDA is completed, FEMA and the state discuss findings and reconcile any discrepancies. FEMA funds 75% of the cost of the PDAs, and the state pays 25% unless there is a determination that no declaration is appropriate, in which case FEMA and the state each pay its own costs. When there is a declaration, the state share is a part of its administrative costs.

FEMA may waive the requirement for a joint PDA when the incident is of such unusual severity and magnitude that field damage assessments are not necessary to determine whether supplemental federal assistance is appropriate[65] or when the FEMA RA, in consultation with the state, so determines. Even where the need for supplemental federal assistance is obvious, however, FEMA may request a damage assessment to evaluate unmet needs to be able to better manage the nature of its supplemental assistance. For example, if many disaster survivors are economically living below the federally determined poverty line, currently $22,050 for a family of four,[66] FEMA may seek assistance early from other federal

---

[63] Id. § 206.33(a). The state is expected to verify its initial information, and FEMA may decline a request to participate in a PDA under circumstances that realistically cannot result in an assessment that can support a request for a declaration.

[64] Id. § 206.33(b).

[65] See discussion at II. C. *Expedited Request for Major Disaster.*

[66] Department of Health and Human Services, Administration for Children and Families, 2011/2012. See http://liheap.ncat.org/profiles/povertytables/FY2011/popstate.htm.

agencies (OFAs), such as the Department of Housing and Urban Development (HUD) and the local public housing authority.

IV. Processing Requests for Declarations

The FEMA RA reviews the governor's request for a declaration and the joint PDAs,[67] and submits a report with a formal recommendation to the FEMA Administrator.[68] FEMA Headquarters (HQ) staff, that is, personnel from IA, PA, Hazard Mitigation (HM), and Office of Chief Counsel (OCC), review the governor's request and the Region's report. The Region and FEMA HQ independently review the governor's request and supporting documentation for compliance with the requirements in the Stafford Act and FEMA's regulations. The Administrator reviews the recommendations of the Region and FEMA HQ[69] and formulates FEMA's final recommendation to the President.[70]

A. Evaluation Factors for a Major Disaster or an Emergency Declaration

Under the Stafford Act, in order for the federal government to assist, an incident must be of such severity and magnitude that effective response is beyond the capabilities of the state and affected local governments.[71] Disaster assistance, however, is also part of the mission of many OFAs, including the Department of Health and Human Services, the Environmental Protection Agency, the U.S. Coast Guard (USCG), the SBA, and the U.S. Army Corps of Engineers (USACE).[72] Generally, FEMA will not recommend an emergency declaration when the authority to respond

---

[67] 44 C.F.R. § 206.48. No executive order delegated Stafford Act § 401 and 501, 42 U.S.C. § 5170 and 5191(a) from the President to any agency or department.
[68] 44 C.F.R. § 206.37(b).
[69] For example, evaluation factors include the amount of insurance available to cover losses, but there is no stated percentage of insurance coverage that will trigger or disallow either the IA or PA program. Similarly, there is no required minimum percentage of special needs population necessary to trigger program implementation.
[70] 44 C.F.R. § 206.37(c).
[71] Stafford Act §§ 401 and 501, 42 U.S.C. §§ 5170 and 5191.
[72] The USACE has authority and resources to carry out what is traditionally called "floodfighting," which includes, among other things, sandbagging at low places and at river edges to prevent flooding.

to an incident is within the existing statutory authority of another federal agency unless there are significant unmet needs that other federal assistance does not address and that the Stafford Act could address.[73]

Non-Stafford Act Event

In 2010, the federal government responded to the Deepwater Horizon Oil Spill in the Gulf of Mexico pursuant to the Oil Pollution Act and the National Contingency Plan. FEMA provided support through the USCG National Incident Commander but the President did not declare an emergency or major disaster under the Stafford Act.

In order to recommend an emergency to the President, FEMA evaluates whether emergency assistance under the Stafford Act is necessary "to supplement the State and local efforts to save lives, protect public health and safety, or lessen or avert the threat of a catastrophe."[74]

Under the statute and regulations, FEMA considers the following factors in reviewing a request for a major disaster declaration:[75]

- Whether the situation is of such severity and magnitude that it is beyond the capabilities of the state and local governments and supplemental assistance under the Stafford Act is necessary;[76]

- Whether the request states that federal assistance is necessary to supplement efforts and resources of state and local governments, disaster relief organizations, and insurance;

- Whether the state has made a request within 30 days of the occurrence of the incident unless the requestor has made a request for an extension within the 30-day time period;

- Whether the type of event is appropriate for a major disaster declaration (e.g., a natural event, fire, flood or explosion); if not,

---

[73] 44 C.F.R. § 206.37(d).
[74] Stafford Act § 502, 42 U.S.C. § 5192; 44 C.F.R. §§ 206.37(c)(2) and (d).
[75] Id. § 401, 42 U.S.C. § 5170; 44 C.F.R. §§ 206.48 and 206.37(c)(1).
[76] Id. § 401, 42 U.S.C. § 5170.

FEMA is likely to review the governor's request as an emergency declaration request;

- Whether the governor or acting governor, who should provide written evidence of authority to act for the governor, is requesting the declaration and not a lower level official;

- Whether there is confirmation that the governor has taken appropriate action under state law and directed execution of the state emergency plan;

- Whether the incident meets the per capita indicator for PA;[77]

- Whether there is information about how many residences have sustained major damage or have been destroyed;

- Whether the request contains preliminary estimates of the amount and severity of disaster damage and/or losses, including the impact of disaster damage on affected individuals and the public and private sectors;

- Whether there is a description of the nature and amount of available resources of the state and local governments and disaster relief organizations, such as, but not limited to, cots, food, clothing, and shelter facilities, that have or will be committed to the incident;

- Whether the request contains preliminary estimates of the types and amounts of supplemental federal disaster assistance needed;

- Whether there is an assessment of the extent and type of insurance in effect to cover losses (i.e., how many public facilities and homeowners have flood insurance, homeowner's insurance, and/or personal property insurance in effect);

- Whether there is assistance available from other federal programs and other sources (e.g., if federal-aid highway roads are among the damaged facilities, then the Federal Highway Administration is responsible for repairs);

- Whether there are imminent threats to public health and safety;

---

[77] 44 C.F.R. § 206.48(a)(1).

- Whether there is information regarding the recent disaster history in the state (i.e., the number and severity of disasters that the President has recently declared in the particular state);[78]

- Whether the state and affected local government have undertaken appropriate measures related to hazard mitigation (e.g., the state or tribe must have an approved hazard mitigation plan as a condition of receiving funds for PA Categories C through G and HMGP,[79] but FEMA does not normally consider other relevant mitigation measures to make this determination;

- Whether the governor has certified that the state and local government obligations and expenditures for the current incident will comply with all cost share requirements;

- If debris removal is requested, whether the request contains indemnification and hold harmless clauses; and if the governor is requesting debris removal on private property, whether there is an assurance of needed access authorizations beforehand; and

- If there is a specific request for DFA, whether the necessary certifications are present, including hold harmless, rights of way, payment of non-federal cost share, and coordination.[80]

FEMA will recommend the issuance of a major disaster declaration if it finds the nature and level of impacts warrant supplemental assistance under the Stafford Act from either the PA program or the IA program, or both.[81] Given that the factors do not set forth clear "black and white" tests or bases, the FEMA Administrator's final agency recommendation for a declaration may not always reflect the original Regional Administrator's recommendation. This disparity can be the result of additional realities at play, including an interest in national consistency in the application of these factors as well as other policy considerations. Sometimes FEMA

---

[78] This factor is most likely to be significant if other declared disasters in the same area have already caused damage, which may have been severe, leaving local and state governments' assets depleted.

[79] 44 C.F.R. §§ 201.4 and 201.7.

[80] 44 C.F.R. § 206.208.

[81] Since FEMA provides the HMGP as a percentage of IA and PA funds under the President's major disaster declaration, the HMGP alone is not a basis for recommending a declaration. See Stafford Act §§322(e) and 404(a), 42 U.S.C. §§5165(e) and 5170c(a).

---

receives additional information after the region has submitted its recommendation to HQ that also may alter the outcome.

B. Evaluation Factors - Public Assistance (PA) Program

FEMA must consider six primary factors in evaluating the need for PA.[82] Cost, as outlined in this section, is a primary factor, since federal disaster assistance is contingent on a finding that state and local resources are inadequate and require supplemental assistance under the Stafford Act. FEMA estimates the per capita impact of the disaster by dividing the total estimated cost of eligible federal and non-federal assistance under the Stafford Act by the statewide population.[83] That figure is then compared to a regulatory figure as an indicator that a disaster is of such size that it might warrant federal assistance. FEMA annually adjusts the regulatory state per capita indicator based on the Consumer Price Index.[84] For disasters occurring during fiscal year[85] 2013, the per capita indicator is $1.37.[86]

FEMA also has established a minimum threshold of $1 million in total estimated public assistance disaster damage because FEMA expects that all states, regardless of size, can cover this level of damage using state resources.[87] The Stafford Act prohibits preventing a geographical area from receiving assistance based solely on "an arithmetic formula or sliding scale based on income or population."[88] Thus, in total, FEMA considers the following factors:[89]

---

[82] 44 C.F.R. § 206.48(a)(1)-(6). This list of evaluation factors is essentially those factors which illuminate the first two factors for determining whether FEMA should recommend a disaster declaration to the President.

[83] As of July 2011, FEMA uses 2010 Census population data.

[84] See http://www.bls.gov/cpi/cpifaq.htm.

[85] The federal fiscal year begins on October 1st of the previous year and extends to September 30th of the named year.

[86] 77 Fed. Reg. 61423 (Oct. 9, 2012) FEMA has also established a county per capita indicator which for FY 2013 is $3.39. See 77 Fed. Reg. 61011 (Oct. 5, 2012). FEMA publishes the thresholds annually in the *Federal Register* and on the FEMA Declaration Unit website. http://on.fema.net/programs/orr_programs/declarations/Pages/default.aspx.

[87] 44 C.F.R. § 206.48(a)(1).

[88] Stafford Act § 320, 42 U.S.C. § 5163.

[89] 44 C.F.R. § 206.48(a).

1. The estimated costs of assistance;

2. Localized impacts at county, city, and tribal government levels;

3. Insurance coverage in force;

4. Hazard mitigation measures that contributed to the reduction of damages;

5. Recent multiple disasters within the prior 12 months at the state and local level; and

6. Available assistance programs of OFAs.

In addition to these primary factors, FEMA may consider other relevant factors.[90]Localized Impact Example

2010 Arizona Flooding Disaster (FEMA-1950-DR-AZ)
Declaration Date: December 21, 2010
Incident: Severe Storms and Flooding

In 2010, the President signed a declaration providing assistance to the isolated Havasupai Tribe in the Grand Canyon, which had been impacted by flooding. Even though the state per capita indicator was well under $1.30, the President authorized a declaration for PA where the per capita impact on the tribe was over $3,000.

C. Evaluation Factors – Individual Assistance (IA) Program

FEMA considers the following factors in evaluating the need for the IA program:[91]

1. Concentration of damage, such as a tornado that destroys an entire town;

2. Trauma;

3. Presence of particular populations, such as persons with low income;

4. Voluntary agency assistance availability;

---

[90] Id.
[91] Id. § 206.48(b)(1)-(6).

5. Insurance coverage; and

6. Average amount of individual assistance provided by small, medium, and large states in prior disasters.

Similar to the process of evaluating the level of need for public assistance, and in order to assess whether the event is beyond state and local capabilities to warrant supplemental individual assistance, a primary consideration is the level and anticipated cost of significant damage to homes (see factor 6).

FEMA regulations contain a chart depicting the average amount of assistance provided from July 1994 to July 1999, including the average number of homes identified as having received major damage or having been destroyed, and the average amount of IA provided by size of state.[92] Although these numbers may be indicative of when supplemental individual assistance is appropriate, the numbers are not a required minimum threshold, and, based on other factors, FEMA may recommend such assistance when fewer homes have major damage or more are destroyed than are shown on the chart.

Localized Impact Example

2007 Kansas Tornado Disaster (FEMA-1699-DR-KS) Declaration Date: May 6, 2007

Incident: Severe Storms, Tornadoes, and Flooding

In 2007, a tornado destroyed the community of Greensburg, Kansas, leaving only one building standing. The nearest rental housing was about 100 miles away. In these circumstances, a major disaster was declared even though the number of houses destroyed was less than the average from other disasters.

---

[92] Id. § 206.48(b)(6).

V. Presidential Action on the State Request for Declaration

When a state requests a major disaster declaration, the President may issue either a major disaster or an emergency declaration, or deny the governor's request.[93] When a state requests an emergency declaration, however, the President may only grant the emergency declaration or deny it.[94] The rationale for this result is that although all assistance available under an emergency declaration is available under a major declaration, the reverse is not true. Thus, it is not appropriate for the federal government to determine unilaterally the state's broader potential involvement and commitment than the governor did in the request.[95] If the state requests both an emergency and a major disaster declaration, FEMA will make a recommendation to the President for either a major disaster or an emergency. FEMA promptly notifies the governor in writing as soon as the President grants or denies the declaration request. The agency publishes presidential declarations in the *Federal Register*.

VI. The Declaration

A presidential declaration of an emergency or major disaster generally contains the following elements.

A. Description of the Incident Type

The incident type is such things as tornado, hurricane, flooding, or earthquake.[96] An event that is likely to result in a declaration under the

---

[93] To the extent the Administrator's recommendations to the President in connection with disaster declarations are pre-decisional and deliberate in nature, they are exempt from disclosure, in part or in full, pursuant to the Freedom of Information Act, 5 U.S.C. 552(b)(5). If this information were to be released, it would have a chilling effect in the future for the necessary discussions of FEMA officials to be completely frank, as well as cause unnecessary confusion to the public.

[94] 44 C.F.R. § 206.38.

[95] Similarly, FEMA will not designate areas of the state or types of assistance beyond those the governor requests.

[96] Incident is defined as any condition that meets the definition of major disaster or emergency that causes damage or hardship that may result in a Presidential declaration. 44 C.F.R. § 206.32(e).

Stafford Act generally consists of a single event or storm system.[97] FEMA, generally, does not consider storms that result from a pattern, pressure, or troughs, to be a single event for Stafford Act purposes.

Fire, Flood, or Explosion Regardless of Cause

A major disaster is defined as "any natural catastrophe ... or, regardless of cause, any fire, flood, or explosion." Stafford Act §102(2), 42 U.S.C. § 5122(2). The President's declaration for the 2001 New York World Trade Center Terrorist Attack (FEMA-1391-DR-NY) was for fires and explosions.

Stafford Act assistance will not be approved unless the damage or hardship to be alleviated resulted from the disaster-causing incident.[98] Damage type and incident type are two separate concepts, and issues may arise regarding whether damages can be related back to the declared incident. In some instances it may be necessary to expand the incident type, which is described in more detail in section VII. D of this chapter.

Flood to Fire

1997 North Dakota Red River Flooding Disaster (FEMA-1174-DR-ND)

The declaration was originally for damages resulting from "severe flooding, severe winter storms, heavy spring rain, rapid snowmelt, high winds, ice jams, and ground saturation due to high water tables..." a particularly detailed incident description. The flooding triggered a massive fire in downtown Grand Forks. The incident type was expanded to include damage resulting from fires.

---

[97] See Guide for Federal Coordinating Officers Post Declaration Actions (2011) [hereinafter FCO Guide]. See also Elizabeth Zimmerman, Memorandum on Governor's Request, Regional Summary, Analysis, and Recommendation and Stafford Act Declarable Event (Oct. 1, 2009).
[98] 44 C.F.R. § 206.32(f).

> ### Typhoon Incident Included Explosion and Fire
>
> ### 2002 Guam Super Typhoon Pongsona Disaster (FEMA-1446-DR-GU)
>
> The declaration was for damages resulting from Super Typhoon Pongsona. While the Super Typhoon raged, an explosion and fire erupted at commercial port tank farm in Guam due to a buildup of static electricity caused by extremely high winds rushing through the ventilation system. FEMA provided direct and financial assistance for emergency assistance under the declaration for the explosion and fire that arose from the typhoon without amending the incident type.

In contrast, the following is an example of an extremely narrow incident type.

> ### Specific Incident Designation
>
> ### 2012 Colorado Wildfires (FEMA-4067-DR-CO)
> **Declaration Date**: June 28, 2012
>
> This disaster was declared for the High Park and Waldo Canyon wildfires. While they had already been designated for Fire Management Assistance Grants, the fires reached the severity and magnitude to warrant a major disaster declaration. As the incident was restricted to these two named fires, damage related to other wildfires occurring in Colorado was not eligible for assistance.

B. The Incident Period

The incident period is the time interval during which the incident occurs.[99] In addition, work undertaken in anticipation of the incident is eligible for Stafford Act assistance.[100] As provided for in Paragraph 1 of the standard FSA terms, this means: "reasonable expenses that were incurred in anticipation of *and immediately preceding* such event may be eligible" (emphasis added). FEMA generally interprets this to be a narrow

---

[99] 44 C.F.R. § 206.32(f).
[100] Stafford Act § 424; 42 U.S.C. § 5189b.

time frame. Whether 24, 48, or 72 hours or more, the further out in time, the less likely that FEMA can directly tie activities to the declared disaster in question rather than for seasonal or general preparedness for events that may occur at some time in the future. There is a distinction between general preparedness and activities specifically undertaken in anticipation of and immediately before an event.

An open or "continuing" incident period is not necessary to capture damage that may occur in the future so long as the damage results from the declared incident. For example, a flood event need not have an open incident period in order to capture rising flood waters that will not crest for some days or weeks. The damage that might occur when the floodwaters crest would still result from the declared flooding incident and therefore need not be accounted for and need not occur during the incident period. Although not legally necessary, FEMA's practice in flooding events is initially to indicate the incident period as "continuing" where, for example, flooding is moving downstream to an area and flood waters continue to rise there after the storm ends. Once flood levels peak, FEMA closes the incident period by amending the original declaration and the FSA. Most events, however, identify the close of the incident period in the original declaration and the FSA.

An Incident Period of Long Duration
1990 Hawaii Disaster for lava flow (FEMA-DR-864-DR-HI)
Declaration Date: May 18, 1990
Incident: Lava Flow, Kilauea Volcano
Incident Period: January 24, 1983, to January 27, 1997 (14 years for the lava flow)

C. Designation of the Affected Geographical Areas

The affected geographical areas are those eligible for Stafford Act assistance, such as counties, parishes, or tribal lands. The declaration may designate any area, typically a county, tribal land, independent city, or parish that sustained sufficient damage from an eligible event. The declaration designates each area by type of assistance; these areas are generally those based on eligible damage amounts. In addition to

---

considering localized impacts when reviewing whether to recommend a declaration,[101] for the PA program, FEMA also uses a county per capita indicator to determine whether the impact of a disaster on a county is of sufficient magnitude that it might warrant inclusion of the county in the PA program for that disaster.[102] There is no similar indicator at the county level for the IA program, but FEMA will consider the concentration of damage in a given area.[103] For the HMGP, the governor may request it for particular counties or statewide, regardless of where damage may have occurred. After the issuance of the presidential declaration, new information about damage in additional areas may become available, and FEMA may designate additional areas to the original declaration. FEMA will not, however, designate areas of the state or types of assistance beyond those that the governor requests.

There is no statutory or regulatory requirement that a designated geographic area encompass an entire local government jurisdiction. Areas eligible for assistance may be more narrowly or specifically designated. Declarations are typically, however, designated on a county basis.

Sub Area Designation

2007 California Wildfires Disaster (FEMA-1731-DR-CA)
Declaration Date: October 24, 2007

The original declaration was for wildfires for certain designated counties. The declaration was amended to expand the incident type to include flooding, mud flows, and debris flows directly related to the wildfires. The expanded incident type was limited to those areas within the previously designated counties specifically determined by the FCO to be damaged or adversely affected as a direct result of the compromised watershed conditions and fire-generated debris caused by the wildfires.

---

[101] 44 C.F.R. § 206.48(a)(2).
[102] 77 Fed. Reg. 61011(Oct 5, 2012).
[103] Id. § 206.48(b)(1).

D. Designation of Stafford Act Programs Available for Assistance and the Federal-State Cost Share

FEMA's regulations provide that the Assistant Administrator for the Disaster Assistance Directorate[104] has the authority to determine and designate:

- The types of assistance to be made available initially;[105]
- The areas initially eligible for assistance;[106] and
- Both area and program add-ons after the initial declaration.[107]

In practice, the President initially determines and includes in his declaration the types of Stafford Act assistance to be made available, applicable cost shares, and the geographical areas to be designated. A declaration may be for limited assistance within the major assistance programs.[108] PA may, for example, be designated in its entirety, limited to PA Emergency Work,[109] or designated in stages: first Emergency Work and then Permanent Repair Work.[110] Following the President's declaration, the governor or governor's authorized representative (GAR) may request additional areas or types of assistance[111] for which the relevant RA may provide a recommendation. Pursuant to FEMA regulation, the Office of Response and Recovery may approve additional areas and types of assistance.[112] As with PA, there may also be limited designations of IA programs.

Requests for additional areas or types of assistance after a declaration has been issued must be submitted within 30 days from the termination date of the incident, or 30 days after the declaration, whichever is later. The

---

[104] As a result of reorganization, this position no longer exists, and the authority is now with the Deputy Associate Administrator for the Office of Response and Recovery.
[105] 44 C.F.R. § 206.40(a).
[106] Id. § 206.40(b).
[107] Id. § 206.40(c).
[108] 44 C.F.R. § 206.40(a).
[109] Stafford Act § 403 and 502, 42 U.S.C. § 5170(b) and § 5192.
[110] Id. § 406, 42 U.S.C. § 5172.
[111] 44 C.F.R. § 206.40(c).
[112] Id. § 206.40(b).

30-day period may be extended provided that a written request is made during this 30-day period.[113]

2006 Hawaii Earthquake Disaster (FEMA-1664-DR-HI)

Declaration Date: October 17, 2006

Maui County declared for IA limited to DUA. DUA was then further limited to the communities of Kaupo, Kipahulu, and Hana (already designated for PA, including DFA).

2007 California Severe Freeze Disaster (FEMA-1689-DR-CA)

Declaration Date: March 13, 2007

Assistance Designated: DUA and Food Commodities in the designated areas and any other forms of assistance under the Stafford Act deemed appropriate. Amendment No. 1 authorized both DUA and Food Commodities for Kings, Madera, and Merced Counties; DUA only for Stanislaus County; and HMGP statewide.

E. Designation of the Federal Coordinating Officer (FCO)

The Stafford Act requires the designation of an FCO immediately upon declaration.[114] Current practice is for FEMA to recommend an FCO to the President, who then designates the FCO in the declaration. The FCO is the lead federal official at the incident site and is responsible for assuring that federal assistance is provided in accordance with the declaration, laws, regulations, and the FSA.[115] The FCO makes an initial appraisal of types of relief most urgently needed, establishes necessary field offices, and

---

[113] 44 C.F.R. § 206.40(d).

[114] Id. § 302(a), 42 U.S.C. § 5143(a).

[115] 44 C.F.R. § 206.41(a). *See also* National Response Framework at 67 (2008); FEMA Directive FD 008-1, Section 8 K (2008). For a complete reference to all of the statutory and regulatory authorities of FCOs, see the FEMA Office of Chief Counsel booklet, *Federal Coordinating Officers Statutory and Regulatory Authority*, issued Dec. 18, 2010.

coordinates the relief activities of state and local governments, and non-profit and relief organizations.[116]

F. Delegation of Authority to Regional Administrators (RA)

Pursuant to the Homeland Security Act, FEMA is divided into 10 regional offices, each headed by a Regional Administrator (RA).[117] Appointed by the FEMA Administrator, in consultation with state, local and tribal government officials in that region, the appointee must be a member of the Senior Executive Service (SES).[118] RAs report directly to the Administrator and have statutory responsibilities analogous to the Administrator's, but at the regional level.[119] By regulation, the RA is vested with the authority of the Disaster Recovery Manager (DRM).[120]

In addition to their inherent responsibilities, the RAs have been delegated a number of the Administrator's authorities over the years.[121] These delegations were found in scattered memoranda and instructions.[122] In a major effort to consolidate these delegated authorities into a single comprehensive document, the Administrator issued FEMA Delegation of Authority 0160-1, *Delegation of Authority to the Regional Administrators*, on February 6, 2012, superseding the earlier delegations.[123]

The delegated authorities to the RAs are set forth in a relatively brief delegation and then extensively delineated in the supporting Appendices A-H. The primary grants of authority, however, are contained in

---

[116] Stafford Act § 302(b), 42 U.S.C. § 5143(b), 44 C.F.R. § 206.2(a)(11).
[117] 6 USC § 317.
[118] Id.
[119] Id. and 6 U.S.C. § 314
[120] 44 CFR § 206.2(a)(21).
[121] See Memorandum from the Administrator re: Delegation of Authority (2008); Memorandum from the Administrator re: Delegating Authorities to Regional Administrators (2009); FEMA Instruction No. 1030.2, chg. 3, Delegations of Authority for Personnel Administration (2005); and Memorandum from the FEMA Administrator re: Delegation of Authority to Certain Officers to Approve Gifts of Travel Offered by Non-Federal Entities (2009);
[122] Id.
[123] Delegation of Authority to Regional Administrators, FDA 01601 (2012). FDA 0160-1, p.A-4, §10. http://on.fema.net/employee_tools/forms/Documents/FDA0160-1.pdf. The earlier documents are superseded only as applicable to RAs; delegations within the documents to other officials are unaffected.

Appendices A-D. The remaining appendices essentially list the sources of the authorities delegated.

Specifically, Appendix A addresses the delegation of management, financial, gift, personnel, travel, public and congressional affairs, Freedom of Information Act, and tribal coordination authorities.[124] Appendix B deals with Response and Recovery, delegating specific authorities regarding Pre-Declaration activities, Title III, Title IV, Title V, and Title VI in the Stafford Act.[125] Appendix C is dedicated to Federal Insurance and Mitigation authorities.[126] These include authorities related to national flood insurance, environmental and historic preservation, dam safety, flood hazards, and earthquake hazards reduction.[127] Appendix D delegates authorities under an array of preparedness-related statutes, executive orders, regulations, and grant programs.[128] These include, among others, the National Hurricane Program, National Terrorism Alert System Agency Implementation, destruction of stockpiled lethal chemical agents and munitions, and radiological emergency preparedness at commercial nuclear power plants.[129]

The delegated authorities are limited to use within the RA's region and to regional assets, whether equipment or personnel.[130] All delegations may be redelgated by the RA unless otherwise prohibited by law, executive order, regulation, or the terms of the delegation itself.[131] There are general and specific reservations and limitations spread throughout the delegation and appendices. The Administrator has directed that going forward, FEMA directives, instructions, memoranda, and other internal issuances regarding delegations to RAs should be designated as interim pending their incorporation into this delegation.[132] The Chief Counsel is charged with an agency-wide annual review of the delegation and, as

---

[124] Id. at pp. A-7 through A-14.
[125] Id. at pp. B-1 through B-9.
[126] Id. at C-1 through C-7.
[127] Id.
[128] Id. at D-1 through D-7.
[129] Id.
[130] Id. At p. A-1, 2 § 3.
[131] Id. at p. A-3, §3.
[132] Id. at p. A-5, §11.

necessary, incorporating any changes and submitting the updated document for the Administrator's signature.[133]

G. Delegation of Authority to the Disaster Recovery Manager (DRM)

The RA designates a DRM to exercise the Administrator's authority in a major disaster or emergency,[134] including expenditure authority from the DRF.[135] In delegating DRM authority, the RA has broad discretion in determining which authorities the DRM may perform, may hold back certain authorities, sets conditions on the exercise of certain authorities, and communicates management expectations. Normally, for a declared emergency or disaster, the RA designates the FCO as the DRM. Following the designation as the DRM and delegation of authority, the FCO possesses not only the independent authority to "coordinate" disaster relief, but also the RA's authority to expend funds from the DRF, and thus is able to approve public assistance, individual assistance, and hazard mitigation, and issue "mission assignments" to OFAs.[136]

The regulations do not prevent other officials from receiving DRM authority.[137] Other lower level employees may be provided DRM authority by the RA or FCO if the FCO has been provided the authority to redelegate DRM authority. For example, the Infrastructure Branch Director at the Joint Field Office (JFO) may be provided DRM authority for PA, and the Human Services Branch Director may be provided DRM authority for IA. In addition, the RA may designate a Federal Disaster Recovery Coordinator as the DRM in addition to, or independent of, the FCO (see discussion in section H). When a JFO closes, DRM authority is usually provided to a staff member at the Regional Office for closeout purposes (typically, the Response or Recovery Division Director).

---

[133] Id.

[134] Id. § 206.41(b); FEMA Directive FD 008-1, Section VIII L (2008); FEMA Instruction 8600.4, § 7, *Roles and Responsibilities of the Disaster Recovery Manager* (Oct. 10, 1986) [hereinafter FEMA Instruction 8600.4].

[135] The DRF is the FEMA appropriation that funds Major Disaster and Emergency Declarations, Fire Management Grants, the Disaster Readiness and Support (DRS) account, and the Surge accounts. *See* Chapter 2, *Readiness and Pre-Declaration Activities*, for a discussion of the DRS and Surge accounts. DRM authority is an inherently governmental function that cannot be exercised by a contract employee.

[136] *See* Chapter 4, *Response*, for a discussion of mission assignments.

[137] 44 C.F.R. § 206.41(b).

H. Delegation of Authority to the Federal Disaster Recovery Coordinator (FDRC)

The focus of the Federal Disaster Recovery Coordinator (FDRC) is on long-term recovery.[138] The concept of the FDRC was introduced by the National Disaster Recovery Framework (NDRF).[139] Facilitating disaster recovery coordination and collaboration between federal, tribal, state, and local governments; the private sector; and voluntary, faith-based, and community organizations is a primary FDRC responsibility.[140] The FDRC becomes a juncture for incorporating recovery and mitigation considerations into the early decision making processes of a large-scale disaster or catastrophic incident, taking on the role of a deputy to the FCO in these areas.[141]

The FDRC, unlike the FCO, is not a statutorily required appointment when a declaration is made and has no inherent powers upon appointment. The official must be delegated whatever authorities are deemed necessary to the particular disaster or incident. FDRC authority is derived from at least two sources: the statutory authority granted to the FCO under the Stafford Act[142] and the authority of the DRM established by federal regulations.[143] Additional authorities found in the Post-Katrina Emergency Management Reform Act (PKEMRA) may also be delegated at the Administrator's discretion (e.g., recovery and mitigation actions and administration of grant programs).[144]

The FDRC's reporting chain and scope of authorities is entirely a policy matter, provided the FDRC acts within the scope of the Administrator's and/or RA's delegated authorities for disaster recovery. As described in the NDRF, the FDRC may serve, for example, as one of the FCO's deputies until the FCO is demobilized. If the FCO is demobilized and a continued need for an FDRC is identified, the RA may appoint the FDRC to continue

---

[138] National Disaster Recovery Framework 29 (2011); available at http://www.fema.gov/pdf/recoveryframework/ndrf.pdf.
[139] Id. at 1.
[140] Id. at 29.
[141] Id.
[142] 42 U.S.C. §5143
[143] 44 C.F.R. §206.41(b)
[144] 6 U.S.C. §314

coordinating disaster recovery, including approving expenditures from the DRF, provided the RA delegates DRM authority to the FDRC.

VII. FEMA-State Agreement (FSA)

The FSA[145] or FEMA-Tribe Agreement (FTA)[146] states the understandings, commitments, and conditions under which FEMA will provide and coordinate federal disaster assistance. The governor or tribal leader and the RA, or designee, sign the agreement that imposes legally enforceable obligations on FEMA, the state, local governments, tribes, and/or private non-profit organizations.[147]

The FSA contains the following terms and conditions:

- The incident period;

- Areas designated;

- The type and extent of federal assistance the declaration is making available;

- The cost sharing provisions;

- FEMA and state responsibilities, including the grant management regulations in 44 C.F.R. Part 13;

- The grant conditions, including:

    o 2 C.F.R. Part 215, Uniform Administrative Requirements for Grants and Agreements with Institutions of Higher Education, Hospitals, and Other Non-Profit Organizations, OMB Circular A-110;

    o 2 C.F.R. Part 220, Cost Principles for Educational Institutions, OMB Circular A- 21;

---

[145] All references to the FSA apply equally to FTAs when an Indian tribal government has such an agreement as a direct grantee.
[146] 44 C.F.R. § 206.201(e) and 206.431. Although a tribe cannot directly request a declaration, once the state has received a declaration, tribes within designated geographic designations may act as grantee for PA and/or HMGP Stafford Act assistance.
[147] 44 C.F.R. § 206.44.

- 2 C.F.R. Part 225, Cost Principles for State and Local Governments, OMB Circular A-87;

- 2 C.F.R. Part 230, Cost Principles for Non-Profit Organizations, OMB Circular A-122;

- 45 C.F.R. Part 74, Appendix E, Principles for Determining Costs Applicable to Research and Development Under Grants and Contracts With Hospitals;

- 48 C.F.R. section 31.2, Federal Acquisition Regulation, Contracts with Commercial Organizations;

- OMB Circular A-133, Audits of States, Local Governments, and Non-Profit Organizations;

- 31 C.F.R. section 205.6, Funding Techniques; and

- Certifications agreeing to maintaining a Drug-Free Workplace, 44 C.F.R. Part 17, and New Restrictions on Lobbying, 44 C.F.R. Part 18.

- The governor's (or tribe's) authorized representative (GAR), who is the corresponding state official to the federal DRM and who the governor authorizes to sign all needed documents in order to receive federal assistance, including subgrants; and

- Any special terms and conditions consistent with the declaration, such as the fact that assistance is contingent upon having an approved mitigation plan.

The standard FSA and FTA templates may not be altered or amended in the field. States and tribal governments frequently request changes in standard terms, but neither agreement is open to negotiation. The Office of Chief Counsel in FEMA headquarters in Washington must review and recommend appropriate action concerning any request to change or alter a provision in the FSA or FTA.

FEMA may not provide funding or DFA through a mission assignment to any grantee or other recipient until the state or the tribe signs the FSA or FTA, except where it is necessary to provide essential emergency services or housing assistance under the Individual and Households Program.[148] An additional implication for a state or a federally-recognized tribe is that if either does not have an approved mitigation plan, it may decide not to sign the FSA or FTA until it is within 30 days of having an approved mitigation plan so as not to jeopardize its eligibility for certain categories of FEMA's PA program (Categories C through G), (see Chapter 5, *Public Assistance*, for a discussion of these categories) and the HMGP (see Chapter 7, *Hazard Mitigation*, for a discussion of mitigation issues).

A. State Coordinating Officer (SCO)

After a declaration, the President will request the specific governor to designate an SCO to coordinate state and local disaster assistance efforts with those of the FCO who is acting for the federal government.[149] Sometimes, the governor indicates the SCO in his or her request for a declaration. Typically, the SCO and the FCO sit near one another at the Joint Field Office and consult frequently on virtually all disaster-related issues affecting state and local governments. See next section for a discussion of the duties of the other state official, the governor's (or tribe's) authorized representative[150] (GAR) or (TAR), which may be the same person as the SCO and the corresponding state official to the federal DRM.

B. Governor's Authorized Representative (GAR)

In the FSA, the governor will designate a GAR, who will be empowered to execute all necessary documents for disaster assistance on behalf of the state.[151] The FSA will also include designations of one or more alternate GARs. While the GAR is generally empowered to act on behalf of the governor, there are a number of actions that, under the Stafford Act or FEMA regulations, must be carried out by the governor. Table 1 outlines which Stafford Act declaration and post-declaration actions must be carried out by the governor and which may be performed by the GAR.

---

[148] Id. § 206.44(a).
[149] Stafford Act § 302(c), 42 U.S.C. § 5143(c).
[150] 44 C.F.R. § 206.41(d).
[151] 44 C.F.R. §206.2(a)(13).

Table 1: Governor/GAR Declaration Authorities

	Stafford Act Declaration Action Authorities	
Action	**Governor**	**Governor's Authorized Representative (Y/N)**
Request a declaration	§401 and §501 of the Stafford Act	No, governor only per §401 and §501 of the Stafford Act
Request an extension of time to request a declarations	44 CFR 206.35(a) & 44 CFR 206.36(a)	No, governor only per 44 CFR 206.35(a) and 44 CFR 206.36(a)
Execute the FSA	44 CFR 206.44(a)	No, governor only under 44 CFR 206.44(a)
Execute amendments to the FSA	44 CFR 206.44(a)	Yes, per 44 CFR 206.44(c) *except for amendments to Exhibit A: State Certification Officers*, see 44 CFR 206.41(c) and (d)
Request add-on assistance and areas	44 CFR 206.40(c)	Yes, per 44 CFR 206.40(c)
Request an extension of time to request add-on assistance and areas	44 CFR 206.40(d)	Yes, per 44 CFR 206.40(d)
Request an adjustment of the cost share	44 CFR 206.47 provides the circumstances under which FEMA may recommend a PA cost share adjustment, without specifying requirements for a state cost share adjustment request.	Yes. 44 CFR 206.47 provides the circumstances under which FEMA may recommend a PA cost share adjustment, without specifying requirements for a state cost share adjustment request.

Action	Governor	Governor's Authorized Representative (Y/N)
Request amendment of (close, expand, reopen, etc.) the incident period	There is no statute or regulation on requests to amend a declaration's incident period; however, 44 CFR 206.44(c) refers to amendments to the FSA to include *inter alia* amending the incident period. Such modification would be triggered by an amendment to the declaration.	Yes. There is no statute or regulation on requests to amend a declaration's incident period; however, 44 CFR 206.44(c) refers to amendments to the FSA to include *inter alia* amending the incident period. Such modification would be triggered by an amendment to the declaration.
Request amendment of the incident type	There is no statute or regulation on requests to amend a declaration's incident type; however, 44 CFR 206.44(b) and (c) refer to the terms and conditions of the FSA, including the incident and modifications to those terms. Such modification would be triggered by an amendment to the declaration.	Yes. There is no statute or regulation regarding requests to amend a declaration's incident type; however, 44 CFR 206.44(b) and (c) refer to the terms and conditions of the FSA, including the incident, and modifications to those terms. Such modification would be triggered by an amendment to the declaration.
Request a state share loan	44 CFR 206.45(a)	No, governor only per 44 CFR 206.45(a)
Appeal: major disaster or emergency declarations	44 CFR 206.46(a)	No, governor only per 44 CFR 206.46(a)
Appeal: partial denial of add-on assistance or areas requested	44 CFR 206.46(b)	Yes, 44 CFR 206.46(b)
Appeal: denial of advance of state share	44 CFR 206.46(c)	No, governor only under 44 CFR 206.46(c)

C. Amending the Declaration and the FSA

The Declarations Unit in FEMA HQ handles all amendments to the declaration. Amendments to the FSA generally follow amendments to the declaration but not always.[152] The governor or the GAR or Alternate GAR (AGAR) may sign amendments to the FSA on behalf of the state, except for an amendment naming a new GAR or AGAR. The governor must sign the latter because only the governor has the authority to sign the delegation appointing a new GAR to the position. Thus, in addition to the governor, the GAR can request an extension of the incident period, an amendment to the cost share, and the addition of an incident type.

Use of the correct format and contents of amendments to the FSA and the declaration is critical in order to avoid inadvertent substantive changes to the original agreement. For example, when the state proposes, and FEMA agrees, to add new geographic areas such as counties, parishes or tribal lands, to the original declaration, FEMA personnel restate all of the disaster areas to avoid inadvertently eliminating the eligibility of the areas previously declared in the amendment. The FEMA Declarations Unit website contains FSA amendment templates.[153]

D. Common Amendments to the Declaration and the FSA

1. Requests for Additional Programs, and Additional Eligible Areas

The governor or the GAR may request additional Stafford Act programs or the addition of areas based on verified damage assessments of unmet needs beyond state and local capabilities.[154] The state must submit

---

[152] The declaration names the FCO; however, the FCO is not named in the FSA and therefore does not need to be amended when an FCO's appointment is terminated and another person is appointed. The GAR is not appointed in the declaration but is appointed in the FSA (Attachment A) by the governor. Changes to the GAR appointment are reflected in the FSA but not the declaration.

[153] http://on.fema.net/programs/orr_programs/declarations/Pages/default.aspx.

[154] 44 C.F.R. § 206.40(c).

requests within 30 days from the termination date of the incident, or 30 days after the declaration, whichever is later.[155]

2. Amending the Incident Period

The declaration and the FSA establish the incident period based on official information which the appropriate federal agency provides, such as, the National Weather Service (NWS) for a weather-related event or the United States Geological Survey (USGS) for an earthquake.

When the effects of the incident are ongoing, the initial declaration and the FSA may state that the incident period is "continuing." If so, the FCO is responsible for monitoring and evaluating weather conditions to determine when to recommend closing the incident period. FEMA will consult with the state and establish the closing date in an amendment to the FSA and the declaration and publish the amended date in the Federal Register.[156] If there is sufficient justification based on official data, FEMA may reopen the incident period. Requests to reopen an incident period, or to include new damage under an existing declaration in which the incident period is still open, can be controversial. In either case, FEMA bases its determination on whether a meteorologically-connected event, that is, one that is part of the same storm system, caused the subsequent damage.[157] The NWS has previously explained to FEMA that a discrete weather system will generally affect the same geographic area for a period of no more than two or three days, whereas broader meteorological phenomena, such as weather patterns, troughs, and pressures, might result in multiple storm systems over a longer period of time, from days to weeks.

---

[155] Id. § 206.40(d).
[156] Id. § 206.44(c).
[157] *FCO Guide* states that "There must be a finding that the events are connected meteorologically (same storm system), damage from the new event is of the severity and magnitude that warrants a separate declaration, the same areas are impacted again, and there are three days or less between storms."

Understanding Storm Events

For example, a series of severe storms may impact an area over three successive days resulting in tornadoes, heavy rain, and flooding. If the NWS determines that these storms were part of the same meteorological system, then the storms may be combined into one disaster declaration. The declaration may be initially made with a "continuing" incident period.

Ten days later another storm system in the same area causes additional damage, and the state requests that FEMA cover the new damage under the existing declaration. Without further analysis, the existing declaration cannot simply include the new damage where the incident period is still open or "continuing," nor could new damage reopen a closed incident period. FEMA must determine whether the new storm

system causing damage was a continuation of the initial event, or a separate, unrelated event. Given that the storm conditions occurred 10 days apart, it is extremely unlikely that the later storm system was part of the same meteorological system. If the determination is that the second storm is a separate event, the state must request and qualify for a new declaration based solely on the damage from the new event

3. Request to Adjust Cost Share

This chapter discusses cost shares and the request to adjust a cost share[158] in section IX, *Federal and State Cost Share and Adjustments.*

4. Expansion of Incident Type

A governor may request an expansion of the incident type based on sufficient justification from an incident-appropriate agency (e.g., official reports from the NWS or the USGS, and supporting damage assessments). The governor should address the request to the President and submit it through the RA or FCO.[159]

---

[158] 44 C.F.R. § 206.47. Stafford Act § 319, 42 U.S.C. § 5162, also authorizes loans of the non-federal share to eligible applicants. *See* 44 C.F.R. § 206.45.
[159] *FCO Guide.*

Expansion of the incident type is rare but may be necessary when an expedited governor's request results in a declaration prior to the completion of PDAs and the identification of all applicable damage types. The initial request for declaration may contain one incident type, such as "severe storms and flooding," but subsequent PDAs may reflect damage, which mudslides or landslides caused, during the storm. In order for damage that mudslides or landslides caused to be eligible for assistance, FEMA must expand the incident type specified in the initial declaration to include them.

Fires to Flooding/Mudslides

2003 California Wildfires Disaster (FEMA -1498-DR-CA)
Declaration Date: October 27, 2003
Original Incident Type: Wildfires

Amendment 3 dated January 14, 2004: The incident period was reopened from December 2, 2003, through and including February 2, 2004, and the incident type expanded specifically for flooding, mudflow, and debris flow directly related to the wildfires. During the expanded incident period, only those areas within the designated areas specifically determined by the FCO to be damaged or adversely affected as a direct result of the compromised watershed conditions and fire-generated debris caused by the wildfires could be considered eligible for assistance.

Disaster Facts: On October 27, 2003, the President declared a major disaster for California for wildfires. The incident period, which was initially established as October 21, 2003, and continuing, was subsequently closed effective December 2, 2003, after all the fires were 100% contained. On December 25, 2003, flash floods and mudflows from one day's rain along Lyle Creek and Waterman Canyon caused the loss of 15 lives. The rain amounts were not particularly heavy or unusual; however, they occurred in an area that had suffered a loss of vegetation and created hydrophobic soil conditions from the wildfires, which made the soil conditions very vulnerable in a rain event. Insufficient time had lapsed from the wildfires themselves to allow for vegetative growth.

Similar amendments were made to wildfire disasters FEMA-1005-DR-CA declared in 2005 and FEMA-1731-DR-CA declared in 2006.

VIII. Federal Assistance under Major Disaster and Emergency Declarations

The Stafford Act authorizes very broad actions under either a major disaster[160] or an emergency[161] declaration, but there are significant differences in the activities and programs available under the different types of declarations. Table 2 provides a summary.

Table 2: Summary of Federal Activities and Programs - Emergency v. Major Disaster Declaration

Purpose of Declaration Type	Emergency Declaration	Major Disaster Declaration
Immediate versus Longer Term and Broader Assistance	Intended **for immediate and short-term assistance** essential to save lives, protect public health, safety, and property;[162] may include IA under section 408[163]	• Includes broad range of response and recovery assistance. May include IA, PA, and HM, or a combination.[164]
Emergency Work and Permanent Work in Public Assistance	Provide PA grants to state and local governments for Debris Removal and Emergency Work only – Section 502[165]: • Debris removal • Emergency protective measures • Cost share: 75% federal, 25% state; state may request increase	• Provide PA grants to state and local governments, which may include only Debris Removal – Sections 403[166] and 407[167] and Emergency Protective Measures – Section 403[168]; may also include permanent work – Section 406[169] • Cost share: 75% Federal, 25% state; state may request increase

---

[160] Stafford Act § 402, 42 U.S.C. § 5170a.
[161] Id. § 502, 42 U.S.C. § 5191.
[162] 44 C.F.R. § 206.63.
[163] Stafford Act § 502, 42 U.S.C. § 5192 (a)(6).
[164] Id. §§ 401 - 427, 42 U.S.C. §§ 5170-5189e.
[165] Id. § 502, 42 U.S.C. § 5192.
[166] Id. § 403, 42 U.S.C. § 5170b.
[167] Id. § 407, 42 U.S.C. § 5173.
[168] Id. § 403, 42 U.S.C. § 5170b.
[169] Id. § 406, 42 U.S.C. § 5172.

Table 2, continued

Purpose of Declaration Type	Emergency Declaration	Major Disaster Declaration
Hazard Mitigation	HMGP is *not authorized* under an emergency declaration	• HMGP – Section 404[170] is usually included in all major disaster declarations to provide grants to reduce risk from future hazards • Amount available is based on percentage of total eligible IA and PA under the declaration • Cost share: up to 75% federal contribution
Other Stafford Act Disaster Assistance	Food Commodities – Section 413 Emergency Communications – Section 418 Transportation Assistance to Individuals and Households – Section 425	• Disaster Unemployment Assistance – Section 410[171] • Benefits and Distribution – Section 412[172] • Food Commodities – Section 413[173] • Disaster Legal Services – Section 415[174] • Crisis Counseling Assistance – Section 416[175] • Community Disaster Loans – Section 417[176] • Emergency Communications – Section 418[177] • Emergency Public Transportation – Section 419[178] • Transportation Assistance to Individuals and Households – Section 425[179] • Disaster Case Management – Section 426[180]

[170] Id. § 404, 42 U.S.C. § 5170c; 44 C.F.R. Part 206, Subpart N (44 C.F.R. §§ 206.430-206.440).
[171] Id. § 410, 42 U.S.C. 5177.

Purpose of Declaration Type	Emergency Declaration	Major Disaster Declaration
Amount of Funding and Notifications	Assistance under Emergency Declaration limited to $5 million but may be increased when needed, and FEMA must report increase to Congress.[181]	No caps on funding although subject to availability of funds

IX. Federal and State Cost Share and Adjustments

Federal and state cost shares under the Stafford Act vary by program:

- PA programs under emergency work,[182] debris removal,[183] and permanent work[184] are at least 75% federal cost share.

- Housing assistance under the Stafford Act is 100% federally funded.[185]

- Other Needs Assistance is set at a 75% federal cost share and may not be increased; the state is required to provide the funds for the non-federal share.[186]

- For HMGP, FEMA can provide up to 75% of the total eligible costs.[187]

---

[172] Id. § 412, 42 U.S.C. 5179.
[173] Id. § 413, 42 U.S.C. 5180.
[174] Id. § 415, 42 U.S.C. 5182.
[175] Id. § 416, 42 U.S.C. 5183.
[176] Id. § 417, 42 U.S.C. 5184.
[177] Id. § 418, 42 U.S.C. 5185.
[178] Id. § 419, 42 U.S.C. 5186.
[179] Id. § 425, 42 U.S.C. 5189c.
[180] Id. § 426, 42 U.S.C. 5189d.
[181] Id. § 503(b), 42 U.S.C. 5193(b).
[182] Stafford Act § 403(b) and (c)(4), and 503(b), 42 U.S.C. §§ 5170b(b) and (c)(4) and 5193(b).
[183] Id. § 407(d), 42 U.S.C. § 5173(d).
[184] Id. § 406(b), 42 U.S.C. § 5172(b).
[185] Id. § 408 (g)(1), 42 U.S.C. § 5174 (g)(1); 44 C.F.R. § 206.110(i)(1).
[186] Id. § 408 (g)(2), 42 U.S.C. § 5174 (g)(2); 44 C.F.R. § 206.110(i)(2).
[187] Id. § 404(a), 42 U.S.C. § 5170c (a).

The Stafford Act is silent on how the non-federal cost share for PA and the HMGP should be addressed.[188] States may provide all, some, or none of these non-federal cost shares for its subgrantees. However, states must certify that state and local government obligations and expenditures will comply with all applicable cost sharing requirements of the Stafford Act.[189]

The governor or the GAR may request an increase in the federal share to 90% for PA programs when disaster damage in the state is so severe that federal obligations under the Stafford Act meet or exceed the statewide per capita threshold.[190] The statewide per capita threshold for calendar year 2013 is $133.[191]

Rare Use of Less Than Statewide Impact

It is extremely rare to consider a per capita indicator for anything other than statewide impact. However, on two occasions the President has considered per capita impacts on tribes when making cost share adjustments. In 2010, the Chippewa Cree Tribe of the Rocky Boy Reservation received a 100% federal share adjustment for a disaster in which the estimated per capita impact on the tribe was over $7,000. Similarly, in 2011, the President adjusted the cost share to 90% for the Havasupai Tribe for a disaster in which the per capita impact on the tribe, based upon actual obligations, was over $790. In both situations, state law prevented the tribes from receiving financial assistance from their respective states.

If the severity of the disaster so warrants, FEMA may recommend up to 100% in federal funding for emergency work and debris removal for a limited period in the initial days of a major disaster.[192] Generally, a limited period in the initial days of the disaster means FEMA will limit the

---

[188] See 48 U.S.C. § 1469a(d); 44 C.F.R. § 206.47(c-d), 206.48(b); FEMA Recovery Policy 9523.9 (June 9, 2006) for guidance.
[189] Id. § 401, 42 U.S.C. § 5170.
[190] 44 C.F.R. § 206.47(b)
[191] Id. 44 C.F.R. § 206.47(b)(4): 78 Fed. Reg. 9935 (Feb 12, 2013)
[192] FEMA Recovery Policy 9523.9, 100% Funding for Direct Federal Assistance and Grant Assistance, (2006) [hereinafter FEMA RP 9523.9]; http://www.fema.gov/pdf/government/grant/pa/9523_9.pdf.

period of 100% funding to the first 72 hours following the disaster declaration, or an applicant's selected 72-hour period.[193] The President may determine to extend this period based on the gravity and scope of the disaster.[194] FEMA considers the impact of major disaster declarations in the requesting state in the prior 12-month period to determine whether to recommend a cost share adjustment.[195]

The governor or GAR should address the state's request to the President and submit it through the RA. Only the President may adjust the cost share. FEMA will review the governor's request and supporting documentation and make a recommendation based on the particular circumstances. A cost share adjustment may also be required by an act of Congress.[196]

As described previously, under the Stafford Act, only the PA program federal cost share can be adjusted above 75%. However, if the declaration is for an insular area (American Samoa, Guam, the U.S. Virgin Islands, and the Commonwealth of the Northern Mariana Islands), the cost share for PA, Other Needs Assistance and the HMGP are mandatorily waived if the respective non-federal share is under $200,000.[197] Whenever the cost share in any cost sharing context in an insular area is more than $200,000, any cost sharing arrangement becomes discretionary.[198] FEMA's practice is to apply the PA cost share adjustment criteria[199] for Other Needs Assistance and the HMGP when it is triggered for PA.

---

[193] Id.

[194] Id.

[195] 44 C.F.R. § 206.47(c) and (d).

[196] See US Troop Readiness, Veterans' Care, Katrina Recovery, and Iraq Accountability Appropriations Act, 2007 (Pub. L. 110-28), Sec 4501: "... the Federal share of assistance, including direct Federal assistance, provided for the States of Alabama, Florida, Louisiana, Mississippi, and Texas in connection with Hurricanes Katrina, Wilma, Dennis, and Rita under sections 403, 406, 407, and 408 of the Stafford Act shall be 100 percent of the eligible costs under such sections..."

[197] 48 U.S.C. § 1469a(d) note. See also Pub. L. 96-205, Title VI, §601, 94 Stat. 90; as amended (1983); Pub. L. 98-213, §6, 97 Stat. 1460; (1984); Pub. L. 98-454, Title VI, §601(b), 98 Stat. 1736 (1984).

[198] Id.

[199] 44 C.F.R 206.48(b).

Insular Areas Cost 90% Share and 100 % Floating Cost Share Adjustment

2009 American Samoa Earthquake and Tsunami Disaster (FEMA-1859-DR-AS)

Declaration Date: September 29, 2009

Incident: Earthquake, Tsunami, and Flooding

Amendment dated January 15, 2010:

The declaration was amended to authorize federal funds for all categories of PA, HM, and the Other Needs Assistance at 90 percent of total eligible costs, and further authorize PA (Categories A and B), including DFA, at 100 percent of total eligible costs for 30 consecutive days.

Application:

- For DFA for Categories A and B, the 30 consecutive day period for 100% was established as starting on September 29, 2009, the declaration date.

- For grant assistance, each applicant could establish a consecutive 30-day time period that could be different for Category A and Category B work and could begin no sooner than September 29, 2009, the commencement date of the Incident Period.

- Each applicant was required to provide its designated commencement dates to the GAR in writing by a specified date or be subject to a 30 consecutive day period of September 29, 2009, through October 28, 2009, for Category A and Category B work.

Eligible work outside the designated 30 consecutive day periods was subject to the 90% federal, 10% non-federal cost share.

Another Floating Cost Share Example

Please note the differences from the previous example, which was a no-notice event declared immediately:

2008 Iowa Flooding Disaster (FEMA-1763-DR-IA)

Declaration Date: May 27, 2008

Incident: Severe Storms, Tornadoes, and Flooding

Incident Period: May 25, 2008, to August 13, 2008

Amendment dated June 11, 2009:

The declaration was amended to authorize Federal funds for debris removal and emergency protective measures (Category A and B), including DFA, under the PA program, at 100 percent of the total eligible costs for 14 consecutive days.

Application:

- For DFA, for Categories A and B, the 14 consecutive day period for 100% was established as starting on May 27, 2008, the declaration date.

- For grant assistance, each applicant could establish a consecutive 14-day time period that could be different for Category A and Category B work, and that could begin no sooner than the date of the state, county or local declaration of emergency for the affected area.

- Eligible work outside the designated 14 consecutive day periods was subject to a previously established 90% federal cost share.[200]

---

[200] *See* FEMA Recovery Policy 9523.9 (2006) for guidance. http://www.fema.gov/pdf/government/grant/pa/9523_9.pdf.

X. Appeals

A. Denial of Declaration Request

The governor may appeal the denial of a request for a declaration within 30 days after the date of the denial letter. The governor should submit this one-time appeal to the President through the RA. The appeal must include additional information supporting the request for declaration.[201]

B. Partial Denial of Requested Areas or Types of Assistance Requested

When the President denies the type of assistance or geographical areas requested for declaration, the governor or the GAR may appeal. On some occasions, the President does not designate or authorize areas while additional PDAs are pending. This one-time appeal, including any justification or additional supporting information, must be submitted within 30 days of the date of the denial letter. The governor or GAR submits the appeal through the RA to FEMA's Deputy Associate Administrator for Response and Recovery.[202]

C. Denial of Advance of Non-Federal Share

The governor may appeal the denial of a request to advance the non-federal share within 30 days of the date of the denial letter. The governor must submit this one-time appeal in writing through the RA to the Deputy Associate Administrator for Response and Recovery.[203]

FEMA may extend any of the 30-day appeal deadlines, provided the governor submits a written request within the original 30-day time period and there exists legitimate reasons for the delay.[204]

---

[201] 44 C.F.R. § 206.46(a).
[202] Id. § 206.46(b); Id. § 206.37.
[203] Id. § 206.46(c).
[204] Id. § 206.46(d).

XI. State/Tribal Hazard Mitigation Plans

Hazard mitigation measures are actions taken to reduce the risk or potential for loss of life or damage to property due to natural disasters. We discuss the details of the Hazard Mitigation program in detail in Chapter 7.

The Stafford Act requires states to have an approved Standard or Enhanced State Hazard Mitigation Plan in place at the time of a disaster to be eligible for all non-essential assistance.[205] Thus, if FEMA has not approved a state plan, FEMA may not authorize Stafford Act permanent repair or HM funding.[206] In the event a state's HM plan lapses during an ongoing disaster, with the exception of emergency work, FEMA may not provide any further assistance for PA permanent repair work and HM projects until it approves an updated plan.

An Indian tribal government acting as a direct grantee under the PA or HM program must have an approved Tribal Mitigation Plan in order to receive non-emergency assistance under the Stafford Act.[207] All states currently have mitigation plans, but not all federally-recognized Indian tribes have such a plan.

States and Indian tribal governments applying directly to FEMA for assistance that do not have a FEMA approved plan in effect at time of declaration have a limited number of days in which to develop a state or tribal mitigation plan, respectively, and to obtain FEMA approval of the plan, in order to have HMGP and PA categories C through G authorized under the declaration.[208]

---

[205] Emergency Work, the IA programs, and Community Disaster Loans are exempt from this restriction. 44 C.F.R. § 201.4(a).

[206] Id. § 206.434(b). See also id. § 201.4, Standard State Mitigation Plans and § 201.5, Enhanced State Mitigation Plans.

[207] Tribal Mitigation Plan requirements are set forth in 44 C.F.R. § 201.7.

[208] See 44 C.F.R. § 201(c)(6); FEMA Mitigation Planning Memorandum (MT-PL) #1: Disaster Declaration Procedures After May 1, 2005 for States Without an Approved State Mitigation Plan (2005); FEMA Mitigation Planning Memorandum (MT-PL) #2: Implementation Procedures for States, Territories, and Indian Tribal Governments Without an Approved State Mitigation Plan - Follow-up Guidance (2005). FEMA is reviewing a

Local governments also must have an approved mitigation plan in order to receive HMGP project grants.[209] RAs may grant an exception, however, in extraordinary circumstances, such as for small and impoverished communities.[210]

XII. Fire Management Assistance Declaration

Entirely distinct from the President's emergency or major disaster declarations, the Stafford Act authorizes FEMA to make Fire Management Assistance declarations.[211] The Stafford Act authorizes federal assistance[212] for the "mitigation, management, and control of any fire or fire complex on public or private forest land or grassland that is burning uncontrolled and threatens such destruction as would constitute a major disaster."[213] The Administrator has authorized RAs to approve requests for fire management assistance declarations.[214] A state may request a Fire Management Assistance Grant (FMAG) from an RA at any time (24 hours a day); decisions are frequently made based on facts the RA receives by telephone. Requests must be submitted while the fire is burning uncontrolled.[215]

The Stafford Act authorizes fire management assistance for fires "on public or private forest land or grassland."[216] FEMA will approve declarations for fire management assistance when the RA[217] determines that a fire or fire complex threatens such destruction as would constitute a major disaster.

---

revised policy at time of publication. Please coordinate with HQ OCC concerning current policy.

[209] 44 C.F.R. §§ 201.6(a)(1) and 206.434(b).

[210] Id. § 201.6(a)(3).

[211] Stafford Act § 420, 42 U.S.C. § 5187.

[212] Assistance may include certain grants, equipment, supplies, personnel, and essential assistance under 42 U.S.C. § 5170b. See 44 C.F.R. Part 204, especially, § 204.42.

[213] 44 C.F.R. § 204.22.

[214] Memorandum to the Regional Administrators from the FEMA Administrator (2010). See also DHS Management Directive 9001.1.

[215] 44 C.F.R. 204.22

[216] Stafford Act § 420, 42 U.S.C. § 5187. FEMA regulations inaccurately do not contain this limiting language. See 44 C.F.R. Part 204.

[217] Id. § 204.51(c).

This authority is not available for typical structure fires; if, however, in spite of the FMAG's fire control and response measures, the fire ultimately causes damage that warrants assistance under the PA and/or the Individuals and Households Program, a major disaster declaration request may follow a FMAG declaration. FEMA must carefully evaluate such requests to ensure additional supplemental assistance under the Stafford Act is appropriate, where emergency protective measures and response costs are already available under an FMAG declaration. Presidential emergency declarations are not appropriate for fires on grasslands or forest lands, as noted previously, because this emergency declaration provision in the Stafford Act is tailored specifically to those fires and because of the unique state and federal framework for wildfire response. FEMA expects to issue a new guide on fire management assistance in the coming months.

XIII. Tribal Requests for a Major Disaster or Emergency Declaration under the Stafford Act – *New*

The Sandy Recovery Improvement Act of 2013 (SRIA), amended the Robert T. Stafford Disaster Relief and Emergency Assistance Act (42 U.S.C. 5121 et. seq.) to allow federally-recognized tribes to seek Stafford Act assistance from the President directly in the event of an emergency or major disaster.[218] This was an important change in the law that corrected a long standing anachronism within the Stafford Act, which defined federally-recognized tribes only as local governments, ignoring the sovereignty of tribes and standing in the way of government-to-government relations between the Tribes and the Federal Government.

SRIA:

- Amends the Stafford Act to provide for an option for the Chief Executive of a federally recognized Indian tribe to make a direct request to the President for a major disaster or emergency declaration. The amendment provides that Tribes may elect to receive assistance under a State's declaration, provided that the

---

[218] Sandy Recovery Improvement Act of 2013, Pub. L. No. 113-2, § 1110, Tribal Requests for a Major Disaster or Emergency Declaration under the Stafford Act (2013).

President does not make a declaration for the Tribe for the same incident.[219]

- Authorizes the President to establish criteria to adjust the non-federal cost share for an Indian tribal government consistent to the extent allowed by current authorities.[220]

- Requires FEMA to consider the unique circumstances of tribes when it develops regulations to implement the provision.[221]

- Amends the Stafford Act to include federally recognized Indian tribal governments in numerous references to state and local governments within the Stafford Act.[222]

---

[219] Id. at § 1110(a) and (b). *See also* Stafford Act §§401(b) and 502 (c), 42 U.S.C. 5170(b) and 5192 (c).

[220] Id. at § 1110(a). *See also* Stafford Act §401(c), 42 U.S.C. 5170(c).

[221] Id. at § 1110(e).

[222] Id. at § 1110(d). *See also* Stafford Act §103, 42 U.S.C. 5123.

CHAPTER 4
Response
Table of Contents

Response

I. Introduction

An effective, coordinated response is crucial for maintaining the public's trust. Response operations must be proactive, scalable and nimble. The failure or perceived failure to respond immediately and effectively will set a negative tone for the life of the operations. The FEMA statutory mission includes a mandate that it "develop a Federal response capability that, when necessary and appropriate, can act effectively and rapidly to deliver assistance essential to saving lives or protecting or preserving property or public health and safety in a natural disaster, act of terrorism, or other man-made disaster."[1]

FEMA works with state, tribal, and local governments; other federal partners; non-governmental organizations; and the private sector to utilize fully the nation's resources and take immediate actions to save lives, protect property, and meet basic needs in declared major disasters and emergencies.[2] To accomplish its response mission, FEMA maintains operational facilities in Washington, D.C., in the 10 FEMA regional offices, and at temporary disaster field locations that a Federal Coordinating Officer (FCO) may establish near active major disaster or emergency sites.[3]

This chapter discusses FEMA's disaster response authorities, organizational structures, and activities and the rapid interface with recovery operations, as the trend in disaster operations is for the immediate initiation of recovery activities while robust response operations are ongoing.

---

[1] Homeland Security Act § 503(b)(2)(C), 6 U.S.C. § 313(b)(2)(C); *See also* Stafford Act §§ 403(a) & 502(a), 42 U.S.C. § 5170b(a) & § 5192(a); 44 C.F.R. §§ 206.201(b) & 206.225.
[2] Homeland Security Act § 503(b)(2)(B), 6 U.S.C. § 313(b)(2)(B).
[3] Stafford Act § 302(b)(2), 42 U.S.C. § 5143(b)(2); FEMA Publication 1 [hereinafter Pub. 1] at 30 (Nov. 2010).

II. Response Authorities

FEMA has significant legal authorities in the Stafford Act and the Homeland Security Act to undertake response activities to save lives, protect public health and safety, and prevent damage to improved public or private property.[4] FEMA administratively categorizes activities under these statutory provisions as "emergency work,"[5] which includes "debris removal" and "emergency protective measures."[6] Emergency work includes response activities and actions taken to pre-position staff and equipment before an incident and, during and after a major disaster or emergency declaration, to employ emergency equipment, personnel and supplies; evacuate survivors out of harm's way; provide rescue, food, water, shelter, and emergency medical care; remove debris; and restore critical public services.[7]

The Stafford Act authorizes FEMA to provide assistance to state, tribal,[8] and local governments, and to certain non-profits to carry out these activities[9] either through direct assistance, which includes in-house resourcing or mission assignments to other federal agencies (OFAs), or financial assistance through public assistance grants. Recipients of

---

[4] Stafford Act §§ 402, 403, 407, 502 & 503; 42 U.S.C. §§ 5170a, 5170b, 5173, 5192, & 5193. Additional authorities for FEMA to respond are in the Homeland Security Act, §§ 503, 504 & 507, 6 U.S.C. §§ 313, 314 & 317.

[5] PUBLIC ASSISTANCE GUIDE, FEMA 322 [hereinafter PA GUIDE] at 29, ¶ 2 (June 2007), "Debris removal and emergency protective measures are considered 'emergency work.'" See also, id. at 67, which describes the emergency work categories.

[6] Id. at 71; see also PUBLIC ASSISTANCE DIGEST, FEMA 321 [hereinafter PA DIGEST], at 46 (2008). See also Chapter 5, Public Assistance, explaining that the Public Assistance (PA) program calls debris removal "Category A" and emergency protective measures "Category B."

[7] Stafford Act, §§ 403 & 502, 42 U.S.C. 5170b & 5192; Homeland Security Act § 504(a)(9)(C), 6 U.S.C. § 314 (a)(9)(C). Pub. 1, at 30. In addition, the Post Katrina Emergency Management Reform Act of 2006, Pub. L. No. 109-295 (2006) [hereinafter PKEMRA] § 632, 6 U.S.C. § 721, directed FEMA to coordinate with appropriate other federal agencies to provide evacuation technical assistance to state, local, and tribal governments, including preparation of hurricane evacuation studies, and assistance in developing plans for, among other things, evacuation zones, evacuation clearance times, and shelter capacity.

[8] Under the Stafford Act, tribes are included within the definition of local government. Stafford Act, § 102(7), 42 U.S.C. § 5122. Although the Stafford Act thus does not distinguish tribes apart from local governments, FEMA policy is to distinguish tribes from local governments where possible. See, e.g., FEMA Tribal Policy (June 29, 2010), <http://www.fema.gov/pdf/government/tribal/fema_tribal_policy.pdf>.

[9] Stafford Act § 403(a)(4), 42 U.S.C. § 5170b (a)(4).

---

response assistance must be eligible applicants[10] and own or operate an eligible facility.[11] Moreover, the work for which they seek reimbursement must meet the general work eligibility requirements,[12] the public interest requirement for debris removal,[13] and the requirements for emergency work.[14] The chapter on *Public Assistance* discusses the details of these eligibility requirements.

The Stafford Act also allows FEMA to direct other agencies to use their authorities and resources to assist states[15] and, in another provision, to direct other agencies to assist with a variety of emergency measures.[16] Yet another section permits FEMA to direct other agencies to assist with debris removal.[17] Further, in an emergency declaration, if existing emergency measures are inadequate, FEMA may take actions and direct other agencies to lessen or avert the threat of a catastrophe.[18] In some instances, FEMA directs other agencies to assist or support FEMA in providing response assistance; when it does so, FEMA issues a mission assignment for federal operational support or one to advise FEMA or the state with technical assistance. This chapter discusses these types of mission assignments in the following section.

---

[10] 44 C.F.R. § 206.222.

[11] Id. § 206.221.

[12] Id. § 206.223(a).

[13] Id. § 206.224. There is a public interest requirement for public and private property debris removal. While it is generally presumed that there is a public interest in removing debris from public property, a more detailed finding is required for private property to meet the public interest requirement.

[14] Id. § 206.225.

[15] Stafford Act § 402, 42 U.S.C. §§ 5170a.

[16] Id. § 403, 42 U.S.C. §§ 5170b.

[17] Id. § 407, 42 U.S.C. §§ 5173.

[18] Id. § 502, 42 U.S.C. §§ 5192.

III. Direct Assistance and Mission Assignments

For a major disaster, the Stafford Act authorizes FEMA to direct any agency[19] to utilize its existing authorities and resources in support of state and local assistance response and recovery efforts;[20] and to "provide assistance that is essential to meeting immediate threats to life and property," including debris removal.[21] For an emergency, the Stafford Act authorizes FEMA to direct any agency to utilize its existing authorities and resources in support of state and local emergency assistance efforts.[22] State, tribal, and local governments typically perform or arrange for the performance of emergency work, described previously, and then apply to FEMA for financial reimbursement for the costs of that work. However, when a state, tribal, or local government is incapable of performing or arranging for emergency work, it may make a request[23] for FEMA to arrange for the provision of the work,[24] subject to a state cost share.[25] FEMA administratively categorizes the execution of such work as "Direct Federal Assistance" (DFA).[26] FEMA's regulation requires states to submit requests for DFA to the Regional Administrator.[27] FEMA's current

---

[19] "Executive Agency" is defined as: an Executive department, a Government corporation, (or) an independent establishment. 5170a(1). 5 U.S.C. § 105. For example, the U.S. Postal Service is considered an "executive agency" because it is legally defined as an "independent establishment of the United States of the executive branch of the Government of the United States", and is controlled by Presidential appointees and the Postmaster General. 39 U.S.C. § 201. Accordingly, FEMA could mission assign the Postal Service during a disaster to perform tasks such as transportation or distribution of commodities or supplies to disaster survivors.

[20] Stafford Act § 402(1), 42 U.S.C. § 5170a(1).

[21] Id. § 403(a), 42 U.S.C. § 5170b(a). PKEMRA, § 681, added FEMA's authority under the Stafford Act to direct another agency in support of recovery efforts. See also Stafford Act § 304, 42 U.S.C. § 5147, which essentially provides that FEMA may use the DRF to reimburse federal agencies for expenditures in the immediate anticipation of or after a major disaster or emergency declaration. Federal agencies may deposit any funds they receive as reimbursement for services or supplies they furnish to the credit of their own appropriation(s) currently available for such services or supplies rather than having to turn these funds over to the U.S. Treasury.

[22] Stafford Act § 502(a)(1), 42 U.S.C. § 5192(a)(1).

[23] The request must be consistent with the procedures at 44 C.F.R. § 206.208.

[24] Id.

[25] Stafford Act § 403(b), 42 U.S.C. § 5170b(b).

[26] 44 C.F.R. § 206.208(a); see also PA GUIDE, at 76-78.

[27] 44 C.F.R. § 206.208(b). This regulation does not reflect that the National Response Coordination Center (NRCC) at FEMA Headquarters, an RRCC in each FEMA region, or a

---

regulations limit the execution of DFA to emergency work and debris removal.[28] Since FEMA promulgated these regulations, however, Congress expanded FEMA's authority in the Stafford Act to also authorize the direction of other agencies in support of recovery efforts.[29] FEMA has not promulgated new regulations or guidance on how it will execute this authority, nor has it determined whether it will use a tasking document similar to a mission assignment or some other form.

To effectuate its authority to direct OFAs to provide disaster assistance to state, tribal, and local governments in responding to major disasters or emergencies,[30] FEMA administratively created the "mission assignment."[31] A mission assignment is a "work order" that FEMA issues to another federal agency, directing the other agency to complete a specified task and setting forth funding, other managerial controls, and guidance.[32] The mission assignment executes an exception provided by the Stafford Act to the Economy Act, which ordinarily governs the means by which one agency obtains supplies or services from another agency.[33]

When tasking another agency to execute DFA, the Stafford Act provides that FEMA may direct the agency "with or without reimbursement."[34] If FEMA funds the mission assignment, the funding comes from the Disaster Relief Fund (DRF). Many other agencies have their own statutory authorities that may be utilized in disaster or emergency response and recovery. FEMA regulation provides that the FEMA Regional Administrator may not approve a request for DFA for work that "falls within the statutory authority of another Federal agency" and is to refer

---

Joint Field Office, which an FCO establishes, all process Mission Assignments for DFA, especially in the beginning of a disaster. This chapter discusses all of these terms.

[28] 44 C.F.R. § 206.208(a).

[29] PKEMRA, § 681; Stafford Act § 402(1), 42 U.S.C. § 5170a(1).

[30] Stafford Act §§ 402(1), 403(a), 407, & 502(a)(1); 42 U.S.C. §§ 5170a(1), 5170b(a), 5173 & 5192(a)(1); 44 C.F.R. §§ 206.5 & 206.208.

[31] Mission Assignment form, O.M.B. No. 1660-0047, <http://on.fema.net/components/orr/response/Pages/MissionAssignment.aspx>.

[32] 44 C.F.R. § 206.2(a)(18). Congress later clarified this definition which was codified at 6 U.S.C. § 741(c). See Mission Assignments webpage: <http://on.fema.net/components/orr/response/Pages/MissionAssignment.aspx>.

[33] See 31 U.S.C. § 1535; Federal Acquisition Regulation, 48 C.F.R. § 17.502-2(b) ("The Economy Act applies when more specific statutory authority does not exist").

[34] Stafford Act § 402, 42 U.S.C. § 5170a.

that work to the appropriate agency for action.[35] Although FEMA, in its coordinating role, may still issue a non-reimbursable mission assignment to another federal agency to ensure coordination with the scope of the response effort, informal coordination without a mission assignment is often sufficient. FEMA's denial of funding for work that falls under the authority of another agency has been a frequent source of conflict in previous disasters. In particular, the issue often arises because the other federal agency represents to FEMA that it has inadequate funding in its budget for the particular work or task. Because this issue is primarily a legal one, when it arises, the FEMA Office of Chief Counsel (OCC) is the appropriate FEMA office to resolve it.

Examples of Mission Assignments

In response to the Space Shuttle Columbia explosion, FEMA mission-assigned the U.S. Forest Service (USFS) to tag the location of shuttle debris fragments and the Environmental Protection Agency (EPA) to check all debris fragments for toxicity. Neither agency had the specific independent authority to carry out these activities in response to this event, thus, FEMA reimbursed each agency.

A. Types of Mission Assignments

All mission assignments must be in writing, or if initially made orally, confirmed in writing.[36] Though not in regulation, FEMA's mission assignment form allows for three types of mission assignments with different criteria for eligibility and reimbursement:

- Federal Operations Support (FOS);
- Technical Assistance (TA); and
- Direct Federal Assistance (DFA).[37]

---

[35] 44 C.F.R. §§ 206.208(c)(2) & 206.8(b); *see also* 44 C.F.R. § 206.37(d).

[36] 44 C.F.R. § 206.7.

[37] Mission Assignment form, O.M.B. No. 1660-0047, <http://on.fema.net/components/orr/response/Pages/MissionAssignment.aspx>.

The entire statement of work for a mission assignment is not necessarily determined at the time of the event. The Post-Katrina Emergency Reform Act (PKEMRA)[38] required FEMA to develop pre-scripted mission assignments (PSMAs).[39] These are "draft" mission assignments negotiated with various federal agencies to provide specific assets and personnel at the time of a declared major disaster or emergency in order to assist state, tribal, and local governments.

1. Federal Operations Support (FOS)

FOS is technical, operational, or logistical support by a federal agency or department to support FEMA or another responding agency. FEMA may activate FOS in order to place assets in position in order to respond before a major disaster or emergency declaration.[40] FOS permits FEMA to activate OFAs and assure they are in place, ready to assist the state once a declaration occurs.

The Stafford Act does not explicitly authorize FEMA to direct OFAs for purposes of supporting FEMA or another federal agency. Such work is required, however, for FEMA and the federal government to support state and local assistance response and recovery efforts. This work is also thus a "necessary expense"[41] in order for FEMA to carry out its mission and does not constitute a form of direct assistance for which a state or local cost share would be required. The work instead facilitates administrative operational activity at the federal level necessary later to deliver state-requested DFA and is 100% federally funded.

---

[38] PKEMRA, Pub. L. No. 109-295 (2006).

[39] Id. at § 653, 6 U.S.C. § 753(c).

[40] FEMA Office of Chief Financial Officer, Directive 125-2, Disaster Relief Fund (DRF) – Pre-Declaration Surge Funding [hereinafter OCFO – Pre-declaration Directive] (June 22, 2011), which lists those particular activities that FEMA may fund before the President makes a Stafford Act declaration, http://on.fema.net/components/ocfo/policy/Documents/directives/FD125-2.pdf. See also Readiness and Pre-declaration Activities chapter.

[41] UNITED STATES GENERAL ACCOUNTABILITY OFFICE (GAO), I PRINCIPLES OF FEDERAL APPROPRIATIONS LAW [hereinafter GAO REDBOOK](3rd ed.) 4-22 & 23.

> **Examples of FOS**
>
> Mission assignments to appropriate agencies assigned to the National Response Coordination Center (NRCC) and the Regional Response Coordination Center (RRCC) to staff the Emergency Support Functions (ESFs); mission assignments issued to the Department of Agriculture (USDA) or the U.S. Forest Service (USFS) to establish an emergency responder support camp to house federal disaster workers; mission assignments to the Department of Defense (DOD) to transport DHS and/or FEMA personnel and equipment to be ready to evacuate medical patients.

2. Technical Assistance (TA)

The Stafford Act provides authority for technical assistance (TA) to state, tribal, and local governments in major disaster and emergency declarations.[42] TA is technical expertise that federal agencies provide to FEMA or that FEMA provides itself, or through OFAs, to state, local, or tribal governments that lack the knowledge and skills to analyze needed eligible work related to the disaster or emergency. Pursuant to the Mission Assignment Standard Operating Procedure, TA is 100% federally funded and, if it is for a state, local, or tribal government rather than for FEMA, the state must request it. TA costs, in the context of mission support, usually are a minimal expense, typically involving between one and four experts, and thus allow state, local, or tribal governments to respond more effectively and efficiently to the incident, ultimately saving the federal government and the other governmental entities substantial costs.

Clearly a state would prefer a TA mission assignment, since it is 100% federally funded, to a DFA mission assignment that is generally cost-shared. FEMA must assure that it correctly categorizes the type of mission assignment. For example, a mission assignment for bridge inspectors to provide damage assessments to augment state and local resources would be for DFA. FEMA, however, would consider a mission assignment to

---

[42] Stafford Act, §§ 402 & 502, 42 U.S.C. 5170a(3) & 5192(a)(3); and § 403(a)(3)(H), 42 U.S.C. 5170b ("technical advice").

provide advice on demolition of a dam, when the state lacks the necessary expertise, to be TA. Importantly, if the state were able to contract for the TA work, FEMA would reimburse under a project worksheet at the cost share rate for the underlying work. It is thus critical that FEMA confirm requested TA is, in fact, beyond state and local knowledge, skills, and contracting capability.

Examples of TA Mission Assignments

Mission assignment to the U.S. Army Corps of Engineers (USACE) to provide technical oversight to a state when writing debris removal contracts; mission assignment to deploy radiological experts to provide assistance in assessment, containment, or decontamination.

3. Direct Federal Assistance (DFA)

DFA[43] consists of goods or services that FEMA, another federal agency, or a contractor provides to state and local jurisdictions that lack the capability to perform or contract for eligible emergency work. DFA thus can provide emergency protective measures to save lives, protect public health and safety, protect property, and implement debris removal for state and local governments. FEMA's regulations require the completion of mission assignments for DFA within 60 days of the date of declaration of the major disaster or emergency, unless extended by the Regional Administrator.[44]

---

[43] 44 C.F.R. § 206.208; PA GUIDE, at 76-78; PA DIGEST, at 36; *See also* FEMA Standard Operating Procedure No. 2600-007, *Financial Processing of Mission Assignments* at 25 (March 17, 2011).
http://on.fema.net/components/ocfo/policy/Documents/SOPs/Financial%20Processing%20of%20Mission%20Assignments.PDF.
[44] 44 C.F.R. § 206.208(d).

FEMA may provide DFA after a declaration, and DFA is limited to the following types of activities: [45]

- Debris removal;
- Emergency work and protective measures;
- Emergency communications; and
- Emergency public transportation.

In addition, FEMA may task the USACE to build temporary housing unit group sites for disaster survivors through existing PSMAs pursuant to direct assistance authorities.[46]

Response to Recovery Timeline

The effort to construct group sites when no alternate temporary housing is available is an example of an effort begun in the response timeframe to assist with recovery issues.

Public Assistance (PA) eligibility requirements and the cost share provisions of the Stafford Act and the FEMA-State Agreement (FSA) apply to DFA. The chapter on *Public Assistance* discusses PA eligibility requirements; the chapter on *Declarations* discusses cost share requirements.[47]

Incidental Benefits to the Private Sector through DFA

FEMA may authorize DFA to state and local governments and certain non-profit private entities when these entities lack the capability to perform or to contract for eligible emergency work and/or debris removal and request that work be accomplished by a federal agency.[48] The Stafford Act

---

[45] Id. § 206.208(a).

[46] Stafford Act § 408, 42 U.S.C. 5174. This type of construction for temporary housing is 100% federally funded. *See* the *Individual Assistance* chapter for further details.

[47] 44 C.F.R. § 206.203(b).

[48] Stafford Act, §§ 402(1) and 502(a)(1) (codified as amended at 42 U.S.C. §§ 5170a and 5192(a)(1)). As described in these sections, FEMA may direct any federal agency to perform work necessary to "support...State and local assistance response and recovery efforts, including precautionary evacuations" (§ 402(1)), or to "support...State and local emergency assistance efforts to save lives, protect property and public health and safety,

and its implementing regulations do not, however, authorize FEMA to provide DFA to private for-profit entities directly in response to a request for assistance, nor does it authorize federal assistance exclusively for economic recovery. In limited circumstances, private commercial entities may be indirect or incidental beneficiaries of DFA. When FEMA determines a private organization lacks the capability to perform a task on its own and the assistance is a direct benefit to the federal government and/or would address an immediate threat to the community at large, and is beyond state and local capability, FEMA may authorize assistance through a privately owned, for-profit entity. By contrast, DFA would not be appropriate in situations where assistance is requested for certain businesses or industries based on a perceived importance of the asset to the state or local economy. In each case, this will be a very fact-specific analysis and subject to the prior approval of OCC.

Example of DFA to the Private Sector

FEMA has provided generators to for-profit hospitals in response to disasters in cases where there would otherwise be a lack of emergency health care for a community if the hospital were without power

---

4. <u>Processing DFA Requests</u>

As the chapter on Declarations discusses, until the state or the tribe signs the FSA or FEMA-Tribe Agreement, except where it is necessary to provide essential emergency services or housing assistance under the Individuals and Households program, FEMA may not provide DFA to any grantee or other recipient. If FEMA approves the request for DFA, FEMA will task the appropriate federal agencies through a mission assignment to perform the work or to obtain a contract to perform the work.

The governor generally provides certain assurances in the declaration request. These are a statement explaining why the state, local, and/or

---

and lessen or avert the threat of a catastrophe, including precautionary evacuations." (§ 502(a)(1)); *see also* 44 C.F.R. § 206.208.

---

tribal government is unable to perform or contract for the work[49] and a written agreement that the state or tribe will:

a. Provide, without cost to the United States, all lands, easements, and rights-of-way necessary to complete approved work;

b. Hold harmless and save the United States free from damages due to the requested work and indemnify the federal government against any claims arising from such work;

c. Provide reimbursement to FEMA for the non-federal share of the cost of the work; and

d. Assist the performing federal department or agency in all support and local jurisdictional matters.

There may be occasions, however, where the grantee may submit a request for DFA[50] to FEMA without having included these assurances in the state's declaration request and before FEMA and the state or tribe has signed either an FSA or FEMA-Tribe Agreement. If the state is legally unable to provide rights-of-way, easements, and indemnification, an eligible applicant must agree in writing to meet these requirements.[51]

B. Pre-Scripted Mission Assignments (PSMAs)

FEMA had been developing PSMAs before Congress passed PKEMRA in 2006, but PKEMRA specifically directed FEMA[52] to develop PSMAs with federal agencies having responsibilities under the National Response Framework (NRF) in areas that include logistics, communications, mass care, health services, and public safety. Since PKEMRA, FEMA has worked with OFAs and developed over 250 PSMAs. By developing some provisions of mission assignments ahead of time (e.g., statements of work and cost estimates, which can be time consuming), PSMAs may facilitate a more rapid response.

---

[49] 44 C.F.R. § 206.208(b)(3).
[50] Id. § 206.201(e).
[51] Id. § 206.208(b).
[52] PKEMRA § 653, 6 U.S.C. § 753.

PSMAs are not automatic or self-executing documents. The statement of work, dollar amount, and timeline serve only as a guideline or template; FEMA, with the OFA, often revises them as needed to fit the specific need. The decision to issue a mission assignment remains with FEMA.

Some examples of FEMA's PSMAs include agreements with these agencies:

- Department of Health and Human Services (HHS) for medical care and support, including establishing temporary medical facilities for disaster survivors using the National Disaster Medical System (NDMS);

- DOD for aero-medical patient evacuation;

- U.S. Coast Guard (USCG) for search and rescue support in flooded areas;

- EPA to collect household hazardous waste; and

- USACE for debris removal and to oversee and secure contracts for the removal of debris, logistics, and water.

A detailed example of a PSMA is the one that FEMA has with the USACE under which USACE provides emergency residential roof covering ("Blue Roof" program) for holes and leaks in a homeowner's roof after a major disaster or emergency. Emergency residential roof covering provides individuals and households protection from the elements and allows them to shelter in place rather than requiring them to relocate to a shelter or other temporary housing arrangement.[53]

---

[53] Emergency Residential Roof Covering, Interim Policy (Sep. 6. 2005).

IV. Response Organizational Structure and Response Teams

A. National Response Framework (NRF) and Emergency Support Functions (ESFs)

The Homeland Security Act requires the FEMA Administrator to consolidate federal response plans into a single, coordinated national response plan, now known as the National Response Framework (NRF),[54] and last updated in January 2008.[55] Responsibility for management and maintenance of the NRF falls under the FEMA National Integration Center.[56] FEMA and all other agencies use the NRF to organize the federal government's response to presidentially declared events under the Stafford Act and for non-Stafford Act events. The NRF "builds upon the National Incident Management System (NIMS), which provides a consistent template for managing incidents."[57] In addition, Homeland Security Presidential Directive #5 (HSPD-5) combines the investigative and responsive elements of federal agencies (called "crisis management and consequence management") into a single approach.[58] These three documents provide the basis for organizing federal emergency response plans in order to manage all domestic incidents—not only natural disasters, but also man-caused events, such as terrorist attacks.[59]

The design of the NRF permits its use at any time in incidents or events of all sizes, through its organization of many of the federal government's agencies into Emergency Support Functions (ESFs).[60] These ESFs, described in Table 1, provide assistance in specified practical areas. Each

---

[54] Homeland Security Act, § 502(a)(6), 6 U.S.C. § 313(a)(6). This National Response Framework (NRF) expanded upon the Federal Response Plan, which FEMA first developed in 1992, <http://biotech.law.lsu.edu/blaw/FEMA/frpfull.pdf> and <http://www.disasters.org/emgold/frp.htm>.

[55] NRF see < http://www.fema.gov/emergency/nrf>. A revised NRF is scheduled to be issued in early 2013.

[56] Homeland Security Act, § 509(b)(1), 6 U.S.C. § 319(b)(1).

[57] NRF, at 1. NIMS (Dec. 2008) provides a unifying system of definitions for local, county, state, tribal, and federal governments. Thus, all levels of government use the same term for the same type of equipment, location, or team in an incident so that all levels of government can communicate with one another more effectively, <http://www.fema.gov/pdf/emergency/nims/NIMS_core.pdf>.

[58] HSPD-5 at ¶ 16, <Homeland Security Presidential Directive # 5>.

[59] NRF, at 7; HSPD-5, ¶¶ 1 and 3.

[60] NRF, at 1.

function has a coordinating agency with management oversight and one or more primary and support agencies with significant authorities, roles, resources, or capabilities to support particular tasks. FEMA coordinates the ESFs through the NRCC and the applicable RRCC. Not all incidents requiring federal support, however, result in the activation of ESFs.

In addition to activating agencies after an event, FEMA may deploy assets and capabilities through the coordinating agencies in charge of each appropriate ESF into an area when an incident is imminent but not declared and where resources and assets will be necessary to prepare for the expected event.[61] FEMA issues mission assignments to obtain resources and capabilities from across the federal government in support of the state.

Example of Pre-Declaration Mission Assignments

A hurricane is approaching the coastline of a state, and the state requests assistance with a mass evacuation and sheltering of persons. In this instance, the NRCC might request activation of standby FEMA contracts related to transportation, and analysis from ESF #1 (Transportation), ESF #6 (Mass Care, Housing, and Human Services), and ESF #8 (Public Health and Medical Services). If the President issues a pre-disaster emergency declaration[62] and FEMA later sets up a JFO after a presidential major disaster declaration, the FCO may then integrate these ESFs into a single branch or group within the JFO's Operations Section to ensure effective coordination of evacuation and sheltering services.

---

[61] OCFO – Pre-declaration Directive. *See also* chapter on *Readiness and Pre-Declaration Activities* for a further discussion of these early activities.

[62] Stafford Act §§ 501-503, 42 U.S.C. §§ 5191-5193; 44 C.F.R., Part 206, Subparts B, C; FEMA Policy 010-4, *Pre-Disaster Emergency Declaration Requests* (May 18, 2012).

Table 1: Emergency Support Functions (ESFs) and Coordinating Department

ESF Coordinator	Department	Activities
ESF #1– Transportation	Department of Transportation	• Federal and civil transportation support • Transportation safety • Restoration/recovery of transportation infrastructure • Movement restrictions • Damage and impact assessment
ESF #2 – Communications	DHS (National Communications System)	• Coordination with telecommunications industry • Restoration/repair of telecommunications infrastructure • Protection, restoration, and sustainment of national cyber and information technology resources
ESF #3 – Public Works and Engineering	Department of Defense (USACE)	• Infrastructure protection and emergency repair • Infrastructure restoration • Engineering services, construction management • Critical infrastructure liaison
ESF #4 – Firefighting	Department of Agriculture (USFS)	• Firefighting activities on federal lands • Resource support to rural and urban firefighting operations
ESF #5 – Emergency Management	DHS (FEMA)	• Coordination of incident management efforts • Issuance of mission assignments • Resource and human capital • Incident action planning • Financial management
ESF #6 – Mass Care, Housing, and Human Services	DHS (FEMA)	• Mass Care • Disaster housing • Human services
ESF #7 – Logistics Management and Resource Support	General Services Administration and DHS (FEMA)	• Resource support (e.g., facility space, office equipment and supplies, contracting services)

ESF Coordinator	Department	Activities
ESF #8 – Public Health and Medical Services	Department of Health and Human Services	• Public health • Medical • Mental health services • Mortuary services
ESF #9 – Search and Rescue	DHS (FEMA)	• Life saving assistance • Urban search and rescue
ESF #10 – Oil and Hazardous Materials Response	EPA/ USCG	• Oil and hazardous materials (e.g., chemical, biological, radiological) response • Environmental safety and short- and long-term cleanup
ESF #11 – Agriculture and Natural Resources	Department of Agriculture	• Nutrition assistance • Animal and plant disease/pest response • Food safety and security • Natural and cultural resources and historic properties protection and restoration
ESF #12 – Energy	Department of Energy	• Energy infrastructure assessment, repair, and restoration • Energy industry utilities coordination • Energy forecast
ESF #13 – Public Safety and Security	Department of Justice	• Facility and resource security • Security planning and technical and resource assistance • Public safety/security support • Support to access, traffic, and crowd control
ESF #14[63]		
ESF #15 – External Affairs	DHS (FEMA)	• Emergency public information and protective action guidance • Media and community relations • Congressional and international affairs • Tribal and insular affairs

---

[63] ESF-14 Long-Term Community Recovery and Mitigation has been replaced by the National Disaster Recovery Framework (NDRF), as discussed in the next section. This change will be reflected in the next NRF update, scheduled for release in early 2013.

B. National Disaster Recovery Framework (NDRF)

FEMA has learned that recovery and recovery planning can commence almost as soon as response activities do, and the quicker a dedicated effort is underway for an area to recover, the earlier the community can begin to do so. FEMA has worked with a number of OFAs to develop the National Disaster Recovery Framework (NDRF), a structure for the whole community to address recovery issues.[64] The NDRF aligns with the NRF. The NRF primarily addresses actions during disaster response. Like the NRF, the NDRF seeks to establish an operational structure and to develop a common planning framework. The NDRF replaces the NRF Emergency Support Function #14 (ESF #14) - Long-Term Community Recovery. Key ESF #14 concepts are expanded in the NDRF and include recovery-specific leadership, organizational structure, planning guidance, and other components needed to coordinate continuing recovery support to individuals, businesses, and communities.[65] The design of the NDRF brings in several new concepts including the Federal Disaster Recovery Coordinator, the state or tribal Disaster Recovery Coordinator, the local Disaster Recovery Manager, and Recovery Support Functions (RSFs). While similar to the NRF positions and functions, these personnel and functions are to focus strictly on recovery issues.

C. National Response Coordination Center (NRCC)

The Homeland Security Act requires the FEMA Administrator to maintain and operate an NRCC.[66] The NRCC is the national-level coordinating center for FEMA's operations and the focal point for national resource coordination during an incident.[67] The NRCC's mission is to maintain situational awareness of ongoing operations and emerging events that have the potential to require federal resources, and to identify, mobilize, deploy, and coordinate federal resources in support of state governments or OFAs in response to incidents.

---

[64] NDRF http://www.fema.gov/pdf/recoveryframework/ndrf.pdf
[65] Id. at 2.
[66] Homeland Security Act § 504(a)(17), 6 U.S.C. § 314(a)(17).
[67] National Incident Support Manual (NISM), Change 1-Jan 2013 at 7, available at: http://on.fema.net/components/orr/response/training/Documents/FEMA%20National%20Incident%20Support%20Manual%20012913.pdf

---

FEMA executes its statutory responsibility to operate an NRCC through a variety of policy and guidance documents. The NRCC conducts operations at four activation levels reflecting increasing threat levels as described in Table 2. NRCC staffing levels vary by activation level. The NRCC remains at Level IV (Watch-steady state) until an event occurs or there is evidence of a coming event that may require additional federal assets to aid in the response. The NRCC does not follow the Incident Command System (ICS) of the NIMS because the requirements for ICS at the field level are significantly different from the support coordination requirements of the NRCC staff. The National Response Coordination Staff (NRCS), as well as the Chief of the NRCS, receive support from the following sections: Situational Awareness, Planning Support, Resources Support, and Center and Staff Support.

Table 2: NRCC Activation Levels and Corresponding Staffing

NRCC Activation Level	Staffing
Level I-extensive damage, likely declaration with major federal assistance	NRCC Watch and Activation Teams, all ESFs, supporting agencies, and other representatives.
Level II-moderate damage that will likely result in a declaration	NRCC Watch and Activation Teams, with selected ESFs and selected supporting agencies.
Level III-minor to average level/breadth of damage that may result in a declaration	NRCC Watch and selected members or sections from NRCC Activation Team.
Watch-steady state	NRCC Watch maintains situational awareness with normal office staffing.

D. Regional Response Coordination Centers (RRCCs)

The Homeland Security Act requires each FEMA Regional Administrator to maintain and operate an RRCC.[68] Similar to their national-level counterpart, the NRCC, the RRCCs are 24/7 coordination centers that expand to interagency facilities staffed by ESF personnel in anticipation of or immediately following a serious incident in the particular region.[69]

A regional office activates its RRCC to coordinate regional response efforts, establish federal priorities, and implement local federal program support. The RRCC establishes communications with the affected state emergency management agency; deploys regional teams to assess the impact of the event, gauge immediate state needs, and makes preliminary arrangements to set up field facilities; and provides information to the NRCC on the disaster situation and federal response. The NRCC supports the RRCC efforts by deploying national assets when needed. RRCC operations transfer to the Joint Field Office (JFO) after it is established.

E. Joint Field Offices (JFOs)

Following a major disaster or emergency declaration, the Stafford Act charges the FCO with establishing field offices.[70] The primary one is the JFO—a temporary federal facility that provides a central location for the coordination of federal, state, tribal, and local governments, as well as private sector and non-governmental organizations, with primary responsibility for response and recovery. The JFO does not provide services to the public.[71] Instead, as the primary field structure, the JFO provides the organizing structure to integrate diverse federal authorities and capabilities and coordinate federal response and recovery operations.[72]

---

[68] Homeland Security Act § 504(c)(2)(H), 6 U.S.C. § 317(c)(2)(H).

[69] NRF, at 61.

[70] Stafford Act § 302(b)(2), 42 U.S.C. § 5143(b)(2).

[71] NRF, at 52. It is clear from the text of the NRF that the JFO is not a location where individual applicants may seek assistance.

[72] See, Joint Field Office Activation and Operations, Standard Operating Procedures, Version 8.3 (Interim Approval, April 2006) http://www.fema.gov/pdf/emergency/nrf/NRP_JFO_SOP.pdf < see also NISM, Change 1, Jan 2013, http://on.fema.net/components/orr/response/training/Documents/FEMA%20National%20Incident%20Support%20Manual%20012913.pdf (2013).

At the JFO, the Unified Coordination Group, consisting of the FCO, the State Coordinating Officer (SCO), and senior officials from other entities with jurisdictional authority and operational responsibility for some aspect of an incident, leads the coordination of activities.[73] Staff with the appropriate delegated authority within the NRCC, the RRCC, and the JFO, all may issue mission assignments.

FEMA may also deploy attorneys, called Deployable Field Counsel, to JFOs. These attorneys from the FEMA OCC provide the command staff with legal advice, as needed.

In a large disaster, the FCO may establish satellite Area Field Offices (AFOs) as well. These AFOs provide a federal and state presence, essentially mini-JFOs, in local areas that the disaster hit especially hard. As an example, after Hurricanes Ike and Gustav, when FEMA established the JFO in Austin, Texas, FEMA also established an AFO in the Port Arthur and Beaumont, Texas, area to assure that the local citizens had sufficient state and federal support personnel who could immediately address the severe local circumstances.

F. Federal Coordinating Officers (FCOs)

With the declaration of a major disaster or emergency, "the President shall appoint an FCO to operate in the affected area."[74] The Stafford Act charges the FCO with performing an initial appraisal of the types of relief most needed, establishing field offices, coordinating the administration of relief, and taking other such action consistent with his or her delegation and authority to provide assistance.[75]

While the President is not limited in choosing an FCO from FEMA, traditionally FEMA provides FCOs for Stafford Act major disasters and emergencies.[76] All FEMA FCOs are members of the FCO cadre that is part

---

[73] NRF, at 62-63; *see also* NISM, at 7.
[74] Stafford Act, § 302(a), 42 U.S.C. § 5143(a).
[75] Id. § 302(b), 42 U.S.C. § 5143(b).
[76] 44 C.F.R. § 206.41(a). *See also* 44 C.F.R. § 206.42, which lists the responsibilities of FCOs after a Stafford Act declaration; NRF, at 67, which states the President chooses an FCO based upon the recommendations of the FEMA Administrator and the DHS Secretary. *See also*, Department of Homeland Security Appropriations Act, 2010, Pub. L. No. 111-83, §

of the Office of Federal Disaster Coordination (OFDC) within the Office of Response and Recovery (ORR) at FEMA Headquarters (HQ). The Director of the OFDC reports directly to the Associate Administrator for ORR. The mission of the OFDC is to lead, train, equip, and manage FEMA's FCOs to ensure their availability for rapid deployment in response to any disaster; deliver training to develop and sustain professional competencies; and coordinate assignments to meet the on-scene needs of FEMA and its emergency management partners.[77] FEMA assigns its FCOs to particular regions; the FCOs receive their delegated authority to expend funds[78] from the Regional Administrator.

G. Federal Disaster Recovery Coordinators (FDRCs)

While disaster-impacted jurisdictions must necessarily and immediately focus on emergency response activities, the decisions made very early after a disaster influence recovery. In large-scale disasters and catastrophic incidents where a federal role may be necessary, the Federal Disaster Recovery Coordinator (FDRC) is a focal point for incorporating recovery and mitigation considerations into the early decision-making processes.[79]

The FDRC derives his or her authority from at least two sources: the statutory authority granted to "Federal coordinating officers" (FCO) under the Stafford Act[80] and the authority of the Disaster Recovery Manager (DRM) established by federal regulations.[81] The Administrator may also choose to delegate to the FDRC additional authorities found in the Post-Katrina Emergency Management Reform Act4 as circumstances warrant.[82] The Administrator and Regional Administrators may delegate to the FDRC all authorities typically delegated to an FCO, including the authority to coordinate disaster recovery, administer disaster relief programs funded

---

522, for possible additional officials that may be appointed and the requirements related to such officials.

[77] Office of FCO Operations, Directive FD 008-1 (Dec. 3, 2008), that describes the operation of the FCO program,
http://on.fema.net/components/orr/fcoo/Pages/default.aspx.

[78] See the chapter on *Declarations* for a discussion of this Disaster Recovery Manager authority. See also 44 C.F.R. §206.2(8).

[79] NDRF at 29.

[80] 42 U.S.C. § 5143.

[81] 44 C.F.R. § 206.2; 206.41.

[82] *See e.g.*, 6 U.S.C. §§ 313-314.

---

from the DRF, and direct federal agencies to utilize their authorities and resources in support of state and local recovery efforts.

Typically when an FDRC is first appointed, the FDRC will work as a deputy to the FCO for all matters concerning disaster recovery.[83] The FDRC is responsible for facilitating disaster coordination and collaboration between the federal, tribal, state and local governments; the private sector; and voluntary, faith based and community organizations. The FDRC may take over the lead from the FCO, when the FCO demobilizes, to continue management of federal recovery resources for those incidents that require continued significant interagency disaster recovery coordination.[84]

FDRC's will generally be FEMA employees, and the OFDC is responsible for their training and management. The NDRF structure may be used, however, for recovery from any type incident, including those that do not result in a Stafford Act declaration. In those situations, OFAs may find it appropriate to appoint one of their own employees as an FDRC. Such an appointment is done under the specific agency's own authority and does not transfer any authority from FEMA to that agency. For example, in the summer of 2012, the Secretary of Agriculture appointed an FDRC to facilitate recovery coordination and collaboration in response to a historic drought impacting much of the nation.

a.   Federal Resource Coordinators (FRCs) for Non-Stafford Act Events

In a situation that does not result in the President declaring a major disaster or emergency under the Stafford Act, but when another federal department or agency, acting under its own authority, requests the assistance of the Secretary of the Department of Homeland Security to obtain support from other federal departments and agencies, DHS may designate an FRC.[85] In these situations, the FRC coordinates support through interagency agreements and Memorandum of Understanding (MOU). Relying on the same skill set, DHS may select the FRC from the FCO cadre or other personnel with equivalent knowledge, skills, and

---

[83] Id.

[84] NDRF at 33.

[85] An FRC was appointed for the 2010 Deepwater Horizon Oil Spill to help coordinate efforts among the various federal agencies in assisting the USCG in responding to the oil spill.

abilities. The FRC is responsible for coordinating the timely delivery of resources to the requesting agency.[86]

H. Disaster Recovery Centers (DRCs)

The FCO's authority to take "such other action" consistent with his or her authority to provide assistance[87] includes working with state and local officials to establish DRCs around the impacted communities. Representatives from federal, state, and local agencies and non-profit organizations that provide disaster relief services staff the DRCs. The DRCs are places where disaster survivors can discuss their needs and register for assistance.[88] In addition to visiting these physical locations, individual applicants for assistance may call 1-800-621-FEMA (3362) to discuss their personal situation with trained FEMA personnel. FEMA may set up these physical centers in buildings that the state, tribal, or local governments provide, or FEMA may bring in a mobile office to perform these functions.[89]

I. Federal Emergency Management Teams

The Stafford Act and the Homeland Security Act authorize FEMA to activate specialized assets and teams[90] to aid in the response effort based on the type and scope of an incident.[91] Some of these teams are subject to FEMA's authority, some are subject to DHS's authority, and some are subject to the authority of other departments. Generally, the senior staff at the NRCC, the RRCCs, or the FCO may activate these specialized emergency support and response teams but additional concurrences may be necessary. This chapter discusses the following specialized response teams:

---

[86] NRF at 68.

[87] Stafford Act § 302(b)(4), 42 U.S.C. § 5143(b)(4).

[88] FEMA Disaster Assistance Policy [hereinafter DAP] 9430.1, *Disaster Recovery Center Services and Providers* (Oct. 12, 2008).

[89] See discussion of MVOCs in Chapter 2, *Readiness and Pre-declaration Activities*, Section VII.

[90] Stafford Act, § 303, 42 U.S.C. § 5144; 44 C.F.R. § 206.43. *See also* 6 U.S.C. § 317(f) requiring the establishment of regional strike teams authorized under the Stafford Act § 303, 42 U.S.C. § 5144, and detailing the composition of the teams.

[91] NRF, at 61.

- Incident Management Assistance Teams (IMATs);
- Hurricane Liaison Team (HLT);
- Mobile Emergency Response Support (MERS);
- Urban Search and Rescue (US&R);
- NDMS teams;
- Nuclear Incident Response Team (NIRT); and
- Domestic Emergency Support Team (DEST).

1. Incident Management Assistance Teams (IMATs)

IMATs[92] are highly mobile, responsive forces of qualified and experienced federal emergency management personnel and resources that can immediately deploy in support of any all-hazard incident response in the nation. While state and local responders are, of course, the first on the scene of an incident, IMATs are often the earliest federal presence there. An IMAT rapidly deploys as an experienced, cohesive team to an incident or incident-threatened venue to lead or support a prompt, effective, and coordinated federal response in support of state, tribal, territorial, and local officials. Although, FEMA may deploy an IMAT in anticipation of an event and before the President issues a declaration, FEMA may not authorize the IMAT to provide grant or direct assistance and is limited to providing FOS until the President issues a declaration. In addition, FEMA may name the IMAT lead as an FCO once the President has issued a declaration. FEMA, through IMATs, has a cadre of full-time[93] staff entirely focused on exercising, analyzing, and executing disaster response operations. Currently, FEMA has three national IMATs and a regional

---

[92] PKEMRA § 633, 6 U.S.C. § 317, amending the Stafford Act § 303, 42 U.S.C. § 5144, requiring that three national response teams be set up.
[93] Previously, federal on-scene teams were a combination of full-time staff pulled from other duties and temporary federal employees.

IMAT in each FEMA region.[94] FEMA is currently conducting a pilot program aimed at restructuring and reorienting its IMAT teams.[95]

2. Hurricane Liaison Team (HLT)

On June 1 of each year, FEMA activates the HLT to be ready when 1) a hurricane threatens the United States or its territories and 2) the National Hurricane Center (NHC) deems it requires such assistance. The HLT is a small, specialized team of FEMA staff and National Weather Service (NWS) meteorological and hydrologic experts that supports hurricane response operations by facilitating the rapid and accurate exchange of information between the NHC in Miami; the National Oceanic and Atmospheric Administration/National Weather Service (NOAA/NWS); and federal, state, tribal, and local government officials.[96] The HLT communicates about the progress and threat level of a storm with appropriate federal, state, and local officials to assist them in their decision-making. The team also organizes and facilitates video and/or teleconferences with the NHC, FEMA, and OFAs; state emergency operations centers; weather prediction centers; and river forecast centers.[97]

---

[94] 6 U.S.C. § 317(c)(2)(D) and (f). PKEMRA § 633 (Pub. L. No. 109-295, 6 U.S.C. § 721), in amending § 303 of the Stafford Act, 42 U.S.C. § 5144, also required that FEMA establish a "Target Capability Level" for each team. An FCO leads each team, the FCO leading a Type I team is in the federal government's Senior Executive Service (SES), and these teams have the most experience and the most training. National IMATs are Type I teams, and a member of the SES leads the team, while Regional IMATs are Type II teams, and their leader is a GS-15.

[95] See, Memo from Administrator Craig Fugate re Management Assistance Team Pilot Program (February 2, 2013).

[96] NRF, at 62.

[97] See Hurricane Liaison Team Operations Manual, < http://on.fema.net/components/orr/fcoo/Documents/DHS_FEMA_HLT_Ops_Manual.pd f >.

---

3. Mobile Emergency Response Support (MERS)

The MERS[98] provides rapid operational, communications, and logistics support to federal, state, tribal, and local responders in their efforts to save lives, protect property, and coordinate response operations.[99] The MERS directly supports and meets the needs of federal, state, tribal, and local emergency managers and responders, not disaster victims. MERS units are available for immediate deployment and equipped with self-sustaining elements of assistance. MERS assistance falls into the following three broad categories:

1. Operations Support

   - Situation and event reporting and briefing;
   - Data collection and display;
   - Interagency coordination;
   - On-site security (facility, equipment, and personnel), planning, and supervision; and
   - Law enforcement coordination.

2. Communications Support

   - Telecommunications transmission systems, including satellite, high frequency, microwave line of sight, and local area networks;
   - Communications equipment and assets, including radios, computers, phone and video systems; and
   - Technician and operator communications.

3. Logistics Support

   - Power generation and distribution; heating, ventilation and cooling (HVAC); fuel transportation and distribution, and potable water;

---

[98] *See* DEC MERS briefing (2011)at <
http://on.fema.net/components/orr/response/disaster_comms/mers/Pages/default.aspx
>; *see also* MERS Fact Sheet at
<http://www.fema.gov/pdf/media/factsheets/2010/dod_dec.pdf>.
[99] *See* Mobile Operations Capability Guide for Emergency Managers and Planners at
<http://www.fema.gov/emergency/mers/index.shtm>.

- Experienced personnel in facility management, acquisition support, warehouse operation, transportation management, and property accountability; and

- Emergency operation vehicles.

MERS stages units in six strategic locations and can support multiple field operating sites at the same time.[100] The six MERS detachment locations and the FEMA region(s) they cover are:

1. Bothell, WA (Regions IX and X);
2. Denton, TX (Regions VI and VII);
3. Denver, CO (Regions V and VIII);
4. Maynard, MA (Regions I and II);
5. Thomasville, GA (Regions III and IV); and
6. Frederick, MD (National Capitol Region).

The legal issues generally associated with MERS operations include:

- Security for transportation and the storage of equipment, which is generally handled with FEMA security staff and, depending upon whether MERS stores the equipment in an actual structure, the Federal Protective Service;

- Whether the particular jurisdiction allows red or blue lights on emergency response vehicles at a disaster site;

- Whether staging areas have proper arrangements for use of the property; and

- Whether there are any DOT or state transportation regulations to which MERS must adhere.

---

[100] NRF, at 62.

4. Urban Search and Rescue (US&R)

The US&R System, first created by FEMA administratively and then codified by PKEMRA,[101] provides the framework for structuring local emergency services personnel into integrated response task forces.[102] US&R teams provide urban search and rescue and life-saving assistance to state, tribal, and local authorities when activated for incidents or potential incidents requiring a coordinated federal response.[103] FEMA's US&R regulations[104] have three parts. The first gives an overview of the authority for the program. The second provides for its steady state preparedness programs, and the third describes US&R's activities when actually performing as teams at an incident. In addition, the FEMA US&R Program has a robust library of policies, which are on its internal website.[105]

There are many participants in the National US&R System. During its steady state, preparedness phase, the organization of US&R System falls into four categories:

1. FEMA – establishes policy and leads the coordination of the national system;

2. Sponsoring Agency – a state or local government that has executed an Memorandum of Agreement (MOA) with DHS and/or FEMA to organize and administer a Task Force;

3. Task Force – an integrated US&R organization of multi-disciplinary resources with common communications and a leader, organized and administered by a Sponsoring Agency and meeting DHS and/or FEMA standards; and

4. Participating Agencies – a state or local government, nonprofit organization, or private organization, which has an executed

---

[101] PKEMRA, § 634, 6 U.S.C. § 722, confirmed FEMA's authority to establish the US&R.
[102] NRF, at 62.
[103] *See* Urban Search and Rescue, Overview, <http://www.fema.gov/about-urban-search-rescue>.
[104] 44 C.F.R. § 208.
[105] Only an appropriate member of the FEMA US&R program may grant access to this site.

agreement with a Sponsoring Agency to participate in the National US&R Response System.[106]

FEMA's US&R system consists of three main operational elements:

1. FEMA – establishes policy, leads the coordination of the national system, and provides the senior federal leadership for deployed US&R Task Forces through ESF-9;

2. Task Forces – the 28 FEMA US&R Task Forces spread throughout the continental United States, which FEMA trained and equipped to handle structural collapse; and

3. Incident Support Teams (IST) – support the US&R Task Forces in accomplishing their mission through logistical, electronic, and coordination expertise. They are drawn from members of the 28 US&R Task Forces who, when assigned a role on an IST, take on that role rather than their regular US&R Task Force membership.

Since FEMA issued regulations covering US&R teams working in the United States and its territories, the legal issues associated with US&R teams have included questions largely related to international aid, such as:

- Whether all international teams have available a previously negotiated MOU with the U.S. Agency for International Development (USAID);

- Whether the use of any other teams when used internationally requires execution of a MOU;

- To what extent international teams are federalized when activated, that is:

  o Eligibility of teams for Workers' Compensation

  o What is the salary of the individual members, and are they covered under the Federal Tort Claims Act?

  o What does FEMA pay for and what does the sponsoring agency pay for?

---

[106] 44 C.F.R. § 208.2.

FEMA, or often the requested team, resolves these issues through the development of MOUs and interagency agreements with the requesting agency.

5. Nuclear Incident Response Team (NIRT)

NIRTs[107] are teams with specific expertise to provide a rapid response to nuclear accidents or incidents. They are generally composed of trained personnel with specialized equipment from the Department of Energy (DOE)/National Nuclear Security Administration and the EPA. They can assess situations and advise local, state, and federal officials on the scope and magnitude of response needs. When activated, the NIRT provides DHS and/or FEMA with expert technical advice and support in disaster response operations on the following types of issues:

- Nuclear weapons accidents;
- Radiological accidents;
- Lost or stolen radioactive material incidents; and
- Acts of nuclear terrorism.

Assets and capabilities of the NIRT include, for example:

- Aerial Measuring System - Airborne radiological sensing and surveying; and

- Federal Radiological Monitoring and Assessment Center - Operational and logistical management for radiological consequence management.[108]

FEMA assists the NIRT by establishing standards and certifying when the NIRT meets those standards; conducting joint and other exercises, and training and evaluating performance; and providing funds to the DOE and the EPA, as appropriate, for homeland security planning, exercises and training, and equipment.

---

[107] 6 U.S.C. § 312; see generally, 42 U.S.C § 5144; 44 C.F.R. § 206.43; see also <http://www.phe.gov/Preparedness/support/medicalassistance/Pages/default.aspx#ndms>,and<http://www.phe.gov/preparedness/pages/default.aspx>.
[108] Department of Homeland Security, Management Directive 9400 (Mar. 25, 2003).

The NIRT operates subject to the direction, authority, and operational control of the Secretary of DHS. NIRT assets deploy at the direction of the Secretary of DHS in connection with an actual or threatened terrorist attack, major disaster, or other emergency in the United States. The legal issues regarding control of these assets are resolved through FEMA HQ with a U.S. Secret Service liaison, detailed to FEMA to coordinate NIRT activities, and by working closely with DOE and DHS to assure clear roles and responsibilities of the multiple agencies involved with the NIRT.

6. Domestic Emergency Support Team (DEST)

The DEST[109] is a specialized interagency team designed to provide expert advice, guidance and support to the Federal Bureau of Investigation (FBI) On-Scene Commander (OSC) during a Weapons of Mass Destruction incident or credible threat. The DEST is comprised of members from the following agencies: FBI, FEMA, DOD, HHS, EPA, and DOE. FEMA manages the DEST in support of the FBI. While no legal issues apparently exist at this time with this team, when activated, there are likely to be questions regarding who receives information this team acquires.

The DEST consists of "crisis and consequence management"[110] components and augments the FBI's Joint Operations Center with tailored expertise, assessment, and analysis capabilities, providing the FBI OSC with expert advice and guidance in the following areas:

- Interagency crisis management assistance;
- Information management support;
- Enhanced communications capability;
- Contingency planning for consequence management support;

---

[109] 6 U.S.C. § 314 (a)(3)(B); see generally, 42 U.S.C § 5144; 44 C.F.R. Part 206.43.
[110] As explained earlier, these terms mean that both investigative and response functions work together. See also, NRF, at 1. NIMS (Dec. 2008) provides a unifying system of definitions for local, county, state, tribal, and federal governments. Thus, all levels of government use the same term for the same type of equipment, location, or team in an incident so that all levels of government can communicate with one another more effectively, <http://www.fema.gov/pdf/emergency/nims/NIMS_core.pdf>.

- Explosive devices and their components; chemical, biological, and nuclear weapons/devices and their components, as well as radiological dispersion devices; and
- Technical expertise and equipment to operate in a contaminated environment to conduct threat sampling, take measurements, and collect tactical intelligence and evidence.

7. National Disaster Medical System (NDMS)

NDMS is a coordinated interagency effort among the HHS, DOD, Department of Veterans Affairs (VA), DHS/FEMA, state and local governments, and private sector institutions and medical professionals to provide medical response, patient evacuation, and hospitalization during disasters and emergencies.[111] Under the NRF, NDMS serves as a component of ESF #8, Public Health and Medical Services.[112] NDMS supplements state and local medical resources.

NDMS, formed in 1984 as part of the Public Health Service within HHS, began with medical professionals who were strictly volunteers. HHS has managed NDMS since its inception, except from 2003–2006 when Congress transferred it to DHS.[113] PKEMRA, as of January 1, 2007, however, transferred NDMS back to HHS.[114] In the absence of a Stafford Act declaration, the authority to activate NDMS rests with the Assistant Secretary for Preparedness and Response in HHS. When the President issues a Stafford Act declaration, however, FEMA may mission assign HHS to deploy NDMS teams. The following NDMS teams have significant roles in disaster response activities:[115]

- Disaster Medical Assistance Team (DMAT);
- Disaster Mortuary Operations Response Team (DMORT);
- National Veterinary Response Team (NVRT); and
- National Medical Response Team (NMRT).

---

[111] 42 U.S.C. § 300hh-11(a)(2); Stafford Act § 303, 42 U.S.C. § 5144.
[112] NRF, at 59; *see* NRF ESF #8 Annex <http://www.fema.gov/emergency/nrf/#>
[113] 6 U.S.C. § 314.
[114] PKEMRA, Pub. L. 109-295 (2006). *See also* Conference Report on H.R.5441 (House Rept. No. 109-699), Department of Homeland Security Appropriations Act, 2007, Title III, Public Health Programs, 72 Cong. Rec. H 7789 (Sept. 28, 2009).
[115] <http://www.phe.gov/Preparedness/responders/ndms/teams/Pages/default.aspx>.

Medical Licensure

The issue of medical licensure frequently arises in major disasters or emergency declarations when local medical authorities are overwhelmed and require assistance from out-of-state medical professionals. State authorities establish medical licensing requirements. The Stafford Act is silent on medical licensing, and FEMA has no authority to authorize licensure. During Hurricanes Katrina and Rita, HHS set up a licensure process that allowed doctors practicing under HHS auspices and licensed in one state to practice as a volunteer in another state with the same protection as other federal employees. Out-of-state medical professionals not affiliated with HHS who volunteer to assist in a jurisdiction in which they are not licensed must consult state licensing authorities for their requirements.

Legal issues that may arise include the scope of services that NDMS provides and the reimbursement of such services.

a.) Disaster Medical Assistance Team (DMAT)

DMAT[116] is a rapid response medical team consisting of physicians, nurses, and medical technicians sent to the site of declared events to supplement local medical care until FEMA or HHS mobilize other federal or contract resources, or the situation resolves itself. With logistics and administrative personnel support, DMATs deploy to disaster sites with sufficient supplies and equipment to sustain themselves for a period of 72 hours while providing medical care at a fixed or temporary medical care site. The HHS activates DMAT personnel for a period of two weeks. The statute authorizing NDMS provides that team members, such as the DMATs, become federal employees when HHS activates them to provide medical care during an event, and therefore, they have protection from liability in the event of a malpractice claim.[117]

The medical care that DMATs provide includes primary and acute care; triage of mass casualties; resuscitation and stabilization; advanced life support; patient reception at staging facilities; and preparation of sick or

---

[116] <http://www.phe.gov/Preparedness/responders/ndms/teams/Pages/dmat.aspx>
[117] 42 U.S.C. § 300hh-11(c)(1).

injured patients for evacuation. The ability of the DMATs to provide the same type of care that an eligible non-profit hospital can provide is limited and thus, once the DMAT stabilizes a patient, the DMAT staff works to "regulate" or move the patient to an out-of-area full service hospital. This process can involve legal issues and questions related to reimbursement for far off available facilities. In mass casualty incidents, DMATs provide high-quality medical care despite the adverse and austere environment often found at a disaster site. When it is necessary to evacuate disaster survivors to a different locale to receive definitive medical care, HHS may activate DMATs to support the movement of patients to an appropriate hospital.

b.) Disaster Mortuary Operational Response Team (DMORT)

HHS deploys DMORTs[118] to provide victim identification and mortuary services in disasters and emergencies. The DMORTs work under the guidance of local authorities, including coroners, medical examiners, law enforcement, and emergency managers, to provide TA and personnel to assist with the recovery, identification, and processing of deceased victims. Teams consist of funeral directors, medical examiners, coroners, pathologists, forensic anthropologists, medical records technicians and transcribers, fingerprint specialists, forensic odontologists, dental assistants, x-ray technicians, and support staff. The DMORTs can also assist with maintaining temporary morgue facilities and helping address mortuary concerns in unique situations, including deaths from chemical, biological, or radiological events.

In Louisiana, following Hurricanes Katrina and Rita, FEMA utilized the DMORTs to identify remains so that the state and local entities could reinter caskets, which the floodwaters had disinterred. Initially, there was a legal issue regarding whether the caskets came from a public or non-profit church cemetery, where FEMA would have had the authority under the Stafford Act to assist these cemeteries, as compared to a private cemetery where FEMA would be unable to assist the state to reinter the bodies. After Hurricane Floyd in 1999 (FEMA-DR-1292), there was controversy in North Carolina about whether FEMA should pay for grave markers for disinterred remains.

---

[118] <http://www.phe.gov/Preparedness/responders/ndms/teams/Pages/dmort.aspx>.

c.) National Veterinary Response Team (NVRT)

HHS deploys NVRTs[119] to provide veterinary health care and public health assistance following disasters or emergencies. Like other emergency response teams, NVRTs supplement the efforts already underway by state and local veterinary and public health resources. NVRTs are comprised of veterinarians, veterinarian pathologists, veterinary technicians, microbiologists, virologists, epidemiologists, toxicologists, and various scientific and support personnel.

NVRT capabilities include:

- Assessment, treatment, and stabilization of animals;
- Animal disease surveillance;
- Zoonotic[120] disease surveillance;
- Public health assessments;
- TA related to food and water quality; and
- Animal decontamination.

The legal issues associated with NVRTs include determining the degree to which they are necessary and coordinating with the USDA and non-profit organizations who wish to use dogs available to them.

d.) National Medical Response Team (NMRT)

NMRTs[121] provide medical care for victims following a nuclear, biological, and/or chemical incident. NMRTs are comprised of health, medical, and hazardous materials professionals supported by logistics and administrative staff. The NMRT capabilities include:

- Agent detection;
- Sample collection;
- Mass casualty decontamination;
- Medical triage and emergency care of contaminated patients; and

---

[119] <http://www.phe.gov/Preparedness/responders/ndms/teams/Pages/nvrt.aspx>.
[120] A zoonotic disease is a disease that can infect both animals and humans.
[121] 42 U.S.C. §§ 300hh-11(c)(1)(A); the Pandemic and All-Hazards Preparedness Act, Pub. L. No. 109-417, § 2811(c)(1)(A) (2006); Defense Against Weapons of Mass Destruction Act of 1996, Pub. L. No. 104-201,§§ 1412, 1414(b) (1996); see generally, 42 U.S.C. § 5144; 44 C.F.R. Part 206.4, <http://nmrt-ncr.com/mission.html>.

- Medical care to stabilize victims for transportation to tertiary care facilities that are able to manage hazardous materials.

J. Defense Support of Civil Authorities (DSCA)

A DOD directive defines DSCA as support provided by military and DOD personnel and assets "in response to requests for assistance from civil authorities for special events, domestic emergencies, designated law enforcement support, and other domestic activities."[122] The NRF also uses this term.[123] This section describes the elements of DSCA.

1. National Guard (NG)

The National Guard (NG) is the present day version of the original state militia concept in the Constitution.[124] When the NG is working for the governor of a state, it is in "State Active Duty" status, the state determines the pay and benefits of their NG personnel, and they are considered state employees for benefits and liability purposes. Each state has its own militia law governing this status.[125]

NG members and units may be placed into "federal service" by being ordered to active duty in their reserve component status or called into federal service in their militia status under various sections of Title 10 of the United States Code.[126] In this role, NG forces are under the command of the President. When in federal service, NG members are relieved from duty in the NG of their state and consequently are removed from state

---

[122] Department of Defense Directive No. 3125.1.

[123] DoD Directive No. 3025.15. *See* NRF, at 11, note 12.

[124] U.S. CONST. art. I, § 8, cl. 15 & 16; art. II, § 1 & amend. II, for references to the militia. The Constitution empowered Congress to "provide for organizing, arming, and disciplining the militia." However, recognizing the militia's state role, the Founding Fathers reserved the appointment of officers and training of the militia to the states. Today's National Guard remains a dual state-federal force. *See also Perpich v. Department of Defense*, 496 U.S. 334, 342 (1990).

[125] For example, Arizona Constitution, art. 5, § 3; A.R.S. § 26-101 (governor as commander-in-chief of state military forces when not in federal service); A.R.S. § 26-121 (composition of militia); A.R.S. § 26-172 (mobilization of militia for emergencies and when necessary to protect life and property).

[126] 10 U.S.C. §§ 101(c); 331-335; 12301-12304; & 12406.

command and control.[127] A limited exception allows selected NG members to be placed on active duty without being relieved from duty in the NG of the state.[128] This exception allows an NG member to be under the President's command and concurrently under a governor's command for specified matters.

Alternatively, NG members may be ordered to perform training or operational duty in support of operations or missions at the request of the President or Secretary of Defense.[129] In that capacity, members train for their federal military missions according to the congressionally established disciplines in Title 32, United States Code, under state control as members of their respective states' militia. They can also perform operational missions such as disaster response in the United States. NG members in this "state status" receive federal pay and benefits from funds appropriated to DOD and are considered federal employees for purposes of the Federal Tort Claims Act[130] but are under the governor's command and control.

2. Posse Comitatus

The primary statutory restriction on the participation of military personnel in civilian law enforcement activities[131] is the Posse Comitatus Act (PCA).[132] The PCA provides that "Whoever, except in cases and under circumstances expressly authorized by the Constitution or Act of Congress, willfully uses any part of the Army or the Air Force as a posse comitatus or otherwise to execute the laws shall be fined . . . or imprisoned . . . or both." The term "posse comitatus" means the power of the county and refers to the authority of the sheriff to call to his aid the male population

---

[127] 32 U.S.C. § 325.

[128] Id.

[129] 32 U.S.C. §§ 502(a) & (f). See also 32 U.S.C. §§ 901-904, authorizing DOD funding to governors for NG units engaged under section 502(f) in "homeland defense activities" which is an activity "undertaken for the military protection of the territory . . . of the United States . . . as being critical to national security, from a threat or aggression."

[130] Federal Tort Claims Act, 28 U.S.C. §§ 1346(b), 2671-2680.

[131] This section describing posse comitatus is liberally taken or copied from portions of the U.S. Army, The Judge Advocate General's School publication, Domestic Operational Law Handbook for Judge Advocates (July 20, 2009), Chapter 4 "Military Support to Civil Law Enforcement." This is an overview only, and those not fully familiar with this concept should consult legal counsel for specific application.

[132] 18 U.S.C. § 1385.

of the county above the age of 15 to assist in capturing escaped felons and keeping the peace.

The prohibitions of the PCA apply to the enforcement of federal, state, or local law by members of the Army or Air Force unless otherwise authorized by the Constitution or by federal statute.[133] The PCA makes unlawful the willful use of "any part of the Army or Air Force" absent constitutional or statutory authority. Although not expressly applicable to the Navy and Marine Corps, a DOD directive extends the prohibitions of the PCA to restrict similarly the use of Navy and Marine Corps personnel without proper approval of the Secretary of Defense or Secretary of the Navy.[134] Thus, the NG may support state law enforcement while in "State Active Duty" or in Title 32 status without violating the prohibitions in the *posse comitatus* statute. If the federal government uses Title 10 forces to preserve order without carefully following PCA provisions, however, commanding officers may violate *posse comitatus*.

a.) Possible consequences of a violation of the PCA include the following:

i). Criminal sanctions. Willful violations subject the military member to imprisonment for not more than two years or a fine of $10,000 or both.

ii). Inability to convict offenders. A court may rule that evidence obtained because of a violation of the PCA is inadmissible against a defendant in a criminal prosecution. While a violation of the PCA alone is not determinative, important factors include the seriousness of the violation and the frequency of such violations.

iii). Civil liability. Military members whose conduct violates the PCA may not be acting within the scope of their employment, and thus they may be exposed to personal liability for their actions in a civil suit.

---

[133] *See* the Insurrection Act, 10 U.S.C. §§ 331-335, and 10 U.S.C. Chapter 18, *Military Support for Civilian Law Enforcement Agencies.*
[134] DoD Directive No. 5525.5, DoD Cooperation with Civilian law Enforcement Officials (Jan.15, 1986).

b.) The PCA does not prohibit the following activities involving direct assistance by military personnel:

i). **Military Purpose Doctrine**. Actions taken for the primary purpose of furthering a military or foreign affairs function of the United States, regardless of incidental benefits to civilian authorities, do not violate the PCA. Commanding officials must use this provision with caution. Actions under this provision may include the following: actions related to the commander's inherent authority to maintain law and order on a military installation or facility; protection of classified military information or equipment; protection of DOD personnel, DOD equipment, and official guests of DOD; and, other actions undertaken primarily for military or foreign affairs purposes.

ii). **Sovereign authority**. Actions taken under the inherent right of the U.S. government, a sovereign national entity under the Constitution, to ensure the preservation of public order and the carrying out of governmental operations within its territorial limits, by force if necessary, do not violate the PCA. The proper exercise of this authority is available only for unusual circumstances and in only two circumstances:

- Emergency. When prevention of the loss of life or wanton destruction of property and restoration of governmental functions and public order requires prompt and vigorous federal action, including use of military forces. When sudden and unexpected civil disturbances, disasters, or calamities seriously endanger life and property and disrupt normal governmental functions so much that duly constituted local authorities are unable to control the situation, actions will include use of military forces; and

- Protection of federal property and functions. When the need for protection exists, and duly constituted local authorities are unable or decline to provide adequate protection to protect federal property and functions, federal action may or will include the use of military force.

iii). **Statutory Authority**. Actions taken under express statutory authority to assist civilian officials in execution of the laws do not violate the PCA.

3. Base Commander Authority

Base commanders and a DOD component have the delegated authority to provide immediate assistance to civil authorities to save lives, prevent human suffering, and mitigate great property damage in the event of a civil emergency or attack.[135] In addition, the Stafford Act also provides that a governor of a state may request the Secretary of Defense to use DOD resources to perform emergency work, which is essential for life and property. If the President grants the request, DOD may perform the work for no more than 10 days.[136]

4. Dual Status Command

Recognizing the growing scope of state and federal military domestic missions following 9/11, Congress amended Title 32 in the 2004 National Defense Authorization Act, permitting NG commanders to retain their state commissions after they received orders to active duty. This change allows NG officers to command both federal and state forces simultaneously (dual-status) to preserve unity of command at the operational level. Within months of this legislative change, three national special security events implemented dual-status command arrangements and did so in support of the U.S. Customs and Border Protection's border patrol during Operation Winter Freeze. These operations were coordinated extensively among USNORTHCOM, the National Guard Bureau, and the NG and viewed as successful examples of state and federal military cooperation. Building on this momentum, in 2005, Congress again amended Title 32, authorizing the Secretary of Defense to "provide funds to a governor to employ National Guard units or members to conduct homeland defense activities."

---

[135] DOD Directive No. 3125.1 § ¶ 4.5.
[136] Stafford Act, § 403(c), 42 U.S.C. § 5170b(c).

Unfortunately, federal military support of civil authorities since 9/11 is proving to be more complicated than anticipated. The national consternation caused by the uncoordinated NG and federal military response in the aftermath of Hurricane Katrina makes this point clear. To be sure, the military performed superbly at the tactical level, but, according to the Executive Office of the President, at the strategic and operational level, "lack of an integrated command structure for both active duty and National Guard forces exacerbated communications and coordination issues during the initial response."[137]

In a large-scale event, in order to assure a unified command and control among the regular Army forces and NG forces, the President may authorize one officer to be in command of both forces and thus be in duty status in both the Army and the NG.

5. Military Reservists

As of July 2012, the Secretary of Defense may involuntarily order units and individuals of the Army, Navy, Marine Corps, and Air Force Reserves to active duty for up to 120 days "when a governor requests federal assistance in responding to a major disaster or emergency."[138] Since this authority is specific to assistance in responding to a major disaster or emergency under the Stafford Act, FEMA will reimburse DOD for all costs (salary and travel) if DOD activates non-National Guard reservists for disaster response activity in response to a FEMA mission assignment request.[139] FEMA will pay travel and per diem of federal military personnel assigned to respond to disasters or emergency areas designated by FEMA.[140]

Figure 4a outlines the status of military forces, including command and control, funding, location of duty, mission types, and support to law enforcement under State Active Duty (SAD) and Titles 10, 32, and 14 of the U.S. Code.

---

[137] THE WHITE HOUSE, THE FEDERAL RESPONSE TO HURRICANE KATRINA: LESSONS LEARNED at 43 (Feb. 23, 2006), http://library.stmarytx.edu/acadlib/edocs/katrinawh.pdf.
[138] National Defense Authorization Act for FY2012, 10 U.S.C. § 12304a.
[139] 44 C.F.R. § 206.8(c).
[140] Id § 206.8(c)(3).

Figure 4a: Status of Military Forces

	State Active Duty (SAD)	Title 32	Title 10	Title 14
Command and Control	Governor	Governor	President	Commandant of the US Coast Guard
Location of Duty	In accordance with State Law	U.S.	Worldwide	Worldwide. Law Enforcement jurisdiction upon High Seas and waters over which U.S. has jurisdiction
Funding	State Funds	Federal	Federal	Federal
Mission Types	In accordance with State Law (riot control, emergencies)	Training and/or other federally authorized missions	Overseas Training and other missions as assigned	Uniformed armed service with broad law enforcement powers
Military Discipline	State Military Code	State Military Code	State Military Code	UCMJ
Support to Law Enforcement	Yes, within authority extended by state law	Yes, within authority extended by state law	As limited by Federal law Posse Comitatus Act	Yes
Indemnity for Accidents	State	Federal	Federal	Federal

V. Response Activities

The first to respond to the scene of any disaster, whether a house fire or a tornado, will be neighbors, local emergency responders, and voluntary agency relief groups. This sense of community and drive to rally together in times of need is woven into the fabric of this country and is one its greatest strengths in times of need.

FEMA and OFAs support and supplement state and local responsibilities for their citizens. This is the continuum of delivery—state, local, and tribal governments respond and FEMA reimburses them for their costs. FEMA provides coordinating and technical assistance and, if state, local, and tribal governments are overwhelmed, FEMA tasks other agencies to provide direct assistance through mission assignments, often through negotiated PSMAs. Thus, response activities in field operations fall into several categories—those that FEMA assigns as missions to OFAs, those that relief organizations and the private sector implement, those that FEMA staff engage in,[141] and, most importantly, those that state and local governments implement for which FEMA may later reimburse them. This chapter discusses mission assignments and DFA in the section on *Direct Assistance and Mission Assignments*. In addition, various OFAs have the authority to respond to emergencies, and they coordinate with the rest of the federal government through FEMA and the NRCC/RRCC structure. The remainder of this chapter discusses these various categories.

A. Use of and Coordination with Relief Organizations

Relief organizations usually arrive at a disaster location before federal assistance is present and will remain long after. The Stafford Act also authorizes FEMA to utilize the personnel and facilities of relief organizations such as the American Red Cross (ARC), The Salvation Army (TSA), the Mennonite Disaster Service (MDS), and others to distribute medicine, food, supplies, or other items and to restore and reconstruct community services, housing, and essential facilities.[142] FEMA has written agreements with many of these organizations so that the FCO may coordinate disaster relief activities with those activities of the state, local, and tribal governments.[143] Any written agreement must include assurance that the non-profit will implement the use of federal facilities, supplies, and services in a non-discriminatory manner and will not duplicate benefits to recipients of federal assistance.[144] The authority to use federal facilities, supplies, and services is only triggered if there is a major disaster or emergency. [145] FEMA has also developed a system to use these relief

---

[141] FEMA personnel are also on many of the teams discussed in *Response Organizational Structure and Response Teams* in this chapter.

[142] Stafford Act, § 309, 42 U.S.C. § 5152(a); 44 C.F.R. § 206.12(a).

[143] Id. § 309, 42 U.S.C. § 5152(b); 44 C.F.R. § 206.12(b).

[144] Id.

[145] Id.

organizations to distribute items that others have donated to FEMA to disaster applicants.[146] FEMA may utilize invitational travel under the Federal Travel Regulations to provide transportation support for relief organization personnel who are engaged in coordinated relief operations, particularly for remote or insular areas.[147]

Partnering with Relief Organizations

In the 2010 Alaska major disaster declaration, FEMA, the State of Alaska and several relief organizations, including the MDS, and Samaritan's Purse (SP), partnered to purchase, assemble, and furnish log cabins for disaster victims in a very remote village. FEMA purchased the log cabin kits under the Stafford Act's Federal Assistance to Individuals and Households program (see the chapter on Individual Assistance). The MDS volunteers oversaw the assembly and construction, and SP provided necessary furnishings and appliances. FEMA also provided logistical (transportation) support under the Stafford Act's emergency assistance program, called "Essential Assistance" in the statute. Stafford Act §§ 402, 403, 407, 502, 503; 42 U.S.C §§ 5170b(a), 5192(a); 44 C.F.R. §§ 206.201(b) & 206.225.

As of December 2010, FEMA had MOUs with the following relief organizations: Adventist Community Services; ARC; Church World Service; Feeding America; MDS; Operation Hope; National Council on Independent Living; North American Mission Board (Southern Baptists); National Voluntary Organizations Active in Disaster; Committee on Relief; TSA; and United Methodist Committee on Relief.[148] These organizations provide services such as establishing and operating shelters, providing meals to survivors and, as needed, providing donated clothing to disaster survivors.

---

[146] FEMA Standard Operating Procedure, Processing, Distribution and Disposal of Donated and Federally-Purchased Goods Controlled by FEMA [hereinafter Donated Goods SOP] (Annex, FEMA 6150-1) (August 20, 2008).

[147] Travel expenses and reimbursements are subject to the Federal Travel Regulation, 41 C.F.R. Chapters 301-304.

[148] Information from FEMA's Voluntary Agency Liaison.

Donated goods, which FEMA receives, are processed, distributed, and disposed of pursuant to a standard operating procedure.[149] GSA regulations also have a significant influence on how FEMA may dispose of supplies and equipment that FEMA purchases.[150]

B. Use of State and Local Assets

State, tribal, and local governments are, of course, on scene well before federal assets. When they agree, FEMA may use their assets to provide supplemental aid to assist in responding to the incident.[151] The authority to accept state and local services and facilities is only in furtherance of FEMA's supplemental role.[152] For example, affected state, local, and tribal governments typically provide space at no cost for use as DRCs, discussed previously, where disaster survivors could access a broad range of relief programs and organizations.

C. Hiring Temporary Personnel

The Stafford Act authorizes FEMA to hire temporary personnel, experts, and consultants to perform services under the Stafford Act.[153] PKEMRA directed FEMA to develop a Surge Capacity Force of trained and deployable personnel under Stafford Act authorities.[154] The Incident Workforce Management Office (IWMO) in the Response Directorate, ORR, oversees employee readiness and deployment for the agency, including the internal Surge Capacity Force (full-time FEMA employees who do not typically deploy, and the centrally managed Disaster Generalist Cadre of Reservists), as well as the external DHS Surge Capacity Force.[155] FEMA also has an arrangement with AmeriCorps and the Corporation for National and Community Service (CNCS), creating FEMA Corps, a unit of 1,600 members within AmeriCorps, National Civilian

---

[149] *Donated Goods SOP.*
[150] 41 C.F.R. § 102-35 through 102-38.
[151] Stafford Act, § 306(a), 42 U.S.C. § 5149 (a).
[152] *Id.*
[153] *Id.* § 306(b), 42 U.S.C. § 5149(b). *See* FEMA Disaster Reserve Workforce: http://on.fema.net/components/msb/occhco/dwd/Pages/default.aspx; *see, also, Thiess v. Witt,* 100 F.3d 915 (Fed. Cir. 1996).
[154] PKEMRA § 624, 6 U.S.C. § 711.
[155] These issues are discussed in more detail in the *Human Capital* chapter.

Community Corps (NCCC) that is solely devoted to disaster preparedness, response, and recovery.[156] *See* the chapter on *Human Capital* for further discussion of temporary disaster personnel and FEMA Corps.

D. Acquisition and Distribution of Potable Water for Staff

There are numerous recurring legal issues at the JFO, such as using appropriated funds to purchase potable[157] or bottled water for staff in field offices.[158] As a rule, without specific statutory authority, appropriations are not available for personal expenses. The Comptroller General normally considers bottled water to be a personal expense of the government employee.[159] There are several Comptroller General decisions, however, addressing when federal agencies may use appropriated funds to purchase bottled water for employees in federal facilities. An agency may use appropriated funds, however, to provide a work site with potable water, as well as clean air, sufficient light, and certain facilities such as restrooms.[160] Specifically, federal agencies may use appropriated funds to purchase bottled water upon a showing of necessity, either because the available water, if consumed, poses a health risk or because water is not available.[161]

---

[156] *See* http://www.fema.gov/fema-corps.

[157] Water that meets the standards for drinking purposes of the state or local authority having jurisdiction, or water that meets the standards prescribed by the U.S. Environmental Protection Agency's National Primary Water Regulations (40 CFR 141). This definition is found in the following Occupational Health and Safety Administration Standards: General Industry 1910.141(a)(2), Construction 1926.51(a)(6) and the Agriculture Field Sanitation 1928.110(b).

[158] While this edition of the DOLR covers one such recurring issue, DOLR 3.0 (forthcoming FY 2013) may cover other issues, such as badging, security, JFO leases, donated space, clothing, the DHS logo, cold weather gear, and others.

[159] Department of the Army-Use of Appropriations for Bottled Water, Comp. Gen. File No. B-310502 (Feb 4, 2008), <http://www.gao.gov/decisions/appro/310502.htm>. The Army Corps of Engineers could use appropriated funds to provide bottled water to its employees working in remote work sites without access to potable water.

[160] Department of the Army, Military Surface Deployment and Distribution Command-- Use of Appropriations for Bottled Water, Comp. Gen. File No. B-318588 (Sep. 29, 2009),

[161] *Id.*

When water otherwise available to agency employees is unwholesome or is otherwise not potable, the government may view the purchase of bottled drinking water as a necessity.[162]

Consequently, FEMA may use appropriated funds to purchase bottled water for employees at FEMA JFOs or in the field when the command staff, usually the safety officer, has determined that it is necessary because the available water supply is inadequate or the available water is not potable.[163] There must be factual support for this determination. There is no requirement for specific approval from FEMA OCC for such purchases.

E. Accepting Gifts and Donations

Private companies, organizations, individuals, and even foreign governments may offer to donate goods and services to FEMA after a disaster.[164] Gifts and donations can raise legal and ethical issues. This section discusses only gifts/donations offered to FEMA as an entity to further the purposes of the Stafford Act, not gifts to individual FEMA employees. See the chapter on Ethics for further discussion of gifts to FEMA employees.

The Stafford Act authorizes the FEMA Administrator to accept donations and gifts of services, money, or property in furtherance of the purposes of the Stafford Act, i.e., to alleviate the suffering and damage caused by disasters.[165] The Administrator has delegated or redelegated such gift acceptance authority to various FEMA officials. The scope of such delegations varies depending on factors such as whether the source of the gift is a domestic or international entity or whether the gift involves the

---

[162] Decision Concerning Army Officer's Appeal of Claims Group's Denial of Claim for Reimbursement for Purchase of Bottled Water, Comp. Gen. File No. B-236330 (Aug 14, 1989), < http://www.gao.gov/assets/500/496278.pdf >.

[163] See U.S. Agency for International Development, Purchase of Bottled Drinking Water, Comp. Gen. File No.B-247871 (Apr. 10, 1992), <http://redbook.gao.gov/11/fl0054092.php>. The water available through the agency's office was discolored, had an unusual odor and taste, and contained elevated levels of lead.

[164] 42 U.S.C. § 5201.

[165] Stafford Act § 701(b), 42 U.SC. § 5201(b). See also Stafford Act § 621(d), 42 U.S.C.5197(d) (The Director [now called the Administrator] may accept gifts of supplies, equipment, and facilities and may use and distribute those gifts for emergency preparedness purposes under Stafford Act Title VI, Emergency Preparedness).

use or transfer of real property or facilities. Nonetheless, FEMA officials exercising delegated authority must consult with the OCC before accepting any bequests, gifts, or donations offered to FEMA.[166] Note that offers of gifts and/or donations received by any FEMA official not specifically authorized in the sub-delegation must be sent to the Administrator for acceptance.

1. Gifts and Donations from Domestic Sources

FEMA Directive 112-3, Agency Gift Acceptance and Solicitation, establishes FEMA's policy and responsibilities for accepting and soliciting gifts from domestic sources. The Gift Acceptance and Solicitation Directive does not apply to gifts to individuals; use of state, tribal, or local government or relief or disaster assistance facilities for Stafford Act purposes; certain travel expenses; volunteer services; foreign gifts; or gifts accepted by the U.S. General Services Administration (GSA) under its own authorities for use by FEMA.

With the exception of gifts of real property or facilities, the following are authorized agency officials who may accept or solicit gifts and/or donations to FEMA from domestic sources: the Administrator, the Deputy Administrator, Deputy Administrator for Protection and National Preparedness, Associate Administrator for Response and Recovery, Associate Administrator for Mission Support, Associate Administrator for Policy and Program Analysis, the Chief Counsel, the Chief Financial Officer, the Deputy Associate Administrator for Response and Recovery, the Assistant Administrators for both the Response and Recovery Directorates, the Superintendent of the Emergency Management Institute, the Superintendent of the Center for Domestic Preparedness, the Regional Administrators, and FCOs appointed for declared events. In addition, the Administrator of the United States Fire Administration and the Associate Administrator of the Federal Insurance and Mitigation Administration are delegated authority to accept gifts for the purposes of the Fire Prevention and Control Act and the Earthquake Hazards Reduction Act, respectively. The authority to accept or solicit gifts of real property or facilities is

---

[166] Id. at 2.

reserved for the Administrator, Deputy Administrator, and Regional Administrators.

The process for accepting or soliciting gifts subject to FEMA Directive 112-3 is as follows:

- The prospective donor must fill out the relevant sections of the FEMA Gift Donation Agreement, FEMA Form 112-13-0-2.

- An authorized agency official, with the assistance of a FEMA Ethics Counselor, must analyze the gift by completing the Checklist for Reviewing Gift Donations or Solicitations (FEMA Form 112-13-0-1). The Checklist guides agency officials in making a determination of whether or not the proposed gift or donation reflects poorly on the agency, compromises the agency's integrity, attaches prohibited conditions on the gift or requires the agency to act outside of its mission and duties, requires the expenditure of appropriated funds, provides the donor with some benefit, or creates a conflict of interest or the appearance of a conflict of interest.

- Both the authorized agency official and the Ethics Counselor must sign the Gift Donation Agreement to signify that the agreement is complete and that the agency will accept the gift.

- For gifts of facilities subject to FEMA Directive 112-13, OCC will assist in development, review, and approval of Interagency Agreements, Memorandums of Understanding, Memorandums of Agreement, License Agreements, and Use Agreements, as necessary. Gifts involving use of a facility accepted by GSA under its authorities on behalf of FEMA may be accepted pursuant to the policies and procedures established by GSA in lieu of FEMA's policies for gift acceptance and solicitation.

Example of Donation Issue

In August 2011, Hurricane Irene caused major damage and disruption to telecommunications systems from North Carolina and through the Mid-Atlantic region all the way north through the New England states. A communications company offered to donate telecommunications services, including networking, wireless access, phone, videoconferencing, and radio interoperability, to any government entities (federal, state, or local) that needed it in responding to Hurricane Irene. The question was whether FEMA could accept this offer of donated telecommunications services from the company. Services are specifically included in items that FEMA may accept for donation under Stafford Act. As part of its offer, however, the company requested that the accepting entity agree to provide food, fuel, and shelter for its employees who would be providing the donated services. FEMA declined the donation because the agency does not accept gifts and/or donations that may result in a conflict of interest or the appearance of a conflict of interest.[167]

2. Gifts and Donations from International Sources

FEMA may accept gifts and/or donations from international sources pursuant to its gift acceptance authority under the Stafford Act.[168] The AARR delegated this authority to the Deputy AARR; the Assistant Administrator, Response Directorate; and the Chief and Deputy Chief of the NRCS.[169] Typically, the NRCS Chief or Deputy or their senior management, in consultation with OCC, will determine whether to accept an international offer of assistance.

---

[167] *See also* 5 C.F.R. § 2601.203-.204; Ethical Implications of Emergency Response Conf. Report, *Agency Gift Acceptance* (June, 2006) at http://www.oge.gov/DisplayTemplates/SearchResults.aspx?query=Ethical%20Implications%20of%20Emergency%20Response%20Conf.%20Report,%20Agency%20Gift%20Acceptance%20(June,%202006)

[168] *See* Stafford Act § 701(b), 42 U.S.C. § 5201(b).

[169] Memorandum from the Associate Administrator for Response and Recovery, *Sub-delegation of Gift Acceptance Authority* (Aug. 30, 2011). This delegation does not include Stafford Act Title VI preparedness gift acceptance authority under § 621(d), 42 U.S.C. 5197(d).

Generally, the federal government expects to have the resources to respond to a domestic disaster without the need of international assistance and has an interest in avoiding an unanticipated influx of goods, which may interfere with ongoing response and recovery operations. Thus, typically the Department of State (DOS) will refer foreign offers of assistance for domestic disaster events to non-governmental organizations.

In response to what some may characterize as catastrophic disasters, however, the federal government may receive offers of assistance from another country or international organization where DHS and/or FEMA and DOS make a decision in principle to accept international assistance. The International Assistance System Concept of Operations governs offers and receipt of goods and services from foreign governments and international organizations.[170] This includes when and how FEMA coordinates with the DOS for communicating acceptance and denials of offers; how FEMA may task USAID Office of Foreign Disaster Assistance (OFDA) for logistics support in receiving and distributing donations; and procedures for ensuring compliance with entry-into-country requirements.

F. Federal Advisory Committee Act

The Federal Advisory Committee Act and its implementing regulations govern the establishment, operation, and termination of advisory committees within the executive branch.[171] A Federal Advisory Committee is defined as any committee, board, commission, council, conference, panel, task force, or other similar group, established by statute or established or utilized by the President or by an agency official, for the purpose of obtaining advice or recommendations for the President or on issues or policies within the agency official's responsibilities.[172]

---

[170] International Assistance System Concept of Operations, SBU version (Oct. 26, 2009).
[171] 5 U.S.C. App. and 41 C.F.R. Parts 101-6 and 102-3.
[172] 5 U.S.C. App. § 3. 41 C.F.R. 102-3.25.

Federal Advisory Committees must be chartered before they can meet and expire two years after their charter dates unless they are renewed prior to those dates.[173]

1. Federal Advisory Committee meetings must be announced in the *Federal Register* and open to the public unless specifically exempt by law in consultation with the Office of Chief Counsel and the Department of Homeland Security Committee Management Office.

2. The documents a Federal Advisory Committee prepares must also be available to the public, subject to the exclusions contained in the Freedom of Information Act

3. Minutes must be prepared for each Federal Advisory Committee meeting.

4. Federal Advisory Committee membership must be fairly balanced.[174]

One example of a Federal Advisory Committee within FEMA that is subject to the provisions contained in FACA is the National Advisory Council established by the Homeland Security Act of 2002, as amended by the Post-Katrina Emergency Management Reform Act of 2006.[175]

For more specific information on legal issues arising from FEMA's interactions with the private sector, please consult OCC's "Framework for Private Sector Engagement," which is available at: http://on.fema.net/components/oocc/Pages/main.aspx.

Meetings where FACA does not apply:

- Town halls/public forums seeking individual input
- Meetings with state or local officials in their official capacities
- Meetings with a single non-federal group or entity
- Meetings organized by a non-federal group or entity where FEMA does not fund the meeting, set the agenda, or invite the participants

---

[173] 5 U.S.C. App. §§ 9-10. The committee's charter is filed with the head of the agency or department.
[174] 5 U.S.C. App. §§ 5 and 10. 41 C.F.R. 102-3.70, 102-3.75, 102-3.55, 102-3.150, 102-3.155 and 102-3.175. Designated Federal Officers must approve all meetings and agendas as well as attend the meetings. 41 C.F.R. 102-3.120.
[175] 6 U.S.C. § 318.

G. Evacuation and Sheltering

FEMA coordinates the delivery of federal mass care[176] and emergency assistance when local, tribal, and state response and recovery needs exceed the capabilities of these entities. As a part of the NRF and its ESFs, FEMA works with support entities, including many OFAs and non-profit organizations.[177] In ESF #6 FEMA works to assist, as needed, with evacuation and sheltering in partnership with the ARC. ESF #6 includes two components related to mass care and emergency assistance:[178]

- Mass care includes sheltering, feeding, emergency first aid, bulk distribution of emergency items, and collecting and providing information on survivors to family members; and

- Emergency assistance includes evacuation support (registration and tracking of evacuees); reunification of families; aid and services to special needs populations; evacuation, sheltering, and other emergency services for household pets and service animals; support to medical shelters; coordination of donated goods and services; and coordination of voluntary agency assistance.[179]

FEMA may provide reimbursement to state and local governments for eligible costs related to their mass care and emergency assistance under a major disaster or emergency declaration.[180] Eligible costs for mass care and emergency assistance include facility costs, supplies and commodities, emergency medical services, durable medical equipment (DME), and emergency costs for household pets and service animals.[181] All persons in the disaster area are eligible to receive shelter, food, and other basic

---

[176] FEMA and ARC are co-leads for the mass care component of ESF #6 pursuant to an MOA between FEMA and ARC. FEMA and ARC coordinate with states in planning and executing mass care services.

[177] Support agencies include the Departments of Agriculture, Defense, Health and Human Services, Housing and Urban Development, Interior, Justice, Labor, Transportation, Treasury, and Veterans Affairs; the General Services Administration; the Small Business Administration; the U.S. Postal Service; the ARC; the Corporation for National and Community Service; and the National Voluntary Organizations Active in Disaster.

[178] NRF Emergency Support Function #6 Annex, at ESF #6-2; *see* http://www.fema.gov/pdf/emergency/nrf/nrf-esf-06.pdf.

[179] Two other components in ESF #6, housing and human services, come into play in IA. *See* the chapter on *Individual Assistance*.

[180] Stafford Act §§ 403 or 502, 42 U.S.C. §§ 5170b or 5192.

[181] DAP9523.15, *Eligible Costs Related to Evacuations and Sheltering* (Apr. 6, 2007); PA GUIDE, at 62.

commodities; there are no individual eligibility requirements for life-saving and life-sustaining assistance. FEMA may also reimburse states outside of the declared area, called "host-states," that incur evacuation and sheltering costs for evacuees from declared areas for their eligible costs when the impact state has requested DFA[182] and FEMA has entered into an agreement with the host state to provide the service.[183]

The National Shelter System (NSS), which non-profit organizations originally developed and which became a federal asset in 2009,[184] is a database of over 60,000 government-owned and private non-profit facilities throughout the United States, such as previously inspected schools and churches that may be utilized as general population shelters. The ARC manages sheltering operations in approximately 75% of disasters; however, local and tribal governments, other non-profit agencies, or contractors through FEMA's Individual Assistance Technical Assistance Contracts (IA-TACs) may also operate shelters.[185]

FEMA maintains the NSS database with the name, location, and types of facilities for each shelter. FEMA is negotiating separate agreements with the states and with ARC through which they may access the NSS database. The NSS allows authorized users to identify, track, analyze, and report shelter data in a consistent and reliable manner. Emergency shelters must also accommodate individuals with disabilities and functional needs.

1. Accommodating Individuals with Disabilities and Functional Needs during Evacuations and in Shelters

The Stafford Act[186] and federal civil rights laws[187] prohibit discrimination against individuals with disabilities in the provision of publicly funded

---

[182] 44 C.F.R. § 206.208(c)(3); DAP 9523.18, *Host-State Evacuation and Sheltering Reimbursement* (July 23, 2010) http://www.fema.gov/pdf/government/grant/pa/9523_18.pdf.
[183] 74 Fed. Reg. 6,020 (Nov. 20, 2009).
[184] *See* http://on.fema.net/programs/orr_programs/recovery_programs/ia_programs/Documents/National%20Shelter%20System.pdf.
[185] *See* chapter on *Individual Assistance* for a discussion of FEMA's IA-TAC contracts.
[186] PKEMRA, (Pub. L. No. 109-295) amended the Stafford Act, adding persons with disabilities to § 308, 42 U.S.C. 5151, prohibiting discrimination in the provision of disaster assistance, and adding durable medical equipment to § 403(a), 42 U.S.C. § 5170b(a), as essential assistance.

services, programs, or activities. In addition, FEMA has a Disability Coordinator to ensure that the access and functional needs of individuals with disabilities are being properly addressed in emergency preparedness and disaster relief.[188] FEMA *Guidance on Planning for Integration of Functional Needs Support Services in General Population Shelters* ("FNSS Guidance")[189] supports state, tribal, local, and federal government efforts to integrate individuals who have access and functional needs into every aspect of emergency shelter planning and response. FNSS was developed and approved in conjunction with a number of partners, including the Department of Justice.[190]

Functional Needs Support Services (FNSS) are services that enable individuals to maintain their independence in a general population shelter. Children and adults requiring FNSS may have physical, sensory, mental health, cognitive, and/or intellectual disabilities affecting their ability to function independently without assistance. Others who may also have access and functional needs include but are not limited to women in late stages of pregnancy, elders, and individuals needing bariatric equipment or communication assistance. FNSS includes:

- Reasonable modification to policies, practices and procedures;
- Durable medical equipment (DME);
- Consumable medical supplies (CMS);
- Personal assistance services (PAS); and
- Other goods and services as needed.

---

[187] The Rehabilitation Act of 1973 § 504, as amended, 29 U.S.C. § 794; the Americans with Disabilities Act of 1990, as amended by the ADA Amendments Act of 2008 ("ADA"), 42 U.S.C. §§ 12101-12213; and the Architectural Barriers Act of 1968, 42 U.S.C. §§ 4151-4157. *See* < http://www.fema.gov/accommodating-individuals-disabilities-provision-disaster-mass-care-housing-human-services > for summaries of applicable civil rights laws.

[188] Homeland Security Act § 513, 6 U.S.C. § 321b.

[189] *Guidance on Planning for Integration of Functional Needs Support Services in General Population Shelters* (Nov. 2010).

[190] FNSS Review Panel members included FEMA, HHS, DHS, Department of Justice, ARC, the National Council on Disability, the National Council on Independent Living, the National Disability Rights Network, the Center for Disability and Health Policy, the Rhode Island Department of Health, the Florida Division of Emergency Management Statewide Disability Coordinator for Emergency Management, and the California Emergency Management Agency Office of Access and Functional Needs.

Examples of specific needs addressed by planning for FNSS in general population shelters include the following:

- Access to effective communication during shelter registration and while applying for disaster-related benefits and services;

- Access to necessary medications;

- Availability, modification, and stabilization of universal/accessible sleeping accommodations (cots, beds, and/or cribs);

- Access to orientation and way-finding for people who are blind or have low vision;

- Assistance for individuals with cognitive and intellectual disabilities;

- Access to an air conditioned and/or heated environment (for example, for those who cannot regulate body temperature);

- Availability of food and beverages appropriate for individuals with dietary restrictions (for example, persons with diabetes or severe allergies to foods);

- Providing food and supplies for service animals (for example, dishes for food and water, arrangements for the hygienic disposal of waste; and, if requested, portable kennels for containment);

- Accessible transportation for individuals who use a wheelchair or other mobility device;

- Assistance with activities of daily living.

The FNSS Guidance identifies key considerations that shelter planners should consider when planning for shelter set-up, shelter operations, and transitioning survivors from shelters back into the community. The FNSS Guidance includes over 35 operational tools consisting of examples and excerpts taken from a variety of state and local jurisdictional documents as tools and templates for local, tribal, state, and federal emergency sheltering planners.

In addition, FEMA publishes a reference guide called *Accommodating Individuals with Disabilities in the Provision of Disaster Mass Care, Housing, and Human*

Services.[191] Further, the Department of Justice (DOJ) developed the *ADA Guide for Local Governments: Making Community Emergency Preparedness and Response Programs Accessible to People with Disabilities*[192] and an ADA Checklist for Emergency Shelters.[193] The ADA Checklist provides informal guidance to assist in understanding the ADA and DOJ regulations for ADA accessibility standards.[194] The standards address facility features such as:

- Passenger drop off areas with wheelchair/mobility device accessibility;

- Accessible parking spaces and entrance to shelters;

- Interior hallways and corridors wide enough for mobility devices;

- Accessible ramps with handrails;

- Elevators large enough to accommodate mobility devices;

- Accessible routes to accessible sleeping areas, restrooms and bathing areas (minimum dimensions required for turning mobility devices);

- Accessible telephones when public telephones are provided, including text telephones or TDY devices for individuals who are deaf, hard of hearing, or who have a speech disability;

- An accessible route at least 36" wide and without steep slopes to accessible tables and seating; and

- A backup power supply to provide refrigeration for medication, operation of supplemental oxygen and breathing devices, and battery charging for power wheelchairs and scooters.

---

[191] See http://www.fema.gov/accommodating-individuals-disabilities-provision-disaster-mass-care-housing-human-services.
[192] See http://www.ada.gov/emergencyprepguide.htm.
[193] See http://www.ada.gov/shleterck.htm.
[194] 28 C.F.R. Part 36, Appendix A.

> **Court Ruling on Emergency Preparedness for Disabled Residents**
>
> A federal district court ruling found, as a matter of law, that the City of Los Angeles excluded individuals with disabilities from participation in the city's emergency preparedness program in violation of the ADA, the Rehabilitation Act, and state statutes that prohibit discrimination against individuals with disabilities in state and local government programs and in programs receiving federal financial assistance. This Los Angeles case illustrates the importance of assuring that local governments plan to meet the access and functional needs of individuals with disabilities in an emergency or major disaster. [195] The nondiscrimination principles apply to other levels of government.

2. Household Pets and Service Animals

A lesson learned from Hurricane Katrina in 2005 was that individuals with household pets and service animals refused to evacuate without their pets or service animals, and there were few, if any, provisions to evacuate and shelter the animals. In 2006, Congress passed two identical statutes to address this issue, both of which amended the Stafford Act to authorize rescue, care, shelter, and essential needs for household pets and service animals as eligible emergency assistance.[196]

FEMA defines the types of household animals covered by these statutes through policy. A household pet is a domesticated animal, such as a cat, dog, bird, rabbit, rodent, or turtle traditionally kept in the home for pleasure. A service animal, on the other hand, has a regulatory definition in the ADA implementing regulations.[197] FEMA policy defines service

---

[195] *Communities Actively Living Independently and Free v. City of Los Angeles,* U.S. Dist. LEXIS 118364 (C.D. CA. Feb. 10, 2011). Although Los Angeles County entered a consent decree with the plaintiffs to address the need of disabled individuals in the County's emergency planning and preparedness, the City of Los Angeles continued to fight the lawsuit, resulting in this decision.

[196] The Pets Evacuation and Transportation Standards Act of 2006, § 4, Pub. L. No. 109-308, 120 Stat. 1725; PKEMRA, (Pub .L. No. 109-295) § 689(b)(D), amending § 403 of the Stafford Act, 42 U.S.C. § 5170b(a)(3)(J).

[197] The revised Title II Regulations of the ADA define "service animal" as "any dog that is individually trained to do work or perform tasks for the benefit of an individual with a disability, including a physical, sensory, psychiatric, intellectual, or other mental

animal more broadly than the current ADA regulations because the policy is based on a previous version of the regulations. FEMA policy provides that "a service animal is any guide dog or signal dog or other animal individually trained to provide assistance to an individual with a disability."[198] The policy also provides for the following:

- State and local governments outside the designated disaster area may seek reimbursement under mutual aid protocols through the affected and supported state(s);

- State and local governments are the only eligible applicants for sheltering and rescuing household pets and service animals; contractors and private non-profit organizations (PNPs) can be reimbursed for sheltering and rescuing household pets and service animals through a state or local government;

- State and local governments may conduct sheltering operations for pets directly, or may contract with other sheltering providers for such services. Eligible congregate pet sheltering costs may include the reasonable costs for:
  - Facilities;
  - Supplies and commodities;
  - Eligible labor;
  - Equipment;
  - Emergency veterinary services;
  - Transportation;
  - Shelter safety and security;
  - Cleaning and restoration;
  - Removal and disposal of animal carcasses; and
  - Cataloging/tracking system for pets.

Service animals will be sheltered with their owners; however, household pets may be sheltered in separate congregate pet shelters.

---

disability." See 28 C.F.R. § 35.104 and § 35.136 for the current definition of "service animal" and additional regulations regarding service animals.
[198] DAP 9523.19, Eligible Costs Related to Pet Evacuations and Sheltering (Oct. 24, 2007).

---

3. National Emergency Family Registry and Locator System (NEFRLS)

The mass evacuation of hundreds of thousands of Gulf Coast residents after Hurricane Katrina separated many survivors, including children, from their families. No adequate mechanism existed at the time to collect information on all those displaced and to reunite them with their families. As a result, Congress directed that FEMA establish the NEFRLS[199] to help reunify families separated after an emergency or major disaster.

NEFRLS is a web-based system that facilitates the reunification of families separated because of a declared event. Activated during a declared disaster or emergency, NEFRLS enables displaced adults to register voluntarily over the Internet or by phone with their name, current location of residence, and other information that others seeking to locate them could use. The design of the system protects individual privacy and complies with laws that protect "personally identifying" information, including the Privacy Act.[200]

Upon registration, FEMA provides a standard Privacy Act statement. The registrant either views it online or FEMA call center staff read it to the registrant. After acknowledging the Privacy Act statement, registrants provide personally identifiable information (PII) to NEFRLS, including their name and current location. A third party contractor verifies the registrant's actual identity, and the registrant can name up to seven individuals authorized to view his or her PII. Only authorized searchers may access the registrant's information, and a third party must also authenticate the searchers' identities. NEFRLS refers displaced children to the National Child Locator Center, discussed in the following section.

---

[199] PKEMRA, Pub .L. No. 109-295)§ 689c, 6 U.S.C. § 775.
[200] 5 U.S.C. § 552(a) *et seq.*

4. National Emergency Child Locator Center (NECLC)

PKEMRA[201] mandates the NECLC in order to assist state, local, and tribal governments, as well as law enforcement agencies, to track and locate children separated from their parents or guardians because of a declared event.

In collaboration with the National Center for Missing and Exploited Children (NCMEC), NECLC is a clearinghouse for information about children displaced in a declared event, and it assists law enforcement in locating these children.[202] During a major event with large numbers of displaced people, the NECLC will operate a telephone bank and a website for information about displaced children; deploy staff, called "Adam teams," to shelters to help ensure the safety of displaced children; and coordinate reunification efforts with local law enforcement and human service agencies.[203]

In addition to the MOA, discussed previously, FEMA signed an MOU in February 2007 with the NCMEC, the ARC, the DOJ, and the HHS to facilitate the identification and reunification of children with their families. In March 2011, FEMA signed an agreement with NCMEC to be able to work with them as soon as the need arises.

5. Firearms and Evacuations

The Stafford Act provides that an official may require the temporary surrender of a firearm as a condition for entry into any mode of transportation used for rescue or evacuation during a major disaster or

---

[201] Id. § 689b, 6 U.S.C. § 774.

[202] See MOA between DHS/FEMA and FBI. See MOA between FEMA and the FBI (Jan. 8, 2007). The MOA grants the FBI Crimes against Children Unit limited access to FEMA's Privacy Act-protected Disaster Recovery Assistance Files for the purpose of assisting locating children missing as a result of a declared event, http://ia.fema.net/contents/bpas/benefits/documentation/DOJ%20CACU%20MOA_Missing%20Kids_1-07.pdf. FEMA also amended its Disaster Recovery Assistance Files, FEMA/REG-2, adding a new routine use, permitting FEMA to disclose information to a federal or state law enforcement authority authorized to investigate or coordinate locating missing children or reuniting families. 71 Fed. Reg. 38,408 (July 6, 2006).

[203] See FEMA IA Division Fact Sheet: < http://on.fema.net/programs/orr_programs/recovery_programs/ia_programs/Documents/National%20Emergency%20Child%20Locator%20Center-IA%20Fact%20Sheet.pdf

emergency, if the official returns the temporarily surrendered firearm at the completion of such rescue or evacuation.[204] An official is a federal officer or employee, civilian or military, or <u>any</u> person operating under color of federal law or receiving federal funds, among other situations,[205] while supporting relief after a declaration of major disaster or emergency. FEMA has not issued a policy on this provision, but if these governmental entities determine that other federal, state, or local laws do not already apply, FEMA may assist financially state, tribal, or local governments who use this provision.[206] Many private transportation companies, however, already disallow firearms on their carriers.

Example of Private Firearm Regulations

Many bus companies do not permit the open display of firearms on a bus and require them to be in the baggage compartment.[207]

---

6. Providing Access to Essential Service Providers

A provision in the Stafford Act requires that federal officials may not restrict access to disaster areas where the service provider, such as the electric company or a communications company, seeks to restore service.[208] In order to assure that these providers are able to carry out their work and that, inadvertently, state and local officials do not restrict them, all levels of government can effectively coordinate through the JFO. A recurring problem in disasters is utility repair crews having difficulty accessing the disaster area due to road blocks established by local law enforcement. The private sector in the past has asked FEMA to intervene to solve the problem. FEMA, however, has no authority to override local law enforcement. As a solution, a best practice that FEMA has developed in the past few years is for FEMA to encourage governors or other suitable state official to issue to the private sector a letter on letterhead that asks the local law enforcement to let them pass through critical access points.

---

[204] Stafford Act, § 706(b), 42 U.S.C. § 5207(b).
[205] Id. § 706(a), 42 U.S.C. § 5207(a).
[206] Id. § 403, 42 U.S.C. § 5170b(a)(3)(I).
[207] <http://www.greyhound.com/en/docs/greyhound_prohibited_items_list.pdf>.
[208] Stafford Act § 427, 42 U.S.C. § 5189(e).

> **Example of Resolution of Provider Access to Disaster Sites**
>
> Texas issued a letter during Hurricane Ike to allow communications providers access to disaster sites, and the process resolved many otherwise contentious problems.

H. Debris Removal

The Stafford Act authorizes FEMA to provide assistance for debris removal[209] through a mission assignment to another federal agency or through direct grants to an eligible applicant for the cost of removing debris or wreckage resulting from a major disaster or emergency from publicly or privately owned lands and waters. The chapter on *Public Assistance* discusses debris removal in detail.

I. Emergency Protective Measures

Depending upon the particular circumstances, including who has legal responsibility and whether that person or entity is an eligible applicant, FEMA may fund costs for emergency protective measures to protect lives or improved property. Examples include construction of temporary berms, levees, and dikes; bracing or shoring damaged structures to prevent further damage; providing temporary facilities; boarding windows and doors; or covering the roof to prevent further damage.[210] The chapter on *Public Assistance* discusses eligibility in detail.

---

[209] Id. §§ 403(3)(A), 407 and 502(a)(5), 42 U.S.C. § 5170b(3)(A), 42 U.S.C. § 5173 & 42 U.S.C. § 5192(a)(5); *see also* 44 C.F.R. § 206.224. Additional resources: DAP 9523.4, *Demolition of Private Structures* (July 18, 2007); DAP, 9523.5 *Debris Removal form Waterways*, (March 29, 2010); DAP 9523.9, *100% Funding for Direct Federal Assistance and Grant Assistance* (June 9, 2006); DAP 9523.11 *Hazardous Stump Extraction and Removal Eligibility* (May 15, 2007); DAP 9523.12 *Debris Operations-Hand Loaded Trucks and Trailers*, (May 1, 2006); DAP 9523.13 *Debris Removal From Private Property*, (July 18, 2007). FEMA 325, Debris Management Guide (July 2007). http://www.fema.gov/pdf/government/grant/pa/demagde.pdf.
[210] PA GUIDE at 74.

J. Distribution of Commodities: Food, Water, Ice

FEMA maintains pre-positioned critical disaster relief assets and supplies in strategically located distributions centers within and outside the continental United States.[211] Life-saving and life-sustaining commodities include water, tarps, meals, cots, blue roofing sheeting, blankets, hygiene kits and generators intended to sustain lives and prevent further property damage during an emergency or disaster. See the *Initial Response Resources* section in the *Readiness and Pre-Declaration Activities* chapter,

Based on lessons learned from prior hurricane response operations, as well as enhanced relationships with logistics partners at all levels of government, in 2007, FEMA announced that it would no longer purchase, distribute, or store ice as one of the basic response commodities. Instead, FEMA may reimburse eligible applicants for the costs of purchasing and distributing ice as an emergency protective measure or may use agreements with other entities to augment local supplies.[212]

K. Restoration of Power in the Aftermath of a Disaster

The loss of electric power caused by a disaster poses a tremendous threat to public health and safety. Individuals may have to function without heat, cooling, light, food, and water. Additionally, emergency service providers such as hospitals cannot function without electric power or fuel for generators. The loss of power also impedes efforts to respond to and recover from a disaster, as emergency work is difficult or impossible in areas without power, and other critical infrastructure assets, such as communications, may be compromised and frustrate response efforts. Therefore, it is imperative that power be restored as soon as possible following a disaster.

Unlike other emergency response functions, the private sector has the lead in power restoration efforts. Emergency Support Function 12, led by the Department of Energy, works with the private sector after a loss of power

---

[211] PKEMRA (Pub .L. No. 109-295)§ 636. *See* Logistics Management Directorate Fact Sheet (Revised Sept. 2010).
[212] FP 203-075-1, Purchase and Distribution of Ice, (currently pending as of January 2013).

due to a disasters to coordinate and assist in power restoration efforts.[213] FEMA plays a critical coordination role, issuing mission assignments necessary to assist in power restoration and providing generator support from FEMA assets, contracted assets, and mission assignments.

The *Power Restoration Primer*, found at *Appendix D* provides a brief overview of this complex area, describing the nature of the electricity distribution system, commonly known as "the Grid," and describes how federal agencies, states, municipalities, and the private sector work together to regulate, maintain, and restore electric power.

L. Emergency Communications

FEMA may establish temporary communications systems and make them available to state and local government officials and others deemed appropriate during or in anticipation of an emergency or major disaster.[214] The Homeland Security Act provides that to the maximum extent feasible, the Secretary of DHS will use private sector networks for emergency response.[215] FEMA may only provide emergency communications through DFA; FEMA does not have authority to reimburse an applicant for its costs unless it is an eligible applicant with eligible costs under the FEMA PA program. A temporary emergency communications system could be a mobile radio system or cellular telephones meant to supplement that portion of a community's communication system that is inoperable. It does not replace or expand the pre-disaster system. The expectation is that the community will repair the damaged system on an expedited basis; federal assistance will end when there is no longer an emergency need.[216]

Example of Communications Equipment Resolution

In 2006, FEMA loaned hand-held radio communication equipment to the New Orleans Police Department in anticipation of a threatening tropical storm/hurricane.

---

[213] NRF, ESF # 12, Energy.
[214] Stafford Act, §§ 418 & 424, 42 U.S.C. §§ 5185 & 5189b. Note that section 418, does not include the provision of "assistance" to state, tribal or local governments.
[215] Homeland Security Act § 519, 6 U.S.C. § 321h.
[216] PA GUIDE at 75.

M. Emergency Public Transportation

When a major disaster damages essential portions of a community's transportation system and disrupts the vital functions of community life, FEMA may provide temporary public transportation, through DFA, to stores, post offices, schools, major employment centers, and other places that will assist the community in returning to its normal pattern of life.[217] As with emergency communications, FEMA does not have authority to give a grant to an applicant to set up an emergency transportation system.[218]

Example of Emergency Transportation Issue

In Louisiana, after Hurricane Katrina, FEMA issued a mission assignment to the U.S. Department of Transportation to contract for bus service to provide for emergency transportation in Baton Rouge because of the influx of disaster survivors to Baton Rouge who did not have cars. FEMA could not provide financial assistance to Louisiana to set up the bus service because of the limits of FEMA's statutory authority.[219]

N. Accelerated Assistance

Once the President has declared a major disaster or emergency under the Stafford Act, FEMA may provide accelerated federal assistance and federal support "where necessary to save lives, prevent human suffering, or mitigate severe damage even in the absence of a specific request" from the state.[220] Congress added this language in PKEMRA in response to criticisms of the federal response to Hurricane Katrina where allegations surfaced that the federal government would not assist Louisiana until the state made a specific request for the particular type of assistance the state desired. FEMA has no examples of this situation occurring. The language

---

[217] Stafford Act § 419, 42 U.S.C. § 5186; PA GUIDE at 75.
[218] Id.
[219] Id.
[220] Stafford Act §§ 402(5) & 502(a)(7), 42 U.S.C. §§ 5170a(5) & 5192(a)(7). FEMA must promptly notify and coordinate with the State "to the fullest extent practicable."

of the provision is not limited with respect to time, and because it allows FEMA to act unilaterally without the consent of the governor and is limited to those circumstances where "necessary to save lives, prevent human suffering, or mitigate severe damage," it is clear that application of this authority is limited to those circumstances where a rapid response is critical.

In any event, FEMA must promptly notify and coordinate with the state to the fullest extent practicable. This is particularly important if the federal declaration requires the state to pay a 25% share of the cost and the state has not requested the work nor knows the nature and scope of expenses ahead of time.

Example of Accelerated Assistance in a Major Disaster or Emergency

Following Hurricane Sandy in 2012, FEMA utilized its authority to provide accelerated assistance, perhaps for the first time, to provide fuel to first responders and emergency workers in the initial days of the response, on occasion in the absence of a specific state request, when there was a significant shortage of commercially available gasoline and where the President had already approved a 100% federal cost share for certain power restoration and transportation work.

O. Responder Support Camps

FEMA may establish responder support camps to provide essential services such as lodging, meals, and laundry to individuals who are part of the response efforts when those essential services are not otherwise available in the disaster area.[221] FEMA has advance contracts currently in place for the construction and operation of responder support camps covering different regions of the country.[222] FEMA establishes support camps for federal, state, local, and tribal responders and approved volunteers. They are not suitable for disaster survivors or pets.[223]

---

[221] Stafford Act § 403(a)(3)(D), 42 U.S.C. § 5170b(a)(3)(D).
[222] See FEMA Responder Support Camps, Concept of Operations (May 19, 2009).
[223] Id. at 4.

FEMA may determine that it is necessary to the response effort to allow other individuals associated with the response effort to utilize the support camp. An example would be employees of a private sector utility company working to restore electricity. These response workers may stay at the camp provided they reimburse/pay FEMA the cost, generally based on per person/per day fees.

Responder support camps raise several issues, including:

- Whether teenagers or children should be allowed access;

- Whether local or federal law enforcement should resolve security and/or law enforcement issues; and

- Whether federal employees should be required to stay at base camps or forfeit per diem for lodging and meals.

The FCO, along with FEMA HQ or the Regional Administrator, may resolve these issues depending upon the situation presented in consultation with the state, tribal, and local governments the federal government is assisting.

CHAPTER 5
Public Assistance
Table of Contents

Page

Public Assistance

Part One: Public Assistance Eligibility

I. Introduction

The Stafford Act authorizes federal assistance for state, tribal, and local governments, and certain private non-profit (PNP) entities to respond to and recover from emergencies and major disasters. FEMA has administratively combined these authorities under the umbrella of its Public Assistance (PA) program. The PA program provides a broad range of assistance. First, it provides direct services and financial assistance for emergency protective measures, such as emergency evacuation, sheltering,[1] and debris removal. This assistance, which is generally considered "Response," is discussed in Chapter 4. The PA program also provides financial assistance for the permanent restoration of facilities, which is generally considered "Recovery." This chapter is divided into two parts: Part One discusses eligibility requirements, categories of work, special categories of projects, mitigation, codes and standards, duplication of benefits considerations, public notice requirements, and appeals procedures; Part Two of this chapter covers project administration and grants administration. It also covers Fire Management Assistance Grants (FMAGs) as a form of special funding.

Both parts of this chapter discuss the legal authorities, regulations, and policies governing the PA program, including the Stafford Act[2] and its implementing regulations.[3] It includes many of FEMA's PA program

---

[1] *See* also discussion in Chapter 2, *Readiness and Pre-Declaration Activities*, and Chapter 4, *Response*.

[2] *See* Stafford Act §§ 403, 406, 407, 502, and 503; 42 U.S.C. §§ 5170a, 5172, 5173, 5192, and 5193, respectively.

[3] The applicable regulations include 44 C.F.R. §§ 206.31 – 206.67 (Emergency Assistance) and 44 C.F.R. §§ 206.200 – 206.253 (Basic Public Assistance); 44 C.F.R. §§ 207.1 – 207.10 (Management Costs). Other relevant regulations include: 44 C.F.R. Part 9 (Floodplain Management and Protection of Wetlands); 44 C.F.R. Part 13 (related to grants

---

policies, which explain and assure basic consistency in the discretion FEMA has to manage the PA program. In addition, the FEMA PA Guide, PA Policy Digest, Disaster Assistance Policies (DAPs), Recovery Policies (RPs),[4] and other publications, though not legal authorities, serve to further clarify PA program administration and practices in the field.[5] The Stafford Act provides broad, flexible authorities to provide financial assistance and limited direct assistance under the PA program with few monetary caps. Limitations on funding derive from eligibility determinations. There is a constant tension between establishing clear, consistent policies and guidance for all hazards, program-wide implementation, and the application of these policies to unique, disaster-driven fact patterns.

II. Eligibility – In General

The PA program places eligible work into project categories, which must meet eligibility requirements to be eligible for FEMA funding. Eligibility determinations commence when the "applicant" (a state, tribal, or local government or certain non-profit organizations) submits a Request for Public Assistance (RPA)[6] and continue through project formulation, financial obligation, and financial and programmatic closeout process.

---

administration and costs); and 44 C.F.R. Part 75 (Exemption of State-Owned properties under Self-insurance Plan).

[4] FEMA's PA policies are called the "9500 Series Policy Publications" and are available on FEMA's public website at <http://www.fema.gov/9500-series-policy-publications >. As noted in the text, these policies are abbreviated DAP and RP.

[5] PUBLIC ASSISTANCE GUIDE, FEMA 322 (2007) [hereinafter PA GUIDE]; PUBLIC ASSISTANCE POLICY DIGEST, FEMA P-321 (2008) [hereinafter PA DIGEST]; PUBLIC ASSISTANCE APPLICANT HANDBOOK, FEMA 323 (2010) [hereinafter PA HANDBOOK]; PUBLIC ASSISTANCE DEBRIS MANAGEMENT GUIDE, FEMA 325 (2007) [hereinafter PA DEBRIS GUIDE]; Public Assistance Program Fact Sheet, FEMA 328; El Programa Asistencia Publica, FEMA 328S. *See also* PA appeals data base on FEMA's public website at:
<http://www.fema.gov/appeals/viewAppeal.do?action=Init&viewType=brief&appealId= 2356>.

[6] 44 C.F.R. § 206.202(c). The RPA is the beginning of the project grant application. PA GUIDE, at 92.

To be eligible for PA, a project (or "item of work") must meet the following foundational requirements. It must:

- Be required as a result of the declared event;[7]

- Be located within the designated disaster area;[8] and

- Be the legal responsibility of an eligible applicant at the time of the disaster.[9]

In addition, the applicant's project must also meet specific eligibility requirements for the following four essential elements that FEMA staff should review in this order: (1) the applicant,[10] (2) the facility,[11] (3) the work,[12] and (4) the costs.[13]

---

[7] 44 C.F.R. § 206.223(a)(1); the PA HANDBOOK, uses the term "damage" instead of "work" to illustrate these general requirements; identifying and verifying the disaster "damage," however, is part of the analysis of eligible work. *See* Section II, Subsection C(1), *Work Eligibility, Direct Result of the Disaster* in this chapter.

[8] Evacuation and sheltering support provided outside the declared state is also eligible pursuant to 44 C.F.R. § 206.223(a)(2) and 44 C.F.R. § 206.208(c)(3). *See also* FEMA DAP 9523.15, *Eligible Costs Related to Evacuation and Sheltering* (2007), < http://www.fema.gov/9500-series-policy-publications/952315-eligible-costs-related-evacuations-sheltering >.

[9] 44 C.F.R. § 206.223(a)(3). FEMA interprets the third bullet as including "at the time of the disaster," although this phrase is not in the regulations. Locking in legal responsibility at the time of the disaster discourages applicants from assuming responsibility for work merely because federal funding is available. It is a fundamental cost principle that costs claimed under a federal award must conform and be consistent with policies and procedures that apply to other activities of the applicant when federal funding is not involved. *See, e.g.,* OMB Circular A-87, Basic Guidelines, at 1.e. It may be possible for an eligible applicant to transfer legal responsibility after a disaster to another eligible applicant (such as from a town to a county), but all such decisions regarding legal responsibility are likely to require further legal analysis and review of statutory authority, contracts, government organizations, and the applicant's supporting documentation.

[10] 44 C.F.R. § 206.222.

[11] Id. §§ 206.221, 206.223(b), 206.223(c), and 206.226.

[12] Id. §§ 206.224-226. Eligibility determinations are also made as to types and location of debris. *See* PA DEBRIS GUIDE, at 21-40.

[13] Id. § 206.228 and § 13.36.

A. Applicant Eligibility

1. State, Tribal, and Local Governments

State,[14] tribal,[15] and local[16] governmental entities are eligible applicants. States include: any state of the United States, the District of Columbia, Guam, the Virgin Islands, Puerto Rico, American Samoa, and the Commonwealth of the Northern Mariana Islands. Local governments include counties, municipalities, cities, towns, townships, local public authorities, school districts, special districts, intrastate districts, councils of government,[17] regional or interstate government entities, and agencies or instrumentalities of a local government. Evaluating applicants under the special district subcategory can be complex, as local governments across the country create various districts for financing purposes that blend public and private interests, and thus, may require a more in-depth review of their legal status as a local government entity and their responsibility for the requested work.[18] The statutory definition of local government also includes rural communities, unincorporated towns or villages, or other "public entity" for which an application for assistance is made by a state or political subdivision of the state.[19]

Indian tribal governments[20] now have a number of avenues through which they may pursue Public Assistance. Until recently, tribal entities were defined by the Stafford Act as "local governments" and were therefore prevented from requesting a declaration directly from the federal government. However, in January 2013, Congress amended the Stafford Act to allow Indian tribal governments to directly request emergency or

---

[14] *See* Stafford Act § 102(4), 42 U.S.C. § 5122(4).
[15] See *id.* § 102(7)(B), 42 U.S.C. § 5122(7)(B).
[16] *See id.* § 102(7), 42 U.S.C. § 5122(7).
[17] Such a council is eligible even if it is a non-profit corporation under state law. *Id.*
[18] *See* Section II, Subsection C(3), *Work Eligibility, Legal Responsibility* in this chapter.
[19] Stafford Act § 102(7)(C), 42 U.S.C. § 5122(7). "Public entity" is defined as "an organization formed for a public purpose whose direction and funding are provided by one or more political subdivisions of the State." 44 C.F.R § 206.221(g). *See also* § 206.223(c) regarding facilities belonging to a public entity.
[20] 44 C.F.R. § 206.201(i) provides: *Indian tribal government* means any federally recognized governing body of an Indian or Alaska Native tribe, band, nation, pueblo, village, or community that the Secretary of the Interior acknowledges to exist as an Indian tribe under the Federally Recognized Tribe List Act of 1994, 25 U.S.C. 479(a).

---

major disaster declarations from the President.[21] A tribal government[22] may choose to submit its own request for a Presidential emergency or major disaster declaration. or it may opt to pursue assistance through a state declaration. Under a state declaration, an Indian tribal government has the option to apply for PA disaster funding as a direct grantee, or it may act as a subgrantee of the state.[23] Unique issues may arise with respect to tribal ownership and control of certain entities and structures on tribal lands, including corporate or development commissions, federally owned facilities, gaming partnerships, and private/public small businesses.[24]

The Stafford Act and its implementing regulations do not authorize FEMA to provide direct federal or grant assistance to private for-profit entities. However, in limited circumstances, private commercial entities may be indirect or incidental beneficiaries of Direct Federal Assistance (DFA) when FEMA determines a private organization lacks the capability to perform an activity on its own that would address an immediate threat to the community at large and is beyond state and local capability. See Chapter 4, Response, section on Incidental Benefits to the Private Sector through DFA.

---

[21] Disaster Relief Appropriations Act of 2013, Pub. L. No. 113-2, § 1110(c)(3). (2013)
[22] 44 C.F.R. § 206.201(i) provides: Indian tribal government means any federally recognized governing body of an Indian or Alaska Native tribe, band, nation, pueblo, village, or community that the Secretary of the Interior acknowledges to exist as an Indian tribe under the Federally Recognized Tribe List Act of 1994, 25 U.S.C. 479(a)
[23] 44 C.F.R. § 206.201(e). See discussion this Chapter, Part Two: Public Assistance and Grants Management Process.
[24] Id. Exec. Order 13175, Consultation and Coordination with Indian Tribal Governments (Nov. 6, 2000), 3 C.F.R. 2001 Comp., p. 304; President's Memorandum, Tribal Consultation (2009); FEMA Tribal Policy (2010).

2. PNP Organizations

Certain PNPs, as defined in the Stafford Act, are eligible for PA if they own or operate a facility that provides essential governmental type services to the general public.[25] PNP applicant and facility eligibility determinations are intertwined.[26]

- The regulations require, as a condition to funding, that an eligible PNP provide a letter from the U.S. Internal Revenue Service[27] ruling that it is a 501(c),[28](d),[29]or (e)[30] exempt organization or has satisfactory evidence from the state that it is a non-profit organization doing business under state law.[31]

- The PNP must be legally responsible for the disaster-related repairs.[32]

B. Facility Eligibility

After FEMA determines that the applicant as an entity is eligible for PA, consideration must then be given to the facility for which the applicant requires assistance, if there is a facility at issue.[33] Permanent work assistance for repair, restoration, reconstruction, or replacement is

---

[25] 44 C.F.R. §§ 206.222(b) and 206.221(e)

[26] 44 C.F.R. §§ 206.222(b) and 206.223(b); Stafford Act § 102(10(B); 42 U.S.C. § 5122(10)(B); DAP 9521.3, PNP Eligibility

[27] *See* Internal Revenue Service regulations at 26 U.S.C. § 501(c), (d), and (e); *see also* 44 C.F.R. § 221(f).

[28] 26 U.S.C. § 501(c), *List of exempt organizations.*

[29] *Id.* at § 501(d), *Religious and apostolic organizations.*

[30] *Id.* at § 501(e), *Cooperative hospital service organizations.*

[31] 44 C.F.R. § 221(f).

[32] 44 CFR § 223(a)(3). While this is true of all projects regardless of the applicant status, PNP projects are more likely to involve leased facilities, shared facilities, joint venture relationships, and/or mixed use facilities requiring apportionment of costs. *See* PNP *Facilies* section in this chapter.

[33] PA for emergency work, *see* Chapter 4, more often than not involves the provision or reimbursement of a service (sheltering, food, search and rescue) and not a particular facility. Emergency work assistance is available, however, to protect improved property, Stafford Act §§ 403 and 592, 42 U.S.C. §§5170b and 5192. "Improved property" is defined as a structure, facility or item of equipment built, constructed or manufactured. 44 C.F.R. §§ 206.221(d).

---

available for eligible facilities.[34] "Facility" is defined as "any publicly or privately owned building, works, system, or equipment, built or manufactured, or an improved and maintained natural feature. Land used for agricultural purposes is not a facility."[35]

1. Public Facilities

Public facilities include the following facilities owned by a state or local government:[36]

a. Any flood control, navigation, irrigation, reclamation, public power, sewage treatment and collection, water supply and distribution, watershed development, or airport facility;

b. Any non-federal aid street, road, or highway;

c. Any other public building, structure, or system, including those used for educational, recreational, or cultural purposes; and

d. Any park.

Under certain conditions, public beaches may be an improved and maintained feature and thereby an eligible facility for sand replacement.[37]

---

[34] Stafford Act § 406, 42 U.S.C. §5172; 44 C.F.R. §§ 206.201(j) and 226.

[35] 44 C.F.R. § 206.201(c); but see DAP 9524.2, Landslides and Slope Failures, at VII.A.4, which provides "[i]ntegral ground refers to 'natural or improved ground' upon which an eligible facility is located and which is essential to support the structural integrity and utility of the facility." See also 44 C.F.R. § 206.221(e) and (h) for more specific definitions of various types of facilities.

[36] Stafford Act § 102(9), 42 U.S.C. § 5122(9); 44 C.F.R. § 206.221(h). FEMA's practice is to provide PA for leased facilities if the applicant can establish legal responsibility for disaster-related repair or replacement of the damaged facility.

[37] 44 C.F.R. § 206.226(j); FEMA PUBLIC ASSISTANCE FACT SHEET 9580.8, Eligible Sand Replacement on Public Beaches.

"Any Other Public Building"

In determining whether a facility falls within the "any other public building" category, FEMA will examine whether the facility is used to provide services of a governmental nature. For instance, if a city's development authority purchases some residences to restore and re-sell as part of its urban renewal program, these residences it owns, if damaged in a Stafford Act event, would not be eligible facilities under the PA program because they are not providing services of a governmental nature.

On tribal lands, many tribal members live in tribally-owned housing. In such circumstances, FEMA may consider the housing a public facility; therefore, assistance for the repair of this housing may come under the PA program rather than the Individual Assistance (IA) program for owner occupied housing.[38]

2. PNP Facilities

Pursuant to the Stafford Act, the following types of facilities, when owned or operated[39] by a PNP entity, may be eligible for PA funding: education, utility, irrigation, emergency, medical, rehabilitation, and temporary or permanent custodial care facilities.[40] The Stafford Act also includes certain additional facilities that provide essential services of a governmental nature to the general public, including museums, zoos, performing arts facilities, community arts centers, libraries, homeless shelters, senior citizen centers, rehabilitation facilities, shelter workshops,

---

[38] Stafford Act § 408(c)(2) and (3), 42 U.S.C. § 5174(c)(2) and (3).

[39] Stafford Act § 406(a)(1)(B), 42 U.S.C. § 5172(a)(1)(B). *See also* 44 C.F.R. §206.222(b), which tracks the Stafford Act language of "own or operate." Note, however, that there is a discrepancy in 44 C.F.R. §206.223(b) that provides that a PNP facility must be owned *and* operated by a PNP organization in order to be eligible. This regulatory language would appear to be *ultra vires*. FEMA practice and policy has been to implement the terms of the Stafford Act and determine eligibility based on whether an applicant with an appropriately documented PNP status owns *or* operates a PNP defined facility, recognizing that some PNPs may operate out of leased facilities. Also note that the legal responsibility eligibility requirement still applies and may lead to a determination of ineligibility if the PNP operator-applicant is not legally responsible for disaster-related repairs or replacement of the facility.

[40] Stafford Act § 102(10)(A), 42 U.S.C. § 5122(10)(A).

---

and facilities that provide health and safety services of a governmental nature.[41] The specific facility types are further defined in FEMA's regulations, which also address whether administrative and support facilities are included.[42]

a.) Open to the General Public

Certain types of PNP facilities have additional restrictions or eligibility requirements. The Stafford Act specifies that the eligible additional facilities must provide essential services of a governmental nature to the general public.[43] FEMA policy provides that a PNP facility is likely to meet this requirement if it is open to the general public, and membership fees, if any, are nominal and can be waived due to inability to pay.[44] The policy also lists factors that would likely lead to a determination that a facility does not serve the general public: a membership fee that would exclude access by a significant portion of the community or that clearly exceeds what would be considered an appropriate fee based on reasonable assumed use of the facility; membership is limited to a certain number of people; membership is limited to a defined group of individuals who have a financial interest in the facility (e.g., a condo association); or membership discriminates against discrete classes of people or is limited to a geographic area that is more restrictive than the community from which the facility could normally be expected to draw users.[45]

Facilities owned or operated by homeowners' associations can present challenges. Such associations are generally formed as non-profit

---

[41] Id. § 102(10)(B), 42 U.S.C. § 5122(10)(B). FEMA's policy regarding PNP facility eligibility provides the following examples of health and safety services of a governmental nature: low income housing, alcohol and drug treatment centers, residences and other facilities offering programs for battered spouses, animal control facilities directly related to public health and safety, facilities offering food programs for the needy, daycare centers for children, and daycare centers for individuals with special needs. DAP 9521.3, *Private Nonprofit (PNP) Facility Eligibility* [hereinafter DAP 9521.3, *PNP Eligibility*] at VII.B.4 (2007), http://www.fema.gov/public-assistance-9500-series-policy-publications/private-nonprofit-facility-eligibility-0

[42] 44 CFR § 206.223(e)(1) – (7).

[43] FEMA regulation further specifies that "[a]ll such facilities must be open to the general public." 44 C.F.R. § 206.221(e)(7).

[44] DAP 9521.3, *PNP Eligibility*, at VII.C.1.

[45] DAP 9521.3, *PNP Facility*, at VII.C.2.

corporations to provide services, including managing, maintaining, and governing the use of property within a housing subdivision. Membership is restricted to property owners, and access to facilities may be restricted to members and their guests. Eligibility of facilities owned or operated by a homeowners' association depends on the type of facility and whether it is required to be open to the general public. Museums, zoos, community centers, libraries, homeless shelters, senior citizen centers, rehabilitation facilities, shelter workshops, irrigation facilities, and facilities that provide health and safety services of a governmental nature must be open to the general public in order to be eligible for PA.[46] Accordingly, an association would not be eligible for assistance for those types of facilities if access is restricted to association members. However, an association may be eligible for assistance for its eligible educational, medical, custodial care, emergency, and utility facilities even if use of those facilities is restricted to association members.[47] Debris removal from roadways owned by an association may be eligible for emergency access purposes if performed under the auspices of an eligible state or local government[48]; however, permanent repair of private roads owned or operated by an association would not be eligible because roads are not eligible PNP facilities.[49]

b.) Requirement by non-critical services PNPs to apply to SBA for permanent work

The Stafford Act requires that all PNP facilities not deemed to provide critical services apply to the Small Business Administration (SBA) for a disaster loan.[50] Critical services are defined to include "power, water (including water provided by an irrigation organization or facility), sewer services, wastewater treatment, communications, education, and emergency medical care."[51] A PNP that provides critical services is not required to apply for an SBA loan and may directly apply to FEMA for

---

[46] Stafford Act § 102(10)(B), 42 U.S.C. §5122(10)(B), 44 C.F.R. 206.221(e)(3) and (e)(7).
[47] PA DIGEST, at 68.
[48] Stafford Act §§ 403(a)(3) and 502(a), 42 U.S.C. §§ 515170b(a)(3) and 5191(a), 44 C.F.R. 206.224.
[49] Id. § 102(10), 42 U.S.C. §5122(10)(B), 44 C.F.R. 206.221(e).
[50] Id. § 406(a)(3)(A)(ii); 42 U.S.C. § 5172(a)(3)(A)(ii); 44 C.F.R. §§ 206.221 and 206.226(c)(1).
[51] Id. § 406(a)(3)(B), 42 U.S.C. § 5172(a)(3)(B); 44 C.F.R. § 206.226(c)(1).

assistance with eligible emergency or permanent work. A PNP that does not meet that definition may still apply for eligible emergency work but will need to first apply to SBA for a disaster loan for its permanent work. It is recommended that the PNP apply for the SBA loan for permanent work at the same time it submits its RPA in order to meet both programs' filing deadlines. If the PNP organization does not receive a loan from SBA, or if it receives a loan in an amount lower than the disaster damage, it may then be eligible for PA funding.[52]

c.) PNP Mixed-Use Facilities

PNP organizations offer so many types of services that FEMA has published policy guidance to assist in determining eligibility.[53] Eligibility issues can be multi-tiered and complex. Funding will depend on whether the facility is an eligible type and whether the PNP has legal responsibility for the facility's repair.[54] PNPs may share facilities with for-profit or other entities that are not eligible for PA, and a facility may be partially used for eligible services and partially used for ineligible services. Overall facility eligibility is based on the primary use of that facility. A facility must have over 50% of its space dedicated to eligible uses for the facility to be eligible as a whole. Common spaces are not included in the calculation. When a space is used for purposes both eligible and ineligible for PA funding, the primary use of that space is determined by looking at the time used for each activity. FEMA considers damage to the entire facility, however, and assistance is provided in proportion to the space dedicated to eligible services.[55]

---

[52] DAP 9521.3, PNP Facility, at VII.F.2.
[53] PA DIGEST, at 21; for example, DAP 9521.3, PNP Facility; DAP 9521.1, Community Center Eligibility [hereinafter DAP 9521.1 PNP Community Center](2008), <http://www.fema.gov/9500-series-policy-publications/95211-community-center-eligibility>; DAP 9521.2, PNP Museum http://www.fema.gov/public-assistance-9500-series-policy-publications/private-nonprofit-museum-eligibility.
[54] DAP 9521.3, PNP Facility, at VII.B. and E.
[55] DAP 9521.3, PNP Facility, at VII.D.

Example of Eligible and Ineligible Work

"TEAM," a PNP, operated a homeless shelter and food pantry. In the aftermath of Hurricane Katrina, TEAM distributed groceries to individuals affected by the disaster. The increased demand as a result of the storm depleted TEAM's food stocks. TEAM requested reimbursement for replenishment of its stock. FEMA established on second appeal that TEAM was an eligible PNP; however, distributing groceries to disaster-affected individuals was not within the definition of eligible work.[56] If a state or local government had contracted with such a PNP, however, to provide these emergency services, the state or local government may have been eligible for FEMA reimbursement.

i). Primary Use

Facilities with mixed uses must be primarily used for eligible activities to qualify for FEMA assistance. "Primarily used" means that over 50% of the facility space is used for eligible activities. Where the same space is used for both eligible and ineligible purposes, eligibility is determined by the amount of time the facility is used for eligible versus ineligible services.[57] FEMA will evaluate damage to the entire facility, but will prorate assistance based on the percentage of space or time used for eligible purposes. Contents within an ineligible space will not be eligible for any assistance.[58]

Example of Eligible Museum

A botanical center whose mission was to carry-out scientific and educational services in the field of botany was initially determined not to meet the eligibility criteria of a PNP educational facility. However, FEMA determined on second appeal that the facility's primary use was to preserve and exhibit its collection to the general public. Thus, the botanical center met the definition of an eligible PNP museum.[59]

---

[56] *See* 44 C.F.R. § 206.223; *FEMA Appeal Brief, FEMA-1604-DR-MS, Together Everyone Achieves More, Inc.* (TEAM). < http://www.fema.gov/appeal/219054
[57] PA Digest, at 100; DAP 9521.3, *PNP Facility*, at VII.D.
[58] PA Guide, at 19-20.
[59] Second Appeal Brief; FEMA-1306-DR-FL, Montgomery Botanical Center (2001), < http://www.fema.gov/appeal/218795>.

d.) Types of Non-Profit Mixed Use Facilities

i). Community Centers

A community center as an "essential governmental service facility" must be open to the general public.[60] In order to be considered open to the general public, a facility must be available to the public on a non-discriminatory basis, and any access fees should be reasonable. A facility with a high initiation or usage fee, or high annual dues, would not be eligible.[61]

Community center facilities, including attached structures and grounds, that are established and primarily used as a gathering place for social, educational enrichment, and community service activities are eligible for assistance.[62]

Eligible activities include:

- Social – such as board meetings, senior citizen meetings, or community picnics;

- Educational – such as seminars on personal finance, stamp collecting, or gardening;

- Community service – such as organizing clean-up projects, local government meetings, rehabilitation programs, or blood drives.[63]

In determining eligibility, FEMA looks to the primary purpose of the facility by reviewing the organization's charter, bylaws, amendments, and other documented evidence of use. A community center need not be used exclusively for community activities; however, the majority use should be for eligible functions.[64] Those facilities not eligible as community centers for public assistance include those established or primarily used for

---

[60] 44 C.F.R. § 206.221(e)(7).
[61] DAP 9521.1, Community Center, at 2.
[62] Id.
[63] PA DIGEST, at 21. DAP 9521.1, Community Center, at 1-2.
[64] Id. at 2. For examples and analyses of community center issues, see the Appendix to DAP 9521.1.

---

political, athletic, religious, recreational, vocational or academic training, conferences, or similar activities.[65]

A facility primarily used for religious activities is not considered an eligible community center. Just because a community center is operated by a religious institution, however, does not automatically make it ineligible. In addition to worship services, many religious institutions conduct a variety of secular activities that benefit the community. A key to distinguishing between the religious and secular activities is the nature of the activities. Worship, proselytizing, and religious instruction are inherently religious. Bingo, bake sales, and other fundraising activities undertaken for the benefit of a religious institution would not be eligible. On the other hand, if fundraising is intended to help the community at large, such as to assist the homeless, the activity could serve an eligible purpose.

Facilities primarily established or used for political or similar activities are also not eligible community centers. This includes partisan political activities, advocacy and lobbyist groups, and any other groups that primarily serve to promote a political campaign, candidate, agenda, philosophy, or cause. Finally, facilities primarily established or used for athletic, recreational, vocational training, conferences, or similar activities are not eligible community centers.[66]

ii). Church Schools

FEMA may not fund repairs or reconstruction for a facility used primarily for religious functions. A church school may be eligible for assistance, however, if the school is an eligible education institution.[67] The buildings must be primarily used for secular education, and the few religious classes in the curriculum must not be sufficient to change the primary purpose of secular education. FEMA assistance will be based on

---

[65] Id.

[66] DAP 9521.1, Community Center, at 5. Recreational, vocational or academic training, and conference facilities were specifically listed as examples of ineligible facilities in the Supplementary Information section of the final rule revising 44 CFR §206.221(e). See 58 Fed. Reg. 47,992 (1993).

[67] 44 C.F.R. § 206.221(e)(1).

the proportion of the total time that such spaces are used for eligible purposes.[68]

iii). Charter Schools

One section of the Stafford Act defines PNPs to include any PNP educational facility;[69] while, another section[70] defines a local government to include, among other things, a school district. FEMA recognizes a charter school, as defined in the Elementary and Secondary Education Act of 1965[71] as a local government applicant (not as a PNP) for purposes of public assistance, including permanent repair, restoration, and replacement. A charter school applicant must provide documentation to FEMA establishing that, pursuant to state law, an authorized chartering agency has given its approval to operate a charter school.[72]

e.) Mixed Ownership

An eligible PNP organization may own a facility and use a portion of that facility for eligible services but lease the remaining portion for other purposes not considered eligible under the PA program. In other situations, a facility may be partially owned by an eligible PNP and an ineligible organization. Reimbursement in either case depends upon the percentage of ownership, amount of space occupied by the applicant, and amount of space dedicated to eligible services. The PNP must own more than 50% of the facility, in addition to the requirement that at least 50% of the space be dedicated to eligible services. Again, funding will be based on the percentage ownership by the PNP, as well as the percentage of space dedicated to eligible services.[73] A guideline for determining the eligible costs for such facilities is set out in FEMA's Policy.[74]

---

[68] DAP 9521.3, PNP Eligibility, Appendix.
[69] Stafford Act § 102(10), 42 U.S.C. § 5122(10).
[70] Id. § 102(7), 42 U.S.C. § 5122(7).
[71] Elementary and Secondary Education Act of 1965, 20 U.S.C. § 7221i. now called the No Child Left Behind Act, Pub. L. No. 107-110 (2002).
[72] DAP 9521.5, Eligibility of Charter Schools (2006); website: http://www.fema.gov/public-assistance-9500-series-policy-publications/95215-eligibility-charter-schools http://www.fema.gov/9500-series-policy-publications
[73] DAP 9521.3, at VII.E.
[74] DAP 9521.3, PNP Facility.

---

3. Federally-Owned Facilities

Federal agencies are not eligible applicants for their facilities under the PA program.[75] The Stafford Act does authorize the President to authorize any federal agency to repair, reconstruct, restore, or replace any facility owned by the United States that is damaged or destroyed by a major disaster if he determines that the action "...is of such importance and urgency that it cannot reasonably be deferred..." pending the enactment of an appropriation.[76] The President did not delegate this authority in his first executive order delegation to the then FEMA Director,[77] nor did the President do so under the various subsequent executive orders to the FEMA Administrator or to the Secretary of Homeland Security.[78] This authority resides with the President and the individual agency that has a facility damaged or destroyed by a major disaster. The practical effect of this provision is that when a federally-owned facility is damaged in a major disaster, the agency need not wait for an appropriation from Congress but can instead proceed with repair and restoration if the President has determined that the urgency of the situation requires immediate action; and the agency may use funds appropriated to the agency for another purpose to effectuate the repairs.

---

[75] *See* 44 C.F.R.§206.222.

[76] Stafford Act § 405, 42 U.S.C. § 5171(a); 44 C.F.R. § 206.226(a)(1).

[77] EXEC. ORDER 12148, *Federal Emergency Management* (1979), 44 Fed. Reg. 43,239 (1979), 3 C.F.R. 1979 Comp., p. 412.

[78] EXEC. ORDER 12673, *Delegation of Disaster Relief and Emergency Assistance Functions* (Mar. 23, 1989), 54 Fed. Reg. 12571 (1989), 3 C.F.R. 1989 Comp., p.309, delegated all functions vested in the President under the Stafford Act to the Director of the FEMA except those functions in Sections 401 and 501(declaration of major disasters and emergencies), Section 405 (repair, reconstruction, restoration, or replacement of federal facilities), and Section 412 (food coupons and distribution). EXEC. ORDER No. 13,286, 68 Fed. Reg. 10619 (2003), 3 C.F.R. (2003) Comp. at 166, subsequently amended EXEC. ORDER 12673, to reflect creation of the Department of Homeland Security (DHS) and the transfer of certain functions to the Secretary of DHS.

> **Example of FEMA's Authority Regarding Federal Facility Funding**
>
> Hurricane Katrina severely damaged the federal courthouse in New Orleans. FEMA had no authority to provide assistance, and the President did not authorize triggering section 405 of the Stafford Act in the absence of an appropriation from Congress. Stafford Act § 405, 42 U.S.C. § 5171(a); 44 C.F.R. § 206.226(a)(1). Congress ultimately appropriated funds to the U.S. courts for the courthouse repair.

Although federal agencies are not eligible for FEMA PA as discussed previously, there are circumstances where a federally-owned facility that is operated and maintained by a local government may be eligible for assistance because the local government has the legal and financial responsibility for the operation, maintenance, and repairs for the facility. A review of the operations and maintenance agreement executed between the parties would be necessary to determine who has the legal responsibility to repair a damaged facility. Examples include roads constructed by the U.S. Forest Service and the Bureau of Indian Affairs, and reservoirs and water delivery systems constructed by the U.S. Bureau of Reclamation.[79]

4. Active Use at Time of Disaster

In order to be eligible for assistance, a facility must be in active use at the time of the disaster.[80] This requirement also applies to a facility that is partially occupied and partially inactive. Inactive portions would not be eligible, although certain exceptions may apply.[81] When the ineligible repairs would benefit a non-active portion, the assistance will be prorated. For PNP facilities, over 50% of the facility must be in active use for an eligible purpose at the time of the disaster.[82] FEMA will consider exceptions upon evidence that the facility was temporarily inoperative for repairs or remodeling; was unoccupied for a short time between tenants;

---

[79] PA Guide, at 23; *see also* discussion in Section II, Subsection C(3),*Work Eligibility, Legal Responsibility.*in this chapter.
[80] *See id.* § 206.226(k)(2).
[81] Id.
[82] DAP 9521.3, *PNP Facility,* at VII.D.1 and 2.

or was shown to be in active use in an approved budget; or it can be demonstrated that there was intent to begin use within a reasonable amount of time. In any case, the facility must have been eligible when it was in use.

5. Alternate Use[83]

If, at the time of the disaster, an applicant is using a facility for purposes other than the use for which it was originally designed, FEMA limits the eligible cost of work to restore the facility to the lesser of (1) the cost of restoring the facility to its original design and capacity, or (2) the cost of restoring the facility to the immediate pre-disaster alternate use.[84] Another consideration is whether the facility is eligible based on pre-disaster use. PA funding is for the purpose of repairing, restoring, and replacing facilities that serve a public purpose.

In the case of a PNP, the primary purpose of the facility is relevant to an eligibility determination. For example, a church might be used as a homeless shelter, while its primary purpose remained as a church. It would be ineligible based on the primary or majority use. Facilities with mixed activities (eligible and non-eligible) may be eligible if the facility has over 50% of its space dedicated to eligible uses.[85]

C. Work Eligibility

For all PA, response or recovery, there must be an eligible item of work or project. As stated, eligible work[86] must be (1) required as a direct result of the disaster; (2) located within the designated disaster area (except for sheltering and evacuation activities); and (3) the legal responsibility of an eligible applicant at the time of the disaster.[87]

---

[83] This term is not to be confused with "alternative project" which is a form of permanent repair project discussed later in this chapter.
[84] *See* 44 C.F.R. § 206.226(k)(1).
[85] DAP 9521.3, *PNP Facility*, at VII.D.1.
[86] 42 U.S.C. §§ 5170b and 5172; 44 C.F.R. §§ 206.223.
[87] 44 C.F.R. § 206.223(a)(1) – (3).

1. Direct Result of the Disaster

Those provisions of the Stafford Act that have been incorporated as the authority for the PA program require that the needed assistance arise from the declared event. For example, emergency work authorized by section 403 of the Stafford Act must "result from the major disaster,"[88] and permanent work authorized by section 406 of the Stafford Act must be for a facility "damaged or destroyed by a major disaster."[89] The President's declaration establishes an incident period which "is the time interval during which the disaster-causing incident occurs."[90] Generally, only disaster-related damage incurred during the incident period is eligible for Stafford Act assistance; however, reasonable costs incurred for emergency protective measures in anticipation of the incident may also be eligible.[91] This may include activities such as sandbagging and constructing temporary levees to protect the community from flooding.[92] Similarly, protective measures to alleviate or lessen threats may be performed after the incident period closes because the need for this work arises from the declared event. For instance, the cost of a temporary berm to prevent a water saturated hillside from encroaching into buildings may be eligible even though constructed after the incident period closed.[93]

2. Designated Area

As discussed in Chapter 3, *Declarations*, an emergency or major disaster declaration designates the counties, cities, or tribal areas that are eligible for assistance. Eligible work must be located within these geographic boundaries, except for emergency evacuation and sheltering costs incurred by Host-States.[94] An eligible applicant located within the designated area therefore cannot receive assistance for its damaged eligible facilities

---

[88] Stafford Act § 403(a), 42 U.S.C. § 5170b.

[89] Id. § 406(a), 42 U.S.C. § 5172(a).

[90] 44 C.F.R. § 206.32(f).

[91] Stafford Act § 424, 42 U.S.C. § 5189b; 44 C.F.R. § 206.32(f). *See also* Chapter 3, *Declarations*.

[92] DAP 9524.3, *Rehabilitation Assistance for Levees and other Flood Control Works* (2009).

[93] Pre-disaster damage or deferred maintenance, i.e., neglect, of a building would not be eligible for PA funding, as this work did not arise from the event that resulted in the declaration.

[94] 44 C.F.R. § 206.223(a)(2).

---

located outside the designated area, even if such damage can be related to the same disaster event.[95] Such circumstances are relatively rare. More common is where a community may be split between two political jurisdictions with one declared and the other not, creating frustration for those in the undeclared portion of the community.

3. Legal Responsibility

An eligible applicant must be legally responsible for the item of work or project for it to be eligible for disaster assistance funding.[96] The legal responsibility to repair a facility usually resides with the owner of the facility, unless the owner has transferred that responsibility to another party by lease or other legal instrument. Legal responsibility for government-owned facilities is usually straightforward. Leased facilities, however, require more careful examination. A lessee's repair responsibility, if any, for disaster-related damage to a leased facility will be provided for in the facility lease agreement. A lessee's obligations for general maintenance and repair (usually stemming from the tenant's operation and use of the leased premises and ordinary wear and tear), standing alone, do not directly address the issue of extraordinary repairs resulting from disaster-related damage and cannot be construed to obligate a tenant to make extraordinary repairs required in order to address partial or total destruction resulting from an "act of God." Such a clause, however, coupled with an all-perils casualty insurance requirement and nominal rental obligation, for example, may provide sufficient support for a determination that lessee is legally responsible for repairs. A lessee may be responsible for its improvements only or the lessor may be responsible for common area damage.

A building may be the legal responsibility of an eligible applicant, but some or all of the contents may be the legal responsibility of an ineligible applicant. For example, the replacement of leased hospital equipment may be the legal responsibility of a contractor to the hospital. In such instances, replacement of the equipment is not eligible under the PA program.

---

[95] See 44 C.F.R. § 206.223(a)(2); PA GUIDE, at 30, discussing a designated disaster area.
[96] 44 C.F.R. § 206.223(a)(3). See discussion in PNP Facilities, Lease Agreements in this chapter.

In the event of damage to a facility under construction, legal responsibility for the damage must be examined carefully as FEMA must determine which entity—eligible applicant or contractor—is legally responsible for repairs.[97] Repair work is eligible if (a) the construction contract places responsibility to repair damage on the eligible applicant during construction, or (b) the eligible applicant had accepted the construction work as complete prior to the disaster.[98] State law may place requirements on scope of contractor liability for such damage in public contracts in order to manage contract costs.[99]

An eligible PNP applicant must be legally responsible for disaster-related repairs whether it owns a facility or leases it. An eligible PNP applicant that leases an asset of an ineligible applicant and uses it for eligible services may be eligible for PA funding. The lease must pre-date the disaster and must clearly specify that the eligible applicant is responsible for losses and major damage to the facility, not just maintenance or minor repairs.[100] Lease agreements are often poorly drafted, and they are not always clear as to whether the lessor or lessee is legally responsible for losses and major damage to the facility. Legal review in such circumstances will be necessary. In some instances, the answer as to who has legal responsibility may turn on which party in the lease is required to carry insurance, such as an all-perils or commercial property policy, to protect the facility.

---

[97] 44 C.F.R. § 206.223(a)(3).

[98] Stafford Act § 406(e)(4), 42 U.S.C. § 5172(e)(4).

[99] For example, California law provides that construction contracts of public agencies will not require the contractor to be responsible for the cost of repairing or restoring damage to work, determined to have been proximately caused by an act of God (3.5 or higher earthquake or tidal wave), in excess of 5 percent of the contracted amount, subject to exceptions. Cal. Pub. Cont. § 7105, <http://law.onecle.com/california/public-contract/7105.html>.

[100] Id. at 8.

Example of a PNP Lease Agreement Issue

FEMA determined a medical foundation was an eligible PNP; however, the foundation did not have legal responsibility for repairs to the office building that the earthquake damaged. At the time of the disaster, a for-profit entity affiliated with the medical foundation was the facility lessee and had legal responsibility pursuant to the lease for repairs to the space. Thus, the Inspector General recommended that funds paid to the foundation for repairs to the facility be disallowed.[101]

Example of a Determination of Concurrent Legal Responsibility

When a number of towns in the Commonwealth of Massachusetts were impacted by declared disasters FEMA-4028-DR, Tropical Storm Irene, and FEMA-4051-DR, severe storm and snowstorm, in 2011, several of the towns requested the assistance of the Massachusetts Emergency Management Agency (MEMA) for the performance of debris removal and emergency protective measures within the towns' respective jurisdictions. While towns in Massachusetts are typically eligible applicants for debris removal and emergency protective measures because they have legal responsibility for performing such work within their jurisdictions, a determination was made that under Massachusetts' Civil Defense Act, MEMA had concurrent legal responsibility to perform debris removal and emergency protective measures in any town in the commonwealth. It was therefore determined that FEMA could reimburse MEMA for its eligible contractor costs for the debris removal and emergency protective measures, as long as the towns in which the work was performed did not also seek such reimbursement, since Section 312 of the Stafford Act prohibits FEMA from reimbursing two applicants for performing the same work. Stafford Act § 312, 51 U.S.C. § 5155.

---

[101] DHS, OFFICE OF INSPECTOR GENERAL, AUDIT REPORT, NUMBER W-02-03 (2002), *Facey Medical Foundation, Mission Hills, CA.*

D. Eligible Costs

Eligible applicants with eligible work will seek FEMA grant funding for associated costs. In determining the eligibility of these costs, FEMA, like all federal agencies, follows the Uniform Administrative Requirements for Federal Grant Assistance, including allowable cost principles, which are cited in its regulations at 44 C.F.R. Part 13.[102] These regulations set forth the policies establishing federal grant procurement requirements and allowable costs in the PA program.[103]

Allowable costs must be:

- Reasonable and necessary to accomplish the work;[104]

- In compliance with federal, state, and local requirements for competitive procurement;[105] and

- Reduced by applicable credits, such as anticipated insurance proceeds and salvage values.[106]

---

[102] *See* 44 C.F.R. Part 13, the Uniform Administrative Requirements for Grants and Cooperative Agreements to State and Local Governments; and OMB Circulars A-102, Grants and Cooperative Agreements with State and Local Governments, and A-110. The Uniform Administrative Requirements for Grants and Cooperative Agreements with Institutions of Higher Education, Hospitals, and Other Nonprofit Organizations, 2 C.F.R. Part 215. *See also* Part 2, Subsection II, *Applicant Compliance with Procurement Requirements* in this chapter.

[103] Stafford Act § 406, 42 U.S.C. § 5172(e); 44 C.F.R. §§ 206.228, 206.202(d) and 13.22. Several Office of Management and Budget (OMB) circulars, which are available at 2 C.F.R. Part 225, define allowable costs for different governmental and non-profit entities: Circular A-87 for state, tribal and local governments, < http://www.whitehouse.gov/omb/circulars_a087_2004>; Circular A-122 for PNPs other than institutions of higher education, hospitals and any other organization specifically exempted, < http://www.whitehouse.gov/omb/circulars_a122_2004/ >; Circular A-21 for educational institutions < http://www.whitehouse.gov/omb/circulars_a021_2004/ >; PA GUIDE at 40-67;*See generally*, DAP, <http://www.fema.gov/9500-series-policy-publications

[104] *See, e.g.*, OMB Circular A-87, Basic Guidelines, at 8.

[105] Including 44 C.F.R. § 13.36.

[106] PA GUIDE, at 40. The Stafford Act also requires FEMA to assure there is no duplication of benefit with other available assistance, including insurance. Stafford Act §312, 42 U.S.C. § 5155.

Whether a cost is reasonable can be established through a competitive procurement process, as well as through:

- The use of historical documentation for similar work;

- Average costs for similar work in the area;

- Published unit costs from national cost estimating databases; and

- FEMA cost codes, equipment rates, and engineering and design services curves.

Labor, materials, equipment, and contracts awarded for the performance of eligible work must all meet the test of reasonableness; FEMA will make the final determination as to the reasonableness of cost.[107]

1. Labor, Materials, and Equipment

Labor, materials and equipment[108] may add up to a significant portion of eligible costs. Note that the applicant should determine the extent of disaster-related damage. Random surveys to look for damage are not eligible costs; however, if disaster-related damage is discovered or evident during such a survey, FEMA may pay for inspections to determine the extent of damage and method of repair.[109]

a.) Force Account Labor Costs

Force account labor is labor that an applicant's employees perform rather than a contractor and may be claimed at an hourly rate when those employees perform eligible work. Labor rates include actual wages paid plus fringe benefits. Different eligibility criteria apply depending on an employment status, e.g., temporary versus permanent, and type of work performed.

---

[107] See PA GUIDE, at 40, which discusses eligible costs in detail.

[108] Id. at 42-49.

[109] PA GUIDE, at 55 and 85; PA DIGEST, at 135; PA HANDBOOK, at 16. These costs are part of the applicant's administrative allowance. This issue related to surveys comes up most often in evaluating utilities. See Category F, Utilities.

Generally, FEMA does not pay for straight-time (regular-time) force account labor costs of an applicant's employees performing work on debris removal (Category A) or emergency protective measures (Category B) under Sections 403 and 407 of the Stafford Act.[110] There is an exception for straight-time salaries and benefits of permanently employed personnel for work associated with eligible evacuation and sheltering activity.[111] There is also an exception as discussed later in this section for debris and wreckage removal undertaken in relation to 2012 Hurricane Sandy related federal declarations.

In most cases, an applicant may be reimbursed for overtime costs for permanent employees performing debris removal and emergency work but not regular or straight-time costs.[112] In contrast, when permanent employees perform permanent work on eligible facilities, both regular or straight-time costs and overtime costs are eligible.[113] The PA GUIDE discusses the rules applicable to reassigned employees, backfill employees, temporary employees, force account mechanics, foremen and supervisors, contract supervisions, and National Guard and prison labor.[114]

---

[110] C.F.R. § 206.228(a)(2). Per FEMA Recovery Policy 9525.7 dated November 16, 2006, this prohibition is extended to emergency work conducted under Stafford Act Section 502 and is reflected in declaration and FEMA-State Agreement language.

[111] Id; 44 C.F.R. 206.202(f)(ii)

[112] 44 C.F.R. § 206.228(a)(2); DAP 9525.7, *Labor Costs-Emergency Work* (2006), < http://www.fema.gov/9500-series-policy-publications/95257-labor-costs-emergency-work >.

[113] Id. The difference in treatment between eligible emergency work and permanent force account labor costs stems from the 1993 amendment to the regulations. *See* the preamble to the *Federal Register* for this amendment which is found at 58 Fed. Reg. 47,994 (1993). Section 406(a)(2)(C) of the Stafford Act specifically authorizes base and overtime wages for permanent work but the Act is silent on emergency work. FEMA determined this omission provided it the discretion to determine the scope of eligible force account labor costs for emergency work.

[114] PA GUIDE, at 42-44.

> ### Special Hurricane Sandy Rule for Force Account Labor
>
> In response to Hurricane Sandy[115] in October 2012, FEMA modified its regulations to allow for applicants to receive reimbursement for force account labor costs for employees who performed debris removal work for a 30-day period.[116] This rule is only applicable for emergencies or disasters declared in response to Hurricane Sandy, for work performed under Sections 403, 407, or 502 of the Stafford Act.[117] To be eligible for reimbursement, the hours claimed must be related solely to eligible debris activities resulting from Hurricane Sandy.[118] FEMA will not reimburse an applicant for normally scheduled waste pick-up and disposal activities, even if it is done concurrently with Hurricane Sandy debris removal.[119]

b.) Davis-Bacon Act

The Davis-Bacon Act[120] requires every construction and repair contract in excess of $2,000 to which the federal government "is a party" to pay all laborers and mechanics not less than the locally "prevailing wage," as defined by the Department of Labor.[121] FEMA does not generally contract under the PA program for construction and repair work. Instead, such contracts are typically executed by the PA applicant. The Davis-Bacon Act does not apply to state and local contracts to which the federal government is not a party, including for work completed using PA grant

---

[115] DR-4085(NY). DR-4086(NJ), DR-4087(CT), DR-4089 (RI), DR-4090 (DE),

[116] RP 9580.215, Debris Removal Force Account Labor Costs (November 5, 2012).

[117] Id; C.F.R. § 206.228(a)(2); Stafford Act §§ 403, 407, 502, 42 U.S.C. §§ 5170b, 5173, 5192.

[118] RP 9580.215, Debris Removal Force Account Labor Costs (November 5, 2012).

[119] Id.

[120] Davis-Bacon Act, 40 U.S.C. §§ 3141-3144, 3146, and 3147. The Davis-Bacon Act of Mar. 3, 1931, 40 U.S.C. § 276a-5, repealed and reenacted by Pub. L. No. 107-217, 116 Stat. 1062 (2002), as 40 U.S.C. §§ 3141-3144, 3146, and 3147. Accordingly, the Davis-Bacon citations in the Stafford Act and FEMA's regulation have been superseded. *See also* 44 C.F.R. § 13.36(i)(5).

[121] 29 C.F.R §§ 1.5 and 1.6; U.S. Department of Labor, Davis-Bacon Wage Determination Reference Material. http://74.218.115.26/wp-content/uploads/2010/07/4B-6.-Davis-Bacon-Reference-Material.pdf

---

funds under the Stafford Act.[122] The Davis-Bacon Act does apply to construction and repair contracts awarded by other federal agencies (OFAs) and funded by FEMA for emergency work. For example, if the U.S. Army Corps of Engineers (USACE) is operating under a mission assignment from FEMA and contracts directly for construction of a temporary building, the Davis Bacon Act would apply because the USACE is a federal agency and party to the contract. In addition, some state and local governments have state or local laws requiring a prevailing wage rate, and they incorporate these requirements as part of their normal practice for all of their contracts. In such circumstances, these rates are eligible under the PA program.[123]

Further, the Uniform Administrative Requirements for Federal Grant Assistance require grantee and subgrantee contracts to contain a provision requiring compliance with the Davis-Bacon Act when required by the grant program legislation.[124] Only Stafford Act preparedness grants require a grantee to comply with Davis-Bacon provisions.[125] There is no other program legislation applicable to Stafford Act grants requiring application of Davis-Bacon.

Davis-Bacon Waiver

The Davis-Bacon Act provides that "[t]he President may suspend the provisions of this subchapter during a national emergency."[126] On September 8, 2005, President Bush issued a proclamation suspending the application of the Act to contracts to be performed in the counties included in the Hurricane Katrina disaster area.[127]

---

[122] Davis-Bacon does not apply to FEMA PA grants because the grantees and subgrantees are not "the federal government" and FEMA is not a party to grantee and subgrantee contracts.

[123] PA Guide, at 44; PA Digest at 30.

[124] 44 C.F.R. § 13.36(i)(5).

[125] Stafford Act § 611(j)(9), 42 U.S.C. § 5196(j)(9).

[126] Davis-Bacon Act, 40 U.S.C. § 3147.

[127] Presidential Proclamation 7924, 70 Fed. Reg. 54,227 (2005).

c.) Materials and Equipment

FEMA may reimburse PA applicants for the cost of supplies[128] used to perform eligible work and for ownership and operating costs for applicant owned equipment under one of following:

- FEMA published equipment rates;[129]
- State rates (rates developed using state guidelines); or
- Local rates.[130]

2. Mutual Aid Agreements

a.) Introduction

The Emergency Management Assistance Compact (EMAC) is the interstate mechanism to exchange resources and assistance in the event of a presidential or gubernatorial declared emergency or disaster. EMAC establishes procedures so that a disaster-impacted state can request and receive assistance from other member states quickly and efficiently. EMAC resolves two key issues at the outset: liability and reimbursement.[131] To be eligible for FEMA reimbursement, costs must be consistent with FEMA PA policies, regulations, and procedures.[132] The receiving state is responsible for requesting FEMA assistance.

The National Emergency Management Association (NEMA) administers EMAC in collaboration with FEMA. FEMA reimburses work done pursuant to mutual aid agreements to the extent the specific agreement between the states or entities meets the requirements of FEMA policy on mutual aid agreements and the work meets FEMA eligibility requirements.[133] Reimbursement for these costs is subject to the non-federal cost share for that disaster.

---

[128] PA GUIDE, at 48-49. *See also* OMB Circular A-87 Attachment B, *Scheduled Items of Cost* (2004), http://www.whitehouse.gov/omb/circulars_a087_2004/.
[129] *See* FEMA Schedule of Equipment Rates, http://www.fema.gov/government/grant/pa/eqrates.shtm.
[130] *See* PA GUIDE, at 48-49, for an explanation of state and local rates.
[131] *See* PA GUIDE, at 51; *see also* EMAC website at http://www.emacweb.org/.
[132] Id.
[133] Id.

b.) EMAC Provisions

EMAC is defined by its articles, which constitute the agreement on how emergency assistance will be exchanged among the member states. To join, each member state must agree to standard operating procedures (SOPs) for requesting and providing assistance, each state's legislature must enact EMAC legislation, and the governor must sign articles into law to become a member state. The EMAC agreement consists of thirteen articles. All members of EMAC, by adopting the language of the compact into law, agree to abide by and fulfill the articles of the compact.[134]

The articles define, among other things:

- EMAC's purpose;
- Member state responsibilities;
- Limitations of the agreement;
- License and permit recognition across member states;
- Liability arrangements;
- Compensation and reimbursement; and
- Implementation requirements.

By agreeing to a standard legal process, member states are guaranteed reimbursement for all eligible assistance provided through EMAC. Under the compact, it is the responsibility of states requesting assistance to reimburse the states that provide it. The requesting states also are responsible for the actions of workers from assisting states because the requesting state assumes tort responsibility for out-of-state workers.

c.) How EMAC is Coordinated with the Federal Response

EMAC is first and foremost a state-to-state compact; however, FEMA and EMAC leadership[135] have a long-standing agreement in which NEMA facilitates requests to deploy a team to coordinate EMAC activities with federal personnel whenever requested by FEMA Headquarters (HQ).[136]

---

[134] http://www.emacweb.org
[135] The EMAC Committee of NEMA is the managing body of the Compact and provides overall policy direction for EMAC operations. The committee comprises representatives from each member state, either the state director or his or her appointed representative.
[136] *See* WHO ADMINISTERS EMAC: <http://www.emacweb.org/>.

Upon such a request, an EMAC coordinating team may be deployed to the National Response Coordination Center (NRCC) at FEMA HQ in Washington, DC, or to a FEMA Regional Response Coordination Center (RRCC). To stand up a coordinating team at the NRCC or an RRCC, FEMA contacts the NEMA EMAC Coordinator who coordinates with the NRCC or RRCC, NEMA Executive Director, and the National Coordination Group to determine whether the event is at a level that would make deployment of state resources and such coordination under EMAC necessary and to complete a task order.

d.) FEMA Reimbursement for EMAC Activities

FEMA recognizes mutual aid agreements between requesting and assisting entities and statewide mutual aid agreements where the state is responsible for administering the claims for reimbursement of assisting entities. In addition, FEMA recognizes the standard EMAC agreement as a valid form of mutual aid agreement between member states.

FEMA will reimburse all eligible costs under the PA program incurred by the requesting state through mutual aid agreements between applicants and other entities when these costs are for emergency work[137] and are:

- Requested by a requesting entity or incident commander;[138]
- Directly related to a presidentially declared emergency or major disaster, or declared fire;
- Used in the performance of eligible work; and
- Reasonable costs.

The requesting entity should claim the eligible costs of the assisting entity, pursuant to the terms and conditions of the mutual aid agreement and agree to disburse the federal share of funds to the assisting entity. FEMA will honor the reimbursement provisions in a pre-event agreement to the

---

[137] Stafford Act §§ 403, 407, 420 and 502, 42 U.S.C. §§ 5170b, 5173, 5187 and 5192.
[138] DAP 9523.6, *Mutual Aid Agreements for Public Assistance and Fire Management Assistance* (2007), VII. A. 5. [hereinafter DAP 9523.6, *Mutual Aid*], the ranking official responsible for overseeing the management of emergency planning, logistics and finances of the field response,
http://www.healthlawyers.org/Members/PracticeGroups/THAMC/EmergencyPreparednessToolkit/Documents/V_EMAC/B_FEMAMutualAidPolicy9523_6.pdf

extent the provisions are consistent with its own policies.[139] Work associated with the grantee's responsibilities as the grant administrator, as outlined in FEMA regulations, is eligible.[140] Also, use of EMAC-provided assistance to perform these tasks is eligible mutual aid work.

When a pre-event agreement provides for reimbursement but also provides for an initial period of unpaid assistance, FEMA will pay the eligible costs of assistance after such initial unpaid period.

Examples of eligible emergency work include:

- Search and rescue, sandbagging, emergency medical care, and debris removal;

- Reasonable supervision and administration in the receiving state that is directly related to eligible emergency work;

- Costs to transport equipment and personnel by the assisting entity to the incident site;

- Costs incurred in the operation of the Incident Command System (ICS), such as operations, planning, logistics, and administration, provided such costs are directly related to the performance of eligible work on the disaster to which such resources are assigned;

- State Emergency Operations Center (EOC) or Joint Field Office (JFO) assistance in the receiving state to support emergency assistance;

- Assistance at the NRCC and RRCC, if requested by FEMA (labor, per diem, and transportation);

- Dispatch operations in the receiving state;

- Donations warehousing and management (eligible only upon approval of the Assistant Administrator of the Disaster Assistance Directorate); and

- Dissemination of public information authorized under emergency work.

---

[139] Id.
[140] 44 C.F.R. § 206.202(b).

When a pre-event agreement specifies that no reimbursement will be provided for mutual aid assistance, FEMA will not pay for the costs of assistance. When an agreement makes reimbursement discretionary, FEMA will not pay for the costs of assistance.[141] FEMA will not reimburse costs incurred by entities that "self-deploy" (deploy without a request for mutual aid assistance by a requesting entity), except to the extent those resources are subsequently used in the performance of eligible work at the request of the requesting entity or incident commander. Permanent restoration work is not eligible for FEMA mutual aid reimbursement. Additionally, the reimbursement provisions of a mutual aid agreement must not be contingent on a declaration by the federal government.

Examples of non-eligible work:

- Permanent restoration work;

- Training, exercises, on-the-job training;

- Long-term recovery and mitigation consultation;

- Costs outside the receiving state that are associated with the operations of the EMAC system, except for state EOC or JFO assistance in the receiving state to support emergency assistance and assistance at the NRCC and RRCC, if requested by FEMA (labor, per diem and transportation);

- Costs for staff performing work that is not eligible under the PA program;

- Costs of preparing to deploy or "standing by;"

- Dispatch operations outside the receiving state;

- Tracking of EMAC Incident Cost Accounting and Reporting System resources; and

- Situation reporting not associated with the costs of operating the ICS.

---

[141] DAP 9523.6, *Mutual Aid*, VII. C. 4.

e.) Labor Force Account Reimbursement

The straight- or regular-time wages or salaries of a requesting entity's permanently employed personnel performing or supervising emergency work are not eligible costs even when such personnel are reassigned or relocated from their usual work location to provide assistance during an emergency.[142] Overtime costs for such personnel, however, are eligible. The labor force account costs of an assisting entity will be treated as contract labor, with regular-time and overtime wages and certain benefits reimbursable as eligible costs, provided labor rates are reasonable. The labor force account costs of the assisting entity will not be treated as contract labor if the labor force is employed by the same local or state government as the requesting entity. Straight-time and overtime costs are determined in accordance with the assisting entity's pre-disaster policies, which should be applied consistently in both disaster and non-disaster situations.

In circumstances where an assisting entity is also an eligible applicant in its own right, the determination of eligible and ineligible costs will depend on the capacity in which the entity is incurring costs. An applicant's straight-time wages are not eligible costs when the applicant is using its permanently employed personnel for emergency work in its own jurisdiction.

Requesting and assisting entities may not mutually deploy their labor forces to assist each other so as to circumvent these restrictions. The straight-time or regular-time wages or salaries for backfill personnel incurred by assisting entities are not eligible for reimbursement.[143] However, the overtime portion of the backfill salary is considered an additional cost of deploying personnel who perform eligible work and is eligible for reimbursement by FEMA.

---

[142] *See* 44 C.F.R. § 206.228(a)(4).
[143] Backfill is defined as replacement personnel for those personnel who cannot perform their regular duties because they are performing eligible emergency work in the requesting state. DAP 9523.6, *Mutual Aid*, at VII.A.1.

---

f.) Mutual Aid Agreements Must Be Reduced To Writing

Mutual aid agreements can be pre-disaster standing agreements and made verbally or in writing post-disaster. When the parties do not have a pre-event written mutual aid agreement, or where a written pre-event agreement is silent on reimbursement, the requesting and assisting entities may verbally agree on the type and extent of mutual aid resources to be provided in the current event, and on the terms, conditions, and costs of such assistance. This arrangement must be reduced to writing and executed by an authorized official of both the requesting and assisting entity. The agreement should be consistent with past practices for mutual aid between the parties. A written post-event agreement should be submitted within 30 days of the requesting entity's Applicant's Briefing.[144] Only requesting entities are eligible applicants for FEMA assistance. An assisting entity must submit its claim for reimbursement to a requesting entity that will then pay them. States may be eligible applicants when statewide mutual aid agreements or compacts authorize the state to administer the costs of mutual aid assistance on behalf of local jurisdictions.

g.) FEMA-Required Documentation

Requesting and assisting entities must keep detailed records of the services requested and received, and provide those records as part of the supporting documentation for a reimbursement request. A copy of the mutual aid agreement, whether pre- or post-event must be included in the documentation, as well as a written and signed certification by the requesting entity certifying the types and extent of mutual aid assistance requested and received in the performance of eligible emergency work and the labor and equipment rates used to determine the mutual aid cost reimbursement request. Volunteer labor or the value of paid labor that is provided at no cost to the applicant is not reimbursable. To the extent the assisting entity is staffed with volunteer labor, the value of the volunteer labor may be credited to the non-federal cost share of the requesting entity's emergency work.[145] If a mutual aid agreement provides for an

---

[144] Id. at VII. D. 2.
[145] See DAP 9525.2, Donated Resources (2007), http://www.fema.gov/pdf/government/grant/pa/9525_2.pdf.

initial period of unpaid assistance or provides for assistance at no cost to the requesting entity, the value of the assistance provided at no cost to the requesting entity may be credited to the non-federal cost share of the requesting entity's emergency work.[146] Reimbursement for equipment provided to a requesting entity will be based on FEMA equipment rates, approved state rates, or—in the absence of such standard rates—on rates deemed reasonable by FEMA.[147] Reimbursement for equipment damaged or purchased and used in emergency operations will be based on FEMA policy.[148]

h.) Medical Care

EMAC can be used to provide emergency medical care, and these costs may be eligible for reimbursement as well. Reimbursement claims made by mutual aid providers must comply with applicable FEMA policy.[149] Public or private non-profit medical service providers working within their jurisdiction, however, do not qualify as mutual aid providers.[150]

i.) National Capital Region (NCR) Mutual Aid Agreement

The National Capital Region (NCR) was created pursuant to the National Capital Planning Act of 1952.[151] This Act defined the NCR as the District of Columbia; Montgomery and Prince George's Counties of Maryland; Arlington, Fairfax, Loudoun, and Prince William Counties of Virginia; and all cities in Maryland or Virginia within the geographic area bounded by the outer boundaries of the combined area of said counties. The NCR is the fifth largest economy in the United States.

---

[146] Id.

[147] DAP 9523.6, Mutual Aid, at VII. H.6.

[148] See DAP 9525.8, Damage to Applicant Owned Equipment Performing Emergency Work (2008), < http://www.fema.gov/public-assistance-9500-series-policy-publications/95258-damage-applicant-owned-equipment-performing >; DAP 9525.12, Disposition of Equipment, Supplies, and Salvageable Materials (2008), < http://www.fema.gov/9500-series-policy-publications/952512-disposition-equipment-supplies-salvageable-materials>.

[149] See DAP 9523.6, Mutual Aid; https://www.fema.gov/9500-series-policy-publications/95236-mutual-aid-agreements-public-assistance-fire-management

[150] See DAP 9525.4, Emergency Medical Care and Medical Evacuations (2008) < http://www.fema.gov/9500-series-policy-publications/95254-emergency-medical-care-medical-evacuations >; and DAP 9523.6, Mutual Aid.

[151] 40 U.S.C. § 71.

The Homeland Security Act established the Office of National Capital Region Coordination (NCRC) within the Department of Homeland Security.[152] The NCRC is responsible for overseeing and coordinating federal programs for, and relationships with, state, local, and regional authorities in the NCR. In addition, the NCRC assesses and advocates for resources needed by state, local, and regional authorities in the NCR to implement efforts to secure the homeland.

Mutual aid agreements have existed in the National Capital Region for decades. After 9/11, awareness of the need for updated mutual aid capacities and agreements, including clarification of liability issues, sharpened. Congress enacted legislation addressing mutual aid acceptable to the local and state jurisdictions as part of the Intelligence Reform and Terrorism Protection Act of 2004.[153] The NCR Mutual Aid Agreement represents the general implementing document resulting from the enacted federal legislation[154] and consolidates the 31 existing mutual aid agreements to strengthen communication, coordination, and execution of response efforts. The agreement supports all mutual aid generally provided between and among units of local government, including but not limited to police, fire, emergency management, public health, and public works, including transportation.

Under current law, the federal government has authority to enter into mutual aid agreements with state and local governments in the NCR in order to allow the various jurisdictions to cooperate in the event of an emergency.[155]

---

[152] 6 U.S.C. § 462.
[153] Pub. L. No. 108-458, 118 Stat. 3638, § 7302 (2004).
[154] *See* 42 U.S.C. § 5196 note. *See* Pub. L. No. 108-458, 118 Stat. 3840, title VII, § 7302 (), as amended by Pub. L. No. 110-250, 122 Stat. 2318, § 1 (2008).
[155] *Id.*

3. Deductions for Applicable Credits-Anticipated Insurance and Salvage Values

To avoid a duplication of benefits,[156] FEMA must reduce eligible project costs by any applicable salvage value for materials or equipment. For example, disaster debris, such as timber and mulched debris and scrap metal, may have a market value. FEMA will also reduce eligible project costs by anticipated insurance proceeds. Insurance is a complex topic and is discussed in detail later in this chapter.

III. Categories of Work

After a major disaster or emergency declaration, the Stafford Act authorizes FEMA to provide grant or direct assistance to state, tribal, and local governments, and certain PNPs.[157] Reasonable expenses incurred in anticipation of and immediately preceding the event's incident period may also be eligible for assistance.[158] FEMA has administratively divided disaster-related PA work into two major types: Emergency Work and Permanent Work. These work types are subdivided into seven categories, designated Categories A through G.[159] FEMA calls Categories A and B Emergency Work, and Categories C through G Permanent Work. Only Emergency Work is available under PA for an emergency declaration.[160] This chapter discusses these categories. FEMA characterizes work authorized under Debris Removal[161] as Category A, and Essential Assistance (emergency protective measures)[162] as Category B. FEMA characterizes Repair, Restoration, and Replacement of Damaged

---

[156] Stafford Act § 312; DAP 9525.3, *Duplication of Benefits – Non-Government Funds* (2007) [hereinafter DAP 9525.3, *Duplication of Benefits*] < http://www.fema.gov/public-assistance-9500-series-policy-publications/95253-duplication-benefits---non-government-funds >.
[157] Stafford Act §§ 403, 406, 407 and 502, 42 U.S.C. §§ 5170b, 5172; 5173 and 5192.
[158] Id. § 424, 42 U.S.C. § 5189b.
[159] PA GUIDE, at 66-87; PA DIGEST.
[160] Stafford Act § 502, 42 U.S.C. §5192. The language for the provision of emergency work under an emergency declaration is not identical to that for a major disaster and thus may lead to differences in the scope of eligible work.
[161] Id. § 407, 42 U.S.C. § 5173.
[162] Id. § 403, 42 U.S.C. § 5170b.

Facilities[163] as permanent work (Categories C through G), which is based on the types of facilities to be restored.

A. Emergency Work

Emergency work[164] is work necessary to meet an immediate threat to life and property and is essential to saving lives and protecting public health and safety.[165] The President may authorize FEMA, under an emergency or major disaster declaration, to provide DFA and grant funding for work under Categories A and B (debris removal and emergency protective measures, respectively, as noted earlier).[166] Please refer to Chapter 4, *Response*, for the request process for DFA mission assignments. For emergency work that grantees and subgrantees perform using contractors, they will award contracts using their own procurement procedures, provided these are in conformance with federal grant procurement standards.[167] *See* discussion under *Applicant Compliance with Procurement Requirements* in Part 2, Section II of this chapter.

1. Category A: Debris Removal

Debris removal[168] is a significant activity in most major disasters or emergencies declarations. Indeed, the iconic visual of many disasters

---

[163] Id. § 406, 42 U.S.C. § 5172.

[164] Id. §§ 403 and 502, 42 U.S.C. §§ 5170b and 5192 ; 44 C.F.R. §§ 206.201 (b) and 206.225; Fact Sheet 9580.4, *Emergency Work* (2010) < https://www.fema.gov/9500-series-policy-publications/fact-sheet-emergency-work-contracting

[165] Id. §§ 403 and 502, 42 U.S.C. §§ 5170b and 5192; 44 C.F.R. § 206.225; PA GUIDE; PA DIGEST, at 17 and 46. The Stafford Act defines the scope of what constitutes emergency work most specifically in section 403, which pertains to a major disaster declaration. FEMA relies, however, on this specificity for guidance in authorizing emergency work for emergency declarations under section 502(b) of the Stafford Act, which provides very broad and very general authority for any assistance necessary to save lives, protect property and public health and safety, and to lessen or avert the threat of catastrophe.

[166] Id. § 403 and 502, 42 U.S.C. §§ 5170b and 5192.

[167] Id. 44 C.F.R. § 13.36(b) and 2 C.F.R. 215.40 - 215.48. *See* discussion in Part 2, Section II, *Applicant Compliance with Procurement Requirements* of this chapter.

[168] Stafford Act §§ 403 and 407, 42 U.S.C. §§ 5170b and 5173; 44 C.F.R. § 206 224; PA DEBRIS GUIDE; PA GUIDE, at 2,21,29,50, 66,67-71; PA DIGEST, at 31; RP 9523.4, *Demolition of Private Structures* (2007), < http://www.fema.gov/public-assistance-9500-series-policy-publications/95234-demolition-private-structures >; RP 9523.12, *Debris Operations – Hand Loaded Trucks and Trailers* (2006), < http://www.fema.gov/9500-series-policy-

---

depicts debris strewn devastation. Debris removal is an essential response activity, and it hastens recovery by the community, both psychologically and logistically. PA applicants will generally remove debris themselves through their own labor force or contractors instead of requesting a mission assignment for debris removal. Even in these circumstances, however, FEMA takes an active role in the process of debris removal to include review of contracts for eligible scopes of work and cost reasonableness, monitoring performance, and planning for disposal and salvage.[169] Upon request, FEMA may issue a technical assistance mission assignment to USACE to assist applicants with debris removal procurements, which may involve large dollar amounts, as well as detailed scopes of work and monitoring methodology. FEMA makes all debris removal eligibility determinations, including those for costs and cost reasonableness. The PA Debris Management Guide addresses the most common eligibility issues for various types of debris and recommends supporting documentation.[170]

a.) Debris Removal from Public Property

Two sections of Title IV of the Stafford Act authorize DFA and grant assistance for removal of debris resulting from a major disaster—sections

---

publications/952312-debris-operations-hand-loaded-trucks-trailers>; DAP 9523.11 *Hazardous Stump Extraction and Removal Eligibility* (2007), < http://www.fema.gov/9500-series-policy-publications/hazardous-stump-extraction-removal-eligibility DAP 9523.13 *Debris Removal from Private Property* (2007) [hereinafter *Private Debris Removal*], < http://www.fema.gov/9500-series-policy-publications/952313-debris-removal-private-property >; RP 9524.3 *Policy for Rehabilitation Assistance for Levees and Other Flood Control Works* (2009), < http://www.fema.gov/public-assistance-archived-policies/95243-policy-rehabilitation-assistance-levees-and-other-flood>. *See also*, PA DEBRIS GUIDE, *Appendix G*, Decision Tree; http://www.fema.gov/pdf/government/grant/pa/demagde.pdf FEMA RP 9525.7 *Labor Costs – Emergency Work* (2006), < http://www.fema.gov/9500-series-policy-publications/95257-labor-costs-emergency-work>, *Fact Sheet: Debris Operations – Clarification: Emergency Contracting vs. Emergency Work* (2001), < http://www.fema.gov/9500-series-policy-publications/fact-sheet-emergency-work-contracting> FEMA RP 9580.201 *Fact Sheet: Debris Removal – Applicant's Contracting Checklist* (2006), < http://www.fema.gov/public-assistance-9500-series-policy-publications/debris-removal-applicant%27s-contracting-checklist >; RP 9580.202, *Fact Sheet: Debris Removal – Authorities of Federal Agencies* (2007); *see*, PA DEBRIS GUIDE, Appendix G; DAP 9580.203 Fact Sheet: *Debris Monitoring* (2007), http://www.fema.gov/pdf/government/grant/pa/9580_203.pdf
[169] PA DEBRIS GUIDE.
[170] Id. at 22-31.

---

403 and 407.[171] In the event of an emergency declaration under the Stafford Act, FEMA may also provide assistance for debris removal pursuant to section 407.[172] The statutory standard for debris removal in section 403 is that which is "essential to saving lives and protecting and preserving property or public health and safety."[173] The standard in section 407 is whether debris removal is "in the public interest."[174] By regulation, FEMA has defined debris removal to be in the "public interest" when necessary to:

- Eliminate an immediate threat to lives, public health, and safety;

- Eliminate immediate threats of significant damage to improved public or private property;

- Ensure the economic recovery of the affected community to the benefit of the community at large; or

- Mitigate the risk to life and property by removing substantially damaged structures and associated appurtenances as needed to convert property acquired using FEMA hazard mitigation program (HMP) funds to uses compatible with open space, recreation, or wetlands management practices.[175]

By regulation, therefore, FEMA has essentially collapsed the Section 403 standard for debris removal into the first two prongs of the public interest standard under Section 407.

Debris removal must also meet general work eligibility criteria:

- The debris must have been generated by the major disaster event;

- The debris must be located within a designated disaster area on an eligible applicant's improved property or rights-of-way; and

---

[171] Stafford Act §§ 403(a)(3)(A) and 407, 42 U.S.C. §§ 5170b(a)(3) and 5173.
[172] Id. §§ 501 and 502(a)(6), 42 U.S.C. §§ 5191 and 5192 (a)(6); 44 C.F.R. § 206.63.
[173] Id. § 403(a)(3)(A), 42 U.S.C. § 5170b(a)(3).
[174] Id. § 407, 42 U.S.C. § 5173.
[175] 44 C.F.R. § 206.224 (a).

- The debris removal must be the legal responsibility of the applicant.[176]

Examples of ineligible debris include:

- Debris from an eligible applicant's unimproved property or undeveloped land;

- Debris from a facility that is not eligible for funding under the PA Program, such as a PNP cemetery or PNP golf course; or

- Debris from federal lands or facilities that are the authority of another federal agency or department.[177]

An applicant may conduct debris operations in any manner it deems appropriate, such as through:

- **Force Account Labor.** The applicant may utilize its own labor, equipment, and materials. It is important for the applicant staff to document hours worked by employees and equipment used to complete the eligible work.[178]

- **Mutual Aid Agreements.** The applicant may have agreements with other jurisdictions and agencies for the provision of debris management services in the event of an emergency. *See* earlier discussion in this chapter on *Mutual Aid Agreements*.

- **Contract Services.** An applicant may hire a contractor to perform such work as debris clearance, removal, disposal, reduction, recycling, and/or monitoring. Funding is limited to the scope of work necessary to remove debris that is an immediate threat to life, public health, and safety, or poses an immediate threat of significant damage to improved public or private property. *See Applicant Compliance with Procurement Requirements* in this chapter.

---

[176] Stafford Act §§ 406, 407, 42 U.S.C §§ 5172, 5173; 44 CFR. § 206.223(a)(3); PA DEBRIS GUIDE, at 21.
[177] Stafford Act § 405, 42 U.S.C. § 5171; 44 C.F.R. § 206.226(a)(1) ; PA DEBRIS GUIDE at 22.
[178] Id. at 13; RP 9525.7, *Labor Costs — Emergency Work* (2006), < http://www.fema.gov/9500-series-policy-publications/95257-labor-costs-emergency-work

- **Direct Federal Assistance.** When the impact of a disaster is so severe that neither the state nor local governments can remove debris on their own, including through contract, the state may request that debris removal be performed directly by the federal government.[179] When FEMA approves DFA, it will task or mission assign an appropriate federal agency to perform work.[180] If another federal agency has the authority to provide an applicant with assistance for debris removal operations, FEMA cannot provide funds for that project. Applicants should pursue funding assistance offered through those agencies.[181]

Debris removal may include the clearance of: trees and woody debris; building components and/or contents; sand, mud, silt, and gravel; wreckage produced during conduct of emergency protective measures; and other disaster-related wreckage.[182] Debris that blocks streets and highways is deemed a threat to public health and safety because it blocks passage of emergency vehicles or blocks access to emergency facilities.[183] Debris cleared from roads and highways, including shoulders, ditches, and drainage structures, may also be eligible for the same reason. An eligible applicant must own or be responsible for maintaining the roads.

b.) Debris Removal from Wetlands

Removal of debris or wreckage from a natural stream, flood channel, or waterway may be eligible because it could cause flooding from a future storm that threatens damage to improved property.[184] In such a situation, only the clearance of debris necessary to protect against an immediate threat of damage to improved property or to protect public health and safety will be eligible.[185]

---

[179] 44 C.F.R. § 206.208(a).
[180] PA GUIDE, at 76-78.
[181] PA DEBRIS GUIDE, at 10 and Appendix G; RP 9580.202, *Fact Sheet: Debris Removal – Authorities of Federal Agencies* (2007).
[182] PA GUIDE, at 67; PA DIGEST, at 31.
[183] PA GUIDE, at 68.
[184] RP 9523.5, *Debris Removal from Waterways* (2010), < http://www.fema.gov/9500-series-policy-publications/95257-labor-costs-emergency-work >.
[185] PA GUIDE, at 68.

Under the Emergency Watershed Protection (EWP) Program, the National Resource Conservation Service (NRCS) of the U.S. Department of Agriculture has authority to remove debris from a watershed causing a sudden impairment to the watershed resulting in an imminent threat to life or property. This typically includes debris in channels but also can include debris nearby areas if a future event could create an imminent threat to life or property.[186] NRCS may provide assistance under the EWP when the President declares a major disaster under the Stafford Act, or when an NRCS state conservationist determines that watershed impairment exists.[187]

Because EWP debris removal assistance only is available when a debris-causing watershed impairment creates an imminent threat to life or property, if an applicant does not qualify for EWP Program assistance, it also likely cannot qualify for FEMA debris removal assistance—the work will not satisfy the public interest standard in the Stafford Act.[188]

Generally, FEMA has not provided funding where another federal agency has specific authority to perform the work.[189] However, in October 2012, FEMA revised its policy to allow for limited debris removal from streams where another federal agency (such as NRCS) has authority to do so but does not exercise it.[190] Limited debris removal may be eligible under the PA Program if it is:

- Reasonably necessary to eliminate an immediate threat to life, public health and safety; or located immediately up/down stream of or in close proximity to improved property and which poses an immediate threat of significant damage to that property; and

---

[186] Flood Control Act of 1950 § 50, PL 81-515, 33 U.S.C. § 701b-1; 16 U.S.C. § 22037; 7 CFR Part 624.

[187] 7 CFR § 624.6.

[188] Stafford Act §§ 403, 407, 502, 42 U.S.C. §§ 5170b, 5173, 5192; 44 CFR § 206.224(a).

[189] See, e.g., 44 CFR §§ 206.208(c)(2) (providing that if any part of work requested for a federal mission assignment falls within the statutory authority of another federal agency, FEMA will not approve that portion of the work), and 206.226(a) ("Generally, disaster assistance will not be made available under the Stafford Act when another federal agency has specific authority to restore facilities damaged or destroyed by an event which is a declared major disaster."); and PA GUIDE, at 23-24.

[190] FEMA Recovery Policy RP 9523.5, Debris Removal from Waterways, (October 30, 2012).

- Another federal agency is not providing assistance for the activity.[191]

Example: Vermont Debris Removal

Disaster conditions were such that Vermont didn't have the capability to take the administrative steps necessary to get a project agreement in place with NRCS before completing debris removal work. 33 USC 701b-1 requires that any conservation assistance be made in accordance with plans approved by the Secretary of Agriculture in advance of restoration as a condition of financial assistance. NRCS's regulation, which implements the statute, carries forth this planning requirement at 7 CFR 624.6. It was therefore impracticable and/or impossible for the communities to comply with the requirement. Since this requirement was established by statute, the Vermont project was outside the scope of NRCS' statutory authority, and NRCS lacked the authority to provide the requested reimbursement . As a result, the Vermont projects were not affected by appropriations limitations and could be considered by FEMA for eligibility under either 403 or 407 as appropriate.

---

c.) Debris Removal from Navigable Waterways

USACE has primary responsibility for the removal of debris from federally-maintained navigable channels and waterways.[192] As stated previously, generally FEMA will not provide funding where another federal agency has specific authority to perform a particular type of work otherwise eligible under the PA Program.[193] For FEMA to reimburse an applicant for the removal of vehicles and vessels, the applicant must provide supporting documentation[194] for its funding request. As with other types of debris removal, the removal of debris from waterways must

---

[191] Id. at VII.B.8.

[192] River and Harbor Appropriations Act of 1899, 33 U.S.C. §§ 407, 409 414, 415, 419, 701 et seq.

[193] See, e.g., 44 CFR §§ 206.208(c)(2), and 206.226(a); and PA GUIDE, at 23-24.

[194] Id. § 13.20(b)(6).

be found to be in the public interest.[195] The applicant must demonstrate one of the following in addition to establishing legal responsibility:

- If a threat to life, public health, and safety, the basis of such a determination by the state, county, or municipal government's public health authority or other public entity that has legal authority to make such a determination; or

- If a threat to improved property, the basis of the determination by the state, county, or municipal government that the removal of disaster-generated debris from a navigable waterway is cost-effective. Debris removal is cost-effective if the cost to remove the debris is less than the cost of potential damage to the improved property; or

- If necessary for economic recovery, the basis of the determination by the state, county, or municipal government that the removal of debris from a navigable waterway is necessary to ensure economic recovery of the affected community to the benefit of the community at large.[196]

d.) Boat Retrieval

The retrieval/removal of boats from navigable waters may be necessary where the boats present an obstruction or danger to other vessels, including emergency service providers. FEMA provides funding to eligible applicants to remove sunken vessels from non-federally maintained navigable waterways, the coastal or inland zones, or wetlands, when removal is necessary to eliminate an immediate threat to life, public health and safety, or improved property, or to ensure the economic recovery of the affected community.[197]

The primary issue is the question of who bears the responsibility to remove such a vessel. Under federal law, it is the duty of the owner, lessee, or operator of a sunken craft to immediately remove it from navigable channels; failure to do so is considered abandonment of the

---

[195] 44 C.F.R. § 206.224 (a).
[196] RP 9523.5, at VII.B.1.
[197] Stafford Act §§ 403, 407, 502, 42 U.S.C. § 5170b, 5173, 5192; 44 CFR 206.208, 224.

---

craft, after which the craft is subject to removal by the United States.[198] The owner, lessee, or operator is strictly liable for the full costs of removal.[199]

In cases where the craft is considered abandoned, USACE has primary responsibility for the removal of sunken vessels or other obstructions from federally-maintained navigable waterways under emergency conditions.[200] USACE will remove a vessel using its emergency authorities only if the owner, operator, or lessee cannot be identified or cannot affect removal in a safe and timely manner.[201]

The U.S. Coast Guard (USCG)has primary responsibility for removing, or to destroy, if necessary, abandoned barges greater than 100 tons, and sunken or abandoned vessels "threatening to discharge" hazardous substances or that pose a threat to the public health, welfare, or environment.[202]

USACE and USCG have a Memorandum of Agreement under which the two agencies work together to determine if a sunken vessel either poses a threat to navigation or a pollution threat to public health and safety.[203] If the agencies determine that the threat is to navigation, the USACE will remove the vessel. If the threat is related to pollution, USCG will remove the vessel if it determines that its removal is essential to abate a pollution threat; otherwise, USCG will remove the oil and other hazardous substances while leaving the vessel in place.

---

[198] 33 U.S.C. 409; 33 CFR Part 245.
[199] Id.; 33 CFR Part 245.45.
[200] River and Harbor Appropriations Act of 1899, 33 U.S.C. §§ 407, 409 414, 415, 419, 701 et seq.; 33 CFR Part 245.
[201] Id.
[202] Abandoned Barge Act of 1992 § 20, 46 U.S.C. § 4701 et seq; Federal Water Pollution Control Act, 33 U.S.C. § 1321(c)(1)(B)(iii); Comprehensive Environmental Response Compensation and Liability Act (CERCLA), 42 U.S.C. § 9604(e)(1); 33 C.F.R. Part 153.
[203] Memorandum of Agreement Between the Department of the Army and the U.S. Coast Guard, Marking and Removal of Sunken Vessels and other Obstructions to Navigation, http://publications.usace.army.mil/publications/eng-regs/ER_1130-2-520/a-b.pdf

Key Factors

- If any part of the damaged vessel can be used to identify an owner, the applicant should contact the owner and follow its local ordinances and state laws to demonstrate legal responsibility to remove and dispose of the vessel[204]

- Owners must be given notice of their obligation to remove the boat; if a responsible party cannot be determined, notice is effected through newspaper publication[205]

FEMA may fund the removal and disposal of eligible disaster-generated debris, wreckage, and sunken vessels from the coastal or inland zone, non-federally maintained waterways and wetlands by an eligible applicant if (1) the debris, wreckage, or sunken vessel is the direct result of a presidentially declared disaster, (2) the removal is in the public interest, and (3) another federal agency does not have specific authority to fund the work.[206]

e.) Debris Removal on Federal Aid Highways

On July 6, 2012, the President signed into law the Moving Ahead for Progress in the 21st Century Act (MAP-21).[207] A provision of MAP-21 amended the statutory authorization for the Federal Highway Administration's (FHWA) Emergency Relief Program to remove FHWA's authority to fund debris removal from federal aid highways where Public Assistance funding is available for debris removal under a declared major disaster or emergency. The amendment was effective October 1, 2012. For emergencies or major disasters declared on or after that date, absent special appropriation, FEMA, not FHWA, will have the authority for debris removal from federal aid highways during emergencies or major disasters in jurisdictions where debris removal is authorized under the Stafford Act.

---

[204] *See, e.g.,* 44 CFR §§ 206.208(c)(2), and 206.226(a); PA GUIDE, at 23-24; and FEMA Recovery Policy RP 9523.5.
[205] Id.; 33 CFR Part 245
[206] 44 CFR § 206.223(a), 44 CFR 226.224(a), 44 CFR 206.208(c)(2); Stafford Act § 203, 403, 407, 502, 312. Recovery Policy RP 9523.5
[207] Pub. L. 112-141. (2012).

FEMA applicants still must meet the applicable Public Assistance requirements, including specific debris removal criteria. FHWA will continue to provide debris removal funding, following their procedures and eligibility rules, for events that do not result in Stafford Act declarations, events that are authorized for IA only, or areas that are not designated for PA/Debris Removal. There may be situations where a debris removal work begins before the President has made a determination regarding a Stafford Act declaration, and therefore before the applicant will know which program of federal funding will be available. Applicants in those circumstances should be sure that their actions would meet the requirements of either program. Thorough and accurate documentation is the key to establishment of eligibility under either program.

f.) Removal of Debris from Public Parks and Recreation Areas

Removal of debris from parks and recreational areas that the public uses is eligible when it affects public health or safety or proper utilization of such facilities. Trees frequently constitute a large part of debris in these areas.[208] Stump removal is not eligible unless it is determined that the stump itself poses a hazard.[209]

g.) Debris Removal from Private Property

In general, the cost of debris removal from private property[210] is not reimbursable because it does not typically present an immediate health and safety threat to the general public. Debris removal from private property is, in the first instance, always the responsibility of individual

---

[208] Id.

[209] Id; DAP 9523.11, *Hazardous Stump Extraction and Removal Eligibility* (2007); < http://www.fema.gov/9500-series-policy-publications/hazardous-stump-extraction-removal-eligibility : RP 9580.204, *Documenting and Validating Hazardous Trees, Limbs and Stumps* (2007); < http://www.fema.gov/9580204-documenting-and-validating-hazardous-trees-limbs-and-stumps >.

[210] 44 C.F.R. § 206.224(b) and (c); PA GUIDE, at 69-70; PA DIGEST, at 31; PA DEBRIS GUIDE, at 33-40; DAP 9523.4 *Demolition of Private Structures* (2007), <http://www.fema.gov/public-assistance-9500-series-policy-publications/95234-demolition-private-structures >; DAP 9523.13, < http://www.fema.gov/pdf/government/grant/pa/9523_13.pdf >.

---

private property owners; other sources of funding, such as insurance, are commonly available to cover the cost of work. If private property owners move debris from private property to a public right-of-way, however, the cost of removing this debris may be reimbursed because then the debris may be construed as debris from public property,[211] particularly where the Federal Coordinating Officer (FCO) makes the finding discussed in the next paragraph.

In those extraordinary circumstances where debris on private property threatens public health, safety, or the economic recovery of the community, FEMA may fund such debris removal, but it must be approved in advance by the FCO.[212] The FCO will work with the grantee affected by a major disaster to designate, as appropriate, those areas where debris removal from private property is in the public interest.[213] Any state or local government that seeks reimbursement to remove debris from private property will, prior to commencement of work, submit a written request to the FCO that includes the following information:

- Public Interest Determination[214]

    o   A determination by the state, county, or municipal government's public health authority or other public entity that has legal authority to make a determination that disaster-generated debris on private property constitutes an immediate threat to life, public health, and safety, or is necessary to ensure the economic recovery of the community; or

    o   If a threat to improved property, the basis of the determination that the removal of disaster-generated debris costs less than the cost of potential damage to the improved property; or

    o   If necessary for economic recovery, the basis of the determination by the state, county, or municipal government that the removal of debris is necessary to ensure economic

---

[211] 44 C.F.R. § 206.224; PA GUIDE, at 68-69; PA DIGEST, at 31; PA DEBRIS GUIDE, at 3.
[212] Stafford Act §§ 403 and 407, 42 U.S.C. §§ 5170b and 5173; 44 C.F.R. § 206.224(b); PA DEBRIS GUIDE, at 33; DAP 9523.13, *Debris Removal*.
[213] 44 C.F.R. § 206.224; PA DEBRIS GUIDE, at 34.
[214] *Id.* § 206.224(a); DAP 9523.13, *Debris Removal*, at 3.

recovery of the affected community to the benefit of the community at large.

- Documentation of Legal Responsibility and Authorization[215]

  o The applicant requesting assistance must demonstrate the legal basis as established by law, ordinance, or code upon which it intends to exercise its responsibility to remove disaster-related debris from private property. Governments ordinarily rely on condemnation and/or nuisance abatement authorities to obtain legal responsibility prior to beginning debris removal work. There may be circumstances, however, where the government determines that ordinary condemnation and/or nuisance abatement procedures are too time-consuming to address the immediate public health and safety threat. In such circumstances, applicants may follow other procedures that meet state and local legal requirements for entering private property and removing a health and safety threat.[216]

- The applicant's legal responsibility to take action must be independent of any expectation, or request, that FEMA will reimburse costs incurred for private property debris removal. The applicant must confirm that a legally authorized official has ordered the exercise of public emergency power or other appropriate authority to enter onto private property to remove/reduce threats to life, public health, and safety.[217]

  o A governmental resolution after a disaster by an applicant declaring that debris on private property constitutes a threat to public health and safety does not in itself make the debris removal eligible. The applicant should submit its established, specific legal requirements for declaring the existence of a threat. FEMA will review and determine eligibility.[218]

---

[215] Id. § 206.223(a)(3); DAP 9523.13, at 3.
[216] 44 C.F.R. § 206.225(a)(3); PA DEBRIS GUIDE, at 34 (2007); DAP 9523.13, Debris Removal.
[217] Stafford Act §§ 403(a)(3)(A), 407(b) and 502, 42 U.S.C. §§ 5170b (a)(3)(A), 5173(b) and 5192; 44 C.F.R. §§ 206.223(a)(3) and 206.224(b); PA GUIDE, at 69-71; DAP 9523.13.
[218] PA GUIDE, at 70; DAP 9523.13.

- Indemnification
  - o Before FEMA approves debris removal from private property, the state or local government must agree in writing to indemnify FEMA from any claims arising from such removal.[219] If FEMA approves debris removal from private property, the state and local government must ensure "unconditional authorization" with respect to rights of entry and hold harmless agreements. The applicant is required to properly document all legal processes used to gain access, as well as document applicable scopes of work.[220]
  - o In order to prevent duplication of benefits, the applicant must obtain insurance information from property owners.[221]

- Commercial property
  - o Debris removal from private residential property under the PA program is relatively rare, as the public interest standard is a high bar. It is an even higher bar for commercial property. It is generally expected that commercial enterprises retain insurance and/or have the financial wherewithal to remove their own debris. An FCO may determine, however, in limited and extraordinary circumstances, that the removal of debris from private commercial property is in the public interest, generally for circumstances related to the economic recovery of the community. For example, where the commercial district of a very small town is destroyed, the rebuilding of that district may be so tenuous as to depend on government help with debris removal to facilitate rebuilding. Such circumstances are highly fact dependent and require legal review.[222]

---

[219] Stafford Act § 407(b), 42 U.S.C. § 5173(b); 44 C.F.R. § 206.9; PA GUIDE, at 69-71.
[220] 44 C.F.R. § 206.225(a); PA GUIDE, at 70; DAP 9523.13, Debris Removal.
[221] Stafford Act § 312, 42 U.S.C. § 5155.
[222] 44 C.F.R. § 206.224 (a) and (b).

h.) Environmental and Historic Preservation Review

While debris removal is exempt from the National Environmental Policy Act,[223] FEMA still must follow all applicable federal laws, regulations, and executive orders relating to protecting the environment and historic preservation in conducting and funding disaster debris removal activities. FEMA uses the term "special considerations" for issues such as environmental and historic preservation requirements that affect the scope of work and funding for a project. Applicants should identify these issues as early as possible and provide FEMA with the information necessary for review.[224] Chapter 8, *Environmental and Historic Preservation Laws*, discusses some of these "special considerations" because they apply to PA as well as IA. *See also* Chapter 6, *Individual Assistance*, and Chapter 7, *Hazard Mitigation*.

2. Category B: Emergency Protective Measures

In addition to debris removal, FEMA can provide direct federal and grant assistance for activities before, during, and after a disaster to save lives, protect public health and safety, and prevent damage to improved public and private property.[225] Examples of measures that may be eligible include:[226]

- Warning of risks and hazards;
- Search and rescue;
- Emergency evacuations;[227]
- Provision of shelters and emergency mass care;[228]

---

[223] Stafford Act § 316, 42 U.S.C. § 5159.
[224] *See* 44 C.F.R. Parts 9 and 10; PA GUIDE, at 127-136; PA DEBRIS GUIDE, at 6-10.
[225] Stafford Act §§ 402, 403 and 502, 42 U.S.C. §§ 5170a, 5170b and 5192; 44 C.F.R. §§ 206.201(b) and 206.225; PA GUIDE, at 71-78.
[226] Stafford Act §§ 402, 403 and 502, 42 U.S.C. §§ 5170a, 5170b and 5192; 44 C.F.R. § 206.225; PA GUIDE, at 66 and 71-78; PA DIGEST, at 31 and 46.
[227] DAP 9523.15, *Eligible Costs Related to Evacuations and Sheltering* (2007)[hereinafter DAP 9523.15, *Evacuation and Sheltering Costs*], < http://www.fema.gov/pdf/government/grant/pa/9523_15.pdf>.
[228] *See* PKEMRA § 689, 6 U.S.C. § 773, "Functional Needs Support Services Guidance;" DAP 9523.15, *Evacuation and Sheltering Costs*. http://www.fema.gov/pdf/government/grant/pa/9523_15.pdf

---

- Essential needs for persons affected by the outbreak and spread of an influenza pandemic;[229]
- Protection of an eligible facility;
- Security;
- Food, water, and other essentials at central distribution points;
- Temporary generators for facilities that provide health and safety services;
- Rescue, care, shelter, and essential needs for household pets and service animals if claimed by a state or local government;[230]
- Temporary facilities for schools and essential community services;[231]
- Emergency operations centers to coordinate and direct the response to a disaster;
- Demolition and removal of public and private buildings and structures that pose an immediate threat to the safety of the general public;[232]
- Removal of health and safety hazards;
- Construction of emergency protection measures to protect lives or improved property, such as temporary levees[233] or sandbagging;
- Emergency measures to prevent further damage to an otherwise eligible facility;

---

[229] DAP 9523.17, *Emergency Assistance for Human Influenza Pandemic* (2009), <http://www.fema.gov/sites/default/files/orig/fema_pdfs/pdf/government/grant/pa/9523_17.pdf >.

[230] Stafford Act §§ 403 and 502, 42 U.S.C. §§ 5170b and 5192; 44 C.F.R. §§ 206.223(a) and 225(a); DAP 9523.19, *Eligible Costs Related to Pet Evacuations and Sheltering* (2007), < http://www.fema.gov/9500-series-policy-publications/952319-eligible-costs-related-pet-evacuations-sheltering>.

[231] DAP 9523.3, *Provisions of Temporary Relocation Facilities* (1998), < http://www.fema.gov/9500-series-policy-publications/95233-provision-temporary-relocation-facilities>.

[232] Stafford Act § 403(a)(3)(I), 42 U.S.C. § 5170b (a) (3) (I); 44 C.F.R. § 206.221(c); PA GUIDE, at 26, 38, 66-67, 71, 76; DAP 9523.4, *Demolition of Private Structures* (2007), < http://www.fema.gov/public-assistance-9500-series-policy-publications/95234-demolition-private-structures >.

[233] Where temporary levees have been constructed as an emergency protective measure, the cost of removing them will only be eligible to protect public health and safety or to protect improved public or private property.

- Restoration of access; and

- Inspections if necessary to determine whether structures pose an immediate threat to public health or safety.

Specific eligibility requirements may apply to the provision of emergency communications, public transportation, building inspections, snow removal assistance, Host-State sheltering, demolition, and pet evacuation and sheltering.[234]

Example of Emergency Protective Measures on Private Property: Sheltering and Temporary Essential Power Program (STEP)

In the immediate aftermath of Hurricane Sandy[235] in October 2012, which resulted in extensive and extended power outages in New York and the Northeast, FEMA initiated the Sheltering and Temporary Essential Power (STEP) pilot program to assist state, local, and tribal governments in performing work and services to save lives, preserve public health and safety, and to protect property.[236] STEP provides essential power, heat, and hot water and rudimentary temporary exterior repairs to affected residences, allowing residents to shelter in their homes pending permanent restoration work, thus reducing demand for sheltering options.[237] The STEP pilot program was only available in areas that received major disaster declarations after Hurricane Sandy, and only New York and New Jersey opted to participate.[238] Only residential properties were eligible to receive the emergency temporary repairs under STEP.[239] FEMA administered the program through DFA; reimbursement of applicants who performed the work or contracted for its performance; or a combination thereof.[240] Repairs were capped at $10,000 per residence.[241]

---

[234] PA GUIDE, at 75-78.
[235] DR-4085 (NY), DR-4087 (CT), DR-4086 (NJ).
[236] FEMA Recovery Program /guidance, Sheltering and Temporary Essential Power (STEP), November 16, 2012
[237] Id.
[238] Id.
[239] Id
[240] Id; Stafford Act § 403, 42 U.S.C. § 5170b(a)(3)(B) and (I), 5170b(a)(4)
[241] Id; FEMA Recovery Program /guidance, Sheltering and Temporary Essential Power (STEP), November 16, 2012.

a.) Emergency Communications

Communication capabilities may be damaged by a disaster or an emergency to the extent that government officials are unable to carry out their duties of providing essential community services or responding to the disaster. The Stafford Act authorizes FEMA to provide a temporary emergency communications system through DFA[242] for both emergencies and major disasters, but it does not authorize grant assistance for emergency communications.[243]

b.) Emergency Public Transportation

A community's public transportation system (buses, subways, trains, bridges, etc.) may be damaged by a disaster such that vital functions of community life may be disrupted. The Stafford Act authorizes FEMA to provide DFA for temporary public transportation services[244] to replace those damaged by a major disaster event to assist a community to resume its normal pattern of life. FEMA may also provide temporary public transportation services required due to temporary changes in the location of government facilities or residential areas. Direct federal assistance will be discontinued as soon as the needs have been met. FEMA's costs must be offset by revenue earned from operation of the public transportation.[245] Stafford Act assistance is limited to "an area affected by a major disaster."[246]

FEMA lacks authority to provide grant assistance for permanent repair or replacement work for public transportation systems, which is generally provided by the U.S. Department of Transportation Federal Transit Administration.[247] FEMA may only provide assistance under Direct

---

[242] Stafford Act § 418, 42 U.S.C. § 5185; 44 C.F.R. § 206.225(c); PA GUIDE, at 75.

[243] The authorization of grant or financial assistance must be specific. No special words are required but there must be specific indication that Congress intended to authorize financial assistance. Words typically used to demonstrate grant assistance is authorized include "grants," "contributions," and "financial assistance." II PRINCIPLES OF FEDERAL APPROPRIATION LAW 10-1 to 10-3, 10-37 and 10-70.

[244] Stafford Act § 419, 42 U.S.C. § 5186; 44 C.F.R. § 206.225(d); PA GUIDE, at 75.

[245] 44 C.F.R. § 13.25.

[246] Id.

[247] See, generally, 49 U.S.C., Part 53; http://www.fta.dot.gov/grants.html

---

Federal Assistance, or Public Assistance Category B, Emergency Protective Measures, for restoration public transportation services to assist a community to resume its normal pattern of life or to provide temporary services needed due to changes in the location of government or residential facilities due to the disaster.[248] FEMA assistance ends as soon as the needs have been met.[249]

c.) Building Inspections

The costs of building inspections are eligible as Category B costs if necessary to establish whether a damaged structure poses an immediate threat to life, public health, or safety.[250] The following inspections are not eligible under the PA program because these inspections go beyond the scope of a safety inspection:[251]

- To determine if the building was substantially damaged beyond repair under the National Flood Insurance Program (NFIP);

- To determine if the building should be elevated or relocated; or

- To determine if the repairs are needed to make the building habitable.

When building inspections are required for FEMA-funded permanent repairs, they will be included as permanent repair costs, not emergency protective measure costs.[252] However, costs for such inspections may be eligible under FEMA's Hazard Mitigation Grant Program.[253] *See* Chapter 7, *Hazard Mitigation.*

---

[248] Stafford Act § 419, 42 U.S.C. 5186; 44 C.F.R. § 226(d).

[249] Id.

[250] Stafford Act § 403, 42 U.S.C. § 5170b; PA GUIDE, at 78; DAP 9523.2, *Eligibility of Building Inspections in a Post-Disaster Environment* (2008) [hereinafter DAP 9523.2, *Building Inspections Eligibility*], < http://www.fema.gov/9500-series-policy-publications/95232-eligibility-building-safety-inspections-supporting-emergency >.

[251] Stafford Act § 403; 44 C.F.R. § 206.225; PA Digest, p. 14; PA Guide p. 76; DAP 9523.2 (2008).

[252] Stafford Act § 406; 44 C.F.R. § 206.226; PA GUIDE, at 76; PA DIGEST, at 14; DAP 9523.2, *Building Inspections Eligibility.*

[253] *See* Stafford Act § 203, 42 U.S.C. § 5133; 44 C.F.R Part 206, Subpart N, *Hazard Mitigation Grant Program,* 44 C.F.R. § 206.430 *et seq*; Hazard Mitigation Unified Guidance, (HMAUG)

d.) Snow Removal Assistance

Assistance for snow removal will be provided when the President declares a major disaster in an event that results in a case of a record or near record snowstorm.[254] Such an event may include one or more of the following conditions: snow, ice, high winds, blizzard conditions, and other wintry conditions that cause substantial physical damage or loss to improved property. All eligible costs are authorized over a continuous 48-hour time period[255] to address the most critical emergency needs, provided that:

- The snowfall is of record or near record amount;
- The response is beyond the state and local government capabilities; and
- The action is necessary to save lives, protect public health and safety, and protect improved property.

Applicants may select a 48-hour time period during which the highest eligible costs were incurred. FEMA may extend the eligible time period of assistance by 24 hours in counties where snowfall quantities greatly exceed record amounts. Different applicants in the same designated county may use different 48-hour periods. However, all agencies or instrumentalities of a local government must use the same 48-hour time period.[256]

Eligible emergency protective work includes snow removal, snow dumps, de-icing, salting and sanding of roads, and other activities essential to eliminate or lessen immediate threats to life, public health, and safety. In addition, activities related to the snowstorm such as search and rescue,

---

pp. 54-55.
http://www.fema.gov/library/file;jsessionid=75DAD2EEFE5D5D2C459BB0F9FCE19240.
WorkerPublic2?type=publishedFile&file=final_june_1_2010_hma_unified_guidance_092
52012a_508.pdf&fileid=e68044c0-07e4-11e2-89a0-001cc456982e.
[254] Stafford Act § 403, 42 U.S.C. § 5170b; 44 C.F.R. §§ 206. 35, 36, 48 and 227; PA GUIDE, at 76; PA DIGEST, at 122; DAP 9523.1, *Snow Assistance and Severe Winter Storm Policy* (2009)[hereinafter DAP 9523.1, *Snow Policy 2009*], <
http://www.fema.gov/pdf/government/grant/pa/9523_1.pdf>.
[255] DAP 9523.1, *Snow Policy 2009*.
[256] Id. at VII. F. 3., at 6.

sheltering, and other emergency protective measures are eligible outside of the 48-hour time period where appropriate.[257]

e.) Host-State Sheltering

A "Host-State"[258] is a state or Indian tribal government that provides sheltering and/or evacuation support to evacuees from another state for which the President declared an emergency or major disaster. For purposes of Host-State sheltering, the state that received the declaration and has determined that it must evacuate and shelter its residents and pets is called the "Impact State."[259]

Host-State costs for reimbursement must meet the eligibility requirements for PA Category B, emergency protective measures.[260] Host-States may receive assistance for evacuation and sheltering support provided to evacuees from an impact state in two ways:

- Mutual Aid Agreements[261]
  Assistance may be available through existing mutual aid agreements. *See* earlier discussion in this chapter on *Mutual Aid* Agreements. The Impact State may reimburse the Host-State for 100% of eligible costs incurred in providing evacuation and/or sheltering support. The Impact State may also reimburse the Host-State for straight-time salaries of the Host-State's force account employees who performed eligible work.[262] The Impact State remains obligated to pay the non-federal share of eligible costs of services provided by the Host-State.

---

[257] Id.
[258] 44 C.F.R. § 206.201(g).
[259] Id. § 206.201(h).
[260] Id. § 206.225; DAP 9523.18*Evacuation and Sheltering Costs,* < http://www.fema.gov/9500-series-policy-publications/952318-host-state-evacuation-sheltering-reimbursement >.
[261] DAP 9523.18, *Host-State Evacuation and Sheltering Reimbursement* (2010)[hereinafter DAP 9523.18,*Host-State* 2010], < http://coop.fema.gov/government/grant/pa/9523_18b.shtm >; *Host-State Policy Clarification Memorandum* (2008)[hereinafter *Host-State Policy Clarification Memo*], < http://www.fema.gov/9500-series-policy-publications/memo-952318-host-state-evacuation-and-sheltering-reimbursement >.
[262] 44 C.F.R. § 206.202(f)(1)(ii). This is an exception to allowable overtime costs only for force account labor provided for emergency work set forth in 44 C.F.R. § 206.228(a)(2).

- Direct Reimbursement[263]

  The Impact State makes a DFA request to FEMA for direct reimbursement of a Host-State for evacuation and sheltering support.[264] In deciding whether to award a grant to the Host-State, FEMA will consider whether a Host-State has sufficient capability to meet some or all of the sheltering and/or evacuation needs of an Impact State and whether, if necessary, the Host-State will agree to accept Impact State evacuees via any requested mode of organized transportation. FEMA may reimburse the Host-State for 100% of eligible costs, regardless of the Impact State's cost share obligation under the declaration, provided the Impact State agrees to pay its required non-federal cost share.[265] Straight-time salaries and benefits of a Host-State's permanently employed personnel are eligible for reimbursement.[266]

The statutes, regulations, policies, guidance, and procedures of the PA program apply to reimbursement under the FEMA - Host-State Agreement.[267]

The federal cost share of grant assistance to the Host-State from the Impact State is based on the cost share for Category B, Emergency Protective Measures, approved for the declared event. The Impact State is responsible for the non-federal cost share, if any, of funding FEMA provides to the Host-State. Therefore, Host-States receive 100% reimbursement of their eligible costs.[268]

A grant to a Host-State for sheltering and/or evacuation support is available when the Impact State requests DFA from FEMA.[269] Reimbursing a Host-State for sheltering costs is an exception to the requirement that assistance can only be provided to the areas designated in the major

---

[263] 44 C.F.R. § 206.208; DAP 9523.18; *Host-State Policy Clarification Memo*.
[264] 44 C.F.R. § 206.208.
[265] Id. § 206.202 (f)(2); DAP 9523.18,*Host-State Policy Clarification Memo*.
[266] Id. § 206.202 (f)(1)(ii); DAP 9523.18, *Host-State Policy Clarification Memo*.
[267] Fact Sheet 9580.7, *Host-State Evacuation and Sheltering Frequently Asked Questions* (2010)[hereinafter Fact Sheet, *Host-State*]
<http://www.fema.gov/pdf/government/grant/pa/9580_7.pdf>.
[268] DAP 9523.18, *Host-State 2010*; *Host-State Clarification Memo*.
[269] 44 C.F.R. § 206.208(c)(3).

disaster or emergency declaration. [270] To receive this grant, a Host-State must enter into a FEMA - Host-State Agreement and amend its State Administrative Plan (SAP).[271] The Host-State must also submit an "Application for Federal Assistance" directly to FEMA to apply for cost reimbursement. Upon award, the Host-State assumes the responsibilities of "grantee" with respect to the award.[272]

f.) Demolition

Demolition of unsafe private structures that endanger the public may be eligible as emergency work when the Following conditions are met:[273]

- The structures were damaged and made unsafe by the declared disaster;

- The applicant certifies that the structures have been determined to be unsafe and pose an immediate threat to the public;

- The applicant establishes legal responsibility based on statute, ordinance, or code to exercise its authority to demolish the unsafe structure;

- The applicant obtains rights of entry; and

- The applicant indemnifies the federal government from claims arising from the demolition of the structures.[274]

Demolition of private structures requires approval prior to work. The structures must be found to be unsafe due to the imminent threat of

---

[270] Id. § 206.223(a)(2).

[271] Id. § 206.207.

[272] Id. § 206.202(f)(1).

[273] Stafford Act § 403(a)(3)(E)(which is not restricted to private structures), 42 U.S.C. § 5170b(a)(3)(E); 44 C.F.R. 206.225; DAP 9523.4, Demolition of Private Structures (2007)[hereinafter DAP 9523.4, Demolition], Please note that eligible PA facilities may also be demolished as part of a Section 406 project.
< http://www.fema.gov/public-assistance-9500-series-policy-publications/95234-demolition-private-structures >, PA GUIDE, at 39, 69, 73, 91, 119, 131 and 133; PA DEBRIS GUIDE.

[274] DAP 9523.4, Demolition. Note the PA Digest, incorrectly applies the debris removal public interest standard from 44 C.F.R. § 206.224 to demolition, however, the correct standard is articulated in DAP 9523.4.

---

partial or complete collapse. FEMA will consider alternative measures to eliminate threats to life, public health, and safety posed by disaster-damaged unsafe structures, including fencing off unsafe structures and restricting public access, when evaluating requests for demolition.[275] Local governments must agree to hold the federal government free from damages due to performance of the work. Demolition work also requires state or local certification that the structure is unsafe, as well as having an authorized local official condemn the structure in accordance with state and local law. Demolition costs are also eligible for permanent work assistance when the work is required in support of eligible repair, replacement, or reconstruction of a project.[276]

While the Stafford Act authorizes demolition separately from debris removal, there are situations in which the distinction is a fine line. For example, in the implementation of the Expedited Debris Removal (EDR)[277] pilot program after the southern tornadoes in the spring of 2011, FEMA followed a policy of one wall standing. If a damaged structure only had one wall left standing, it would all be considered debris and the cost of knocking over the standing wall would be considered eligible under the pilot debris program. If a structure had more than one wall standing, it would not be considered debris and it would have to be separately authorized and funded as demolition, which was outside of the purview of EDR. This is also a relevant distinction in terms of eligibility. Debris removal may be authorized when FEMA determines it to be in the public interest, which includes an economic recovery rationale, in addition to protection of health and safety.[278] However, demolition is only authorized as an emergency protective measure where there are immediate threats to life and property and the unsafe structures endanger the public.[279]

---

[275] DAP 9523.4, Demolition, at VII.C.1.b.

[276] PA GUIDE, at 39 and 73; PA DIGEST, at 34; PA DEBRIS GUIDE, at 37-40; DAP 9523.4, Demolition.

[277] Also known as "Operation Clean Sweep" for the April 2011 AL and MS tornado disasters.

[278] 44 C.F.R. § 206.224.

[279] Stafford Act § 403(a)(3)(E), 42 U.S.C. § 5170b(a)(3)(E); 44 C.F.R. § 206.225.

g.) Pet Evacuations and Sheltering

FEMA may provide reimbursement for the costs of rescue, care, shelter, and essential needs for individuals with household pets and service animals, and to the household pets and animals themselves following a major disaster.[280] State and local governments may conduct rescue operations for household pets directly, or they may contract with other providers for such services.

During the initial response phase of a disaster, PNPs or other organizations may assume the responsibility for care of animals. FEMA and the states and localities must be alert to such activity and promptly notify and coordinate with the PNPs, particularly if the FEMA-State Agreement requires a 25% cost share. FEMA policy[281] provides that a state or local government must make a determination that pet evacuation and shelter is "essential to meeting immediate threats to life and property"[282] and then request reimbursement of PNPs and their contractors for sheltering and rescuing household pets and service animals.

Household pet is defined as a domesticated animal, such as a dog, cat, bird, rabbit, rodent, or turtle that is traditionally kept in the home for pleasure rather than for commercial purposes; can travel in commercial carriers; and be housed in temporary facilities.[283] Household pets do not include reptiles (except turtles), amphibians, fish, insects/arachnids, farm animals (including horses), and animals kept for racing purposes.[284] Service animal is defined as a guide dog, signal dog, or other animal individually trained to provide assistance to an individual with a disability, including, but not limited to guiding individuals with impaired vision, alerting individuals with impaired hearing to intruders or sounds,

---

[280] Stafford Act §403(a)(3)(J), 42 U.S.C. § 5170b(a)(3)(J). See also DOLR Chapter 4, *Response*, V.F.2.

[281] DAP 9523.19, *Eligible Costs Related to Pet Evacuations and Sheltering* (2007)[hereinafter DAP 9523.19, *Pet Costs*], http://www.fema.gov/9500-series-policy-publications/952319-eligible-costs-related-pet-evacuations-sheltering.

[282] Stafford Act § 403(a)(3)(J), 42 U.S.C. § 5170b(a)(3)(J).

[283] DAP 9523.19, *Pet Costs*, at VII.A.1.

[284] *Id.*

providing minimal protection or rescue work, pulling a wheelchair, or fetching dropped items.[285]

i). Rescue Costs - Eligible costs for rescue operations for household pets include, but are not limited to, the following:

- Overtime for regular full-time employees;
- Regular time and overtime for contract labor specifically hired to provide additional support required as a result of the disaster; and
- The use of applicant owned or leased equipment (such as buses or other vehicles) to provide eligible pet transportation.

ii). Sheltering Costs – Pet sheltering costs may include, but are not limited to, the reasonable costs for:

- Facilities;
- Supplies and commodities;
- Eligible labor;
- Equipment;
- Emergency veterinary services – to include screening for health and assessing and treating minor illnesses and injuries;
- Transportation;
- Shelter safety and security;
- Cleaning and restoration of a facility and restoration to pre-congregate pet shelter condition;
- Removal and disposal of animal carcasses; and
- Cataloging/tracking system, for the purposes of reuniting pets with their owners.

---

[285] Id. at VII.A.2.

Costs of sheltering/caring for household pets will no longer be eligible for FEMA reimbursement when the pet owner transitions out of emergency sheltering.[286]

B. Permanent Work

Section 406 of the Stafford Act authorizes FEMA to provide grant assistance to states, local governments, and certain PNPs for the repair, restoration, and replacement of damaged or destroyed facilities.[287] FEMA administratively categorizes this work as "permanent work," Categories C-G.[288] Section 406 limits permanent work reimbursement to the cost to restore a damaged facility to its pre-disaster design, function, and capacity in accordance with applicable codes and standards.[289] *See* Codes and Standards section later in this chapter. The three basic criteria for permanent work are:[290]

- Design: FEMA will restore a facility to its pre-disaster design or to a design in accordance with an applicable standard.

- Function: The facility must be restored to the same function that it was performing, or designed to perform, if less costly.

- Capacity: The restored facility must operate at its pre-disaster capacity.

- Current Applicable Codes: If codes dictate a larger area—for example, a square footage requirement per student in a school—FEMA will pay to increase the size of the building.

FEMA may make exceptions to these criteria for Alternate[291] and Improved Projects[292] as discussed later in this chapter.

---

[286] Stafford Act § 403(a)(3)(J), 42 U.S.C. § 5170b(a)(3)(J).

[287] Id. § 406, 42 U.S.C. § 5172.

[288] Id.; 44 C.F.R. §§ 206.226; PA GUIDE, at 3-6, 79-108; PA DIGEST, at 95; PA HANDBOOK, at 15-17.

[289] Stafford Act § 406, 42 U.S.C. § 5172; 44 C.F.R. § 206.226; PA GUIDE, at 79; PA DIGEST, at 95.

[290] PA DIGEST, at 95.

[291] 44 C.F.R. § 206.203(d)(2); PA GUIDE, at 79, 111-112; PA DIGEST, at 5; DAP 9525.13, *Alternate Projects*, (2008), < http://www.fema.gov/9500-series-policy-publications/952513-alternate-projects>.

1. Category C: Roads and Bridges

FEMA will provide reimbursement funding for roads (paved, gravel, and dirt) and bridges[293] that need permanent repair or replacement as a result of damage from a declared major disaster, unless they are federal aid roads or bridges under the authority of the FHWA.[294] Eligible work includes repair to surfaces, bases, shoulders, ditches, culverts, low water crossings, and other features, such as guardrails. Earthwork necessary to ensure the structural integrity of the road may be eligible. Restoration may also include upgrades necessary to meet current codes and standards. Typical standards affect lane width, loading design, and construction materials.[295]

Eligible repair to bridges includes decking and pavement, piers, girders, abutments, slope protection, and approaches. Earthwork to the channel and stream banks is eligible if necessary to ensure the structural integrity of the bridge. Debris removal at the bridge site is also eligible if it could cause further damage to the structure. Eligible work may include upgrades necessary to meet current standards for road and bridge construction. As with roads, typical standards for bridges may affect lane width, loading design, construction materials, and hydraulic capacity.[296]

2. Category D: Water Control Facilities

USACE and the NRCS have primary authority for the repair of flood control works.[297] By regulation, it is also the responsibility of NRCS to coordinate with FEMA in providing assistance in a presidentially declared

---

[292] Id. § 206.203(d)(1); PA GUIDE, at 79,110-111; PA DIGEST, at 71.

[293] Stafford Act § 102 (9)(B), 42 U.S.C. § 5122(9)(B); PA GUIDE, at 79-82; PA DIGEST, at 13 and 118.

[294] 44 C.F.R. § 206.226(a)(1).

[295] PA GUIDE, at 79-82; PA DIGEST, at 118.

[296] PA DIGEST, at 13.

[297] Stafford Act § 102(9)(A, 42 U.S.C. § 5122(9)(A); 44 C.F.R. § 206.221(h); PA GUIDE, at 82-83; PA DIGEST, at 138; DAP 9524.3, *Policy for Rehabilitation Assistance for Levees and Other Flood Control Works* (2009)[hereinafter DAP 9524.3, *Levees*], <http://www.fema.gov/pdf/government/grant/pa/9524_3.pdf>, *as amended*, Memorandum (Aug. 5, 2009) [hereinafter Aug. 5, 2009, Memo], < http://www.fema.gov/public-assistance-9500-series-policy-publications/95243-rehabilitation-assistance-levees-other-flood>. In individual cases, OFAs may dispute their responsibilities for substantive and/or funding reasons. In such an event, FEMA will coordinate with these other agencies to determine responsibility.

---

major disaster area.[298] When OFAs have the specific authority to repair facilities that are also eligible under the Stafford Act, FEMA generally defers to the OFAs.[299] FEMA can help with permanent repairs for other water control facilities, such as:

- Channel alignment
- Recreation
- Navigation
- Land reclamation
- Maintenance for fish and wildlife habitat
- Interior drainage
- Irrigation
- Erosion prevention
- Flood control[300]

The facilities include dams and reservoirs, levees, lined and unlined engineered drainage channels, canals, aqueducts, sediment basins, shore protective devices, irrigation facilities, and pumping facilities. FEMA may limit eligibility for PNP irrigation facilities[301] and for certain facilities built specifically for flood control.[302]

3. Category E: Buildings and Equipment

Buildings, including contents such as furnishings and interior systems, are eligible for repair or replacement.[303] In addition to the building's contents, FEMA will pay for the replacement of pre-disaster quantities of consumable supplies and inventory, such as the replacement of library books and publications.[304] The goods or property of another held in bailment or storage by an applicant are not eligible for reimbursement, as

---

[298] See 7 C.F.R. § 624.5(a).
[299] 44 C.F.R. § 226(a).
[300] PA GUIDE, at 82-83; PA DIGEST, at 138.
[301] 44 C.F.R. § 206.226 (c) and § 206.221(e)(3); PA DIGEST, at 77.
[302] DAP 9524.3, Levees; Aug. 5, 2009 Memo, < http://www.fema.gov/public-assistance-9500-series-policy-http://www.fema.gov/public-assistance-9500-series-policy-publications/95243-rehabilitation-assistance-levees-other-floodpublications/95243-rehabilitation-assistance-levees-other-flood>.
[303] Stafford Act § 102(9) and (10), 42 U.S.C. § 5122(9) and (10); 44 C.F.R. §§ 206.221(e), 206.221(h) and 206.226; PA GUIDE, at 83-85.
[304] 44 C.F.R. § 206.226 (i).

---

they are not the property of the applicant. If disaster-related mud, silt, or other accumulated debris does not pose an immediate threat but its removal is necessary to restore the building, its removal is eligible as permanent work. If it does pose an immediate threat, the work will fall under Category A, debris removal.[305]

If the applicant has insurance coverage for any permanent work facility, FEMA will deduct the amount of insurance proceeds, actual or anticipated, before providing funds for restoration of the facility,[306] which is consistent with the prohibition against duplication of benefits.[307] *See Insurance and Duplication of Benefits* later in this chapter for a further discussion of insurance. If an insurable building damaged by flooding is located in a Special Flood Hazard Area (SFHA) identified for more than one year, FEMA will reduce the PA grant for permanent work by the maximum amount of insurance proceeds the applicant would have received for the building and its contents even if it is not covered by flood insurance.[308] There is a very limited exception for PNP facilities that could not be insured because they were located in a community that was not participating in the NFIP if the community agrees to participate in the NFIP within six months after the disaster declaration date.[309]

4. Category F: Utilities

FEMA will fund the repair or restoration of utilities[310] owned by public and certain PNP entities. Typical utilities include:

- Water treatment plants and delivery systems;

- Power generation and distribution facilities, including natural gas systems, wind turbines, generators, substations, and power lines;

---

[305] PA GUIDE, at 83; PA HANDBOOK, at 15-16.
[306] Stafford Act § 312, 42 U.S.C. § 5155; PA GUIDE, 83, 119-123; PA DIGEST, at 15; DAP 9525.3, *Duplication of Benefits.*
[307] Stafford Act § 312(a), 42 U.S.C. 5155.
[308] Id. § 406(d), 42 U.S.C. § 5172; 44 C.F.R. § 206.252; PA DIGEST, at 15.
[309] 44 C.F.R. § 206.252(b). *See Insurance and Duplication of Benefits* later in this chapter.
[310] Stafford Act § 102, 42 U.S.C. § 5122; 44 C.F.R. §§ 206.221(e)(2) and (h) and 206.226; PA GUIDE, at 10, 18, 21, 54-55, 66, 85; PA DIGEST, at 17 and 135; PA APPLICANT HANDBOOK, at 16; Fact Sheet 9580.6, *Electric Utility Repair – (Public and Private Nonprofit)* (2009) < http://www.fema.gov/9500-series-policy-publications/electric-utility-repair

---

- Sewage collection systems and treatment plants; and

- Communications.

The costs to operate a utility facility or provide service may increase due to the disaster. These costs are usually not eligible for reimbursement and are considered increased operating costs. However, the cost to establish temporary emergency services in the event of a utility shut-down may be eligible as emergency work. The loss of revenue when a utility service is shut down due to the disaster is not an eligible cost for reimbursement.[311]

Emergency power repairs may involve miles and miles of power lines with intermittent damage making it difficult to quantify the work needed for emergency power restoration. Due to the critical nature of restoring power following a disaster and because exigent circumstances do not permit delays related to fully assessing the damage before repair work begins, FEMA may permit "time and equipment" contracts.[312] As more fully discussed in Part Two of this chapter, such contracts should be avoided but may be allowed for work that is necessary immediately after the disaster has occurred when a clear scope of work cannot be developed, it has been determined that no other contract is suitable, and the contract includes a ceiling price that the contractor exceeds at its own risk.[313] Generally, such emergency work is limited to no more than 70 hours; however, power restoration is given special consideration because the type of work is best suited to a "time and materials" or more commonly a "time and equipment" contract than unit price or lump sum contract.[314]

Category F refers to the permanent repair of utility systems. Although work to restore power to customers following disasters is time sensitive akin to emergency work, most of the work performed is permanent in nature because it constitutes a permanent repair to a damaged facility. FEMA categorizes electric utility work as follows:

---

[311] PA GUIDE, at 54.

[312] Rural electrical cooperatives, municipal utilities, and public power districts generally provide the materials used in repairing their systems; accordingly instead of "time and material" contracts, they use "time and equipment" contracts. PA Fact Sheet 9580.6, 9580.6, *Electric Utility Repair*].

[313] 44 C.F.R. §13.36(b)(10); however, there is no analogous section in 2 C.F.R. Part 215 for colleges, hospitals, or non-profits.

[314] PA DIGEST, at 23.

- Temporary work to restore power to all facilities capable of receiving it is Category B, emergency work. In these situations, the utilities make permanent repairs later to bring the damaged components into compliance with appropriate codes and standards.

- Work to restore the damaged facilities to pre-disaster condition in accordance with applicable codes and standards is Category F, permanent work. Utilities may complete permanent repairs immediately after the disaster occurs or after temporary repairs are completed.[315]

Example of Provision of power restoration through %100 federal cost share

In 2012, Hurricane Sandy left countless numbers of residents and businesses in New Jersey, New York, and Connecticut without power. The lack of electricity posed an imminent threat to the public health and safety and property. Due to immediacy and severity of the threat, the President authorized 100% federal cost share, including Direct Federal Assistance, for emergency power restoration for 15 days pursuant to 44 C.F.R. §206.47(d). This assistance was offered after FEMA determined that (1) the power companies were unable to execute the power restoration work themselves in a timely manner; (2) continued interruption/lack of power would result in an immediate threat to the health and safety of the community; and (3) provision of the assistance was beyond state and local capability. Permitted use of this authority was limited to transporting, equipping, and, when necessary, temporarily sheltering power restoration teams and providing equipment and activities necessary for temporary power generation (including pumps and debris removal).

---

[315] Fact Sheet 9580.6, *Electric Utility Repair.*

> **Example of a Three-Stage Power Restoration Project**
>
> The power facility on the Island of Tutuila, American Samoa, suffered major damage in the 2009 earthquake and tsunami disaster disrupting power island-wide. Phase 1 consisted of a Category B mission assignment to the USACE for the temporary placement of generators to provide immediate but limited power. Phase 2 consisted of Category B grant assistance for the lease of a temporary turnkey power facility to provide sufficient, uninterrupted power for the island pending the repair/replacement of the damaged facility. Phase 3 consisted of Category F grant assistance for the permanent repair of the damaged facility.

5. Category G: Parks, Recreational Areas, and Other Facilities

Publicly owned facilities in this category[316] that are generally eligible include:

- Playground and picnic equipment;
- Swimming pools, golf courses, and tennis courts;
- Piers and boat docks;
- Beaches (see criteria later in this section);
- Mass transit, such as rail systems;
- Supporting facilities, such as roads, buildings, and utilities, that are located in parks and recreational areas;
- Golf courses; and
- Fish hatcheries and other facilities that do not fit in Categories C-F.[317]

PNP organizations are not eligible for recreational area restoration or repair.[318]

---

[316] Stafford Act § 102(9) and (10), 42 U.S.C. § 5122 (9) and (10); 44 C.F.R. § 206.221(e)(h); PA GUIDE, at 20, 66 ,68, 74, 86-87; PA DIGEST, at 12 and 92; *FEMA Categories of Work, Reference Topics* at Category G (2008), <http://www.fema.gov/public-assistance-local-state-tribal-and-non-profit/categories-work>.
[317] PA GUIDE, at 86 and 87; PA DIGEST, at 92.
[318] PA GUIDE, at 86; PA DIGEST, at 92.

---

a.) Beaches

Beaches are eligible for permanent repair only if they are improved beaches and have been routinely maintained prior to the disaster.[319] A beach is considered to be an "improved beach" if it has been constructed by the placement of sand to a designed elevation, width, grain size, and slope and has been maintained in accordance with a maintenance program involving the periodic re-nourishment of sand. FEMA requires the following from an applicant before approving assistance for permanent restoration of a beach:

- Design documents and specifications, including analysis of grain size;

- "As-built" plans;

- Documentation of regular maintenance or nourishment of the beach; and

- Pre- and post-storm profiles of the beach.[320]

- The placement of sand on a beach from periodic dredging operations is not considered a regular beach maintenance plan. Such activities are considered maintenance of the channel, not the beach.[321]

b.) Trees and ground cover

Trees and ground cover are not eligible for replacement. This restriction applies to trees and shrubs in recreation areas, such as parks, as well as trees and shrubs associated with public facilities. Grass and sod are eligible only when necessary to stabilize slopes and minimize sediment runoff.[322]

---

[319] 44 C.F.R. § 206.226(j)(2); PA GUIDE, at 74, 86-87; PA DIGEST, at 12.
[320] PA GUIDE, at 86 and 87; PA DIGEST, at 12 and 92; Disaster Assistance Fact Sheet DAP 9580.8, *Eligible Sand Replacement on Public Beaches*, (October 1, 2009).< http://www.fema.gov/pdf/government/grant/pa/9580_8.pdf
[321] DAP9580.8,
[322] DAP 9524.5 *Trees, Shrubs and Other Plantings Associated with Facilities* (2007), < http://www.fema.gov/9500-series-policy-publications/95245-trees-shrubs-other-

ie Stafford Act authorizes FEMA to reimburse the costs of repair and
placement based on the design of the facility as it existed immediately
efore the disaster event but also in "conformity with codes,
iecifications, and standards . . . applicable at the time at which the
saster occurred."[323] Improvements and upgrades are thus eligible
ovided they are required by a properly promulgated code, specification
· standard. Moreover, section 323 of the Stafford Act makes PA funding
r repair and replacement contingent upon the work being carried out in
:cordance "with applicable standards of safety, decency, and sanitation
id in conformity with applicable codes, specification, and
andards...."[324] FEMA may also require safe land use and construction
·actices.[325]

irmanent work, including repairs or replacement, is work performed to
store an eligible facility on "the basis of its pre-disaster design and
irrent applicable standards."[326] Pre-disaster design is defined as "the size
· capacity of a facility as originally designed and constructed or
ibsequently modified by changes or additions to the original design. It
)es not mean the capacity at which the facility was being used at the
ne the major disaster occurred if different from the most recent
esigned capacity."[327] If a facility is eligible for replacement, funding will
: based on the cost to construct the new facility according to the pre-

---

intings-associated-facilities-0 >. Note: This policy was under review at the time of
inting. Check with OCC for updates to this policy.
i Stafford Act § 406(e)(1), 42 U.S.C. § 5172(e)(1).
· Stafford Act § 323 (a)(1), 42 U.S.C. § 5165a(a)(1); 44 C.F.R. § 206.226 and §§
16.400 - 206.402; EXEC. ORDER 12,699 (1990), 55 Fed. Reg. 835 (1990), 3 C.F.R., 1990
)mp., at 269, as amended by EXEC. ORDER 13,286 (2003), 68 Fed. Reg. 10619 (2003), 3
F.R., 2003 Comp., at 166; DAP 9527.4, Construction Codes and Standards (2008) [hereinafter
\P 9527.4 Codes]. < http://www.fema.gov/public-assistance-local-state-tribal-and-non-
ofit/construction-codes-and-standards>. See also Earthquake Hazards Reduction Act of
'77, § 5, Pub. L. No. 95-124, as amended, 42 U.S.C. § 7704(a)(2)(B)(ii); DAP 9527.1,
smic Safety – New Construction (2007) < http://www.fema.gov/public-assistance-9500-
ries-policy-publications/seismic-safety---new-construction >.
i Stafford Act § 323(a)(2), 42 U.S.C. § 5165a(a)(2); 44 C.F.R. § 206.400.
) 44 C.F.R. § 206.201(j).
' Id. § 206.201(k).

---

disaster design and in compliance with current codes for new construction.[328]

Federal, state, and local repair or replacement standards which change the pre-disaster design of facilities must:

- Apply to the type of repair or restoration required;

- Be appropriate to the pre-disaster use of the facility;

- Be found reasonable, in writing, and formally adopted and implemented on or before the disaster declaration date or be a legal federal requirement applicable to the type of restoration;

- Apply uniformly to all similar types of facilities within the jurisdiction; and

- Have been enforced during the time the standard was in effect.[329]

If FEMA determines that a code meets all five of those criteria, the work and associated costs, including any eligible upgrades triggered by the code, may be eligible for funding.[330] Code upgrades that are ineligible pursuant to the five criteria, but which will enhance a facility's ability to resist similar damage in a future event, may be eligible under section 406 hazard mitigation, discussed later in this chapter.[331]

Applicable codes, specifications, and standards[332] include any disaster resistant building code that meets the minimum requirements of the NFIP,[333] as well as being substantially equivalent to the recommended provisions of the National Earthquake Hazards Reduction Program.[334] In addition, the applicant will need to comply with any other applicable

---

[328] DAP 9527.4, *Codes*, VII C 1.b..
[329] 44 C.F.R. § 206.226(d).
[330] Stafford Act § 406(e), 42 U.S.C. § 5172(e); 44 C.F.R. § 206.226(d); DAP 9527.4, *Codes*.
[331] *Id.*
[332] 44 C.F.R. § 206.221(i).
[333] Flood Disaster Protection Act of 1973, 42 U.S.C. §§ 4002, 5154 and 5172; 44 C.F.R. §§ 206.251(d) and 206.400(b).
[334] Earthquake Hazards Reduction Act of 1977, 42 U.S.C. §§ 7701-7709; 44 C.F.R. § 206.400(b).

---

requirements, such as the Coastal Barrier Resources Act;[335] Executive Order 11,988, Floodplain Management; and Executive Order 12,699, Seismic Safety of Federal and Federally Assisted or Regulated New Building Construction.[336] *See* Chapter 8, *Environmental and Historic Preservation Laws.*

Example of a Facility for Which FEMA May Reimburse for Upgrades to Meet Current Codes, but Not for Relocation Costs

A police station in Alabama was destroyed by a tornado in April 2011. The facility could not be rebuilt on the same site, as there was not sufficient square footage on the site to meet Alabama Administrative Code requirements for an on-site sewer treatment system (OSS). Alabama Administrative Code 420-3-1-.09(1)(a). The original facility was on a 2,400-square-foot lot, while the code that had been enacted since the facility's construction required a lot of at least 15,000 square feet to accommodate the OSS. The applicant sought reimbursement from FEMA for the costs of rebuilding the police station, along with the upgraded OSS at a different, larger site, and sought reimbursement for the cost of acquiring the land for the alternate site. It was determined that the costs of the upgraded OSS at the new site were eligible, since the upgrades were required by state standards, which resulted in a change to the pre-disaster design of the police station. 44 C.F.R. § 206.226(d). However, even though the facility was technically being relocated, the land acquisition costs were not eligible because the regulatory criteria for relocation of a facility were not met. 44 C.F.R. § 206.226(g)(i)-(iii).

V. Insurance and Duplication of Benefits

A. Insurance Requirements in PA

There are three key provisions in the Stafford Act, described more fully here, that relate to insurance and the PA program:

---

[335] Coastal Barrier Resources Act, 16 U.S.C. §§ 3501-3510.
[336] EXEC. ORDER 12,699 (1990), *amended by* EXEC. ORDER 13,286 (2003).

- A requirement to obtain and maintain insurance as a condition of receiving PA grant funding;[337]

- A prohibition on duplication of disaster assistance benefits (from any source, including insurance proceeds);[338] and

- Deductions from grant funding for certain uninsured facilities located in an SFHA.[339]

In addition, pursuant to the National Flood Insurance Act (NFIA)[340] and the Stafford Act, facilities damaged by flood that have been located in a Special Flood Hazard Area (SFHA)[341] for more than one year, regardless of whether they have incurred previous flood damage, must be insured under the NFIP.[342]

Typically, FEMA does not require the applicant to have had insurance on a facility before the first request for PA funding. However, facilities located in an SFHA may incur an automatic reduction in the amount of assistance on a first request for PA funding after a flood event. Typically, FEMA does not require the applicant to have had insurance on a facility before the first request for PA funding. However, facilities located in an SFHA may incur an automatic reduction in the amount of assistance on a first request for PA funding after a flood event.[343]

---

[337] Stafford Act § 311, 42 U.S.C. § 5154.

[338] Id. § 312, 42 U.S.C. § 5155.

[339] Id. § 406(d), 42 U.S.C. § 5172(d).

[340] 42 U.S.C. §4012a.

[341] See 42 U.S.C. §§4001 et seq.

[342] National Flood Insurance Act of 1968, Pub. L. No. 90-448, 82 Stat. 572 (codified as amended at 42 U.S.C. §§ 4001-4129); see 42 U.S.C. § 4002(b)(4) (stating congressional intent to require flood insurance in special flood hazard areas), 42 U.S.C. § 4012a(a) (forbidding federal financial assistance "for acquisition or construction purposes in any area that has been identified by the Director as an area having special flood hazards" and where flood insurance under NFIP is available); 42 U.S.C. § 5172(d) (mandating reduction of repair and replacement assistance if facility location in an SFHA for more than one year is damaged or destroyed by flooding and is not covered by flood insurance); See also 44 C.F.R. §§ 206.250(c), 206.252(a).

[343] See 44 CFR 206.250(d) and 206.252(a).

Also, FEMA's regulations exempt applicants from Section 311's "obtain and maintain requirement" when the eligible damage (before any reductions) for a project is less than $5,000.[344]

1. Requirement to Obtain and Maintain Insurance

a.) Effect on future PA grants

The Stafford Act requires that an applicant who receives assistance to repair, restore, and replace damaged facilities obtain and maintain reasonably available, adequate, and necessary insurance to protect against future loss to such facilities.[345] The insurance must, at a minimum, be in the amount of the eligible project costs, including any hazard mitigation measures taken. Regulations implementing insurance requirements differ slightly if the damage was caused by flood.[346] In general, however, if an entity receives PA grants, it is required, as a condition of such receipt, to obtain and maintain insurance in at least the same amount of the eligible cost of that disaster to protect against future loss to such property from the same peril.[347]

---

[344] 44 C.F.R. §§ 206.252(d), 206.253(d). *See also* PA GUIDE, *supra* note 23, at 123. For flood-damaged properties, this waiver stems from section 102 of the Flood Disaster Protection Act of 1973, Pub. L. No. 93-234, (codified as amended at 42 U.S.C. § 4012a(c)(2)). For non-flood-damaged properties, FEMA determined that the section 311 insurance requirement is not cost-effective for PA projects under $5,000. Disaster Assistance; Subpart I—Public Assistance Insurance Requirements, 56 Fed. Reg. 64,560 (Dec. 11, 1991) (to be codified at 44 C.F.R. pt. 206).

[345] *Id.* § 311 (a)(1)-(2), 42 U.S.C. § 5154(a)(1)-(2); 44 C.F.R. § 206.252(d) (facilities damaged by flood) and §206.253(b)-(f) (facilities damaged by disasters other than flood). But *see Insurance "waivers" in this chapter.*

[346] PA Insurance regulations are located at 44 C.F.R. §§ 206.250 - 206.253. Chapter 8 discusses flood insurance more fully; this section primarily deals with non-flood insurance issues. For future PA grant eligibility, however, insurance must be obtained and maintained for facilities located both in and outside of SFHAs. DAP 9580.3, *Insurance Considerations for Applicants* (2008) [hereinafter DAP 9580.3, *Insurance*], < http://www.fema.gov/public-assistance-9500-series-policy-publications/insurance-considerations-applicants>

[347] 44 C.F.R. §§ 206.252(d) and 206.253(b)(1). Note that the language describing applicant-required insurance differs depending on whether the cause of the peril is related to a flood or non-flood event. For a flood event, the applicant must maintain insurance "in the amount of eligible disaster assistance." For a non-flood event, the applicant must maintain insurance "based on the eligible damage that was incurred…" In practice, PA

If an entity does not obtain and maintain the required insurance, the current PA grant will be deobligated.[348] The applicant must submit proof of purchase of the required insurance in the form of a binder or policy to FEMA. If an applicant cannot obtain insurance because the disaster destroyed the facility, the applicant must provide a commitment letter to document the outstanding insurance requirement for the replacement facility. The applicant must then provide proof of insurance for the rebuilt facility to the state as soon as possible after the insurance is purchased. FEMA requires this proof before it can close out a project.

If it is determined that an applicant did not meet this requirement, FEMA may deobligate the PA funds. In addition, if an applicant does not obtain and maintain insurance on a facility as required, that facility will not be eligible for any PA funding in future major disasters.[349] In addition, FEMA may be required to recoup previously provided funding since obtaining insurance was a condition of the previous grant.

Applicants are not required to obtain and maintain insurance on temporary facilities; if applicants purchase such insurance, FEMA will not reimburse the costs of such premiums.[350]

---

treats the differences in language the same in both the flood and non-flood provisions. Insurance required is based on the amount of the PA funding received from FEMA

[348] Stafford Act § 311 (a)(1)-(2), 42 U.S.C. § 5154(a)(1)-(2); 44 C.F.R. § 206.253(b)(f). *See also*, PA Appeal FEMA-1426-DR-GU, *Guam Department of Education Southern High School A/C System* (2010). The applicant claimed that the requirement to obtain and maintain insurance coverage was only applicable to receiving FEMA assistance in future events, not the current one. FEMA disagreed, stating that § 311 of the Stafford Act requires applicants, as a condition of receiving assistance, not only to obtain and maintain such types and extent of insurance as may be reasonably available, adequate, and necessary to protect against future loss, but additionally, 44 C.F.R. § 206.253 states that "Assistance under § 406 of the Stafford Act will be approved only on the condition that the subgrantee obtain and maintain . . . insurance . . . ." In this case the applicant failed to obtain the required insurance coverage and FEMA deobligated the grant funding.

[349] Stafford Act § 311(b); 44 C.F.R. § 206.253(f).

[350] PA GUIDE, at 123.

---

b.) Insurance "waivers"

Federal agencies may promulgate regulations that interpret and implement statutory authority granted to them, but they may not ignore, override, waive, or otherwise act outside that authority.[351] The plain language of the Stafford Act prohibits FEMA from waiving the "obtain and maintain" requirement.[352]

However, FEMA cannot require insurance beyond the type or extent that the state insurance commissioner responsible for regulation of such insurance certifies as reasonable.[353] Generally, the states regulate insurance as intrastate commerce;[354] however, the state insurance commissioner does not regulate the NFIP.[355] As a result, the state insurance commissioner is not "responsible for regulation of" the NFIP, and Section 311's deference to the state insurance commissioner's certification of reasonableness does not apply with respect to flood

---

[351] Cf. *Nat'l Cable & Telecomms. Ass'n v. Brand X Internet Servs..*, 545 U.S. 967, 982-84 (2005) (finding no deference to agency interpretations where court finds statute to be unambiguous) and *Bowen v. Georgetown Univ. Hospital*, 488 U.S. 204, 208 (1988) ("[i]t is axiomatic that an administrative agency's power to promulgate legislative regulations is limited to the authority delegated by Congress.").

[352] 42 U.S.C. § 5154(b).

[353] Stafford Act § 311(a)(2), 42 U.S.C. § 5154(a)(2); 44 C.F.R. § 206.253(b)(1). *See also*, PA Appeal FEMA-1577-DR-CA, *City of Los Angeles* (2008): "In making a determination with respect to availability, adequacy, and necessity . . . the President shall not require greater types and extent of insurance than are certified to him as reasonable by the appropriate state insurance commissioner responsible for regulation of such insurance. For the applicant to receive a waiver of insurance requirements under §311 of the Stafford Act, it must present a certification signed by the California State Insurance Commissioner that flood insurance for its facilities is not reasonably available. The certification must be based on the grounds of availability, adequacy, or necessity for the applicant to receive a waiver. This letter was signed by a DOI (Department of insurance) analyst rather than the California State Insurance Commissioner . . . ." FEMA denied this appeal.

[354] 15 U.S.C. §§ 1011-1015.

[355] *Id.* § 1012(b). *See, e.g., Jacobson v. Metro. Prop. & Cas. Ins. Co.*, 672 F.3d 171, 175-176 (2d Cir. 2012) and *McGair v. Am. Bankers Ins. Co.*, 693 F.3d 94, 99 (1st Cir. 2012) (holding interpretation of insurance policies issued pursuant to NFIP is a matter of federal law.); PA Appeal FEMA-1763-DR-IA, *City of Keokuk, George M. Verity Tow Boat Museum* (Feb. 29, 2010) (denying waiver because FEMA determined flood insurance under NFIP was available); PA Appeal FEMA-1606-DR-TX, *Texas Parks and Wildlife Department* (Feb. 21, 2008) (finding State Insurance Commissioner cannot waive obtain and maintain requirement for flood damage because Congress created NFIP to provide reasonable flood insurance). *See also West v. Harris*, 573 F.2d 873, 881 (5th Cir. 1983) (referring to NFIP as a "child of Congress, conceived to achieve policies which are national in scope...").

---

insurance available under the NFIP.[356] For insurance required above the maximum amount of flood insurance available under the NFIP, a certification from the commissioner could reduce the amount of insurance that an applicant is required to obtain and/or maintain on a facility repaired and/or replaced with a PA grant.[357]

Except for the limited circumstance of the NFIP, FEMA will honor a certification from the commissioner when determining the type and amount of insurance that an applicant is required to purchase as a condition of the grant. Such a certification should include:

- A description of the property to which the certification applies[358]; and

---

[356] 42 U.S.C. § 5154(a)(2). See, e.g., PA Appeal FEMA-1763-DR-IA, City of Keokuk, George M. Verity Tow Boat Museum (2010). The applicant had stated it tried for the past 30 years to obtain flood insurance for the facility and provided a letter from its insurance carrier stating that the facility was uninsurable under the National Flood Insurance Program (NFIP). The facility was a boat that had been dry-docked since 1961, had cables attached to concrete pylons buried in the ground to permanently anchor it, was hard wired for electricity, and had plumbing running to it. FEMA determined that the museum met the definition of a building (found at 44 C.F.R. § 206.251(b)) for purposes of the NFIP and therefore flood insurance under NFIP was available. FEMA denied the appeal. See, e.g., PA Appeal FEMA-1606-DR-TX, Texas Parks and Wildlife Department (2008). The applicant submitted a letter from the Texas Commissioner of Insurance who certified that although insurance was available, the type, amount, and extent of insurance FEMA was requiring was not reasonable and requiring it would be contrary to public policy. The applicant requested that FEMA accept the commissioner's certification, thereby eliminating the requirement that the applicant purchase insurance on its damaged facilities. The applicant also stated, "We find no authority under federal or state law for a FEMA official to overrule the certification of the Texas Insurance Commissioner that certain insurance requirements are not reasonable." In denying the appeal, FEMA stated that § 311 of the Stafford Act requires applicants that receive assistance under § 406 of the Stafford Act to obtain and maintain insurance in the amount of eligible damage to the facilities. FEMA also pointed out that NFIP insurance was reasonably available and that the applicant's request was not consistent with the intent of § 311 of the Stafford Act because Congress created the NFIP to provide flood insurance at reasonable rates throughout the country. Therefore, because NFIP was available, an insurance commissioner cannot certify that flood insurance is not available at a reasonable cost.

[357] The regulatory provision for facilities damaged by flood indicating the Regional Administrator shall not require greater types and amounts of insurance than are certified as reasonable by State Insurance Commission thus applies only to an insurance requirement above the $1,000,000 NFIP coverage limit. 44 C.F.R. § 206.252(d).

[358] Section 311(a)(1) applies the obtain/maintain requirement on a per property basis. 42 U.S.C. § 5154(a)(1). Therefore when applying a determination with respect to the

---

- The commissioner's reasons as to why, based on the facts, the insurance type(s) and limits are unreasonable, [359] including supporting data regarding the availability, adequacy, and necessity of such insurance.[360] Such data could include information regarding the commercial availability of insurance based on types of risks, classification of facilities, extent of coverage limits, and related premium costs.

In practice, it is extremely rare for no amount of insurance to be reasonably available. Often, an insurance commissioner will certify that the full amount that FEMA requires is not reasonably available but will certify a lower amount that is reasonably available. FEMA will then use that lower amount as the amount that the applicant is required to obtain and maintain.

While the commissioner may issue a certification as to the type and amount of insurance that is available, adequate, and necessary to protect the property against future loss, and FEMA may not require an applicant to purchase more insurance than certified, FEMA is not required to fund the difference between the amount of the previous loss and the amount the commissioner deems appropriate.[361] FEMA is never obligated to provide PA. The issuance of a PA grant, including the amount of such a grant, is discretionary.[362] When FEMA applies a certification from an insurance

---

availability, adequacy, and necessity of the types and extent of insurance that is required for that property, this needs to be made on a property by property basis. A statewide, or citywide determination, for example, would not reasonably show that the state insurance commissioner determined that the types and extent of insurance required to cover the "property to be replaced, restored, repaired, or constructed with such assistance" is not reasonably available, adequate or necessary. *Id.* § 5154(a).

[359] *Id. See also id.*§ 5154(a)(2) (requiring certification); 44 C.F.R. §§ 206.253(b)(1), 206.252(d) (establishing basis for type and extent of insurance FEMA requires as a condition of the grant).

[360] 42 U.S.C. § 5154(a)(2) . These considerations are inherent to a finding as to whether FEMA's insurance requirements are reasonable. *See also* 44 C.F.R. § 206.252(d).

[361] *See* 42 U.S.C. 5172 (FEMA "may make contributions" to the state or local government for the repair or replacement of their damaged facilities.) *See also* 42 U.S.C. § 5121(b)(4) (Congress' intent to encourage applicants to protect themselves by obtaining insurance coverage to supplement or replace governmental assistance).

[362] *California-Nevada Methodist Homes v. Fed. Emergency Mgmt. Agency*, 152 F. Supp. 2d 1202 (N.D. Cal. 2001). ("Section 5172 of the Stafford Act provides that the President 'may make contributions' to eligible entities…the 'Grant Approval' section of FEMA's regulations pertaining to the Public Assistance Project does not contain any requirement that FEMA

---

commissioner, the relevant applicant will be eligible for future PA for damage from an event of the same type, provided the damage exceeds the amount of assistance provided for the first event. FEMA funding will be limited to the eligible amount above and beyond the amount of assistance provided in the first disaster.

c.) Blanket Insurance and Insurance Pools

Due to the high cost of insurance, some applicants may request to insure damaged facilities under a blanket insurance policy covering all their facilities or under an insurance pool arrangement between multiple entities covering all their facilities.[363] Such arrangements may be accepted for other than flood damage.[364] If a facility is insured in such a manner and becomes damaged in a future disaster of the same type, eligible costs will be reduced by the amount of the eligible damage sustained in the previous disaster.[365] In practice, FEMA applies this by subtracting an amount of the proceeds from the blanket or pool policy, equal to the amount of FEMA funding received from the prior event, from the amount of eligible costs for the damaged facility.

---

approve eligible costs or any standard for their approval. No regulation under the Public Assistance Project requires FEMA to approve any funding request. Rather, these regulations simply refer to costs that are 'eligible,' i.e., expenses that FEMA could choose to pay. E.g., 44 C.F.R. 206.226.... The decision to fund or not fund repairs necessarily involves the judgment of the decision-maker and is therefore discretionary. Decisions regarding the allocation of resources are precisely the type of action Congress sought to protect.")
[363] 44 C.F.R. § 206.253(b)(2). An insurance pool arrangement is an agreement among a group of entities to pool their resources to jointly fund a deductible for the group of properties they own. For example, multiple school districts could form a pool under a state statute to jointly purchase insurance or re-insurance with a high deductible covering all of their facilities; the deductible is funded jointly by the pool members in the event of damage to any of the covered facilities.
[364] 44 C.F.R. § 206.253(b)(2). Such pools are not available under the NFIP, *see* Standard Flood Insurance Policy, General Property Form, 44 C.F.R. § 61 App. A(2).
[365] 44. C.F.R. § 206.253(b)(2).

d.) Deductibles

FEMA deducts the total insurance proceeds received or anticipated from the total eligible cost of the project.[366] FEMA will not further reduce eligible costs by an insurance deductible.

2. Prohibition on Duplication of Benefits

The Stafford Act duplication of benefits provision requires FEMA to reduce the amount of assistance provided to the applicant by the amount of financial assistance it will receive under any other program, from insurance proceeds, or from any other source.[367] FEMA cannot, therefore, provide disaster assistance for damage or losses covered by insurance, as this would be a duplication of benefits, which is prohibited under the Stafford Act. Therefore, prior to approval of a PA grant for flood or non-flood events, the grantee must notify FEMA of any entitlement to an insurance settlement or recovery.[368] The owners of insured facilities must provide FEMA, through the state public assistance officer, the policies, declarations, insuring agreements, conditions, exclusions, and "Statements of Loss," including settlement information for every facility which the current disaster damaged. The applicant must also provide FEMA a list of all facilities for which PA funding was received previously and for which insurance was previously required to be purchased. Additionally, if a flood caused the damage, the applicant must identify all facilities located in the SFHA.

3. Deduction of Insurance Proceeds from the PA Grant

FEMA is required to deduct all insurance proceeds available for eligible PA grants, regardless of whether the insurance proceeds were for emergency or permanent work.[369] If the applicant has not completed negotiations

---

[366] See 42 U.S.C. 5155, 44 CFR 206.252(c), and 44 CFR 206.253(a). See also memorandum dated February 8, 2013, from Deborah Ingram to FEMA Regional Administrators, rescinding Disaster Assistance Fact Sheet 9580.3.
[367] Stafford Act § 312(a), 42 U.S.C. 5155(a). See also, DAP 9580.3, Insurance.
[368] 44 C.F.R. §§ 206.252(c) and 206.253(a).
[369] See, e.g., PA Appeal FEMA-1603-DR-LA, Housing Authority of New Orleans (2009). The applicant's position was that the Stafford Act does not explicitly authorize insurance reductions for emergency work under § 403, as it does under § 406. The applicant also

with the insurance company at the time it develops the project worksheet (PW), FEMA will estimate the anticipated insurance proceeds and deduct the estimated amount. The final deduction is the actual amount of available insurance.[370] When an insured applicant has not yet received the insurance proceeds, FEMA does have the authority to provide PA funding on the condition that the applicant agrees to repay to FEMA all duplicative assistance eventually received.[371] This authority should rarely be utilized, however, as advancing PA financial assistance against a future insurance recovery may discourage or thwart an appropriate insurance settlement. If FEMA obligates PA funds for work that it subsequently finds to be covered by insurance, FEMA must deobligate the funds.[372] Final accounting will occur at closeout.

Depreciation, defined as, the difference between FEMA eligible costs and final loss valuations that insurers use, is an eligible uninsured loss.[373]

4. Automatic reduction in Special Flood Hazard Areas (SFHAs)

The Stafford Act requires that for any public or PNP facility located in an SFHA identified for more than one year that is damaged or destroyed by flood, PA funding will be automatically reduced by the lesser of the value of the facility on the date of damage, or the maximum amount of NFIP

---

stated that insurance monies received would be insufficient to cover all losses and that it would apply any insurance proceeds received towards permanent work activities, resulting in no duplication of benefits for the emergency work. FEMA stated that § 312(a) of the Stafford Act provides that requirements to reduce insurance proceeds from eligible assistance apply to both emergency and permanent work. In another appeal, FEMA, reaching a similar result, stated that the category of work does not determine the applicability of the requirement for the purchase of insurance. See, PA Appeal FEMA-1426-DR-GU, *Guam Department of Education, Southern High School A/C System* (2010).

[370] There can be a dispute over the meaning of "available." *See* Insurance "waivers" in this chapter. See, e.g., Office of the Inspector General's Audit, 1008-DR-CA *Santa Monica Hospital Medical Center* (2009). The applicant accepted a negotiated settlement of $46.7 million, which was the present value of the $50 million the applicant was eligible to receive over time. For purposes of the PA grant reduction in this case, the OIG was of the opinion that the applicant received the equivalent of $50 million in insurance, and FEMA, in its appeal decision, agreed.

[371] Stafford Act § 312(b)(1), 42 U.S.C. § 5155(b)(1).

[372] Id. § 312(c), 42 U.S.C. § 5155(c).

[373] Id.

proceeds that would have been available to such a facility.[374] The only exception is for PNP facilities that do not have flood insurance because of the local government's failure to participate in the NFIP. To qualify for that exception, the local government must agree to participate in the NFIP within six months of the major disaster declaration date, and the PNP must then purchase the required flood insurance in order to comply with the requirements to obtain and maintain insurance.

B. Allocation between Eligible and Ineligible Work

In the case of an insurance policy that covers eligible and ineligible work, such as a property insurance policy that includes business interruption coverage, FEMA apportions the value of insurance proceeds as follows for purposes of deductions:

- If the applicant's insurance policy specifies the amount of coverage for each type of loss, the proceeds will be apportioned according to the policy limits;

- If the insurer provides a statement of loss that specifies the amount of proceeds per type of loss, that will be used to determine the proceeds for eligible costs;

- If the applicant's policy is silent as to apportionment, the proceeds will be apportioned based on the ratio of the applicant's eligible to ineligible costs. For example, if the applicant's total losses were 60% property damage (PA eligible) and 40% business interruption (PA ineligible), then 60% of the insurance proceeds would be deducted from the total eligible PA funding.[375]

This same apportionment formula applies to the deductible.

---

[374] Stafford Act § 406(d), 42 U.S.C. § 5172(d).
[375] PA GUIDE, at 119; Fact Sheet 9580.3, *Insurance*.

C. Self-Insurance

As discussed previously, the Stafford Act requires applicants to obtain insurance on damaged insurable facilities (e.g., buildings, equipment, contents, and vehicles) in order to receive PA grant funding.[376] Moreover, the applicant must maintain insurance coverage to be eligible for PA funding for any future disasters.[377] The Stafford Act allows states and tribes[378] to satisfy the insurance purchase requirement for state-owned facilities if it maintains a plan of self-insurance.[379] The state must either declare its election to self-insure in writing at the time of acceptance of assistance, or subsequently, and submit an established plan of self-insurance with supporting documentation for approval to FEMA's Assistant Administrator for Recovery.[380] The self-insurance exemption to the Stafford Act's insurance purchase requirement is available only to states and Indian tribal governments. It does not apply to counties, cities, and PNP organizations.

FEMA promulgated regulations with respect to the state acting as a self-insurer for flood insurance under the NFIP.[381] Pursuant to FEMA's regulations, states may satisfy the mandatory insurance purchase requirement by submitting an established plan of self-insurance for

---

[376] Stafford Act § 311(a), 42 U.S.C. § 5154(a).

[377] Stafford Act §§ 311(b), 42 U.S.C. § 5154(b), 401, 501; Disaster Relief Appropriations Act of 2013, Pub. L. 13r-1, H.R. 152 § 1110 (Amending sections 401 and 501 of the Stafford Act to provide for an option for the Chief Executive of a federally recognized Indian tribe to make a direct request to the President for a major disaster or emergency declaration. Amends some other sections of the Stafford Act to incorporate "tribal" into references to state and local governments.

[378] Stafford Act §§ 401, 501; Disaster Relief Appropriations Act of 2013, Pub. L. 13r-1, H.R. 152 § 1110 (401, 501; Disaster Relief Appropriations Act of 2013, Pub. L. 13r-1, H.R. 152 § 1110(updating the definitions of "tribe" in the Stafford Act to reflect the nation-to-nation recognition of tribes by removing federally recognized Indian tribal government from the definition of local government, and defining Indian tribal government in its own right consistent with FEMA's current regulatory definition of the term. The section also provides that combination references to state and/or local government throughout the Stafford Act are deemed to include Indian tribal government.

[379] Id. § 311(c), 42 U.S.C. § 5154(c).

[380] See id. § 311(c), 42 U.S.C. 5154(c); see also DAP 9580.3, at Frequently Asked Questions, Item # 8. The position of "Assistant Administrator for the Disaster Assistance Directorate" referred to in the DAP no longer exists and is replaced in this instance by the Assistant Administrator for Recovery.

[381] 44 C.F.R. § 75.11.

---

approval to the Federal Insurance Administrator.[382] The plan must: 1) constitute a formal policy of self-insurance authorized by statute or regulation; 2) specify that hazards covered by the self-insurance plan include those flood-related hazards covered under the Standard Flood Insurance Policy (SFIP); 3) provide coverage equal to that provided in the SFIP; 4) consist of a self-insurance fund or a commercial policy of insurance for structures and contents; 5) regularly maintain an inventory of structures and contents within designated flood hazard zones; 6) provide a record of prior flood losses (structure and contents) in the five years prior to application; and 7) provide a certified copy of the floodplain management regulations for the state-owned properties located within designated flood hazard zones.[383] It is the state's burden to establish that its self-insurance plan equals or exceeds FEMA's regulatory standards.[384] If approved, the state is exempt from the requirement to purchase flood insurance for state-owned structures and their contents.[385] The Federal Insurance Administrator is required to review the state's plan for continued compliance with regulations and may request updated documentation as part of the review.[386] The Federal Insurance Administrator may revoke the self-insurance certification if it is determined that the plan is inadequate and the state has not corrected the inadequacies within 90 days of the date in which the inadequacies were identified.[387]

D. Private Property Debris Removal and Insurance

Debris removal on private property may be an eligible cost where the public health, safety or economic recovery of the community is threatened and if FEMA approves this work before it begins.[388] Debris removal by an

---

[382] Id. § 75.10.

[383] Id. § 75.11.

[384] Id. § 75.3.

[385] Id. § 75.10. Even though the state is exempt from the obtain/maintain requirement under the NFIP, the state is not guaranteed to receive PA funding if they subsequently apply for PA . The issuance of a PA grant, including the amount of such a grant, is discretionary. *California-Nevada Meth. Homes v. FEMA.*, 152 F. Supp.2d 1202 (N.D. Ca. 2001)http://www.leagle.com/xmlResult.aspx?xmldoc=20011354152FSupp2d1202_112 33.xml&docbase=CSLWAR2-1986-2006

[386] Id. § 75.13(a)-(d).

[387] Id. § 75.13(c).

[388] 44 C.F.R. § 206.224(b); *see also*, 44 C.F.R. 206.208(c)(2)..

---

applicant or by a federal agency through DFA would constitute a duplication of benefits if the private property owner has property insurance which covers debris removal. The state or local government must agree in writing to indemnify FEMA from all claims arising from the private property debris removal. This indemnification must include signed agreements from property owners providing that they will pursue and credit back to FEMA any available insurance proceeds they receive.[389] *See Debris Removal from Private Property* in this chapter for a discussion of private property debris removal.

E. Federally-Assisted Facilities

The Stafford Act's duplication of benefits provision applies not just to insurance but also to any part of a loss for which an applicant will receive assistance from any other program or from any other source.[390] This necessarily includes circumstances where applicants may receive funding to repair facilities from another federal agency.

In addition to the duplication of benefits provision in the Stafford Act, federal appropriations law restricts the government from using a more general funding authority to augment the appropriations that Congress has authorized to address a particular purpose under other, more specific or primary authorities.[391] Consequently, FEMA has promulgated a regulation providing that if another federal agency has specific primary statutory responsibility to provide disaster assistance to certain facilities, FEMA does not provide assistance under the Stafford Act.[392]

Examples of such authority are:

a. United States Army Corps of Engineers (USACE)—has the authority to provide permanent restoration of damaged flood

---

[389] PA GUIDE, at 70.

[390] Stafford Act § 312, 42 U.S.C. § 5155. *See also* Chapter 6, *Individual Assistance*, for a discussion of duplication of benefits.

[391] Application of this principle is based on the authority provided, and it is not affected by the extent to which funds may actually be available. *See, e.g.,* 63 Comp. Gen. 422 (1984); 36 Comp. Gen. 386 (1956). Moreover, general appropriations may not be used as a back-up for a more specific appropriation. 20 Comp. Gen. 272 (1940).

[392] 44 C.F.R. § 206.226(a); *see* discussion of OFAs in PA GUIDE at 23-26.

control works, such as levees, floodwalls, flood control channels, and dams designed for flood control.[393]

b. United States Department of Agriculture - Natural Resource Conservation Service (NRCS)—under the Emergency Watershed Protection Program, also has authority to repair flood control works,[394] similar to the USACE.

c. United States Department of Interior - Bureau of Indian Affairs (BIA)—provides resources, such as road maintenance grants,[395] that may help tribal recovery.

d. United States Department of Transportation - Federal Highway Administration (FHWA)—assists with the repair of federal aid roads and bridges damaged during disasters.[396] Rural or minor collection routes not covered are eligible for FEMA assistance. In July 2012, Congress amended the statutory authorization for the FWHA's Emergency Relief Program to remove FHWA's authority to fund debris removal from federal aid highways where PA funding is available for debris removal under a declared major disaster or emergency[397]. For emergencies or major disasters declared after October 1, 2012, FEMA, not FHWA, will have the authority for debris removal from federal aid highways during emergencies or major disasters in jurisdictions where debris removal is authorized under the Stafford Act.

e. Department of Housing and Urban Development (HUD)—Prior to October 1, 2008, authorized HUD to provide disaster assistance to repair disaster-damaged public housing authority (PHA) facilities.[398] Consequently, FEMA could provide funding for emergency work but not for the permanent repair, replacement, or restoration of disaster-

---

[393] 33 U.S.C. § 701, et seq.

[394] 33 U.S.C. § 701b, Pub. L. No. 81-516, as amended, § 216.

[395] 25 C.F.R. § 170, et seq.; 23 U.S.C. §§ 101(a), 202, 204, 308; 25 U.S.C. § 47; 25 U.S.C. § 450.

[396] 23 U.S.C. § 120(e).

[397] Moving Ahead for Progress in the 21st Century Act (MAP-21), Pub. L 112-141 (July 6, 2012).

[398] Housing Act of 1937 § 9(k), 42 U.S.C. § 1437g(k), as amended.

damaged PHA facilities. Congress changed the law in 2008.[399] FEMA now has authority to fund *both* emergency work and permanent repair of all disaster-damaged PHA facilities <u>unless</u> Congress appropriates funds to HUD for emergency capital needs to repair, restore, or replace certain PHA facilities damaged in presidentially declared major disasters. Alaskan Native and American Indian public housing entities may apply directly to FEMA for disaster assistance, though they are otherwise funded by BIA.[400]

f. United States Department of Education (ED)—notwithstanding FEMA's general prohibition on providing funding where another federal agency has specific authority, there is a specific exception for the repair of elementary and secondary education facilities, which are otherwise eligible for assistance from the Department of Education.[401] The exception does not cover increased operating expenses or replacement of lost revenue.

VI. Hazard Mitigation Measures in PA Permanent Work Projects

Section 406(e) of the Stafford Act authorizes as an eligible cost, the work necessary to conform to codes and specifications, including "hazard mitigation criteria required by the President."[402] The Stafford Act thus allows FEMA to consider PA funding for mitigation measures that would go beyond the scope of work required to return a damaged facility to its pre-disaster design and function.[403] FEMA regulation limits these mitigation measures to restoration projects.[404] These mitigation measures are often called "Section 406 hazard mitigation" after the PA section of the Stafford Act that authorizes them, as distinguished from Hazard Mitigation Grant Program (HMGP) measures authorized by Section 404 of

---

[399] The Housing and Economic Recovery Act of 2008, Pub. L. No.110-289 (2008), repealed Section 9(k) of the Housing Act.
[400] Recovery Fact Sheet 9580.205, *Public Assistance Funding to Public Housing Facilities* (2010) < http://www.fema.gov/library/viewRecord.do?id=6681?id=6681>.
[401] 44 C.F.R. § 206.226(a)(2).
[402] Stafford Act § 406(e)(1)(A)(ii), 42 U.S.C. § 5172(e)(1)(A)(ii).
[403] *See* Stafford Act § 101, 42 U.S.C. 5172, which states the congressional intent to encourage "...hazard mitigation measures to reduce losses from disasters..."
[404] 44 C.F.R. 206.226(e)(1), Hazard Mitigation.

---

the Stafford Act.[405] FEMA may use Section 406 hazard mitigation funding to provide protection to parts of a facility that were damaged and thus became eligible for Section 406 assistance. The HMGP authorized by Section 404 is a stand-alone and much broader program where funding may be provided to undamaged facilities and projects.[406] *See* subsequent discussion for a comparison of the two types of assistance.

This section will discuss the requirements for approval of Section 406 mitigation funding measures as follows: Part A discusses project eligibility requirements; Part B discusses cost-effectiveness requirements; and Part C discusses the key differences between mitigation under Sections 406 and 404 of the Stafford Act.

A. Eligibility

Either the applicant or the state may request that hazard mitigation measures be included in the overall funding of a project.[407] For hazard mitigation measures to be approved, FEMA must review the measures for eligibility, which will be discussed in detail here. Additional factors include ensuring that the measures are technically feasible, compliant with environmental and historic preservation, and cost-effective.[408] The following are requirements and considerations for eligibility under Section 406:

---

[405] *Compare* Stafford Act § 406, 42 U.S.C. § 5172, with Stafford Act § 404, 42 U.S.C. § 5170c, for mitigation measures as a consequence of a major disaster declaration. *See* discussion of the distinctions between §§ 404 and 406 in the section titled *Differences between Section 406 and Section 404 Hazard Mitigation Measures* later this this chapter. *See also* Stafford Act § 203, 42 U.S.C. § 5133, (available as a grant when the President has not made a disaster declaration).

[406] RP 9526.1, *Hazard Mitigation Funding Under Section 406 (Stafford Act)* [hereinafter RP 9526.1, *Hazard Mitigation Funding*] at VI. A. 2, < http://www.fema.gov/95261-hazard-mitigation-funding-under-section-406-stafford-act>

[407] *Id.* at VII.C. and G.

[408] RP 9526.1, *Hazard Mitigation Funding.*

---

1. Disaster Damage

Mitigation measures eligible under Section 406 must be appropriate to the disaster damage and must prevent future damage similar to that caused by the declared event.[409]

2. Applicable Damaged Elements

Mitigation measures under Section 406 must be applied only to the damaged element(s) of a facility.[410] When conducting repairs to a portion of a system, this criterion is particularly important.

Example of when a facility is not eligible for Section 406 mitigation funding

If floodwaters inundate a sanitary sewer, block manholes with sediment, and damage some of the manholes, cost-effective mitigation to prevent blockage of the damaged manholes in future events may be eligible; however, work to improve any undamaged manholes that are part of the system is not eligible. Similarly, raising the height of an existing berm, which was not damaged in an event, but surrounds a damaged facility, does not meet the requirement of being part of a damaged facility, and thus is not eligible for Section 406 mitigation funding. **Note:** While the elevation of the referenced berm is not eligible for Section 406 funding, the work may be eligible under the Section 404 mitigation program.

---

3. Work Needed Greater Than That Eligible

Under Section 406, eligible costs may only include work that is required to return the damaged facility to its pre-disaster design.[411] In repairing the facility to its pre-disaster design, FEMA will include those costs incurred to repair damaged portions of a facility in conformance with current codes and standards. However, FEMA does not consider whole building upgrades required to meet current codes and standards to be

---

[409] Stafford Act § 101, 42 U.S.C. § 5121.
[410] 44 C.F.R. § 206.223(a)(1); 44 C.F.R. § 206.201(k).
[411] Stafford Act § 406(e), 42 U.S.C. § 5172(e); 44 C.F.R. § 206.226.

---

eligible hazard mitigation measures for purposes of the PA Program. Further, if the applicant requests an improved project,[412] which will involve the replacement of the facility on the same site or an alternate site, the cost of mitigation measures is not eligible.[413]

4. Not for Replacement Buildings

Mitigation funding under Section 406 must not be applied to replacement buildings.[414]

B. Determining Cost-effectiveness

Mitigation measures must be cost-effective.[415] Cost-effectiveness is determined by evaluating the cost of mitigation measures under the following categories:[416]

1. 15% of Total Eligible Cost of Eligible Repair Work

Mitigation measures may total up to 15% of the total eligible cost of the repair work on a particular PA project. The total cost to repair the initial damaged facility under the PA Program is calculated against the total cost of the mitigation measures proposed to improve the damaged elements of that facility. If the cost for the mitigation measure is no more than 15% of the total eligible cost of eligible repair work, then the mitigation project is considered cost-effective.[417]

---

[412] 44 C.F.R. 206.203(d)(1); see *Improved Projects* later in this chapter, which discusses "improved projects" in further detail.

[413] Id.; see also, RP 9526.1, *Hazard Mitigation Funding*.

[414] Facilities eligible for replacement are not eligible for mitigation measures under 44 C.F.R. §§ 206.226(e) and 206.226(f)(1). Note also that an applicant may not apply the cost of hazard mitigation measures towards an alternate project under 44 C.F.R. § 206.203(d)(2). The reason for this prohibition is the mitigation measures must be applied to the damaged elements of the facility; whereas, the alternate project is a replacement project used for a different purpose than the pre-disaster facility. One exception, however, may allow applicants to use "funds contributed for alternate projects" towards "hazard mitigation measures." 44 C.F.R. 206.203(d)(2)(iv).

[415] 44 C.F.R. 206.226(e); 44 C.F.R. § 206.228(a).

[416] RP 9526.1, *Hazard Mitigation Funding*, Appendix A.

[417] Id.

---

2. Pre-determined Cost-effective Mitigation Measures

Certain mitigation measures are pre-determined as cost-effective, as long as the mitigation measure does not exceed 100% of the eligible cost of the eligible repair work on the project. Examples of a few such hazard mitigation projects are:[418]

- Protection from high winds. Example: Facilitates in hurricane prone areas may install hurricane straps or clips to their roofs to reinforce the roof and prevent blow off in future events.

- Protection of utilities. Example: Elevation of HVAC and electrical control panels, located in the facilities basement, when the facility is in a flood prone area.

- Protection of drainage crossings and revetments. Example: Replacement of culverts;[419] on improved banks, installation of headwalls and wing walls, as well as gabion baskets, and geo-textile fabric installation on shoulders, to control erosion.

3. Cost-Benefit Analysis (CBA)

For measures that exceed the previously described categories, the applicant or state must demonstrate, through an acceptable CBA methodology, that the measure is cost-effective.[420]

The CBA will be based on a comparison of the total project cost to the proposed projected benefits of the mitigation measures.[421] FEMA takes into consideration certain factors to determine if a hazard mitigation measure is feasible. They are:[422]

---

[418] Id.

[419] However, culverts need to be considered with regard to a total drainage system and should not be upgraded without a watershed hydrology study with an emphasis on downstream effects and NFIP regulations. See RP 9526.1, *Hazard Mitigation Funding*, Appendix A.

[420] RP 9526.1, *Hazard Mitigation Funding* at VII.B.

[421] FEMA determines cost-effectiveness. When FEMA performs a cost-benefit analysis, it employs a qualified FEMA hazard mitigation specialist utilizing the methods in RP 9526.1, *Hazard Mitigation Funding*.

[422] Id. at VII.B.

- Damage to the facility and its damaged contents;
- Emergency protective measures required as a result of that damage;
- Temporary facilities required due to the damage;
- Casualty (loss of life and injury);
- Loss of function; and
- Cost avoidance (damage avoided in the future due to mitigation measures).

Example 1

The applicant increased the cost of a PA project to repair a flood-damaged lift station by adding a hazard mitigation component to improve sanitary drainage. The applicant argued that 1) its drainage improvements mitigated against the floodwaters that damaged the eligible facility; and 2) the cost-benefit analysis was over 1.0, which is considered cost-effective. FEMA denied the appeal because the hazard mitigation project did not directly relate to the damaged elements of the facility, and therefore, the CBA result was irrelevant.[423]

Example 2

A declared disaster damages an eligible facility owned by an eligible applicant, including breaking some but not all of the facilities windows. Section 406 PA hazard mitigation funding may be used to upgrade the disaster-damaged windows with wind resistant windows; however, funding to upgrade undamaged windows would have to come from the Section 404 statewide hazard mitigation program.

C. Differences between Section 406 and Section 404 Hazard Mitigation Measures

The Stafford Act provides for two types of funding for hazard mitigation measures: statewide mitigation programs[424] and mitigation for disaster-damaged facilities.[425] While Section 406 applies to restoration projects

---

[423] Second Appeal Brief, FEMA-1766-DR-IN PA ID # 081-UZMC8-00; Johnson Memorial Hospital PW # 2002; Hazard Mitigation (2010).
[424] Stafford Act § 404, 42 U.S.C. § 5170c.
[425] Id. § 406, 42 U.S.C. § 5172.

administered under the PA Program, Section 404 provides hazard mitigation grants directly to states and local governments to implement long-term hazard mitigation measures after a major disaster declaration through the HMGP.[426]

Program implementation, project application, and funding limits differ between the two programs. The differences between these provisions are illustrated in the following table.

Section 404 Mitigation compared to Section 406 Mitigation		
	404 Hazard Mitigation	**406 Hazard Mitigation**
Implementation	Separate program run by the state.	Implemented for restoration projects through the PA Program.
Project application	Applies to structural measures and to non-structural measures (such as planning, property acquisition, drainage projects).	Must apply to a damaged element of the facility and does not apply to buyouts of affected private property to protect from future risk.
Coverage	Applies throughout the state in most disasters.	Applies to eligible restoration projects upon request.
Funding calculations and limitations	The formula for calculating the HMGP allocation for states with a standard state mitigation plan is based on 15% of the first $2 billion of estimated aggregate amounts of disaster assistance. For amounts greater than $2 billion, a sliding scale is used to make allocation determinations. States with enhanced mitigation plans are eligible for a 20% HMGP formula.	No program-wide limits in funding; proposed hazard mitigation measure(s) must be cost-effective and approved for each eligible restoration project.

---

[426] Chapter 7, *Hazard Mitigation*, discusses § 404 in more detail.

VII. Repair, Replacement, Alternate and Improved Projects

A. Repair or Replacement

The Stafford Act recognizes that disasters may destroy buildings and infrastructure and that replacement of destroyed structures may be essential.[427] FEMA's regulations provide that if disaster damage does not exceed 50% of the cost of replacing a facility, then the facility is repairable.[428] Conversely, if the disaster damage is greater than 50% of the cost of repairing a facility, then the facility is eligible for replacement. Exceptions exist for historic preservation of structures and whether it is possible to meet current codes and standards.[429] The PA Guide explains the process for determining whether replacement may be appropriate.[430] The challenge for FEMA and the applicant is determining what elements of the structure should be included in the cost analysis.[431]

B. Alternate Projects

An applicant has the flexibility to determine that funds to repair an eligible facility damaged by a disaster could be of better use if applied to an alternate project.[432] More specifically, an applicant must have determined that "the public welfare would not be best served by repairing, restoring, reconstructing, or replacing any public facility owned or controlled by the state or local government."[433] An applicant has additional flexibility in being able to apply the funding to multiple projects.[434] All alternate projects must be within the declared disaster area.

---

[427] Stafford Act §§ 406(a), (c), and (e), 42 U.S.C. § 5172(a), (c), and (e).
[428] 44 C.F.R. § 206.226(f). DAP 9524.4, *Repair vs. Replacement of a Facility under 44 C.F.R. §206.226(f) (The 50 Percent Rule)* (2009) [hereinafter DAP 9524.4, 50 Percent Rule]. http://www.fema.gov/9500-series-policy-publications/95244-repair-vs-replacement-facility-under-44-cfr-ss206226f-50-rule.
[429] *Id.* § 206.226(f)(3).
[430] PA GUIDE, at 36-38.
[431] RP. 9526.1, *Mitigation Funding* at VII.B. *See also* DAP 9524.4, 50 Percent Rule.
[432] Stafford Act § 406(c), 42 U.S.C. § 5172(c); 44 C.F.R. § 206.203(d)(2); DAP 9525.13, *Alternate Projects* (2008). http://www.fema.gov/9500-series-policy-publications/952513-alternate-projects
[433] *Id.* § 406(c)(1)(A), 42 U.S.C. § 5172(c)(1)(A).
[434] *Id.* § 406(c)(1)(B)(i) and (ii), 42 U.S.C. § 5172(c)(1)(B)(i) and (ii).

Alternate projects may include:

- repair or expansion of other public facilities;
- construction of new facilities;
- demolition of the original structure;
- purchase of capital equipment;
- funding of cost-effective hazard mitigation measures in the area affected by the disaster;
- funding project shortfalls due to mandatory NFIP reductions on applicant buildings in floodplains; and
- supplemental funds used on an improved project.

Alternate projects for governmental entities are eligible for 90% of the lesser of:

- The approved federal share of the estimated eligible costs associated with repairing the damaged facility to its pre-disaster design; or
- The approved federal share of the actual costs of completing the alternate project.[435]

Alternate projects for PNP entities are eligible for 75% of the lesser of:

- The approved federal share; or
- The approved federal share of the actual costs of completing the alternate project.[436]

C. Improved Projects

When performing permanent restoration work on a damaged facility, PA applicants may decide to make improvements to the damaged facilities while restoring them to their pre-disaster function. For example, an applicant may wish to replace a fire station that had one bay with a new fire station that has three bays, or to lay asphalt on a gravel road. FEMA regulations authorize such "improved projects," i.e., projects that

---

[435] Id. § 406(c)(1)(A), 42 U.S.C. § 5172(c)(1)(A); 44 C.F.R. § 206.203(d)(2)(ii).
[436] Id. § 406(c)(2)(A), 42 U.S.C. § 5172(c)(2)(A); 44 C.F.R.§ 206.203(d)(2)(iii).

---

incorporate improvements while retaining the original pre-disaster function, subject to the limitations discussed in this section.[437]

An applicant may request an improved project for either small or large projects. *See PA Process* later in this chapter for a discussion of small and large projects. The improved facility must maintain the original pre-disaster function and at least the pre-disaster capacity. In addition, federal funds for improved PA projects are limited to the federal share of the estimated costs of repairing or replacing the damaged facility to its pre-disaster design, or the actual costs of completing the improved project, whichever is less.[438] The balance of funding is a non-federal responsibility. This includes any costs required solely because of the improvements (for example, increased costs to comply with codes and standards, or environmental or historic preservation requirements attributable solely to improvements and not to repairs of the original facility). FEMA may also provide assistance with hazard mitigation measures under the PA program for the original facility but not if the improved project involves a completely new facility.

FEMA must approve any project that results in significant change to the pre-disaster configuration of a facility, including a different location, facility footprint, or size, prior to construction to ensure compliance with environmental and historic review.[439] Further, subgrantee applicants must obtain the grantee/state's approval for an improved project prior to the start of construction. The time limits associated with repairing the damaged facility to its pre-disaster condition also apply to improved project construction.

VIII. Appeals under the PA Program

The Stafford Act provides applicants a 60-day right of appeal from any eligibility decision for assistance under the Stafford Act.[440] It requires FEMA to establish regulations that provide for fair and impartial

---

[437] 44 C.F.R. § 206.203(d)(1).
[438] PA Guide, at 111; PA Digest, at 71.
[439] Id. *See also* < http://www.fema.gov/public-assistance-local-state-tribal-and-non-profit/historic-preservation>.
[440] Stafford Act § 423, 42 U.S.C. § 5189(a).

consideration of appeal.[441] A grantee, subgrantee, or applicant (appellant) has the right to appeal any decision or determination regarding a PA application for federal assistance, including eligibility and the amount of assistance.[442] Appellants must comply with the procedures for the appeal process contained in FEMA regulations.[443] There are two levels of appeal: the Regional Administrator (RA) decides the first appeal, and the Assistant Administrator for Recovery decides the second appeal at FEMA HQ.[444] Each level of appeal has independent deadlines that apply. The decision of the second appeal at HQ is FEMA's final administrative decision.

Applicants typically dispute eligibility determinations regarding applicant status (e.g., PNP eligibility, legal responsibility), work (e.g., scope, debris quantity, repair versus replacement, emergency versus permanent, cause of damage), facility (e.g., legal responsibility, PNP owned or operated, public purpose), and costs (e.g., reasonableness, allowable).

FEMA informs the grantee in writing, most frequently in the form of a PW presented to the applicant for signature, or a letter, detailing the determination(s) of the Agency and the basis for each determination. The grantee, in turn, must provide a copy of the written determination to the subgrantee, who then has the right to appeal any determination that it considers unfavorable. Appellants must file appeals within 60 days after receipt of a notice of the FEMA determination that is being appealed.[445]

All appeals must be in writing and must contain documented justification supporting the appellant's position, specifying the monetary figure in dispute and the provisions in federal law, regulation, or policy with which the appellant believes the initial determination was inconsistent.[446] The appellant composes the document, includes supporting documentation, and sends it to the grantee. The grantee will review and forward appeals

---

[441] 44 C.F.R. § 206.206.
[442] Id.
[443] Id.
[444] Id. § 206.206(b). The position of "Assistant Administrator for the Disaster Assistance Directorate" referred to in the regulation no longer exists and is replaced in this instance by the Assistant Administrator for Recovery.
[445] See 44 CFR § 206.206(c)(1).
[446] See 44 CFR § 206.206(a).

from an applicant or subgrantee, with a written recommendation, to the RA within 60 days of receipt.[447]

The subgrantee applicant must send both first and second appeals through the grantee to the RA.[448] It is highly recommended that the Office of the RA date-stamp an appeal upon receipt, but FEMA does not require this practice. The RA has 90 days to "notify the grantee in writing of the disposition of the appeal or of the need for additional information."[449] Once the appellant receives the decision, the appellant has another 60 days to submit a second appeal to the grantee.

At either level of appeal, if needed, FEMA may request additional information.[450] The RA or Assistant Administrator (AA) must notify the grantee of the need for additional information within 90 days of receipt of an appeal and give a date within which FEMA must receive the requested information.[451] Within 90 days of receipt of that information, or following expiration of the period for providing the information, FEMA will notify the grantee in writing of the disposition of the appeal.[452] In first or second appeals involving highly technical issues, FEMA may, in its discretion, submit the appeal to an independent scientific or technical subject matter expert for advice or recommendation.[453] The period for this technical review may be in addition to other allotted time periods. There is no time limit for the period of technical expert review. Once FEMA receives a report from the technical expert, FEMA has 90 days to notify the grantee in writing of the disposition of the appeal.[454]

The second appeal follows the same process as the first appeal; all subgrantee appeals must go through the grantee for review and evaluation before submission to the RA.[455] Therefore, the grantee has 60 days from

---

[447] *See* 44 CFR § 206.206(c)(2).
[448] Id. § 206.206(a).
[449] Id. § 206.206(c)(3).
[450] Id.
[451] Id.
[452] Id.
[453] Id. § 206.206(d).
[454] Id.
[455] Id. § 206.206(a).

submission to review the second appeal before forwarding it to the RA.[456] The RA must then forward it to HQ.

Some FEMA regional offices forward second appeals immediately to HQ with no review, while other regions may review the appellant's materials and make recommendations to HQ when they forward the second appeal. The regulations state that FEMA will notify the grantee of the agency's determination in writing within 90 days following receipt of an appeal. For second appeals, FEMA generally considers "receipt" to mean receipt by HQ, not receipt by the Region.

Where the process outlined in 44 CFR 206.206 is based on a subgrantee as applicant, a grantee may also appeal FEMA determinations on its own PA projects under these procedures.[457]

FEMA must provide a written decision on both first and second appeals.[458] Appeal decisions most often are written in a letter format and are publicly available on FEMA's website for viewing and download.[459]

Appeal timeliness is of utmost importance because applicants rely on FEMA project approval decisions to make key repair or rebuilding choices. FEMA program staff may change field project approval decisions if they determine that the project funding decision was ineligible. The DHS Office of Inspector General may question project funding decisions in audits of FEMA programs. While neither FEMA nor any other agency is bound to make changes the Inspector General recommends,[460] federal funding may only be used for the purpose for which it was appropriated.

In 2009, an arbitration process was implemented to expedite resolution of outstanding FEMA PA projects stemming from Hurricanes Katrina and Rita. This process has been designed to further recovery efforts by

---

[456] Id.

[457] See 44 CFR § 206.206(a).

[458] Id. § 206.206(c)(3).

[459] See the PA appeal database at: <http://www.fema.gov/appeals/search.do;jsessionid=1C2954502C4F95F8288E9EBFEF00DB72.Worker2Public?action=Init>.

[460] See 5 U.S.C. App. 3, Inspector General Act of 1978, Pub. L. No. 95-452 (1978), as amended by Inspector General Act Amendments of 1988, Pub. L. No. 100-504 (1988), as amended by Homeland Security Act, Pub. L. No. 107-296, § 812 (2002).

---

providing final adjudication of disputes arising from PA projects by an independent and neutral panel of arbitrators.

Pursuant to Section 601 of the American Recovery and Reinvestment Act of 2009, Public Law 111-5, 44, CFR § 206.209 establishes procedures for the arbitration to resolve disputed PA applications under the following major disaster declarations: DR-1603, DR-1604, DR-1605, DR-1606, and DR-1607. Section 601 directs the President to establish an arbitration panel under the FEMA PA program to expedite the recovery efforts from Hurricanes Katrina and Rita within the Gulf Coast region.[461] Pursuant to Section 601, the arbitration panel shall have sufficient authority regarding the award or denial of disputed PA applications for covered hurricane damage under Sections 403, 406, or 407 of the Stafford Act for a project if the total amount is more than $500,000.[462]

The relevance of PA appeals to PA arbitration is that eligibility to file a PA appeal is one of the considerations in determining whether an applicant has standing to file a PA arbitration. An applicant or subgrantee may request arbitration of a determination made by FEMA on an application for PA, provided that the total amount of the project is greater than $500,000 and provided that: (1) the subgrantee or applicant is eligible to file an appeal under 44 CFR § 206.206; or (2) the subgrantee or applicant had a first or second level appeal pending with FEMA pursuant to 44 CFR § 206.206 on or after February 17, 2009.[463] A request for arbitration under 44 CFR § 206.209 is in lieu of filing or continuing an appeal under 44 CFR § 206.206.[464] Arbitration is not available for any matter that obtained final agency action by FEMA pursuant to 44 CFR § 206.206 prior to February 17, 2009.[465] Arbitration is not available for determinations for which the applicant failed to file a timely appeal under the provisions of 44 CFR § 206.206 prior to August 31, 2009, or for determinations which received a decision on a second appeal from FEMA prior to February 17, 2009.[466]

---

[461] See http://www.gpo.gov/fdsys/pkg/PLAW-111publ5/html/PLAW-111publ5.htm.
[462] Id.
[463] See 44 CFR § 206.209(b).
[464] See 44 CFR § 206.209(d)(1).
[465] See 44 CFR § 206.209(d)(2).
[466] See 44 CFR § 206.209(d)(2).

In Section 1105 of the Sandy Recovery Improvement Act of 2013 (SRIA), Public Law 113-2, Congress established a PA arbitration pilot program that offers an arbitration option available to applicants nationwide. Applicants may utilize the SRIA arbitration pilot program if (1) the project in question is subject to a non-federal cost share; (2) the amount in dispute is $1 million or more; and (3) the applicant has pursued a first appeal and has received a decision on that first appeal from FEMA.[467] If these criteria are met, an applicant may choose to request arbitration by an independent review panel, or it may choose to file a second appeal. If an applicant requests arbitration, it may not file a second appeal.[468] The arbitration panel's decision is binding.[469] At the time of this writing, FEMA is in the process of developing procedures for this arbitration pilot program. Under the SRIA, applicants may request arbitration up until December 31, 2015.[470]

---

[467] *See* Sandy Recovery Improvement Act of 2013, Pub. L. No. 113-2, § 1105(a)(2) (2013).
[468] *Id.*, § 1105(b)(3)(A).
[469] *Id.*, § 1105(b)(2).
[470] *Id.*, § 1105(c).

Part Two:
Public Assistance and Grants Management Process

I. Steps In the PA Process for the PA Applicant

A. The Grantee, Subgrantee, and Applicant

The grantee is the government to which FEMA awards a PA grant and will generally be the state for which the disaster or emergency was declared; however, a tribal government may choose to be a grantee.[471] The applicant is the state agency, local government, or eligible PNP submitting an application to the grantee for assistance under the grant.[472] Subgrantees are the governments or other legal entities that receive FEMA PA funding through a subgrant from the state.[473] The subgrantee is accountable to the grantee, and the grantee is accountable to FEMA for the use of the funds provided. The terms "applicant" and "subgrantee" are often used interchangeably.[474]

B. The PA Process

FEMA has developed a series of standard operating procedures that provide guidance for the Agency, states, and applicants on each step of the PA process.[475] The PA process begins with the joint Preliminary Damage Assessments (PDAs) by federal, state, and local officials to determine the impact and magnitude of disaster damage and the resulting unmet needs of the public and PNP sectors and the community as a whole.[476] The PDA

---

[471] 44 C.F.R. § 206.201(e).

[472] See 44 CFR § 206.201(a).

[473] Id. § 206.201(o).

[474] The applicant applies for assistance; a subgrantee is the recipient of a subgrant from the grantee for assistance. The PA regulations may refer to applicant or subgrantee depending on the context. The PA appeals regulations found at 44 C.F.R. §206.206 refer to applicant, subgrantee, and grantee. 44 C.F.R. Part 13: Uniform Administrative Requirements for Grants and Cooperative Agreements to State and Local Governments uses the terms grantee and subgrantee.

[475] See PA SOPs 9570.2 through 9570.15 at: <http://www.fema.gov/9500-series-policy-publications >.

[476] 44 C.F.R. § 206.33.

---

findings are an essential element of the governor's request for a declaration.[477] Chapter 3, *Declarations*, discusses PDAs in detail.

One of the first events in the PA process, following a declaration that includes authorization for the PA program, is the applicants' briefing.[478] The state conducts this briefing for all potential PA applicants to explain application procedures, administrative requirements, funding, and program eligibility criteria.[479] FEMA personnel attend the meeting to answer questions about the PA Program.

Each applicant must submit an RPA[480] (as defined in *Eligibility – In General* previously in this chapter) to the grantee notifying FEMA of its intent to apply for PA in order to receive reimbursement for PA eligible costs. The RPA is the official application for FEMA's disaster assistance.

Among other general information, applicants are required to identify themselves on the RPA as a state, local government or PNP, and provide the location of damage. The RPA starts the grant process and opens the case management file, which contains general claim information as well as records of meetings, conversations, phone messages, and any special issues or concerns that may affect funding. The RPA must be submitted to the RA within 30 days after designation of the area where the damage occurred.[481]

At this point in the PA process, FEMA determines whether the applicant is eligible and whether the facility is eligible. Once an applicant files an RPA, FEMA PA staff work with the applicant to identify the scope of eligible work and derive an estimate of associated costs for each project (project formulation). The first meeting between the applicant, the state PA representative, and FEMA is called the kickoff meeting.[482] The kickoff meeting provides a much more detailed review of the PA Program. A

---

[477] Id. § 206.37(b).

[478] PA GUIDE, at 91-92. There may be more than one briefing, depending on size of the declared area and the number of possible applicants.

[479] The state may request INF for emergency work that must be performed immediately and paid for within 60 days after the declaration. *See* discussion of INF later in this chapter.

[480] 44 C.F.R. § 206.202(c), *see* FEMA Form 90-49 at http://www.fema.gov/library/viewRecord.do?id=2658.

[481] *See* 44 CFR § 206.202(c).

[482] PA HANDBOOK, at 21-22.

---

kickoff meeting is held for each applicant. The FEMA Project Specialist, who will be working with the applicant, will also be at this meeting. FEMA's Public Assistance Coordination (PAC) Crew Leader conducts the meeting. The purpose of this meeting is to advise the applicant of eligibility and documentation requirements. The PAC Crew Leader also discusses special considerations, which include insurance issues, hazard mitigation opportunities, and compliance with environmental and historic preservation laws, including floodplain management issues.

An applicant has 60 days from the first substantive meeting, usually the kickoff meeting, to identify and report damaged facilities to FEMA.[483] The PW[484] is the primary form used to document the location of damaged facilities, a description of damage, the scope of work to repair the damage, and a cost estimate.[485] The PW becomes the basis for the FEMA grant. FEMA may determine that PA funding is allowed—in accordance with the Stafford Act, FEMA regulations, and FEMA policies—for a project in whole or in part, or is not allowed for a project in whole or in part.

The RA may extend the 30-day and 60-day time limitations described previously when the grantee justifies and makes a request in writing based on extenuating circumstances beyond the grantee's or subgrantee's control.[486]

During this phase, projects are divided into small and large projects based on the monetary threshold established in the Stafford Act, which is adjusted annually.[487] The threshold for disasters declared on or after October 1, 2011, is $66,400. The Stafford Act provides simplified procedures for small projects.

FEMA or the applicant will prepare a PW for each project, identifying the eligible scope of work and a cost estimate for the eligible work.[488] Applicants may prepare the PW for small projects, but FEMA assigns

---

[483] 44 C.F.R. § 206.202(d)(1)(ii).
[484] FEMA Form 90-9.
[485] 44 C.F.R. § 206.201 (l); PA GUIDE, at 96-97; PA HANDBOOK, at 17-33; PA DIGEST, at 105.
[486] 44 C.F.R. § 206.202(f)(2).
[487] Stafford Act § 422, 42 U.S.C. § 5189; 44 C.F.R. § 206.203(c).
[488] 44 C.F.R. § 206.202(d).

project specialists to assist applicants to prepare large project PWs. When the estimated cost of work on a project is less than $1,000, FEMA does not consider the work eligible for reimbursement under the PA program.[489]

The PW must completely describe the scope of eligible work necessary to repair the damage and the scope of work must correspond to the cause of damage.[490] If part of the work is completed prior to project approval, the PW should separate that documentation from the work remaining.[491]

The PW should also document other information pertinent to the scope of work, for example:

- Eligible codes and standards;
- Evidence of pre-disaster damage;
- Reports of pre-disaster deficiencies;
- Ineligible work, such as maintenance, inactive facilities, responsibilities of OFAs, etc.;
- Hazard mitigation proposals;
- Descriptions of improved project proposals;
- Special equipment or construction needs; and
- Description of the entire complex, if the project is only a part.[492]

While FEMA may base the initial obligation of funds on estimated costs, final costs for all large projects are based on the actual cost of the work done.[493] The three primary methods of determining cost are time and materials, unit costs, and contracts.[494] FEMA uses a cost estimating format (CEF) for large projects[495] to estimate the total cost. The CEF should only be used on large projects that are 90% or less complete. Projects greater than 90% complete are not required to be estimated using the CEF. In the

---

[489] Id. § 206.202(d)(2).
[490] PA GUIDE, at 101.
[491] Id.
[492] Id.
[493] Stafford Act §§ 406(e)(1) and (2), 42 U.S.C. §§ 5172(e)(1) and (2); 44 C.F.R. §§ 13.22, 13.36 and 206.228; PA GUIDE, at 40-41, 51 and 103-108; PA DIGEST, at 108. *See* DAP 9525.1 - 9525.16, all of which discuss *"Allowable Costs"*, http://www.fema.gov/9500-series-policy-publications
[494] PA GUIDE, at 103-104.
[495] 44 C.F.R. § 206.203 (c)(1).

case of projects more than 90% complete, the actual costs of the eligible work are used with an extension of those costs to cover the remaining work.

If the work is complete at the time of the request, reimbursement is based on reasonable actual costs. If the work is not complete, FEMA obligates funds based on estimates. The state is responsible for progress payments to the applicant as actual costs are documented. Final payments will be based on documentation of payroll information, equipment logs, or usage records and by other records, such as invoices, receipts, or work orders prepared by the applicant. Under current regulations, if an applicant's actual costs come in under the CEF estimate, the difference between the estimate and actual costs will be deobligated and returned to FEMA.[496]

Following Hurricane Sandy in 2012, Congress amended the Stafford Act to provide FEMA authority to establish alternative procedures to allow grantees or subgrantees in cases where actual costs are below estimated costs to use all of part of excess funds in permanent repair or replacement work to fund (i) cost-effective activities that reduce the risk of future damage, hardship, or suffering from a major disaster; or (ii) other activities to improve future PA operations or planning; and for emergency and debris removal work projects, to allow grantees or subgrantees to use excess funds for (i) debris management planning; (ii) acquisition of debris management equipment for current or future use; and (iii) other activities to improve future debris removal operations, as determined by the Administrator.[497]

Grantees are responsible for informing subgrantees about the status of their applications, including notification of FEMA approval of subgrantees' PWs and estimates of when FEMA will make payments.[498] Grantees must also pay the full amount due to subgrantees, including the state matching fund contribution, as soon as practicable after FEMA approves payment.[499]

---

[496] 44 CFR §§ 206.207, 206.228; DAP 9529.9
[497] Disaster Relief Appropriations Act of 2013, Pub. L. No. 113-2, § 102. (2013). FEMA is currently in the process of drafting regulations to implement these provisions. Check with OCC for further information.
[498] Id. § 206.200(b)(2)(i).
[499] Id. § 206.200(b)(2)(ii).

The grantee is accountable to FEMA as grant administrator for all funds provided under the PA program, including:

- Providing technical advice and assistance to eligible subgrantees;
- Providing state or tribal support for project identification activities including small and large projects and validating small projects; and
- Ensuring that all potential applicants are aware of PA grant funding availability, and submitting the necessary documents for grant award.[500]

C. State Administrative Plan (SAP)

Before disaster strikes, each state must have in place a comprehensive plan, which it reviews and updates annually as appropriate, under which it will administer FEMA PA grants.[501]

The plan must, at a minimum, include the following details:

- The state agency with primary responsibility for PA program administration;
- The staffing functions and the sources of staff to fill the functions; and
- Management and oversight responsibilities of each staff function.

The SAP must provide comprehensive procedures for each phase of the PA Program from post-incident damage assessments to PA Program closeout.[502] The specific contents required for SAPs are set forth in FEMA regulations.[503] An approved plan must be on file with FEMA before grants will be approved in a future major disaster; further, the grantee must incorporate the administrative plan into its state emergency plan.[504]

---

[500] Id. § 206.202(b).
[501] Id. § 206.207(b).
[502] Id.
[503] Id.
[504] 44 C.F. R. § 206.207(b)(3) and(4).

II. Applicant Compliance with Procurement Requirements

A. Introduction to the Procurement Process

FEMA's review of PA Program grants and those entities which receive PA grants are subject to several federal requirements beyond those in the Stafford Act.[505] These requirements include: the Uniform Administrative Requirements for Grants and Cooperative Agreements to State and Local Governments [hereinafter FEMA's Common Rule];[506] and OMB Circular A-110 (Uniform Administrative Requirements for Grants and Agreements with Institutions of Higher Education, Hospitals, and Other Nonprofit Organizations).[507] These set the minimum requirements for grantee and subgrantee procurement standards for federal grants. The Common Rule contains specific rules applicable to state, tribal, and local procurements involving federal grant funds.[508]

It is virtually inevitable that PA applicants will need to procure goods or services (including construction) as they repair their damaged facilities with PA grant funds. This section reviews the requirements that applicants must follow in acquiring goods and services. As noted previously, the Common Rule does not apply to non-profit organizations, including schools and hospitals, but in reviewing both the Common Rule and OMB Circular A-110, the relevant comparable provisions in the two documents have significant similarities.

---

[505] *See* generally, 44 CFR Part 13, 2 CFR Parts 215, 220, 225, 230; RP 9580.212,*Public Assistance Grant Contracting Frequently Asked Questions.*
[506] *44 C.F.R. Part 13, the Uniform Administrative Requirements for Grants and Cooperative Agreements to State and Local Governments.* These requirements in a similar form are in each federal agency's regulations. On March 12, 1987, the President directed the federal grant-making agencies to issue a grants management common rule to adopt government-wide terms and conditions for grants to states and local governments. In 1988, OMB revised Circular A-102 to include guidance to federal agencies on matters not covered by the Grants Management Common Rule. The attachments to Circular A-102 were replaced by the Grants Management Common Rule. OMB maintains a chart which includes the locations of federal agency codifications of the Common Rule.
[507] OMB Circular A-110 [hereinafter OMB Circular A-110], http://www.whitehouse.gov/omb/circulars_a110/ which is now codified in 2 C.F.R. Part 215.
[508] 44 C.F.R. § 13.36.

B. Procurement Standards for Grantees and Subgrantees

States must use the same policies and procedures for procurements using federal grant funds as they use for procurements using non-federal grant funds.[509] States must also ensure that all purchase orders or other contracts they enter into using PA funds contain any clauses required by federal statute and regulations.[510] Non-state grantees[511] and subgrantees[512] must use their own procurement procedures that reflect state and local procurement and contracting rules, provided that the procurements conform to applicable federal law and standards identified in the Common Rule.[513] Non-profit organizations must follow similar procedures in OMB Circular A-110.[514] If the grantee or subgrantee does not follow these procurement procedures, they risk losing PA program funding.

These procedures and requirements include that the grantee:

- Must have a contract administration system;[515]

- Must have a written code of standards for its employees regarding conflicts of interest;[516]

---

[509] Id. § 13.36(a).

[510] Id.

[511] A grantee is also a "state" as defined in the Stafford Act § 102(4), 44 U.S.C. 5122(4), or an "Indian tribe or authorized tribal organization, or Alaska Native village or organization," as defined in the Stafford Act at §102(7)(B), 44 U.S.C. 5122(7)(B).

[512] States and other grantee requirements for subgrantees are set forth at 44 C.F.R. § 13.37.

[513] Id. § 13.36(b)(1). This section is not applicable to state grantees. See 13.36(a).

[514] 2 C.F.R. Part 215.

[515] 44 C.F.R. 13.36(b)(2). This system ensures that contractors perform in accordance with the terms, conditions, and specifications of their contracts. Verbal agreements between a grantee and a contractor are not appropriate, do not comply with program procedures, and do not normally result in generating program-required documentation. See PA Appeal Jefferson Parish, PA ID # 051-99051-00, FEMA-1603-DR-LA (2008). Applicant and contractor had a sole source, noncompetitive verbal contract for mold remediation/stabilization work. After the work was completed, the Parish signed the contract. The detailed scope of work and cost estimate for the projects that FEMA requires did not exist. FEMA then inspected the facilities and developed the scope of work. This later appeal resulted in Jefferson Parish receiving less than half of its claim for reimbursement. On appeal, the parish was told that it had not complied with federal procurement requirements contained in 44 C.F.R. § 13.36 and had not provided sufficient detail about the scope of work for which it sought reimbursement.

[516] 44 C.F.R. § 13.36. See subsection I, *General Applicant Contract Provisions*.

- Must have a system to assure economical purchases and avoid unnecessary ones;[517]

- Encourage lower prices by using:
  - State and local intergovernmental agreements to obtain common goods and services;[518]
  - Federal excess or surplus property;
  - Value engineering analysis for each item in contracts for large construction projects; [519]

- Use only responsible contractors;[520]

- Must maintain sufficient records to detail a procurement's history, such as;
  - Rationale for the procurement method;
  - Selection of contract type;
  - Contractor selection or rejection; and
  - Basis for the contract price;[521]

- May use time and materials contract only under certain circumstances;[522]

- Must be responsible for settling all contractual and administrative claims; and

---

[517] In addition, where appropriate, the grantees and subgrantees must undertake an analysis concerning lease versus purchase decisions and any other economical approach.
[518] 44 C.F.R. § 13.36 (b)(5).
[519] Value engineering is a systemic and creative analysis of each contract item or task to ensure that its essential function is provided at the overall lower cost. See 44 C.F.R. § 13.36(b)(7).
[520] 44 C.F.R. § 13.36(b)(6-8). Grantees and subgrantees should use only reputable and qualified contractors with a history of integrity, compliance with public policy from their past performance, and the requisite financial and technical resources. FEMA does not endorse, recommend, or approve any contractors, including those in a registry of online debris contractors that FEMA developed to assist state and local governments in identifying and contacting contractor resources.
[521] 44 C.F.R. § 13.36(b)(9).
[522] 44 C.F.R. § 13.36(b)(10). There is no comparable section in 2 C.F.R. Part 215. Note also that FEMA restricts time and materials contracts generally to 70 hours for work immediately after a disaster when a clear scope of work cannot be determined. PA GUIDE, at 53; PA DIGEST, at 23; PA DEBRIS GUIDE, at 99.

- Must have protest procedures:[523]

  o Protest procedures exist to handle procurement disputes, and grantees and subgrantees will usually have protest procedures in their procurement regulations to resolve disputes;

- Grantees and subgrantees must disclose any protests to FEMA;

  o Protesters must exhaust all administrative processes with the grantee before pursuing a protest with FEMA;[524]

  o FEMA's review of a protest is limited to reviewing violations of federal law and violations of the grantee's protest procedures.[525]

In addition, states must ensure that every subgrant contain all clauses that federal statute and executive orders and their implementing regulations require and make certain that subgrantees are aware of applicable federal and state rules and requirements.[526] They must ensure that there is a provision requiring subgrantees to retain records and provide reasonable access to the required records.[527] States must also conform any advances of grant funds to subgrantees to the same standards of timing and amounts that apply to cash advances by federal agencies.[528] All grantees must follow the provisions of the Common Rule[529] and ensure that every subgrant includes a provision for compliance with these provisions as well. Grantees should make every effort to ensure that their subgrantees understand these requirements.

C. Competition Requirements

In general, open and unfettered competition for emergency work (FEMA PA Categories A and B) and permanent work (FEMA PA Categories C-G) is the rule. The grant provisions in the Common Rule set forth a full

---

[523] Id. § 13.36(b)(12)(ii).
[524] Id. § 13.36(b)(12).
[525] Id. § 13.36(b)(12)(ii).
[526] Id. § 13.37(a)(1).
[527] Id. § 13.37(a)(3).
[528] Id. § 13.37(a)(4); see also 44 C.F.R. § 13.20(b)(7), and §13.21(c) and (e).
[529] 44 C.F.R. Part 13.

competition requirement unless an exception authorizes otherwise.[530] Even if a grantee carries out competitive procurement, there can still be situations that FEMA considers restrictive of competition and therefore not in the spirit of full and open competition.

These can include:

- Requiring unnecessary experience and excessive bonding;
- Placing unreasonable requirements on firms in order for them to qualify to do business;
- Noncompetitive pricing practices between firms or between affiliated companies;
- Noncompetitive awards to consultants that are on retainer contracts;
- Organizational conflicts of interest;
- Specifying only a brand name product instead of allowing an equal product to be offered; and
- Any arbitrary action in the procurement process.[531]

OMB Circular A-110 requires that non-profit organizations make awards to a bidder or offeror whose bid or offer is responsive to the solicitation and is most advantageous to the recipient, when the organization considers price, quality, and other factors. In addition, the solicitations must clearly set forth all requirements that the bidder or offeror must fulfill in order to evaluate the offer. The organization may reject any and all bids when it is in the organization's best interests to do so.

D. Reasonable Cost Requirement

A reasonable cost is defined as a cost that, in its nature and amount, does not exceed that which would be incurred by a prudent person under the circumstances prevailing at the time the decision was made to incur the

---

[530] 44 C.F.R. § 13.36(c).
[531] 44 C.F.R. § 13.36(c)(1)(i-vii).

cost.[532] Considerations include evaluating historical costs for similar work in the region, reviewing published unit cost data for the work, and comparing costs with the FEMA Schedule of Equipment Rates and Cost Codes.[533] The source of costs may include the applicant's force account labor, equipment and materials, contracted services, and mutual aid agreements. Regardless of the terms of an applicant's contract, all costs must be reasonable and meet PA Program eligibility rules for PA reimbursement.[534]

FEMA may review proposed or existing contracts for compliance with eligibility rules and reasonableness of costs, but such a review does not constitute approval.[535] Moreover, grantee contractual obligations do not bind FEMA because FEMA is not a party to the contracts; thus, the grantee is responsible for paying for its contracts regardless of whether FEMA reimburses for the costs.[536]

When an applicant fails to use a competitive process, or uses a flawed process in violation of the Common Rule, FEMA may disallow all or part of the costs.[537]

Notwithstanding noncompliance with procurement requirements, however, FEMA may choose to reimburse the applicant for its reasonable costs. FEMA may determine reasonable costs by analyzing the applicant's procurement process, historical documentation, what other applicants in

---

[532] See OMB Circulars A-87, *Cost Principles for State, Local, and Indian Tribal Governments* and A-122, *Cost Principles for Non-Profit Organizations. See also,* discussion about cost principles in *Management Costs* later in this chapter.

[533] FEMA maintains a national unit price listing called "Cost Codes" that FEMA updates and revises to conform to geographical and disaster-specific needs. See PA DIGEST, at 24, < http://www.fema.gov/sites/default/files/orig/fema_pdfs/pdf/government/grant/pa/pd igest08.pdf>.

[534] See, e.g., 44 C.F.R. §§ 206.222, 223, 226, and 228; see also PA Appeal Harrison County, PA, ID # 047-99047-00, FEMA-1604-DR-MS (2008). High winds and heavy rainfall necessitated removing hazardous trees and limbs from public and private property. Applicant properly contracted for this work, but some work was performed on roads outside of its jurisdiction. As such, the applicant did not have legal responsibility for those roads, and the costs were ineligible for reimbursement.

[535] PA GUIDE, at 53.

[536] 44 C.F.R. § 13.36(b)(11).

[537] 44 C.F.R. § 13.43(a).

the same disaster are paying for like work, or published cost codes.[538] The DHS Inspector General has issued a report discussing the importance of only reimbursing costs that are reasonable or otherwise following the Common Rule.[539]

The reasonable cost requirement applies to all contract costs for the performance of eligible work: labor, materials, and equipment. FEMA takes a proactive approach by reviewing and documenting an applicant's procurement and contracting procedures in an effort to communicate risks to reimbursement.[540]

In addition, the Common Rule allows a reasonable profit for the contractor (but not for the grantee or subgrantee). Grantees and subgrantees must negotiate profit as a separate element of the price for each contract in which there is no price competition and in all cases where they perform a cost analysis. To establish a fair and reasonable profit, grantees and subgrantees should consider the complexity of the work the contractor is to perform, the risk that the contractor will bear, the contractor's investment, the amount of subcontracting, the quality of the contractor's record of past performance, and industry profit rates in the surrounding geographical area for similar work.[541] The geographic area served is the state, county, congressional district, and/or metropolitan statistical area where the vendor provides or delivers products and/or services.[542]

---

[538] See also 44 C.F.R. §§ 206.228 and 13.22; PA DIGEST, at 108; PA GUIDE, at 40-41, Office of Management and Budget (OMB) Circular A-87 Cost Principles for State, Local, and Indian Tribal Governments, 69 Fed. Reg. 25,920, 25,980-25,987 (2004); See http://www.whitehouse.gov/omb/circulars_a087_2004/.

[539] DEPARTMENT OF HOMELAND SECURITY, OFFICE OF INSPECTOR GENERAL, Audit Tips for Managing Disaster-Related Project Costs, at 6 – 8 (2011), < http://www.oig.dhs.gov/assets/Audit_Tips.pdf >. The OIG has recommended in audit reports that a complete de-obligation is required if the applicant implemented a flawed procurement process.

[540] PA HANDBOOK, at 21-22.

[541] 44 C.F.R. § 13.36(f)(2).

[542] This information is collected to identify prospective contractors that can deliver emergency supplies and services needed in a specific disaster area. Additional information on Metropolitan Statistical Areas may be found at http://www.whitehouse.gov/sites/default/files/omb/assets/bulletins/b10-02.pdf

---

E. Selection Processes for Procurement

FEMA requires grantees to be able to provide the detail of procurement transactions, including: the rationale for the method of procurement, the selection of contract type, contractor selection or rejection, and the basis for those decisions, as well as the basis for the contract price.[543] The selection procedures should incorporate a clear and accurate description of the technical requirements for the material, product, or service that the grantee or subgrantee wishes to procure. Regulations forbid features that unduly restrict competition and require that the applicant for federal funds identify all technical requirements or specifications.[544] This chapter discusses limited exceptions to this rule. In addition, before receiving bids, grantees must make independent estimates. FEMA may require applicants to submit this cost analysis and other documentation pre-award to FEMA for review.[545] If adequate price competition is lacking, documented cost analysis will be essential to demonstrate price reasonableness.

F. Procurement Methods

FEMA regulations[546] allow the following procurement methods:

1. Procurement by Small Purchase Procedures under $150,000

In procurement by small purchase procedures,[547] the applicant must obtain price or rate quotations from an adequate number of qualified sources.[548]

---

[543] 44 C.F.R. § 13.36(b)(9).
[544] 44 C.F.R. § 13.36(c)(3)(i).
[545] Id. § 13.36(d)(4)(iii).
[546] 44 C.F.R. Part 13.
[547] Id. § 13.36(d)(1). Currently, the maximum is set at $150,000. See 75 Fed. Reg. 53,129 (2010), as authorized under the Ronald Reagan National Defense Authorization Act for FY 2005, Pub. L. No. 108-375, § 807, modifying 41 U.S.C. § 403(11).
[548] Id.

---

2. Procurement by Sealed Bids

In procurement by sealed bids[549] grantees and subgrantees must publicly advertise bids and solicit bids from a number of known suppliers, providing them sufficient time prior to the date set for opening bids. The invitation to bid must be specific and must clearly define items or services clearly so bidders can respond. Grantees and subgrantees must publicly open all bids at the time and place set in the invitation for bids. They may reject any or all bids if there are sound, documented reasons. The lowest responsive and responsible bidder will receive a firm fixed-price (lump sum or unit price) written contract. This sealed bid method is the preferred method for procuring construction if the following are true:

- A complete, adequate, and realistic specification or purchase description is available;

- Two or more responsible bidders are willing and able to compete; and

- The procurement lends itself to a firm fixed price contract and the selection can be made on the basis of price.

3. Procurement by Competitive Proposals

Applicants use procurement by competitive proposals[550] where the competitors' qualifications are of the utmost importance and price is not the critical issue. Fair and reasonable compensation is, however, a factor. Generally, applicants use this method when conditions are not appropriate for the use of sealed bids. For example, applicants use this method in the procurement of qualifications-based procurements, such as architectural or engineering professional services. Normally, more than one source submits an offer, and applicants award either a fixed-price or cost-reimbursement type contract. To use this method, applicants must publicize requests for proposals and identify all evaluation factors and their relative importance. Applicants must solicit proposals from an adequate number of qualified sources. Grantees should have a method for conducting technical evaluations of the proposals and for selecting

---

[549] Id. § 13.36(d)(2).
[550] Id. § 13.36(d)(3).

---

awardees. The responsible firm, whose proposal is most advantageous to the program, when the grantee or subgrantee considers price and other factors, will receive the award.

4. Procurement by Noncompetitive Proposals and Contracting When a Public Exigency or Emergency Exists

Procurement by noncompetitive proposals[551] is procurement through solicitation of a proposal from only one source, or after solicitation of a number of sources, competition is determined inadequate.[552] This method is the least favored method and may only be used if other procurement methods described in 44 CFR Part 13 are infeasible. In other words, all contracts should be competitively bid unless one of the exceptions discussed in this subsection apply.

For this type of procurement to be used, FEMA requires a cost-analysis, that is, the grantee must verify the proposed cost data, projections of the data and evaluation of the specific elements of cost and profit.[553] A cost analysis is important to establish the reasonableness of the proposed contract price, particularly with sole source solicitations, when adequate price competition is limited and the contracts involve professional, consulting or engineering/architectural services.[554] The method and degree of the cost analysis are dependent on the facts surrounding the procurement.

Grantees may use procurement by noncompetitive proposals only when the award of a contract is infeasible under the other methods of procurement described in this chapter and the public exigency or emergency will not permit a delay resulting from the amount of time required to obtain competitive bidding.[555] This situation occurs in the PA program most frequently with emergency debris removal, for instance, trimming and removing dangerous tree limbs or clearing roads for emergency access. It is important not to confuse this type of emergency

---

[551] Id. § 13.36(d)(4).
[552] Id.
[553] Id. § 13.3(d)(4)(ii).
[554] Id. § 13.36(f)(1).
[555] 44 C.F.R. 13.36(d)(4)(i)(B).

contracting with FEMA's division of disaster work into "emergency" and "permanent" work. Performing emergency work (Categories A and B) does not relieve the applicant from the requirements of competitive bidding; not all emergency work is time sensitive to the point where competitive bidding is infeasible.[556] Grantees and subgrantees thus cannot justify awarding a noncompetitive contract simply by using the term "emergency work,"[557] and grantees also should not make noncompetitive bid awards for work lasting for several days or weeks after the disaster or for long-term debris removal. FEMA will determine eligibility for reimbursement based upon a review of the facts.

Only FEMA has the authority to make eligibility decisions. Contractors cannot make eligibility determinations or determine what is appropriate emergency contracting or emergency work.[558]

FEMA may approve reimbursement under a time and materials contract for work that is necessary immediately after a disaster but generally only for the first 70 hours of necessary work immediately after the disaster when a clear scope of work cannot be developed.[559] For example, FEMA may allow limited use of these contracts when necessary debris removal work is needed immediately after a disaster, when a clear scope of work cannot be developed, the work will not exceed 70 hours, and only after it has been determined that no other contract is suitable and the contract contains a ceiling price that the contractor exceeds at its own risk.[560] If the work is to last longer, the grantee or subgrantee should seek

---

[556] Fact Sheet 9580.4, Emergency Work Contracting [hereinafter FS 9580.4, Emergency Contracting] (2008), <
http://wyohomelandsecurity.state.wy.us/Library/DisasterInformationReportsForms/FEM APolicies/EmergencyWorkContracting.pdf>.

[557] See, e.g. Housing Authority of New Orleans, File No. 071-U8M7N-00, FEMA-1603-DR-LA (2000). Eligible debris removal work must be necessary to eliminate an immediate threat to life, public health, and safety. The applicant did not demonstrate that the removal of shrubs and bushes, delivery of mulch, and delivery and placement of sand in ponding areas were necessary to eliminate an immediate threat. Additionally, not being informed of monitoring and documentation requirements is not an argument that will win an appeal.

[558] PA Debris Guide, at 23 and 94; DAP 9580.4, Fact Sheet: Emergency Work Contracting, at 2; RP 9580.201, Recovery Fact Sheet,: Debris Contracting Guidance, at 4.

[559] PA GUIDE, at 53. PA DEBRIS GUIDE, at 99-100.

[560] RP Fact Sheet 9580.201(2010), <
http://regulations.justia.com/regulations/fedreg/2010/06/15/2010-14289.html>.

competitive bids for the work as soon as possible.[561] An applicant should consult FEMA when it is considering using a time and materials contract.

In some cases, a grantee or subgrantee may use an expedited procurement process that allows for shorter time frames for receiving competitive bid proposals where time is of the essence, such as for debris removal.[562] For example, a grantee might develop a scope-of-work, identify contractors that can do the work, and make telephone invitations for bids.[563] In addition, prior to a disaster, grantees may take affirmative steps to expedite the procurement process without jeopardizing potential grant funding, including:[564]

- **Pre-drafted contracts:** Grantees may draft a contract prior to a disaster event. Once the extent of the disaster is known, the contract can then be completed with the appropriate scope of work and advertised in a timely manner.

- **Pre-qualified contractors:** Contractors typically must have insurance, bonding, and licensing prior to an applicant awarding them a contract. Grantees may advertise a request for qualifications for contractors to establish their company as a credible candidate for a contract award. The grantee may then invite the pre-qualified contractors on the list to bid on a contract on an as-needed basis. The pre-qualified contractor can then focus on developing a cost estimate rather than assembling documentation in order to qualify for bidding. This approach may save the grantee time in getting the contract awarded.

- **Pre-event contracts:** A grantee may choose to solicit bids and award contracts in non-disaster times. This approach allows time for a deliberate procurement process and gives applicants flexibility in mobilizing the appropriate resources in anticipation of an event. Pre-event contracts can result in higher costs, and grantees should

---

[561] 44 C.F.R. § 13.36(b)(10); FS 9580.4, *Emergency Work Contracting*. *See also* explanation charts of contract types in PA DEBRIS GUIDE, at 101-103.

[562] DAP 9580.4, Fact Sheet, Emergency Work Contracting, at 1.

[563] FEMA 9580.4, January 19, 2001, Fact Sheet: Debris Operations –Clarification, Emergency Contracting vs. Emergency Work, at 2.

[564] PA DEBRIS GUIDE, at 95.

---

be careful to ensure the proposed scopes of work provide flexibility for a variety of event types and sizes.

G. Procurement Documentation

When grantees and subgrantees follow the proper procurement rules, the process of so doing naturally generates documentation. FEMA requires this documentation.[565] Procurement documentation must be available for review for compliance with applicable federal law. Documentation includes the scope of work or the contract, number of bidders, and each bidder's unit cost or lump sum, and the reasons for disqualifying a bidder.

Before receiving bids, grantees and subgrantees must make independent cost estimates. FEMA may require grantees and subgrantees to submit this cost analysis and other documentation pre-award to FEMA for review.[566] If adequate price competition is lacking, documented cost analysis will be essential to demonstrate price reasonableness.

H. FEMA Review of Grantee and Subgrantee Contracts

FEMA's review of documented procurement activity may take place at various times during the life of a PA project, ranging from pre-award of the contract to closeout of the project. When FEMA believes it is necessary to ensure that the item and/or service specified in the project is the one being proposed for purchase, the grantee must make available to FEMA technical specifications on proposed procurements.[567] This review generally takes place before the grantee or subgrantee even publishes the solicitation, but it can take place afterwards as well.[568] Upon request, the grantee or subgrantee must make available for pre-award review the procurement documents, such as requests for proposals, invitations for bids, responses to the invitations, independent cost estimates, etc. This information is critical, particularly when the grantees' procedures do not comply with Part 13.[569] The grantee or subgrantee must also make

---

[565] 44 C.F.R. § 13.36(c)(3).
[566] Id. § 13.36(d)(4)(iii).
[567] Id. § 13.36(g)(1).
[568] Id.
[569] Id. § 13.36(g)(2)(i).

available the information in the following circumstances when the procurement is over the simplified acquisition threshold:

- When the grantee or subgrantee's procurement procedures fail to comply with the procurement standards in Part 13;

- When the project is awarded without competition, or only one bid is received in response to a solicitation;[570]

- When the procurement specifies a brand name;[571]

- When the contract is awarded to other than the lowest bidder under a sealed bid procurement process;[572] and

- When a proposed contract modification changes the scope of a contract or increases the contract amount by more than the simplified acquisition threshold.[573]

The grantee or subgrantee must provide written justification when there is an exception to full and open competition.

I. General Applicant Contract Provisions

FEMA recognizes three types of contracts for reimbursement:

- **Lump sum**: a contract for work within a prescribed boundary with a clearly defined scope and a total price;

- **Unit price**: contract for work done on an item-by-item basis with cost determined per unit; and

- **Cost-plus-fixed-fee**: either a lump sum or unit price contract with a fixed contractor fee added into the price.

---

[570] Id. § 13.36(g)(2)(ii).
[571] Id. § 13.36(g)(2)(iii).
[572] Id. § 13.36(g)(2)(ii); 41 U.S.C.403(11).
[573] Id. § 13.36(g)(2)(v).

Every applicant contract should be in writing. There are many reasons to spell out contract terms besides avoiding confusion, misinterpretation, mistake, and delay. One of the ancillary benefits of a written contract is that it produces the necessary documentation to assist with writing PWs and can demonstrate price reasonableness to justify FEMA reimbursement. Because FEMA will only pay for reasonable and eligible costs, in the absence of a written contract, it is extremely difficult to quantify reasonable costs and justify eligibility. Minimum documentation for a PW and a contract are described at length in "Elements of a Project Worksheet."[574]

In addition, every contract must contain certain specific items. Federal law requires the following contract terms:[575]

- The administrative, contractual, and legal remedies when contractors breach the contract, including sanctions and penalties for such breach with contracts over the simplified acquisition threshold;[576]

- A process for grantee termination of the contract for cause or convenience and the basis for settlement for contracts over $10,000;

- In contracts over $10,000, provisions assuring that the parties will comply with all applicable federal and state regulations;[577]

---

[574] Fact Sheet: 9580.5, *Elements of a Project Worksheet* (2008), http://www.fema.gov/pdf/government/grant/pa/9580_5.pdf
[575] 44 C.F.R. 13.36(i)(1)-(13).
[576] Currently, the "simplified acquisition threshold" is $150,000. *See* 41 U.S.C. § 403(11).
[577] These include: EXEC. ORDER 11246 (1965), *Equal Employment Opportunity* (1965), 30 Fed. Reg. 12,319 (1965), 3 C.F.R., 1964-1965 Comp. at 339, amended by EXEC. ORDER 11375 (1967), 32 Fed. Reg. 14,303 (1965), 3 C.F.R., 1966-1970 Comp. at 684; 41 C.F.R. Chapter 60; Copeland "Anti-Kickback" Act, 18 U.S.C. § 874; 29 C.F.R. Part 3; Contract Work Hours and Safety Standards Act §§ 103 and 107, 40 U.S.C. §§ 327 and 330; 29 C.F.R. Part 5 for construction contracts grantees award in excess of $2,000 and in excess of $2,500 for other contracts that involve the employment of mechanics or laborers; EXEC. ORDER 11738 (1973), 38 Fed. Reg. 25,161 (1965), 3 C.F.R., 1971-1975 Comp. at 799; Clean Air Act § 306, 42 U.S.C. § 1857(h); Clean Water Act § 508, 33 U.S.C. § 1368; Environmental Protection Agency regulations found at 40 C.F.R. Part 15 for all contracts in excess of $100,000; and compliance with mandatory standards and policies relating to

- FEMA's requirements and regulations pertaining to reporting;

- FEMA's requirements and regulations pertaining to copyrights, rights in data, and patent rights with respect to any discovery or invention arising or developed in the course of or under the contract;

- Access by FEMA, the grantee, subgrantee, the Comptroller General of the U.S. or any of their duly authorized representatives to any contractor books, documents, papers, and records that are directly pertinent to that specific contract for the purpose of audit, examination, excerpts, and transcriptions;

- Terms insuring retention of all required records for three years after final payment is made and all other pending matters are closed; and

- Language indicating that FEMA will only pay FEMA-determined eligible work and a time frame for required reporting and invoices.

J. Contract Prohibitions

1. Conflicts of Interest

The grantee must abide by FEMA's conflict of interest regulations.[578] Grantees and subgrantees must maintain a written code of standards regarding conduct of their employees engaged in procurement. This code of standards shall provide penalties, sanctions, or other disciplinary actions, to the extent that these sanctions do not violate state law. One basic rule is that no employee, officer, or agent of the grantee shall participate in selection, award, or administration of a contract supported by federal funds if a conflict of interest, real or apparent, would be involved.[579] A conflict would arise if the employee, officer or agent, any member of his or her immediate family, his or her partner, or any

---

energy efficiency contained in the state energy conservation plan issued in compliance with the Energy Policy and Conservation Act of 1975, Pub. L. No. 94-163, 89 Stat. 871. *See generally,* 44 C.F.R. §§ 13.36(a) and (i)(3-6,12).
[578] 44 C.F.R. § 13.36(b)(3)(i-iv).
[579] Id. § 13.36(b)(3).

---

organization that employs or is about to employ any of those named has a financial or other interest in the firm the applicant selects for the contract.[580] Further, the grantee's officers, employees, or agents cannot solicit or accept gratuities, favors, or anything of monetary value from contractors, potential contractors, or parties to sub agreements.[581] It is important to note, as well, that ethical violations can rise to the level of criminal prosecution.

2. No Contracts to Suspended/Debarred Entities

Suspension and debarment are administrative tools to address waste, fraud, abuse, poor performance, program noncompliance, or other misconduct. "Debarment" means action taken by a debarring official to exclude a contractor from government contracting and government-approved subcontracting for a reasonable, specified period.[582] A contractor that is excluded is "debarred." "Suspension" means action taken by a suspending official to disqualify a contractor temporarily from government contracting and government-approved subcontracting. A contractor that is disqualified is "suspended."[583] Contracts awarded to suspended or debarred contractors are prohibited.[584] Suspension and debarment actions thus prevent companies and individuals from participating in government contracts, subcontracts, loans, grants, and other assistance programs. The effect of a federal agency's suspension and debarment is government-wide.[585] In short, suspension and debarment actions protect the government from doing business with individuals, companies, or recipients who pose a business risk to the government. The federal government should list entities that are debarred or suspended

---

[580] Id.

[581] Id.

[582] 2 C.F.R. §§ 180.865 and 180.925.

[583] Office of Management and Budget Circular A-102, *Grants and Cooperative Agreements with State and Local Governments* (1994), as amended by, 62 Fed. Reg. 45934 (1997); EXEC. ORDER 12549, *Debarment and Suspension* (1986), 51 Fed. Reg. 6370 (1986), 3 C.F.R. 1986 Comp., p. 189; 44 C.F.R. § 13.35.

[584] Id.

[585] *See* 2 C.F.R. Part 180 and 2 C.F.R. Part 1532; EXEC. ORDER 12549, *Debarment and Suspension*, (1986).

from doing business with the federal government on the Excluded Parties List System (EPLS).[586]

Suspension, for a set period of time determined on a case-by-case basis, may be based on indictments, information, or adequate evidence involving environmental crimes, contract fraud, embezzlement, theft, forgery, bribery, poor performance, nonperformance, or false statements.[587] They are temporary actions that may last up to 18 months and are effective immediately.[588] Debarment may be based on convictions, civil judgments, or fact-based cases involving crimes, contract fraud, embezzlement, theft, forgery, bribery, poor performance, nonperformance, or false statements, as well as other causes.[589] Statutory debarments occur by operation of law following criminal convictions under certain laws, i.e., the Clean Water Act and Clean Air Act.[590] These last until the debarring official certifies that the condition giving rise to the conviction has been corrected. Suspensions and debarments can be extended to include subsidiaries, parent companies, and other individuals.[591]

FEMA is required to establish procedures for the effective use of the EPLS, as well as procedures to provide for effective use and dissemination of the list to assure that grantees and subgrantees at any tier do not make awards to suspended or debarred entities.[592] As of the date of this publication, FEMA has not established these procedures.

---

[586] The purpose of EPLS is to provide a single comprehensive list of individuals and firms excluded by federal government agencies throughout the federal government from receiving federal contracts or federally approved subcontracts and from certain types of federal financial and nonfinancial assistance and benefits. The EPLS is an electronic, web-based system. The user is able to search, view, and download both current and archived exclusions. When a federal agency takes an action to exclude a person under the non-procurement or procurement debarment and suspension system, the agency enters the information about the excluded person into the EPLS; https://www.epls.gov/.
[587] 2 C.F.R. §§ 180.700 and 180.800.
[588] 2 C.F.R. § 180.760.
[589] 2 C.F.R. § 180.800.
[590] See 2 C .F.R. Part 1532.
[591] 2 C..F.R. § 180.625
[592] Office of Management and Budget Circular A-102, § (6)(d), *Grants and Cooperative Agreements with State and Local Governments* (1994), as amended by, 62 Fed. Reg. 45,934 (1997).

3. Prohibited Contract Terms

The Common Rule does not permit applicants to use a cost plus percentage-of-cost contract.[593] Simply calling the percentage on top of the contract an "administrative fee" will also not be acceptable to FEMA.[594]

FEMA disfavors "piggyback" contracts. A piggyback contract occurs when one applicant utilizes a contract awarded by another applicant and simply expands the existing contract to encompass new work. For example, County A may utilize County B's debris removal contract by changing the scope of work to include County A's geographical jurisdiction. Even if County B's contract was competitively awarded, the bids received and contract awarded would not have been based on County A's scope of work. Piggybacking may be legal under applicable state law, but the use of such a contract will jeopardize FEMA funding.[595]

If the applicant uses prohibited contracts or terms, FEMA may deny funding all together or determine what it considers fair, reasonable, and eligible under the circumstances and reimburse accordingly.[596]

4. Prohibition against Discrimination

FEMA does not tolerate discrimination. The Stafford Act requires that all governmental bodies and other organizations involved in the distribution of assistance or supplies or other relief activities comply with all federal and state nondiscrimination regulations.[597] The Stafford Act and its regulations forbid discrimination on the grounds of race, color, religion, nationality, sex, age, disability, English proficiency, or economic status.[598]

---

[593] 44 C.F.R. § 13.36(f)(4).
[594] A markup of 10% on a subcontract constituted a prohibited cost-plus-percentage-of-cost method of contracting, and there was no substantiation of the reasonableness of a 10% profit. PA Appeal *City of Hoisington*, PA ID # 009-32550-00, FEMA-1366-DR-KS (2007).
[595] Piggyback contracts do not meet the requirements of 44 C.F.R. Part 13. RP Fact Sheet 9580.201, *Debris Contracting Guidance*, at 5.
[596] 44 C.F.R. § 13.43(a).
[597] Stafford Act § 308, 42 U.S.C. § 5151.
[598] *Id.*

In addition, the Common Rule favors small firms, minority firms, women's business enterprises, and labor surplus area firms when possible.[599] Affirmative steps to this end include:

- Placing qualified small and minority businesses and women's business enterprises on solicitation lists;

- Assuring that the grantees and subgrantees solicit small and minority business and women's business enterprises whenever they are potential sources;

- Dividing total requirements, when economically feasible, into smaller tasks or quantities to permit maximum participation by small and minority business and women's business enterprises;

- Establishing delivery schedules where the requirement permits which encourage participation by small and minority business, and women's business enterprises;

- Using the services and assistance of the SBA and the Minority Business Development Agency of the Department of Commerce; and

- Requiring the prime contractor, if subcontracts are let, to take these same affirmatives steps as well.[600]

K. Bonds

A bond is a written instrument that a bidder or contractor executes with a second party, generally, an insurance company or a bank, to assure fulfillment of the contractor's obligations to a third party identified in the bond. In the PA Program, the grantee is usually the third party identified in the bond. If the contractor's obligations are not met, the bond assures payment up to the amount of the bond for any loss that the grantee sustains. Whether the bond is for service or construction contracts, it assures the federal government that a prospective contractor is capable of fulfilling the contract requirements. For contracts over the simplified acquisition threshold,[601] after FEMA determines that the grantee has

---

[599] 44 C.F.R. § 13.36(e).
[600] Id.
[601] See generally, 44 C.F.R. §§ 13.36(a) and (i)(3-6,12); 44 C.F.R. § 13.36(b)(3(i-iv).

adequately protected the federal government's interests, FEMA may accept whatever requirements the grantee imposes on the contractor regarding bonds.[602] If FEMA has not made such a determination, however, then, at a minimum, FEMA requires:

- Each bidder must give a bid guarantee equivalent to 5% of the bid price. The "bid guarantee" shall consist of a firm commitment, such as a bid bond, certified check, or other negotiable instrument accompanying a bid as assurance that the bidder will, upon acceptance of his bid, execute such contractual documents as may be required within the time specified;

- A performance bond posted by the contractor for 100% of the contract price. This bond is to secure fulfillment of all the contractor's obligations under the contract; and

- A payment bond by the contractor for 100% of the contract price. This bond assures payment, as the law requires, of all persons supplying labor and materials in the execution of the work required under the contract.[603]

III. Management Costs

A. Introduction

The Disaster Mitigation Act of 2000 amended the Stafford Act by adding a section titled "Management Costs."[604] This amendment authorized FEMA to reimburse grant recipients for indirect costs, administrative expenses, and other expenses not directly chargeable to a specific project incurred by grantees and subgrantees in the management and administration of Stafford Act grants through application of a rate(s).[605] By regulation, FEMA has established rates for determining the amount that FEMA will

---

[602] 44 C.F.R. § 13.36(h).
[603] 44. C.F.R. § 13.36(h)(1)-(3).
[604] Stafford Act § 324(b), 42 U.S.C. § 5165b(b).
[605] Id. § 324b(a), 44 C.F.R. Part 207.

provide to grantees for management costs they incur in managing PA and HMGP grants.[606]

Rates and procedures for reimbursement of management costs are established in 44 CFR part 207. Those regulations are in addition to common federal requirements of grantees and subgrantees consistent with Office of Management and Budget (OMB) circulars and 44 CFR part 13. Part 13 and the OMB circulars are instructions on eligible costs that OMB has established for the funding of grants. Each agency issuing grants and each grantee must adhere to them.[607]

The OMB circulars separate management and administrative costs into two groups—direct and indirect costs. In part 207, FEMA interpreted section 324's language authorizing the payment of "indirect costs, administrative expenses, and other expenses not directly chargeable to a specific project" to apply only to indirect costs. As a result, FEMA's management cost regulation applies only to indirect management costs, while direct management costs are to be billed directly to the PW like any other project cost. The difference between direct and indirect costs, and project and management costs, will be discussed in more detail later in this section.

Because FEMA regulations concerning management cost grants have changed over the years, and will continue to change, earlier but still existing FEMA policies interpreting previous management cost regulations may be obsolete, inaccurate, and inapplicable in a particular disaster;[608]

---

[606] 44 C.F.R. § 207.5. Note that this regulation is called a "Final Interim Rule," and it applies only to declarations after Nov. 13, 2007. At the time of this publication, FEMA is reviewing the rule; readers are advised to review current regulations for changes.
[607] OMB Circular A-110, (2 C.F.R. Part 215) establishes cost principles for institutions of higher education, hospitals, and other PNPs. OMB Circular A-87, (2 CFR Part 225) establishes cost principles for state, local, or Indian tribal governments; OMB Circular A-122 (2 CFR Part 230) applies to private non-profit organizations other than an (1) institution of higher education, (2) hospital, or (3) an organization named in OMB Circular A-122 as not subject to that circular; OMB Circular A-21, (2 C.F.R. Part 220) applies to educational institutions; 48 C.F.R. Part 31 establishes cost principles for for-profit organizations other than a hospital and an organization named in OMB Circular A-122 as not subject to that circular.
[608] DAP 9525.6 *Project Supervision and Management Costs of Subgrantees* (2001) [hereinafter DAP 9526.6] http://www.fema.gov/9500-series-policy-publications/95256-project-supervision-management-costs-subgrantees and DAP 9525.11, *Payment of Contractors for Grant Management Tasks* (2001) [hereinafter DAP 9525.11, *Contractor Payment for Grant Tasks*],

---

however, they may still be instructive for general concepts, such as what are and are not management costs.[609] Therefore, if the declaration was on or after November 13, 2007, the final interim rule (44 CFR 207.1 – 207.8) and the policies in place at the time of the declaration apply.[610] If the declaration was issued before November 13, 2007, the regulation at 44 CFR 207.9 and the policies in effect on the date of the declaration apply.

B. Defining Management Costs

1. What Are Management Costs

In the PA context,[611] "management costs" are those costs that a grantee incurs in requesting, obtaining, and administering the grant.[612] These management costs are separate and apart from project costs, which can

---

http://www.fema.gov/9500-series-policy-publications/952511-payment-contractors-grant-management-tasks have been, for the most part, rendered obsolete for disaster declarations after Nov. 13, 2007. On October 11, 2007, FEMA published the *Management Costs* interim final rule (72 FR 57869) that established the management costs rates for emergencies and major disasters. The interim final rule went into effect on November 13, 2007. See DAP 9525.9.

[609] While DAP 9525.9, *Section 324 Management Costs and Direct Administrative Costs* (Mar. 12, 2008) [hereinafter DAP 9525.9], http://www.fema.gov/public-assistance-9500-series-policy-publications/95259-section-324-management-costs-direct does not state explicitly that it supersedes DAP 9525.6 and DAP 9525.11, these older policies pre-date the 2007 management costs regulation, known as the Final Interim Rule. FEMA published DAP 9525.9 interpreting this 2007 regulation on March 12, 2008. The regulations that are in effect on the date of the event are controlling, *see Durable Mfg. Co v. U.S. Dept. of Labor*, 584 F. Supp. 2d 1092 (7th Cir. 2009). Regarding agency policies, the United States Supreme Court has stated: "While these administrative interpretations are not products of formal rulemaking, they nevertheless warrant respect . . . ." (the court was referring to the publicly available operating instructions for processing Social Security, namely the Social Security Administration's Program Operations Manual System), *Washington State Department of Social and Health Services v. Guardianship Estate of Danny Keffeler*, 537 U.S. 371 (2003). Therefore, it is logical that agency policies in force on the date of the event control as well.

[610] Namely, 44 C.F.R. part 207; DAP 9525.9.

[611] Note that Section 324 of the Stafford Act applies to all grants issued under the authority of the Stafford Act, and 44 CFR part 207 applies to both the PA Program and the HMGP. However, as this chapter addresses only the PA program, we will reference only the application of management costs with respect to PA.

[612] See 44 CFR § 207.2.

---

include some management expenses, but are focused on completing the purpose of the grant, not obtaining the grant itself.[613]

Examples of PA management costs:
The cost to identify and assess damage; photographing and flying over damaged areas; attending the applicant's briefing; maintenance of a disaster administrative office, such as, staff, staff travel, printing, communications, supplies, utility costs, cell phones and other necessary equipment; development, review, and selection of projects; assisting subgrantees in completing forms necessary to request assistance; preparing PWs for small projects; assisting the Project Specialist (Project Officer) in completing PWs for large projects; collecting cost data and developing cost estimates; bid review; invoice review and approval; providing oversight of grant, subgrant, or project cash management, accounting and reporting, including subgrantee accounting and tracking of progress and expenditures for projects; site visits; conducting or assisting FEMA or the subgrantee in environmental consideration reviews; reconciliation of costs and payments; close-out of projects; final inspection; audit compliance; and developing, revising or updating the SAP.[614]

Examples of PA project costs include:
The cost of labor, materials, or equipment to do the repair; additional costs for compliance with codes and standards; costs necessary to obtain permits; costs necessary to comply with environmental or historic preservation laws, regulations and executive orders. In other words, the labor costs involved to hammer nails or dig ditches, draw blue-prints, or develop design services, as well as the wages of a foreperson on the site of a repair project, are all project costs that a grantee can tie to a specific project and thus the grantee should not include them in the calculation of management costs.

---

[613] See e.g. "CEF for Large Projects Instructional Guide V 2.1", Section 11, Part H. September 2009.
[614] 44 C.F.R. §§ 206.207(b), 207.7(b); PA GUIDE, at 63.

For events declared after November 13, 2007, management costs are charged to the PA PW separately from project costs, and are capped at the rates contained in part 207 of FEMA's regulations.[615]

2. What Are *Direct and Indirect* Management Costs

Management costs are separated into two groups—direct and indirect costs—by OMB Circular A-87.[616] As discussed previously, in promulgating its regulations implementing section 324 of the Stafford Act, FEMA interpreted the language "any indirect costs, administrative expenses, and any other expenses not directly chargeable to a specific project" as addressing indirect, not direct, management costs.[617] Direct management costs, which are those "activities and costs that can be directly charged to a project with proper documentation"[618] are charged to the PW the same as any other project costs. Indirect management costs, which are commonly referred to as "management costs" in PA parlance, are those costs that, while properly documented, cannot be attributed to any single project.[619] Indirect costs must comply with 44 CFR part 207 and be addressed in the grantee's approved SAP for PA.[620]

Examples of direct management costs:[621]
Activities to collect damage data, invoices, estimates, and support documentation related to a specific project; travel expenses related to a specific project; activities to evaluate the impact of hazard mitigation measures, insurance coverage, historic preservation, environmental impact, and flood risk for a specific site or project; activities to document funding, scope of work, and other impacts resulting from mitigation,

---

[615] *See* 44 CFR 207.5.
[616] OMB Circular A-87, 2 C.F.R. Part 225.
[617] 44 C.F.R. § 207.2.
[618] *Id.* § 207.6(c).
[619] 44 CFR 207.2.
[620] 44 CFR 206.207(b), and 207.7(b).
[621] *See* DAP 9525.9 "Section 324 Management Costs & Direct Administrative Costs"(2008) http://www.fema.gov/public-assistance-9500-series-policy-publications/95259-section-324-management-costs-direct; Memo on Reasonable Costs (2009) http://www.fema.gov/pdf/government/grant/pa/9525_9_pa_reasonable_costs_memo.pdf; Direct and Direct Administrative Activity List http://www.fema.gov/pdf/government/grant/pa/9525_9_pa_indirect_direct_administrative_activity_list.pdf.

---

alternate, improved, or other funding requests for a specific project; activities related to visiting, surveying, and assessing sites for a specific project; activities related to estimating project costs for a specific project; activities to respond to grant review, inspection, or closure document requests from the grantee for a specific project; preparing new versions of the PW; and activities related to the close out process of a specific PW.

Examples of indirect management costs:[622]
Costs associated with the applicant briefing, kickoff meeting, and preliminary cost estimates; travel and expenses in general, not tied directly to a specific project; assisting subgrantees in completing forms necessary to request assistance; preparing PWs for small projects; assisting the Project Specialist (Project Officer) in completing PWs for large projects; collecting cost data and developing cost estimates; bid review; invoice review and approval; meetings with FEMA and grantee officials regarding the overall program; PA programmatic compliance reviews; and PW exit briefing for the overall program.

C. Management Cost Grants for Events Declared After November 13, 2007 (Interim Rule)

1. The State Administrative Plan (SAP)

Management costs funds are available to PA grantees—state or Indian tribal governments (tribal governments)—that receive PA grants pursuant to presidentially declared major disasters and emergencies. If both a state and a tribal government serve as grantees, each is eligible for management cost grants.[623] Before FEMA provides any management cost grants, however, the SAP for that state must have a process in place for how the state will treat the management costs of its subgrantees and how the state will "pass through" management cost funds to the subgrantee. The grantee has the discretion to decide these details. The SAP must address, in detail, the amount of the grant it will spend while the project is being completed, at closeout, and during audit procedures.[624] The SAP should

---

[622] Id.
[623] Id. § 207.2; DAP 9525.9(VII)(c)(3).
[624] Id. § 207.7(b).

---

also include "the reasonable percentage or amount of pass-through funds for management costs . . . that the grantee will make available to subgrantees, and the basis, criteria, or formula for determining the subgrantee percentage or amount."[625]

2. How Costs Are Calculated

For major disasters, the maximum amount that FEMA will reimburse for management costs cannot exceed 3.34% of the federal share of projected eligible program costs, not including DFA. That percentage is 3.90% for emergency declarations.[626] Regardless of the percentage, the amount of a management cost grant pursuant to a single declaration is capped at twenty million.[627]

Grants for management costs are only for incurred eligible costs. The 3.34% and 3.90% thresholds are figures above which FEMA will not fund incurred costs. Applicants do not automatically receive an additional 3.34% or 3.90% addition to their grant to account for management costs. All management costs must be reasonable and necessary. They must be real or actual costs that the grantee incurs and are connected to an eligible project.[628] The grantee and subgrantee must document all costs expended for management costs. FEMA will deobligate any unused funds, and the grantee must return them to FEMA.[629] FEMA will not pay management costs of less than $1,000.[630] Finally, there is no requirement for a grantee to request management cost funding.

3. The Lock-In Process

The process of determining the management cost amount is known as "Lock-In." The FEMA Office of Chief Financial Officer (OCFO) will

---

[625] Id. § 206.207(b)(iii)(K).
[626] 44 C.F.R. § 207.5(b)(4)(i-iii).
[627] Id. § 207.5(c). The $20 million dollar cap may be waived pursuant to the process in place for changes to the lock-in amount discussed in Subsection (3), *The Lock-In Process*.
[628] See Memo on Reasonable Costs (2009).
http://www.fema.gov/pdf/government/grant/pa/9525_9_pa_reasonable_costs_memo.pdf
[629] 44 C.R.R.§ 207.8(b)(3).
[630] DAP 9525.9, *Management Costs and Direct Administrative Costs* (March 12, 2008).

determine[631] and make available (locked-in) a maximum amount for management costs based on program projections. This lock-in amount acts as a ceiling for all funds available to both the grantee and subgrantees.[632] The lock-in letter is provided to the grantee between 30 and 35 days from the date of declaration. The grantee must then submit an initial management cost funding request, in the form of a PW, to the RA. No additional documentation is needed with this initial request. FEMA must receive this request before it will provide management cost funds.[633] FEMA will then obligate 25% of the locked-in amount to the grantee.[634]

FEMA does not require detailed justification and documentation to support these anticipated management costs until 120 days after the date of the declaration.[635] This window of time alleviates the burden on the grantee and affords it the opportunity to provide a more thorough and accurate picture of the costs. The grantee can also request additional time to submit this documentation in "extraordinary circumstances."[636]

The documentation must include the following:

- a description of activities;
- personnel requirements;
- other management costs;
- grantee's plan for expending the funds;
- grantee's plan for monitoring the funds;
- grantees plan for ensuring sufficient funds are budgeted for grant closeout;
- percentage of funds that will be "passed-through" to subgrantee; and
- the basis, criteria or formula for determining the "pass-through."[637]

---

[631] Id; 44 C.F.R. § 207.4(b)(1);
[632] 44 C.F.R. § 207.5(b).
[633] Id. § 207.7(c).
[634] Id. § 207.5(b)(1).
[635] Id. § 207.7(d).
[636] Id.
[637] 44 C.F.R. § 207.7(d)(1-3); DAP 9525.9, at (VII)(c)(2).

FEMA will deny costs that lack sufficient documentation.[638] After the grantee gives the detailed documentation to FEMA, the agency will approve or reject the request within 30 days. If rejected, the grantee has 30 days to resubmit documentation for reconsideration and approval.[639] FEMA will not obligate the balance of the lock-in costs until it approves the documentation.

At six months from date of declaration, FEMA will revise the lock-in amount and will provide this revised projection to the grantee for its planning purposes.[640] At this time, if the grantee can justify the amount, the grantee can request an interim obligation. The RA and the CFO must both approve such interim funding. If approved, the new amount FEMA obligated will "not exceed an amount equal to 10 percent of the six month lock-in amount, except in extraordinary circumstances."[641]

Finally, 12 months after date of declaration, FEMA will determine the final lock-in amount[642] and give notice to the grantee. Upon notice of this final lock-in amount, the grantee must submit a final management cost funding request to the RA. The grantee must attach any necessary revisions, including supporting documentation to this final funding request.[643] FEMA will then obligate the remaining amount of the grant.[644]

The grantee must document management costs on a "Category Z PW."[645] The grantee must use and attach associated forms, if relevant, to the PW, including appropriate OMB forms.

If the grantee submits a written request with justification to FEMA through the RA, FEMA may change the lock-in amount, extensions to the

---

[638] PA Appeal, *Los Angeles County Courts, Central Jail Arraignment Court Building*, PA ID # 037-91032, FEMA-1008-DR-CA (2009). (Applicant's argument that its regular employees did the work but its financial system did not allow it to track these costs held irrelevant); 44 C.F.R. § 207.7(d)(1).
[639] 44 C.F.R. § 207.7(d).
[640] Id. § 207.5(b)(2).
[641] Id. § 207.7(e).
[642] Id. § 207.5(b)(3).
[643] Id. § 207.7(f).
[644] Id. § 207.5(b)(3).
[645] 44 C.F.R. § 207.7(c)(1); DAP 9525.9, at (VII)((D)(3).

lock-in time-periods and interim obligations of funding, and may even adjust the $20 million cap. [646]

The grantee must retain all supporting documentation, including all source records, for three years from the date of submission of the final financial status report to FEMA.[647] If any litigation, claim, negotiation, audit, or other action involving the records begins before the expiration of the three-year period, the grantee must retain the records until completion of that action and resolution of all issues which arise from it or until the end of the regular three-year period, whichever is later.[648]

4. Grantee Duties

The grantee has primary responsibility for grants management costs activities and accountability of the management cost grant.[649] The grantee has the responsibility to assure and properly document[650] that management cost funding is only used for costs related to the administration of the PA Program. The grantee is responsible for administering the management grant funds and addressing procedures to ensure that the subgrantee properly implements the projects and close-out in accordance with program time frames and guidance.[651] The grantee must make sure it and the subgrantee comply, not only with specific regulations regarding management costs, but also with rules regarding federal agency grants in general.[652] Additionally, there are uniform audit requirements that apply to federal grants in general, including management cost grants.[653] The grantee must also include provisions in its SAP to determine the amount of management cost funding to be passed through to the subgrantee for its costs in administering these projects.[654]

---

[646] Id. § 207.5(e).
[647] Id. §§ 207.8(f) and 13.42.
[648] Id. § 13.42(b)(2).
[649] Id. § 207.8(a).
[650] Id. § 207.6(a).
[651] Id. § 207.4(c)(1).
[652] Id. § 207.4(a); *See Applicant Compliance with Procurement Requirements* earlier in this chapter.
[653] Id. § 207.8(e); *see also* 44 C.F.R. § 13.26.
[654] Id. § 207.4(c)(2).

FEMA's regulations require the grantee to provide quarterly progress reports to the RA.[655] These quarterly reports should address the amount and percentage of management costs expended compared to the percentage of work completed on the disaster.

For major disasters, the grantee has eight years from the date of the major disaster declaration to expend a grant for management costs or 180 days after the latest performance period date of a PW that does not concern management costs, whichever is sooner. For emergencies, that time period is two years or 180 days after the latest non-management cost PW, whichever is sooner.[656] FEMA's CFO may extend these periods upon the written request of the grantee justifying the extension with a recommendation from the RA.[657] The grantee is also responsible for resolving questioned costs that may result from audit findings during the three year-record retention period and returning to FEMA any disallowed costs from ineligible activities.[658] FEMA will deobligate any unexpended management funds. Such funds are not available for another project and the grantee must return them to FEMA.

D. Declarations before November 13, 2007

Many of the general concepts outlined previously, such as the definition of management costs and the responsibilities of the grantee, are equally applicable to PA management costs grants for events declared before November 13, 2007. See, e.g., 44 CFR 207.9(b)(1); DAP 9525.11, Payment of Contractors for Grant Management Tasks; PA GUIDE, at 64-65). For these earlier events, however, the management cost calculation is very different.

For those events declared by the President on or before November 13, 2007, FEMA used three separate methods under two separate authorities to reimburse administrative and management costs for the PA and HMGP programs.

---

[655] Id. § 207.8(c).
[656] 44 C.F.R. § 207.8(b).
[657] Id. § 207.8(3).
[658] Id. § 207.8)(d) and (f).

- A <u>sliding scale</u>, also known as the Statutory Administrative Costs Allowance, was set out in the Stafford Act.[659]

  o Grantees were reimbursed according to the sliding scale for certain enumerated extraordinary costs incurred to manage the grants, such as the costs for project applications, final audits, and damage survey reports. Labor costs (those base wages for an applicant's employees) for grantees were expressly disallowed.

  o Subgrantees were reimbursed according to the sliding scale for necessary costs of requesting, obtaining, and administering federal assistance. Subgrantees' eligible costs were more broad. Activities eligible for reimbursement in this category include overtime labor costs and per diem and travel expenses for state or tribal employees related to identifying and assessing damage, attending grantee and FEMA meetings, completing forms to request assistance, establishing files, collecting cost data, developing cost estimates, and working with FEMA and the grantee during project monitoring, final inspections, and audits. These funds do not cover regular-time labor costs, equipment purchases, contractor assistance, or other costs directly associated with grants administration.[660]

  o The sliding scale was applied to eligible project costs as follows:

Amount (of Total Eligible Costs)	Rate
First $100,000	3 percent
Next $900,000	2 percent plus $3,000
Next $4,000,000	1 percent plus $21,000
Amounts above $5,000,000	0.5 percent plus $61,000

---

[659] *See* 42 U.S.C. 5172(f).
[660] PA DIGEST at 63.

FEMA's computer system automatically calculated the fund amounts when FEMA processed project applications and obligated them to the state. The regulations did not require either the grantee or the subgrantee to submit documentation for these funds, but each was required to keep the documentation and records on how each spent the funds for three years.[661]

- State Management Administrative Costs were those administrative costs incurred by the grantee that were directly attributable to a particular project, but were not explicitly enumerated in section 406(f) of the Stafford Act.[662] Costs eligible for reimbursement using this method included supplies, material, equipment, and office space necessary to manage the disaster, as well as related field expenses. Reimbursement is also available for the regular-time salaries and benefits that state employees incur for conducting applicant briefings, preparing PWs, record keeping, project monitoring, and ensuring subgrantee compliance with laws and regulations, final inspection reports, and audits.[663] Eligible costs do not include overtime, per diem, and travel costs of state employees performing any of the named tasks because these costs are reimbursed through the sliding scale calculation.[664]

FEMA did not reimburse these costs for subgrantees. The subgrantee is not entitled to these funds because the percentage allowance of the sliding scale was meant to reimburse all the subgrantees' necessary costs of requesting, obtaining, and administering federal assistance.

These funds are in addition to the sliding scale funds available to the state for costs incurred in PA grant management.[665] These funds are not used

---

[661] 44 CFR § 13.42 (b). These record retention rules are the same as those applicable to events post-November 13, 2007, including rules about how long to keep records if the grantee, subgrantee, or FEMA is in litigation.
[662] *See* 2 CFR part 225 and 42 U.S.C. 5172(f).
[663] PA DIGEST, at 63.
[664] Id.
[665] Id. §§ 207.9(b)(1)(ii) and 207.9(c)(2).

in the calculation of the sliding scale funding for either the state or the subgrantee.[666]

Costs reimbursed in this category cannot duplicate any of the costs the state already claims in the sliding scale category; the regulations prohibit duplication of costs among the categories. FEMA reimbursed state management administrative costs in accordance with the Common Rule.[667] These costs were subject to the federal-state cost share.

Example: Contractors

Sometimes a state or tribal government will hire a contractor to manage its PA grant program because it lacks the requisite personnel, resources, or expertise to do the work. FEMA allowed all reasonable contractor costs, including straight-time force account labor costs, overtime, travel, per diem, and grantee costs associated with developing work plans for contractors or managing contractor work were eligible as State Management Administrative Costs.[668] If a grantee hired a contractor to run its PA disaster, the sliding scale calculations did not factor in the contractor costs.[669] These contracts between a state or tribal government and a contractor were required to adhere to appropriate federal standards.[670]

---

[666] DAP 9525.11(7)(A)(5), *Contractor Payment for Grant Tasks.*

[667] *See* 44 C.F.R. § 13.22; *see* also OMB Circular A-87, for allowable criteria; DAP 9525.11(6)(D), *Contractor Payment for Grant Tasks,* and 44 C.F.R. § 207.9 (b)(1)(ii).

[668] DAP 9525.11(6)(B), *Contractor Payment for Grant Tasks.* Before these costs will be reimbursed however, FEMA had to approve the state or tribal government's SAP in regards to its use of contractors. The Administrative Plan had to assess the grantee's own capability to manage the grant. There must have been an identified potential need for a significant level of contractor assistance. In addition, the amendments to the plan for each disaster (submitted in accordance with 44 C.F.R. 206.207(b)) had to include all proposed uses of contractors as part of the staffing plan for that disaster, and identify specific contractor functions, cost rates, and contract duration. The plan also was required to include grantee staffing to assure adequate contractor oversight and program management. DAP 9525.11(7)(A)(2).

[669] DAP 9525.11(7)(A)(5), *Contractor Payment for Grant Tasks.*

[670] 44 C.F.R. § 13.36.

The state documented these costs on Category Z PW.[671]

- <u>Finally, Indirect Costs</u>, those costs that could not be directly attributable to a particular project, were reimbursed according to an indirect cost rate agreement.[672] This reimbursement method was only available to grantees. The costs that were reimbursed according to this method were overhead costs, such as electricity, building rent, and water charges.

The indirect cost rate agreement is an agreement between a grantee and its cognizant federal agency specifying the indirect cost rates agreed to for that grantee.[673] To simplify relations between federal grantees and awarding agencies, OMB established the "cognizant agency" concept, where a single agency represents all others in dealing with grantees in certain areas. Other federal agencies must accept the approved rates, unless specific program regulations restrict the recovery of indirect costs. OMB publishes a listing of cognizant agencies.

Under this pre-2007 method, the state could be reimbursed with money using all three of these mechanisms,[674] but the subgrantee could only be reimbursed from sliding scale funds.[675] Further, funds from the sliding scale mechanism were calculated differently for a state than for a subgrantee. Finally, although a state was eligible to recover funds from all three funding mechanisms, it was supposed to address different management costs incurred by the state and not duplicate each other. This system contained weaknesses, however, as there existed "a real potential for excess funding and a financial windfall for state grantees because the two fund sources cover essentially the same activities . . . "[676]

---

[671] Id.

[672] 2 CFR part 225 (OMB Circular A-87).

[673] 44 C.F.R. § 207.9(c). See OMB Circular A-87, Attachment E, regarding state and local indirect cost rate proposals.

[674] Id. § 207.9(b)(1).

[675] Id. § 207.9(b)(2).

[676] See Memorandum for Margaret Young, FEMA Chief Financial Officer and David Garratt, Acting Director for FEMA Recovery Division, from Matt Jadacki, Special Inspector General for Gulf Coast Hurricane Recovery, FEMA Policy for Funding Public Assistance Administrative Costs, Audit Report GC-HQ-06-40 (2006).

IV. Public Notice, Comment, and Consultation Requirements

A. New or Modified Policies

FEMA must provide notice and an opportunity for comment before adopting any new or modified policy governing the PA Program that could result in a significant reduction of assistance.[677] Any policy subject to this requirement applies only prospectively to a major disaster or emergency declared on or after the date on which the policy is adopted.[678]

Example: When FEMA revised its Snow Assistance and Severe Winter Storm Policy,[679] it was determined that the revision would likely result in a significant reduction in assistance. As a result, FEMA published the draft policy for comment,[680] in response to the comments received and to address additional changes to the policy, FEMA published a second proposed revision for comment.[681] FEMA published the final policy in November 6, 2009.[682]

As a matter of practice, FEMA currently publishes notice of all proposed revisions to PA 9500 series policies in the *Federal Register* to allow for public comment.

B. Interim Policies

Before adopting any interim policy under the PA Program to address specific conditions that relate to a declared disaster or emergency, FEMA must solicit, to the maximum extent practicable, the views and recommendations of grantees and subgrantees with respect to the major disaster or emergency if the interim policy is likely to "(A) result in a significant reduction of assistance to applicants with respect to the major disaster or emergency; or (B) to change the terms of a written agreement

---

[677] Stafford Act § 325(a)(1), 42 U.S.C. § 5165c(a)(1).

[678] Id. § 325(a)(2), 42 U.S.C. § 5165c(a)(2).

[679] DAP 9523.1, *Snow Assistance Policy* (2009), <http://www.fema.gov/public-assistance-9500-series-policy-publications/95231-snow-assistance-policy

[680] On September 17, 2002, FEMA published a first proposed revision in the *Federal Register* for comment. *See* 67 Fed. Reg. 58,608 (2002).

[681] 73 Fed. Reg. 43,243 (2008).

[682] 74 Fed. Reg. 57,409 (2009).

to which the Federal Government is a party concerning the declaration of the major disaster or emergency."[683]

These requirements to provide notice, comment, and consultation do not confer a legal right of action on any party.[684]

C. Public Access

The Stafford Act requires FEMA to promote public access to policies governing the implementation of the PA Program.[685] Pursuant to this requirement, FEMA provides the states, tribal, and local governments with more and better information about the PA Program through the Internet, newly published materials, and training opportunities, and the production of a standard applicant's briefing package.[686] Access to all current PA policies is available on FEMA's website.[687]

V. Special Funding Circumstances

A. Immediate Needs Funding (INF) and Expedited Payments

Generally, FEMA completes a PW and obligates the federal share via transfer of funding into Smartlink where it is available for drawdown by the grantee. Where the project scope of work has not already been completed, this obligation is the equivalent of an "advance payment," which is required by the Common Rule [688] if the grantee and subgrantees maintain or demonstrate the willingness and ability to maintain procedures to minimize the time that may elapse between the transfer of the funds and when the grantee or subgrantee disburse the funds.[689] If the grantee or subgrantee maintains methods and procedures for payment to subgrantees and contractors in accordance with the appropriate

---

[683] Stafford Act § 325(b)(1), 42 U.S.C. § 5165c(b)(1).
[684] Id. § 325(c), 42 U.S.C. § 5165c(c).
[685] Id.
[686] PA DIGEST, at Introduction,
[687] See http://www.fema.gov/public-assistance-local-state-tribal-and-non-profit.
[688] See The PA Process earlier in this chapter; 44 C.F.R. § 13.21(c), 44 C.F.R. § 206.204(b).
[689] Id.

Department of Treasury regulations,[690] FEMA may assume the grantees and subgrantees have provided evidence of such willingness and ability.[691] Forms for obtaining these advance payments are on FEMA's website.[692]

1. INF

INF[693] is a variation of the advanced funding FEMA typically provides based on a completed scope of work memorialized in a PW in cooperation with the grantee and subgrantee.[694] With INF, funding is provided, however, for "urgent needs" requiring payment within the first 60 days after a disaster declaration, in a manner that avoids burdening applicants "during peak crisis operations" with completion of the ordinary PW scope of work process.[695] FEMA's INF SOP defines the term "urgent needs" to include debris removal, emergency protective measures, and removal of health and safety hazards.[696] FEMA may authorize INF even if a PDA does not occur;[697] but if a PDA occurs, FEMA will only award an INF amount limited to 50% of the PDA estimate for the needed amount of emergency work.[698] Although FEMA may fund up to 50% of the PDA estimate, it will fund only the federal cost share of the total INF.[699]

---

[690] 31 C.F.R. § 205.

[691] Id.

[692] See RPA Form, http://www.fema.gov/library/viewRecord.do?id=2222
SF 270 Request for Advance or Reimbursement,
Tribal Hazard Mitigation Request for Advance or Reimbursement SF 270, <
http://www.whitehouse.gov/sites/default/files/omb/grants/sf270.pdf; Direct Deposit
Form, SF 1199A, for State, Tribal, and local governments, <
http://www.gsa.gov/portal/forms/download/115702 >.

[693] Not to be confused with INF restrictions, which may be implemented by the FEMA Chief Financial Officer when necessary to extend the Disaster Relief Fund balance.

[694] See 44 C.F.R. § 13.21(c).

[695] Standard Operating Procedure 9570.7, *Immediate Needs Funding* [hereinafter INF SOP] at 2, <http://www.fema.gov/pdf/government/grant/pa/sopinf.pdf>.

[696] Id.

[697] Id. Appendix A at 15. *See* Chapter 3, *Declarations*, for a discussion of Preliminary Damage Assessments.

[698] PA GUIDE, at 91.

[699] INF SOP at 6 and 10.

---

a.) The INF Process

After an incident, FEMA cooperates with the state, tribal, and local governments to conduct a PDA.[700] As Chapter 2 discusses, during the PDA, the applicant identifies emergency work to the PDA team and explains any immediate needs. The PDA team documents these damages and prepares cost estimates. These are the cost estimates the state typically uses to apply for INF. If no PDA occurs, then the state tries to obtain sufficient information from interested subgrantees (for example, local and tribal governments and eligible PNP organizations) to estimate eligible emergency work costs.[701] The state determines whether INF is necessary based on the urgency of the applicants' needs.[702] If the state determines that there is a need for INF, the state notifies FEMA of its intent to request INF[703] and notifies interested applicants of the process for requesting INF and any associated deadlines.[704] Then, the state applies for INF on behalf of applicants by submitting to FEMA a list of eligible applicants and RPA forms for each applicant.[705] The FEMA Public Assistance Officer (PAO) reviews the INF request from the state. If the PAO approves the INF request, then FEMA will draft PWs for the approved INF applicants. Upon such approval and drafting of PW's FEMA places the funds in the state's Smartlink account. The state is then responsible for disbursing the funds to the INF eligible applicants.[706] If the applicants complete the emergency work before FEMA obligates the INF, then the funds the applicant spent on such work is offset by the amount of the INF.[707] The FEMA Public Assistance Coordinator is responsible for reconciling all INF against actual project costs.

---

[700] 44 C.F.R. § 206.33(b); PA GUIDE, at 90; INF SOP at 2. *See* Chapter 3, *Declarations*, for a discussion of Preliminary Damage Assessments.
[701] INF SOP, at 2.
[702] *Id.* at 9, 10 and 15. The state determined percentage of INF is based on the state's assessment of the applicant's need for immediate cash. The maximum allowable percentage is 50%.
[703] *Id.*
[704] *Id.* at 2 and 5.
[705] *Id.*
[706] *Id.* at 2.
[707] *Id.* at 6.

---

b.) INF Eligibility Requirements

In order for a state to be eligible for INF, FEMA requires the following:

- There must be a declared major disaster for a requesting state or for lands under the civil/regulatory control of an Indian tribal government;

- The state[708] or an Indian tribal government, which FEMA has approved as a grantee (hereinafter grantee tribal government), must request INF for PA purposes;[709]

- The state or grantee tribal government must indicate that the INF is for the immediate performance of emergency work that it must pay for within the first 60 days after the major disaster declaration;[710]

- If a PDA occurs, the state or grantee tribal government must include INF eligible emergency work in the PDA; if the state or grantee tribal government does not include the INF eligible emergency work in the PDA, the applicant is not eligible for INF;[711]

- If no PDA occurs, the state or grantee tribal government must obtain sufficient information from interested applicants to estimate eligible emergency work costs;[712] and the state must determine whether an applicants' immediate needs warrant INF.[713]

---

[708] PA GUIDE, at 90; see INF SOP, at 2-3, 5-7, and 12-13.

[709] Neither the INF SOP, nor the PA GUIDE, state that Indian tribal governments may request INF; but see 44 C.F.R. § 206.201(e), "If an Indian Tribal government is the grantee, it will assume the responsibilities of the "grantee" or "State" as described in this part with respect to administration of the Public Assistance program." Note that FEMA published the definition of grantee stated in 44 C.F.R. § 206.201(e) after the agency drafted both the INF SOP, and the PA GUIDE..

[710] PA GUIDE, at 91; INF SOP, at 2, 4, 5, 7, 8, 12, 15.

[711] INF SOP, Appendix A at 16.

[712] Id. at 2.

[713] Id. at 5.

---

c.) INF Exclusions and Limitations

FEMA excludes various types of work from INF, including:[714]

- Work for which the applicant carries insurance;[715]

- Work that includes review for environmental and historic preservation compliance with federal laws, regulations, and executive orders;[716] and

- Debris removal and disposal in Coastal Barrier Resources Act areas.[717]

As noted previously and consolidated here for easy reference, FEMA also restricts the INF program in several ways:

- INF is not available if the applicant cannot perform the emergency and pay for the work within 60 days after the date of the disaster declaration.[718]

- FEMA limits the total amount of INF to 50% of the PDA estimate of emergency work eligible for INF, unless no PDA occurs. If there is no PDA, then FEMA limits INF to 50% of the state or grantee tribal government estimate of the INF eligible emergency work.[719]

- When the state, tribal, and local governments and FEMA perform a PDA, only applicants that the PDA included are eligible to receive INF.[720]

---

[714] Id.; see PA GUIDE, at 91 and 115-136; see previous discussion of Insurance in this chapter.
[715] PA GUIDE, at 115; INF SOP, at 15.
[716] PA GUIDE, at 115; INF SOP, at 2. These cannot be approved for INF because FEMA needs to ensure compliance with applicable federal laws and regulations which is unlikely to occur within the time allowed for otherwise eligible INF. See previous discussion of insurance considerations in this chapter.
[717] PA GUIDE, at 91; INF SOP, at 5.
[718] Id.
[719] See INF SOP, Appendix A at 16.
[720] Id.

---

2. Expedited Payments

In 2006, Congress amended the Stafford Act to require that FEMA provide "expedited payments" for debris removal.[721] These payments are required to be not less than 50% of the initial estimate of the federal share of assistance to be provided not later than 60 days after the estimate and not later than 90 days after the applicant applies for debris removal assistance.[722] Although FEMA already provided advance payments for debris removal within the meaning of the Common Rule, Congress clearly expects that FEMA will provide funding even more quickly for debris removal.

Expedited payments differ from INF in the following four ways:

a. The amount of the expedited payment is based on the federal cost share for debris removal, while INF is limited to 50% of the INF eligible emergency work estimated in the PDA or, if no PDA occurs, 50% of the INF eligible emergency work estimated by the state or tribal government;[723]

b. Expedited payments are limited to applicants that participate in the PDA, whereas, INF does not require that a PDA occur;

c. Expedited payments for debris removal will be made within 60 days after the estimate was made and no later than 90 days after the RPA was submitted;[724] whereas, INF requires that the project be completed and paid for within 60 days after the major disaster declaration;[725] and

d. PWs for expedited payments follow normal processes; whereas, PWs for INF are expedited and labeled INF.[726]

---

[721] Safe Port Act, Pub. L. No. 109-347; Stafford Act § 407(e), 42 U.S.C. § 5173(e).

[722] Stafford Act § 407(e), 42 U.S.C. § 5173(e). This is the work the PA GUIDE refers to as Category A.

[723] See PA GUIDE.

[724] See Stafford Act § 407(e)(2), 42 U.S.C. § 5173(e)(2); PA GUIDE, at 91. There is no provision in statute or regulations on the timing of payments for emergency work (Category B).

[725] PA GUIDE, at 91.

[726] Id.

B. Advance/Loan Payment of Non-Federal Share

The Stafford Act and its implementing regulations authorize FEMA to advance or loan to a state, tribal government, local government, or applicant the portion of PA for which the state or tribal government is responsible pursuant to the cost-sharing provisions of the Stafford Act under the following circumstances:

- The state or Indian tribal government is unable to assume its financial responsibility under such cost-sharing provisions with respect to concurrent, multiple major disasters in a jurisdiction or after incurring extraordinary costs as a result of a particular disaster;

- The damage caused by such disaster(s) are so overwhelming and severe that it is not possible for the applicant or the state to assume immediately its financial responsibility under the Stafford Act;[727] and

- The state and other eligible applicants are not delinquent in payments on any disaster-related debts to FEMA.

Pursuant to the implementing regulations, such a loan must be at the request of the governor. FEMA provides all such loans to the state as grantee.[728] The grantee then distributes the funds to the subgrantees.

FEMA is not authorized to cancel loans or advances of the non-federal share. Any such loan bears interest at a rate that the Secretary of the Treasury determines.[729]

C. Community Disaster Loans (CDLs)

Although a distinct loan program separate from the Public Assistance Program, organizationally, FEMA manages the CDL program out of the Public Assistance Branch of the Recovery Division. The Stafford Act

---

[727] Stafford Act § 319, 42 U.S.C. § 5162.
[728] 44 C.F.R. § 206.45.
[729] Stafford Act § 319(b)(2); 44 C.F.R. § 206.45; 6 C.F.R. § 11.10; 37 U.S.C. § 3717; 31 C.F.R. § 901.9.

authorizes FEMA to make CDLs to help local governments[730] that have incurred significant revenue losses due to a presidentially declared major disaster,[731] necessary for a local government to perform its governmental functions.[732] This section discusses the traditional CDL Program, applicable to all major disasters, and the Special CDL program passed by Congress to address the unprecedented and widespread financial losses suffered by communities across the Gulf Coast states as a result of hurricanes Katrina and Rita in 2005.[733] CDLs may not be used for work eligible under the PA Program but are discussed in this chapter because they are used for local governmental operations and administratively managed within the PA Program.

1. Traditional CDL Program

The CDL Program for local governments began in 1970 as a program of community disaster grants. In 1974, Congress replaced the grant program with a program of community disaster loans. [734]

a.) Eligibility

FEMA may make CDLs available to any local government that:

- Is located within the area declared eligible for assistance;[735]

---

[730] Under Stafford Act § 102(7), "local government" includes virtually any political subdivision of a state, as well as Indian tribes and Alaskan native villages.

[731] The Stafford Act authorizes CDLs only under major disaster declarations; however, 44 C.F.R. § 206.363(b)(1) erroneously refers to major disasters and emergencies. CDLs are not authorized for emergency declarations.

[732] Stafford Act § 417, 42 U.S.C. § 5184.

[733] The Community Disaster Loan Act of 2005, Pub. L. No. 109-88 (2005) authorized FEMA to transfer funds appropriated in the Second Emergency Supplemental Appropriations Act To Meet Immediate Needs Arising From The Consequences Of Hurricane Katrina, 2005, Pub. L. 109-62 (2005), to support up to $1 billion in loan authority to assist communities impacted by Hurricanes Katrina and Rita. Loans issued by FEMA under the 2005 Act are referred to as "Special Community Disaster Loans." Department of Homeland Security Federal Emergency Management Agency, Docket ID FEMA-2005-0051, 44 C.F.R. Part 206, RIN 1660-AA44, Special Community Disaster Loans.

[734] The regulations for the CDL Program are in 44 C.F.R. 206 Subpart K, 44 C.F.R. §§ 206.360- 206.367.

[735] 44 C.F.R. § 206.363(a).

- Suffers a substantial loss of tax or other revenues as a result of a major disaster;[736]
- Has demonstrated need for financial assistance in order to perform its governmental functions;[737] and
- Is not in arrears with respect to any loan payments due on previous loans.[738]

FEMA will consider whether the local government is responsible for providing essential municipal operating services to the community, and whether it maintains an annual operating budget.[739] In addition, state law must not prohibit the local government from incurring indebtedness resulting from a federal loan.[740]

b.) Loan Amount

The loan amount is based on need and shall not exceed:

- 25% of the annual operating budget of the local government for the fiscal year in which the disaster occurs, and shall not exceed $5 million; or
- If the disaster-related loss of tax and other revenues is at least 75% of the local governments annual operating budget, 50% of the annual operating budget for the fiscal year in which the major disaster occurs, and shall not exceed $5 million.[741]

c.) Loan Applications and Loan Administration

The local government must submit its application through the state, which then must certify to FEMA that the local government is legally qualified to assume the proposed debt under state law. FEMA's

---

[736] See 44 C.F.R. § 206.363(b)(2)(i) and (ii) for criteria FEMA uses to assess size of revenue loss.
[737] See Id. § 206.363(b)(3)(i)-(ix) for criteria FEMA uses to assess demonstrated need for financial assistance.
[738] Stafford Act § 417(c)(2), 42 U.S.C. § 5184(c)(2); 44 C.F.R. § 206.363(b)(1).
[739] 44 C.F.R. § 206.363(a)(2).
[740] Id. § 206.363(a)(1).
[741] Stafford Act § 417(b), 42 U.S.C. § 5184(b); 44 C.F.R. § 206.361(b).

---

regulations do not take into account a tribal government as a local government wanting to directly apply to FEMA or a tribal agency applying through the tribal government and not the state. The applicant must justify its application based on need and develop it from financial information contained in its annual operating budget.[742]

If FEMA approves the loan, the applicant and FEMA will execute a promissory note, and FEMA will disburse CDL funds according to the loan schedule in the promissory note.

d.) Loan Terms

The interest rate on the loan is equal to the rate for five-year maturities as determined by the monthly U.S. Treasury Schedule of certified interest rates on the date the promissory note is signed.[743] FEMA may approve the loan only in either the fiscal year in which the major disaster occurred or the following fiscal year, and FEMA may approve only one for any local government for a single disaster.[744] The standard loan term is five years; however, FEMA may extend the loan based on the local government's financial condition.[745]

e.) Use of Funds

The CDL recipient may only use CDL funds for existing governmental functions or to expand those functions to meet disaster-related needs.[746] Local governments may not use CDL funds for capital improvements, for the repair or restoration of damaged facilities, or as the non-federal share of any federal program.[747]

---

[742] The specific requirements for demonstrating the insufficiency of revenues to meet the local operating budget are in 44 C.F.R. § 206.364.
[743] Id. § 206.361(c).
[744] Id. § 206.361(d).
[745] Id. § 206.361(e).
[746] 44 C.F.R. § 206.366(b).
[747] Id. § 206.361(f).

f.) Loan Cancellation

The Stafford Act mandates the cancellation of all or any part of a CDL if the local government's revenues during the three fiscal years after the disaster are insufficient, as a result of the disaster, to meet its operating budget.[748] FEMA regulations set forth the specific requirements for demonstrating the insufficiency of revenues to meet the local operating budget.[749]

The local government must apply for loan cancellation through the governor's authorized representative to the FEMA RA prior to the expiration of the loan. The Assistant Administrator for Recovery will make the determination whether to cancel all or any part of the CDL, and any amount cancelled becomes a grant. The local government must still repay any portion of the loan that is not cancelled.[750]

The existence or cancellation of a CDL has no effect on any other Stafford Act grant or assistance, except that a local government may not be eligible for additional CDLs if they are in arrears on required CDL repayments.[751] FEMA may, however, use another agency's funds awarded to an applicant to offset a delinquent loan from grant funds.[752]

2. Special Community Disaster Loans

Hurricanes Katrina and Rita devastated communities across Louisiana, Texas, Mississippi, and Alabama in August and September 2005. Property tax revenue was lost because people no longer lived in the area; residents who remained were unable to pay taxes due to unemployment; and mass evacuations and limited sheltering options in the region resulted in fewer households purchasing goods and services and, in turn, paying sales tax. Despite the severely depleted tax base, communities still had to provide essential services such as police, medical personnel, teachers, and

---

[748] Stafford Act § 417(c), 42 U.S.C. § 5184(c); the specific requirements for demonstrating the insufficiency of revenues to meet the local operating budget are set forth in 44 C.F.R. § 206.366.
[749] 44 C.F.R. § 206.366.
[750] Id. § 206.366(d).
[751] Stafford Act § 417(c) and (d), 42 U.S.C. § 5184(c) and (d); 44 C.F.R. § 206.361(h).
[752] Administrative offset is available under 44 C.F.R. § 206.367(b)(6).

firefighters—costs not eligible for Stafford Act funding from FEMA under the PA Program or under any other FEMA grant program. Further, the traditional CDL program cap of $5 million per individual loan was too small considering the catastrophic nature of, and years-long recovery from, these disasters.

Realizing the catastrophic nature of Hurricanes Katrina and Rita, the unusual circumstances facing these local communities, and the lack of pre-existing sources of federal funding, Congress passed the Community Disaster Loan Act of 2005 [hereinafter 2005 CDL Act].[753] The 2005 CDL Act authorized FEMA to transfer funds to support up to $1 billion in loan authority to assist Gulf Coast communities that Hurricanes Katrina and Rita impacted. FEMA-issued loans under the 2005 CDL Act are called "Special Community Disaster Loans."

For these Special CDLs, the 2005 CDL Act altered three elements from the traditional CDL program: (1) it removed the $5 million limit on individual loans; (2) it restricted use of the loans "to assist local governments in providing essential service;" and (3) it prohibited loan cancellation.

Congress passed an additional emergency supplemental appropriation in 2006 ("2006 CDL Act");[754] however, certain parts of the 2006 CDL Act program were different from those in the 2005 CDL Act program. The 2006 CDL Act allowed the maximum loan amount to be increased to 50% of the applicant's operating budget the fiscal year of the disaster when applicants demonstrated actual loss in tax revenues of 25% or greater.

The 2006 CDL Act, like the 2005 CDL Act, prohibited loan cancellation. As a result of the 2005 and 2006 CDL acts, FEMA made 152 loans totaling $1,270,501,241 to 109 eligible applicants in Mississippi and Louisiana.

In a 2007 appropriations law,[755] Congress removed the loan cancellation prohibitions that were in the 2005 and 2006 CDL acts. This statutory

---

[753] Pub. L. No. 109-88 (2005).
[754] Emergency Supplemental Appropriations Act for Defense, the Global War on Terror, and Hurricane Recovery, 2006, Pub. L. No. 109-234 (June 15, 2006) ("2006 CDL Act").
[755] The U.S. Troop Readiness, Veterans' Care, Katrina Recovery, and Iraq Accountability Appropriations Act, 2007, Pub. L. No. 110-28, § 4502(a), 119 Stat. 2061 (2007).

change reinstated the Stafford Act requirement that the loans would be canceled to "the extent that revenues of the local government during the full three fiscal year period following the disaster are insufficient to meet the operating budget for the local government, including additional unreimbursed disaster-related expenses of a municipal operating character." FEMA's loan cancellation authority for the Special CDL program is now the same as its authority to cancel CDLs in the traditional CDL program.[756]

D. Fire Management Assistance Grant Program (FMAG)

Although a distinct grant program separate from the PA Program, organizationally, FEMA manages the FMAG program out of the Public Assistance Branch of the Recovery Division. As discussed in Chapter 3, FMAGs may be authorized for the mitigation, management, and control of any fire or fire complex on public or private forest land or grassland that threatens such destruction as would constitute a major disaster.[757] FMAGs are distinct from major disaster or emergency declarations; however, once an FMAG is declared, the program operates in a similar manner to normal PA. The FMAG grantee is generally the state, although an Indian tribal government may elect to serve as grantee.[758] After an FMAG declaration, FEMA and the grantee enter into a FEMA-State (or Tribal) Agreement that states the understandings, commitments, and conditions under which FEMA provides federal assistance.[759] As in the regular PA program, eligible applicants are state agencies, Indian tribal governments, and local governments;[760] and these entities may apply for assistance through the grantee.[761]

---

[756] Stafford Act § 417(c)(1), 42 U.S.C. § 5184(c)(1); 44 C.F.R. § 206.366 (traditional CDL cancellations); 44 C.F.R. § 206.376 (special CDL cancellations).

[757] Stafford Act § 420, 42 U.S.C. § 5187. For more information on FMAG declarations, *see* Chapter 3, *Declarations.*

[758] 44 C.F.R. § 204.3, definition of grantee.

[759] Id. § 204.25.

[760] Unlike the regular PA program, PNPs are not eligible applicants. Entities such as PNP fire departments may receive reimbursement but only through a contract, compact, or similar agreement with an eligible applicant.

[761] 44 C.F.R. § 204.41.

All FMAGs are provided at a 75% federal cost share. Unlike regular PA, there is no mechanism for adjusting the cost share.[762] Eligible costs essentially mirror PA Category B, emergency protective measures.[763] FEMA will reimburse for activities undertaken for the mitigation, management, or control of a declared fire or fire complex.[764] Generally, such work must take place during the incident period of the declared fire; however, certain pre-positioning costs are eligible when the RA approves them.[765] Grantees and applicants are subject to the Common Rule and applicable OMB circulars.[766] Appeals of FMAG eligibility requirements follow the same process as PA appeals.[767]

---

[762] Id. § 204.61.

[763] Direct federal assistance is not available in an FMAG declaration.

[764] Id. § 204.42. This section provides more information regarding specific costs. As with Category B in PA, only overtime costs are eligible force account labor.

[765] Id. § 204.42(e).

[766] Id. § 204.63. The Uniform Requirements are also known as the *Common Rule*. *See Applicant Compliance with Procurement Requirements* in this chapter for a discussion of the Common Rule and the OMB circulars.

[767] 44 C.F.R. § 204.54.

CHAPTER 6
Individual Assistance
Table of Contents

Individual Assistance

I. Introduction

The Stafford Act authorizes a wide variety of assistance to individuals and households affected by a major disaster or emergency.[1] FEMA has implemented this authority through its Individual Assistance (IA) Programs, which include the Individuals and Households Program (IHP), as well as a variety of other programs.[2] This program is a complement to FEMA's Public Assistance (PA) program, in particular its emergency shelter programs, which assist state, tribal, and local governments in their responsibilities to save lives and protect property. See Chapter 4, *Response* and Chapter 5, *Public Assistance,* and Section III of this chapter, *Transition from Section 403 Emergency Assistance (Response) to Section 408 Housing Assistance (Recovery).* The Stafford Act prohibits discrimination in the provision of IA and other relief and assistance activities based on race, color, religion, nationality, sex, age, disability, English proficiency, or economic status.[3]

Not every disaster event rises to the level of a Northridge earthquake,[4] 9/11 terrorist attack,[5] or a Hurricane Katrina[6] in its widespread impact and nationwide attention. For those directly affected by a disaster, however, it is their "Katrina moment." The loss or injury of loved ones, loss of or damage to one's home, and the loss of irreplaceable possessions can have devastating mental, physical, and monetary impacts. Generally,

---

[1] Stafford Act, §§ 408 – 416, 423, 425 and 426; 42 U.S.C. §§ 5174 – 5183, 5189, 5189c and 5189d. The Post Katrina Emergency Management Reform Act of 2006 (PKEMRA) Pub. L. No. 109-295, amended the Stafford Act, among other things, to add Sections 425 and 426.

[2] Stafford Act § 408, *Federal Assistance to Individuals and Households,* 42 U.S.C. § 5174. The IHP program is referred to "section 408 assistance" because it is authorized by section 408 of the Stafford Act.

[3] See Stafford Act § 308, 42 U.S.C. § 5151

[4] FEMA-1008-DR-CA(1994).

[5] FEMA-1391-DR-NY(2001); FEMA-1392-DR-VA(2001).

[6] FEMA 1603-DR-LA(2005), Hurricane Katrina (also declared a major disaster in AL, FL, and MS).

the same IA programs are available and authorized for major disaster declarations whether they are like Katrina or not. There have been circumstances, described in Chapter 3, *Declarations*, where more limited IA assistance has been designated for major disasters presenting economic loss as the primary effect. Scaling up IA is a bit more difficult. There is a monetary cap on the financial assistance available under the IHP. Any scalability of IA to meet disaster survivors' needs will generally be found in the direct assistance elements of IHP and in utilizing its broad emergency work authorities under the PA program for emergency work.

The IA programs are part of the continuum from response to recovery, assisting individuals and households back to self-sufficiency. After a major disaster or emergency, FEMA's assistance under its IA programs is not likely to make the individual or household completely whole, in part because federal disaster assistance is supplemental and is not the same as insurance, which can be much more extensive in its coverage for replacing damaged and destroyed property. Thus, disaster survivors may have higher expectations than the federal government, states, or voluntary organizations can meet regarding financial assistance. However, IA for a major disaster is more holistic in its approach by providing not only financial assistance for temporary housing and repair and replacement of real and personal property for essential needs, but also crisis counseling, free legal services, emergency food stamps, disaster unemployment and case management services. This is in addition to the broad array of services and assistance that may be provided by other federal agencies (OFAs), state, tribal, and local governments and voluntary organizations active in disasters (VOADs).

Managing the expectations of disaster survivors early in the disaster with respect to what federal, state, local, and tribal governments and non-profit organizations can deliver will assist disaster survivors in understanding that their own role in the recovery process is crucial. Disaster survivors can then make informed decisions regarding their individual and/or household recoveries. FEMA provides information to disaster survivors in a multitude of ways: online (fema.gov and Disaster Assistance.gov)[7]; via

---

[7] DisasterAssistance.gov provides disaster survivors with a single source for potential assistance programs, easy access to the application process, application updates, and disaster-related information. It is a primary component of the Disaster Assistance

smart phone application (m.fema.gov); toll free lines (1-800-621-3362 and 1-800-462-7585 TTY); in person at Disaster Recovery Centers, at community town hall meetings, and through Community Relations staff; and through press releases and applicant guides.

Table 6.1: IA Programs Available under a Major Disaster or Emergency Declaration

IA Program	Major Disaster	Emergency
Individuals and Households Program	Yes, 42 U.S.C. §5174(a)(1)	Yes, 42 U.S.C. §5192(a)(6)
Disaster Unemployment Assistance	Yes, 42 U.S.C. §5177(a)	No
Benefits and Distribution ("Food Stamps")	Yes, 42 U.S.C. §5179(a)	No
Food Commodities	Yes, 42 U.S.C. §5180(a)	Yes, 42 U.S.C. §5180(a)
Relocation Assistance	Yes, 42 U.S.C. §5181	No
Disaster Legal Services	Yes, 42 U.S.C. §5182	No
Crisis Counseling	Yes, 42 U.S.C. §5183	No
Transportation Assistance	Yes, 42 U.S.C. §5189c	Yes, 42 U.S.C. §5189c
Disaster Case Management	Yes, 42 U.S.C. §5189d	No
Cora Brown	Yes, 44 C.F.R. §206.181(c)	Yes, 44 C.F.R. §206.181(c)

Improvement Program (DAIP) created pursuant to Executive Order No. 13411 of August 29, 2006, *Improving Assistance for Disaster Victims*, 71 Fed. Reg. 52729 (Sept. 6, 2006). The mission of the DAIP is to ease the burden on disaster survivors by providing them with a mechanism to access and apply for disaster assistance through the collaborative efforts of federal, state, tribal, local, and non-profit partners.

II. The Individuals and Households Program (IHP)

A. In General

FEMA[8] is authorized under Section 408[9] of the Robert T. Stafford Disaster Relief and Emergency Assistance Act[10] (Stafford Act) to provide financial assistance and direct services[11] to individuals and households who, as a result of a major disaster, have necessary expenses and serious needs that they are unable to meet through other means.[12] IHP assistance is also available under an Emergency Declaration, although it is rare.[13]

This is the Individuals and Households Program (IHP), which provides housing assistance (financial and direct) and other needs assistance (financial) for individuals and households.

1. Scope and Amount of IHP Assistance

IHP provides:

- Housing Assistance (HA),[14] including rental assistance (financial assistance);[15] direct assistance for temporary housing;[16] repair

---

[8] The Stafford Act vests this authority in the President. The President has delegated most of the functions vested in him under the Robert T. Stafford Disaster Relief and Emergency Assistance Act, 42 U.S.C. §§ 5121-5207, to the Secretary of Homeland Security. *See* Executive Order No. 13,286, 68 Fed. Reg. 10,619 (Feb. 28, 2003); Executive. Order No. 12,673, 54 Fed. Reg. 12,571 (Mar. 23, 1989); and Executive. Order No. 12,148, 44 Fed. Reg. 43,239 (July 20, 1979). The Secretary of Homeland Security has delegated this authority to the Administrator of FEMA. *See* Delegation to the Administrator of the Federal Emergency Management Agency, DHS Delegation No. 9001.1 (Dec. 10, 2010).

[9] Stafford Act § 408, 42 U.S.C. § 5174.

[10] Pub. L. 93-288, *as amended*, 42 U.S.C. § 5121 *et seq.*

[11] For purposes of housing assistance, the term "direct assistance" is used instead of direct services. *See* generally Stafford Act §408(c),42 U.S.C. § 5174(c); 44 C.F.R. §206.110(a).

[12] Stafford Act §408(a)(1),42 U.S.C. § 5174 (a)(1).

[13] Stafford Act §502(a)(6),42 U.S.C. § 5192(a)(6)..

[14] FEMA determines the appropriate types of housing assistance based on considerations of cost effectiveness, convenience to the individuals and households, and such other factors it determines appropriate. Stafford Act § 408(b)(2)(A); 42 U.S.C. § 5174(b)(2)(A).

[15] Stafford Act § 408(c)(1)(A); 42 U.S.C. § 5174(c)(1)(A).

[16] Stafford Act § 408(c)(1)(B); 42 U.S.C. § 5174(c)(1)(B) for the provision of temporary housing units or for the lease and repair of multifamily rental properties.

(financial assistance),[17] replacement (financial assistance),[18] permanent and semi-permanent construction (financial or direct assistance);[19] and

- Other Needs Assistance (ONA) financial assistance for medical, dental, child care, funeral, personal property, and transportation needs.[20]

Eligible applicants can receive more than one type of housing assistance, including a mix of financial and direct assistance.[21] FEMA will determine the appropriate types of assistance based on considerations of cost effectiveness, convenience to disaster survivors, and suitability and availability of the types of assistance to meet survivor needs in the particular disaster situation.[22] FEMA utilizes temporary housing and repair assistance to the fullest extent possible before other types of housing assistance.[23] An applicant is expected to accept the first offer of housing assistance; unwarranted refusal of assistance may result in the forfeiture of future housing assistance.[24]

The amount of financial assistance available to an individual or household under Section 408 for HA and ONA is subject to a maximum amount per single disaster (or emergency) declaration[25], adjusted annually[26] to reflect changes in the Consumer Price Index for All Urban Consumers (CPI-U).[27] It is $31,900 for declarations issued on or after October 1, 2012 (fiscal

---

[17] Stafford Act § 408(c)(2), 42 U.S.C. § 5174(c)(2).
[18] Stafford Act § 408(c)(3), 42 U.S.C. § 5174(c)(3).
[19] Stafford Act § 408(c)(4), 42 U.S.C. § 5174(c)(4).
[20] Stafford Act § 408(e), 42 U.S.C. § 5174(e); 44 C.F.R. § 206.119.
[21] Id. § 408(b)(2)(B), 42 U.S.C. § 5174(b)(2)(B.
[22] Id. § 408(b)(2), 42 U.S.C. § 5174(b)(2); 44 C.F.R. § 206.110(c).
[23] 44 C.F.R. § 206.110(c).
[24] Id.
[25] Stafford Act § 408(h)(1), 42 U.S.C. § 5174(h)(1); 44 C.F.R. § 206.110(b).
[26] FEMA makes its annual IHP maximum grant adjustment every fiscal year (October 1-September 30) based on changes in the Consumer Price Index for All Urban Consumers (CPI-U) for a preceding 12-month period, which is published by Bureau of Labor Statistics for the Department of Labor. 44 C.F.R. § 206.110(b). The maximum amount does not always increase. It actually decreased from $30,300 to $29,900 for FY 2010 due to a decrease in the CPI-U. See 74 FR 51303 (October 6, 2009).
[27] Stafford Act § 408(h)(2), 42 U.S.C. § 5174(h)(2).

year 2013).[28] For the purposes of this chapter, this dollar amount is called the "max IA grant."[29]

2. Assistance not Income

Federal major disaster and emergency assistance provided to individuals and households under the Stafford Act is not considered income or a resource determining eligibility for federally funded means tested programs such as welfare.[30] Comparable disaster assistance provided by states, tribes, and local governments and by disaster assistance organizations is also not considered income or a resource for these purposes.[31]

Qualified disaster relief payments such as IHP assistance are not considered income for income tax purposes.[32] Qualified disaster relief payments include amounts paid to, or for the benefit of, an individual for personal, family, living, or funeral expenses and repair/replacement of personal residence and contents if those expenses are attributable to a qualified disaster[33] and are not compensated for by insurance or otherwise.[34] Deductions or credits are not allowed for casualty losses and medical expenses specifically reimbursed under qualified disaster relief payments.[35]

IHP assistance is also exempt from garnishment, seizure, encumbrance, levy, execution, pledge, attachment, release or waiver and may not be

---

[28] See 77 FR 61425 (October 9, 2012).
[29] Please note that financial assistance provided under non-408 authorities is not subject to this maximum cap.
[30] Stafford Act § 312(d), 42 U.S.C. § 5155(d); 44 C.F.R. §§ 206.110(f) and 206.191(b)(2).
[31] Stafford Act § 312(d), 42 U.S.C. § 5155(d.
[32] 26 U.S.C. § 139(a) Disaster Relief Payments, which provides that "qualified disaster relief payments" are not included in gross income.
[33] 26 U.S.C. § 139(c)(2), which includes federally declared disasters as defined by 26 U.S.C. §165(h)(3)(C)(i), which provides that that means any disaster determined to warrant assistance by the federal government under the Stafford Act.
[34] 26 U.S.C. § 139(b). See IRS Publication 547 (2012), Casualties, Disasters, and Thefts at http://www.irs.gov/pub/irs-pdf/p547.pdf for a detailed explanation of tax relief for declaring losses and treatment of "qualified disaster relief payments." Please note that disaster unemployment compensation is subject to applicable taxation.
[35] 26 U.S.C. § 139(h).

reassigned or transferred.[36] However, these exemptions do not apply to FEMA recovery assistance fraudulently obtained or misapplied.[37]

B. Assistance Registration Process

Applicants for disaster assistance may access the federal disaster assistance system in a number of ways: online (fema.gov and DisasterAssistance.gov) via smart phone application (m.fema.gov), and via toll free lines (1-800-621-3362 and 1-800-462-7585 TTY).[38] Applications are processed by FEMA through its National Processing Service Centers (NPSCs), which are designed to be a first contact point for disaster survivors seeking assistance. When an applicant initially seeks federal assistance through one of these methods, FEMA enters the pertinent personal and disaster-related information into its National Emergency Management Information System (NEMIS) computer system.[39] Thereafter, applicants can obtain application status online, via smartphone application, by contacting the NPSCs via the FEMA toll free lines, or by visiting a Disaster Recovery Center (DRC).

1. Registration Period

The IHP registration period is 60 days following the date of declaration for IA.[40] The Stafford Act is silent on the application period; however, the IHP regulations provide at 44 C.F.R. § 206.112(a) that "[t]he standard FEMA registration period is 60 days following the date that the President declares an incident a major disaster or an emergency."[41] FEMA interprets this as starting on the date when IA was included in the declaration.

---

[36] 44 C.F.R. §206.110(g).

[37] Id.

[38] In unusual circumstances, applicants may be able to fill out an application for assistance in person by visiting a Disaster Recovery Center (DRC).

[39] FEMA is required to maintain a system, including an electronic database, for purposes of verification, fraud prevention, prevention of duplicative payments, and the provision of instructions to applicants on use of assistance, and for the review and appeal of denied applications. Stafford Act §408(i), 42 U.S.C. § 5174(i).

[40] If the ending date is on a Sunday or federal holiday, it is automatically extended to the next day.

[41] See 44 C.F.R. § 206.112(a). Contrast this language with the PA regulations for applications for assistance found at 44 C.F.R. § 206.202(c), which provides that requests

---

The Regional Administrator or his or her designee may extend the registration period: 1) when the state requests more time to collect registrations from the affected population; or 2) when necessary to establish the same registration deadline for contiguous counties or states for the same declared event.[42] For example, if there is a lengthy incident period or prolonged evacuation, the registration period may be extended to ensure that affected individuals and households have an opportunity to register, or if additional counties are added at a later date, the registration period can be extended to have the same ending date for all add-on counties. In addition, FEMA regulations permit late registration for an additional 60 days for applicants who provide justification for the delay.[43]

2. Housing Inspection and Identification Verification Process

FEMA conducts a housing inspection to confirm that the applicant's primary residence is uninhabitable or inaccessible as a result of the major disaster or emergency. Often the inspection is a basic step to establish applicant eligibility for temporary housing and disaster-related real property damages (housing assistance) and for personal property needs (ONA). The inspectors,[44] while they are at the residence, generally have the applicant sign the Declaration and Release Form, FEMA Form 009-0-03.[45]

---

for PA be submitted "within 30 days after designation of the area where the damage occurred."

[42] 44 C.F.R. § 206.112(b). *See* also 44 C.F.R. § 206.110(k)(2), which provides that the governor's authorized representative may request a time extension for FEMA (see § 206.112) to accept registrations and to process assistance applications from applicants with damaged property in a SFHA located in a non-National Flood Insurance Program (NFIP) participating community if the community qualifies for and enters the NFIP during the six-month period following the declaration. Further discussion regarding the NFIP is found in the section titled National Flood Insurance Coverage Requirement later in this chapter.

[43] 44 C.F.R. § 206.112(c). *See*, for example, FEMA memorandum, *Extension of Registration Periods for Late Applications*, (Sept. 26, 2008)(permitting late registration without written justification after Hurricanes Gustav and Ike); <http://ia.fema.net/contents/policy/memos.asp>.

[44] These are generally contract inspectors, not FEMA employees. FEMA does maintain a small number of in-house inspectors who may conduct quality control inspections.

[45] *See* http://on.fema.net/employee_tools/forms/Pages/fema_forms.aspx.

All applicants must pass the basic identification requirements for IHP and sign the Declaration and Release Form before FEMA considers them eligible for IHP or ONA.

3. Period of Assistance

FEMA may provide IHP assistance for a "period of assistance" not to exceed 18 months from the date of declaration.[46] This primarily affects continued assistance for temporary housing assistance.[47] The Assistant Administrator for Recovery may extend this period if he/she determines that due to extraordinary circumstances, an extension would be in the public interest.[48]

Repair and replacement assistance is generally provided as a one-time payment. Rental assistance is generally provided for an initial period of one, two, or three months. To be considered for additional rental assistance, applicants must demonstrate that they have spent any previous assistance from FEMA as instructed, and they must demonstrate efforts to re-establish permanent housing.[49] Additional assistance is generally provided for one, two, or three months at a time.

C. Access to Records and Privacy Act Protections

When an event forces mass evacuations, sheltering, and ongoing displacement of disaster survivors from their homes, FEMA is often the only governmental entity with current information and the ability to quickly contact or locate disaster survivors because they have registered for assistance and provided current contact information. In addition, during disasters, FEMA frequently receives requests to provide applicant

---

[46] Although Stafford Act Section 408 only refers to an 18-month temporary housing assistance, FEMA's implementing regulations apply this period of assistance to all of IHP. See Stafford Act §408(c)(1)(B)(iii), 42 U.S.C. §5174(c)(1)(B)(iii) and 44 C.F.R. §206.110(e).

[47] See 44 C.F.R. §§206.114(b)(3) and (4) and 206.117(b)(1)(ii)(G)(1).

[48] 44 C.F.R. §206.110(e). Please note that the regulations refer to the "Assistant Administrator for the Disaster Assistance Directorate." The Disaster Assistance Directorate or "DAD" has been replaced by the Recovery Directorate within the Office of Response and Recovery.

[49] 44 C.F.R. § 206.114(b)(1)-(4).

---

information to non-profit organizations or government agencies seeking to provide additional forms of disaster assistance, or for law enforcement purposes.

This leads to many requests for personally identifiable information (PII)[50] from FEMA's NEMIS database on disaster survivors. The Privacy Act of 1974[51] regulates the federal government's collection, maintenance, use, and dissemination of individually or personally identifiable information, or PII.[52] FEMA may only release PII from its disaster assistance files with the consent of the individual,[53] under an exception in the Privacy Act, or under a published "routine use."[54] Under the Privacy Act, a routine use is a use "for a purpose which is compatible with the purpose for which it was collected."[55]

The Stafford Act requires FEMA to provide access to its IHP electronic records (NEMIS database) to states if: (1) the purpose is to make available additional state and local assistance, and (2) the information pertains only to individuals located in the requesting state.[56] This is considered a "congressionally mandated" routine use for purposes of release of PII from FEMA's IHP records.[57]

---

[50] PII includes name, address, social security number, FEMA registration identification number, drivers' license number, financial account numbers, citizenship or immigration status, medical information, or any other personally identifying symbol or data.

[51] 5 U.S.C. § 552a; see also 6 C.F.R. Part 5, Subpart B for the DHS Privacy Act Regulations and 44 C.F.R. § 206.110(j) for FEMA's IHP regulations regarding application of the Privacy Act.

[52] 5 U.S.C. § 552a(b).

[53] FEMA does not have a standard authorization or consent form for release of information to third parties. However, it does have available guidance on consent forms and a sample consent form that can be adapted for use. See FEMA Written Consent-Third Party Request Job Aid Directive and Sample Letter (2011).

[54] 5 U.S.C. § 552a(b).

[55] Id. at § 552a(a)(7).

[56] Stafford Act § 408(f)(2), 42 U.S.C. § 5174(f)(2). See also 44 C.F.R. § 206.110(j)(2).

[57] See OMB Privacy Act Guidance, 40 Fed. Reg. 28,948 (July 9, 1975) at 28,956-58.

IHP SORN Revisions

FEMA is required to publish its routine uses in the *Federal Register*, in a Privacy Act System of Records Notice (SORN).[58] Please note that FEMA recently amended its IHP SORN and its processes to provide a more streamlined manner to provide access to states, pursuant to the Stafford Act, to make additional assistance available to disaster survivors while protecting PII under the Privacy Act.[59] *Please consult with the FEMA OCC for guidance regarding implications of the new SORN for purposes of PII disclosures and processing requests.*

The law governing disclosure of information under the Privacy Act is complex, and there can be significant civil and criminal penalties for violations. Field staff who receive a request for applicant information from FEMA's disaster assistance files should consult with FEMA's OCC. *See* also the Information Management Chapter for a more detailed discussion of the Privacy Act.

D. Eligibility for IHP

The general eligibility criteria for an individual or household to receive IHP assistance are:

- U.S. citizenship, non-citizen national, or qualified alien status;

- Necessary expenses and serious needs directly related to a declared disaster;

- Insurance or other forms of disaster assistance cannot meet the disaster-related needs.

---

[58] Id. § 552a(e)(4).
[59] 78 Fed. Reg. 25,282 (April 30, 2013).

---

1. Citizenship and Immigration Status Requirements for Federal Public Benefits

In 1996, Congress passed the Welfare Reform Act,[60] which provides that aliens who are not qualified aliens are not eligible for federal public benefits.[61] A federal public benefit includes any retirement, welfare, health disability, public or assisted housing, post-secondary education, food assistance, unemployment benefits, or any similar benefit for which payments or assistance are provided to an individual, household, or family eligibility unit by an agency of the United States or by appropriated funds of the United States.[62] Stafford Act and other disaster assistance programs to which this restriction applies include IHP, disaster unemployment assistance (DUA),[63] Small Business Administration (SBA) disaster loans,[64] and the Cora Brown Fund.[65] As a result, disaster survivors must certify that they are U.S. citizens, non-citizen nationals of the United States, or qualified aliens to receive assistance under IHP.

The citizen[66] or qualified alien eligibility requirement does not apply to the following short-term, non-cash, in-kind federal emergency disaster relief programs:[67]

- Emergency assistance;[68]
- Disaster legal services; [69]
- Crisis counseling;[70] and

---

[60] The Personal Responsibility and Work Opportunity Reconciliation Act Of 1996 [Hereinafter Welfare Reform Act], Title Iv, Pub. L. No. 104-193, 110 Stat. 2105 (Aug. 22, 1996). See 8 U.S.C., Chapter 14 - Restricting Welfare and Public Benefits for Aliens, 8 U.S.C. §§ 1611- 1646.
[61] 8 U.S.C. § 1611(a).
[62] 8 U.S.C. § 1611(c).
[63] Stafford Act § 410, 42 U.S.C. § 5177.
[64] See SBA discussion later in this chapter.
[65] 44 C.F.R. § 206.181
[66] Encompasses both U.S. citizen and non-citizen national of the United States status for purposes of this discussion.
[67] Welfare Reform Act, 8 U.S.C. § 1611(b)(1)(B).
[68] Stafford Act §§ 403 and 502, 42 U.S.C. §§ 5170b and 5192. Emergency assistance includes search and rescue, medical care, shelter, food, water, hazard clearance, and reducing threats to life, property, and public health or safety.
[69] Id. § 415, 42 U.S.C. § 5182.
[70] Id. § 416, 42 U.S.C. § 5183.

- Disaster food stamps (Disaster Supplemental Nutrition Assistance Program, or D-SNAP).[71]

While the citizen/qualified alien eligibility requirement does not apply to emergency shelter, which is considered short-term, non-cash, in-kind federal emergency disaster relief provided under Stafford Act Sections 403 or 502,[72] FEMA considers IHP assistance (financial or direct) provided under Stafford Act Section 408, a "federal public benefit" because it involves either financial payments or a temporary housing unit (THU) for up to 18 months. Consequently, some survivors who are eligible for congregate emergency sheltering may be ineligible when assistance transitions to temporary housing direct assistance under IHP.

After Hurricanes Katrina and Rita, for example, FEMA paid for tens of thousands of people to stay in hotels and motels under emergency assistance (discussed in Chapter 4, *Response*). The transition to IHP was difficult because many could not meet the eligibility requirement because they were not U.S. citizens or qualified aliens, which the Welfare Reform Act requires of recipients of federal public benefits.[73] *See* the discussion in Transition from Section 403 Emergency Assistance (Response) to Section 408 Housing Assistance (Recovery) later in this chapter.

---

[71] Id. § 412, 42 U.S.C. § 5179. *See* Disaster SNAP Guidance, May 18, 2012, Figure 1. Comparison of Eligibility Standards for SNAP and D-SNAP, Restricted Eligibility Categories, Page 3, at <http://www.fns.usda.gov/disasters/response/D-SNAP_Handbook/guide.htm>. This is in contrast to the restrictions provided for the regular program, Supplemental Nutritional Assistance Program (SNAP), 7 C.F.R. §273.4.
[72] 42 U.S.C. §§ 5170b or 5192.
[73] 8 U.S.C. § 1611(c); *See also* Stafford Act § 408(c)(1)(B)(i), 42 U.S.C. § 5174(c)(1)(B)(i)..

In 2002, in New Mexico, the federal government carried out a controlled burn that was part of the 10-year Bandelier National Monument plan for reducing fire hazard within the monument. Unfortunately, the government lost control of the burn due to high winds and drought conditions in the area, and the fire destroyed the homes of a number of scientists from other countries who were working at the Los Alamos National Laboratory. The scientists, who were lawful residents in the United States and often homeowners, were ineligible for Stafford Act IHP assistance because they were not "qualified aliens" due to the nature of their visas. However, the Cerro Grande Fire Assistance Act,[74] which was administered by FEMA, was enacted to provide an expedited claims process for 'injured persons', including individuals—regardless of citizenship or immigration status[75]—who suffered losses resulting from the Cerro Grande Fire.

a.) Status Definitions

A **U.S. citizen** is a person born in one of the 50 states, the District of Columbia, Puerto Rico, Guam, the U.S. Virgin Islands, or the Northern Mariana Islands; a person born outside of the United States to at least one U.S. parent; or a naturalized citizen.[76]

A non-citizen national of the United States is a person born in an outlying possession of the United States (American Samoa or Swain's Island) on or after the date the United States acquired the possession, or a person whose parents are U.S. non-citizen nationals.[77] U.S. citizens are nationals of the United States; however, not every national of the United

---

[74] Pub. L. 106-246, 114 Stat. 584.

[75] 44 C.F.R. § 295.50.

[76] See 8 U.S.C §§ 1401-1504.

[77] See 8 U.S.C § 1408. The term 'national of the United States' means (A) a citizen of the United States, or (B) a person who, though not a citizen of the United States, owes permanent allegiance to the United States. As a general matter, a U.S. non-citizen national is a person born in an outlying possession of the United States (American Samoa or Swain's Island) on or after the date the United States acquired the possession, or a person whose parents are U.S. non-citizen nationals (subject to certain residency requirements).

States is a U.S. citizen, although owing permanent allegiance to the United States.[78]

Qualified alien is a complex definition under federal immigration law.[79] It includes aliens[80] under the following categories:

- Legal permanent resident ("green card" holder)[81]

- An asylee,[82] refugee,[83] or an alien whose deportation is being withheld[84]

- Alien paroled into the United States for at least one year[85]

- Alien granted conditional entry (per law in effect prior to April 1, 1980)[86]

- Cuban/Haitian entrant[87]

- Battered alien spouse, battered alien children, the alien parent of battered children, and alien children of battered parents who fit certain criteria[88]

- Victim of a severe form of trafficking[89]

Many categories of aliens lawfully present in the United States, however, are not considered qualified aliens, including but not limited to temporary tourist visa holders; foreign students; temporary work visa holders; and habitual residents such as citizens of the Federated States of Micronesia and the Republic of the Marshall Islands.

---

[78] 8 U.S.C. § 1101(a)(22).
[79] *See* 8 U.S.C. § 1641.
[80] Any person not a citizen or national of the United States. 8 U.S.C. §1101(a)(3).
[81] 8 U.S.C. § 1641(b)(1).
[82] *Id* at § 1641(b)(2).
[83] *Id* at § 1641(b)(3).
[84] *Id* at § 1641(b)(5).
[85] *Id.* at § 1641(b)(4).
[86] *Id.* at § 1641(b)(6).
[87] *Id.* at § 1641(b)(7).
[88] *Id.* at § 1641(c).
[89] *Id.* at § 1641(c)(4).

b.) Household Eligibility

FEMA requires applicants for federal disaster assistance to sign a Declaration and Release Form declaring whether they are a U.S. citizen, non-citizen national, or a qualified alien.[90]

If the applicant does not meet these criteria, the household may still apply for and receive IHP assistance if:

- Another adult household member meets the eligibility and signs the form; or

- The applicant is the parent/guardian of an eligible minor child residing in the household so that the applicant can sign the form on behalf of the minor.[91]

One member of a household who meets the citizenship or qualified alien requirement qualifies the entire household for assistance.

Example of Household Eligibility

An eligible child born during the incident period for the declared event may qualify the household for assistance.

---

c.) Collection of Citizenship and Immigration Status Information

Applicants have repeatedly raised concerns regarding the release of immigration status information that FEMA collects in the application registration process. The information that FEMA collects as part of the registration process is protected under the Privacy Act;[92] however, as

---

[90] FEMA Form 009-0-03, Declaration and Release. Please note that FEMA Form 009-0-04 is the Spanish language form of the Declaration and Release. For copies of these forms, *see* http://on.fema.net/employee_tools/forms/Pages/fema_forms.aspx. FEMA's process for compliance with the Welfare Reform Act has been designed to meet the statutory requirements while not unduly slowing down the application process and provision of disaster relief assistance.

[91] Id.

[92] As provided in the Privacy Act Statement for Declaration and Release Form 009-0-01, information may be disclosed as generally permitted under the Privacy Act of 1974, as

provided in the Declaration and Release Form, FEMA is a component of DHS, and that information may be subject to sharing within the DHS, including but not limited to the U.S. Immigration and Custom Enforcement (ICE).[93] FEMA only collects that information necessary to qualify one member of the pre-disaster household. FEMA does not require applicants to declare their specific subcategory of qualified alien status[94] and does not collect citizenship/immigration status information regarding other household members, including the parent/guardian who applies on behalf of a qualifying child.[95]

2. Disaster-Related Necessary Expenses and Serious Needs

As noted in the Introduction to this chapter, federal disaster assistance is not the same as insurance and does not compensate survivors for all disaster-related losses. IHP is intended to meet basic disaster-related necessary expenses and serious needs[96] for housing,[97] and for food, lost personal property (such as basic furniture), and medical, dental, funeral and transportation expenses.[98] A necessary expense is defined as a cost associated with acquiring an item or items, obtaining a service, or paying for any other activity that meets a serious need.[99] A serious need is defined as the requirement for an item or service that is essential to an applicant's ability to prevent, mitigate, or overcome a disaster-related hardship, injury, or adverse condition.[100]

---

amended, 5 U.S.C. § 552a(b). This includes using this information as necessary and authorized by routine uses published in DHS/FEMA-008 Disaster Recovery Assistance Files System of Records Notice, 74 Fed. Reg. 48,763 (Sept. 24, 2009) and upon written request, by agreement, or as required by law.

[93] Declaration and Release Form 009-0-3.

[94] Id.

[95] See Application/Registration for Disaster Assistance, Form 009-0-01 and Declaration and Release Form 009-0-03.

[96] Stafford Act §408(a)(1), 42 U.S.C. §5174(a)(1); 44 C.F.R. §206.110(a).

[97] Stafford Act §408(c), 42 U.S.C. §5174(c).

[98] Stafford Act §408(e), 42 U.S.C. §5174(e).

[99] 44 C.F.R. §206.111 Definitions.

[100] Id.

a.) Disaster-related

An applicant who has incurred a disaster-related necessary expense or serious need in a declared state may be eligible for assistance without regard to the applicant's residency in that state. However, that disaster-related expense or need must be attributable to an area of the declared state designated for federal disaster assistance.[101] For purposes of Housing Assistance, that means the applicant's pre-disaster primary residence be located in a designated area. For purposes of Other Needs Assistance (personal property losses, medical, dental, funeral, etc.), that means that the loss occurred in a designated area irrespective of residence in the state or location of primary residence. For example, someone visiting a designated area whose vehicle is damaged or destroyed or who suffers an injury as a result of the disaster, may be eligible for ONA. An out of the state applicant who is "next of kin" may be eligible for ONA for funeral costs of someone whose death is attributed to the disaster.

b.) Displacement or Uninhabitable Pre-disaster Primary Residence for Housing Assistance

Eligibility for Housing Assistance (temporary housing, repair or replacement,[102] and permanent or semi-permanent housing construction)[103] but not ONA is limited to applicants with disaster-related housing needs who are displaced from their pre-disaster primary residence or whose pre-disaster primary residence is uninhabitable or, in the case of individuals with disabilities, rendered inaccessible or uninhabitable as a result of damages caused by the declared event.[104]

i). Pre-disaster Primary Residence

FEMA defines primary residence as 1) the dwelling where the applicant normally lives during the major portion of the calendar year, or 2) the

---

[101] *See* 44 C.F.R. § 206.40 Designation of affected areas and eligible assistance (b) Areas eligible to receive assistance and 206.2 (a)(6). Designated area: any emergency or major disaster-affected portion of a state which has been determined eligible for federal assistance.

[102] Only owner-occupants and not renters are eligible for repair or replacement assistance. *See* Stafford Act §408(c)(2)(A) and 3(A), 42 U.S.C. §5174(c)(2)(A) and (3)(A).

[103] Stafford Act §408(c)(1)-(4), 42 U.S.C. §5174(c)(1)-(4).

[104] Stafford Act §408(b)(1), 42 U.S.C. §5174(b)(1). *See also* 44 C.F.R. § 206.113(b)(8).

dwelling that is required because of proximity to employment, including agricultural activities that provide 50 percent of the household's income.[105] This includes any residence where the applicant "lived in the home more than six months of the year, or the applicant lists it as the address of his or her Federal Tax Return, or the applicant files a homestead exemption, or the applicant uses it as a voter registration address..."[106] Issues may arise regarding pre-disaster primary residence when an applicant is the process of moving from one residence to another and the move is interrupted by the disaster event. Questions of whether a damaged residence is a vacation or secondary home and not an eligible primary residence may also arise, especially in Sunbelt areas such Arizona or Florida with sizable "snowbird" populations. There may also be issues regarding whether student housing is an applicant's primary residence. *See* text box regarding IHP Eligibility for Students in Dorms at the end of this section.

ii). Displacement

A displaced applicant is one whose primary residence is uninhabitable, inaccessible, made unavailable by a landlord (to meet the landlord's own disaster housing need) or not "functional"[107] as a direct result of the disaster and who has no other housing available in the area, such as a secondary home or vacation home within a "reasonable commuting distance"[108] to the disaster area.[109] An applicant with adequate rent-free housing accommodations will not be eligible for housing assistance.[110] An applicant who owns available rental property that meets the applicant's temporary housing needs will also not be eligible for housing assistance.[111] An applicant who evacuated the residence in response to official warnings as a precautionary measure and who is able to return to

---

[105] 44 C.F.R. §206.111.
[106] *See* Application/Registration for Disaster Assistance, Form 009-0-1, page 2: Application/Registration for Disaster Assistance Instructions, note 16.
[107] Meaning an item or home that is capable of being used for its intended purpose. 44 C.F.R. §206.111.
[108] *See* 44 C.F.R. §206.111.
[109] *See* 44 C.F.R. §§206.111 and 206.113(a)(8)-(9) and (b)(3).
[110] Id at 206.113(b)(2).
[111] Id at 206.113(b)(3).

the residence immediately after the disaster incident will not be eligible for temporary housing assistance.[112]

iii).Uninhabitable

A residence (dwelling)[113] is considered "uninhabitable" for purposes of housing assistance if it is not:

- safe, i.e., secure from disaster-related hazards or threats to occupants;[114]
- sanitary, i.e., free of disaster-related health hazards;[115] or
- fit to occupy[116]
- as a result of disaster-related damages.[117]

The habitability for an owner-occupied residence is assessed at the time of the incident, while it is assessed at the time of the inspection for a renter occupied residence. It is presumed that an owner-occupant (eligible for all forms of housing assistance) whose residence is damaged will commence repairs immediately and will thus have incurred eligible out-of-pocket repair expenses by the time of the inspection, while a renter who is not eligible for repair or replacement assistance will not have such out-of-pocket expenses at the time of inspection. A renter may, however, be able to establish out-of-pocket temporary housing expenses because of displacement while repairs were made by the landlord to the residence prior to the inspection.

There has been one significant case on the habitability of an applicant's primary residence. In *La Union Del Pueblo Entero (LUPE) v. Fed. Emergency Mgmt. Agency*,[118] LUPE applicants sought disaster housing assistance after Hurricane Dolly. FEMA denied housing assistance because FEMA

---

[112] Id at 206.113(b)(4).
[113] Id at 206.111.
[114] Id.
[115] Id.
[116] Id.
[117] Stafford Act §408(b)(1), 42 U.S.C. §5174(b)(1).
[118] La Union Del Pueblo Entero (LUPE) v. Fed. Emergency Mgmt. Agency, 2008 U.S. Dist. LEXIS 102978 (S.D. Tex. Dec. 17, 2008); motion denied by, injunction granted at LUPE v. FEMA, 2009 U.S. Dist. LEXIS 40368 (S.D. Tex. May 13, 2009); vacated by, remanded by LUPE v. FEMA, 608 F.3d 217, 2010 U.S. App. LEXIS 11242 (Fifth Cir. Tex. 2010).

determined the damage was not a result of the storm; thus, any damages present were pre-existing. Among other claims, the LUPE applicants challenged the sufficiency of FEMA's regulations governing housing repair assistance and claimed that the regulations should state with particularity the criteria used to determine whether damage was disaster-related.

Initially, the District Court for the Southern District of Texas enjoined FEMA to: (1) publish definite and ascertainable criteria, standards, and procedures for determining eligibility for relief assistance; and (2) reconsider LUPE applicants' applications for housing assistance under the new criteria, standards, and procedures. On appeal, the Fifth Circuit determined that in creating FEMA's program, *Federal Assistance to Individuals and Households*,[119] Congress required FEMA to promulgate standards and criteria for housing assistance through regulations but did not require any level of specificity in the regulations. The court further found that FEMA had discretion to decide how specific its regulations would be and noted that responding to disasters requires a degree of flexibility that the regulations appropriately recognize. Accordingly, the Fifth Circuit concluded that the district court had abused its discretion in issuing the preliminary injunction, and remanded the case to the district court for further proceedings.

Concurrently, FEMA is currently in the process of revising its repair, replacement, and housing construction assistance regulations to help clarify the eligibility criteria for assistance.[120]

iv). Inaccessible

A residence is considered "inaccessible" if, as a result of the incident, the applicant cannot reasonably be expected to gain entry to his or her pre-disaster residence due to the disruption or destruction of access routes or because of other impediments to access or restrictions placed on movement by a responsible official due to continued health, safety, or security problems.[121]

---

[119] Stafford Act § 408, 42 U.S.C. § 5174; 44 C.F.R. §206.111.
[120] *See* Notice of proposed rulemaking; Housing Assistance due to Structural Damage; Docket ID FEMA-2010-0035; RIN No. 1660-AA68. See also
[121] 44 C.F.R. §206.111.

IHP Eligibility for Students in Dorms

IHP assistance, Housing, and ONA for students living in campus-affiliated housing or dormitories (on or off campus) during a disaster must be addressed in an appropriate manner to minimize or prevent duplication of benefits when processing student disaster-related unmet needs. Issues may be raised regarding insurance coverage (including coverage on a parent's homeowner's policy), continuing school obligation to provide housing,[122] and whether the housing can be considered the primary residence of the student.

1. Temporary Housing Assistance: IHP may provide Housing Assistance, such as Rental Assistance, when a student's primary residence is damaged or destroyed.

    a. In most cases, a dormitory or student housing is considered temporary and does not meet the definition of a primary residence; therefore, Rental Assistance is not initially provided unless the student can establish independent status.[123]

    b. Students living in off-campus/non-school-affiliated housing may be eligible for rental assistance if displaced from their pre-disaster primary residence.

2. ONA: all students who reside in dormitories or student housing at a college, university, or other institutions of higher learning may be eligible for ONA, irrespective of whether such housing is considered their primary residence.

    a. Students, regardless of roommate status, may be eligible for uninsured damaged personal property even though their school living arrangement is not their primary residence. If found eligible, assistance is limited to those items an individual student brought with them to school and excludes items provided by the school.

    b. Students may be eligible for medical, dental, funeral, transportation, and moving and storage expenses without regard to the type of pre-disaster housing.

---

[122] Please note that temporary facilities and permanent repair/replacement of damaged school housing may be provided under the PA program.

[123] "Independent status" refers to financial independence from parent(s) and/or guardian(s) such as to indicate that the student: does not have primary residence elsewhere and is responsible for his or her own living expenses: is at least age 24 by December 31 of the award year; was married prior to the disaster; is in a masters or doctorate program; has legal dependents; is an orphan or ward of the court; is on active military duty; is a military veteran; or has documented determination of independent status by a financial aid administer.

---

3. Unmet Needs - Insurance Coverage and Other Sources of Funding

IHP provides assistance to eligible individuals and households for their uninsured or under-insured disaster-related necessary expenses and serious needs that they are unable to meet through other means.[124] Assistance through other means includes monetary or in-kind contributions from voluntary or charitable organizations, insurance, other governmental programs, or any sources other than those of the applicant.[125] FEMA considers most of its assistance to be primary unless a disaster survivor has insurance that will meet those needs. *See* discussion on Duplication of Benefits Prohibition and the Sequence of Delivery later in this chapter.

a.) Applicants without Insurance

FEMA may provide assistance to applicants who do not have insurance for most of their verified housing losses up to the maximum allowable grant for the fiscal year without requiring the applicant to seek assistance from other sources, such as SBA.[126] In addition, if an applicant's eligible disaster-related losses exceed the amount of IHP repair or replacement assistance, the applicant may apply for a loan from the SBA to help with additional needs, including additional repair or replacement costs. The SBA considers FEMA IHP assistance already provided to the applicant in order to avoid a duplication of benefits prohibited under Stafford Act. *See* Section VIII, Other Needs Assistance (ONA) and FEMA's Interface with the Small Business Administration (SBA).

---

[124] Stafford Act § 408(a)(1), 42 U.S.C. § 5174(a)(1) and 44 C.F.R. § 206.110(a).
[125] 44 C.F.R. § 206.111.
[126] *See* discussion on Other Needs Assistance later in this chapter. In ONA, funeral, dental, and medical are not dependent on an applicant going to SBA for a loan first before seeking assistance from FEMA. All other ONA categories require that the disaster survivor go to SBA first for such items, such as clothing, household items, moving and storage, and essential tools. FEMA calls the latter categories "SBA dependent" because the applicant must go to SBA first.

---

b.) Applicants with Insurance

Under certain conditions set forth in FEMA regulations,[127] FEMA may provide assistance to applicants who have insurance. For example, if an applicant's insurance settlement is delayed, FEMA may provide assistance if the applicant agrees to repay FEMA from insurance proceeds that the applicant receives later. In addition, FEMA may provide assistance when insurance proceeds are less than the maximum amount of assistance FEMA can authorize and the disaster survivor continues to have necessary expenses or serious needs.[128]

E. The Duplication of Benefits Prohibition and the Sequence of Delivery

The Stafford Act includes a specific provision prohibiting the duplication of federal benefits.[129] Every agency in the federal government must assure that no one receives duplicate assistance for any part of a loss for which the individual or business has received financial assistance under any other program, from insurance, or from any other source.[130]

FEMA's implementing IHP regulations provide that FEMA will not provide IHP assistance when any other source has already provided such assistance or when such assistance is available from any other source. In the instance of insured applicants, FEMA will provide IHP assistance only when:

- Payment of the applicable benefits are significantly delayed;
- Applicable benefits are exhausted;
- Applicable benefits are insufficient to cover the housing or other needs; or
- Housing is not available on the private market.[131]

---

[127] 44 C.F.R. § 206.113(a)(2) – (6).
[128] At this time, if the insurance settlement is, for example, $50,000, but the verified loss is $55,000, FEMA's regulations do not allow it to provide funds above the maximum amount of assistance for the fiscal year at issue. Id. at 206.113(a)(4) and (a)(6).
[129] Stafford Act § 312, 42 U.S.C. § 5155.
[130] Id.
[131] 44 C.F.R. § 206.110(h).

The duplication of benefits prohibition essentially means that FEMA must coordinate individual assistance with other entities, as well as taking insurance coverage into consideration. Two of the most important are the SBA and non-profit voluntary organizations. *See* Section VIII, Other Needs Assistance (ONA) and FEMA's Interface with the Small Business Administration (SBA). FEMA's IA regulations provide a sequence of delivery scheme to allow each indicated agency or organization to deliver its assistance without regard to duplication later in the sequence.[132]

The usual order for delivery of services is:[133]

- Volunteer agencies' emergency assistance; homeowner and personal property insurance (including flood insurance); and FEMA emergency assistance;
- Housing assistance pursuant to section 408 of the Stafford Act;
- SBA and Farmers Home Administration (FHA)[134] disaster loans;
- ONA pursuant to section 408;
- Voluntary agencies' "additional assistance" programs and unmet needs committees; and
- The "Cora Brown Fund."

The sequence order thus determines what other resources the agency or organization must consider before it provides assistance.[135] In very large disasters, FEMA may provide rental assistance to eligible disaster survivors within 72 hours because it appears from the level of devastation that the disaster survivors will receive their insurance assistance significantly later.[136] The Stafford Act prohibits disaster survivors from collecting reimbursement from two different sources for the same loss, or a

---

[132] 44 C.F.R. § 206.191(d)(3)(i).

[133] 44 C.F.R. § 206.191(d)(2).

[134] As of this publication date, we are unaware of any FHA loans made to disaster survivors.

[135] *Id.*

[136] FEMA does not immediately provide funds for insurable losses, such as repair or replacement housing assistance, to disaster survivors who indicate that they have home insurance when they register for FEMA assistance. If they say they do not have insurance and turn out to be mistaken, which is when duplication with insurance is most likely to arise. Moreover, housing assistance, including repair or replacement assistance, will ordinarily not happen until there is a FEMA housing inspection.

"duplication of benefits."[137] If disaster survivors receive an insurance settlement greater than the amount they receive from FEMA for the same type of damage or loss, they must return their FEMA assistance because they have received duplicate benefits in violation of the Stafford Act prohibition.[138] While this result may initially seem unfair, Congress clearly determined that it was not appropriate for disaster survivors to be reimbursed twice for the same loss.

Military Basic Allowance Housing (BAH)

The survivor's receipt of an unrestricted housing allowance, such as Basic Allowance Housing (BAH) from the military, does not create a duplication of benefits under Section 312, preventing their receipt of Stafford Act housing benefits.

F. National Flood Insurance Coverage Requirement

Disaster applicants seeking housing repair or replacement assistance or seeking ONA for damaged property located in a designated Special Flood Hazard Area (SFHA)[139] are subject to National Flood Insurance Reform Act of 1994 (NFIRA) flood insurance requirement to obtain and maintain flood insurance.[140] A flood insurance "obtain and maintain" requirement is generated when disaster assistance for flood-damaged real and personal property is provided to applicants whose flood-damaged property is located within an SFHA.[141]

Disaster assistance for flood damaged insurable real and personal property located in an SFHA will not be provided unless the community where the property is located is participating in the National Flood Insurance Program (NFIP) at the time of the declaration.[142] However, the state may ask for an extension of time for FEMA to accept IHP applications and

---

[137] 42 U.S.C. § 5155.
[138] Id.
[139] See 42 U.S.C. § 5154(a) and 44 C.F.R. § 206.110(k) and 206.113(b)(7).
[140] NFIRA, as amended, Pub. L. No. 102-125; 42 U.S.C. § 4001-4129.
[141] The Flood Disaster Protection Act of 1973, Pub. L. No. 93-134; 42 U.S.C. §§ 4001-4129.
[142] See 44 C.F.R. §§ 206.110(k)(2) and 206.113(b)(7) ;

process applications if the community qualifies for and enters the NFIP during the six months following the declaration.[143]

The NFIRA requirement applies only to real and personal property that is in a designated SFHA and that can be insured under the NFIP.[144] Homeowners' insurance virtually never includes flood insurance. ONA recipients may be eligible for Group Flood Insurance Policy (GFIP) coverage to meet their initial obtain and maintain flood insurance requirements for their flood damaged property. *See* discussion in Group Flood Insurance Policy (GFIP) later in this chapter for more information.

An applicant who had a prior NFIRA requirement for any reason is ineligible for future federal assistance for flood-damaged real and personal property if he or she did not obtain and maintain flood insurance.[145] The applicant may only be eligible for medical, dental, funeral, transportation, uninsurable real property, and rental assistance and any loss that was not flood related.[146]

III. Transition from Section 403 Emergency Assistance (Response) to Section 408 Housing Assistance (Recovery)

As discussed in Chapter 4, *Response* and in Chapter 5, *Public Assistance*, the Stafford Act authorizes emergency sheltering and other emergency assistance to meet life threatening needs.[147] FEMA provides or funds prolonged emergency sheltering and other emergency assistance as part of its PA program in extreme situations when such assistance is requested by the state and the affected local communities. There is no formal application to FEMA by individuals and households for such assistance, although in some cases, assistance is only provided to IHP registered applicants. These programs help form a bridge from immediate, short-term mass care and sheltering assistance provided by affected communities

---

[143] Id.
[144] Id.
[145] Flood Disaster Protection Act, of 1973, Pub. L. 93-234, 42 U.S.C. § 4106(a). *See also,* 44 C.F.R. § 206.110(k) and 206.113(b)(8).
[146] 44 C.F.R. § 206.113(b)(7).
[147] Stafford Act § 403(a)(3), 42 U.S.C. §5170b(a)(3).

---

and voluntary agencies to IHP's longer term housing assistance for IHP eligible applicants.

A. Emergency Sheltering Programs

FEMA has several PA Emergency Assistance Programs that may provide prolonged sheltering assistance to evacuees, immediate temporary repairs to residences to allow occupants to shelter in place, or debris removal from private property:

- Transitional Sheltering Assistance: for extended sheltering through hotel lodging for IHP eligible applicants who are unable to return to their communities because they are inaccessible or uninhabitable.

- Blue Roof Program: temporary repairs to damaged roofs to allow sheltering in place pending permanent repairs.

- Sheltering and Temporary Essential Power (STEP) Program: to provide essential, temporary repairs and power restoration for residences to allow sheltering in place pending permanent repairs.[148]

- Private Property Debris Removal: clearance of disaster-related debris creating a public health and safety hazard.

In general, these programs, which provide direct assistance instead of financial assistance for emergency sheltering and public safety concerns, are not considered a duplication of benefits for IHP assistance.

B. Hurricanes Katrina and Rita (2005) Emergency Shelter and Temporary Housing Assistance Litigation

In 2005, hundreds of thousands of Gulf Coast residents fled Hurricanes Katrina and Rita, and many had nowhere to go. FEMA funded shelter to more than 100,000 evacuees in hotels and motels. This type of assistance can be very costly and can be financially and mentally stressful on

---

[148] STEP is a pilot program for the 2012 Hurricane Sandy declarations for New York, New Jersey, and Connecticut (FEMA-4085/4086/4087-DR).

---

survivors because of the lack of adequate cooking and laundry facilities and living in close quarters.

As the post-disaster circumstances stabilized and emergency conditions ended, FEMA began winding down the emergency sheltering program in order to transition eligible applicants to IHP.[149] Not all individuals in the sheltering program met the eligibility criteria for IHP assistance such as temporary housing assistance, and FEMA so notified them. Several groups sued FEMA, challenging various aspects of the transition from emergency sheltering to IHP.

1. Litigation on Transitioning to Temporary Housing Assistance

In *McWaters v. FEMA*,[150] disaster assistance applicants alleged that FEMA violated statutory and constitutional requirements in administering temporary housing assistance under IHP.

On June 16, 2006, the district court dismissed most of the plaintiffs' claims in its final order, but the court ruled that applicants for disaster assistance who meet the statutory eligibility criteria[151] have a constitutionally-protected property interest in the receipt of housing assistance under the Due Process Clause of the Fifth Amendment of the U.S. Constitution.[152] Nonetheless, the court ruled that the plaintiffs failed to prove that FEMA unconstitutionally deprived them of that interest. Instead, the court found that the significant delays in processing Katrina-related applications for housing assistance were inevitable due to the magnitude of the disaster and the multitude of applications for temporary housing assistance. Therefore, the court found no constitutional violation on which the plaintiffs could sue FEMA.

---

[149] Alternative Dispute Resolution (ADR) may be useful when terminating emergency shelter assistance for individuals. ADR has been successfully used to help survivors develop transition plans to more permanent living arrangements.

[150] 408 F. Supp. 2d 221 (E.D. La. 2006), *modified*, McWaters v. FEMA, 408 F. Supp. 2d 221; *dismissed in part, injunction granted*, McWaters v. FEMA, 436 F. Supp. 2d 802 (E.D. La. 2006).

[151] "…[I]ndividuals and households who are displaced from their primary pre-disaster residences or whose primary pre-disaster residences are rendered uninhabitable …" Stafford Act § 408(a)(2), 42 U.S.C. § 5174(a)(2).

[152] McWaters v. FEMA, 436 F. Supp. 2d 802, 816-818 (E.D. La. 2006).

The court required FEMA to provide evacuees with two weeks' notice prior to terminating their temporary housing assistance. In addition, the court permanently enjoined FEMA from requiring that applicants for temporary housing assistance apply for a loan from the SBA as a prerequisite of applying for or receiving temporary housing assistance, and from improperly communicating to applicants about SBA loan requirements.[153]

2. Litigation on Denial of Temporary Housing Assistance

In *Ass'n of Cmty Orgs. for Reform Now (ACORN) v. FEMA*, ACORN, acting for FEMA disaster applicants that Hurricanes Katrina and Rita affected, filed a class action complaint against FEMA. Specifically, the lawsuit targeted FEMA's transition of disaster applicants from the Stafford Act's emergency assistance program for shelter housing to the Stafford Act's temporary housing assistance program. ACORN sought injunctive relief. The Court denied ACORN's request for a temporary restraining order.

On November 29, 2006, the district court issued an order granting ACORN's motion for a preliminary injunction, determining, among other things, that FEMA's temporary housing assistance ineligibility notices contained cryptic, often conflicting, numeric codes that were meaningless without the explanation provided in a separate application guide, whose language was vague and non-individualized and thus the notices did not provide sufficient notice under the Fifth Amendment of the Constitution. FEMA appealed the November 29 order to the D.C. Circuit Court of Appeals. On December 22, 2006, the appellate court stayed the requirements that FEMA immediately restore short-term emergency sheltering assistance benefits and pay short-term emergency sheltering assistance that the applicable evacuees otherwise would have received

---

[153] Note that this district court's finding of a constitutionally-protected property right in the receipt of disaster housing assistance conflicts with a subsequent Fifth Circuit Court of Appeals decision in *Ridgely* v. *FEMA* [hereinafter *Ridgely*]. The Fifth Court of Appeals in *Ridgley* held that the Stafford Act and FEMA's implementing regulations alone do not create a constitutionally protected property right. *See Ridgely*, 2007 U.S. Dist. LEXIS 38461 (E.D. La. May, 2007); *injunction granted in part, Ridgely*, 2007 U.S. Dist. LEXIS 43009 (E.D. La. June 2007); *vacated in part, remanded, Ridgely*, 512 F.3rd 727 (Fifth Cir. La. 2008); *later proceeding, Ridgely*, 2010 U.S. Dist. LEXIS 136368 (E.D. La. Dec. 2010).

from September 1, 2006, through November 30, 2006. The circuit court denied the motion for stay pending appeal in all other respects

IV. Temporary Housing: Financial Assistance

One of FEMA's basic principles is to provide assistance to disaster applicants as soon as possible after a declared disaster. When a disaster survivor registers for assistance with FEMA and has met the basic requirements for eligibility, FEMA, after a housing inspection, may provide funds to assist with housing repair or replacement and/or for rental assistance as temporary housing assistance.[154] Temporary housing and repair assistance are to be utilized to the fullest extent practicable before other types of housing assistance.[155]

FEMA applicants can receive financial assistance to reimburse lodging expenses and/or rental assistance for up to 18 months[156] or the program maximum,[157] whichever occurs first. FEMA bases the amount of assistance on the Department of Housing and Urban Development (HUD) fair market rent (FMR) for the county within the declared disaster area where the primary residence is located.[158]

While FEMA determines rental assistance with reference to HUD's FMR, FEMA's rental assistance need not be identical to HUD's FMR. Federal courts upheld FEMA's broad discretion in calculating what FMR it will use in affected localities in *Watson v. FEMA*.[159]
If applicants are unable to make use of financial assistance, FEMA may provide direct assistance.[160]

---

[154] Stafford Act § 408(c)(1)(A), 42 U.S.C. § 5174(c)(1)(A).
[155] 44 C.F.R. § 206.110(c).
[156] The President may extend the housing program beyond 18 months if he finds that "due to extraordinary circumstances, an extension would be in the public interest." Stafford Act § 408(c)(1)(B)(ii), 42 U.S.C. § 5174(c)(1)(B)(ii).
[157] As noted, in FY 2013, that amount is $31,900.
[158] *See* 44 C.F.R. § 206.117(b)(1)(i)(B).
[159] *Watson v. FEMA*, C.A. No. H-06-1709, 2006 U.S. Dist. Lexis 34414 (S.D. Tex.); injunction granted, *Watson v. FEMA*, 438 F. Supp. 2d 638 (S.D. Tex.); vacated, motion denied, *Watson v. FEMA*, 2006 U.S. App. Lexis 29392 (Fifth Cir Sept 6, 2006).
[160] Stafford Act § 408(c)(1)(B), 42 U.S.C. § 5174(c)(1)(B).

A. Continued Assistance

After the individual or household receives an initial amount of rental assistance, FEMA may provide additional assistance if the survivor continues to require housing assistance and the applicant has developed a plan for obtaining permanent housing and is working towards that plan.[161] This process is called "recertification." Applicants are required to provide verifiable rental receipts, express an ongoing need for housing assistance, and demonstrate action towards achieving housing self-sufficiency in order to receive recertification.[162]

B. Utility Costs and Security Deposits

In response to Hurricane Katrina and issues relating to utility costs and security deposits, the Post Katrina Emergency Management Reform Act (PKEMRA)[163] amended the Stafford Act to allow for the payment of utility costs, excluding telephone service, and for the inclusion of security deposits. [164] FEMA's regulations regarding utility costs and security deposits were issued in 2002 and have not been revised to reflect these PKEMRA changes.[165]

---

[161] *See* 44 C.F.R. § 206.114(a) and (b)(1) – (5), Criteria for Continued Assistance.
[162] *Id. See* Fact Sheet: Conversion from Emergency Sheltering to Traditional Housing Assistance 1 (May 2006).
[163] Pub. L. 109–295, 120 payment of the deposit. The occupant must reimburse the full amount of the deposit when the temporary housing period ends.
[163] Stafford Act § 408(b)(1), 42 U.S.C. § 5174(b)(1).
[163] *See* 44 C.F.R. § 206.111; Stafford Act § 408(b)(1), 42 U.S.C. § 5174(b)(1).
[163] Stafford Act § 408(c)(1)(B)(i), 42 U.S.C. § 5174(c)(1)(B)(i).
[163] Stafford Act § 408(b)(1), 42 U.S.C. § 5174(b)(1). 408(b)(2)(A), 42 U.S.C. § 5174(b)(2)(A).Stat. 1355 (2006).
[164] *Id.* at § 689d(1) and (2). *See* Stafford Act § 408(c)(1)(A)(i) and (ii), 42 U.S.C. § 5174(c)(1)(A)(I and (ii)).
[165] 44 C.F.R. § 206.117(b)(1)(C) and (D). *See* 67 FR 61452, Sept. 30, 2002; 67 FR 62896, Oct.9, 2002. Pursuant to these regulations, the disaster survivor is responsible for utility costs and security deposits unless they are included in the rent. The disaster survivor occupant is also responsible for housing security deposits except in extraordinary circumstances when the Regional Administrator or his/her designee may authorize payment of the deposit. The occupant must reimburse the full amount of the deposit when the temporary housing period ends.

DOLR Chapter 6: Individual Assistance

> **CAUTION:**
> FEMA's procedures and practices in this area are in the process of
> review and revision at this writing. Reader is advised to check with the
> program area for any recent changes.

V. Temporary Housing: Direct Assistance

After most disasters, survivors are able to return to their homes within
hours or a few days once the immediate danger has passed. When an
event has significantly damaged or destroyed homes and rental resources
are unavailable, however, survivors may need some form of direct
housing assistance. The Stafford Act authorizes both financial assistance
and direct housing assistance for individuals and households who are
displaced from their pre-disaster primary residence[166] when that residence
is uninhabitable or inaccessible because of the declared event.[167] When
there is an insufficient supply of available housing for survivors, FEMA
may choose to implement a direct housing mission.[168] Housing missions
are extremely expensive. Beyond the financial commitment, they require
a significant commitment of time and personnel for much longer than the
usual disaster mission. An in-depth examination of the alternatives to a
direct housing mission is appropriate before direct housing for survivors
is undertaken.

A. Direct Housing Operations Program (DHOP)

FEMA developed its approach to provide housing for disaster survivors
based on cost effectiveness and what best meets the needs of the particular
households:[169] This discussion focuses on the authorities provided under
IHP for the provision of temporary housing units by lease or purchase
found in Stafford Act § 408(c)(1)(B)(i)[170] and does not address the new

---

[166] Stafford Act § 408(b)(1), 42 U.S.C. § 5174(b)(1).
[167] *See* 44 C.F.R. § 206.111; Stafford Act § 408(b)(1), 42 U.S.C. § 5174(b)(1).
[168] Stafford Act § 408(c)(1)(B)(i), 42 U.S.C. § 5174(c)(1)(B)(i).
[169] Stafford Act § 408(b)(1), 42 U.S.C. § 5174(b)(1). 408(b)(2)(A), 42 U.S.C. §
5174(b)(2)(A).
[170] Stafford Act § 408(c)(1)(B)(i); 42 U.S.C. § 5174(c)(1)(B)(i).

Lease and Repair of Rental Units for Temporary Housing authority provided for in § 408(c)(1)(B)(ii).[171]

- Maximize available housing resources;[172]
- Employ innovative forms of interim housing;
- Use manufactured and alternative interim housing; and finally,
- Under certain circumstances, authorize permanent or semi-permanent construction.[173]

FEMA's decisions, in concert with the state or tribe, concerning overall housing options, such as whether to use THUs or to rely on Rental Assistance alone, are generally made for all of the households in a particular area. For example, in Hurricanes Ike and Gustav, FEMA and the state of Texas decided to use THUs in the Beaumont and Port Arthur areas because there were insufficient rental resources available. Applicants in much of the rest of Texas received rental assistance because rental resources were available.

The Stafford Act requires that FEMA work to use existing housing resources before providing THUs.[174] If local housing resources are inadequate or if the community is unsafe for survivors, FEMA may, with the support of state and local partners, provide THUs to eligible individuals and households. Although FEMA bears the entire cost of providing disaster housing, the most successful recoveries from disasters occur when state and local partners fully support a direct housing mission.

---

[171] Stafford Act § 408(c)(1)(B)(ii); 42 U.S.C. § 5174(c)(1)(B)(ii).

[172] Maximizing available housing resources includes:
- Emergency shelters;
- Transitional shelters funded under Section 403 of the PA program;
- Rapid temporary roof repairs utilizing the U.S. Army Corps of Engineers Blue Roof Program or providing tarps to the states for distribution to disaster survivors;
- Financial assistance for rent;
- Financial assistance for repair and replacement of damaged residences; cataloguing vacant rental properties;
- Host-State Housing Protocol, permitting FEMA to facilitate rental assistance payments directly to property owners.

[173] *See* Stafford Act § 408(c)(4), 42 U.S.C. § 5174(c)(4) and the discussion later in this chapter.

[174] Stafford Act § 408(c)(1)(B)(i); 42 U.S.C. § 5174 (c)(1)(B)(i).

FEMA may place the THUs on the survivor's private property, on a pre-existing commercial pad, a group site which local officials approve and may provide and which FEMA constructs and maintains or, as a last resort, on a group site provided by FEMA.[175] One reason group sites are a last resort is because they take the survivors out of their neighborhoods and essentially create a new temporary neighborhood. This also involves many management considerations, including visitors, noise complaints, laundry facility availability, drug use, and safety and security. FEMA will take on the role of landlord for the duration of the housing mission, a role for which it may not be well-suited or prepared.

1. DHOP Implementation

a.) Direct Housing Operations Unit (HQ-DHOPS)

Once it has been determined a direct housing mission is required, the HQ-DHOPS in the Housing Branch of the HQ Recovery Directorate provides support in the field, including developing operating procedures for direct housing, tracking THU inventory levels, tracking ongoing housing operations, and developing THU specifications. DHOPS staff at the Joint Field Office (JFO) is responsible for coordinating the direct housing mission at the disaster, with support from regional and HQ-DHOPS as necessary. FEMA uses IA-TACs (Individual Assistance Technical Assistance Contracts) for some housing mission functions.

b.) Identification and Verification of Housing Resources

FEMA uses several methods to identify housing resources, including phone calls to apartment complexes, identification of available units by FEMA staff and partners during field operations, and contacts with local real estate agents and/or leasing agents. FEMA may request OFAs, such as HUD and the United States Department of Agriculture (USDA), to assess whether the units they manage may be available and appropriate for temporary disaster housing. With the assistance and cooperation of OFAs, including HUD and USDA, FEMA also maintains the "Housing Portal," a

---

[175] Id. § 408(d)(1)(A)(iii), 42 U.S.C. § 5174(d)(1)(A)(iii). *See also* 44 C.F.R. §206,117(b)(ii)(E).

web-based tool for tracking identified rental resources and making them available to the public.

c.) FEMA Contractor Support-Individual Assistance Technical Assistance Contracts (IA-TAC)

FEMA maintains IA-TACs with four contractors to provide a full range of technical assistance in support of IA programs, including direct housing missions.

The IA-TAC technical support may include:

- Housing mission planning;
- Disaster housing unit staging and management;
- Site assessments;
- Facilities management;
- THU haul, install, and deactivation;
- Group site/facility design;
- Coordinating housing resources;
- Performing needs assessments;
- Supporting applicant pre-placement interviews;
- Supporting Preliminary Damage Assessments;
- Performing shelter and mass care operations and management; and
- Providing unit assignment and occupancy support.

2. Temporary Housing Unit (THU) Placement

FEMA regulations provide four options for placing THUs:[176]

- Commercial sites - FEMA may lease vacant pads in existing commercial sites provided a site inspection determines the pads are suitable for THUs. These locations must meet floodplain management and other environmental compliance requirements, which are addressed in this section.

---

[176] Stafford Act § 408(d)(1)(A)(iii), 42 U.S.C. § 5174(d)(1)(A)(iii). *See also* 44 C.F.R. §206,117(b)(ii)(E).

- Private sites - provided by the disaster survivors; placement on a private site is cost-effective, reduces the risk of further damage, and facilitates applicant repair of the damaged dwelling. FEMA requires a private site feasibility inspection, separate from the previously discussed home inspection, to ensure that all necessary utilities are operational and that the unit will fit in the space available.

- Group site provided by the state or local government may include publicly owned park land with adequate utilities availability. Note that if cost-effective and timely, FEMA may undertake activity to develop the group site, including installation or repairs to essential utilities.

- FEMA-developed group sites on property FEMA leases and develops to accommodate THUs.

3. Environmental and Other Site Considerations

Prior to placing THUs on any private or commercial site, FEMA must comply with several federal, state, and local requirements.[177]

a.) State and Local Codes and Ordinances

State laws and local codes may prohibit locating mobile homes or smaller park models on certain property or in certain areas. FEMA will work with city, tribal, county, and state officials to seek waivers of these provisions.

Example of Waiving Local Codes

After Hurricane Ike in 2008 FEMA worked with local officials from Texas Gulf Coast communities where waivers of local ordinances were necessary to permit placement of THUs near disaster-damaged residences so disaster survivors could more quickly rebuild their properties.

---

[177] 44 C.F.R. § 206.117(b)(1)(ii)(C); *See* Chapter 8, *Environmental and Historic Preservation Laws.*

b.) National Environmental Policy Act (NEPA)

Executive Order 11,991[178] directs federal agencies to evaluate and inform the public about the environmental impacts of their activities pursuant to the National Environmental Policy Act (NEPA).[179] FEMA is the only federal agency with a statutory exclusion from compliance with NEPA for some of its activities. *See* Chapter 8, *Environmental and Historic Preservation Laws*, for a more detailed discussion of NEPA. Pursuant to several sections of the Stafford Act, disaster assistance, "which has the effect of restoring a facility substantially to its condition prior to the disaster or emergency," is exempt from compliance with NEPA requirements.[180]

Temporary housing at group sites is not exempt from compliance with NEPA.[181] In practice, this lack of an exemption means that FEMA must prepare an Environmental Assessment (EA)[182] prior to creating a group site for THUs. When FEMA places THUs on private residential sites, it does not normally do an EA.[183]

c.) Flood Plain Management and Protection of Wetlands

Executive Orders 11,988 (Floodplain Management) and 11,990 (Protection of Wetlands) require that FEMA avoid adverse impacts to floodplains and wetlands to the maximum extent possible in carrying out temporary housing activities.[184] FEMA's implementing regulations contain different requirements for placing THUs on group sites compared

---

[178] Exec. Order No. 11991, 42 FR 26967,

[179] 42 U.S.C. § 4231, *et seq.*

[180] Stafford Act § 316, 42 U.S.C. § 5159. These are: § 402, 42 U.S.C. § 5170a (General Federal Assistance); § 403, 42 U.S.C. § 5170b (Essential Assistance); § 406, 42 U.S.C. § 5172 (Permanent Work); § 407, 42 U.S.C. § 5173 (Debris Removal); § 422, 42 U.S.C. § 5189 (Simplified Procedures); and § 502, 42 U.S.C. § 5192 (Federal Emergency Assistance).

[181] Stafford Act § 408(c)(1)(B), 42 U.S.C. § 5174(c)(1)(B)..

[182] An EA is a concise public document discussing the purpose and need for the proposed action; a description of the proposed action; alternatives considered; environmental impact of the proposed action and alternatives; listing of agencies and persons consulted; and a conclusion of whether to prepare a much more detailed and lengthy Environmental Impact Statement. 44 C.F.R. § 10.9.

[183] 44 C.F.R. § 10.8(d)(xix)(D).

[184] 44 C.F.R. §§ 9.1 to 9.3.

to private or commercial sites.[185] *See* Chapter 8, *Environmental and Historic Preservation Laws*, which discusses floodplain requirements in detail.

d.) Coastal Barriers Resources Act (CBRA)

The Coastal Barriers Resources Act (CBRA)[186] established the Coastal Barrier Resources System (CBRS), comprised of undeveloped coastal barriers along the Atlantic, Gulf, and Great Lakes coasts. The law encourages the conservation of hurricane-prone, biologically rich coastal barriers by restricting federal expenditures that encourage development, such as federal flood insurance through the NFIP. CBRA is applicable to IHP repair/replacement assistance, and FEMA interprets the statute not to permit FEMA to locate a THU on an applicant's home site within the CBRS or other protected area. *See* Chapter 8, *Environmental and Historic Preservation Laws*, for a more detailed discussion of the CBRA.

e.) National Historic Preservation Act

FEMA activities must comply with its federal responsibilities set forth in the National Historic Preservation Act.[187] While assistance under IHP will generally not affect historic properties and will therefore be exempt from historic review, ground disturbing activities and construction related to direct housing assistance,[188] replacement housing,[189] and permanent

---

[185] *See* C.F.R. Part 9. The regulations provide that FEMA should analyze "group sites" using the 8-step process set forth in 44 C.F.R. §§ 9.6 to 9.12. Note that elevation to the base flood level is required. 44 C.F.R. § 9.11(d)(3). FEMA should analyze "private or commercial sites" using a modified process under 44 C.F.R. § 9.13(d); elevation up to the base flood level is required "to the fullest extent practicable" and in a manner consistent with the NFIP, 44 C.F.R. § 9.13(d)(4)(i) and (ii). FEMA Disaster Assistance Policy (DAP) 9453.3, Abbreviated Decision Process for the Placement of Mobile Homes, Travel Trailers, and Other Readily Fabricated Dwellings (Oct. 17, 2008), details the analysis and procedures for placing THUs on private or commercial sites in compliance with 44 C.F.R. § 9.13. For group, private or commercial sites, FEMA must analyze and minimize potential harm to both THU occupants and to the floodplains. FEMA must also meet any more restrictive state or local floodplain management standards for both group, individual or commercial sites. See 44 C.F.R. § 9.11(d)(6) and 44 C.F.R. § 9.13(d)(4)(ii).
[186] *CBRA*, Pub. L. No. 97-348, 16 U.S.C. § 3501, *et seq.*
[187] National Historic Preservation Act §§ 106, 16 U.S.C. § 470f and 110, 16 U.S.C. § 470h-2.
[188] *See* 44 C.F.R. § 206.117(b)(1)(ii).
[189] *Id.* § 206.117(b)(3).

---

housing construction[190] may require review under this statute.[191] One approach to assist with this requirement is to work with the state to establish a programmatic agreement regarding how it will work with FEMA to deal with historic preservation issues as they arise.[192]

FEMA must comply with state historic preservation laws as well. In the past, a federal district court enjoined FEMA where FEMA was alleged not to have properly consulted with the State Historic Preservation Officer.[193]

4. THU Safety

a.) A Case Study: Hurricane Katrina

As noted earlier, FEMA issued approximately 140,000 manufactured homes, travel trailers, and park model trailers to survivors in the unprecedented direct housing mission after Hurricanes Katrina and Rita in 2005. FEMA intended to house survivors in large mobile home sites set up across the Gulf Coast, but state and local officials wanted survivors located in or very near their devastated communities to encourage rapid rebuilding and recovery efforts. FEMA modified the housing plan to accommodate state and local concerns by placing THUs on survivors' private property wherever feasible. In many cases, private property lot sizes were too small to accommodate a mobile home, so FEMA provided smaller travel trailers instead. As a result, the majority of THUs used in the direct housing mission after Katrina and Rita were travel trailers.

Mobile homes are intended for long-term occupancy, and the HUD regulates their construction and safety, including formaldehyde emissions from the materials used to construct a mobile home. Travel trailers are smaller, transportable, and intended for occasional recreational use. There is no formaldehyde regulation or standard governing residential air quality for travel trailers.

---

[190] Id. § 206.117(b)(4).
[191] Id. § 206.110(m).
[192] 16 U.S.C. § 470.
[193] *Haynes Blvd. Preservation Association v. Julich*, 143 F. Supp. 2d 628 (E.D. La. 2001).

Formaldehyde is a chemical commonly found in many construction materials, home furnishings (e.g., fabrics and carpet), household products (e.g., nail polish, antiseptics, medicines, paper towels, cosmetics, etc.), and tobacco products. Formaldehyde-based resins are used as adhesives in composite wood products that are incorporated into travel trailers and mobile homes. Formaldehyde is an eye, nose, and throat irritant, and it may have an irritating odor.

FEMA received a number of complaints about formaldehyde fumes. FEMA took extraordinary steps to assist applicants to relocate from travel trailers, including providing:

- • Direct Lease Agreements;
- • Emergency Food Supplemental Assistance;
- • Emergency Furniture Assistance;
- • Emergency Lodging Assistance for Occupants in Direct Housing;
- • Emergency Pet Management and Sheltering; and
- • Emergency Packing, Transport, and Storage of Personal Property Assistance.

Disaster survivors filed approximately 90,000 administrative claims with FEMA, alleging personal injury from formaldehyde exposure. Plaintiffs filed over 1,600 lawsuits against the United States, FEMA's IA-TACs, and THU manufacturers, alleging personal injury and negligence. The United States has been dismissed as a defendant in virtually all lawsuits on the bases of the discretionary function exception under the Federal Tort Claims Act,[194] application of state Good Samaritan provisions (which preclude liability), and lack of misrepresentation by a government agent. Procedurally, claims have been denied for the failure of the plaintiff to exhaust administrative remedies in a timely fashion. A multidistrict litigation class action was also filed in Alabama, Mississippi, and Texas and was subsequently dismissed. The dismissal of the action against the United States in all three states has been affirmed by the Fifth Circuit Court of Appeals as of April 2013.[195]

---

[194] 28 U.S.C. § 2680(a).
[195] In Re: FEMA Trailer Formaldehyde Products Liability Litigation (Louisiana Plaintiffs), No 12-30635, (Fifth Cir. April 9, 2013)

FEMA's new THUs meet the most recent HUD standard for formaldehyde in their construction. In addition, FEMA coordinates with HUD and private industry during periodic review and revision of FEMA's specifications for manufactured homes. FEMA maintains specifications for northern and southern manufactured homes to ensure availability of units with the appropriate vapor barrier configurations, roof loads, wind loads, and thermal zone ratings.

b.) Formaldehyde Standards for Composite Wood Products Act

In July 2010, Congress passed the Formaldehyde Standards for Composite Wood Products Act,[196] establishing national standards for formaldehyde emissions from various wood products of the type used in travel trailers based on similar standards adopted by the California Air Resources Board. The new standards will become effective six months after the Environmental Protection Agency (EPA) adopts regulations for testing and enforcement. At the time of printing, EPA had promulgated regulations on this subject, expected to publish in the *Federal Register* in May 2013.[197] Please contact OCC for further details. The law also requires HUD to update its regulations for formaldehyde emission levels of products installed in manufactured homes. As of May 2013, HUD is currently in the process of reviewing its regulations for formaldehyde emission levels in manufactured housing[198]

FEMA's new THUs meet the most recent HUD standard for formaldehyde in their construction. In addition, FEMA coordinates with the HUD and private industry during periodic review and revision of FEMA's specifications for manufactured homes. FEMA maintains specifications for northern and southern manufactured homes to ensure availability of units with the appropriate vapor barrier configurations, roof loads, wind loads, and thermal zone ratings.

---

[196] Pub. L. 111-199 (2010), 15 U.S.C. § 2601 *note.*
[197] http://yosemite.epa.gov/opei/rulegate.nsf/byRIN/2070-AJ92?opendocument, http://yosemite.epa.gov/opei/rulegate.nsf/byRIN/2070-AJ44?opendocument.
[198] https://www.federalregister.gov/articles/2013/04/10/2013-08265/notice-of-a-federal-advisory-committee-meeting-manufactured-housing-consensus-committee-structural.

---

5. Special and/or Functional Needs

FEMA's and the federal government's ability to provide assistance to those with some physical or mental issues in a disaster continue to improve. *See* Chapter 4, *Response*, and its section on Evacuation and Sheltering. Accommodating those disaster survivors needing special assistance is an important part of FEMA's mission. PKEMRA made several changes to the Stafford Act affecting individuals with disabilities or functional needs.[199] In addition, FEMA must comply with several other federal laws, such as the Rehabilitation Act[200] and Americans with Disabilities Act (ADA)[201] in providing disaster assistance to individuals with disabilities or functional needs.

Section 504 of the Rehabilitation Act of 1973 ("Section 504") prohibits discrimination against individuals with disabilities in the programs, services, and activities of federal agencies, and in programs receiving federal financial assistance.[202] "disability" is a legal term that should be construed in favor of coverage. An individual with a disability has a physical or mental impairment that limits one or more major life activities, has a record of such impairment, or is regarded as having such an impairment.[203] Examples of "major life activities" are functions such as caring for oneself, walking, seeing, hearing, talking, breathing, and learning.[204] Individuals with disabilities may have access and functional needs that must be met to provide an equal opportunity to participate in or benefit from agency programs, services, and activities in accordance with Section 504.

With respect to FEMA's disaster assistance programs and activities, a "qualified individual with a disability" will usually mean an individual with a disability who meets the essential eligibility requirements for participation in or receipt of benefits from the program or activity.[205] If any of the agency programs or activities require the participants to achieve

---

[199] PKEMRA, Pub. L. 109-295 § 689.
[200] Rehabilitation Act, 29 § 701 *et seq.*
[201] Americans with Disabilities Act (ADA), *as amended*, 42 U.S.C. § 2101 *et seq.*
[202] 29 U.S.C. § 794.
[203] 44 C.F.R. § 16.103
[204] 44 C.F.R. § 16.103.
[205] 44 C.F.R. § 16.103

a certain level of accomplishment, then a "qualified individual with a disability" will mean an individual with a disability who meets the essential eligibility requirements and can achieve the purpose of the program or activity without modifications that would cause a fundamental alteration in the program or activity.[206] If modifications that do not cause a fundamental alteration in the program or activity are necessary for a qualified individual with a disability to participate in the program or activity, then the agency is required to provide those modifications.

Two other provisions in § 16.130 are worth noting. First, the agency may not provide qualified individuals with disabilities with different or separate aids, benefits, or services unless it is necessary to provide aids, benefits, or services that are as effective as those provided to other individuals.[207] Second, while the agency is allowed to provide separate or different programs or activities for individuals with disabilities, the agency may not deny a qualified individual with a disability the opportunity to participate in programs or activities that are not separate or different.[208] This means that the agency may be required to make reasonable accommodations so that individuals with disabilities may participate in programs and activities that are not separate or different. As an example, while state and local governments are technically permitted to create separate shelters for people with disabilities, under the ADA, they are still required to ensure that people with disabilities can benefit from shelter programs that are not "separate or different." Under the ADA (and Section 504), people with disabilities have the right to access government programs and services alongside the rest of the community.[209]

The notion of "program accessibility" is present throughout FEMA's Section 504 implementing regulations. One aspect of program accessibility is ensuring that individuals with disabilities are not physically excluded from FEMA programs because the program is located at a facility with architectural barriers. The regulations prohibit the agency from selecting facilities that have the effect of excluding individuals with

---

[206] 44 C.F.R. § 16.103.
[207] 44 C.F.R. § 16.130 (b)(1)(iv).
[208] 44 C.F.R. § 16.130 (b)(2).
[209] For a detailed discussion of the ADA and Section 504 requirements of state and local governments with respect to sheltering, please see the Order for Summary Judgment in *CALIF v. City of Los Angeles*, No. CV 09-0287 CBM (Central District of California 2011).

disabilities from programs or activities conducted by the agency.[210] This means that the agency must choose facilities that are architecturally physically accessible. The Architectural Barriers Act of 1968 requires access to buildings designed, built, altered, or leased with federal funds, such as post offices, social security offices, prisons, and national parks. It also applies to non-government facilities that have received federal funding, such as certain schools, public housing, and mass transit systems.[211]

Another aspect of "program accessibility" is "effective communication." FEMA is required to engage in "effective communication" with individuals with disabilities.[212] Effective communication is communication that is comparable in content and detail to communication with members of the public who do not have disabilities. Auxiliary aids and services may be necessary to achieve effective communication.[213] The agency is required to give primary consideration to the request of the individual with the disability to determine what type of auxiliary aid or service is necessary to achieve effective communication.[214] Sign language interpreters, video remote interpreting services, computer assisted real-time translation, amplifying devices, magnifying devices, and alternate formats of printed materials such as Braille and large print are auxiliary aids that may be used to provide effective communication.

The ability to provide a menu of options to meet the communication needs of individuals with disabilities requires advanced planning. When providing "effective communication," the agency is not required to take any action that would result in a fundamental alteration of the program or activity or that would result in undue financial and administrative burdens.[215] Practically speaking, the "undue burden" standard is difficult to meet, especially for federal agencies, which have relatively abundant financial resources. When giving legal advice on the requirement to provide "effective communication," the "undue burden" standard should

---

[210] 44 C.F.R. § 16.149.
[211] 42 U.S.C. §§ 4151 et seq.
[212] 44 C.F.R. § 16.160.
[213] 44 C.F.R. § 16.160 (a)(1).
[214] 44 C.F.R. § 16.160 (a)(1)(i).
[215] 44 C.F.R. § 16.160 (d).

typically be disregarded. It would be rare (or impossible) to come across an instance where FEMA was not obligated to provide effective communication to someone seeking disaster assistance. Instances where the agency should plan for effective communication include Disaster Recovery Centers, public meetings, home inspections, and any other situations where FEMA personnel are interacting with the public. In addition, FEMA must ensure effective communication with survivors who register for disaster assistance over the telephone (NPSCs). Some tools available to NPSC operators are video relay service interpreters and TDD (Telecommunications Device for the Deaf).[216]

6. Ongoing Operations: Revocable License and Recertification of Eligibility

If FEMA determines that it is appropriate to assign a THU to an individual or household, the applicant must sign a Form 90-69D-Receipt for Government Property, a revocable license to occupy the unit.[217] The license contains the following conditions for continued occupancy:

- Acknowledgement that the unit is federal property provided as a discretionary benefit and that the government retains the right to revoke the license to use the unit at any time after written notice;

---

[216] Practice point: The National Center for Law and Economic Justice (NCLEJ) filed a complaint with the Civil Rights and Civil Liberties Office in 2007 claiming that FEMA failed to communicate effectively with Hurricane Katrina evacuees who were deaf or hard of hearing in violation of Section 504. One element of the complaint stated that FEMA representatives would not communicate with survivors using a video relay service interpreter without a consent form. After NCLEJ filed this complaint, FEMA issued internal guidance clarifying that relay operators are not third party intermediaries and that a consent form is not required to communicate with FEMA using video relay services. Interpreters are tools for effective communication, not third parties.

[217] For Lease and Occupancy Agreements, see FEMA Disaster Assistance Policy (Interim) 9451.5 [hereinafter DAP 9451.5], *Termination of Leases and Occupancy Agreements under Direct Assistance (Temporary Housing Units)*, Attachment A, Section A, 8-9, <http://ia.fema.net/contents/policy/terminations.asp>. See also *Termination of Leases and Occupancy Agreements under Direct Assistance (Temporary Housing Units)*, Standard Operating Procedure (SOP), February, 2009. For forms applicable to license revocation, <http://ia.fema.net/contents/policy/terminations_SOP.asp>. Note: DAP 9451.5, § III, states that it applies only to Lease and Occupancy Agreements and that a separate policy will cover termination of revocable licenses under direct assistance in IHP. Several Notice of Revocation forms applicable to License Revocations, however, are online. <http://ia.fema.net/contents/policy/terminations_SOP.asp>.

- The duty to meet all FEMA program eligibility criteria for continuing to occupy the unit;

- The duty to obtain and occupy permanent housing at the earliest possible time;

- The duty to comply with any enforcement or removal action;

- The duty to assign to FEMA any insurance benefits for temporary lodging that the applicant receives or to which he or she is entitled;

- Acknowledgement that the applicant will be responsible for damages to the unit or charges for enforcement actions; and

- The duty to comply with all rules listed in the license, all park or group site rules, and relevant ordinances for private property sites.

FEMA regulations require that all recipients of temporary housing assistance establish a permanent housing plan to obtain and occupy permanent housing at the earliest possible time.[218] FEMA monitors applicants' progress toward completion of their permanent housing plan through a periodic recertification process to ensure that they have a verifiable continued need for FEMA-provided temporary housing assistance.[219] Recertification caseworkers meet periodically with applicants to review their progress in achieving their permanent housing plan.[220]

The Stafford Act limits the period during which FEMA may provide direct housing assistance to 18 months, beginning on the date of declaration, unless FEMA determines that an extension is warranted due to extraordinary circumstances.[221]

FEMA has previously used lease agreements to house disaster survivors when it established a housing mission. Many states, however, have statutes preventing a landlord from ending a lease until the lease term has

---

[218] 44 C.F.R. § 206.114(a). *See also* 44 C.F.R. § 206.111. *Permanent housing plan* means a realistic plan that, within a reasonable timeframe, puts the disaster survivor back into permanent housing that is similar to their pre-disaster housing situation.
[219] Id. at § 206.114(b)
[220] Id.
[221] Stafford Act, § 408(c)(1)(B)(ii); 42 U.S.C. § 5174(c)(1)(B)(ii).

ended. Such laws might compel FEMA to continue its temporary housing mission long past the congressionally mandated length of temporary housing. FEMA now uses a revocable license to clarify that the relationship between the FEMA and the disaster survivor is temporary and not one of landlord-tenant and that the disaster survivor should be working to move into a permanent housing situation in anticipation of the end of the housing program.

7. Ending the Direct Housing Mission

a.) License Revocation

The Stafford Act and FEMA regulations authorize FEMA to terminate direct housing assistance to individuals and households living in FEMA THUs.[222] FEMA may initiate termination action for reasons that include, but are not limited to:

- Ineligibility under IHP;[223]
- Refusal of rental assistance;[224]
- Fraud or misrepresentation;[225]
- General violations;[226]
- Major violations;[227]

---

[222] 42 U.S.C. § 5174(b), (i) and (j); 44 C.F.R. § 206.117(b)(ii)(G). Prior to Dec. 7, 2007, FEMA required eligible applicants for direct housing units to sign a Lease and Occupancy Agreement; for disasters after that date, the applicant signs a Receipt for Government Property/Revocable License.

[223] Examples of program ineligibility include: failure to establish or work toward a permanent housing plan; failure to respond to recertification requests; abandonment of the unit; failure to verify identity/citizenship status; primary residence not damaged

[224] 44 C.F.R. § 206.117(b)(1)(ii)(G)(2).

[225] 44 C.F.R. § 206.117(b)(1)(ii)(G)(3).

[226] Id. § 206.117(b)(1)(ii)(G)(4). General violations include: unauthorized pets, guests or vehicles; parking violations; failure to keep premises clean and sanitary; excessive noise disturbing other occupants; and violation of lease/rental agreement. For General Violations applicable to Lease and Occupancy Agreements, see DAP 9451.5, Attachment A, Section E. < http://ia.fema.net/contents/policy/terminations.asp>; for Notice of License Revocation for General Violation, see <http://ia.fema.net/contents/policy/terminations_SOP.asp>.

[227] Major violations or immediate threats to health and safety include criminal acts, or a non-criminal act that threatens the immediate health or safety of the occupant or other persons in the area. For Leases and Occupancy Agreements, see DAP 9451.5, Section VIII.

- Expiration of assistance period;[228]
- Failure to pay rent after 18 months.[229]

The currently available termination policies, procedures, and forms, including required notices and rights to appeal, are set forth in DAP 9451.5 and on the IA website.[230]

b.) Program Termination

The Stafford Act authorizes direct housing for 18 months following the date of declaration; [231] the Assistant Administrator for Recovery may extend that period if it is in the public interest due to extraordinary circumstances.[232] The Regional Administrator or his or her delegated Disaster Recovery Manager must submit the request for extension to the Assistant Administrator for Recovery, preferably at least 90 days prior to the end of the assistance period to allow sufficient time for review and determination.

FEMA may charge up to FMR for continued THU occupancy after the 18-month period, and failure to pay rent is grounds for terminating further direct housing assistance.[233] FEMA calculates FMR for a THU based on the HUD FMR for rental resources in the county or parish where the unit is located, and based on the size of the unit.[234] FEMA considers the ability to

---

J. and Attachment A, Section F, 10-11. For Notice of Revocation for Major Violation, see < http://ia.fema.net/contents/policy/Termination%20SOP%20FINAL%20(013009).pdf >.

[228] Stafford Act § 408(c)(1)(B)(ii), 42 U.S.C. § 5174(c)(1)(B)(ii); 44 C.F.R. § 206.110(e).

[229] Stafford Act § 408(c)(1)(B)(iii), 42 U.S.C. § 5174(c)(1)(B)(iii); 44 C.F.R. § 206.117(b)(1)(ii)(F-G); FEMA Recovery Policy (Interim) IA06-17.*Disaster Housing Rent Collection* (March 17, 2006) sets forth the policy on determining the rent to be charged.

[230] DAP 9451.5; http://ia.fema.net/contents/policy/terminations.asp

[231] Stafford Act § 408(c)(1)(B)(iii), 42 U.S.C. § 5174(c)(1)(B)(ii).

[232] Stafford Act § 408(c)(1)(B)(iii), 42 U.S.C. § 5174(c)(1)(B)(iii); 44 C.F.R. § 206.110(e).

[233] Stafford Act § 408(c)(1)(B)(iii), 42 U.S.C. § 5174(c)(1)(B)(iii); 44 C.F.R. § 206.117(b)(ii)(F-G).

[234] FEMA Recovery Policy (Interim) IA06-17, *Disaster Housing Rent Collection* (Mar. 17, 2006). *See also*, discussion of financial assistance, *above*.

pay in adjusting the amount of rent based on adjusted monthly household income.[235]

Terminating direct housing missions following large disasters can be very challenging when some individuals and households experience great difficulty transitioning back to self-sufficiency after the trauma of a major disaster. FEMA has taken unique and creative measures to encourage and assist the remaining survivors in transitioning out of THUs.

8. Disposing of THUs - Sales and Donations

a.) Sales to THU Occupants

FEMA may sell the units that it has purchased for use as temporary disaster housing to the individual or household occupying the unit at a price that is "fair and equitable" if the occupant lacks permanent housing and has a site for the THU that complies with local codes and ordinances and regulations applicable to floodplain management and wetland protection.[236] A THU occupant purchasing his or her unit must agree to obtain and maintain hazard insurance and flood insurance if the unit will be located in an SFHA.[237]

b.) Other Methods of Disposal

At the conclusion of a direct housing mission, FEMA sends used THUs to a temporary housing storage area, where FEMA personnel or contractors inspect them based on guidance from the Logistics Management Directorate to determine if the units should be disposed of or can be reused. The Stafford Act and FEMA regulations and policy set forth certain requirements for disposal of THUs through sale or donation,[238] but all of

---

[235] Id. See 44 C.F.R. § 206.117(b)(ii)(F).
[236] 44 C.F.R. § 206.118(a)(1)(i). FEMA considers "fair and equitable" to be fair and equitable to both the applicant and the government.
[237] Stafford Act § 408(d)(2)(A)(iv), 42 U.S.C. § 5174(d)(2)(A)(iv); 44 C.F.R. § 206.118(a)(1)(iii).
[238] Stafford Act § 408(d)(2), 42 U.S.C. § 5174(d)(2); 44 C.F.R. § 206.118; FEMA Recovery Policy 9455.1, *Temporary Housing Unit Donations Directive*, (Aug. 16, 2006); Recovery Policy 9455.2 (Interim) *Sale of Temporary Housing Units to Occupants* (Apr. 19, 2007).

FEMA's "sales" to persons who were not occupants of the temporary housing go through the General Services Administration (GSA), the U.S. government's agency with full authority and an established process to sell personal property.[239]

FEMA may also sell, transfer or donate THUs to a state or local government or a voluntary organization for the sole purpose of providing temporary housing to survivors after a disaster or emergency, if the receiving entity agrees to certain conditions.[240] FEMA's policy on donated housing units sets forth the respective costs of the parties and requires that the recipient sign an agreement with FEMA setting forth the conditions of the transfer, including a commitment that it will use the units for a minimum period of time as temporary housing for disaster survivors.[241] FEMA may also sell THUs to any person, and, as noted previously, accomplishes such sales through GSA, which has the process in place to sell this type of property.

B. Disaster Housing Assistance Program (DHAP)

The purpose of DHAP is to leverage HUD's expertise in administering federal housing programs in assisting eligible low-income disaster survivors to find temporary housing solutions that will help them transition to non-disaster, self-sufficient housing. FEMA and HUD initiated DHAP through an Interagency Agreement (FEMA-HUD IAA) in 2007 as a pilot program to assist survivors of hurricanes Katrina and Rita transition to self-sufficiency.

Under DHAP, when FEMA determines that disaster survivors need housing assistance beyond that provided under IHP guidelines for temporary housing, it refers those survivors to HUD, which in turn utilizes its local Public Housing Authorities (PHAs) for delivery of DHAP services. The

---

[239] Personal property is essentially everything that is not real estate. The Federal Management Regulations govern the disposal of personal property. See 41 C.F.R. Ch. 201, et seq.

[240] The receiving agency must agree to comply with the non-discrimination provisions of Stafford Act § 308, 42 U.S.C. § 5151, and to purchase hazard and flood insurance. 42 U.S.C. 5174(d)(2)(B)(ii); 44 C.F.R. § 206.118(a)(2)(1).

[241] FEMA Recovery Policy (Interim) 9455.1, *Temporary Housing Unit Donations* (Aug. 16, 2006).

PHAs, with FEMA funding, provide continued housing assistance, security and utility deposits, lease termination payments, and access to DHAP service resources that can assist recipients on the road to self-sufficiency.

HUD provides rental assistance and case management services to displaced disaster survivors who have not previously received HUD assistance. The PHAs contact landlords and ensure the necessary documents are in place so that families will continue to receive uninterrupted assistance payments through DHAP. The PHAs, through separate contractual arrangements with landlords, make rental payments on behalf of eligible survivors, paying the higher of the FMR rate or the PHA payment standard.

DHAP recipients must sign an agreement with their landlord to pay a portion of their rent in preparation towards non-disaster funded housing when DHAP ends. For Katrina and Rita DHAP, the PHAs implemented the incremental rent transition by reducing the monthly rental subsidy by $50 for the third rent subsidy payment after the rental contract was in effect. The subsidy was decreased incrementally by an additional $50 each month until the recipient's participation in DHAP ended, or the rent subsidy amount equaled $0, or the program ended with the final subsidy payment, whichever occurred first. Recipients could request a hardship waiver of this requirement. Under the FEMA-HUD agreement, DHAP participants worked with "service connectors" to develop an exit strategy from DHAP assistance to non-disaster funded housing. DHAP service connectors established a needs assessment and individual development plan with non-disaster funded housing as the final goal, and service connections related to the needs and goals. DHAP service connectors referred program participants to case management providers for holistic case management services, including FEMA supported case management providers. We discuss Case Management Services later in this chapter.

DHAP is a possible option for presidentially declared disasters, where FEMA authorizes temporary housing and FEMA's recertification process determines that a need exists for long-term assistance. Following FEMA's initial recertification, the FEMA Assistant Administrator for Recovery may determine the best categories of candidates for DHAP, and how, for example, providing FEMA's financial assistance to some survivors while providing DHAP assistance to others may improve the overall assistance to survivors, allowing the greatest number of survivors to meet their long-term housing needs.[242]

The original Katrina/Rita DHAP pilot program was scheduled to end in February 2009. Prior to that date, DHS Secretary Janet Napolitano announced a six-month transition program to ensure families had an opportunity to move on to self-sufficiency or to obtain a HUD Housing Choice Voucher[243] that allowed them to rent housing from private landlords. The program ended October 31, 2009, after assisting 37,000 families. Approximately 12,000 of those families obtained a Housing Choice Voucher.[244]

In 2008, DHAP for Hurricanes Ike and Gustav was instituted to assist the disaster survivors from those hurricanes. On February 5, 2010, FEMA Administrator Craig Fugate extended DHAP-Ike until May 27, 2010, giving approximately 11,000 families displaced by Hurricanes Ike and Gustav more time to transition to longer-term housing solutions.

VI. Repair and Replacement Assistance (Financial Assistance)

A. General Eligibility

IHP Housing Assistance provides financial assistance for the repair or replacement of non-insured/underinsured owner-occupied primary residences made uninhabitable or destroyed by a declared disaster event.[245]

---

[242] FEMA-HUD IAA, p. 6-50, at 5.
[243] The HUD Housing Voucher program provides a form for families to present to landlords in order to rent suitable housing. Details are available on the HUD website: http://portal.hud.gov/hudportal/HUD?src=/program_offices/public_indian_housing/programs/hcv;
http://portal.hud.gov/hudportal/HUD?src=/program_offices/public_indian_housing/programs/hcv/forms/guidebook.
[244] HUD Lauds Housing Authorities, HUD Staff as Disaster Housing Program for Families Displaced by Hurricanes Katrina and Rita Ends, RealEstateRama. <
http://www.disasterlegalaid.org/news/article.288964-
HUD_Lauds_Housing_Authorities_Hud_Staff_As_Disaster_ Program_For_Fam >
[245] Stafford Act § 408(c)(2) and (3), 42 U.S.C. § 5174(c)(2) and (3).

The maximum amount of assistance available to an applicant (individual/household) for either repair or replacement assistance per declaration is the IHP maximum amount of assistance for the fiscal year in question.[246] The subcap maximum amounts provided for in the IHP repair/replacement regulations[247] refer to statutory caps previously contained in the Stafford Act.[248]

Applicants who receive repair or replacement assistance will be subject to NFIP flood insurance requirements to obtain and maintain flood insurance if their property is located in a SFHA.[249] *See* National Flood Insurance Coverage Requirement discussion earlier in this chapter.

Applicants for repair or replacement assistance are subject to the National Environmental Policy Act (NEPA) and other environmental laws.[250] *See* discussion on Environmental and Other Site Considerations earlier in this chapter. Projects funded with replacement assistance may be subject to National Historic Preservation Act requirements for ground disturbing activities and construction.[251]

Cases that are eligible for Home Repair or Replacement and have FEMA verified losses that exceed $20,000.00 should be reviewed to ensure that the total IHP award includes funds for Rental and/or Funeral Assistance (ONA), if required.[252] Funds required for Rental and/or Funeral Assistance should be granted before funds for Home Repair or Replacement.[253]

---

[246] For disasters declared in FY 2013 (Oct 1, 2012-Sept. 30, 2013), this amount is $31,900. *See* Stafford Act § 408(h), 42 U.S.C. § 5174(h).
[247] 44 C.F.R. § 206.117(b)(2)(iv) and (b)(3).
[248] Prior to the 2006 Post Katrina Emergency Reform Act (PKEMRA) amendments to Stafford Act § 408(c)(2) and (3), there was a $5,000 maximum allowable repair assistance amount and a $10,000 maximum allowable replacement assistance amount.
[249] 44 C.F.R. § 206.110(k).
[250] 44 C.F.R. § 206.110(l).
[251] 44 C.F.R. § 206.110(m).
[252] Processing Procedure Manual, Housing Assistance Guidance, II.R.4., Processing Repair/Replacement Housing Grants Over $20K (Jul. 19, 2011).
[253] Id.

1. Repair Assistance

IHP repair assistance is available for the repair of owner-occupied private residences, utilities, and residential infrastructure, including private access routes that have damaged by a declared event.[254] The purpose is to repair the home to a safe and sanitary living or functioning condition, not to return a home to its condition before the disaster.[255] FEMA may provide up to the IHP maximum for home repair; then the applicant may apply for a Small Business Administration disaster loan for additional repair assistance.[256] *See* the discussion in The Duplication of Benefits Prohibition and the Sequence of Delivery earlier in this chapter.

Applicants are responsible for obtaining all permits or inspections applicable to that state or as local building codes require.[257]

Applicants who meet all of the following criteria (as verified by an inspection) may be eligible for repair assistance:

- Owner-occupant;[258]

- Primary residence damaged by the disaster,[259] with habitability repairs required;[260] and

- • No insurance or underinsured for the cause of damage or delayed insurance proceeds if the applicant agrees to repay the IHP assistance.[261]

FEMA may also provide assistance for eligible hazard mitigation measures that reduce the likelihood of future damage to damaged residences, utilities, or infrastructure.[262] However, funds for specific mitigation items are not generally awarded as a part of the initial repair assistance,

---

[254] Stafford Act § 408(c)(2)(A)(i), 42 U.S.C. § 5174(c)(2)(A)(i).
[255] Id.
[256] *See* Stafford Act § 408(c)(2)(B), 42 U.S.C. § 5174(c)(2)(B).
[257] 44. C.F.R. § 206.117(b)(2)(v).
[258] 44. C.F.R. § 206.117(b)(2)(i).
[259] Id.
[260] 44. C.F.R. § 206.113(a)(8). *See* also previous discussion in text in Displacement or Uninhabitable Pre-disaster Primary Residence for Housing Assistance.
[261] 44. C.F.R. § 206.113(a)(2)-(7).
[262] Stafford Act § 408(c)(2)(A)(ii), 42 U.S.C. § 5174(c)(2)(A)(ii); 44 C.F.R. § 206.117(b)(2)(iii).

unless requested by the Disaster Recovery Manager and approved by Headquarters. FEMA has built into repair line items funds for good construction practices that may incorporate mitigation measures, such as strapping water heaters or oil tanks that need replacing, and elevating electrical panels that need replacing.

2. Replacement Assistance

IHP Replacement Assistance is available for the replacement of owner-occupied private residences damaged by a declared event.[263]

Applicants who meet all of the following criteria (as verified by an inspection) may be eligible for replacement assistance:

- Owner-occupant;[264]
- Primary residence destroyed by the disaster;[265] and
- No insurance or underinsured for the cause of damage.[266]

Replacement assistance may be approved for applicants whose damages are less than the statutory limit for the respective declaration in extraordinary circumstances when FEMA determines it is more appropriate than other forms of Housing Assistance.[267]

B. Owner-Occupied Primary Residence

Owners are eligible for the full spectrum of IHP assistance, including repair or replacement assistance for owner-occupied private residences[268] and ONA for their personal property. "Owner-occupied" means that the residence is occupied by 1) the legal owner; 2) a person without formal

---

[263] Stafford Act § 408(c)(3)(A), 42 U.S.C. § 5174(c)(3)(A).
[264] 44 C.F.R. § 206.117(b)(3).
[265] Id. FEMA may also consider residences condemned under state law/local ordinances as destroyed.
[266] 44 C.F.R. §§ 206.110(a), 44. C.F.R. § 206.113(a)(2)-(7).
[267] 44 C.F.R. § 206.117(b)(3), Please note that the $10,000 subcap limit is no longer valid.
[268] Stafford Act § 408(c)(2)(B) and (c)(3)(B), 42 U.S.C. § 5174(c)(2)(B) and (c)(3)(B). Because they do not own their residence, renters may receive ONA but not repair or replacement assistance for the residence where they were living.

title who does not pay rent but is responsible for the payment of taxes or maintenance; or 3) a person with lifetime occupancy rights with formal title vested in another.[269] Proof of ownership and ownership or occupancy rights may be an issue in island or insular area disasters because of family compounds, adverse possession, hereditary family lands, and cultural traditions. There may also be an issue on tribal lands where the land is owned or controlled by the tribe or held in trust by the United States while the dwelling is owned by the occupant. Therefore, deeds or mortgage documents may not always be available or applicable, so FEMA may accept other suitable documentation to establish ownership.[270]

C. Eligible Costs

1. Repair Assistance

Repairs to the primary residence or replacement of items must be disaster-related and must be of average quality, size, and capacity, taking into consideration the needs of the occupant. Repairs to the primary residence are limited to restoration of the dwelling to a safe and sanitary living or functioning condition and may include the following repair and replacement items:[271]

- • Structural parts of a home (foundation, outside walls, roof); [272]
- • Windows, doors, floors, walls, ceilings, cabinetry;[273]
- • Septic or sewage system; [274]
- • Well or other water system;[275]
- • Heating, ventilating, and air conditioning system;[276]

---

[269] 44 C.F.R. § 206.111.
[270] For example, FEMA generally used certifications by the Village Matai or Chief for disasters in American Samoa to establish ownership and occupancy to the damaged dwelling where the land is held communally. FEMA also works with tribal governments to obtain certifications for dwellings on tribal lands.
[271] 44 C.F.R. 206.117(c)(2).
[272] Id. § 206.117(c)(2)(i)
[273] Id. § 206.117(c)(2)(ii) and (v).
[274] Id. § 206.117(c)(2)(iv).
[275] Id. § 206.117(c)(2)(iv).
[276] Id. § 206.117(c)(2)(iii).

- • Utilities (electrical, plumbing, and gas systems);[277]
- • Entrance and exit ways from the home, including privately owned access roads and bridges;[278] and
- • Blocking, leveling and anchoring of a mobile home and reconnecting or resetting its sewer, water, electrical and fuel lines and tanks.[279]

2. Eligible Replacement Assistance Costs

The amount of replacement assistance for an eligible applicant will be limited to the lesser of the following:[280]

- The statutory maximum;[281]
- The total amount of verified disaster-related damages to the dwelling; or
- The actual cost of the replacement dwelling.

Applicants who receive replacement assistance may either: (1) replace their dwelling in its entirety for the statutory maximum or less; or (2) use the assistance as a down payment on a new permanent residence that is greater in cost than the statutory maximum.[282]

---

[277] Id. § 206.117(c)(2)(iii).
[278] Id. § 206.117(c)(2)(vi).
[279] Id. § 206.117(c)(2)(vii).
[280] Id. §§ 206.117(b)(3) and (c)(3).
[281] As discussed in the text, the IHP statutory subcap for replacement assistance was repealed under PKEMRA in 2006; however, the IHP regulations have not been revised to reflect this change, and they still refer to the $10,000 subcap. See 44 C.F.R. § 206.117(b)(3). The maximum statutory cap is now the IHP maximum financial assistance amount, which, for FY 2013, is $31,900.
[282] 44 C.F.R. § 206.117(b)(3). As discussed in the text and in the previous footnote, the maximum statutory cap is now for replacement is the IHP maximum financial assistance amount, which, for FY 2013, is $31,900 and not the $10,000 subcap referred to in the regulations.

VII. Permanent or Semi-Permanent Construction

FEMA may provide financial assistance or direct assistance to individuals or households to construct permanent or semi-permanent housing in insular areas[283] outside the continental United States and in other locations in cases in which

- no alternative housing resources are available; and

- the types of temporary housing assistance FEMA normally deploys, such as rental assistance, temporary sheltering assistance, or providing THUs directly to applicants are unavailable, infeasible, or not cost-effective.[284]

This type of assistance occurs only in very unusual situations, in locations specified by FEMA, where no other type of housing assistance is possible. Construction must be consistent with current minimal local building codes and standards where they exist, or minimal acceptable construction industry standards in the area. Construction will aim toward average quality, size, and capacity, taking into consideration the needs of the occupant.[285]

If the home is located in a SFHA, the homeowner must comply with flood insurance purchase requirements and local flood codes and requirements.[286]

VIII. Other Needs Assistance (ONA) and FEMA's Interface with the Small Business Administration (SBA)

ONA[287] provides financial help to both owners and renters with other serious or necessary disaster-related unmet needs, separate and distinct from housing assistance. Much of what ONA covers, including specific

---

[283] Insular Areas include American Samoa, Guam, the U.S. Virgin Islands, the Commonwealth of the Northern Marianas. *See* 48 U.S.C. § 1469a.

[284] Stafford Act § 408(c)(4), 42 U.S.C. § 5174(c)(4); 44 C.F.R. § 206.117(b)(4). *See also* IA Fact Sheet: *Assistance to Individuals and Households* (September 30, 2008).

[285] 44 C.F.R. § 206.117(c)(3).

[286] Stafford Act § 408(c)(3)(B), 42 U.S.C. § 5174(c)(3)(B). *See also* 44 C.F.R. § 206.110(k)(3).

[287] Stafford Act § 408(e), 42 U.S.C. § 5174(e).

personal property, is agreed upon with the states, which must pay a cost share.[288] There are lists of ONA-eligible expenses, as well as amounts to be awarded—all worked out in advance with each affected state.[289] Needs must be serious or necessary, as well as disaster-related, to be eligible for ONA. A "serious need" for an item or service is present if the item or service is essential for an applicant to prevent, reduce, or overcome a disaster-related hardship, injury, or adverse condition.[290] This assistance takes the form of additional financial payments or the reimbursement of disaster-related expenses. A "necessary expense" means the cost associated with acquiring the item or service.[291] FEMA provides only financial assistance (not direct assistance) under the ONA program, and it is cost-shared between the federal and state governments at a 75% to 25% rate.[292]

The categories of assistance available under ONA include medical, dental, child care,[293] and funeral items or services, as well as personal property, transportation, and other expenses.[294] An additional category, referred to as miscellaneous items or services, which the state determines in consultation with FEMA, gives the state the flexibility to provide needed assistance in a manner or of a type not spelled out in the regulations, as long as this need is also serious or necessary and related to the disaster.[295]

A. Treatment of Insurance

To ensure that the federal government does not provide duplicate benefits, disaster applicants must provide FEMA with information about any insurance proceeds received for damage incurred in the disaster. Specifically, ONA assistance may be available if an applicant or household receives real property insurance proceeds in an amount less than the

---

[288] Id. § 408(g)(2)(B), 42 U.S.C. § 5174(g)(2)(B).
[289] See 44 C.F.R. § 206.119.
[290] 44 C.F.R. § 206.111.
[291] Id.
[292] Stafford Act § 408(e).Stafford Act § 408(f)(1) and (g)(2), 42 U.S.C. § 5174(f)(1) and (g)(2).
[293] See Stafford § 408(e)(1) which was amended by Section 1108 of SRIA, Pub. L. 113-2, 127 Stat. 4 (2013), to include child care expenses.
[294] 44 C.F.R. § 206.119(b.
[295] 44 C.F.R. § 206.119(b)(2)(ii).

$31,400 maximum IHP grant,[296] and the proceeds are insufficient to cover the applicant's necessary expenses or serious needs.[297] However, if the applicant's insurance proceeds for a particular ONA category and cause of damage exceed the FEMA maximum grant award for the same category and cause of damage, the applicant is ineligible for assistance in that category. In that circumstance, the applicant may still be eligible for an award in another ONA category.

B. SBA Loan Eligibility

The categories of ONA assistance break down into "SBA dependent" or non-SBA dependent groupings. Because applicants may be eligible to receive low-interest, long-term loans from SBA to help with personal property, transportation, and storage and moving expenses, FEMA calls these programs "SBA dependent."[298] Unless FEMA finds that the individual or household will not be able to pass SBA's income test, the applicants must first apply to the SBA for a loan for these expenses before requesting assistance from ONA.[299] If approved, SBA loans eliminate the need for ONA grants and thus avoid the issue of duplication of benefits to applicants.[300] If applicants do not meet SBA's income test, FEMA may immediately process applicants who apply for SBA dependent categories of assistance in the ONA program.

C. ONA Eligibility Processing Procedures and FEMA/SBA Cross Referrals

The Small Business Act authorizes the SBA to provide a Physical Disaster Loan to assist disaster survivors with permanent housing repair or replacement, or to assist with needs arising from the loss of personal

---

[296] In accordance with Section 408 (h) of the Stafford Act, the maximum IHP award limit is adjusted by FEMA at the beginning of each federal fiscal year to reflect changes in the Consumer Price Index.

[297] 44 C.F.R. § 206.113(a)(4).

[298] See page 25 of http://on.fema.net/programs/orr_programs/recovery_programs/npscs/training/Documents/2_Processing_Criteria_and_Reference_Materials.pdf.

[299] 44 C.F.R. § 206.119(a).

[300] See 44 C.F.R. § 206.191(d)(2).

property.[301] An applicant must meet a minimum income test, which the SBA establishes, to be eligible for this loan. FEMA determines whether the applicant meets that minimum income standard in instances where the applicant initially contacts FEMA rather than the SBA.[302] FEMA first refers the applicant to SBA if it determines that the individual's or household income does, in fact, meet SBA minimum income guidelines, and the applicant requires financial assistance for personal property, transportation, or moving and storage needs (SBA dependent categories).[303] At the same time, FEMA assesses whether the applicant requires assistance with disaster-related funeral, medical, and dental expenses. ONA is the sole source of possible aid in these categories, and FEMA provides assistance for these purposes without regard to whether a disaster survivor may obtain an SBA loan. SBA refers the applicant back to FEMA for assistance with unmet needs once it denies an applicant's disaster loan application or if the amount it provides under the loan is insufficient to meet the applicant's disaster damage needs.[304]

FEMA may concurrently or at a later date refer an applicant for potential additional assistance from the SBA for home repair or replacement if FEMA is unable to meet all of the applicant's needs. For these categories, FEMA grant assistance would be provided before an SBA loan.

D. SBA Application Dependent ONA Categories

FEMA awards assistance for different types of disaster-related personal property expenses as determined by a standardized, line item list. A state may request that an item be added or deleted (zeroed out) from a particular category of personal property. FEMA then approves or disapproves the item for that given disaster.[305]

---

[301] The Small Business Act § 7(b)(1); 15 U.S.C. § 631, et seq.
[302] SBA, Office of Disaster Assistance, Standard Operating Procedures [hereinafter SBA SOP], Chap. 6-2, ¶ 59(b)(6).
[303] Processing Procedure Manual [hereinafter PPM], General Topic Guidance, I.S.1., *SBA Information* (2010). *See* <https://dosharepoint.fema.net/ia/PPM/PPM.aspx>.
[304] 44 C.F.R. § 206.119(a).
[305] *SBA Information* at 2.

1. Clothing

FEMA's goal with respect to clothing assistance is to provide the minimum amount of assistance to meet the needs of a household.[306] If a household member at the time of the inspection has damaged clothing but still has clothing available to meet his or her essential needs, FEMA does not provide a clothing award.[307] This includes seasonal clothing.[308] ONA thus bases its clothing awards on the amount of undamaged clothing the individual possesses, and not the amount of clothing damaged.[309]

If the inspector verifies that an individual has adequate undamaged clothing, that individual is not eligible for clothing assistance.[310] Volunteer agencies often provide clothing to individuals; however, FEMA considers such clothing expendable so there is no duplication of benefits issue. Therefore, the applicant's household is still eligible for clothing assistance if they received some clothing from a voluntary agency before applying to the IHP.[311]

2. Appliances

FEMA may provide assistance under ONA for repair or replacement of household items, furnishings, or appliances.[312] Assistance with appliances begins with an initial inspection report. The inspector assesses the damaged appliances and makes the determination of Not Affected (by the disaster), Insured, Landlord-owned (meaning owned by someone other than the applicant),[313] Repair (X), or Replace (Z). FEMA does not provide financial assistance to repair or replace items that are not affected by the declared disaster event, or for landlord-owned items (in cases involving rental property). FEMA delays payment for insured items until there is an insurance settlement so a determination can be made regarding whether there continues to be unmet needs.

---

[306] PPM, ONA Guidance Job Aids, III.O.7.b. ja., *ONA Clothing Processing Job Aid* at 1 (2010).
[307] Id.
[308] PPM ONA Guidance, III.O.7., *ONA Personal Property*, at 5.
[309] *ONA Clothing Processing Job Aid* at 1 (2010).
[310] Id.
[311] NEMIS, *Other Needs Assistance Reference Guide*, [hereinafter *ONA Reference Guide*], at 3.
[312] 44 § 206. 119(c)(1)(ii).
[313] PPM ONA Guidance Job Aids III O.7.f. ja Landlord-owned processing

---

FEMA has determined line item limits that represent the number of that type of appliance necessary to meet the needs of a household.[314] The agency determines an applicant's need for a particular appliance based on the line item limit compared to the number of that particular appliance the applicant has that is not affected, insured, or landlord owned.[315] For example, the line item limit FEMA established for a window air conditioner is two.[316]

The only age-related line items are toys for household members under age 17, high chairs, cribs, playpens, and strollers. Car seats are not age-related, but a dependent requiring this item must reside in the household.[317]

ONA uses specific line items based on the Americans with Disabilities Act (ADA)[318] to address personal property that is specific to applicants with disabilities. These items are eligible for repair or replacement only if owned by the applicant or household prior to the disaster and currently consist of:

- ADA accessible raised toilet seat;
- ADA accessible refrigerator;
- ADA accessible washer;
- ADA accessible bed; and
- ADA accessible computer.[319]

3. Home Furnishings

ONA also provides assistance for household items and furnishings damaged or destroyed in disasters.[320] Under ONA, the level of damage to furniture within specific rooms of a residence, as recorded by inspection, determines eligibility for assistance.[321] The four specific rooms eligible

---

[314] PPM, ONA Guidance Job Aids, III.P.2.j.a., *ONA Appliance Processing Job Aid* (2010).
[315] *ONA Personal Property* at 3.
[316] *Id.*
[317] *Id.* at 5.
[318] The Americans with Disabilities Act of 1990, 42 U.S.C § 12101 *et seq.*,
[319] *ONA Personal Property* at 43.
[320] 44 C.F.R. § 206.119(c)(ii).
[321] *ONA Personal Property* at 4.

under this category are kitchen, bathroom, living room, and bedrooms.[322] The ONA program has pre-determined the composition of each room and comprised a standardized personal property room list.[323] Neither the number nor the composition of the four rooms can be changed or added to, nor may FEMA modify the prices assigned by the contractor to the rooms.[324] Rooms the landlord or other non-dependent household members furnished are ineligible.[325]

4. Essential Tools

ONA covers equipment or tools required by an employer as a condition of employment or items required as a condition of an applicant's or dependent household member's education.[326] FEMA considers items used in self-employment, such as tools or equipment, a business expense and therefore not eligible for assistance under this category.[327] FEMA must verify all damage through an on-site inspection.[328] The following are included on the list of eligible items:[329]

- Schoolbooks and supplies are eligible if a school requires the applicant to supply these items for educational courses or schooling, including homeschooling, trade school courses, and college.

- Uniforms are eligible when the applicant is responsible for their replacement.

- ONA covers computers if required by the employer, the applicant is responsible for replacement, and a power surge did not cause the damage.

Occupational tools do not have a set award amount. Receipts up to $800, or the maximum allowable amount, whichever is less, determine the

---

[322] Id at 5.
[323] *ONA Appliances Job Processing Job Aid.*
[324] Id. at 6.
[325] *ONA Personal Property* at 6.
[326] 44 C.F.R. § 206.119(c)(iii).
[327] *ONA Personal Property* at 8, 9.
[328] Id.
[329] PPM, ONA Guidance Job Aids, III.O.7.eja. *ONA Essential Tools Processing Job Aid*, (2010).

---

amount paid. In addition, if the item was not verified at inspection, ONA requires a statement from the employer on company letterhead verifying the necessity and type of tool required, an itemized list of the replacement cost for each tool required, and the place of potential purchase, including a verifiable statement, estimate, or bill stating that the disaster caused the damage.[330]

5. Stored Personal Property

In general, personal property stored away from the damaged dwelling, such as at a public storage facility, is viewed as "non-essential" and not eligible for ONA.[331] The concept is that if the applicant does not need the items for everyday use, then they are not presently essential. ONA may, however, pay for damaged personal property items stored away from the home if FEMA determines the item(s) to be a serious need or necessary expense.[332] Since stored items are most often located away from the damaged dwelling, the initial inspection does not process them as part of the applicant's claim. Instead, the applicant submits a letter explaining the essential need for the stored personal property.[333] The agency then reviews the damage listed with a case-by-case determination of those items chosen for payment.[334] A claim under this heading does not include clothing stored within the damaged dwelling.[335]

Landlord-Owned Property

Landlord-owned property (non-occupant owned) is not eligible for reimbursement or replacement.[336]

---

[330] ONA Personal Property at 10.
[331] 44 C.F.R. § 206.120(5).
[332] PPM, ONA Guidance, III.O.8, ONA Stored Personal Property at 1 (2009).
[333] Id.
[334] ONA Stored Personal Property Job Aid.
[335] ONA Reference Guide, at 22.
[336] ONA Personal Property at 4; PPM, ONA Guidance Job Aids, O.7.f.ja., ONA Landlord-Owned Processing Job Aid at 1 (2009).

6. Transportation

Disaster-related transportation expenses, as verified by an inspector or a mechanic, are eligible for assistance under ONA.[337] The program pays for the repair, replacement, and the cost of an estimate of a car, van, truck, motorcycle, boat, or bike, or other vehicles that the state designates for a particular disaster.[338] The program may also pay for other transportation related expenses incurred as a result of a disaster, such as ferry fees or subway fares.[339] However, FEMA has not currently have a process in place to capture these costs. The state may also establish the amount of the award at the time of the disaster.

Eligibility for the award depends on several conditions:

- The damaged vehicle must comply with state laws regarding vehicle registration, inspection, and/or insurance requirements prior to the disaster.

- The SBA either denies a loan, determines the applicant is ineligible for a loan due to income, or the applicant receives an SBA loan that is insufficient to cover his or her other needs related to necessary expenses and serious needs.

- The applicant does not have comprehensive vehicle insurance or has insufficient comprehensive vehicle coverage.[340]

- In general, the applicant has no other useable or working vehicle or is able to justify the need for a second household vehicle.[341]

7. Moving and Storage Expenses

ONA assists applicants with expenses incurred when moving personal property items into storage to avoid additional storm damage.[342] Damage to the primary residence must be present and confirmed by an on-site

---

[337] 44 C.F.R. § 206.119(c)(2)(ii).
[338] PPM, ONA Guidance, III.O.9., *ONA Transportation & Second Vehicle Requests* (2010).
[339] Id.
[340] 206.119 (c)(2)
[341] *ONA Reference Guide* at 26.
[342] 44 C.F.R. § 206.119(c)(5).

inspection, and the move back must be to the same residence.[343] As mentioned, moving and storage expenses are "SBA dependent" and thus the applicant must first apply and fail to qualify for an SBA loan or receive loan proceeds insufficient to meet his or her needs, before qualifying for this award. [344] Further, there cannot be a duplication of insurance benefits.[345]

E. Non-SBA Application Dependent ONA Categories

The following categories of assistance are non-SBA dependent, i.e., there is no requirement that the applicant seek assistance from the SBA in the form of a loan before qualifying for these classes of ONA. FEMA reimburses the applicants for these ONA items based upon receipts for appropriate expenditures rather than advancing fixed amounts.

1. Funeral Expenses

ONA provides financial aid to an individual or household that experiences unexpected, uninsured expenses associated with the death of an immediate family member attributed to a declared national disaster event.[346] FEMA processes claims for funeral expenses somewhat differently in a given disaster depending upon whether the ONA program is operating under a joint, state, or FEMA Option. A state chooses which option to use, which in turn determines whether the state, FEMA, or both handle the processing of ONA claims during the disaster. Under the FEMA Option, the NPSC Coordination Team (NCT) processes all funeral cases.[347]

The state establishes the maximum dollar amount for funeral expenses at the time of the disaster. In catastrophic events or unusual circumstances, the NCT consults with the state's ONA representative to determine if the

---

[343] PPM, ONA Guidance, III.O.7, *ONA Personal Property* at 10; III.O.6, *ONA Moving and Storage)* at 1. (2009).
[344] Id.
[345] Id.
[346] PPM, ONA Guidance, III. O.2., *ONA Funeral Processing Guidelines* (2009).
[347] PPM, ONA Guidance Job Aids, III.O.2.ja., *ONA Funeral Processing Job Aid FEMA Option*, at 1 (rev. Jan. 17, 2011).

state seeks to exceed the maximum limit cost.[348] Under all of the options and in all circumstances, the Federal Coordinating Officer (FCO) and the State Coordinating Officer (SCO) must approve all payments for funeral expenses. The NCT handles processing of these costs after the SCO and FCO review and forward them.[349]

ONA is available for the following types of funeral expenses for each death caused by a disaster:

- Cost of the casket
- Mortuary services
- Transportation of the deceased and/or up to two family members into the area to identify the decedent (if required by state/local authorities)
- Two death certificates
- Burial plot
- Interment or cremation
- Cost of re-interment if disinterment is caused by the declared disaster or occurs in a family cemetery on private property.[350]

The ONA program has established rules to ensure that duplication of benefits does not occur. FEMA subtracts from funeral expenses both Veteran Affairs and social security benefits, as well as assistance from voluntary agencies. On the other hand, life and accidental death insurance fall under the category of family resources and therefore inure to the benefit of the survivors, and FEMA does not consider them a duplication of benefits.[351]

FEMA's eligibility policy also requires a death certificate for the decedent and documentation from an authoritative state or local entity (e.g., medical examiner, attending physician) attributing the death or the underlying cause of the death to the declared emergency or major disaster

---

[348] ONA Reference Guide at 31.
[349] Individuals and Households Program —Funeral Assistance (Interim Policy) [hereinafter Interim Policy on Funeral Assistance].
[350] ONA Funeral Processing Guidelines (2009); Interim Policy on Funeral Assistance
[351] Id. at 31.

event. The applicant must be the official next of kin and provide proof of unmet funeral expenses.[352]

2. Medical and Dental Expenses

Medical and dental expenses that occur as a result of a disaster are eligible for assistance.[353] Incurred costs eligible for reimbursement include hospital visit(s) and the cost of any medication associated with the disaster-related injuries. There is no specified maximum amount for these expenses other than the overall statutory limit for the IHP maximum. Initial dental or medical expenses totaling less than $50 are not eligible.[354] All applicants must submit a claim for insurance, Medicaid, or Medicare, if applicable, and provide FEMA with information regarding benefits received and/or expected.

Applicants must submit appropriate documentation of their expenses, indicating that they are necessary and disaster-related.[355] FEMA does not reimburse for medical insurance deductibles that are included in a submitted invoice; however, co-pays are a reimbursable expense.[356]

3. Miscellaneous or Other Expenses

The costs associated with certain items purchased or leased *after* the start of the disaster incident period are eligible for reimbursement. Those items are limited to humidifiers, dehumidifiers, generators, and chainsaws, although additional items may be determined eligible at the time of disaster.[357] Applicants must acquire the equipment within 30 days of the incident start date. The program may provide reimbursement for items purchased or leased beyond the 30 days from the incident start date if disaster survivors can show a safety or sanitary need exists or if they purchase the items within an extended incident period.[358] Note that ONA

---

[352] *ONA Reference Guide* at 31.

[353] *ONA Reference Guide*, at 33.

[354] PPM, Job Aids, ONA Guidance Job Aids, III.0.4.ja., *Medical and Dental Processing Job Aid* at 1.

[355] *ONA Reference Guide* at 33.

[356] PPM, Job Aids, ONA Guidance Job Aids, III.0.4.ja., *Medical and Dental Processing Job Aid* at 1.

[357] PPM, ONA Guidance, III.0.5, *ONA Miscellaneous/Other* at 1.

[358] *ONA Reference Guide*, at 35.

addresses damaged items owned prior to the disaster as personal property claims.

Applicants for Miscellaneous/Other have several eligibility requirements to meet in order to qualify for assistance. First, an on-site inspection provides the basis of assistance. Verification of expenses also may occur during this initial inspection, but it is not required. Verification of occupancy is required, however, as applicants residing in secondary homes are not eligible for assistance under this category.[359]

As an alternative to on-site verification, verifiable receipts submitted for post-disaster purchase or rental of eligible items may also suffice.[360] The applicant's award amount is based on FEMA's line item pricing or the actual amount on the submitted receipt, whichever is less. Assistance awarded cannot exceed the line item price.[361]

FEMA processes these four items of equipment under two separate categories of assistance, identified as Personal Property and Miscellaneous Expense of the ONA provision of IHP. The procedures are different under each category, and the distinction is significant[362] with generators and chainsaws.

Child Care Expenses Added

As part of the Sandy Recovery Improvement Act of 2013 (SRIA), child care was specifically added to the ONA eligible expenses authorized in Stafford Act § 408(e)(1). Please look to DOLR 3.0 for a discussion of this authority.[363]

---

[359] PPM, ONA Guidance, III.0.5, *ONA Miscellaneous/Other* at 1.
[360] Id.
[361] Id.
[362] PPM, ONA Guidance III.0.3., *ONA Generator* (2010) at 1-3
[363] *See* § 1108 of the SRIA, Pub. L. 113-2, 127 Stat. 4 (2013) which amends Stafford Act § 408(e)(1) to add child care as an eligible expense under ONA.

F. FEMA/Joint/State Program Administration

FEMA provides the states with three administrative options[364] for processing ONA in each state: FEMA,[365] joint, or state.[366] By November 30 of each year,[367] every state must choose one of these options, which will be executed if the state receives a declaration in the following year. To administer ONA directly, either alone or jointly with FEMA, a state must have a FEMA-approved State Administrative Plan (SAP), describing in detail the staffing schedule, assignment of responsibilities, and program procedures.[368] The state may submit amendments to the Regional Administrator in writing at any time during non-disaster periods.[369]

FEMA provides 75% percent of the funding for ONA, and the states provide 25% percent, regardless of which entity administers the program.[370] If a state administers the ONA program, it may receive 5% of the costs of the program as an administrative fee.[371]

The state must select its administration option prior to the disaster declaration. Once the President declares a disaster, however, the state has three days to amend the SAP[372] with respect to those items that the state is willing to include as eligible items under the IHP program.

G. Group Flood Insurance Policy (GFIP)

The Group Flood Insurance Policy (GFIP) refers to a flood insurance policy established under NFIP regulations.[373] FEMA may pay $600 under

---

[364] For a comprehensive discussion of FEMA's role and the state's role under the different administrative options, see IHP Disaster Processing Procedures: Regions, Headquarters and the National Processing Service Centers [hereinafter IHP Disaster Processing Procedures] (Dec. 7, 2007).
[365] 44 C.F.R. § 206.120(a) and (b).
[366] Id. § 206.120(b).
[367] Even if the state does not plan to make any changes, the state must submit a letter to FEMA stating that its SAP is still current by November 30 to document the submission requirement. See id. § 206.120(c)(2).
[368] Id. § 206.120(d).
[369] Id.
[370] Stafford Act § 408(g)(2), 42 U.S.C. § 5174(g)(2).
[371] See 44 C.F.R. § 206.120(a).
[372] Id. § 206.120(c)(3)(ii).
[373] Id. §§ 206.119(d) and 61.17

ONA[374] for three years of flood insurance for eligible ONA recipients of assistance for flood damaged property (personal and real) located in an SFHA on which FEMA places a first-time flood insurance requirement.[375] Please also refer to the National Flood Insurance Coverage Requirement discussion earlier in this chapter.

The original purpose of the GFIP was to provide a temporary means for the grant recipients—often low-income persons or those on fixed incomes—to have flood insurance coverage for a period of three years following a flood loss. Disaster survivors under the program must buy and maintain their own flood insurance at the end of the three years in order to be eligible for future disaster aid to repair flood loss damage.[376] Owners of dwellings must maintain coverage at the address of the flood-damaged property for as long as the address exists.[377] For renters, coverage must remain on the contents for as long as the renter resides at the flood-damaged rental unit.[378]

Applicants who have not exceeded the IHP maximum are eligible for a GFIP upon referral to ONA for personal property assistance.[379] The GFIP will also cover their IHP Housing Assistance repair/replacement flood insurance coverage requirement. Also, there must be no previous flood insurance requirement for the property, and the applicant must ultimately receive an ONA award for flood damage.[380] Applicants who are non-compliant with a prior flood insurance requirement will be ineligible for future flood insurable real and/or personal property assistance.[381] Applicants who are non-compliant, called "NCOMPs," but who receive an

---

[374] Id. at §§ 206.119(c)(6)(i) and (d)(2).

[375] NFIRA, NFIP, and GFIP Understanding their Interrelationships and Effects in the IHP [hereinafter NFIRA, NFIP and GFIP] at 9 (Oct. 2006).

[376] Even if the state does not plan to make any changes, the state must submit a letter to FEMA stating that its SAP is still current by November 30 to document the submission requirement. See id. § 206.120(c)(2).

[377] 44 C.F.R. § 206.110(k)(3)(i)(A).

[378] NFIRA, NFIP and GFIP at 9; 44 C.F.R. § 206.110(k)(3)(i)(B).

[379] 44 C.F.R. § 206.119(d)(1).

[380] 44 C.F.R. § 206.119(d).

[381] Id.

HA referral are eligible for rental assistance and direct housing assistance (THUs) because neither is subject to the NFIRA restriction.[382]

IX. Additional Individual Assistance (IA) Programs

In addition to the two primary IA Programs, HA and ONA, FEMA is authorized to implement, fund, and make available additional federal disaster assistance programs to families and individual survivors of presidentially declared disasters. A state may ask for these programs as part of its declaration request.

A. Disaster Case Management Services (DCM)

1. Description

The Stafford Act authorizes Disaster Case Management Services (DCM) in major disasters, through direct or financial assistance, to state or local government agencies or qualified private organizations to provide disaster survivors with case management services to identify and address unmet needs.[383] When a state requests, FEMA may authorize DCM in order to identify and assist disaster survivors who continue to have significant disaster-caused unmet needs after they have exhausted their personal resources, insurance, and immediate disaster-related grant benefits. DCM uses a spectrum of services to provide clients with the support they need to establish and successfully complete their own long-term recovery goals and be well on their way to self-sufficiency, without further need of assistance through FEMA.

---

[382] NFIRA, NFIP and GFIP, at 19.
[383] Stafford Act § 426, 42 U.S.C. §5189d.

2. Requirements for DCM Implementation[384]

- The governor of an impacted state may request DCM in one of two ways: 1) as part of the state's Request for a Presidential Disaster Declaration that includes Individual Assistance, or 2) via a written request to the FEMA FCO within 15 days of the date of declaration.

- The major disaster declaration must include IA.

- A DCM Assessment Team must deploy to the disaster area to conduct a comprehensive assessment of the state's disaster case management resources available to implement DCM while identifying the gaps in service that exists due to the disaster.

a.) DCM Assessment Team

The DCM Assessment Team is a rapid deployment assessment team comprised primarily of FEMA staff, the state/tribe, and other partners. An assessment team will deploy only if: 1) there is a request for DCM as a part of a Request for a Presidential declaration that includes Individual Assistance, or 2) the designated FCO receives a written request for DCM within 15 days of the date of declaration. Thereafter, FEMA, in cooperation with the SCO, will determine when the Assessment Team will deploy.

The purpose of the team is to conduct a comprehensive assessment of the state's disaster case management resources available to implement DCM while identifying the gaps in service that exists due to the disaster. The DCM Assessment Team will work in daily coordination with FEMA HQ.

3. Program Management and Operation

FEMA's Human Services/Community Services Branch, Recovery Directorate oversees FEMA's DCM Services programs. The DCM contains two programs—Immediate Disaster Case Management (IDCM) and state

---

[384] For more details on the DCM Program and Grant Application process, please see The Disaster Case Management Program Guidance at:
http://on.fema.net/programs/orr_programs/recovery_programs/ia_programs/Documents/DCM%20PG%20FINAL%203-8-13.pdf.

DCM Grant Program. The disaster case management assessment will provide the basis for determining the best alternative for delivery of Immediate DCM services and/or a state DCM Grant Program.

a.) Immediate Disaster Case Management (IDCM)

Immediate Disaster Case Management is designed to provide for rapid deployment and implementation of DCM services following an IA declaration. IDCM staff will be responsible for providing outreach, initial triage, and DCM services. The IDCM services support state, local, and non-profit capability for disaster case management, augmenting and building capacity where none exists. IDCM staff will be deployed based on the results of the Assessment Team report and concurrence with the FCO, FEMA HQ, and the Individual Assistance Branch Director (IABD). Services will begin within five days of notification from FEMA that IDCM services are needed. IDCM may last up to 90 days. Immediate Disaster Case Work services administered by FEMA staff may be provided through invitational travel to voluntary agencies; mission assignment to other federal agencies; or implementation of an Interagency Agreement, a contract, and/or a state DCM Grant Program application approved by FEMA.

b.) State DCM Grant

The state DCM Grant is a federal grant that makes funds available to the state to implement a Disaster Case Management Program (DCMP) by utilizing providers to offer DCM services for long-term disaster-caused unmet needs. The state DCM Grant application must be submitted within 60 days from the date of declaration. A long-term DCMP shall not exceed 24 months from the date of the declaration. Technical assistance for the development of the state DCM Grant application may be requested, in writing, to the IABD in the JFO. The first draft of the grant application may be submitted to FEMA within 45 days of the date of declaration for technical review and negotiation. A state may elect to only apply for a state DCM Grant. The final DCMP grant application must be submitted by the state within 60 days of the presidential declaration.

B. Crisis Counseling Assistance and Training

1. Overview

The Stafford Act authorizes the Crisis Counseling Program (CCP) to provide supplemental funding to states for the provision of services and training to alleviate mental health issues experienced by survivors that are caused or aggravated by a declared disaster or its aftermath.[385] The program may only be authorized for major disaster declarations.[386] The assistance provided is immediate, short-term, and at no cost to the disaster survivor. This program is for counseling and not treatment.[387] CCP is available to state mental health authorities through two separately funded grants:

- Immediate Services Program (ISP) – provides funding for services up to 60 days following the disaster declaration date and is intended to help the state or local mental health agency respond to and meet the immediate mental health needs of disaster survivors by providing screening, diagnostic, and counseling techniques, as well as outreach services such as public information and community networking.

- Regular Services Program (RSP) – provides funding for up to nine months following the disaster declaration date and assistance to persons affected by a presidentially declared disaster by providing funding, for crisis counseling, community outreach, consultation, and education services.

2. Program Monitoring and Administration

FEMA administers CCP at the federal level through a partnership with the Health and Human

---

[385] Stafford Act § 416, 42 U.S.C. § 5183; 44 C.F.R. § 206.171.
[386] 44 C.F.R. § 206.171(d).
[387] http://www.fema.gov/txt/media/factsheets/2011/dad_crisis_counseling.txt

Services Substance Abuse and Mental Health Services Administration (SAMHSA); state mental health agencies administer it locally.[388] SAMHSA's Center for Mental Health Services (CMHS) Emergency Mental Health and Traumatic Stress Services Branch works with FEMA to provide technical assistance, consultation, and training for state and local mental health personnel, and to provide grant administration, and program oversight.

For ISP, SAMHSA provides technical assistance to state and local mental health agencies, but monitoring responsibilities remain with FEMA. In contrast, FEMA has designated SAMHSA as the federal authority responsible for project management, including monitoring, of all RSPs. FEMA or SAMHSA destroy participant records at the conclusion of a CCP.

3. <u>Eligibility</u>

a.) Individuals

To be eligible for either crisis counseling program, an individual must be a resident of the designated disaster area or must have been located in the area at the time the disaster occurred.[389]

b.) The State

The purpose of CCP assistance is to supplement available state and local government resources. Therefore, a state's application for CCP grant funds must demonstrate that services are required because of the severity and magnitude of the disaster and that the need for crisis counseling and training in the affected area is beyond the capacity of state and local resources.[390]

ISP and RSP funding are separate. A state may request funding for either or both programs, depending on need, by application to FEMA, copied to CMHS. The application for ISP must be submitted no later than 14 days

---

[388] See generally, http://www.samhsa.gov/dtac/proguide.asp
[389] 42 U.S.C. § 5183; See 44 C.F.R. § 206.171(c).
[390] 44 C.F.R. § 206.171(f) (1)(i) and (f)(2); 44 C.F.R. § 206.171(g)(1)(i) and (g)(2).

following the declaration of a major disaster.[391] The application for RSP must be submitted no later than 60 days after the presidential declaration.[392]

For initial and continued eligibility, CCP Grant awards are contingent upon the state's performance of the following additional conditions:[393]

- Submission of an application describing the state's plan for services and budget needs;

- Documentation of the needs and manner in which the program addresses the needs of the affected population; the types of services offered and coordination of services offered if other agencies are involved; training for project staff; and a detailed expense report;

- Provision of regular progress and financial status reports; and

- Participation in at least one site visit by FEMA and SAMHSA during the grant period. (If any questionable activities are noted or observed, corrective action is immediately taken, up to disallowing the costs.) CMHS audits CCP grants under the direction of SAMHSA.[394]

C. Disaster Legal Services (DLS)

1. Program Description

The Stafford Act authorizes Disaster Legal Services (DLS)[395] assistance to provide free, non-fee-generating legal services, including legal advice, counseling, and representation to low-income individuals who are unable to secure adequate legal services but require such services as a result of a declared disaster. The low-income standard is not based on income *per se* but on the applicant's financial ability to secure adequate legal services, regardless of whether that insufficiency existed prior to or as a result of

---

[391] 44 C.F.R. § 206.171(f)(1).
[392] 44 C.F.R. § 206.171(g)(1).
[393] 44 C.F.R. § 206.171(g)(3).
[394] 44 C.F.R. § 206.171(k).
[395] Stafford Act § 415, 42 U.S.C. § 5182, and 44 C.F.R. § 206.164

the disaster.[396] Note that this policy is not considered to be in violation of the Stafford Act nondiscrimination requirement regarding economic status.[397]

Following a major disaster declaration, FEMA, through a Memorandum of Agreement between FEMA and the Young Lawyers Division (YLD) of the American Bar Association (ABA), provides free legal services to disaster victims for the securing of Stafford Act benefits and for other disaster-related claims.[398]

YLD coordinates with a range of participating attorneys, law firms, non-profit legal services providers, Legal Services Corporation recipients, state and local bar associations, and pro bono organizations to provide legal assistance under the DLS Program.[399] The FEMA IA staff coordinates with the YLD DLS National Director and the YLD District Representative for the impacted state. The YLD District Representative may request that OCC Field Counsel staff participate in disaster specific DLS volunteer attorney trainings and consult on applicant cases.

2. Forms of DLS Assistance

DLS assistance includes legal counseling and advice, referral to appropriate sources of legal services, and legal representation. The Regional Administrator or his or her representative refers cases that may generate a fee to private attorneys through lawyer referral services.[400]

---

[396] 44 C.F.R. §§ 206.164(a) and (b).

[397] Stafford Act § 308(a), 42 U.S.C. § 5151(a

[398] 44 C.F.R. § 206.164 (c) and (e) See also, Memorandum of Understanding with American Bar Association,
http://www.americanbar.org/content/dam/aba/migrated/disaster/docs/fema_aba_agree ment_11_07.authcheckdam.pdf.

[399] It is not unusual for a Legal Aid group or the state bar association to operate the DLS hotline.

[400] 44 C.F.R. § 206.164(b).

The assistance that participating lawyers typically provide include:

- Assistance with insurance claims, such as life, medical, property, etc.;
- Counseling and advice with respect to landlord/tenant problems;
- Drafting powers of attorney;
- Replacement of wills and other important legal documents destroyed in a disaster;
- Estate administration, including guardianships and conservatorships;
- Assistance with home repair contracts and contractors;
- Assistance in consumer protection matters, remedies, and procedures;
- FEMA appeals; and
- Other disaster-related actions against the government.

3. Conditions and Limitations

- DLS is for low-income survivors of presidentially declared disasters only;
- Legal representation is limited to non-fee generating cases[401] and legal issues related to or arising from the declared disaster;[402]
- FEMA funds the administrative costs of the DLS program coordinated through the YLD;
- Should it be necessary for FEMA to pay attorneys to provide disaster legal services, the Regional Administrator shall determine the amount of compensation and, at his or her discretion, may pay for related administrative costs requested;[403] and
- DLS assistance is subject to FEMA's policies of non-discrimination.

---

[401] A "fee generating case" is defined in the C.F.R. as "one which would not ordinarily be rejected by local lawyers as a result of its lack of potential remunerative value." 44 C.F.R. § 206.164(b). This would include cases where attorneys might expect to receive a percentage of a court or jury award or settlement.
[402] 44 C.F.R. § 206.164(e).
[403] 44 C.F.R. § 206.164(d).

D. Disaster Unemployment Assistance (DUA)

1. General Purpose and Overview

The Stafford Act provides for special federally funded weekly benefits and re-employment services to workers and self-employed individuals whose employment has been lost or interrupted as a direct result of a declared major disaster and who are <u>not</u> eligible for regular state unemployment insurance benefits.[404] The purpose of Disaster Unemployment Assistance (DUA) is to temporarily provide for replacement of a portion of the survivor's income for basic necessities.[405] There have been disaster declarations that have provided very limited IA (e.g., including DUA but not IHP) for designated areas.[406] *See* Chapter 3, *Declarations.* FEMA has delegated federal responsibility for DUA implementation and administration to the Secretary of Labor, U.S. Department of Labor (DOL).[407] DOL oversees the program in coordination with FEMA.[408]

At the state level, unemployment insurance (UI) agencies administer DUA under agreements with the Secretary of Labor.[409] FEMA provides funds to the Secretary of Labor, or his or her designee, who makes funds available to these agencies for direct payment of DUA benefits to individuals and reimbursement of state administrative costs.[410] DUA benefits are for individuals not covered under regular state or federal unemployment compensation programs and are not payable instead of or in addition to other UI programs.

---

[404] Stafford Act § 410; 42 U.S.C. § 5177.

[405] *See* 20 C.F.R. §625.

[406] Examples include: 2001 Florida Severe Freeze Disaster, FEMA-1359-DR-FL (DUA and HM); 2006 Hawaii Earthquake Disaster, FEMA-1664-DR-HI (Maui County for IA, limited to DUA, DUA further limited to the communities of Kaupo, Kipahulu, and Hana); and 2007 California Severe Freeze Disaster, FEMA-1689-DR-CA (DUA and Food Commodities).

[407] C.F.R. § 206.141.

[408] *See* 20 C.F.R. §625.

[409] The state agency is required to make available upon request a copy of the Agreement to any individual or organization for inspection and copying

[410] DOL DUA Fact Sheet, <http://workforcesecurity.doleta.gov/unemploy/disaster.asp>.

2. Eligibility

In order for disaster survivors to receive this assistance, the disaster declaration must authorize DUA assistance for families and individuals.[411] DUA benefits are generally available to any unemployed or self-employed individual who lived, worked, or was scheduled to work in the disaster area at the time of the disaster and as a direct result of the declared disaster, experienced a loss (total, partial, part-total) of employment or self-employment because:[412]

- The job or place of employment no longer exists;
- The individual is unable to reach the place of work;
- The individual is unable to work due to damage to the place of work;
- The individual is unable to work because of physical or mental injury caused by the disaster;
- The individual has become the breadwinner or major economic support for the household and is seeking work because the former head of household died as a direct result of the major disaster; or
- The individual lost a majority of income or revenue because the employer business or self-employed business was damaged, destroyed, or closed by the federal government.[413]

In addition, eligibility for DUA requires that the applicant:

- Cannot be eligible for, or is already receiving, regular UI, or is eligible for regular UI waiting week credit, which is the first week when one has fulfilled all of the requirements for UI;
- Has had a week of unemployment following the first date of the disaster incident period;

---

[411] See generally, 20 C.F.R. § 625.4.
[412] See DOL DUA Fact Sheet, above.
[413] See 44 CFR 206.141. Economic loss due to damage to property or crops does not automatically entitle an individual to DUA. Individuals with this type of loss should contact their state or local UI Agency office.

- Is able and available for work, unless injured as a direct result of the disaster; and

- Has not refused a suitable offer of employment.[414]

Save for a few limited exceptions, once an applicant's unemployment is no longer directly attributable to the declared disaster, the applicant's entitlement to DUA benefits ends.[415]

3. Benefit Duration and Amounts

DUA benefits are payable to individuals only for weeks of unemployment in the Disaster Assistance Period, which begins with the first day of the week following the incident period opening date, and for up to 26 weeks after the declaration date,[416] as long as the individual's unemployment continues to be a direct result of the declared disaster event.[417]

a.) Weekly Financial Benefits

State law determines the maximum weekly benefit amount for unemployment compensation in the state where the disaster occurred.[418] However, the minimum weekly amount is half (50%) of the average benefit amount in the state. The DUA benefit provision in the Stafford Act specifically provides that "assistance for a week of unemployment shall not exceed the maximum weekly amount authorized under the unemployment compensation law of the state in which the disaster occurred."[419] This provision also prohibits payment of DUA benefits for any week of unemployment for which an unemployed individual qualifies for unemployment compensation or waiting period credit under any federal or state law.[420]

---

[414] *See* 20 C.F.R. § 625.13(b)(2). Some states also require that an individual search for work as a requirement for DUA benefits.
[415] *See* 20 C.F.R. § 625.4(d).
[416] Stafford Act §410(a), 42 U.S.C. § 5177. 20 C.F.R. § 625.7.
[417] 20 C.F.R. § 625.4(d).
[418] 20 C.F.R. § 625.11.
[419] Stafford Act § 410(a), 42 U.S.C. § 5177(a).
[420] *Id.*

b.) Re-employment Services

Re-employment Services assistance under DUA usually refers to counseling, job search assistance, and referrals to suitable work opportunities and job training.[421] All DUA applicants, as well as any other individuals who are unemployed as the result of a declared disaster, must be afforded employment services to assist them in obtaining suitable work as soon as possible.

4. Filing Time Limits

The applicant must file an initial application for DUA benefits within 30 days after the first date following the state workforce agency announcement regarding availability of DUA, unless the applicant has good cause to file after the 30-day deadline.[422] States must accept applications filed within the 30-day application period as timely and may accept applications filed later than 30 days after the announcement date as timely if the state determines that the applicant had good cause for the late filing.[423] The states determine good cause on a case-by-case basis. Thus, without a good cause exception, an applicant must file before the end of the 30-day period; if the assistance period expires on a weekend or holiday in the major disaster area, the 30-day time limit must be extended to the next business day.[424] An applicant will not be able to receive any DUA benefits if filed after the twenty-sixth week following the disaster declaration date.[425]

---

[421] Id. § 410(b), 42 U.S.C. § 5177(b); 20 C.F.R. § 625.3
[422] 20 C.F.R. § 625.8(a).
[423] Id.
[424] Id.
[425] Stafford Act § 410(a), 42 U.S.C. § 5177(a).

---

5. Additional Legislative Authorities

a.) Appeals

The Stafford Act controls appeals of DUA determinations authorizing states and other jurisdictions 60 days to appeal a Stafford Act disaster assistance determination.[426]

b.) Citizenship/Immigration Status Requirement

Because the Welfare Reform Act of 1996 affects the authority of the federal government to provide cash benefits to disaster survivors, individuals who wish to receive DUA benefits must provide proof of identity and demonstrate their status as U.S. citizens, U.S. nationals, or qualified aliens.[427]

E. Food Benefits and Commodities – Direct and Indirect

Ensuring that disaster survivors and emergency responders have access to food[428] is one of the most immediate concerns following a major disaster or emergency, and it is critical to FEMA's effective management of the federal disaster response and recovery efforts. The Stafford Act provides for this critical need following a disaster through the ready and convenient availability of adequate food stocks in order for immediate mass feeding and distribution of food to disaster survivors anywhere in the United States[429] This section pertains only to food and not to water.

---

[426] See Stafford Act § 423, 42 U.S.C. § 5189(a); 20 C.F.R. § 625.10, et seq.; 44 C.F.R. § 206.115
[427] Welfare Reform Act, Pub. L. No. 104-193, 8 U.S.C. § 1611; See also Social Security Act § 303(f), 42 U.S.C. § 503(f); 20 C.F.R. § 603.1(b).
[428] Stafford Act § 413, 42 U.S.C. § 5180; 44 C.F.R. § 206.151.
[429] Id. This section, § 413(b), authorizes the Secretary of Agriculture to use Title 7 appropriated funds as a means of ensuring proper § 413 implementation and compliance.

---

1. Direct Distribution of Food

The USDA receives direct funding from Congress to purchase food commodities necessary to provide adequate food supplies for use in any area of the United States in the event of a major disaster or emergency in that area.[430]

2. Mass/Congregate Feedings

Congregate feeding involves the feeding of large groups of persons, typically in designated local shelters, schools, churches, community centers, soup kitchens and/or mobile kitchens. In accordance with the Stafford Act, and to fulfill its National Response Plan functions, the USDA's Food and Nutrition Service (FNS) donates foods that USDA purchased to maintain and replenish available food stocks in every state and some U.S. territories.[431] In the event of a declared emergency or disaster, and where the state has requested and been granted food commodities as part of an IA request, state agencies may receive and distribute USDA donated foods.

In the case of a presidentially declared disaster, if a non-profit disaster organization, such as the American Red Cross (ARC)[432] or The Salvation Army (TSA) wishes to use USDA donated commodities for congregate feeding, that organization must first submit an application to the state for review and approval.[433]

If, as a result of a presidentially declared disaster, the state is providing congregate feeding, it has authority, without prior FNS approval, to

---

[430] 7 U.S.C. § 612(c). *See* Pub. L. No. 74-320 § 32 (Aug. 24, 1935), and Department of Agriculture Appropriations Act, FY 2000, Pub. L. No. 106-78 (2000), (Individual Hardship Cases), authorizing the USDA to provide commodities acquired in connection with the USDA's § 32 operations and as authorized by 15 U.S.C. § 714(c) and 7 U.S.C. § 612(c), to individuals in case of hardship, as the Secretary of Agriculture determines.

[431] *See* Stafford Act § 413(b), 42 U.S.C. § 5180. FNS is the designated primary agency for ESF-11 (food), as outlined in the NRP.

[432] The ARC is the primary disaster relief organization responsible for coordinating feeding in a state where a disaster occurs.

[433] The application submission and review procedure is different depending on whether there is a residentially declared disaster or a "situation of distress." For a situation of distress, responsibility for approval of the application lies with the FNS.

---

immediately release state or local stocks of USDA-donated food to disaster relief organizations for the congregate feeding of disaster survivors at shelters and other state-approved mass feeding sites.[434] Although prior approval for release is not required, the state must notify the FNS Regional Office of the release of USDA food stocks within 24 hours and forward pertinent information, including but not limited to projections of the number of persons and meals expected to be served, length of time, and type of commodities needed. The state determines how long food disaster survivors need commodities assistance during the duration of the disaster, and FNS guarantees replacement of the commodities used.[435]

The specific FNS program providing commodities will depend on the needs of the disaster organization, the scale of the disaster, accessible inventories, and available funding. FNS suggests that, whenever possible and if available, states first use commodities provided through the National School Lunch Program, since those items are available in sizes appropriate for feeding large groups and easier for disaster organizations to use in preparing congregate meals, and they are easier for FNS to replace or reimburse.

3. Food Stock Direct to Household Distribution

In certain very limited instances, the circumstances may make it impossible or impracticable to effect congregate feeding at shelters or other centrally located mass distribution sites, necessitating a short-term direct to household distribution of commodities. In such instances, the state may distribute food directly to households and FNS will, at the state's request, replace the USDA foods used. The state must:

- Request and receive prior approval from FNS Headquarters for the distribution of foods directly to households for preparation and consumption at home;

---

[434] According to the FNS, congregate feeding may continue as long as it is needed in a residentially declared major disaster or emergency. In congregate feeding, the disaster organization prepares meals in large quantities and serves them cafeteria-style in a central location. U. S. Department of Agriculture, Food and Nutrition Service, USDA Foods Program Disaster Manual [hereinafter USDA Disaster Food Manual](Apr. 2011), at 3.
[435] USDA Disaster Food Manual, at 31.

- Comply with the duration timeline set by FNS Headquarters for household distribution of commodities;

- Take reasonable steps to prevent households from participating in other individual household food assistance programs, such as FNS' food stamps or Supplemental Nutrition Assistance Program (SNAP)[436]; and

- Collect and maintain household information as part of the distribution.

4. Food Commodities Stock Replacement or Reimbursement

FNS will replace, or reimburse the state for, USDA commodities used pursuant to a disaster declaration if the state provides appropriate documentation with its commodity replacement request. The FNS has no authority to replace commodities that are lost, destroyed, contaminated, or otherwise rendered unusable in a disaster due to flooding, fire, wind, power outage, or other cause. The state will have to apply to FEMA for financial assistance for the loss.[437]

5. Food Commodities to Pacific Island Jurisdictions

The Secretary of Agriculture has the authority to donate surplus commodities to the Republic of the Marshall Islands and the Federated States of Micronesia. These commodities are available from the FNS, but FEMA must mission assign (usually through GSA) the transportation of commodities to the disaster-affected jurisdiction from Guam, Hawaii, or other area where the USDA stipulates it has procured commodities available.

---

[436] FNS Supplemental Nutrition Assistance Program, <http://www.fns.usda.gov/snap>.
[437] Id.

F. Benefits and Distribution[438]– Disaster Supplemental Nutrition Assistance Program (D-SNAP)

1. General Program Purpose And Description

In addition to the USDA authorities discussed previously, the Stafford Act authorizes distribution of coupon allotments through electronically issued food coupon or food stamp benefits of the USDA FNS.[439] This is the Disaster-Supplemental Nutrition Assistance Program (D-SNAP). [440] USDA FNS can authorize the issuance of disaster food assistance as a standalone program, even in the absence of a presidentially declared disaster and wider grant of IA.

When grocery stores or other regular commercial channels of food supply have been restored following a disaster, individuals determined eligible by a state Department of Welfare or similar social service agency may receive food assistance via D-SNAP benefits.

- The state may not automatically authorize the disaster food assistance program. The state must ask permission from the FNS to implement the program.

---

[438] Formerly called Food Coupons and Distribution. *See* the Food and Nutrition Act of 2008 § 4115, Pub. L. No. 110-246 (2008).

[439] Stafford Act § 412, 42 U.S.C. § 5179. The Welfare Reform Act of 1996, Pub. L. No. 104-193, 8 U.S.C. § 1611, mandated that all states convert from paper coupon systems to an electronic benefit transfer (EBT) system before October 1, 2002. EBT systems issue and redeem benefits using cards, electronic funds transfer networks, and point-of-sale technology in authorized retail food stores. In FY 2004, the Food Stamp Program converted 100% to EBT in all state agencies, including U.S. territories and the District of Columbia. Additional web sources:
<http://www.fns.usda.gov/disasters/response/faq.htm>
<http://www.fsa.usda.gov/Internet/FSA_File/section32_and_related_laws.pdf>.

[440] Stafford Act § 412, 42 U.S.C. § 5179. The normal food assistance that FNS provides, the "food stamp program", is now referred to as SNAP (Supplemental Nutrition Assistance Program). D-SNAP (Disaster SNAP) is the disaster food assistance program through which FNS provides assistance under section 412 of the Stafford Act. SNAP and D-SNAP are now fully electronic.

2. Eligibility Procedures and Requirements

The D-SNAP program[441] provides grants to individuals via the state and includes direct payments restricted to food purchasing through electronic benefits. Households found to be in need of food assistance receive allotments of electronic food stamp benefits they can use to buy food in authorized food stores. The eligible household allotment varies according to household size, income, and allowable deductions; the state or U.S. territory agency responsible for federally aided public assistance programs, through local welfare officials determines the household allotment.

a.) State Responsibilities

The state must request and receive approval from FNS prior to implementing a disaster food assistance program and issuing D-SNAP benefits to households affected by a disaster.[442]

If FNS approval is granted:

- FNS provides on-site guidance for establishing and operating the disaster program and ensures that an adequate supply of food stamp debit cards is available;

- Commercial channels of food distribution must be restored prior to distribution of electronic food benefits to households; and

- The responsible state and or local service agency determines the eligibility of households to receive disaster food coupons and provides these benefits to eligible households.

b.) Applicant Eligibility

Applications and eligibility determinations are managed by the state or its designee. Generally, to be eligible for this Stafford Act assistance, the disaster survivor must be a member of a low-income household in a

---

[441] *See* Disaster Food Stamp Program Guidance, <http://www.fns.usda.gov/disasters/response/D-SNAP_Handbook/guide.htm>.
[442] *See* 7 C.F.R. §§ 271-283. *See* Food Stamp Act of 1977, *as amended*, Pub. L. No. 95-113, 7 U.S.C. §§ 2011-2036.

---

disaster area unable, due to the disaster, to purchase adequate amounts of nutritious foods.[443]

Non-qualified aliens, ineligible students and disqualified household members who do not qualify for the SNAP program may qualify for this D-SNAP disaster food assistance.[444] Persons already participating in SNAP at the time of the disaster may be eligible for D-SNAP and benefits as a supplement to their normal food benefits.

3. Duplication of Emergency Food Benefits

A household cannot receive both D-SNAP benefits and direct food distributions at the same time. States must take reasonable steps to prevent households from participating in both the D-SNAP and direct to household food distribution programs, and they must collect and maintain household information as part of the distribution.

G. Relocation Assistance

1. Description

The Uniform Relocation Act (URA)[445] provides protection and relocation assistance to individuals whose property the federal government acquires or who are otherwise displaced from their residence as a result of federally funded projects,[446] by ensuring that displaced persons will be treated fairly and equitably and receive assistance in relocating from the property they occupy.[447]

---

[443] *See Id*; Stafford Act § 412, 42 U.S.C. § 5179.

[444] All applicants who apply for assistance under Stafford Act § 412 are required to adhere to the policies which agencies develop when administering the programs for compliance with the Welfare Reform Act, Pub. L. No. 104-193, 8 U.S.C. § 1611.

[445] Uniform Relocation Assistance and Real Property Acquisitions Policies Act of 1970 (URA), 42 U.S.C. § 4601, *et seq.*; 49 C.F.R. Part 24. *See also* Stafford Act § 414, 42 U.S.C. § 5181; 44 C.F.R. § 206.161.

[446] Typically, the federal government or a state exercises eminent domain for a federally funded project.

[447] The URA defines a "displaced person" as: "Any person (individual, family, partnership, association, or corporation) who moves from real property, or moves personal property

This statute applies to renters,[448] as well as owners of property. Those who are "lawfully present" in the United States may benefit from the URA,[449] rather than the stricter standard in the Welfare Reform Act.[450] *See* Section II(B) *Assistance Registration Process.* The assistance the URA provides is actual out-of-pocket moving expenses and any reasonable increase in rent and utility costs.[451]

The Stafford Act provides that if an individual is eligible for housing relocation assistance from the federal government, the fact that the individual is unable to occupy the residence from which the individual is relocating because of a presidentially declared major disaster will not prevent the individual from being entitled to relocation assistance.[452]

Relocation Assistance under the URA may become an issue following disasters when communities acquire, demolish, or relocate at-risk properties through Hazard Mitigation Grant Program (HMGP) funds. *See* Chapter 7, *Hazard Mitigation,* for more information on property acquisition programs. HMGP property owners who choose to sell their properties to the community as a result of a FEMA property acquisition or buyout program using HMGP funds do so voluntarily and are not eligible for relocation assistance.[453] However, tenants of residential properties acquired by localities through FEMA property acquisition projects who are forced to leave their homes involuntarily may be eligible for assistance under the URA.[454]

---

from real property as a direct result of (1) the acquisition of the real property, in whole or in part, (2) a written notice from the Agency of its intent to acquire, (3) the initiation of negotiations for the purchase of the real property by the Agency, or (4) a written notice requiring a person to vacate real property for the purpose of rehabilitation or demolition of improvements, provided the displacement is permanent and the property is needed for a federal or federally assisted program or project." 42 U.S.C. § 4601(6).

[448] 49 C.F.R. § 24.101(a)(2).
[449] *See* 42 U.S.C. § 4605(a); 49 C.F.R. § 24.208.
[450] Welfare Reform Act, Pub. L. No. 104-193, 8 U.S.C. § 1611;
[451] 49 C.F.R § 24.204(c)(2).
[452] *Id.*; 44 C.F.R. § 206.161; *see also* 49 C.F.R. § 24.403(d), Additional rules governing replacement housing payments, which includes very similar language.
[453] *See* Hazard Mitigation Assistance Unified Guidance (HMAUG), pp. 89-80 (2010); http://www.fema.gov/library/viewRecord.do?id=4225 *See also,* URA *Relocation Assistance for Tenants Fact Sheet,* http://www.fema.gov/pdf/government/grant/resources/hbf_ii_3.pdf.
[454] *Id.*

2. Guidance and Policies

The U.S. Department of Transportation is the designated federal lead agency for the URA and has delegated lead agency responsibility to the Federal Highway Administration (FHWA).[455] The regulations for the URA contain a provision similar to but more expansive than the provision in the Stafford Act,[456] stating that the federal government will deny no person a replacement housing payment solely "because the person is unable to meet the occupancy requirements for a reason beyond his or her control, including: (1) A disaster, an emergency, or an imminent threat to the public health or welfare, as determined by the President."[457]

a.) Constructive Residential Occupancy

The FHWA has interpreted both the Stafford Act and FHWA's own regulations to mean that, upon a determination of "constructive residential occupancy," URA residential relocation benefits and payments "will be provided to otherwise eligible residentially displaced persons without regard to their inability to meet prescribed occupancy requirements."[458] The finding of "constructive residential occupancy" is a determination that, if the disaster or emergency event had not occurred, the residential occupant would have occupied the property within the URA's occupancy requirements until the federally funded project displaced it. The FHWA, in accordance with of the Stafford Act and FHWA's own regulations,[459] recommends that the following factors be considered in making the determination of "constructive residential occupancy:"[460]

---

[455] See generally 49 C.F.R. § 24.2(16).
[456] Stafford Act § 414, 42 U.S.C. § 5180.
[457] 49 C.F.R. § 24.403(d).
[458] FHWA Memorandum, Uniform Act Eligibility in Areas Affected by Hurricane Katrina (Oct. 6, 2005) [hereinafter FHWA Uniform Act Memo]; <http://www.fhwa.dot.gov/realestate/katrinaguid.htm>. Although specifically issued "to provide guidance concerning Uniform Act eligibility . . . for those projects located within areas impacted by Hurricane Katrina," the memo addresses the failure in general to meet Uniform Act occupancy standards due to displacement caused by the occurrence of all presidentially declared disaster or emergency events.
[459] See FHWA Uniform Act Memo.
[460] Id.

- The claimant's actual occupancy of the dwelling just prior to the displacing disaster or emergency event;

- The existence of a lease or other legal tenancy covering a tenant's right to occupancy prior to and through the disaster or emergency event;

- An owner's legal right to return to the evacuated property, rebuild, and occupy a dwelling; and any other factors indicating whether the claimant would have been in occupancy at the time of residential displacement by the federally funded acquisition project except for the occurrence of the disaster or emergency event.

b.) Eligibility Caveats

As mentioned previously, the occupancy provision applies only to occupants of residential properties, including manufactured home occupants, and does not apply to businesses.[461]

Residential displacement must be involuntary; that is, property owners not subject to an exercise of eminent domain, who choose to sell their properties in connection with a FEMA or state property acquisition project, and who act voluntarily, are not eligible for Uniform Relocation Act assistance. Tenants involuntarily displaced by voluntary sales might be eligible.

Except for physical occupation as of the date of displacement by the federally funded project, all URA eligibility requirements continue to apply.[462]

H. Transportation Assistance to Individuals and Households

Historically, FEMA did not have a suitable system to reimburse survivors for transportation and related expenses when they relocated in advance of a "notice" event. As a result, in part, Congress passed PKEMRA,[463] which

---

[461] Id.
[462] Id.
[463] PKEMRA, Pub. L. No. 109-195, 6 U.S.C § 701-797. Sec 889(f).

included a new provision to the Stafford Act, *Transportation Assistance to Individuals and Households*.[464] It allows FEMA to pay for returning an evacuee to his or her home to oversee reconstruction or repair of the home and to finally return home. This provision authorizes the federal government to support the return home of evacuees and provides transportation assistance to disaster survivors displaced from their residences, including assistance needed to move among temporary shelters or to return to the original residence. FEMA has not yet issued a policy or regulations to implement this provision of the Stafford Act.

I. Cora Brown Fund

The Cora Brown Fund is a specific account that FEMA administratively established under the Stafford Act's gift acceptance and use authority,[465] and it is the only continuing account under this authority to administer cash awards for long-term unmet needs. Grants from the Cora C. Brown Fund[466] (the Fund) are made possible by the late Cora C. Brown of Kansas City, Missouri who, upon her death in the late 1970s, bequeathed a portion of her estate to the United States to be used expressly for the relief of human suffering caused by natural disasters and not caused or attributed to by war or acts of war. FEMA interprets this requirement to exclude terrorist attacks, so the Fund was unavailable for assistance associated with the September 11, 2011, attacks.[467]

The Fund is meant to provide disaster assistance of last resort as a final step in the IA sequence of delivery, for use when all other avenues of obtaining assistance have been exhausted. Fund amounts are modest, between $2,000 and $10,000.[468]

Eligible Fund recipients are the survivors (individuals, families, groups, or their agents)[469] of presidentially declared natural disasters or emergencies

---

[464] Stafford Act § 425, 42 U.S.C. § 5189c.
[465] Stafford Act § 701(b), 42 U.S.C. § 5201(b); 44 C.F.R. § 206.181. *See* <http://www.fema.gov/pdf/rebuild/ltrc/recoveryprograms229.pdf>.
[466] Id.
[467] *See* 44 C.F.R. § 206.181(a).
[468] Id. § 206.181(c)(1).
[469] For example, an award for a service to a "group" of disaster survivors occurred when Cora Brown funds were applied for and awarded directly to Louisiana and Mississippi so

---

not caused by or attributable to war. The Fund has certain restrictions, however. It is available only for presidentially declared major disasters or emergencies, only in designated areas , and only after a recommendation by the appropriate Regional Administrator. The ultimate authority to use the fund is at the discretion of the Associate Administrator for Response and Recovery, or his or her designee.[470] Funds must be used in a manner consistent with other federally mandated disaster assistance or insurance programs.[471]

X. Appeals

Applicants may appeal any FEMA decision regarding eligibility or the amount of assistance awarded within 60 days after notification of the award or denial of assistance.[472] FEMA must decide the appeal within 90 days of receiving notice of the appeal.[473] The applicant (or a designee) must send in a written appeal, sign it, and give the reasons for an appeal. If the designee files the appeal, the applicant must provide a statement giving that person the authority to do so.[474]

The Regional Administrator or a designee has the authority to make the appeal decision, except in cases of ONA appeals, where the state has chosen the option to administer ONA.[475] In virtually every declared disaster, the Regional Administrator delegates the processing of appeals for HA and ONA to the Recoupment and Appeals Department of the NPSC using the NEMIS system.[476] When the state chooses to administer ONA, the appropriate state official receives and reviews the initial decision and

---

that those "agent" states could continue providing Stafford Act § 426 Phase I Case Management services to individuals and families affected by the 2005 hurricanes. Id. §§ 206.181(a) and (c)(4).

[470] 44 C.F.R. § 206.181(c)(1).

[471] For example, "to comply with the Flood Disaster Protection Act of 1973 . . . any [Cora Brown Fund] award for acquisition or construction purposes shall carry a requirement that any adequate flood insurance policy be purchased and maintained." Id. § 206.181(c)(6).

[472] Id. § 423, 42 U.S.C. § 5189a; 44 C.F.R. § 206.115(a).

[473] 44 C.F.R. § 206.115(f).

[474] Id. § 206.115(b).

[475] 44 C.F.R. § 206.115(c).

[476] Except where a state has determined to manage the ONA program without FEMA assistance. See id. § 206.120.

---

makes the appeal determination.[477] The appropriate FEMA or state official notifies the applicant of the receipt of the appeal.[478] The decision of the appellate authority is final,[479] which means that the applicant must then file suit in federal district court under the Administrative Procedures Act,[480] if the applicant wishes to contest the decision.

The federal regulations implementing the right to appeal list the decisions that applicants may appeal. They include:[481]

- Eligibility for assistance, including recoupment;
- The amount and/or type of assistance;
- The cancellation or rejection of an initial or late application;
- The denial of continued housing assistance;
- FEMA's intent to collect rent from occupants of a housing unit provided by FEMA;
- The termination of direct housing assistance;
- The denial of a request to purchase or the sales price of a FEMA-provided housing unit; and
- Any other eligibility-related decision.

During the appeal process, it may be necessary for applicants to submit additional supporting documentation within the applicable appeal period in order for FEMA to process the appeal. A failure to supply this information will result in a denial of the appeal without having FEMA examine the underlying circumstances which may be involved.[482] When FEMA receives a complete appeal request, FEMA may resolve the appeal either based on an additional inspection or on documentation that the applicant has submitted.[483] Although all decisions can be appealed, FEMA and/or the state may not have the authority to resolve an appeal in the applicant's favor. These situations include, for example, where FEMA

---

[477] 44 C.F.R. § 206.115(c).
[478] Id. § 206.115(e).
[479] Id. § 206.115(f).
[480] 5 U.S.C. § 706.
[481] 44 C.F.R. § 206.115(a).
[482] See PPM, Cross Topic Guidance, IV.A.1., Appeal Processing Guidance (2011) at 3.
[483] See 44 C.F.R. § 206.115 and PPM, Cross Topic Guidance, IV.A.1., Appeal Processing Guidance (2011) (due to be updated in August 2013).

denied assistance to an applicant who lived in an undesignated county or where the applicant had already reached the IHP limit of assistance.

A. General Program Requirements for Appeals

Initially, applicants must meet the general program requirements of identity, lawful residency, and disaster-related necessary expense.[484] Applicants denied assistance for failure to include these general requirements have the right to appeal this decision and must provide the necessary documentation, such as a signed Declaration and Release, Form 009-0-3, within the designated appeal period.[485]

There are instances where an applicant appeals an assistance determination but fails to meet or comply with status, time frame, or information requirements. A failure to provide timely or complete information in an appeal will likely result in a denial of the appeal without an examination of the underlying circumstances involved.[486] Thus, applicants who do not appeal for further assistance within the 60-day time frame are ineligible for additional assistance. Applicants who appeal for further assistance who do not submit the required Declaration and Release, Form 009-0-3, proof of insurance, proof of occupancy, ownership, or identity when required to do so are also ineligible for additional assistance.[487]

Beyond these general eligibility requirements, FEMA handles appeals under the various categories of assistance in similar ways. One distinction in processing appeals arises in the categories of HA and ONA—specifically for personal property and transportation assistance. These are the only two categories that may warrant Appeal Inspections.[488] A separate Appeal Inspection is required if any of the following three situations occur:

---

[484] 44 C.F.R. § 206.113.
[485] See 44 C.F.R. § 206.115(a).
[486] See PPM, Cross Topic Guidance, IV.A.1., Appeal Processing Guidance at 3 (2011).
[487] NPCS Verification Requirements Chart: "PPM, Cross Topic Guidance, IV.V.2.ja., Verification Requirements Chart (2012)." (September 2011)
http://on.fema.net/programs/orr_programs/recovery_programs/npscs/training/Docum ents/4_Eligibility_Determination.pdf.
[488] PPM, Cross Topic Guidance, IV.I.7.a.ja., "Inspection: Types of Inspection and How to Request One" at 1 (2012).

- The applicant appeals the results of the initial home inspection and submits estimates, receipts, or other documentation, and the original inspection noted "deferred maintenance" as a basis for denial;

- In the appeal letter, the applicant identifies damages not addressed in the initial inspection; or

- A FEMA Correction Inspection cannot remedy damages not addressed in the initial inspection if 180 days have passed since the initial inspection.[489]

B. Category Specific Verification Appeals

Applicants must meet program category specific verification requirements to be eligible for assistance.[490] The applicant may present these verifications at the time of inspection or submit them to FEMA by mail or fax. Listed here are some of the specific requirements and their designated categories:[491]

- Occupancy – All HA categories, Personal Property, Moving and Storage, Misc/Other Expenses
- Ownership – Repair Assistance, Replacement Assistance, Permanent Housing Construction, Transportation
- Primary Residence – All HA categories, Personal Property, Moving and Storage, Misc/Other Expenses
- Insurance/Lack of Insurance – All HA and ONA categories except Misc/Other
- Vehicle Registration – Transportation

Applicants denied for specific verification requirements have the right to appeal this decision and must provide the necessary documentation within the appeal period.[492]

---

[489] Id. at 1, 3 (2012).

[490] PPM, Cross Topic Guidance, IV.V.2.ja., Verification Requirements Chart

[491] 44 C.F.R. § 206.113; PPM, Cross Topic Guidance, IV.V.2.ja., Verification Requirements Chart (2012)."

[492] 44 C.F.R. § 206.115 and PPM, Cross Topic Guidance, IV.A.1., Appeal Processing Guidance (2011).

These documents may include but are not limited to the following:

- Contractor's statement
- Insurance settlement or denial
- Deed, title
- Utility bill, tax documents, driver's license
- Receipts, estimates

XI. Recovering Improper Payments – Recoupment

A. Legal Authority

Federal law requires that every federal agency shall collect claims of the United States government for money or property arising out of the activities of the agency.[493] In addition, every agency must periodically review all of its activities and programs to identify those which may have significant improper payments. Further, the President issued an executive order that demonstrated a commitment to reducing payment errors and eliminating waste, fraud, and abuse in federal programs.[494] The order stated that "executive departments and agencies should use every tool available to identify and subsequently reclaim the funds associated with improper payments."[495]

Thorough identification of improper payments promotes accountability at executive departments and agencies; it also makes the integrity of federal spending transparent to taxpayers. Reclaiming the funds associated with improper payments is a critical component of the proper stewardship and protection of taxpayer dollars. The executive order declared that the federal government will not tolerate waste, fraud, and abuse by entities receiving federal payments, and reclaiming these funds underscores that commitment.[496] Moreover, FEMA may not violate appropriations statutes, which require that each federal agency only use funds for the purposes for

---

[493] The Debt Collection Act of 1996, Pub. L. No. 104-34; 31 U.S.C. § 3711(a).
[494] EXEC. ORDER 13250, Reducing Improper Payments (Nov. 20, 2009).
[495] Id.
[496] Id.

which Congress appropriated the funds.[497] DHS regulations set forth the department-wide procedures for the collection of debts.[498] DHS further notified FEMA that it should pursue debt collection "aggressively" and administer appropriate collection processes.[499]

Moreover, FEMA regulations require recipients of assistance to return funds to FEMA and/or the state when FEMA or the state determines that the assistance was provided erroneously, that the applicant spent the funds inappropriately, or that the applicant obtained the assistance through fraudulent means.[500]

B. Effect on FEMA and Disaster Survivors

FEMA has a significant number of individuals and households that may owe a debt to the government as a result of overpayments these individuals and households received following a disaster for a variety of reasons. FEMA calls the process of recovering these funds "recoupment." One common reason for an overpayment is duplication with insurance benefits that are received after FEMA provides assistance. If disaster survivors receive FEMA financial assistance that is a duplication of benefit or otherwise receive the funds for an ineligible purpose, FEMA is legally required to collect these funds, and federal law imposes no statute of limitations on how many years back the government may go.[501]

---

[497] See 31 U.S.C. § 1301(a) (This is only one part of a three-element rule. To determine whether appropriations are legally available, the elements of purpose, time, and amount must be observed. In addition to ensuring that the purpose of the expenditure was within the bound of Congress' intention, the agency must ensure that the obligation occurs within the time limits applicable to the appropriation. In addition, the obligation and expenditure must be within the amount Congress has established. 31 U.S.C. § 1502; 31 U.S.C. § 1341. See also General Accountability Office, Principles of Federal Appropriations Law, p. 4-6 (3rd Ed. 2004)).

[498] See 44 C.F.R. § 206.191(f); 6 C.F.R. Part 11 (adopting the Department of Treasury regulations at 31 C.F.R. §§ 900-903).

[499] Memorandum from the DHS Chief Financial Officer to the FEMA Chief Financial Officer (Mar. 10, 2010).

[500] 44 C.F.R. § 206.116.

[501] 31 USC 3716 (e)(1).

C. Litigation on Recoupment

In *Ridgely v. FEMA*,[502] plaintiffs filed litigation on behalf of disaster applicants from hurricanes Katrina and Rita, alleging that FEMA violated the Stafford Act, the Administrative Procedure Act and the Fifth Amendment of the Constitution with respect to its: (1) distribution of temporary housing assistance (approximately 110,000 disaster applicants); and, (2) recoupment procedures (approximately 124,000 disaster applicants). With respect to recoupment, in particular, plaintiffs alleged FEMA's process provided inadequate explanation for the reasons for recovery and failed to provide a meaningful hearing. On June 14, 2007, the district court certified the class and entered a preliminary injunction against FEMA on constitutional due process grounds, prohibiting FEMA from terminating temporary housing assistance or moving forward with any recoupment until it put new procedures in place.

FEMA complied with the preliminary injunction related to recoupment, ceased all recoupment, and withdrew its previous recoupment notices until it could alter its procedures for recoupment. FEMA recognized it could do a better job with respect to the clarity of its notices advising applicants of why they had a debt and of their appeal rights. Following the termination by FEMA of its recoupment actions, the district court dismissed this portion of the complaint as moot. Recoupment actions for all disasters were on hold until March 15, 2011, when the Agency published its revised recoupment guidelines and processes. FEMA changed its recoupment procedures to provide for an oral hearing where the matter cannot be decided based on the documents alone (for example when there is a question of credibility or veracity). OCC's Alternative Dispute Resolution Division provides the oral hearings.

FEMA appealed the preliminary injunction as it related to the temporary housing assistance class. On January 4, 2008, the Fifth Circuit vacated the preliminary injunction because it determined that FEMA's statute and regulations, standing alone, do not create a property interest in temporary

---

[502] *Ridgely v. FEMA*, 2007 U.S. Dist. LEXIS 38461 (E.D. La. May 25, 2007); injunction granted at *Ridgely v. FEMA*, 2007 U.S. Dist. LEXIS 43009 (E.D. La. June 13, 2007); vacated in part, remanded in *Ridgely v. FEMA*, 512 F.3d 727, 2008 U.S. App. LEXIS 130 (Fifth Cir. La. 2008); later proceeding at *Ridgely v. FEMA*, 2010 U.S. Dist. LEXIS 136368 (E.D. La. Dec. 13, 2010).

housing assistance that require such due process. However, the Fifth Circuit determined that there was still a possibility that FEMA created a property interest based on its implementation of the statute and regulations post-Katrina, and remanded it back to the district court for a hearing on the merits of that issue. FEMA settled the action, and the court approved the settlement on December 13, 2010.

FEMA Disaster Assistance Recoupment Fairness Act of 2011 (DARFA)

From March 2011 to December 2011, FEMA mailed nearly 90,000 Notices of Debt for debts arising from Hurricanes Katrina and Rita and considered thousands of appeals and requests for compromise. Some members of Congress subsequently expressed concern about the fairness of FEMA's debt collection where the debt resulted from FEMA error and when a significant amount of time passed before FEMA notified the survivor of the debt. Consequently, in December 2011, Congress passed the FEMA Disaster Assistance Recoupment Fairness Act of 2011, or DARFA (Consolidated Appropriations Act, 2012, Pub. L. No. 112-74 § 565 (2011)). This Act authorizes FEMA to waive certain debts arising from improper payments to disaster survivors for disasters declared between August 28, 2005, and December 31, 2010, based on an equity and good conscience standard. FEMA subsequently waived more than 17,000 debts pursuant to this authority before it expired in March 2013.[503]

---

[503] *See,* Memorandum of Law from Chief Counsel Brad Kieserman re Expiration of DARFA Authority on March 26, 2013.

XII. Catastrophic Housing Annex to 2012 Federal Interagency Response Plan-Hurricane

In August 2012, FEMA released The Catastrophic Housing Annex[504] to the Federal Interagency Response Plan-Hurricane[505] (the Annex). The Annex describes concepts and options for how FEMA may provide temporary housing for up to 500,000 eligible households to help disaster survivors recover and transition into sustainable housing.[506]

The Annex serves as a guide to assist FEMA and our Federal, state and local partners with both pre-disaster planning efforts and post-disaster planning and operations. FEMA understands that every disaster will be unique in scope and magnitude. The needs of a particular community will continue to drive the response and recovery actions, and not all options outlined in the Annex may be appropriate for the particular event or community.

Recovery support to the most heavily impacted area would emphasize sheltering/temporary housing solutions provided in locations outside of the impacted area, except for those activities that provide life-sustaining support to essential personnel. This concept is intended to help mitigate rapid depletion of limited resources and ensure disaster survivors are assisted as quickly and effectively as possible.

The Annex adopts a Zone Approach, which categorizes the affected area into four zones based on the degree of damage. Zone 1 encompasses the most heavily impacted area, where response efforts will initially focus on life-saving and limited life-sustaining support. Since resources are

---

[504] Catastrophic Housing Annex (August 12, 2012).
http://www.fema.gov/library/viewRecord.do?id=6506. *See also*, Stafford Act §§ 301, 403, 406, 408, 611, Pub. L. 93-288, 42 U.S.C, 5121-5207; Homeland Security Act § 503, 6 U.S.C. 311-321j; Post-Katrina Emergency Reform Act (PKEMRA) § 653, 682, Pub L. 109-295, 6 U.S.C. § 701 *et seq*. No 81-774, 6 U.S.C. § 701 *et seq*; Pet Evacuation and Transportation Standards Act (PETS Act), Pub.L. No. 109-308; Stafford Act §§ 611(e)(4), 613(g), 42 U.S.C. § 5196(e)(4), 5196b(g); Defense Production Act of 1950 (DPA), *as amended*, 50 U.S.C. § 2061 *et seq*; Department of Homeland Security Delegation No. 9001.1 "Delegation to the Administrator of the Federal Emergency Management Agency", December 10, 2011.
[505] Federal Interagency response Plan-Hurricane (August 2011, rev July 2012) http://on.fema.net/components/orr/response/training/Documents/FIRP-Hurricane%20July%202012.pdf.
[506] Catastrophic Housing Annex (August 12, 2012).

---

expected to be limited or non-existent within the most heavily impacted area (e.g., Zone 1), relocation will likely be essential to meet the needs of disaster survivors. As response activities are ongoing, recovery activities will initially focus in Zone 4, where housing options, infrastructure, and wrap-around services are more readily available, and will move inward toward Zone 1. As recommended in the Annex, emphasis on recovery support would initially be directed at the least impacted areas, and progress inward toward the most heavily impacted area as accessibility allows.

The following factors, among others, can be considered to help define zones:

- Are utilities functioning? If not, how long until expected restoration?
- Are police/fire protection sufficiently staffed to provide support to disaster survivors in temporary housing, or will additional personnel be needed?
- Are transportation routes clear of debris?
- Are transportation options (including accessible transportation) available for disaster survivors without privately-owned vehicles?
- Are businesses such as grocery stores, pharmacies, and banks open?
- Are schools open?
- Are medical facilities open?

The Annex provides a deliberative re-evaluation of standard timelines to meet the needs of disaster survivors following a catastrophic hurricane. The standard timelines for sheltering, temporary housing, and sustainable housing must be assessed differently for a catastrophic disaster based on the magnitude, complexity, availability of resources, and disaster-specific situation.

CHAPTER 7
Hazard Mitigation
Table of Contents

Hazard Mitigation

I. Introduction

Hazard mitigation is any sustained action taken to reduce or eliminate long-term risk to people and property from natural hazards and their effects. This definition distinguishes actions that have a long-term impact from those that are more closely associated with immediate preparedness, response, and recovery activities. Hazard mitigation is the only phase of emergency management specifically dedicated to breaking the cycle of damage, reconstruction, and repeated damage. FEMA provides federal assistance for hazard mitigation under six statutorily authorized grant programs. Two programs, the Hazard Mitigation Grant Program (HMGP) and the Public Assistance (PA) program,[1] provide hazard mitigation assistance following the President's major disaster declaration. The remaining programs, the Pre-Disaster Mitigation (PDM)[2] program, the Flood Mitigation Assistance (FMA) program,[3] provide hazard mitigation assistance on an annual basis, pending appropriations. This chapter discusses only the HMGP.

The HMGP[4] provides funding to states, territories, tribal governments, local governments, and eligible private non-profits (PNPs) to implement hazard mitigation measures following a Presidential major disaster declaration. HMGP funded projects typically have a 75% federal share and require a 25% non-federal cost share or match.[5]

---

[1] Stafford Act § 406; 42 U.S.C. § 5172(c)(1)(B)(iii), (c)(2)(B)(iii); 44 C.F.R. § 206.226(e). *See* Chapter 5, *Public Assistance*, for further details.
[2] Stafford Act § 203; 42 U.S.C. § 5133.
[3] 42 U.S.C. § 4104c; 44 C.F.R. Part 79.
[4] Stafford Act § 404, 42 U.S.C. § 5170c; 44 C.F.R. Parts 80 and 206, subpart N. All of the HMGP policies are available at:
http://www.fema.gov/government/grant/hma/policy.shtm#mitigation
[5] If an area falls under the Insular Areas Act (*America Samoa, Guam, the U.S. Virgin Islands, and the CNMI*), the non-federal cost share for PA, ONA or HMGP is mandatorily waived under

---

The key purpose of the HMGP is to ensure that the opportunity to take critical mitigation measures to reduce the risk of loss of life and property from future disasters is not lost during the reconstruction process following a disaster. The HMGP is available, when authorized under a Presidential major disaster declaration, in the areas of the state that the governor requests and designates in the declaration. The amount of HMGP funding available to the applicant is based upon a percentage of the estimated total federal assistance to be provided by FEMA for disaster recovery under the Presidential major disaster declaration. Eligible HMGP projects commonly include, but are not limited to, the acquisition and demolition or relocation of at-risk structures to create open space; elevation of structures subject to flood risk; structural retrofits to reduce risk of seismic and wind damage; and minor localized flood reduction projects.[6]

II. Availability of HMGP Assistance

A. HMGP and the Major Disaster Declaration

HMGP assistance is only available following a declared major disaster.[7] A major disaster will not be declared solely to provide HMGP but is only available if PA or Individual Assistance (IA) is designated for the major disaster.[8] A governor must request HMGP assistance in the disaster declaration in order for HMGP assistance to be available.[9] A governor may request that HMGP assistance be available throughout the entire state or

---

$200,000. If the cost share is $200,000 or more, any cost sharing arrangement becomes discretionary under 48 U.S.C. 1469a(d). *See also* Cost Sharing, Hazard Mitigation Assistance Unified Guidance 12 (2010), Part III B.

[6] Hazard Mitigation Assistance Unified Guidance 12 (12010) (hereinafter FY 2011 HMAUG).

[7] 42 U.S.C. § 5170c(a): "The President may contribute up to 75 percent of the cost of hazard mitigation measures which the President has determined are cost-effective and which substantially reduce the risk of future damage, hardship, loss, or suffering in any area affected by a major disaster."

[8] *See* 42 U.S.C. § 5170c(a) which provides for HMGP allotted funding based on Stafford Act grant funding (IA and PA) for the major disaster, thus making HMGP funding dependent on the provision of the IA and/or PA programs.

[9] *See* 44 C.F.R. §§ 206.36(c)(4), 206.40(a); FY 2011 HMAUG 49.

---

only in specific jurisdictions, regardless of whether the underlying disaster occurred only in certain jurisdictions within a state.[10]

B. Mitigation Planning Requirement

1. Mitigation Plans

The mitigation planning process includes the identification of hazards and assessment of risk, which leads to the development of a comprehensive mitigation strategy for reducing risks to life and property. The mitigation strategy section of the plan identifies a range of specific mitigation actions and projects being considered to reduce risks to new and existing buildings and infrastructure. This section includes an action plan describing how identified mitigation activities will be prioritized, implemented, and administered.[11]

Mitigation plans are the foundation for effective hazard mitigation. A mitigation plan is a demonstration of the state's and/or community's commitment to reduce risks from natural hazards. Mitigation plans also serve as a strategic guide for state and local decision-makers as they commit resources available to mitigate against natural hazards in their community.

2. State Mitigation Plan Requirement

Applicants for HMGP funding must have a FEMA-approved state or tribal (standard or enhanced) mitigation plan[12] at the time of the disaster declaration and at the time FEMA obligates HMGP funding to the grantee in order to receive a FEMA obligated HMGP award.[13] States and tribal

---

[10] FY 2011 HMAUG 49.
[11] *See* 44 C.F.R. §§ 201.4(c), 201.5(b), 201.6(c); FY 2011 HMAUG 15.
[12] Local Multi-hazard Mitigation Planning Guidance http://www.fema.gov/library/viewRecord.do?id=3336, State Multi-hazard Mitigation Planning Guidance- http://www.fema.gov/library/viewRecord.do?id=3115, Tribal Multi-Hazard Mitigation Planning Guidance http://www.fema.gov/library/viewRecord.do?id=4135
[13] *See* 42 U.S.C. §§ 5165(a) & 5170c(a); 44 C.F.R. §§ 201.4(a) & 206.431 (definition of "Standard State Mitigation Plan", "Tribal Mitigation Plan" and "Enhanced State Mitigation Plan.")

governments acting as grantees must also have an approved mitigation plan (standard or enhanced) in order to be eligible to receive non-emergency Stafford Act assistance, such as PA categories C - G, with a major disaster declaration.[14]

States and tribal governments applying directly to FEMA for assistance that do not have a FEMA approved plan in effect at time of declaration have a limited number of days in which to develop a state or tribal mitigation plan, respectively, and to obtain FEMA approval of the plan, in order to have HMGP and PA categories C through G authorized under the declaration.[15]

3. Local Mitigation Plan Requirement

HMGP subapplicants for mitigation projects must have a FEMA-approved local or tribal mitigation plan at the time of obligation of funds. For HMGP, the FEMA Regional Administrator (RA) may grant an exception to the local or tribal mitigation plan requirement in extraordinary circumstances, when an appropriate justification is provided.[16] If this exception is granted, a local or tribal mitigation plan must be approved by FEMA within 12 months of the award or final approval of the project subgrant to that community.[17] Further guidance regarding what constitutes "extraordinary circumstances" can be found in FEMA guidance.[18]

---

[14] 44 C.F.R. §§ 201.4(a) & 206.226(b). See Chapter 5, Public Assistance, for further details.
[15] See 44 C.F.R. § 201.4(a) & 201.7(a); FEMA Mitigation Planning Memorandum (MT-PL) #1: Disaster Declaration Procedures After May 1, 2005 for States Without an Approved State Mitigation Plan (Apr. 13, 2005); FEMA Mitigation Planning Memorandum (MT-PL) #1A: Implementation Procedures for States, Territories, and Indian Tribal Governments Without an Approved State Mitigation Plan - Follow-up Guidance (May 2, 2005). Editor's note: A Revised Policy Is under Review at Time of Publication. Please Coordinate With FEMA Headquarters Office of Chief Counsel For Current Policy.
[16] 44 C.F.R. § 201.6(a)(3).
[17] Id.
[18] See 44 C.F.R. § 201.6; FY 2011 HMAUG 19-20.

C. HMGP Funding Allocation

FEMA allocates HMGP funding based on a percentage of the estimated total federal assistance provided by FEMA pursuant to the major disaster declaration, which includes IA and PA, excluding administrative costs, for that Presidential major disaster declaration.[19] Generally, the state or tribal applicant is allocated up to 15% of such assistance or 20% of such assistance if it has an enhanced mitigation plan at the time of declaration.

For extremely large disasters, where the estimated aggregate disaster assistance under PA and IA exceeds $2 billion, the HMGP allocation is up to 15% of the first $2 billion of the estimated aggregate amount of disaster assistance; up to 10% for the next portion of the estimated aggregate amount more than $2 billion and up to $10 billion; and 7.5% for the next portion of the estimated aggregate amount more than $10 billion and up to $35.333 billion.[20] Applicants with a FEMA-approved state or tribal enhanced mitigation plan are eligible for HMGP funding not to exceed 20% of the estimated total federal assistance under the Stafford Act, up to $35.333 billion of such assistance, excluding administrative costs authorized for the disaster.[21]

D. HMGP Funding Allocation Lock-in

To account for refinements to the estimated amounts of PA and IA under the major disaster declaration, FEMA estimates the amount of HMGP funding allocated under the declaration at defined times following the major disaster declaration based on PA and IA estimates at those times. The HMGP funding allocation estimated ceiling will be established initially within 90 days of the disaster declaration. Six months after the disaster declaration, the estimated ceiling will be reevaluated and the lock-in ceiling will be established. The lock-in may reflect an increase or a decrease from the 90 day estimated ceiling. The six month lock-in represents the minimum amount of HMGP funding that will be made available to a state for a given major disaster declaration. Twelve months after the disaster declaration, FEMA conducts a final review of the lock-in

---

[19] *See* 42 U.S.C. § 5170c(a); 44 C.F.R. § 206.432(b); FY11 HMAUG 5.
[20] Id.
[21] *See* 42 U.S.C. § 5165(e); 44 C.F.R §§ 201.5(a), 206.432(b)(1); FY 2011 HMAUG 5.

ceiling and calculates the final amount of HMGP funds that will be available. The final lock-in amount may be greater than, but will not be less than, the lock-in ceiling calculated six months after the disaster declaration.[22] In rare circumstances, when a catastrophic disaster results in major fluctuations in projected federal expenditures, FEMA may, at the request of the grantee, conduct an additional review 18 months after the major disaster declaration. If the resulting review shows that the amount of funds available for HMGP is greater than previously calculated, the final lock-in amount will be adjusted accordingly, but will not be less than the lock-in ceiling calculated twelve months after the major disaster declaration.[23]

E. State Administrative Plan (SAP) Requirement

The state must have an approved SAP for administration of the HMGP, in accordance with FEMA's HMGP regulations, before it can receive HMGP funds.[24] The SAP is a procedural guide that details how the grantee will administer the HMGP. The SAP may become an annex or chapter of the state's overall emergency response and operations plan or comprehensive mitigation program strategy. At a minimum, the SAP must: designate the state agency that will act as grantee; identify the State Hazard Mitigation Officer; identify staffing requirements and resources, including a procedure for expanding staff temporarily following a disaster, if necessary; and establish procedures to guide implementation activities, including grantee management costs and distribution of subgrantee management costs.[25]

F. Management Costs

FEMA regulations establish the amounts, allowable uses, and procedures for HMGP management costs.[26] Management costs include indirect costs, administrative expenses, and any other expenses not directly chargeable to a specific project that are reasonably incurred by a grantee or subgrantee

---

[22] FY 2011 HMAUG 51.
[23] Id. at. 52.
[24] 44 C.F.R § 206.433(d); FY 2011 HMAUG 49.
[25] 44 C.F.R §§ 206.437 & 206.439(b); FY 2011 HMAUG 49; see also 44 C.F.R. Part 207.
[26] Id. Part 207.

---

in administering and managing a HMGP grant award.[27] Eligible applicant or subapplicant management cost activities may include:

- Solicitation, review, and processing of subapplications and subgrant awards;

- Subapplication development and technical assistance to subapplicants regarding engineering feasibility, benefit cost analysis, and environmental and historical preservation documentation;

- Geo-coding mitigation projects identified for further review by FEMA;

- Delivery of technical assistance (e.g., plan reviews, planning workshops, training) to support the implementation of mitigation activities;

- Managing grants (e.g., quarterly reporting, closeout);

- Technical monitoring (e.g., site visits, technical meetings);

- Purchase of equipment, per diem and travel expenses, and professional development that is directly related to the implementation of Hazard Mitigation Assistance (HMA) programs; and

- Staff salary costs directly related to performing the activities listed here.[28]

HMGP management costs are at a rate of 4.89% of the HMGP ceiling.[29] Management costs are outside of and separate from the HMGP ceiling amount. FEMA calculated management costs are based on the federal share of eligible mitigation activities and therefore represent the federal contribution towards applicant management costs; the applicant contributes the balance of such costs. FEMA will establish the amount of

---

[27] Id. § 207.2.
[28] FY 2011 HMAUG 16.
[29] 44 C.F.R. § 207.5(b)(4)(ii).

funds that it will make available for management costs by a lock-in, which will act as a ceiling for management cost funds available to a grantee, including its subgrantees. FEMA will determine, and provide to the grantee, management cost lock-in estimates at 30 days, 6 months, and 12 months from the date of declaration, or upon the calculation of the final HMGP lock-in ceiling, whichever is later.[30] At the point of notification on the final lock-in amount(s), the grantee must submit a final management cost funding request to the RA. Any necessary revisions to supporting documentation must be attached to the final funding request.[31]

Upon receipt of the 30-day lock-in, grantees may request that FEMA obligate 25% of the estimated lock-in amount(s) to the grantee. No later than 120 days after the date of declaration, the grantee must submit documentation to support costs and activities for which the projected lock-in for management cost funding will be used. In extraordinary circumstances, FEMA may approve a request by a grantee to submit support documentation after 120 days.[32]

III. HMGP Eligibility

A. Eligible Applicants/Grantees and Subapplicants/Subgrantees

Generally, the state where the President has declared a major disaster acts as both the applicant and grantee for HMGP assistance.[33] A tribal government may choose to be a grantee, or it may act as a subgrantee under the state. A tribal government acting as a grantee will assume the responsibilities of a "state" for the purposes of administering the grant.[34] Subapplicants and subgrantees can include state agencies, tribal governments, local governments, or PNPs, as outlined in §206.433.[35] A

---

[30] Id. § 207.5(b).

[31] 44 C.F.R. § 207.7(f)

[32] 44 C.F.R. § 207.7; FY 2011 HMAUG 52-53.

[33] 44 C.F.R. § 206.431, "Generally, the State for which the major disaster is declared is the grantee. However, an Indian tribal government may choose to be a grantee, or it may act as a subgrantee under the State. An Indian tribal government acting as a grantee will assume the responsibilities of a "state," under this subpart, for the purposes of administering the grant."; §§ 206.433(a), 206.434(a).

[34] Id.

[35] 44 C.F.R. §§ 206.431, 206.434(a).

subgrantee, including tribal governments acting as a subgrantee, is accountable to the state grantee.[36]

B. Project Eligibility Requirements

HMGP regulations establish the minimum criteria for a project to be eligible for a Hazard Mitigation program grant.[37] These criteria include requirements that the project, at a minimum:

- Conform to approved state and local mitigation plans.[38] The project must address a risk identified in both the state and local mitigation plan.

- Conform to Floodplain Management and Protection of Wetlands and Environmental Considerations regulations.[39] Compliance with these requirements must be done prior to a project grant award and project implementation.

- Is feasible and independently solves a problem rather than merely identify or analyze hazards or problems.[40] The proposed project must be technically feasible based on accepted engineering practices and must be implemented to result in actual risk reduction (e.g., studies and plans not part of actual project implementation do not affect risk and are not eligible).

- Be cost-effective and substantially reduce the risk of future damage, hardship, loss, or suffering resulting from a major disaster.[41] To be cost-effective, the future benefits from damages avoided must be equal or greater to the cost of the proposed project.

---

[36] 44 C.F.R § 206.431.
[37] 44 C.F.R. § 206.434(c).
[38] See FY 2011 HMAUG 19-20.
[39] See FY 2011 HMAUG 20-21; 44 C.F.R. Parts 9 and 10. This includes compliance with all applicable environmental planning requirements, including but not limited to NEPA, NHPA, ESA, EOs 11990 and 11988 (including FEMA's implementing regulations and program guidance).
[40] See FY 2011 HMAUG 18-19.
[41] Id.

Some other eligibility considerations include the following:

- HMGP acquisition and construction projects sited within a Special Flood Hazard Area (SFHA) are eligible only if the jurisdiction in which the project is located is a participating community in the National Flood Insurance Program (NFIP). There is no NFIP participation requirement for HMGP projects located outside of the SFHA.[42]

- Costs associated with implementation of an activity but incurred prior to grant award are not eligible. Similarly, mitigation activities initiated or completed prior to award are not eligible; FEMA will not reimburse them.[43]

Further information regarding these eligibility criteria can be found in FEMA's HMA Unified Guidance.[44]

C. Common Eligible Activities

The following are some of the commonly encountered HMGP project activities. This listing of project activities is not exclusive. Further information regarding eligible project activities not listed may be found in FEMA's HMA Guidance.

1. Hazard Mitigation Planning Grants

Up to 7% of the grantee's HMGP ceiling may be used for mitigation planning activities. Planning activities funded under HMA are designed to develop State, Tribal and local mitigation plans and plan updates that meet the planning requirements outlined in 44 CFR Part 201. A mitigation planning subgrant award must result in a mitigation plan adopted by the

---

[42] 42 U.S.C. § 4106(a); FY 2011 HMAUG 21.
[43] 44 C.F.R. 206.439(b); FY2011 HMAUG 27-28.
[44] See FY 2011 HMAUG 18-20.
[44] 44 C.F.R. 201.3(c)(4); FY 2011 HMAUG15; See "Scope of Work" requirements at HMAUG 31.

jurisdiction(s) and approved by FEMA prior to the end of the period of performance (POP).[45]

2. Property Acquisition and Structure Demolition or Relocation for Open Space (Buyout)

The acquisition and relocation of at-risk property and the subsequent deeding of that property as open space (acquisition) is a common activity under the HMGP and is often referred to as a buyout. Property acquisition and the Relocation for Open Space program involves the acquisition of at-risk property from willing sellers at fair market value (or pre-disaster fair market value for structures damaged during a declared disaster) and the demolition or relocation of structures on the property to convert the property to open space use in perpetuity in order to restore and/or conserve the natural floodplain functions.[46]

Properties eligible for acquisition include those where:

- The property will be acquired from a willing, voluntary seller. The applicant must submit a voluntary statement of interest from the property owner with the application. Also, the subapplicant must inform the property owner that the federal government will not use eminent domain authority for open space purposes.[47]

- The property contains a structure that an event may or may not have damaged or destroyed. If the property does not contain a structure, there is no at-risk property to mitigate, and the application will be ineligible for assistance.[48]

- The applicant or subapplicant must arrange to extinguish all incompatible easements or encumbrances.[49] Incompatible easements/encumbrances include those that would conflict with

---

[45] 42 U.S.C.§ 5165(d); 44 C.F.R. Part 201.
[46] FY 2011 HMAUG 74; Stafford Act § 404(b); 42 U.S.C. § 5170c(c); 44 C.F.R. Part 80.
[47] 44 C.F.R. § 80.13(a)(4); FY 2011 HMAUG 77-78.
[48] See 44 C.F.R. § 80.11(b).
[49] 44 C.F.R. § 80.17(b).

---

the open space and floodplain purposes designations for the property.[50]

- The property is not contaminated with hazardous materials at the time of acquisition, other than incidental demolition or household waste. In order to determine whether hazardous materials are present, the subapplicant must meet the requirements of the Environmental Protection Agency's "all appropriate inquiries" rule, including contracting with an appropriate qualified environmental professional for a Phase I Environmental Site Assessment Process, as defined by that rule, or by conducting an inquiry and providing a declaration certifying the inquiry and evaluation.[51]

- The property is not part of an intended, planned, or designated project area for which the land is to be acquired by a certain date, and/or where there is an intention to use the property for any public or private future use inconsistent with the open space deed restrictions and FEMA acquisition requirements (examples of inconsistent land use include buildings, roads, and flood control structures).[52] In addition to general assurances to this effect, the subapplicant must demonstrate that it has coordinated with the U.S. Army Corps of Engineers (USACE) and state transportation authority to ensure that there is no planned future use for that property for flood control or for highway/transportation projects.[53]

Some special project implementation requirements include:

- Use of FEMA model deed language including conservation provisions to limit the use of property to open space in perpetuity.[54]

- Offers based on pre-event fair market value must use recognized methodologies and then offset by available amounts of duplicated benefits.[55]

---

[50] 40 C.F.R. Part 312; 44 C.F.R. § 80.17(a).
[51] FY 2011 HMAUG 83.
[52] Id. at 75.
[53] 44 C.F.R. § 80.13(b); FY 2011 HMAUG 78-80.
[54] 44. C.F.R. §§ 80.13(a)(3); 80.17(e); 44 C.F.R. 206.434(e)(1); FY2011 HMAUG 75-77.
[55] 44 C.F.R. § 80.17(c); FY2011 HMAUG 85-89. *See* Duplication of Benefits, III.E.

- Tenants who must relocate as a result of acquisition of their housing are entitled to assistance as required by the Uniform Relocation Assistance and Real Property Acquisition Policies Act of 1970 (URA), as amended.[56]

Acquisition brings forth additional requirements and further information may be found in applicable FEMA regulations at 44 CFR Part 80, as well as in FEMA's HMA Guidance.[57] Because of the special aspects of this project type, such as voluntary requirements, permanent implications of open space, and limited future land uses, it is important that FEMA and the state ensure applicants fully understand the project during the applicant briefings.

3. Structural Elevation

Structural elevation[58] projects are those that physically raise the lowest floor of the structure above Base Flood Elevation, or higher if FEMA or local ordinance requires in order to limit future damage to the structure due to flood waters.[59] Structural elevation takes form through a variety of methods, including elevation on continuous foundation walls or on open foundations, such as piles, piers, posts, or columns, and elevating on fill. FEMA requires that buildings proposed for elevation be structurally sound and capable of being elevated safely.

All projects seeking to elevate buildings or other structures must meet the NFIP design standards, and FEMA encourages applicants and sub-applicants to comply with American Society of Civil Engineers/Structural

---

[56] 42 U.S.C. 4601 et seq.; 49 CFR Part 24. Owners participating in FEMA-funded property acquisition and structure demolition or relocation projects are not entitled to relocation benefits because the voluntary program meets URA exceptions. URA relocation benefits to displaced tenants include moving expenses, replacement housing rental payments, and relocation assistance advisory services. A person who is an alien not lawfully present in the United States, is generally not eligible to receive URA relocation benefits or relocation advisory services. 49 C.F.R. § 24.208. This is a different standard than the "qualified alien" standard used for IA and other mitigation assistance considered Federal public benefits pursuant to 8 U.S.C. § 1611.
[57] FY 2011 HMAUG 74-96.
[58] Id. 141-142.
[59] Id. 139.

Engineering Institute guidelines.[60] The following represents a few examples of generally allowable costs associated with structure elevation projects:

- Engineering services for design, structural feasibility analysis, and cost estimate preparation;
- Disconnection of all utilities;
- Physical elevation of the structure and subsequent lowering and attachment of the structure onto a new foundation;[61]
- Costs for repair of lawns, landscaping, sidewalks, and driveways if damaged by elevation activities; and
- Documented reasonable living expenses (except food and personal transportation) incurred during the period for owners displaced by the elevation construction.

4. Seismic Retrofit Projects

Mitigation projects undertake seismic retrofitting[62] with the goal of reducing the risk of death, serious injury, and property damage during a future earthquake event. Typically, eligible mitigation projects accomplish this by securing, bracing, or isolating architectural elements, mechanical equipment, and building contents. Some common examples of non-structural retrofitting seismic mitigation include the provision of secure attachments for:

- Exterior facade panels or brick masonry;
- Architectural ornaments, roof parapets, and chimneys;
- Heavy interior partition walls;
- Utility and mechanical equipment/systems, such as, heating, ventilation, air conditioning, water/sewer, gas, electric, ductwork, pipes, motors, pumps, and fans;

---

[60] Id.

[61] Mitigation Reconstruction, which is sometimes used, for example, when a structure cannot withstand traditional elevation, is authorized only under the SRL grant program, and is not an eligible HMGP activity. Mitigation reconstruction activities are permitted only in certain areas and subject to funding caps. See FY 2011 HMAUG 127.

[62] Sample Engineering Case Study, Seismic Non-structural Retrofitting 1, http://www.fema.gov/library/viewRecord.do?id=1865.

- Communication equipment and distribution; and
- Drop ceilings and pendant lighting.

5. Wind Shutters

Wind shutters[63] installed over windows and other openings protect buildings and contents from the damaging effects of hurricanes and other high wind events; however, normal shutter design does not typically protect buildings against extreme wind events such as strong or violent tornadoes. Typically, wind shutters are constructed of wood, plastic, or metal, and are most effective for facilities along or near the coast that are subject to frequent hurricanes and other high wind storms. Although wind shutter materials and systems can vary, the general information required for a complete grant application is fairly uniform.

6. Wildfire Mitigation

Wildfire mitigation projects are those projects that mitigate the risks to residential and non-residential structures, including commercial and public facilities, from uncontrolled wildfires. These projects must be located in, adjacent to, or co-mingled with the built environment and provide protection to life and the built environment from future wildfire hazard.[64] Wildfire projects under consideration by FEMA must contain a preliminary operations plan assuring the maintenance of wildfire mitigation measures. Before the performance of any project activities, FEMA must receive from the grantee final affirmation that the mitigation plan meets or exceeds local codes and is in conformance with appropriate fire-related codes.[65] Eligible wildfire mitigation projects include:

- Defensible space activities, including the creation of perimeters around residential and non-residential structures through the removal or reduction of flammable vegetation, including vertical clearance of tree branches. Specifically, this involves minimizing

---

[63] Sample Engineering Case Study, Wind Shutters 1, http://www.fema.gov/library/viewRecord.do?id=1864.
[64] FEMA Mitigation Policy MRR-2-08-1, *Wildfire Mitigation Policy for the Hazard Mitigation Grant Program (HMGP) and Pre-Disaster (PDM) Mitigation Program* (2008); FY11 HMAUG 99-102.
[65] Id.

the volume of combustibles (e.g., surface litter such as dry leaves, pine needles, dead and dying foliage, and trees, and removal of propane tanks) in the safety zone around the structure. The description of requested defensible space activities must accompany each property.

- Structural protection through ignition-resistant construction, defined as the use of non-combustible technologies and materials in the construction of new and pre-existing structures. These activities are eligible as a mitigation project when a property owner has previously created and agrees to maintain a defensible space, and the subapplication includes both the defensible space and ignition-resistant construction projects as part of the same project subapplication.

- Hazardous fuels reduction activities, including community-level vegetation management activities such as vegetation removal, clearing, and/or thinning, and vertical clearance of tree branches.[66]

7. Safe Rooms

Safe room projects include residential, non-residential, and community safe rooms built for the purpose of the immediate protection of life and safety resulting from structural and building envelope protection.[67] Due to the nature of the hazard to the population presented by extreme winds, safe room mitigation projects must meet stringent design and population criteria for approval. For example, in hurricane events emergency planners expect the general population to leave the area of anticipated impact and seek shelter elsewhere. For hurricane threats FEMA will only consider funding extreme wind mitigation projects designed for a specific population who cannot remove themselves from harm's way during a hurricane. With respect to tornadoes, the public receives little or no warning prior to impact, and therefore they must seek immediate life saving shelter. This limits the potential occupancy of tornado residential,

---

[66] Id. For further information regarding eligible wildfire mitigation activities, see FEMA Mitigation Policy MRR-2-08-1, *Wildfire Mitigation Policy for the Hazard Mitigation Grant Program (HMGP) and Pre-Disaster (PDM) Mitigation Program* (2008).
[67] FY 2011 HMAUG 103-113.

nonresidential, and community safe rooms to on-site occupants only, or to those within close proximity.[68]

Additionally, FEMA provides HMGP funds exclusively for safe room projects designed to achieve "near-absolute protection." Any lower threshold of protection exposes safe room occupants to a greater degree of risk than is acceptable. This higher design criterion makes general population evacuation and recovery centers ineligible for extreme wind mitigation projects, since communities design such structures to provide longer-term services and housing for people leaving the anticipated impact area. The requirement that safe rooms provide "near absolute protection" against extreme winds for two hours for tornado events and 24 hours for hurricanes also militates against using general population shelters and long-term recovery centers as event-only safe room projects. This is the required level of design criteria, which all applicants must meet.

8. Other Projects

Up to 5% of the grantee's HMGP ceiling may be used for mitigation measures that are difficult to evaluate against traditional program cost effectiveness criteria (i.e., the "5% Initiative"). For Presidential major disaster declarations due to tornadoes and high winds, an additional 5% of the grantee's HMGP ceiling may be used to fund hazard mitigation measures (e.g., warning systems) to address the unique hazards posed by tornadoes. Some project activities are not eligible as stand-alone activities, and are eligible only when included as a functional component of other eligible mitigation activities. For example, some purchases of real property, easements, generators, or studies (such as engineering or drainage surveys) integral to the implementation of a mitigation project are eligible only when the purchase is required for completion of an eligible mitigation project.[69]

---

[68] Id. For further information regarding eligible wildfire mitigation activities, see FEMA Mitigation Policy MRR-2-08-1, *Wildfire Mitigation Policy for the Hazard Mitigation Grant Program (HMGP) and Pre-Disaster (PDM) Mitigation Program* (2008).
[69] FY 2011 HMAUG 12, 16, 25.

D. Duplication of Programs

FEMA will not provide HMA assistance for activities where FEMA determines that more specific authority for the activity lies with another federal agency or program.[70] Other authorities include other FEMA programs (for example, IA and PA) and programs of other federal agencies (OFAs), USACE, and the Natural Resources Conservation Service (NRCS). FEMA HMA statutory authorities are mostly general authorities, in that they allow for a wide range of mitigation activities. Other federal authorities may be more specific if that statutory authority specifically enumerates a particular activity as eligible, whereas HMA authorities do not reference the particular activity. Also, if another federal authority is more specific, it must be used to the exclusion of HMA grant program authorities, regardless of the appropriated level of funds under either program.[71] For example, FEMA may not use HMA funds for certain large flood control works, which fall under the more specific authority of other agencies (USACE, NRCS) or for the construction of interoperable communications towers, which fall under more specific FEMA preparedness authorities. FEMA may disallow or recoup amounts that duplicate other authorities.

E. Duplication of Benefits

FEMA cannot provide HMA assistance where funds are reasonably available for the same purpose as the proposed HMA project, regardless of source, otherwise the HMA funds would provide a duplication of benefits (DOB) available to the applicant and/or subapplicant.[72] Sources of potential duplication may include funds received by or available to applicants or subapplicants from other sources for the same purpose, such as benefits received from insurance claims, other assistance programs (including previous project or planning grants and subgrants from HMA programs), legal awards, or other benefits associated with properties or damage that may be subject to litigation.

---

[70] 44 C.F.R. § 206.434(f); FY 2011 HMAUG.

[71] UNITED STATES GENERAL ACCOUNTABILITY OFFICE, 1 PRINCIPLES OF FEDERAL APPROPRIATIONS LAW, [hereinafter GAO REDBOOK] 2-21 (3rd ed. 2004).

[72] 42 U.S.C. § 5155; 44 C.F.R. § 79.6(d)(7); FY 2011 HMAUG 11.

FEMA will treat benefits that are reasonably available as a duplication of benefits, even if the benefits were not sought or received. Accordingly, applicants, subapplicants, and potential recipients of HMA funds must notify the grantee and FEMA of all benefits that they receive or anticipate from other sources for the same purpose, and also must seek all such benefits reasonably available to them. FEMA will reduce the total amount of eligible costs by the amount of reasonably available benefits prior to calculating the required non-federal cost share, as the federal cost share is based on the total eligible costs after deductions for duplications of benefits.[73]

The most common sources of DOB are IA repair funds and insurance benefits reasonably available to the applicant, subapplicant, or ultimate recipient of HMA funds for the same purpose as the HMA grant. DOB is particularly an issue for open space acquisition projects, where the purpose of the HMA grant is to compensate the owner for the value of the property loss as a result of the disaster. FEMA allows payment of pre-event value for the structure; however, the amount of funds available to the property owner from other sources to repair or compensate for the property loss must be offset from the pre-event property value to avoid a DOB. Generally, FEMA will not consider repair assistance or insurance proceeds provided for damaged structures as a DOB if the applicant or subapplicant uses the proceeds to repair the damaged structure prior to acquisition.

FEMA may also consider loan assistance from the Small Business Administration (SBA) to be a DOB, as SBA funds may be available to the recipient of HMA funds for mitigation activities. Additionally, a settlement or judgment associated with structures subject to an HMA application is a DOB if the judgment or settlement is reasonably available for the same purpose as the HMA grant. Note that if a structure associated with an HMA application is subject to ongoing litigation and FEMA has already made the grant award, any resulting settlement or judgment may result in a deduction from the grant award or recoupment of awarded funds.

---

[73] FY 2011 HMAUG 11 & 88. Rules governing matching or cost sharing requirements can be found at 44 C.F.R. § 13.24.

F. Income Tax Implications

The Internal Revenue Code excludes amounts received as a "qualified disaster mitigation payment" from gross income. [74] A qualified disaster mitigation payment is defined as any amount paid pursuant to the Stafford Act or the National Flood Insurance Act that benefits property owners through the mitigation of their structures.[75]

It does not include payments for acquisition or disposition of property.[76] If homeowners sell or otherwise transfer property to the federal government, a state or local government, or an Indian tribal government under a hazard mitigation program (e.g., under a buyout program), they can choose to postpone reporting the gain if they buy qualifying replacement property within a certain period of time.[77] Taxpayers cannot increase the basis of their property by the amount of the grants[78] and cannot take deductions or credits for expenditures made with grant funds.[79]

IV. Grants Management

A. Non-Federal Cost Share

HMGP funded projects have a federal cost share of no greater than 75% federal share and require a 25% non-federal cost share or match.[80]

1. Satisfying the Non-Federal Cost Share with other Federal Funds

In general, an applicant may not meet the non-federal cost share requirement with funds from OFAs, unless the respective authorizing

---

[74] 26 U.S.C. § 139(g)(1). See also http://www.irs.gov/Businesses/Small-Businesses-&-Self-Employed/FAQs-for-Disaster-Victims---Mitigation-Payments
[75] 26 U.S.C. § 139(g)(2).
[76] Id.
[77] See IRS Publication 547 (2011), Casualties, Disasters, and Thefts at http://www.irs.gov/publications/p547/ar02.html#en_US_2011_publink1000225406
[78] 26 U.S.C. § 139(g)(3).
[79] 26 U.S.C. § 139(h).
[80] Stafford Act § 403, 42 U.S.C. § 5170c(a); 44 C.F.R. § 206.432(c).

statute explicitly allows some federal funds to be used as a cost share for other federal grants. Federal funds that are used to meet a non-federal cost share requirement must meet the purpose and eligibility requirements of both the federal source program and the HMGP grant program.[81]

Examples of such federal funds that applicants may use as a non-federal cost share for HMGP activities include U.S. Department of Housing and Urban Development Community Development Block Grant funds; certain Department of the Interior Bureau of Indian Affairs assistance; and federal loan assistance, such as U.S. SBA loans.[82]

---

2. Non-Federal Cost Share and ICC Funds

Applicants may use NFIP Increased Cost of Compliance (ICC) claim payments to contribute to the HMGP non-federal cost share requirement, so long as the applicant makes the claim within the time frames allowed by the NFIP. ICC coverage provides for the payment of a claim for the cost to comply with state or community floodplain management laws or ordinances after a direct physical loss by flood. When a building covered by a Standard Flood Insurance Policy under the NFIP sustains a flood loss and the state or community declares the building as substantially or repetitively damaged, ICC will help pay up to $30,000 for the cost to elevate, flood proof, demolish, or relocate the building.[83] ICC payments can only be used for costs that are eligible for ICC benefits; for example, ICC cannot pay for property acquisition but can pay for structure demolition or relocation. FEMA cannot provide HMGP funds for the same costs as ICC funds; if the ICC payment exceeds the required non-federal share, FEMA will reduce the HMGP award to the difference between the cost of the activity and the ICC payment.[84]

---

[81] See 2 GAO REDBOOK, 10-93.
[82] FY 2011 HMAUG 9-10.
[83] NFIP Increased Cost of Compliance – Guidance for State and Local Officials, FEMA Pub. No. 301, 1-3 (2003).
[84] FY 2011 HMAUG 10.

3. Global Match

"Global Match" is an optional way that a state or tribal government HMGP grantee may satisfy the 25% non-federal match requirement on a program-wide basis, as opposed to a project-by-project basis. In other words, the grantee satisfies the non-federal cost share by providing an equivalent of the required 25% non-federal cost share for the overall amount of HMGP grant award for that disaster. Instead of contributing a non-federal share for each HMGP project, it contributes more than 25% for some HMGP projects and less than 25% for other HMGP projects.

There is no difference in the HMGP grant approval and award process. Only mitigation projects that FEMA approves as eligible HMGP project subgrants are part of the HMGP grant. However, in accounting for the non-federal share of HMGP projects under a global match arrangement rather than on an individual project basis, FEMA tracks the non-federal contributions towards eligible project costs under the overall HMGP grant award until the applicant meets the non-federal share of the overall HMGP grant award. The grantee implements individual HMGP projects either wholly with non-federal funds or with a non-federal cost share greater than the 25% required. FEMA adds these non-federal contributions together until the value of HMGP project costs funded with the non-federal funds satisfies the 25% non-federal match required for the overall amount of HMGP funding made available to the grantee. As a result, FEMA may wholly fund other individual HMGP projects with federal funds or fund them with more than a 75% contribution in federal funds. The overall HMGP grant award, comprised of all the HMGP project subgrants, however, meets the requirement of a non-federal cost share of at least 25%.

B. Grantee Monitoring of Projects

The state serving as grantee has the primary responsibility for managing HMGP funded projects, in accordance with the SAP, applicable regulations, and Office of Management and Budget (OMB) circulars.[85]

---

[85] 44 C.F.R. § 206.437(a)(4)(vii); 44 C.F.R. Parts 13, 206 and 207, 2 C.F.R. §215 (OMB Circular A-102), 2 C.F.R. §220 (OMB Circular A-21), 2 C.F.R. §225 OMB Circular A-87),

The governor's authorized representative (GAR) is the person who serves as the grant administrator for all funds provided under the HMGP. He or she is the individual empowered by the governor to execute, on behalf of the state, all necessary documents for disaster assistance.[86]

The GAR does not have to seek approval from the FEMA RA for project cost overruns that do not require additional federal funds or that the grantee can meet by offsetting cost under-runs on other projects. The GAR also must certify that the grantee and/or subgrantee incurred reported costs in the performance of eligible work, that the approved work was completed, and that the mitigation measure is in compliance with the provisions of the FEMA-State Agreement.[87] This area is a source of continuing concern due to recurring post disaster scrutiny that reveals a failure to understand the reporting requirements on the part of grantees. As a result, it is important that the requirements are clearly set forth on the front end of the implementation process as to the quarterly reporting component and the offset measures associated with funding shortfalls. There should be no misunderstanding of what these requirements are by either the grantee or grantors, and all issues need to be addressed in a timely manner between the grantor and grantee.

Grantees shall also submit quarterly progress reports to FEMA indicating the status and completion date for each measure funded. The grantee must describe and include in the report any problems or circumstances affecting completion dates, scope of work, or project costs that the grantee expects to result in noncompliance with approved grant conditions.[88]

C. Closeout

Under FEMA's general grant regulations, the grantee has up to 90 days after the expiration or termination of the grant to submit all financial, performance, and other reports required as a condition of the grant.[89]

---

2 C.F.R. §230 (OMB Circular A-122), 48 C.F.R. §§ 31.1, 31.2, 44 C.F.R. §13.26 (OMB Circulars A-133 and A-110).
[86] FY 2011 HMAUG 150; 44 C.F.R. § 206.2(a)(13).
[87] See 44 C.F.R. § 206.438(b), (d).
[88] 44 C.F.R. § 206.438(c).
[89] See id. § 13.50.

FEMA may grant an extension of this time period upon request.[90] The grantee maintains the complete closeout records file for at least three years from the submission date of its single or last expenditure report. The closeout process includes the following steps:

The grantee receives and processes cost adjustments or returns unobligated funds to FEMA;

- The grantee submits a closeout letter to FEMA with supporting documentation;

- The grantee verifies that statements of work have been completed as approved and all environmental and historic preservation requirements have been satisfied; and

- The grantee notifies FEMA that the grant is ready for final closeout.[91]

D. Appeals

An eligible applicant, subgrantee, or grantee may appeal any determination previously made related to an application for or the provision of federal assistance according to the following procedures.[92]

1. Format and Content

The applicant or subgrantee will make the appeal in writing through the grantee to the RA. The grantee shall review and evaluate all subgrantee appeals before submission to the RA. The grantee may make grantee-related appeals to the RA. The appeal shall contain documented justification supporting the appellant's position and specifying the monetary figure in dispute and the provisions in federal law, regulation, or policy with which the appellant believes the initial action was inconsistent.[93]

---

[90] Id. § 13.50(b).
[91] FY 2011 HMAUG 46.
[92] 44 C.F.R. § 206.440.
[93] Id. at § 206.440(a).

2. Levels of Appeal

a. The RA will consider first appeals for hazard mitigation grant program-related decisions.

b. The Assistant Administrator for the Mitigation Directorate will consider appeals of the RA's decision on any first appeal.[94]

3. Time Limits

a. Appellants must make appeals within 60 days after receipt of a notice of the action that is being appealed.

b. The grantee will review and forward appeals from an applicant or subgrantee, with a written recommendation, to the RA within 60 days of receipt.

c. Within 90 days following receipt of an appeal, the RA (for first appeals) or Assistant Administrator for the Mitigation Directorate (for second appeals) will notify the grantee in writing of the disposition of the appeal or of the need for additional information. A request by the RA or Assistant Administrator for the Mitigation Directorate for additional information will include a date by which the information must be provided. Within 90 days following the receipt of the requested additional information or following expiration of the period for providing the information, the RA or Assistant Administrator for the Mitigation Directorate will notify the grantee in writing of the disposition of the appeal. If the decision is to grant the appeal, the RA will take appropriate implementing action.[95]

4. Technical Advice

In appeals involving highly technical issues, the RA or Assistant Administrator for the Mitigation Directorate may, at his or her discretion, submit the appeal to an independent scientific or technical person or group having expertise in the subject matter of the appeal for advice or

---

[94] Id. at § 206.440(b).
[95] Id. at § 206.440(c).

---

recommendation. The period for this technical review may be in addition to other allotted time periods. Within 90 days of receipt of the report, the RA or Assistant Administrator for the Mitigation Directorate will notify the grantee in writing of the disposition of the appeal.[96]

---

[96] Id. at § 206.440(d).

CHAPTER 8
Environmental and Historic Preservation Laws
Table of Contents

Environmental and Historic Preservation Laws

Several environmental and historic preservation laws and regulations apply to FEMA activities and programs under the Stafford Act, such as temporary housing;[1] repair, restoration, and replacement of damaged facilities;[2] and hazard mitigation.[3]

I. National Environmental Policy Act (NEPA)

A. Overview

The National Environmental Policy Act (NEPA)[4] established an environmental policy based on encouraging harmony between people and the environment; preventing damage to the environment; protecting human health and welfare; and enriching our understanding of the nation's ecological systems and natural resources.[5] NEPA is a procedural law requiring that federal agencies consider the environmental impact of proposed actions, including adverse consequences and reasonable alternatives, prior to making decisions or taking actions that may "significantly affect the quality of the human environment".[6] "Significantly" as used in NEPA includes considerations of both context and intensity.[7]

NEPA does not prevent an agency from taking action that may negatively impact the environment. It does not dictate a specific outcome. NEPA requires that federal agencies incorporate environmental considerations in

---

[1] Stafford Act § 408, 42 U.S.C. § 5174(c)(1)(B).
[2] Id. § 406, 42 U.S.C. § 5172.
[3] Id. § 404, 42 U.S.C. § 5170c.
[4] National Environmental Policy Act (NEPA), Pub. L. 91-190, 42 U.S.C. §§ 4321-4347.
[5] Id. § 4321, See also EXEC. ORDER No. 11,991, 42 Fed. Reg. 26,967 (May 24, 1997).
[6] Id. § 4331(2)(c).
[7] 40 C.F.R. § 1508.27.

---

planning and decision-making and provide opportunity for public input in order to make fully informed decisions.[8]

NEPA created the Council on Environmental Quality (CEQ) to advise the President on the nation's progress in achieving NEPA policy objectives; to review and evaluate federal programs and activities for compliance with those policies; and to conduct research, investigations, and studies relating to ecosystems and environmental quality.[9] CEQ regulations create a framework for integrating the NEPA process early in project planning; encouraging interagency consultation and cooperation; and identifying significant environmental issues requiring further analysis.[10] In addition to CEQ regulations, each federal agency adopts its own environmental review procedures tailored to its mission and areas of responsibility.[11]

B. Disaster Assistance and NEPA

NEPA applies to the following types of actions:

- Direct actions conducted by FEMA, such as construction of FEMA facilities, staging areas, etc.

- Indirect actions that are subject to FEMA control and responsibility, such as projects and programs that FEMA funds partially or entirely.

- Actions that require a federal permit or other regulatory decision to proceed (e.g., a permit from the U.S. Army Corps of Engineers [USACE] or the Environmental Protection Agency [EPA]).

FEMA integrates environmental policies into its mission of disaster response and recovery, mitigation, and preparedness.[12] FEMA provides guidance to local, state, and federal partners on environmental

---

[8] Id.

[9] 42 U.S.C. § 4343; 40 C.F.R. §§ 1500-1508. See also EXEC. ORDER 11,991, 42 Fed. Reg. 26,967 (May 24, 1977).

[10] CEQ regulations are located in 40 C.F.R. §§ 1500-1508. See also EXEC. ORDER 11,991, 42 Fed. Reg. 26,967 (May 24, 1977).

[11] 42 U.S.C. § 4332; 40 C.F.R. § 1507.3; FEMA's environmental review regulations are in 44 C.F.R. Part 10. See also DHS Management Directive 023-01 and DHS Instruction 023-01-00 delegating NEPA responsibilities to DHS component agencies (April, 19, 2006).

[12] 44 C.F.R. § 10.4(a).

---

requirements and engages in a review process to ensure that FEMA-funded activities (e.g., selection of temporary housing sites, debris management, repair and construction of infrastructure, and hazard mitigation projects) comply with federal environmental laws, regulations, and executive orders; protect people; and avoid or minimize adverse impacts to the environment.[13]

C. Process

1. Levels of Review

There are four possible outcomes or levels of NEPA review. A statutory exclusion means no NEPA review is required; the degree of potential environmental impact determines the level of review and documentation required for the other three categories, listed from least amount of analysis and documentation to most comprehensive:

- Statutory Exclusion ("STATEX")
- Categorical Exclusion ("CATEX")
- Environmental Assessment (EA)
- Environmental Impact Statement (EIS)

2. Requirements for Environmental Review

At the outset of the NEPA review process, FEMA must determine the level of analysis required for the proposed action.[14] FEMA first considers the following threshold questions:[15]

a. Does the action normally not require either an EA or an EIS because a statute or regulation excludes it from NEPA review? FEMA does not need to prepare either an EA or an EIS if a statute or regulation excludes the proposed action further from NEPA review. We list and discuss statutory and categorical exclusions in the next section.

---

[13] See DHS/FEMA, Federal Insurance and Mitigation Administration, Environmental Responsibilities: Integrating Environmental Compliance into FEMA's Mission (2010), <http://www.fema.gov/library/viewRecord.do?id=2051>.
[14] 44 C.F.R. § 10.8.
[15] Id. § 10.8(a).

b. If there is no statute or regulation that excludes the action from further NEPA review, does the proposed action "normally require" an EIS? FEMA considers the following criteria in determining whether an action would normally require an EIS:[16]

- Actions resulting in extensive change in land use or a commitment of a large amount of land;

- Action resulting in a land use change that is incompatible with the existing or planned land use of the surrounding area;

- Actions that may affect many people;

- Actions that may have controversial environmental impacts;

- Action that will affect wildlife populations or important natural resources;

- Actions that will result in major adverse impact on air or water quality;

- Actions that would adversely impact a property listed, or eligible to be listed, on the National Register of Historic Places;

- Action that is one of several cumulative impacts that are considered significant;

- Actions that may pose a threat to the public.

If any of these criteria are present, FEMA may prepare an EA first in order to determine if a full EIS is necessary, or FEMA may proceed directly to preparing a full EIS.[17]

If the action is not excluded from preparation of an EA or EIS and does not appear to require an EIS, FEMA prepares the analysis and documentation for an EA.

---

[16] Id. § 10.8(b)(2).
[17] Id. § 10.8(b)(3).

3. Statutory Exclusions ("STATEX")

The Stafford Act excludes many FEMA response and recovery activities from NEPA compliance.[18] The statutory exclusions from NEPA, commonly called "STATEX", include the following types of Stafford Act assistance:

- General Federal Assistance[19] and Essential Assistance[20] following a major disaster declaration;

- Emergency Assistance[21] under an emergency declaration;

- Debris Removal[22] under an emergency or major disaster declaration; and

- Repair, Restoration, and Replacement of Damaged Facilities (Permanent Work under the Public Assistance [PA] Program),[23] provided that the repair or replacement has the effect of restoring the facility substantially as it existed before the disaster or emergency occurred.[24]

Actions taken and assistance provided under these Stafford Act provisions are exempt from NEPA requirements.

An exemption under NEPA does not relieve FEMA of the responsibility to comply with other federal or state environmental laws and regulations. Applicable state laws may include a state endangered species act or state burial laws if human remains are unearthed. FEMA program staff should consult with the Office of Chief Counsel (OCC) regarding compliance with other federal and state laws aside from NEPA.

---

[18] Stafford Act § 316, 42 U.S.C. § 5159; 44 C.F.R. § 10.8(c).
[19] Id. § 402, 42 U.S.C. § 5170a.
[20] Id. § 403, 42 U.S.C. § 5170b.
[21] Id. § 502, 42 U.S.C. § 5192.
[22] Id. § 407, 42 U.S.C. § 5173.
[23] Id. § 406, 42 U.S.C. § 5172.
[24] Id. § 316, 42 U.S.C. § 5159; 44 C.F.R. § 10.8(c)(2). Thus, alternate and improved PA projects are clearly not within the scope of the statutory exemption.

---

4. Categorical Exclusions ("CATEX")

Federal agencies may exclude certain activities from the requirement to prepare an EA or an EIS based on their experience that the activities do not have a significant effect on the human environment, unless there are extraordinary circumstances present that may result in a significant environmental effect.[25] Only actions in the list FEMA has codified may be treated as a categorical exclusion, or "CATEX." FEMA has created the following CATEXs:[26]

- Administrative actions in support of operations (personnel, travel, and procurement of supplies);

- Preparation, revision, and adoption of regulations, directives, manuals, and other guidance documents related to actions that qualify for categorical exclusions;

- Studies that involve no commitment of resources other than manpower and associated funding;

- Inspection and monitoring activities and enforcement of codes and standards;

- Training activities and exercises at existing facilities;

- Procurement of goods and services for support of day-to-day and emergency operational activities and the temporary storage of goods other than hazardous materials, as long as it occurs on previously disturbed land or existing facilities;

- Acquisition of properties and the associated demolition and removal or relocation of structures;

- Acquisition or lease of existing facilities where planned uses conform to past use or local land use requirements;

- Acquisition, installation, or operation of utility and communication systems that use existing distribution systems or facilities;

- Routine maintenance, repair, and grounds-keeping activities at FEMA facilities;

---

[25] 40 C.F.R. § 1501.4(a)(2), and § 1508.4.
[26] 44 C.F.R. § 10.8(d)(2).

- Planting of indigenous vegetation;

- Demolition of structures and other improvements or disposal of uncontaminated structures and other improvements to permitted off-site locations;

- Physical relocation of individual structures where FEMA has no involvement in the relocation site selection or development;

- Granting of community-wide exceptions for flood-proofed residential basements meeting the requirements of the National Flood Insurance Program (NFIP);

- Repair, reconstruction, restoration, elevation, retrofitting, upgrading to current codes and standards, or replacement of any facility in a manner that substantially conforms to the pre-existing design, function, and location;

- Improvements to existing facilities and the construction of small scale hazard mitigation measures in existing developed areas with substantially completed infrastructure;

- Actions conducted within enclosed facilities where all airborne emissions, waterborne effluent, external radiation levels, outdoor noise, and solid and bulk waste disposal practices comply with existing laws and regulations;

- Emergency activities under the Stafford Act;[27]

- Debris removal;

- Temporary housing under Stafford section 408,[28] except placing multiple mobile homes or other readily fabricated dwellings on a site, other than a private residence, not previously used for such purposes;

- Disaster Unemployment Assistance; Disaster Legal Services; Crisis Counseling; emergency communications; emergency public transportation; Fire Management Assistance grants; and Community Disaster Loans.

---

[27] Stafford Act §§ 402 & 403, 42 U.S.C. §§ 5170a & 5170b.
[28] Id. § 408, 42 U.S.C. § 5174.

5. Extraordinary Circumstances

Categorical exclusions do not apply when there are extraordinary circumstances present that may result in a significant environmental impact.[29] In such a case, FEMA prepares an EA, unless the potential impact can be mitigated below a level of concern. Extraordinary circumstances include:

- Greater scope or size than customary for the type of activity;

- A high level of public controversy;

- Potential for degradation of already environmentally compromised area;

- Use of unproven technology with possible adverse effects and environmental risks;

- Presence of threatened or endangered species or critical habitat, or other protected resources (e.g., archeological, historical, cultural);

- Presence of hazardous or toxic substances at levels that exceed federal, state, or local regulations or standards;

- Possible impact on critical resources such as wetlands, coastal zones, wilderness areas;

- Adverse effects on human health or safety;

- Potential violation of law or regulation protecting the environment; and

- Potential for significant cumulative impact when combined with other past, present, and reasonably foreseeable future actions.

---

[29] 44 C.F.R. §10.8(d)(3).

> ### Example Of Extraordinary Circumstances
>
> The demolition of a building would normally fall within a categorical exclusion;[30] however, if that building is historic or located within a historic district, the demolition action would require an EA because of extraordinary circumstances. In another example, if the extraordinary circumstance is the presence of an endangered species, say, a bird that nests at the building, modifying the construction schedule to avoid the nesting period may mitigate the impact, removing the extraordinary circumstances so that the project, subject to the revised construction schedule, may be treated as a CATEX.

FEMA periodically reviews and revises the list of categorical exclusions based on agency experience with activities that do not have a significant impact on the human environment.

6. Documenting Categorical Exclusions

FEMA must prepare and maintain an administrative record supporting its determination that a proposed action meets the criteria for a categorical exclusion.[31] This requirement is critical since anyone may challenge the agency's decision in a later lawsuit.

When FEMA plans to take a number of similar actions or fund a number of similar projects that meet the criteria for a CATEX, it can streamline the documentation by preparing a "programmatic CATEX." A programmatic CATEX describes the type of action or project covered and any conditions that might apply. For example, FEMA prepared a programmatic CATEX for elevation of residential structures in California. The elevation actions fit within a CATEX,[32] and the programmatic CATEX was conditioned on the actions being substantially within the existing footprint, using accepted techniques for elevation and access, and no extraordinary circumstances could apply.

---

[30] *Id.* § 10.8(d)(2)(xii).

[31] *See* Citizens to Preserve Overton v. Volpe, 401 U.S. 402 (1971); Camp v Pitts, 411 U.S. 138 (1973).

[32] 44 C.F.R. § 10.8(d)(2)(xv).

7. Environmental Assessments (EAs)

If a proposed action is not statutorily or categorically excluded from NEPA review (and an EIS is not required), FEMA must prepare an EA.[33] This level of analysis and documentation is typical of, for example, group housing sites, improved public assistance projects, and some hazard mitigation projects. An EA is a concise document briefly discussing:[34]

- The purpose and need for the proposed action;
- Description of the proposed action;
- Alternatives considered;
- Environmental impact of the proposed actions and the alternatives;
- Listing of agencies and persons consulted; and
- A conclusion whether to prepare an environmental impact statement.

FEMA regulations specify the format and contents of an EA.[35] To the extent practicable, FEMA must involve relevant environmental resource agencies (such as U.S. Fish and Wildlife Service, USACE, and state historic preservation officers), applicants, and the public in the process of preparing an EA.[36] FEMA must inform the public when a project and its alternatives are initially being developed and after the completion of the EA when the Finding of No Significant Impact (FONSI) is signed.[37] CEQ regulations and FEMA regulations do not require any specified length of time for public notice, nor do they define exactly what type of public notice vehicle should be used—newspapers, direct mail, state clearinghouse, posting a notice, local media, etc. In determining the public notice vehicle and timeframe, FEMA considers the scope and nature of the project, the location of the project, the likelihood of public interest, the need to act quickly, the potential for controversy, etc.[38] Under certain circumstances, FEMA might set an accelerated timeline to prepare an EA; for example, due to the pressing need to provide temporary housing after

---

[33] Id. § 10.8(e).
[34] 40 C.F.R. § 1508.9
[35] 44 C.F.R. § 10.9(b).
[36] Id. § 10.9(c).
[37] 40 C.F.R. §1506.6.
[38] 44 C.F.R. §10.9(c) and 40 C.F.R. §1506.6.

a disaster, FEMA might establish a 72-hour timeline to prepare an EA for that action.

FEMA's regulation[39] that implements Executive Order 11988 on Floodplain Management and Executive Order 11990 on Protection of Wetlands requires public notice as well.[40] One public notice can serve to satisfy both this part and the public notice requirement of Part 10, which implements NEPA.

There are two possible conclusions to an EA:

a. FEMA may issue a FONSI if the agency determines, on the basis of the EA, that that there is no significant impact on the quality of the human environment;[41] or

b. FEMA may determine that the proposed action is a major action that will have a significant impact and, therefore, a full EIS is required.[42]

If a proposed action will have a significant impact, FEMA may incorporate environmental mitigation measures to lessen the impact so that the agency can issue a FONSI.[43] Such mitigation includes minimizing the impacts to the environment by limiting the degree or magnitude of the action; rectifying the impact by repairing, rehabilitating, or restoring the affected environment; reducing or eliminating the impact over time; and/or compensating for the impact by replacing or providing substitute resources.[44] Revising the project scope or implementation to incorporate such mitigation measures allows FEMA to proceed with an EA rather than the more extensive analysis and documentation of an EIS.

8. Environmental Impact Statements

NEPA requires an environmental impact statement (EIS) for major federal actions significantly affecting the quality of the human environment.[45]

---

[39] Id. Part 9.
[40] Id. §9.8.
[41] Id. § 10.9(e).
[42] Id. § 10.9(d).
[43] 40 C.F.R. § 1508.20.
[44] Id.
[45] 42 U.S.C. § 4332(2)(C); 40 C.F.R. § 1508.18(a): FEMA regulations incorporate the CEQ definitions in 40 C.F.R. § 1508.

Actions include new and continuing activities, including projects and programs entirely or partly funded, conducted, assisted, or approved by federal agencies.[46] Most FEMA actions are appropriately addressed by STATEX, CATEX, or EA; thus, an EIS is not commonly necessary.

Federal actions tend to fall within one of the following categories:

- Approval of specific projects, such as construction activities in a defined geographical area, including actions approved by permit;

- FEMA funding for a project under any FEMA program (PA, Hazard Mitigation, and IA) that would require an analysis of whether an EA or EIS is required, unless a statute or regulation exempts the action;

- Adoption of formal plans that prescribe uses of federal resources, upon which future agency actions will be based;

- Adoption of programs; allocating agency resources to implement a specific statutory program or directive; and

- Adoption of official policy, rules, regulations, and interpretations.

NEPA requires that an EIS include:[47]

- The purpose and need for the action;
- The affected environment;
- Alternatives to the proposed action;
- The environmental impact of the proposed action;
- Any adverse environmental effect which cannot be avoided if the proposal is implemented;
- The relationship between short-term and long-term effects; and
- Any irreversible and irretrievable commitment of resources that would be involved in the proposed action.

The lead federal agency[48] prepares a draft EIS[49] and solicits comments from other federal agencies with jurisdiction or expertise on the environmental issues, state and local environmental agencies, affected tribes, and the public. The draft EIS should disclose and discuss all major

---

[46] 40 C.F.R. 1508.18(a).
[47] 42 U.S.C. § 4331(C); 40 C.F.R. Part 1502.
[48] 40 C.F.R. § 1508.16.
[49] Id. § 1502.9(a).

points of view on the environmental impacts of the proposed action and alternatives.

Federal agencies should prepare the draft EIS concurrently with and integrated with environmental impact analyses and related surveys and studies required by other environmental laws and executive orders.[50]

The final EIS should respond to comments submitted on the draft EIS and indicate the agency's response to the issues raised.[51] Agencies must prepare a Record of Decision (ROD), which is a concise public record stating their decision, the alternatives considered, and whether they adopted all practicable means to avoid or minimize environmental harm.[52]

9. Emergencies and Alternative Arrangements

CEQ regulations provide that if emergency circumstances require federal agencies to take action that may have significant environmental impact without complying with NEPA regulations, the federal agency taking the action should consult with CEQ about "alternative arrangements."[53] Alternative arrangements are limited to actions necessary to control the immediate impacts of an emergency; all other actions remain subject to NEPA review.

FEMA regulations provide that when Regional Administrators (RAs) must take immediate action with significant environmental impact to address an emergency, they must notify the Environmental Officer (EO) of the emergency as soon as practicable so that the EO may consult with CEQ. In no event, however, shall the RA delay emergency action necessary to preserve human life in order to comply with CEQ regulations.[54]

---

[50] Id. § 1502.25.
[51] Id. § 1502.9(b).
[52] Id. § 1505.2.
[53] Id. § 1506.11; 44 C.F.R. § 10.13.
[54] 44 C.F.R. § 10.13.

Example of CEQ Alternative Arrangements

In 2005, Hurricane Katrina caused widespread devastation to the critical infrastructure in the New Orleans Metropolitan Area (NOMA), including police and fire stations; schools; hospitals and health facilities; government and court administration buildings; and jails and detention centers. DHS, FEMA, and CEQ worked together to establish Alternative Arrangements under CEQ and FEMA regulations to enable timely action on PA grant applications in order to restore safe and healthful living conditions in NOMA, while complying with NEPA requirements to the extent possible. The Alternative Arrangements covered only critical infrastructure projects essential in providing the basic life, health, and safety sustaining services within the NOMA for infrastructure damaged as a result of Hurricane Katrina.[55]

10. FEMA Roles and Responsibilities

FEMA RAs are primarily responsible for applying NEPA policy and procedures to agency activities within their regions, including: preparing EAs and EISs and submitting them to the EO and the OCC; preparing administrative records of all categorical exclusions (discussed later in this chapter); and preparing a concise public record of their decisions.[56] FEMA's Regional Environmental Officers (REOs) perform many of these functions for the RAs. For activities within the jurisdiction of other FEMA organizational units (for example, Hazard Mitigation or the NFIP), the head of the office or directorate or administration is responsible for ensuring compliance with NEPA policy and regulations.[57]

The EO is responsible for providing assistance in the preparation of EAs and EISs; reviewing EAs to determine whether to issue a FONSI or if an EIS is required; reviewing changes to FEMA's categorical exclusions; reviewing proposed draft and final EISs; publishing required notices in the Federal Register; providing FEMA's comments to other agencies' EISs; and

---

[55] See <http://www.fema.http://www.fema.gov/new-orleans-metropolitan-area-infrastructure-projects-6>.
[56] 44 C.F.R. § 10.5(a)(1) through (a)(10).
[57] Id. § 10.5(c).

acting as liaison for environmental issues with CEQ and other federal, state, and local agencies.[58]

FEMA's OCC provides advice and assistance on complying with regulatory requirements; reviews all changes to FEMA's categorical exclusions; reviews all FONSIs; and reviews all proposed draft and final EISs.[59]

Case Example

In *National Trust for Historic Preservation v. U.S. Dep't of Veterans Affairs*,[60] the National Trust for Historic Preservation ("Trust") challenged FEMA and the U.S. Department of Veterans Affairs ("VA") under NEPA, alleging that FEMA and the VA failed to consider adverse effects of the proposed construction of two medical centers in New Orleans. Hurricane Katrina seriously damaged both Charity Hospital and the Veterans Affairs Medical Center in New Orleans in 2005. FEMA, the VA, the State of Louisiana, and the City of New Orleans decided to complete a joint, tiered[61] NEPA analysis consisting of a Programmatic Environmental Assessment (PEA) and a subsequent site-specific assessment. The first tier involved evaluating site selection, acquisition, and site preparation; and the second tier would evaluate design, construction, and operation after the parties selected the respective sites. The VA and FEMA were co-lead agencies for conducting the PEA. The state and the city were designated cooperating agencies. Based on the first tier assessments, the mid-city location emerged as the favored site for both facilities, and both FEMA and the VA issued FONSIs.[62]

The Trust challenged FEMA's EA, claiming that the PEA unlawfully used segmentation and did not consider connected actions in the same document, that the PEA's cumulative or indirect impact analysis was legally inadequate, that the tiering of the project was unlawful and arbitrary and capricious, and the reliance on generalized mitigation measures to avoid preparing an EIS was arbitrary and capricious. They

---

[58] *Id.* § 10.5(b).
[59] *Id.* § 10.5(d).
[60] 2010 U.S. Dist. LEXIS 32015 (E.D. La. March 31, 2010).
[61] 40 C.F.R. § 1508.28: "Tiering" refers to a multi-phase environmental review process in which general matters are addressed in a broad environmental impact statement followed by narrower later statements or analyses that address specific issues.
[62] 44 C.F.R. § 10.9(e).

---

claimed that FEMA improperly segmented the project into separate phases and failed to consider all connected actions, such as the later stages of the project. The court found in FEMA's favor and stated that improper segmentation occurs only when an agency artificially segments a project to avoid compliance with NEPA on that project. Furthermore, the court found that FEMA's consideration of impacts was sufficient, that the tiering was lawful and appropriate, and that the mitigation measures relied upon to reduce the impacts below the level of significance were not arbitrary and capricious.[63]

II. Coastal Barrier Resources Act (CBRA)

A. Overview

The CBRA[64] protects ecologically sensitive and geologically vulnerable barrier islands along the coasts of the United States, including the Atlantic Coast, the Gulf Coast, and Great Lakes. These areas make up the Coastal Barrier Resources System (CBRS) units and otherwise protected areas (OPAs).[65] CBRA protects coastal areas that serve as protective barriers against forces of wind and tidal action caused by coastal storms, and serve as habitat for aquatic species.

CBRA prohibits federal flood/disaster insurance coverage in CBRA zones and prohibits new federal expenditures and financial assistance for development in CBRA zones. Its purpose is to prevent loss of life, protect natural resources, and prevent wasteful federal expenditures.[66]

---

[63] *See* 44 C.F.R. § 10.5(a)(1) through (a)(10)..
[64] 16 U.S.C. §§ 3501-3510 (CBRA).
[65] *Id.* at § 3503.
[66] *Id.* at § 3501(b).

Any area that that the law designates as part of the CBRS is:

- Disqualified for disaster assistance and federal flood insurance, except for certain aspects of individual and emergency assistance, such as rental assistance and debris removal; and

- Prohibited from receiving any new federal expenditures, including financial assistance for development, except in some cases.

The Department of Interior's U. S. Fish and Wildlife Service (USFWS) administers CBRA.[67] Any project proposed in a CBRA area requires consultation with USFWS even if one of the exceptions applies. Consultation with USFWS results in consistent determinations.[68] FEMA informs USFWS of proposed disaster assistance actions on a designated CBRA unit, and USFWS makes comments about the appropriateness of that action and whether or not the action is consistent with the purposes of CBRA.

B. Recovery Assistance and CBRA

FEMA generally does not provide recovery assistance in CBRA areas;[69] however, certain types of publicly owned facilities may be eligible for permanent repair assistance (but not expansion) after consultation with USFWS:

- Replacement, reconstruction, or repair, but not the expansion of roads, structures, or facilities that are essential links in a larger network or system. An "essential link" means that portion of a road, utility, or other facility originating outside the system unit but providing access or service through the unit and for which no alternative route is reasonably available.[70]

- Restoration of existing channel improvements and related structures, such as jetties.

---

[67] Id. at § 3503(b).
[68] Id. at § 3505.
[69] 44 C.F.R. § 206.344.
[70] Id. § 206.342(b).

- Repair of energy facilities that are functionally dependent on a coastal location.[71]

Other disaster assistance that may be available in CBRA areas after consultation with USFWS, and provided such assistance is consistent with the purposes of CBRA, includes:

- Emergency actions essential to saving lives and the protection of property and the public health and safety.

- Special purpose facilities, such as navigational aids and scientific research facilities.

- Repair of facilities for the study, management, protection, and enhancement of fish and wildlife resources and habitats.

- Repair of nonstructural projects for shoreline stabilization that are designed to mimic, enhance, or restore natural stabilization systems.[72]

C. Other Disaster Assistance and CBRA

FEMA <u>cannot</u> provide Hazard Mitigation Assistance for construction, reconstruction, retrofit, or purchase of any structure, appurtenance, facility, or related infrastructure. FEMA <u>may</u> provide assistance for emergency actions essential to saving lives and protecting property and public health and safety under the Stafford Act.[73] These emergency actions include:

- Debris removal from public property.

- Emergency restoration of essential community services, such as electricity, water, and power.

- Provision of access to a private residence.

---

[71] Id. § 206.345(a).
[72] 44 C.F.R. §206.345(b).
[73] Stafford Act §§ 402, 403 & 502, 42 U.S.C. §§ 5170a, 5170b, & 5192.

- Provision of emergency shelter by providing emergency repair of utilities, provision of heat in the season requiring heat, or provision of minimal cooking facilities.

- Relocation of individuals or property out of danger, such as moving a mobile home to an area outside of the CBRS.[74]

While FEMA's regulations also allow for certain types of IA in CBRA areas—home repairs to private owner-occupied primary residences to make them habitable, housing eligible families in existing resources in the CBRS, and mortgage and rental payment assistance[75]—FEMA determined that those provisions are inconsistent with the language and intent of CBRA and are therefore unauthorized.[76]

FEMA issued a policy in 1997 to specifically address the provision of IA in CBRA areas. The policy stated that FEMA will only provide emergency shelters under section 403 of the Stafford Act, and assistance for necessary expenses and serious needs related to medical, dental, and funeral expenses, and limited transportation expenses. In addition, social service programs such as Crisis Counseling, disaster unemployment, and Disaster Legal Services would be available within CBRA areas.[77] A fact sheet FEMA published in 2008, however, clarified the policy and includes rental assistance as available to applicants in CBRA areas as long as they rent outside of the CBRS or OPA. Further, the fact sheet specifies that assistance to repair or replace personal property may be awarded if an applicant proves that they have permanently relocated outside the CBRS or OPAs.[78]

---

[74] Id. at § 3505(a)(6)(E), 44 C.F.R. § 206.346(a).

[75] Id.

[76] Memorandum from John P. Carey, General Counsel, to William C. Tidball, Associate Director (Aug. 2, 1996).

[77] Response and Recovery Directorate Policy No. 4430.150A, Human Services Disaster Assistance Programs: Limitations imposed by the Coastal Barrier Resources Act and amending legislation (June 16, 1997).

[78] Disaster Assistance Directorate Fact Sheet, *Disaster Assistance in Coastal Barrier Resources Systems and Other Protected Areas* (Sept. 2008).

D. Process

If an applicant proposes any disaster assistance-funded action on the Atlantic or Gulf Coasts or the Great Lakes, FEMA must first review the location to determine if the action is on or connected to the CBRS unit. FEMA Flood Insurance Rate Maps identify the CBRS units.[79] FEMA program staff generally determines if the action is on or connected to a CBRS unit. If an action is determined to be on or connected to a unit of the CBRS, it is subject to consultation.[80] FEMA's Environmental and Historic Preservation (EHP) staff would then consult with USFWS for determinations of consistency. For emergency actions, however, such as those five listed previously in subsection C, FEMA has conducted advance consultations so the agency may approve those actions without additional consultation.[81] For these actions, FEMA simply notifies USFWS as soon as practicable of emergency projects the agency has approved.[82]

Example of FEMA Monitoring

In 1999, FEMA had a proposed project on North Topsail Beach, North Carolina, to replace 280 linear feet of water main and to repair several leaks elsewhere along the same main. One problem was that FEMA did not know what North Topsail Beach planned to do with the directly connected water main repair/replacement in the adjacent CBRA zone (CBRS unit). FEMA was concerned that the county might use FEMA funds to directly or indirectly subsidize more development in CBRA zones. FEMA monitored to ensure that upgrades were not done with FEMA funds and violations of CBRA were avoided.

---

[79] 44 C.F.R. § 206.347(a)(1).
[80] Id. § 206.347(a)(3).
[81] Id. § 206.347(b)(1).
[82] Id. § 206.347(b)(2).

III. Comprehensive Environmental Response, Compensation, and Liability Act (CERCLA)

A. Overview

The CERCLA of 1980[83] is more commonly known as the Superfund. It authorizes the federal government to respond directly to releases or threatened releases of hazardous substances that may endanger public health or the environment and to address the nation's abandoned hazardous waste sites. The name Superfund applies to both this federal environmental program and the fund established under the act.[84] Congress passed CERCLA in the wake of the discovery of toxic waste dumps such as Love Canal and Times Beach. It allows the EPA to clean up such sites and to compel responsible parties to perform cleanups or to reimburse the government for cleanups.[85]

1. Definitions

a. Hazardous substances: any element, compound, mixture, solution, or substance which, when released into the environment, may present substantial danger to the public health or welfare or the environment.[86]

b. Release: any spilling, leaking, pumping, pouring, emitting, emptying, discharging, injecting, escaping, leaching, dumping, or disposing into the environment (including the abandonment or discarding of barrels, containers, and other closed receptacles containing any hazardous substance or pollutant or contaminant). The term does not include spills in the workplace, exhaust fumes from vehicles or aircraft, nuclear emissions, or the normal application of fertilizer.[87]

---

[83] 42 U.S.C. §§ 9601-9675.
[84] U.S. EPA, Superfund, Basic Information <http://www.epa.gov/superfund/about.htm> (2011).
[85] Id.
[86] 42 U.S.C. § 9601(14).
[87] Id. § 9601(22).

---

2. Scope of Coverage

CERCLA covers releases of hazardous substances, site investigation, and cleanup. Some examples include leaking underground storage tanks, mine tailings, old landfills, and drycleaners. More specifically, Superfund does the following:

a. Establishes prohibitions and requirements concerning closed and abandoned hazardous waste sites;

b. Provides for liability of persons responsible for releases of hazardous waste at these sites; and

c. Establishes a trust fund for cleanup when the federal government cannot identify a responsible party.[88]

CERCLA does not cover oil spills in navigable waters, which fall under the jurisdiction of the Oil Pollution Act of 1990.[89] This act imposes liability for removal costs and damages resulting from an incident in which facilities and vessels discharge oil into navigable waters or adjoining shorelines.[90]

B. Disaster Assistance and CERCLA

CERCLA broadly defines removal as the "cleanup or removal of released hazardous substances from the environment," "the disposal of the removed material," as well as taking other necessary actions to "prevent, minimize, or mitigate damage to the public health or welfare ..."[91] The definition of removal thus may also include emergency assistance provided under what is now the Stafford Act.[92]

If a presidentially declared disaster occurs at or near a Superfund site, FEMA examines closely the potential for duplication of benefits. CERCLA

---

[88] U.S. EPA, SUPERFUND: LAWS, POLICY, AND GUIDANCE, CERCLA OVERVIEW (2011), [hereinafter CERCLA OVERVIEW] <http://www.epa.gov/superfund/policy/cercla.htm>.
[89] 33 U.S.C. §§ 2701-2761.
[90] See EPA Oil Pollution Act of 1990 Overview, http://http://www.epa.gov/oem/content/lawsregs/opaover.htm
[91] 42 U.S.C. § 9601(23).
[92] Id.

---

specifically provides for Superfund cleanup and site remediation, and EPA has specific authority for this activity. There may, however, be emergency assistance that FEMA can provide to address immediate threats to life and safety.

Example of Duplication of Benefits

In the spring of 2008, a tornado virtually destroyed the town of Picher, Oklahoma, which sat atop the Tar Creek Superfund site. The President issued a disaster declaration for the area. EPA had initially placed Tar Creek on its National Priorities List (NPL) in 2003 after testing showed that dust from abandoned lead and zinc mining wastes caused elevated levels of lead in the blood of town residents, especially children. Recognizing the risks to human health involved, EPA, through its Superfund authority, had already tentatively offered buyout and relocation assistance to a number of Picher households before the tornado struck.

FEMA offered home repair and replacement assistance to eligible residents, including those who had received or accepted buyout offers from Superfund. The question was whether the repair/replacement assistance from FEMA would duplicate benefits from EPA for buyouts. FEMA determined that it would be a duplication of benefits prohibited under section 312 of the Stafford Act.[93] Therefore, those who had received buyout payments, or for whom Congress had already appropriated funds for buyout payments, were ineligible for IA repair/replacement grants. Residents who had not yet received buyout payments or who did not participate in the buyout program were eligible for repair or replacement assistance under IA.

---

[93] 42 U.S.C. § 5155.

C. Process

CERCLA authorizes the EPA to take response actions to actual and threatened releases of hazardous substances,[94] and pollutants or contaminants[95] anywhere in the U.S., unless such release or potential release is in a coastal zone, Great Lakes waters, ports, or harbors.[96]

Response takes the form of two kinds of actions:

a. Short-term removals, where the EPA authorizes actions to address releases or threatened releases requiring prompt response; and

b. Long-term remedial response actions that permanently and significantly reduce the dangers associated with releases or threats of releases of hazardous substances that are serious but not immediately life threatening. The EPA conducts remedial response actions only at sites listed on EPA's NPL.[97]

The NPL is a CERCLA-mandated list of national priorities among the sites of known or threatened releases of hazardous substances, pollutants, or contaminants throughout the U.S.

If the EPA determines that an actual or threatened release of a hazardous substance, pollutant, or contaminant presents an "imminent or substantial endangerment to health or the environment,"[98] then the agency may issue an abatement order to the potentially responsible party (PRP) to compel removal or remedial measures. Alternatively, the EPA may request a federal district court to issue such an order.[99] If the EPA issues an

---

[94] Id. § 9601(14).

[95] Id. § 9601(33).

[96] 42 U.S.C. § 9604(a) authorizes "the President" to take action pursuant to the CERCLA. EXEC. ORDER 12,580 §§ 2(f) and (g), 52 Fed. Reg. 2923 (Jan. 29, 1987), delegates CERCLA's presidential authority to the EPA and the Coast Guard depending on the location of a release or potential release; under § 2(d), response authority for releases and potential releases lies with the Department of Defense and the Department of Energy at their respective facilities.

[97] See CERCLA OVERVIEW, note 88.

[98] 42 U.S.C. § 9606(a).

[99] Id.

---

administrative abatement order against a PRP and it fails to obey, then the agency may sue or move to obtain injunctive relief against the PRP.[100]

IV. Endangered Species Act (ESA)

A. Overview

The ESA of 1973[101] protects endangered and threatened species and their critical habitats. Congress passed the ESA as a result of growing concern over the disappearance of plant and animal species. The ESA applies to everyone, but there are different rules that govern a private individual or group's actions and the federal government's actions. The National Marine Fisheries Service has jurisdiction over species in the ocean; the USFWS has jurisdiction over all other species. Throughout this section, the term "Services" may refer to either Service or both.

1. Definitions

a. Endangered Species: an animal or plant in danger of extinction.[102]

b. Threatened Species: an animal or plant likely to become endangered within the foreseeable future.[103]

c. Critical Habitat: specific geographic areas (defined by legislation) essential for the conservation and management of threatened and endangered species.[104]

d. Take: to harass, harm, pursue, hunt, shoot, wound, kill, trap, capture, or collect, or to attempt to engage in any such conduct.[105]

---

[100] Id. § 9606(a) & (b)(1).
[101] 16 U.S.C. §§ 1531-1544.
[102] Id. § 1532(6).
[103] Id. § 1532(20).
[104] Id. § 1532(5)(A).
[105] Id. § 1532(19).

---

2. Requirements for General Public

It is unlawful for anyone to "take" an endangered species.[106] While there is no affirmative permit requirement, any person whose action might fall within the definition of "take" should obtain a permit from the appropriate Service. If the Services discover action within the meaning of "take" and the party responsible has not obtained a permit, penalties can include fines and imprisonment.[107] In order to obtain a permit, an applicant must develop a conservation plan that specifies what impact the proposed action will likely have on the species and what steps the applicant will take to mitigate and minimize those impacts.[108] The Services may then grant an incidental take permit.[109]

3. Requirements for Federal Government

The ESA[110] requires all federal agencies to consider the effects of their actions on listed species and their critical habitats. Federal agencies must consult with the Services to insure that any action funded, authorized, or carried out by the agency is not likely to jeopardize the continued existence of any endangered or threatened species or result in the destruction or adverse modification of habitat.[111] FEMA must determine if its actions have the potential to affect listed species. There are four possible determinations FEMA could make after analyzing an action's potential to impact species.

- No effect;
- May affect, not likely to adversely affect;
- May affect, likely to adversely affect; or
- Will affect, will jeopardize continued existence.

Agencies can make *no effect* determinations without coordination with the Services. An agency could make a *no effect* determination if there were no species or habitat in the affected area or if an action is not of the type that

---

[106] Id. § 1538(a)(1).
[107] Id. §§ 1540(a) and (b).
[108] Id. § 1539(a)(2)(A).
[109] Id. § 1539(a)(2)(B).
[110] ESA § 7, 16 U.S.C. § 1536.
[111] Id. § 1536(a)(2).

could impact species (for example, the purchase of flashlights). All other determinations require consultation with the Services.

If an action is determined by the Services or by FEMA to be likely to adversely affect or jeopardize species, FEMA must prepare a Biological Assessment (BA). A BA describes in detail the proposed action's potential to affect species and any mitigating measures FEMA plans to take.[112] FEMA submits the BA to the Services which then prepare a more detailed analysis called a Biological Opinion (BO). If a BO concludes that there will be jeopardy to the species, it will include Reasonable and Prudent Alternatives (RPAs): actions that the Services believe that FEMA could take to avoid jeopardy.[113] During a consultation, FEMA may not make any irreversible or irretrievable commitments of resources that would have the effect of foreclosing the formulation or implementation of RPAs.[114]

B. Disaster Assistance and ESA

1. In General

FEMA is required to consult with the Services for any disaster assistance action that has the potential to affect species. Consultation may be formal or informal. One exception is for emergency actions. For immediate measures taken to protect life and property in a declared emergency or major disaster, FEMA must notify the Services, but consultation may take place after FEMA takes the action or after the emergency is over.[115] The Services may prescribe conditions or conservation measures to mitigate the effects of the action. The Services may refuse to consult, however, if they do not consider the action to be an emergency. A variety of different organizations and agencies have sued FEMA under the ESA.

---

[112] Id. § 1536(c).
[113] 50 C.F.R. § 402.14(h).
[114] 16 U.S.C. § 1536(d).
[115] Id. § 1536(p).

2. Case Examples

In *Virgin Island Tree Boa v. Witt*,[116] plaintiffs sued FEMA under the ESA over temporary housing constructed on the island of St. Thomas, Virgin Islands, for survivors of Hurricane Marilyn in 1995. The plaintiffs sought to prevent the continued construction of temporary housing at Estate Nazareth on St. Thomas, claiming that such construction would harm the endangered Virgin Islands tree boa. FEMA had prepared an EA pursuant to NEPA requirements. In doing so, it had consulted with the USFWS. The Service identified the tree boa as being an endangered species that might be present at the project site. FEMA's consultation with the Service consisted of telephone discussions and an exchange of correspondence; together, FEMA and the Service devised measures to mitigate any potential effects of the project so that the effects would be below the level of significance. The Service determined that no further consultation was necessary. The court held in FEMA's favor and found that the consultation met the requirements of the ESA and that the mitigation measures were adequate.

In *Florida Key Deer v. FEMA*,[117] various wildlife organizations alleged that FEMA violated the ESA in its administration of the NFIP in the Florida Keys and jeopardized the existence of 10 endangered species. The 11th Circuit Court of Appeals upheld the lower court's finding that the ESA,[118] applied to FEMA's provision of flood insurance under the National Flood Insurance Act of 1968 (NFIA).[119] The court ruled, however, that this section of the ESA did not require FEMA to analyze independently the USFWS's proposed reasonable and prudent conservation alternatives, unless new information arose during the time between the alternatives' proposal and its adoption. The 11th Circuit held that another section[120] of the ESA required FEMA to develop species- and location-specific conservation programs to protect the listed species. Although FEMA's discretion in developing such programs was broad, the law did not permit total inaction. Because FEMA failed to fulfill its obligations under this

---

[116] 918 F. Supp. 879 (D.V.I. 1996).
[117] 522 F.3d 1133 (11th Cir. 2008).
[118] ESA § 7(a)(2), 16 U.S.C. § 1536(a)(2).
[119] 42 U.S.C. §§ 4001-4129.
[120] ESA §7(a)(1), 16 U.S.C. § 1536(a)(1).

section[121] of the ESA, the 11th Circuit upheld the district court's decision to enjoin FEMA from issuing flood insurance for new developments in suitable habitats of the listed species in a particular county.

C. Process

FEMA's REOs and the EHP staff review FEMA's actions to determine when consultation with the Services is required. If an action has the potential to affect species, the EHP staff may either call the Services for an informal consultation or send a coordination letter. The letter would describe the proposed action and FEMA's analysis of its potential effects and ask for the Services' opinion or concurrence. If the Services concur with FEMA's determination that an action is not likely to adversely affect species, then the consultation is complete. The Services could also concur with conditions. For example, they might determine that the action would not be likely to adversely affect species if FEMA took the action during certain months or maintained certain vegetation. If the Services do not concur with a finding that an action is not likely to adversely affect species, consultation continues and FEMA and the Services look for ways to minimize effects on the species and habitat. FEMA often performs the ESA analysis as part of a larger NEPA review.

D. Designation of Non-Federal Representative

A federal agency can designate a non-federal representative to conduct informal consultation with the Services or to prepare a Biological Assessment. If a grant applicant prepared a Biological Assessment for FEMA, FEMA would have to independently review and evaluate it and ensure that it met all requirements since FEMA bears the ultimate responsibility for compliance with section 7 of the ESA.[122]

---

[121] ESA § 7(a), 16 U.S.C. § 1536(a).
[122] 50 C.F.R. § 402.08.

V. National Historic Preservation Act (NHPA)

A. Overview

The National Historic Preservation Act[123] (NHPA or "the Act") established a national policy for preserving the nation's historic and prehistoric resources, and created the Advisory Council on Historic Preservation (Advisory Council) to advise the President and Congress, government agencies at all levels, and the public on historic preservation issues. The Act also created the National Register of Historic Places (National Register), a list of districts, sites, buildings, structures, and objects significant in American history, architecture, archaeology, engineering, and culture maintained by the Department of the Interior.[124]

1. Definitions

Undertaking: a project, activity, or program funded in whole or in part under the direct or indirect jurisdiction of a federal agency, including those carried out by or on behalf of a federal agency; those carried out with federal financial assistance; and those requiring a federal permit, license, or approval.[125]

Historic property: any prehistoric or historic district, site, building, structure, or object included in, or eligible for inclusion in, the National Register. This includes artifacts, records, and remains that are related to and located within such properties. The term also includes properties of traditional religious and cultural importance to an Indian tribe or Native Hawaiian organization and that meet the National Register criteria.[126]

Area of Potential Effects (APE): the geographic area or areas within which an undertaking may directly or indirectly cause alteration in the character or use of historic properties.[127]

---

[123] 16 U.S.C. §§470-470a-2.
[124] 16 U.S.C. § 470a(a)(1)(A).
[125] 36 C.F.R. § 800.16(y).
[126] Id. § 800.16(l)(1).
[127] Id. § 800.16(d).

---

2. Requirements

Two sections of NHPA create responsibilities for federal agencies:

a.) One section requires that federal agencies:

    i.) Consider the effects of proposed federally funded actions or undertakings on historic properties prior to approving or expending federal funds; and

    ii.) Provide the Advisory Council the opportunity to comment on the proposed actions.[128]

This section sets forth a process. It requires FEMA to consider ways to avoid, minimize, or mitigate potential adverse effects to a historic resource, but it does not require preservation or restoration of a resource.

b.) Another section requires integration of historic preservation into agency processes:

This section requires federal agencies to integrate historic preservation into the agency programs[129] and to consult with federal, state, and local agencies, tribes, Native Hawaiian organizations, the private sector, and interested members of the public on historic preservation-related activities.[130]

NHPA also provided for the creation of state historic preservation programs and the designation of state historic preservation officers (SHPOs) and tribal historic preservation officers (THPOs) to maintain inventories of historic properties and operate historic preservation programs within their jurisdictions.[131] The SHPO/THPO is FEMA's primary contact for historic preservation issues at a disaster.

---

[128] NHPA § 106, 16 U.S.C. § 470f; 36 C.F.R. § 800.16(d).
[129] Id. § 470h-2(a).
[130] Id. § 470h-(2)(a)(2)(D)-(E).
[131] Id. § 470a(b).

B. Disaster Assistance and the NHPA

Many of FEMA's disaster assistance activities are undertakings under section 106. For example, any assistance FEMA provides for projects that include construction, renovation, relocation, repair, or demolition would be undertakings. Some programs that trigger section 106 review include but are not limited to PA; Hazard Mitigation Grant Program; temporary housing under the Individuals and Households Assistance Program; and Fire Management Assistance Grants.

C. Process

FEMA's EHP staff coordinates historic preservation reviews with its other environmental reviews pursuant to NEPA.[132] A project found not to have significant environmental effects under NEPA could still have adverse effects under NHPA section 106. If applicants for FEMA assistance take actions affecting properties that are subject to environmental and historic reviews prior to completion of those reviews, FEMA may deny disaster assistance funds for those properties.

FEMA must consult with several different parties in making findings and determinations during the section 106 process: the SHPO; the THPO if a tribe has assumed section 106 responsibility for tribal lands; a tribe or Native Hawaiian organization that attaches religious and cultural significance to affected historic properties; local governments in the affected area; the applicant for FEMA assistance; and individuals or organizations with a particular interest in the undertaking.[133]

The Advisory Council may choose to participate in the process as well. The Advisory Council has established criteria for its involvement in individual undertakings.[134] If it appears that one or more of the criteria exist, FEMA should notify the Advisory Council of the undertaking.

---

[132] Id. § 800.2(a)(4) and § 800.8.
[133] Consulting parties are defined in 36 C.F.R. § 800.2(c).
[134] 36 C.F.R. 800, Appendix A. See also 36 C.F.R. § 800.2(b).

FEMA must also solicit and consider the views of the public regarding the undertaking.[135]

Steps in the section 106 process:

1. Initiate the review process/Define an undertaking

FEMA must determine:

a. whether the proposed federal action is an undertaking, and

b. whether it is the type of activity that has the potential to cause effects[136] on historic properties.

If FEMA has not signed a Programmatic Agreement with the state where the project is located, then FEMA must conduct the review in accordance with the Advisory Council's regulations.[137] If FEMA has signed a Programmatic Agreement with the affected state, the review will follow the stipulations outlined in that agreement.[138]

Early in the process, FEMA should identify the appropriate SHPO, THPO, and/or all other consulting and interested parties.[139]

2. Identify Historic Properties

FEMA in consultation with the SHPO/THPO determines the "area of potential effects"[140] and gathers information on historic properties in the area through background research, oral history interviews, and field investigations and surveys.[141] After the identification and evaluation process, FEMA will make one of two findings:

---

[135] 36 C.F.R. § 800.2(d).
[136] Effect means an alteration to the characteristics of a historic property qualifying it for inclusion in or eligibility for the National Register. Id. § 800.16(i).
[137] See 36 C.F.R. §§ 800.3 to 800.7.
[138] Id. § 800.3(a)(2).
[139] Id. § 800.3.
[140] Id. § 800.16(d).
[141] Id. § 800.4(b); § 800.16(d).

---

a.   Finding of no historic properties present or that will be affected by the undertaking.
     FEMA must provide documentation of the finding to the
     SHPO/THPO, notify all consulting parties, and make the
     documentation available to the public before approving the
     undertaking. If the SHPO/THPO does not object to the finding
     within 30 days, FEMA has fulfilled its section 106 responsibilities and
     may proceed with the undertaking. If the SHPO/THPO objects to the
     finding, there will be further consultations.[142]

b.   Finding that there are historic properties that may be affected. FEMA must notify
     all consulting parties and begin the process to determine whether the
     undertaking may result in any adverse effects to the identified historic
     properties.[143]

3. Assess Adverse Effects

FEMA coordinates with the SHPO/THPO and any tribe or Native Hawaiian
organization that attaches religious or cultural significance to the
identified properties to assess whether the undertaking has the potential to
create adverse effects.[144] Generally, there would be an adverse effect when
the undertaking may alter any of the characteristics that qualify a historic
property for inclusion in the National Register. Examples include:[145]

- Physical destruction to part or all of the property;

- Alteration of the property, including repair, restoration,
  stabilization, hazardous material remediation, and provision of
  handicapped access that is not consistent with standards for
  treatment of historic properties;[146]

- Removal of the property from its historic location;

- Change in the character of the property's use or physical features
  within the property's setting that contribute to its historic
  significance.

---

[142] Id. § 800.4(d)(1).
[143] Id. § 800.4(d)(2).
[144] Id. § 800.5(a).
[145] Id. § 800.5(a)(2).
[146] See 36 C.F.R. Part 68.

---

a.) Finding of no adverse effect.

FEMA may propose a finding of "no adverse affect" when the criteria are not met or the undertaking is modified to avoid adverse effects. FEMA must notify all consulting parties of the proposed finding and provide them with the supporting documentation. If neither the SHPO/THPO nor any consulting party has objected within 30 days, FEMA may proceed with the undertaking.[147]

If the SHPO/THPO or a consulting party objects to the finding, FEMA will consult with the objecting party to resolve the disagreement or request that the Advisory Council review the findings. If the Advisory Council objects to the finding of no adverse effect, FEMA must consider the Advisory Council's objection in making its final determination regarding the undertaking. After FEMA has considered and documented its consideration of the Advisory Council's objection, however, FEMA may proceed with the undertaking.[148]

b.) Finding of adverse effect.

If FEMA finds that an undertaking will have an adverse effect on a historic property, the agency must continue consultations with the SHPO/THPO and consulting parties to develop and evaluate alternatives or modifications to the undertaking that may avoid, minimize, or mitigate the adverse effect.[149]

c.) Resolve Adverse Effects.

Following the required consultations, FEMA will sign a Memorandum of Agreement (MOA) governing the undertaking and ensure that the undertaking is carried out in accordance with its provisions.[150] This MOA will contain treatment measures to minimize or mitigate the potential impacts of FEMA's action. The SHPO/THPO will also sign the MOA if they agree to the resolution; if the SHPO/THPO does not agree to the

---

[147] 36 C.F.R. § 800.5(b).
[148] Id. § 800.5(d). See 36 C.F.R. § 800.11(e) for required documentation.
[149] Id. § 800.6(a).
[150] Id. § 800.6(c).

proposed resolution, FEMA must invite the Advisory Council to join the consultation. The Advisory Council may sign the MOA.[151]

4. Programmatic Agreements

Federal agencies may establish an alternative section 106 review process in a Programmatic Agreement signed by the agency, the Advisory Council, and the affected state or tribal government.[152] Programmatic Agreements create expedited review processes in advance of a disaster that are applicable to all individual undertakings covered by the agreement.[153]

FEMA uses Programmatic Agreements to integrate section 106 considerations into agency programs, and to expedite the review by establishing key processes prior to a disaster, including:

- Establishing coordination and scoping activities at the beginning of disaster response;
- Defining and excluding routine activities from the review process;
- Shortening timeframes for various review activities;
- Addressing tribal and state needs; and
- Delegating some review functions to the state or tribal historic preservation officer.

5. Exemption for Certain Emergency Activities

Advisory Council regulations encourage agencies to develop procedures for taking historic properties into account during operations that respond to disasters or emergencies or other immediate threats to life or property.[154] In addition, FEMA may expedite the section 106 review of certain other emergency activities.

---

[151] Id. § 800.6(c)(1)(iii).
[152] 16 U.S.C. § 470h(2)(l); 36 C.F.R. § 800.14(a).
[153] See FEMA Policy 9560.3, Programmatic Agreement - Historic Review (May 2002), <http://www.fema.gov/public-assistance-local-state-tribal-and-non-profit/95603-programmatic-agreement-historic-review
[154] 36 C.F.R. § 800.12(a).

Certain emergency activities are exempt from compliance with section 106 in the event of a major natural disaster or imminent threat to national security, including immediate rescue and salvage operations.[155] Most assistance to individuals and households under Stafford Act section 408 is exempt from the provisions of section 106, including funding for home repair and replacement; content replacement; personal property; and transportation and healthcare expenses. This exemption does not apply to ground disturbing activities and construction related to temporary housing,[156] replacement housing,[157] and permanent housing construction.[158]

Case Example

In *Friends of St. Frances Xavier Cabrini Church v. FEMA* (*"Cabrini"*),[159] a historic preservation group in New Orleans challenged FEMA's actions in the section 106 review process for a PA project following Hurricane Katrina. Holy Cross College ("Holy Cross") in the Lower Ninth Ward of New Orleans sustained severe damage from Hurricanes Katrina and Rita. Holy Cross applied for PA funds to construct a new campus several miles away on the site of Cabrini Church and the St. Frances Xavier Cabrini and Redeemer School ("school") in the Gentilly neighborhood of New Orleans, which also suffered serious hurricane damage. Cabrini Church was eligible for listing in the National Register of Historic Places and would have to be demolished in order to build a new Holy Cross school campus at that site.

A Programmatic Agreement was in effect among FEMA, the SHPO, the Louisiana Office of Homeland Security and Emergency Preparedness, and the Advisory Council on Historic Preservation (ACHP) covering FEMA funded undertakings in the State of Louisiana. The agreement required FEMA to follow a four-step process. FEMA conducted the review and determined that the undertaking would have an adverse effect on Cabrini Church because it would result in its demolition.

---

[155] 16 U.S.C. § 470h-2(j). 36 C.F.R. § 800.12.
[156] 44 C.F.R. § 206.117(b)(1)(ii).
[157] Id. § 206.117(b)(3).
[158] Id. § 206.117(b)(4).
[159] 728 F. Supp. 2d 820 (E.D. La. 2010).

The Friends of St. Francis Xavier Cabrini Church (Friends of Cabrini) and the ACHP urged FEMA to include the Ninth Ward location of the existing Holy Cross campus within the APE of the undertaking because of the "reasonably foreseeable" effects to the existing school and the surrounding community. FEMA and the SHPO, however, defined the APE to include only the Gentilly site of the Cabrini Church and school, excluding the Holy Cross campus in the Lower Ninth Ward. They did this because it was uncertain at the time what FEMA funded work an applicant might propose for the Ninth Ward site. FEMA planned to conduct the appropriate review whenever Holy Cross submitted proposed project plans for the Ninth Ward site. Section 106 allows for such "phased identification and evaluation" where alternatives under consideration consist of large land areas or if the agency official provides for it in the MOA.[160] FEMA later did a section 106 review for the Holy Cross site when Holy Cross informed FEMA of its plans for the site.

Friends of Cabrini brought suit, claiming that FEMA violated section 106 by improperly defining the undertaking and the APE. They claimed that FEMA should have considered both the sites together as part of a single section 106 process. They further claimed that FEMA did not consult with the public and various interest groups prior to making funding determinations in violation of NHPA. The court reviewed the record of extensive meetings and consultations involving FEMA, the SHPO, the Advisory Council, and various consulting parties, as well as extensive and overwhelmingly supportive public comment on the issue. The court held in FEMA's favor and determined that FEMA had complied with section 106.

---

[160] 36 C.F.R. § 800.4(b)(2).

CHAPTER 9
Information Management
Table of Contents

CHAPTER 9

Information Management

I. Introduction

Effective emergency management operations are dependent on data collection and assessment in all lifecycle phases. This may include hazard assessments, contingency planning, location of evacuees, personal information of applicants, damage assessments, proprietary information in acquisition matters, and multimillion dollar grant determinations. A responsibility incumbent on any emergency manager is the collection and proper maintenance of information relating to individuals receiving disaster assistance. Parties inside and outside the federal government often seek sensitive information regarding survivors' identity, location, receipt of benefits, and other data held by FEMA. These parties could be other agencies, states, the local sheriff, the individual's attorney or insurance company, the media, politicians, or other individuals. They may request information through the release of agency records and/or testimony from agency personnel.

FEMA has the responsibility to collect and preserve sensitive information in a proper manner. This means FEMA must control access to and release of it. This chapter discusses FEMA's responsibility with respect to sensitive information and reviews what types of document and/or testimony requests FEMA may receive. Section II briefly explains FEMA's duty to manage records. Section III and IV examine the requirements under the Privacy Act and the Freedom of Information Act, respectively. Section V covers requests for records in litigation, specifically subpoenas, Touhy requests, and service of process. Section VI concludes this chapter by detailing how to preserve records for litigation.

II. Records Management

The Federal Records Act of 1950, as amended,[1] establishes the framework for records management programs in federal agencies. The Federal Records Act requires every federal agency to establish a records management program, designate a records officer, schedule records, and conduct training. The primary agency for records management oversight is the National Archives and Records Administration (NARA),[2] which administers federal law defining federal records[3] and record management policies;[4] and regulates and approves the disposition of federal records.[5]

A. Definitions of a Federal Record

A record may be anything created or received in the course of agency business.

1. Records or Federal Records

44 U.S.C. § 3301 defines "records" as follows:

> [A]ll books, papers, maps, photographs, machine readable materials, or other documentary materials, regardless of physical form or characteristics, made or received by an agency of the United States Government under federal law or in connection with the transaction of public business and preserved or appropriate for preservation by that agency or its legitimate successor as evidence of the organization, functions, policies, decisions, procedures, operations or other activities of the Government or because of the informational value of the data in them.[6]

---

[1] Federal Records Act of 1950, as amended, codified at 44 U.S.C. chapters 29, 31 and 33.
[2] See 44 U.S.C. Chapter 21.
[3] 44 U.S.C. § 3301.
[4] 44 U.S.C. § 3102.
[5] 44 U.S.C. §§ 3106, 3302 and 3308.
[6] 44 U.S.C. § 3301. See also, 36 C.F.R. § 1222.10 for an explanation of the definition.

Federal records are categorized based on function and use. There are two types of federal records: (1) Administrative records, defined as those relating to the internal administration or housekeeping activities of the office;[7] and (2) Program records, defined as those documenting FEMA mission activities.[8]

2. Documentary Materials

"Documentary materials" is a collective term that refers to recorded information, regardless of the medium or the method or circumstances of recording.[9]

3. Non-Records

Not all documents are considered records. For example, extra copies of documents maintained solely for convenience or reference would not be considered records. Other examples of non-records include library references or stocks of agency publications. Another example is an individual's personal papers. Personal papers are limited to materials belonging to an individual that are not used to conduct agency business and are solely for an individual's own affairs—or used exclusively for that individual's convenience. These files should be clearly designated as personal papers and kept separate from agency records.

B. Record Keeping Responsibilities

Federal records belong to the United States, not to individuals. Given this fact, all FEMA employees and contractors, regardless of their position, are responsible for records management.[10] This includes responsibility for identifying records and applying the appropriate records schedule, following FEMA's retention instructions contained in the records

---

[7] NARA Bulletin 99-04, Attachment A, *available* at http://www.archives.gov/records-mgmt/bulletins/1999/99-04-a.html#records.
[8] Id.
[9] Id. *See also*, 36 C.F.R § 1220.18.
[10] 36 C.F.R. § Part 1220; NARA Bulletin 99-04

---

schedule, and ensuring the safekeeping of federal records until the
designated destruction period.[11]

C. Destruction, Disposition and Retention of Federal Records

Federal records have a proscribed lifecycle depending on the applicable
laws, rules, regulations, and business needs.[12] That lifecycle includes:

1. Creation: When the record is made or received by FEMA.

2. Maintenance and use: The storage, retrieval, and handling of
   federal records.

3. Disposition: Final action taken regarding records dictated by
   FEMA's record schedule.

Federal records may not be destroyed except in accordance with the
procedures described in Title 44, Chapter 33, of the United States Code.[13]
These procedures allow for records destruction only under the authority
of a records disposition schedule approved by the Archivist of the United
States.[14] The National Archives and Records Administration (NARA)
issues a General Records Schedule (GRS) that gives descriptions of records
that are common to most federal agencies and authorizes disposals for
temporary records.[15] FEMA is responsible for developing its own record
schedule, with the Archivist's approval, for agency-specific records.
FEMA's Records Disposition Schedule[16] is a mandatory[17] instruction of
what to do with records (and non-record materials) no longer needed for
current government business. Like other records schedules, it indicates
how long a document must be kept before it is transferred to a Federal

---

[11] Id.
[12] See C.F.R. Parts 1223-1227; NARA Bulletin 99-04.
[13] 44 U.S.C. § 3301 et seq.
[14] Id.
[15] 44 U.S.C. § 3303a(d); 36 C.F.R. Parts 1220; 1227. See also
http://www.archives.gov/records-mgmt/grs; FEMA Records Schedule,
http://dhsconnect.dhs.gov/org/comp/mgmt/General Records
Schedulecao/rpm/Pages/RM_GRS.aspx
[16] FEMA Manual 181-1-1b located at:
http://on.fema.net/components/msb/ocao/orm/Documents/FEMA_Records_Disposition
_Schedule_v17.pdf
[17] See 36 CFR Subpart C, § 1222.34 b for what constitutes unlawful destruction.

Records Center, destroyed, or transferred to NARA for permanent preservation.

Records may not be removed from the legal custody of federal agencies or destroyed[18] without regard to the provisions of FEMA's records schedule. Any unauthorized destruction, alienation, or mutilation of records should be reported to Headquarters and/or FEMA's Agency Records Officer.

III. The Privacy Act

A. Overview

The Privacy Act of 1974[19] and supporting regulations[20] control the collection, maintenance, use, and dissemination of individually or personally identifiable information (PII) by federal agencies.[21] The Privacy Act requirements apply to the PII of FEMA applicants, National Flood Insurance Program (NFIP) policyholders, employees (including contractor employees), and vendors. DHS Management Directive 0470.2 requires that all agency personnel who have access to PII in the course of their duties be knowledgeable about the provisions and requirements of the Privacy Act and privacy provisions of the Homeland Security Act.[22] The Privacy Act provides that no agency shall disclose[23] any agency

---

[18] Criminal Penalties for Unlawful Disposal of Records: The maximum penalty for the willful and unlawful destruction, damage, or alienation of Federal Records is a $2,000 fine, 3 years in prison, or both. 18 U.S.C. § 2071.

[19] 5 U.S.C. § 552a, *as amended*.

[20] 6 C.F.R. § 5.20 *et seq.* These regulations apply to all DHS components including FEMA. FEMA also has Regulations implementing the Privacy Act at 44 C.F.R. Part 6.

[21] DHS defines personally identifiable information "…as any information that permits the identity of an individual to be directly or indirectly inferred, including any information which is linked or linkable to that individual regardless of whether the individual is a U.S. citizen, lawful permanent resident, visitor to the U.S., or employee or contractor to the Department." DEPARTMENT OF HOMELAND SECURITY, HANDBOOK FOR SAFEGUARDING SENSITIVE PERSONALLY IDENTIFIABLE INFORMATION, 4 (2008). PII includes information such as name, address, phone number, and social security number.

[22] Department of Homeland Security Management Directive 0470.2, *Privacy Act Compliance,* (2005).

[23] "Disclose" includes by any means: written, oral, electronic or mechanical. Privacy Act, 5 U.S.C. § 552a(b), *as amended*.

---

record[24] which is contained in a system of records by any means of communication to any person, or to another agency, except pursuant to a written request by, or with the prior written consent of the individual to whom the record pertains unless disclosure is pursuant to one of several enumerated exceptions.[25]

Examples of PII include:

- Names;
- Social security numbers; and
- Home addresses.

Prior to collecting any PII that will be entered into a system of records, federal agencies are required to provide a Privacy Act Statement.[26] The statement must provide why the information is being collected and how the information will be used.

Once this information is collected, FEMA may only release PII from its systems of records either with the consent of the individual or if there is an exception in the law[27] or regulation.[28] The statute also requires that each agency that maintains a system of records collect only such information about an individual that is relevant and necessary to accomplish the purpose.[29] Whenever possible, agencies are required to collect information directly from an individual when the information will be used to determine eligibility for a federal benefit.[30]

---

[24] A "record" means any item, collection, or grouping of information about an individual that is maintained by an agency, including but not limited to his education, financial transactions, medical history, and criminal or employment history and that contains his name, or the identifying number, symbol, or other identifying particular assigned to the individual, such as a finger or voice print or a photograph. 5 U.S.C. § 552a(a)(4).

[25] 5 U.S.C. § 552a(b).

[26] Id. § 552a(e)(3).

[27] Id. § 552a(b)(1-12).

[28] 6 CFR § 5.20 (e). This regulation allows each agency in DHS to retain its prior exempted authorities as an interim solution. The FEMA regulatory exemptions are found at 5 CFR § 6.86 and 6.87.

[29] 5 U.S.C. § 552a(e)(2).

[30] Id. at 552a(e)(2).

B. Exceptions

There are exceptions in both the statute and regulations that override the basic premise of the law, which is no disclosure without consent of the individual to whom the information pertains. Exceptions in the statute authorize access to PII by FEMA employees[31] and contractors[32] who have the "need the know" the information in order to access the information to perform their jobs. These exceptions apply to the PII of FEMA employees, disaster assistance applicants, and (NFIP) policy holders, for example. Another statutory exception allows agencies to share information compiled for the purpose of determining suitability or eligibility for employment.[33]

Another exception is the "routine use" exception, which allows agencies to create "routine uses" through publication in instances where the sharing of the information is permitted routinely as part of the Agency's mission. These are customized t to the specific records maintained by the Agency.[34] In addition, there may be statutory authorizations outside of the Privacy Act for release of PII. Guidance issued by the Office of Management and Budget (OMB) after Congress enacted the Privacy Act made clear that agencies should not interpret or apply the Privacy Act in a manner that frustrates a statutory mandate to disclose PII.[35] The guidance notes that "the conditions of disclosure language" in the Privacy Act make "no specific provision for disclosures expressly required by law," and described such disclosures as "congressionally-mandated 'routine uses.'"[36] The OMB guidance directed agencies, nonetheless, to establish these types of routine uses pursuant to subsections (e)(11) and (e)(4)(D) of the Privacy Act,[37] for the apparent purpose of notifying members of the public how agencies would use their PII, consistent with the statute's purpose.

---

[31] Id. at 552a(b)(1). The regulations allow access to all DHS employees, not just those working for FEMA. This is because intra-agency sharing is allowed for those with a need to know. *See* 5 U.S.C. § 552a(b)(1).
[32] Id. at 552a (m).
[33] Id. at 552a(k)(5).
[34] Id. at 552a(b)(3).
[35] 40 Fed. Reg. 28,948, 28,954 (July 9, 1975).
[36] Id. at 28,954.
[37] Id.

The term "routine use" means the disclosure of a record that is compatible with the purpose for which it is collected.[38] Each agency that maintains a system of records must publish a System of Records Notice ("SORN") in the *Federal Register* describing the character and type of each System of Records, and listing the routine uses or circumstances under which the agency may disclose the information without the prior written consent of the individual to whom the record pertains.[39] This system allows for significant flexibility, as FEMA can modify the routine uses without the need for a full regulatory process.

FEMA maintains many systems of records,[40] including:

- Disaster Recovery Assistance (Individuals and Household Assistance) files;
- National Emergency Family Registry and Locator System files; and
- National Flood Insurance Program files.

The most frequent requests for information arise in connection to applicant information from FEMA's Disaster Recovery Individuals and Households Assistance files. This typically involves state access to PII in FEMA Disaster Recovery Assistance Files.

SORN REVISION ALERT

In 2013, FEMA revised the SORN for the Disaster Assistance Application Files,[41] and is currently engaged streamlining its procedures for providing access to states as authorized by the Stafford Act. Please consult with OCC if you have any questions regarding the SORN and procedures for disclosure of records from this system of records.

FEMA's routine uses also permit limited disclosure of applicant information under certain circumstances to certain other specific outside

---

[38] Id. at § 552a(a)(7).
[39] Id. at 552a(e)(4).
[40] For a list of FEMA SORNs see:
<http://www.dhs.gov/files/publications/gc_1185458955781.shtm#4>.
[41] *Disaster Assistance Recovery Files System of Records*, 78 Fed. Reg. 28,252 (April 30, 2013).
http://www.gpo.gov/fdsys/pkg/FR-2013-04-30/pdf/2013-10173.pdf

eeds and preventing the duplication of benefits to the applicants by the federal government and other entities.

ll requests for applicant information require legal review and concurrence by OCC before disclosure.[42] In addition, prior to releasing PII to a non-FEMA entity, Individual Assistance (IA) personnel must check the information to ensure that it does not contain metadata.[43]

The IA website contains templates for request letters under several different routine uses that the agency may provide as an example of a proper request. The website also contains sample response letters from FEMA to requesters. FEMA may also memorialize information sharing through Information Sharing Access Agreements (ISAAs). Please consult with OCC before using any of the sample letters or ISAA templates to ensure you are using the most updated forms.

The Privacy Act requires that FEMA maintain an accounting of information it discloses under the routine uses.[44] There are potentially significant penalties for the unauthorized release of information.[45]

Legally Sufficient Consent by the Individual to Whom the Record Pertains

In addition to the statutory and regulatory exception that permits disclosure, PII can be released upon receipt of consent by an individual to whom the record pertains. A legally sufficient consent to disclose Privacy Act-protected information must be obtained in writing and must describe the record sought in enough detail to enable agency personnel to locate the records. Individual seeking their own records or authorizing the release of their records to a third party must verify their identity by providing:[46]

Id.
System information (i.e., detailed logs automatically created by a computer detailing who is doing what and when on the computer, commonly referred to as "metadata").
5 U.S.C. § 552a(g)(i).
See Section H, infra.
See DHS Privacy Act Regulations at 6 C.F.R. Part 5, subpart B.

- their full name;
- current address; and
- date and place of birth.

The individual must sign and notarize the request[47] or submit it pursuant to federal statute[48] permitting statements made under penalty of perjury as a substitute for notarization. FEMA does not require a specific consent form as long as the necessary elements are present. When the applicant authorizes the release of information to a third party, such as a non-profit agency providing additional disaster relief, the applicant must identify what records may be released and to whom.[49] A sample statement is provided here.

Sample Release Statement

I, Jane Jones, born on April 1, 1948, in Brooklyn, NY, and [previously or currently] residing at 111 Elm Street, Tupelo, Mississippi, 43456, consent to have the contents of my FEMA disaster application file number xxxxxxxx disclosed to Sam Smith, Esq., 123 Lake Drive, Las Vegas, Nevada 12345. I declare and affirm *under penalty of perjury* that the statements made herein are true and correct to the best of my knowledge, information, and belief.

In the past, for applicants' convenience, FEMA field offices provided Release of Information forms authorizing the release of applicant information. FEMA does not distribute this as a required form because it does not meet the requirements set out in 6 C.F.R. § 5.21 for requesting access to records and may violate the Paperwork Reduction Act at 44 U.S.C. § 3501.

---

[47] 6 C.F.R. § 5.21(d).
[48] 28 U.S.C. § 1746.
[49] 6 C.F.R. § 5.21(f).

D. Consent Form Distinguished From Declaration and Release Form

The Privacy Act requires that FEMA inform disaster assistance applicants about the law's requirements.[50] FEMA provides this information as part of the application process. Applicants must sign a Declaration and Release form, FEMA Form (FF) 009-0-3,[51] acknowledging that as a condition of accepting their application, FEMA may share their information in accordance with the Privacy Act, and FEMA may obtain information about them from other sources, such as banks, financial institutions, and insurance companies. Some applicants or FEMA field staff may think that this Declaration and Release is also the applicant's legal consent authorizing FEMA to disclose their information to a third party; it is not. The Declaration and Release form is not the same thing as an applicant's consent to release his or her information; it is FEMA's required notice to the applicant about how FEMA may use the person's personal information, and it acknowledges and signifies that the applicant is aware that FEMA will use the information from the application in such fashion.

E. State Access to PII in FEMA Disaster Recovery Assistance Files

The Stafford Act mandates in Section 408 the disclosure of information about persons receiving Individuals and Household Program (IHP) assistance to State governments:

Access to records

> In providing assistance to individuals and households under this section, the President shall provide for the substantial and ongoing involvement of the States in which the individuals and households are located, including by providing to the States access to the electronic records of individuals and households receiving assistance under this section in order for the States to make available any

---

[50] 5 U.S.C. § 552a(e)(3).
[51] Please see http://www.fema.gov/pdf/assistance/process/00903.pdf. The Spanish language form is FF 009-0-4.

---

additional State and local assistance to the individuals and households.[52]

The statute requires that FEMA provide access to information about "individuals and households receiving assistance" under the IHP to States. Although the statute does not affirmatively require direct disclosure to local governments, the statutory text expressly intends the State to use FEMA's information "to make available any additional...local assistance to individuals and households."[53] Thus, Congress contemplated that the States would share and coordinate the information with local government programs. Indeed, the statute appears to mandate the sharing of PII with States with only two restrictions: (1) the purpose must be to make available additional State and local assistance and (2) the information pertains only to individuals located in the requesting State.[54]

Thus the Stafford Act provides for a congressionally-mandated routine use[55] for disclosure of IHP information to States in order for the states to provide additional state and local assistance to survivors and also to avoid a duplication of benefits.[56] States must protect any applicant information they receive from FEMA as required in the Privacy Act, and the state shall not further disclose the information.[57] FEMA may grant the state access to its electronic records or, , electronic "excerpts" of applicant records, and/or databases drawn from NEMIS..

The FEMA-State Agreement contains a specific requirement that the state protect any PII provided to it[58] and that the state will indemnify the federal government for any unauthorized disclosure.

---

[52] Stafford Act § 408(f)(2), 42 U.S.C. § 5174(f)(2). *See also* 44 C.F.R. § 206.110(j)(2) for FEMA's implementing regulations.

[53] Id.

[54] Id.

[55] 40 Fed. Reg. 28,948, 28,954 (July 9, 1975).

[56] Stafford Act §§ 408(f)(2) and 312, 42 U.S.C. §§ 5174(f) and 5155.

[57] 44 C.F.R. §206.110(j).

[58] For example, paragraph 3 of the FEMA-State Agreement for FEMA-4031-DR-NY(citation correct?) reads in part: "Under Section 408, the State may obtain disaster applicant information to provide applicants with other State and local assistance. The applicant information is protected under the federal Privacy Act, 5 U.S.C, §552a. A state receiving disaster applicant information is receiving "personally identifiable information" and must protect it in the same manner that the Privacy Act requires FEMA to protect it."

F. Applicant Access to Records

One purpose of the Privacy Act is to give individuals access to records
about themselves that the government maintains in a System of Records.[60]
This includes both IA applicants and employees. Specifically, any agency
must allow an individual to review and copy records pertaining to the
individual.[61] The agency must also provide a process by which an
individual may submit an amendment to the record.[62] However the
Privacy Act also authorizes agencies to exempt certain types of records
(law enforcement) from such disclosure, even to the subject of the
records.[63] Under DHS regulations, FEMA may deny access to employee
investigative files (especially witness statements/affidavits) in order to
avoid anyone impeding the investigation, tampering with witnesses or

---

[59] *Marchand and Richmond v. Foti*, Docket No 540,093, Sec. 23, Civil District Court, Orleans
Parish, La (2005).(unfamiliar with/unable to verify – not sure this unpublished case can
be cited to cover all states in all instances. DMN)
[60] 5 U.S.C. § 552a(d); 6 C.F.R. § 5.21.
[61] 5 U.S.C. § 552a(d)(1).
[62] Id. at 552a(d)(2).
[63] Id. at §§ 552a (j), (k).

evidence, or avoiding detection or apprehension.[64] Any FEMA field office that receives a request for access to investigative records involving employee disciplinary action should consult with FEMA OCC.

G. Additional PII Considerations in the Field

DHS provides extensive guidance on safeguarding PII.[65] FEMA employees should be familiar with the records in their paper files and computers and keep only what is essential. Agency staff should protect information by locking files, not storing electronic PII on a common drive, and by shredding or deleting paper and electronic files containing PII that they no longer need.[66] A Privacy Act Cover Sheet should be used when any document containing PII is transferred or is placed where it could be viewed by an unauthorized person. Special care must be given when maps that provide the location of FEMA IA applicants are created to insure that the map is not specific to the point where an individual residence could be identified. In addition to disaster assistance applicant information, FEMA must also protect employee and contractor PII at FEMA field offices.

H. Security Breaches and Penalties

Access to PII by FEMA employees carries significant responsibilities to protect against a breach or unauthorized disclosure. A breach is "the loss of control, compromise, unauthorized disclosure, unauthorized acquisition, unauthorized access" to PII, whether physical or electronic.[67]

---

[64] See DHS/ALL-018 - Department of Homeland Security Grievances, Appeals, and Disciplinary Action Records System of Records, 73 Fed. Reg. 61882 (2008); 74 Fed. Reg. 4256 (August 24, 2009); 6 C.F.R. Part 5, subpart B, and Appendix C. www.gpo.gov/fdsys/pkg/FR-2008-10-17/html/E8-24741.htm

[65] See DHS Privacy Incident Handling Guide (PIHG). http://www.dhs.gov/xlibrary/assets/privacy/privacy_guide_pihg.pdf

[66] FEMA Directive 262-2, Information Transmitted via Email (2010), provides specific safeguards for protecting PII and sensitive PII transmitted via email. (think this Directive as a DIFFERENT TITLE – DMN)

[67] OMB Memorandum: Safeguarding Against and Responding to the Breach of Personally Identifiable Information (2007).

Examples of security breaches include:[68]

- A FEMA employee laptop containing personally identifiable information about FEMA employees is misplaced, lost, or stolen;
- A FEMA contractor releases the home addresses of individuals insured under the National Flood Insurance Program to an unauthorized third party outside of FEMA;
- An Excel spreadsheet document containing confidential and sensitive information regarding Equal Employment Opportunity charges that employees have filed is placed on a widely accessible computer drive;
- A FEMA contractor prepares envelopes to FEMA reservist employees with his or her addresses and social security numbers on the outside of the envelopes.

The statute also provides for civil penalties, as well as criminal penalties, and a fine of up to $5,000.00 per occurrence for a willful disclosure.[69]

FEMA has incurred significant costs in prior disasters to remedy security breaches involving the release of PII at FEMA's Joint Field Offices (JFOs) during disasters. For example, an employee of a state contractor placed 30,000 names and addresses on the Internet. FEMA in order to mitigate the breach, sent letters to each affected individual and paid for identity theft protection because of the unauthorized release of PII. As a result of this incident, FEMA amended the FEMA-State Agreement to clarify that if a state or its agents or contractors releases PII in an unauthorized manner, the state would be responsible for paying for any mitigation measures FEMA takes as a result.

1. Reporting a Breach or Unauthorized Release of PII

All FEMA employees have a duty to report any potential or confirmed breach in the proper handling of Privacy Act-protected information to their supervisor immediately on learning of the potential breach. The

---

[68] For additional examples, see DHS *Privacy Incident Handling Guidance (PIHG)*, Version 2.1 (2007), Appendix A, 4.
[69] 5 U.S.C. § 552a(i).

Department of Homeland Security's Privacy Incident Handling Guidance (PIHG)[70] establishes strict time-sensitive procedures that DHS personnel must follow upon the detection or discovery of a suspected or confirmed incident involving PII.[71] The PIHG applies to all DHS personnel and to all federally-held information in an unclassified environment such as a JFO, including "information in both electronic and paper format, personal and personally identifiable information, and information maintained in a system of records as defined by the Privacy Act."[72]

2. <u>Summary of PIHG Reporting Requirements</u>

a.) First Stage – Discovery and Notification

Upon discovering that PII or any equipment containing PII has been or may have been exposed, misplaced, mishandled, or stolen, the employee must immediately notify:

- His or her immediate Program Manager/Supervisor;
- The IT Helpdesk (if the loss involves IT equipment or matters of cybersecurity); and
- The FEMA Privacy Office at FEMA-Privacy@fema.dhs.gov or 202-212-5100.[73]

The PIHG establishes strict time-sensitive reporting requirements and the DHS/FEMA employee and contractor must <u>immediately</u> report any suspected or confirmed breach of privacy data.

---

[70] See PIHG, DHS Privacy Incident Handling Guidance (PIHG), Version 2.1, Appendix A, 4 (2007).

[71] OMB requires agencies to report all privacy incidents to the United States Computer Emergency Readiness Team (US-CERT) within one hour of discovering the incident, as mandated by OMB Memorandum 06-19, entitled Reporting Incidents Involving Personally Identifiable Information and Incorporating the Cost for Security in Agency Information Technology Investments, July 12, 2006, (M-06-19), and OMB Memorandum M-07-16, entitled Safeguarding Against and Responding to the Breach of Personally Identifiable Information, OMB M-07-16, (2007); see also Appendix B for the Privacy Incident Report Template. The one-hour time requirement commences when the DHS Chief Information Security Officer (DHS CISO) is notified of the incident. PIHG, at 6.

[72] PIHG at 7.

[73] Id.

b.) Second Stage – Reporting and Investigating

The Program Office should gather the following from the individual who discovered the potential incident and provide an initial incident report and/or written statement describing what occurred, including:

- The name of the FEMA office where the incident occurred;

- Name, phone number, and email address of the employee/contractor who discovered the incident and/or who is responsible for the incident;

- Date and time of the incident and brief description of the circumstances surrounding the potential loss of PII;

- Summary of the type of PII potentially at risk (e.g., full names, social security numbers, account numbers, etc.). NOTE: Only provide the data element categories. (Do not disclose the specific PII data in the report);

- Number of people potentially affected and the estimate or actual number of records exposed;

- Whether the exposure was internal (within DHS) or external;

- If the data was subject to external exposure, a statement about whether it was disclosed to the federal government or the public;

- In certain cases, a police report.

c.) Third Stage – Initial Response

- The Program Office must designate a point of contact (POC) to coordinate with the FEMA Privacy Office throughout the life-cycle of the incident;

- The FEMA Privacy Office and the OCC will develop an incident-specific remediation plan, including, for example, immediately shutting down access to a system, removing a file from a computer network, or turning off a fax or copy machine;

- The FEMA Privacy Office will provide guidance to the Program POC throughout the incident life-cycle;

- The Program Office is responsible for implementation of the remediation actions.

d.) Fourth Stage – Remediation

Remediation of an incident may include the following actions:

- **Notification to affected individuals:** In most cases, incidents warrant notification to the affected individuals. DHS guidance recommends notification by telephone call and certified mail. In these cases, the FEMA Privacy Office will provide the Program Office POC with an approved notification letter and call script template. The Program Office must personalize each letter and follow through with notification in a timely manner.

- **Credit Monitoring:** When Sensitive PII (SPII) has been compromised, FEMA Privacy will provide the Program Office with a Statement of Work (SOW) template and a Blanket Purchase Agreement (BPA) to procure ID theft protection/credit monitoring services. The Program Office must follow through with this action in a timely manner, as the affected individuals may want to enroll in these services immediately.[74]

- **Training:** As a result of most PII incidents, the FEMA Privacy Office will recommend Privacy Awareness/Safeguarding PII training for the involved employee or contractor. Please contact the FEMA Privacy Office to schedule such training.

I. Key Contacts

You can reach the FEMA Privacy Office at FEMA-Privacy@fema.dhs.gov, or by telephone at (202) 212-5100.

---

[74] *See PIHG.*

IV. Requests for Records in Litigation

This section provides guidance where a FEMA employee is served with a subpoena or other request for information or a summons and complaint. This section first addresses what an employee should do if he receives a subpoena. Next, this section gives a brief description of *Touhy* regulations, which cover release of information to a third party by an employee. This section finishes by offering guidance on what to do when served with process.

A. Subpoenas

Occasionally, attorneys deployed to a JFO will receive notification from security that the JFO has received a subpoena. Regardless of where the subpoena originates,[75] the attorney should immediately notify the Federal Coordinating Officer (FCO). It may be appropriate for the attorney to recommend that all solicited hard copy and media records be segregated. The attorney may also want to advise named parties to seek private counsel, especially if they are coming to the attorney seeking advice and guidance. Lastly, the attorney should apprise Headquarters OCC, Field Counsel, and/or Regional Counsel.

Receiving a subpoena may cause concern regarding the procedures for complying on the part of JFO staff, the department from which the information is being requested, or the individual being called upon to testify. The JFO attorney will serve as the on-scene legal expert and reach back to Regional Counsel or to Headquarters OCC. These lines of communication are essential. Responding to a subpoena may require a

---

[75] The subpoena may originate from Congress, the United States Attorney, a private party, as a *Touhy* request (see below), or from another agency. In matters involving Congressional subpoenas, protocol is to accept service and notify OCC immediately. *See* 44 C.F.R. § 5.83. If it comes from another agency, it is an administrative subpoena; most federal agencies have authority to issue these. Although agencies cannot enforce compliance directly, they can request the Attorney General's assistance or simply seek enforcement in the judiciary. For more information on administrative subpoenas, see the Department of Justice's "Report to Congress on the Use of Administrative Subpoena Authorities by Executive Branch Agencies and Entities," *available at* http://www.justice.gov/archive/olp/rpt_to_congress.htm#b8.

significant amount of resources, depending on what information the subpoena solicits.

Subpoenas typically come in two forms, depending on what information it solicits. A subpoena *duces tecum* solicits the production of documents, while a subpoena *testificandum* requires witness testimony. The form will also determine the nature of the response. All responses must be timely, even if the response is merely to inform the moving party of the need for more time to respond.

B. *Touhy* Requests

One particular type of subpoena FEMA may be likely to encounter is a "Touhy (TOO-ee) request." This is a request made to the agency for documents or testimony from a third party whose request is not part of a lawsuit in which FEMA, DHS, or the United States is a party. This is a relatively non-adversarial request made to an agency. This type of request is reviewed by the OCC. Broadly speaking, the Chief Counsel may provide the documents and/or testimony sought, provide a portion of the requested material, or provide none of the requested material. FEMA and DHS Touhy regulations guide the Chief Counsel in deciding what to release.[76] However, if the request is for PII, additional steps may be needed prior to release of the information, such as an applicant's consent for the information or for a court order balancing the privacy interest with the need for the public to know the requested information.[77]

By statute, "the head of an Executive department ... may prescribe regulations for the government of his department, the conduct of its employees, the distribution and performance of its business, and the custody, use and preservation of its records, papers and property."[78] Such regulations are valid and have the force of federal law.[79] Pursuant to the foregoing authorities, both DHS and FEMA have promulgated regulations (Touhy regulations) addressing matters such as employees providing testimony in litigation, their responding to subpoenas *duces tecum*, and

---

[76] 44 C.F.R. §§ 5.80-89; 6 C.F.R §§ 5.41-49.
[77] *See* 44 C.F.R. §§ 6.20-21.
[78] 5 U.S.C. § 301.
[79] Touhy v. Ragen, 340 U.S. 462 (1951); *Boske v. Comingore*, 177 U.S. 459. (1900).

other legal demands of agency employees.[80] DHS regulations control where FEMA regulations are silent. [81]

FEMA's *Touhy* regulations require it to remain neutral in private litigation. Indeed, "[i]t is FEMA's policy and responsibility to preserve its human resources for performance of the official functions of the Agency and to maintain strict impartiality with respect to private litigants. Participation by FEMA employees in private litigation in their official capacities is generally contrary to this policy."[82]

FEMA has promulgated regulations addressing subpoenas for testimony in private litigation. These regulations state the following:

> No FEMA employee shall testify in response to a subpoena or other demand in private litigation as to any information relating to material contained in the files of the Agency, or any information acquired as part of the performance of that person's official duties or because of that person's official status, including the meaning of Agency documents.[83]

The prohibitions may, however, be waived where "necessary to promote a significant interest of the Agency or for other good cause."[84]

C. Service of Process

Service of process is a procedure to provide legal notice to a person of a court or administrative body's jurisdiction over that person and to provide the person an opportunity to respond to a proceeding before that court or administrative body. Like subpoenas, service of process is frequently encountered at the JFO, Regional Office, and Headquarters levels. When the attorney is alerted that a process server has arrived, he should ask himself the following questions: What type of action is it? Does it involve the agency or an individual FEMA employee? If it involves an

---

[80] *See* 6 C.F.R. § 5.41, *et seq.* and 44 C.F.R. § 5.80, *et seq.*, respectively; *see, specifically*, 6 C.F.R. § 5.41(b) and 44 C.F.R. § 5.80(d).
[81] *Id.*
[82] *See* 44 C.F.R. § 5.81(b).
[83] *See* 44 C.F.R. § 5.87(a).
[84] *See* 44 C.F.R. § 5.89.

---

employee, does the action relate to that employee's personal capacity or representative capacity?

When one is served with process, he or she will receive two documents—a summons and a complaint. When FEMA is the intended party, the recipient should refuse service and instead refer these to OCC at FEMA headquarters.[85]

FEMA cannot accept service of process for an individual employee acting in his or her personal capacity. When employees are served at work by an official process server (i.e., a sheriff or U. S. Marshall), OCC will notify the employee and he or she can elect to accept or decline service at work.[86] Where the server is a private individual, he or she is subject to the provisions regarding access to federal facilities and typically will be denied entrance.[87]

Where a process server arrives at a field operation, FEMA will direct him or her to serve the applicable Regional Administrator's office or Headquarters.[88] Whether Headquarters or the Regional Administrator is appropriate depends upon whether the subpoena seeks documents or testimony of employees located at Headquarters, or whether it seeks documents or employee testimony from regional offices or JFOs. Regardless of whether the individual or records are at a field office, the process server is limited to serving only the Regional Office or Headquarters. It is incumbent on FEMA personnel to contact Field Counsel, Regional Counsel, or OCC in Headquarters and notify them of the likelihood of being served and the name(s) of the parties. The attorney may notify the process server that the agency has not yet been adequately served, and any notes the attorney or other staff take down are strictly for informational purposes.

---

[85] 44 C.F.R. § 5.83. If the documents or the employee from whom testimony is sought is located at the Regional Office, the Regional Administrator is to be served. Id.
[86] 44 C.F.R. § 5.80(c).
[87] 41 C.F.R. § 102-74.375.
[88] 44 C.F.R. § 5.51, 5.83

V. Litigation Holds: Preservation of Agency Records

In matters where litigation becomes reasonably likely, FEMA personnel may have a duty to preserve and produce potentially relevant information. This duty has become increasingly important as electronically stored information (ESI) has become prevalent in virtually all organizations, including FEMA. Changes in the Federal Rules of Civil Procedure and recent court decisions[89] have re-emphasized attorneys' roles in meeting discovery obligations and complying with preservation orders.

This is a broad overview of the requirements for information[90] preservation in litigation and how these issues may impact field operations within FEMA. It is not intended to be, and should not be interpreted as, an independent source of rights of, or obligations to, parties in litigation with FEMA or any other individuals or entities. The specific guidelines for document preservation in individual cases will vary and will be generally outlined by OCC.

A. General Duties and Obligations

FEMA has a duty to preserve and produce information relevant to any litigation to which it is a party.[91] It also has a duty to preserve potentially relevant information "[o]nce a party reasonably anticipates litigation."[92] The mere fact that litigation is a general possibility is ordinarily not enough to trigger preservation obligations. There must be some specific set of facts and circumstances that would lead to a conclusion that

---

[89] To understand the attorneys' role in meeting discovery obligations and complying with preservation orders, *See* Fed. R. Civ. Pro. 26. *See generally Pension Committee of the University of Montreal Pension Plan v. Banc of America Securities*, 685 F. Supp. 2d 456 (S.D.N.Y. 2010).

[90] The term "information" refers to traditional "hard copy," paper information and ESI that pertain to a matter under litigation or for which litigation is reasonably likely to ensue.

[91] The duty to produce is necessarily derivative of FEMA's responsibilities to produce information pursuant to discovery requirements. *See* Fed. R. Civ. Pro. 26. *See also* ABA Civil Discovery Standards, as amended through August 2004. Similar duties arise when FEMA receives or otherwise becomes aware of a subpoena *duces tecum* in a proceeding in which it is not a party.

[92] *Zubulake v. UBS Warburg LLC*, 220 F.R.D. 212, 218 (S.D.N.Y. 2003); *Silverstri v. Gen. Motors Corp.*, 271 F.3d 583, 591 (4th Cir. 2001) (stating that "[t]he duty to preserve material evidence arises not only during litigation but also extends to that period before the litigation when a party reasonably should know that the evidence may be relevant to anticipated litigation.").

---

litigation is probable or should otherwise be expected. When FEMA has a duty to preserve information because of pending or reasonably anticipated litigation, an attorney for the OCC will issue a FEMA OCC Litigation Hold Notice. This notice will direct potential witnesses, record/data custodians, and other key individuals to preserve any information relevant to the matter.

B. Type of Information

The Litigation Hold Notice should define the scope of the information relevant to the litigation. This information may include "writings, drawings, graphs, charts, photographs, sound recordings, images, and other data or data compilations in any medium from which information can be obtained."[93]   It may also include all relevant electronic documents and data. This may include but is not limited to:

- Electronic correspondence (e.g., email messages, voicemail messages, and instant messaging dialogs);

- Electronic business documents (e.g., word processing documents, spreadsheets, personal and shared calendars, and FEMA policies and procedures);

- Computer databases information (e.g., financial and human resources databases); and

- System information (i.e., detailed logs automatically created by a computer detailing who is doing what and when on the computer, commonly referred to as metadata).

C. Impact of Litigation Holds

Litigation holds will vary, depending on the nature and/or scope of the litigation and the location, nature, and quantity of potentially relevant information. FEMA has a duty to preserve all information that may be potentially relevant to the litigation, which means that routine record/information destruction schedules are suspended. Procedures must be developed to ensure that routine destruction processes do not

---

[93] Federal Rule of Civil Procedure, Rule34(a), Fed. R. Civ. P. 34(a).

delete or destroy relevant information before it is captured and preserved for litigation. This duty to preserve does not supersede or replace other pre-existing obligations to maintain or preserve documents, and it does not authorize the destruction of documents when any other law, regulation, or procedure requires their preservation.[94]

The attorneys within the OCC have a professional responsibility to work with their clients, potential witnesses, record/data custodians, and other key individuals to take the necessary steps to identify, preserve, and produce relevant information, and to make it available in a proper format.[95] ESI, for example, should be preserved in its originally created or "native" format and should include any related metadata to ensure the integrity of the information.

OCC attorneys assigned to locations where relevant evidence exists (i.e., Deployable Field Counsel, Regional Counsel, and Reservists from the Field Attorney Cadre) may identify a need to preserve evidence, or may be asked to assist with the preservation effort. The assigned attorney will arrange for the capture and preservation of relevant information and work with the record custodians and managers in the affected divisions to ensure that routine destruction procedures (including the routine deletion of electronic information) do not lead to the inadvertent loss of such information. If an employee will remain in possession of the information, counsel will work to develop steps to ensure the preservation of data. Such an employee may be required to contact counsel if he or she transfers positions, is released from a deployment, or leaves FEMA, to ensure that relevant documents and ESI are preserved.

---

[94] General record keeping requirements are set forth in FEMA Manual 181-1-1b, Records Management, File Maintenance and Records Disposition, and FEMA Directive 181-1, FEMA Records Management Program. DHS has also issued a Records Management Directive and a Records Management Handbook, both of which are applicable to FEMA employees. Those documents can be found at
http://on.fema.net/components/msb/ocao/orm/Documents/FEMA_Records_Disposition_Schedule_v17.pdf and
https://www.dhs.gov/xlibrary/assets/foia/mgmt_directive_0550_1_records_management.pdf, respectively.
[95] See ABA Model Rules of Professional Conduct (Model Rules) Rule 3.4 (2002).

Counsel may wish to utilize the template *Notice to Preserve Documents and Electronically Saved Information*[96] and *Litigation Hold Compliance Checklist*[97] and should refer to the FEMA OCC E-Discovery Protocol.[98] In addition, counsel should coordinate with the Office of the Chief Information Officer (OCIO) on all litigation holds. The OCIO will be able to assist in identifying, gathering, and storing ESI.

When the need for a litigation hold no longer exists, the assigned litigation attorney should consult with managers of the affected organizations on the necessary procedures to remove the litigation hold.

Questions or comments about this protocol may be directed to Mr. Joshua Stanton, Associate Chief Counsel for Mission Support, OCC, at (202) 646-3961.

---

[96] https://esw.fema.net/esw/OCC/RRLD/Shared%20Documents/
Litigation%20Hold%20Letter%20Final%206-16-12.pdf
[97] https://esw.fema.net/esw/OCC/RRLD/Shared%20Documents/
Draft%20Litigation%20Hold%20Checklist%2006-17-12.pdf
[98] FEMA OCC E-Discovery Protocol, https://esw.fema.net/esw/OCC/default.aspx

CHAPTER 10
Human Capital
Table of Contents

Human Capital

I. Introduction

One of FEMA's greatest resources and strength is its employees. FEMA employees are dedicated to the mission and are called upon to work after hours, on weekends, and on holidays on disaster operations. They may be deployed with little notice for extended periods of time to disaster sites both within the continental United States (CONUS) and outside the continental United States (OCONUS) in sometimes austere circumstances. FEMA's hiring authorities allow it to surge its workforce for disaster related purposes dramatically with limited term employees, Reservists, and Local Hire employees in addition to its permanent full-time (PFT) staff. [1] FEMA may also call upon volunteers DHS agency wide to assist as part of a surge capacity force.[2] This allows FEMA to scale its workforce as necessary and allows it to staff multiple operations with minimal notice.

During the pre-event phase. FEMA may primarily depend on its Headquarters' and Regional PFTs and Cadre of On-Call Response Employees (COREs). It will also deploy its Reservists Cadres as it readies for and begins to engage in the response phase. As it sets up its disaster operations, such as its Initial Staging Bases, Joint Field Offices (JFOs), and Disaster Recovery Centers, it will also seek to hire locally in the affected communities. As the recovery phase ramps up, the PFTs and many COREs return to their headquarters and regional offices while a dedicated staff of Reservists and Local Hires focus on the disaster specific operations with regional support. Long-term recovery operations may result in hiring field office COREs to replace Reservists and Local Hires. Closeout operations then fold back to the regions and regional PFTs and COREs.

---

[1] Stafford Act § 306(b)(1), 42 U.S.C. 5149(b)(1) provides for FEMA non PFT employee positions.
[2] Post Katrina Emergency Reform Act (PKEMRA) §624, 6 U.S.C. §711.

This chapter will address the various matters that may arise in the JFO workplace that impact employees. The issues addressed range from basic employment matters to more complex employee rights issues.

II. Terms of Employment, General

A. Employee Classifications and Job Categories

1. Employee Classifications

Federal Emergency Management Agency (FEMA) employees are divided into two basic categories: Title 5 Employees (TITLE 5) and Stafford Act Employees (SAE). SAEs are further subdivided COREs, Reservists and Local Hires.[3]

a.) TITLE 5 Employees

TITLE 5 employees are appointed to positions in the "competitive service" or "excepted service" under the Office of Personnel Management (OPM) regulations covering federal agencies and employees.[4] Appointees perform a variety of disaster and non-disaster-related functions consistent with the all-hazards mission of the agency. TITLE 5 employees are entitled to the full range of benefits, including health and life insurance, retirement, Thrift Savings Plan (TSP), and annual and sick leave. Different hiring rules apply, depending on whether the employee is appointed to a competitive service or an excepted service position; however, both are hired under statutes in Title 5 of the United States Code, and regulations promulgated by OPM.[5]

---

[3] CORE Reservist, and local hire hiring authority is pursuant to Stafford Act § 306(b)(1) 42 U.S.C. 5149(b)(1).
[4] Title 5 of the United States Code and the Code of Federal Regulations are the main statutes and regulations that address TITLE 5 employees.
[5] *See* 5 U.S.C §§ 2102, 2103; Id.

b.) Stafford Act Employees – SAE

i). CORE – Cadre of On-Call Response/Recovery Employees

COREs perform ongoing disaster recovery operations at a fixed site facility. CORE appointments are for four-, two-, or one-year terms. Work schedules are typically full time. CORE appointments may be terminated at any time it is determined that the program or the work to be performed is eliminated. COREs are covered by the Civil Service Retirement System (CSRS) or the Federal Employees Retirement System (FERS) and may elect coverage under the Federal Employee Group Life Insurance (FEGLI) program. Employees may also elect to participate in the TSP, the Federal Long-Term Care Insurance Program, and the Flexible Spending Account (FSA). Employees assigned to a regular work schedule earn annual and sick leave.

ii). Reservists

The FEMA Disaster Assistance Employee (DAE) program was reconstituted as the Reservist Program in June 2012. The DAE program ends on December 31, 2012. The Reservist Program is authorized pursuant to Section 306 of the Stafford Act.[6] Guidance for the Reservist Program can be found in FEMA Directive 010-6, *FEMA Reservist Program*. FEMA provides Reservists with time-limited intermittent appointments in the excepted service. The appointment does not confer federal competitive status on the appointee. Reservists' appointments do not exceed 24 months and expire biennially on the last day of the sixth pay period of each even-numbered year (the "NTE date").[7]

FEMA pays Reservists only for those periods when they are activated by the Incident Workforce Management Office (IWMO) and work or are in a travel or training status. At all other times, Reservists remain FEMA employees in a non-pay status. Reservists are paid only for those hours that they work unless authorized by applicable agency directives. Reservists are not entitled to night shift differential payment and do not

---

[6] 42 U.S.C. § 5149(b)(1).
[7] FEMA Directive 010-6, at Chapter IX.B.1.

receive severance pay.[8] Reservists are not entitled to civil service retirement by virtue of their employment as Reservists.[9] However, by FEMA policy, Reservists earn sick leave[10] and are entitled to holiday pay and administrative leave.[11] In addition to the previously mentioned federal equal protection laws, Reservists are entitled to reasonable accommodations,[12] and Reservists who sustain injuries or illnesses while in the performance of duty may be eligible for benefits under the Federal Employees Compensation Act (FECA).[13]

In December 2012, the OPM approved FEMA's request to provide Federal Employees Health Benefits (FEHB) to its Reservists.[14] In early 2013, FEMA will provide all Reservists with the opportunity to enroll in a health benefits plan under FEHB each time they enter pay status, such as during deployments. Once enrolled, Reservists will be able to maintain coverage while they remain in pay status and will receive a 31-day extension of coverage after entering non-pay status.[15]

iii).Local Hires

Local hires are hired under the authority of Section 306 of the Stafford Act.[16] Local hires are not specifically addressed in the new FEMA Reservist Program Guidance, FEMA Directive 010-6. New guidance regarding Local Hires is under development. If you have specific questions regarding Local Hires, contact Headquarters OCC.

---

[8] Id. at Chapter VIII.A.1.

[9] Id. at Chapter VIII.B.1.

[10] On July 31, 2009, FEMA Administrator Fugate issued an interim policy authorizing sick leave for actively deployed Disaster Reservists. See 2009 Disaster Reservist Sick Leave Pay Policy, http://xa.yimg.com/kq/groups/16279885/607894126/name/Memo+-+Disaster+Reservist+Sick+Leave+Pay.pdf

[11] FEMA Directive 253-4, April 7, 2010; FEMA Manual 253-4-1 (2010).

[12] Section 501 of the Rehabilitation Act of 1973 and in accordance with FEMA Manual 1430.1.

[13] FEMA Directive 010-6 Revision Number: 01 at Chapter VIII.B.2.

[14] FEMA Deputy Administrator's Memorandum Regarding Federal Employees Health Benefits Program (FEHBP) dated December 17, 2012.

[15] Please refer to FEMA's FEHBP Health Care Coverage Frequently Asked Questions for additional information and updates at http://www.fema.gov/reservist-program/federal-employees-health-benefits-program-fehbp-health-care-coverage

[16] 42 U.S.C. § 5149 (b) (1).

2. Job Categories and Status

There are two categories of jobs in the federal government: 1) competitive service and 2) excepted service.

Competitive service jobs are under OPM's jurisdiction and subject to the civil service laws passed by Congress to ensure that applicants and employees receive fair and equal treatment in the hiring process.[17] Competitive service jobs are filled according to a merit system based on an application and interview process.[18] The competitive service has to follow OPM hiring rules, pay scales, and so on. Veteran's preferences apply to competitive service hiring.[19]

Excepted service jobs consist of all positions in the executive branch specifically exempted from the competitive service or the senior executive service (SES). Excepted service is a special authority used by the federal government that allows agencies to use a streamlined hiring process rather than hiring through the traditional competitive process.[20] This authority allows agencies to help meet an unusual or special hiring need.

Competitive status is a person's basic eligibility for assignment (by transfer, promotion, reassignment, demotion, or reinstatement) to a position in the competitive service without having to compete with members of the general public in an open competitive examination.[21] When a vacancy indicates that status candidates are eligible to apply, career employees and career-conditional employees who have completed their probationary period may apply.[22] Appointments in the excepted service (such as CORE appointments) do not enable the employee to earn competitive status.[23] A TITLE 5 employee will obtain career tenure after three years of continuous creditable service and can apply for federal jobs

---

[17] 5 U.S.C. § 2102; 5 C.F.R. Part 212.
[18] Each agency is responsible for writing its own merit promotion plan in accordance with 5 C.F.R. Part 335. FEMA's merit promotion plan can be found on the agency's website within FEMA Manual 3100.1.
[19] *See* 5 CFR Part 211 44 s211 .101-103 for veterans' preferences in federal hiring
[20] 5 U.S.C. § 2103.
[21] 5 U.S.C. § 212.301; 5; 5 C.F.R. 1.3, (c)
[22] 5 C.F.R, § 315.302.
[23] 5 C.F.R, § 315.201; 5 C.F.R, § 315.301.

---

under merit promotion procedures.[24] For three years prior to gaining career tenure, a TITLE 5 employee is considered to be a career conditional employee.[25]

Career conditional status allows a person who leaves the federal government eligibility to apply for another federal position under merit promotion procedures for three years from the separation date.[26] After three years, the person is ineligible to apply under merit promotion procedures and must apply through delegated examining procedures open to all U.S. citizens, as if the person never worked for the federal government in a permanent full-time position.[27]

B. Stafford Act Employees (SAEs)

Stafford Act Employees (SAEs) are appointed to federal employment under the authority of Section 306 (b)(1) of the Stafford Act. In performing any services under this act, any federal agency is authorized to appoint and fix the compensation of such temporary personnel as may be necessary, without regard to the provisions of Title 5, United States Code, governing appointments in the competitive service. [28]

SAEs are considered to be "excepted service" employees. However, the personnel rules (for example, the hiring regulations) promulgated by OPM for Title 5 excepted service employees do not apply.[29] For example, veterans' preference rules under the Veterans Employment Opportunities Act are not applicable to hiring of SAEs.[30] Their pay and benefits are set by FEMA as a matter of policy, which the Federal Circuit upheld in *Thiess v. Witt*:[31]

---

[24] 5 C.F.R, § 315.201(a).
[25] 5 C.F.R § 315.201.
[26] 5 C.F.R. Part 315, Subpart H; 5 C.F.R. § 315.401 (b).
[27] Id.
[28] 42 U.S.C. § 5121 *et seq.*
[29] Id.
[30] *See Broughton v. DHS*, 2005 MSPB LEXIS 3558 (2005).
[31] Thiess v. Witt, 100 F. 3d 915 (Fed. Cir. 1996) (holding that the Stafford Act gave FEMA the authority to set the compensation of SAE, and upholding FEMA's decision to preclude Disaster Assistance Employees (DAE) from accruing annual leave, sick leave and holiday pay).

"[T]he plain text of § 5149(b) (1) excludes the statutory obligations of title 5 for appointments in the competitive service. In implementation of the national purpose of facilitating the hiring of short-term, temporary personnel in emergency situations, **§ 5149(b)(1) authorizes the agency to appoint temporary personnel and fix their compensation, and specifically exempts the agency from the provisions of title 5 that apply to appointments in the competitive service.** These provisions include the general schedule pay terms, classification requirements, leave and holiday provisions, and other aspects of title 5, all directed to permanent appointments. An example of the legislative history confirms that the purpose was to authorize the agency to 'temporarily employ additional personnel without regard to civil service laws . . . .' Conf. Rep. No. 91-1752, 91st Cong., 2d Sess., reprinted in 1970 USCCAN 5498, 5500."

The Disaster Relief Act is specific to authorizing and facilitating governmental action in response to emergencies and disasters. Thus, the statutory provision authorizing the agency to fix compensation for temporary disaster relief employees would take precedence over the Leave Act,[32] as the statute states.[33]

FEMA's SAE hirings are subject to federal laws prohibiting discrimination in hiring on the basis of a protected class, such as race, color, sex, disability, religion, national origin, and veteran status.[34] These include: the Uniform Services Employment and Reemployment Rights Act of 1994 (prohibiting discrimination against veterans);[35] Title VII of the Civil Rights Act (Title VII);[36] the Age Discrimination in Employment Act;[37] the

---

[32] Leave Act, 5 U.S.C. § 6301 et seq.

[33] See D. Ginsberg & Sons, Inc. v. Popkin, 285 U.S. 204, (1932) ("Specific terms prevail over the general in the same or another statute which otherwise might be controlling."); VE Holding Corp. v. Johnson Gas Appliance Co., 917 F.2d 1574 (Fed. Cir. 1990). It is a standard rule of construction that "a specific statute controls over a general one 'without regard to priority of enactment.'" Bulova Watch Co. v. United States, 365 U.S. 753, (1961) (quoting Townsend v. Little, 109 U.S. 504, 512, (1883))."

[34] 42 U.S.C. § 2000ff, et seq. (prohibiting discrimination on the basis of race, color, religion, sex, national origin, age, disability, or information); see also 29 C.F.R. § 1614.101.

[35] See 38 U.S.C. § 4311.

[36] 42 U.S.C. § 2000e, et seq.

[37] 29 U.S.C. § 621, et seq.

Equal Pay Act;[38] the Rehabilitation Act;[39] and the Genetic Information Nondiscrimination Act.[40] In addition, discrimination on the basis of sexual orientation is prohibited by executive order.[41]

C. Re-employed Annuitants and Federal Annuitant Waivers[42]

An "annuitant" is "a current or former civilian employee who is receiving, or meets the legal requirements and is applying or has announced intention to apply for, an annuity under subchapter III of chapter 83 or chapter 84 of Title 5, United States Code, based on his or her service."[43]

Annuitants under the Federal Employees' Retirement System (FERS) and under the CSRS are generally subject to termination of their annuity or an annuity offset on re-employment into federal service if they serve in an appointive or elective position.[44] The re-employed annuitant's pay is reduced in "an amount equal to the annuity allocable to the period of actual employment."[45]

FEMA and other agencies may, at that agency's discretion, request OPM approval for an exception from the re-employed annuity provisions of 5 U.S.C. §§ 8344 and 8468, or request a delegation of authority from OPM to grant an exception.[46] Specifically, an agency head may:

- On a case-by-case basis, request OPM approval for an individual annuitant's re-employment without reduction or termination of the individual's annuity to meet temporary needs based on an emergency or other unusual circumstance or when the agency has

---

[38] 29 U.S.C. § 206(d).
[39] 29 U.S.C. § 791, et seq.
[40] 42 U.S.C. § 2000ff, et seq. (prohibiting discrimination on the basis of race, color, religion, sex, national origin, age, disability, or genetic information).
[41] Executive Order 11478, as amended by 13087.
[42] 5 U.S.C., Part 553.
[43] 5 C.F.R. § 553.102(b).
[44] See 5 U.S.C. § 8344 (for CSRS annuitants); 5 U.S.C. § 8468 (for FERS annuitants).
[45] Id.
[46] 5 U.S.C. §§ 8344(i) and 8468(f); 5 C.F.R. Part 553.

encountered exceptional difficulty in recruiting or retaining a
qualified candidate for a particular position;[47] or

- Request OPM to delegate to the agency the authority to approve
individual exceptions on a case-by-case basis in situations resulting
from emergencies posing immediate and direct threat to life or
property or from other specific circumstances.[48]

"In deciding whether to request an exception or grant an exception under
delegated authority, each agency is expected to weigh fiscal responsibility
and employee equity and should consider such factors as availability of
funds" and other criteria set out in 5 C.F.R. Part 553.[49]

On January 11, 1995, FEMA received a delegation from OPM to issue
annuitant waivers, limited to the first 120 days of a presidentially-declared
disaster,[50] requiring issuance on an individual, case-by-case, basis, and
requiring a statement from the individual indicating that he or she will
not accept the job without the waiver.[51]

Exceptions to the salary offset provisions authorized by OPM or by an
agency by delegation under Part 553 apply only to the particular
individual for whom it was authorized and only while that individual
continues to serve in the same or a successor position. [52] The exception
terminates upon the individual's assignment to a different position unless
a new Part 553 exception is authorized.

Annuitants re-employed with full salary and annuity under an exception
granted in accordance with 5 C.F.R. Part 553 are not considered
employees for purposes of 5 U.S.C., Chapter 83, subchapter III or 5
U.S.C., chapter 84 (Federal Employees' Retirement System); may not elect
to have retirement contributions withheld from their pay; may not use

---

[47] 5 C.F.R. §§ 553.201(a), (c), (d), (e) and (f).
[48] 5 C.F.R. § 553.202(a).
[49] 5 C.F.R. § 553.103(a).
[50] "Where an annuitant works under a single disaster for the 120-day period, the annuitant
must complete a second waiver in order to work under a different disaster for another 120
days.
[51] OPM Delegation Letter, January 11, 1995.
[52] 5 C.F.R. § 553.103(b).

any employment for which an exception is granted as a basis for a supplemental or recomputed annuity; and may not participate in the TSP.[53]

In addition to delegated authority described, the FEMA Administrator may issue waivers to annuitants appointed to temporary (one year or less) positions if they are performing certain specified functions and where it is determined that the annuitant's employment is necessary to:

- Fulfill functions critical to the mission of the agency or any component of that agency;

- Assist in the implementation or oversight of the American Recovery and Reinvestment Act of 2009, or the Troubled Asset Relief Program under Title I of the Emergency Economic Stabilization Act of 2008;

- Assist in the development, management, or oversight of agency procurement actions;

- Assist the Inspector General for that agency in the performance of the mission of that Inspector General;

- Promote appropriate training or mentoring programs of employees;

- Assist in the recruitment or retention of employees; or

- Respond to an emergency involving a direct threat to life or property or other unusual circumstances.[54]

This authority also has significant hour limitations. Waiver of the annuitant offset may not exceed 520 hours of service performed by that annuitant during the period ending six months following the individual's annuity commencement date; 1,040 hours of service performed by that annuitant during any 12-month period; or a total of 3,120 hours of service performed by that annuitant.[55]

---

[53] 5 C.F.R. § 553.203.
[54] 5 U.S.C. § 8344(l)(2) and 8468(i)(2), as amended by the October 28, 2009 National Defense Authorizations Act (NDAA). Subsections A, C, E, F and G are most relevant to FEMA employees.
[55] 5 U.S.C. §§ 8344 (l)(3) and 8468(i)(3).

D. The FEMA Qualification System

The FEMA Qualification System (FQS)[56] establishes the system for qualification and certification for the FEMA incident workforce through experience, training, and demonstrated performance, as required pursuant to the Homeland Security Act of 2002.[57] FQS requires FEMA employees who work in incident management and support positions to be formally certified for these positions. Qualification and certification processes provide consistent standards for every field position at FEMA while also professionalizing the entire emergency management workforce. By establishing qualification standards that are consistent across the agency, FQS helps ensure that FEMA employees have the knowledge, skills, and experience to perform in their incident management and incident support positions. FQS also helps employees by providing a pathway for career development and goal achievement.

FQS requirements apply to all FEMA employees who work on disasters and emergencies in incident management and incident support positions. These include CORE employees and Reservists (formerly known as Disaster Assistance Employees) appointed under the Stafford Act; employees who are part of the Incident Management Assistance Teams (IMATs), the Mobile Emergency Response Support (MERS), and the Federal Coordinating Officers (FCOs); and other permanent full-time (TITLE 5) and temporary full-time (TFT) employees covered under the provisions of Title 5, United States Code, who are required or volunteer to work in incident management and incident support activities during disasters and emergencies.

E. FEMA Corps

FEMA Corps is a partnership between FEMA and the Corporation for National and Community Service (CNCS) to establish a FEMA-devoted unit of service corps members within National Civilian Community Corps

---

[56] http://www.fema.gov/fema-qualification-system; *See* FEMA Qualifications System (FQS) Guide (2012), https://www.fema.gov/library/viewRecord.do?id=5896.
[57] Homeland Security Act of 2002 § 510; Pub. L. 109-295, § 624 (2006), 6 U.S.C. §§ 320 and 711.

(NCCC) solely devoted to disaster management operations.[58] AmeriCorps NCCC is a full-time, team-based, residential national service program for men and women between the ages of 18 and 24. The initial term of agreement between FEMA and CNCS runs through February 15, 2017, and the parties have the option to extend the agreement.[59]

FEMA Corps will support up to 1,600 additional members annually within AmeriCorps NCCC. Member service assignments will focus on disaster response and recovery activities, providing support in areas ranging from working directly with disaster survivors to supporting Disaster Recovery Centers.

Members will NOT be considered FEMA employees for any purpose, and each member will be placed in a team of 8–12 members and supervised by a FEMA Corps team leader. While members will be assigned to disaster management operations within a FEMA organizational model, team leaders will be responsible for the direct supervision of their members. FEMA managers will provide technical direction and feedback related to their duties and ensures that members carry out their service assignments safely. Deployment priority will be based on operational needs; FEMA Corps members will be deployed concurrently with Reservists and will augment, not replace, Reservists.

The first 480 FEMA Corps members began their training in August 2012. Members began deploying to disasters such as Hurricane Sandy in the fall of 2012. Recruiting and training will continue until the full complement of 1,600 members is active.

The training, experience, and educational opportunities provided to members will improve their knowledge, skills, and abilities for future careers in emergency management and related fields. Members will be assigned one of the following FQS positions as trainees: PA Project Specialist, Disaster Recovery Center Specialist, IA Applicant Services Program Specialist, Mass Care/ Emergency Assistance Specialist, Voluntary

---

[58] Interagency Agreement between the Corporation for National and Community Service and the Federal Emergency Management Agency, March 2, 2012.
http://www.fema.gov/library/viewRecord.do?fromSearch=fromsearch&id=5620
[59] http://www.fema.gov/fema-corps

Agency Liaison (VAL) Specialist, IA Reports Specialist, Logistics Specialist, Logistics System Specialist, or Community Relations Specialist. FEMA Corps members will be given FQS Position Task Books.

As mission needs dictate, FEMA Corps teams will be deployed via the Automated Deployment Database (ADD). Each Member will be issued a smart phone and a laptop and be given access to the FEMA network.

F. Employment – Monitoring Performance

1. Reservists

The performance of Reservists is managed by their supervisors who refer recommendations for adverse personnel actions against Reservists, to include discipline or termination, to the Reservist Program Managers (RPMs) for review and coordination with OCC, Office of the Chief Component Human Capital Officer (OCHCO) and the IWMO. Supervisors must ensure that the reasons for any such action are documented and that the recommendation for the proposed action and documentation are forwarded to the RPM for review and coordination with OCCHCO, IWMO, and OCC.[60]

FEMA's Administrative Grievance Manual 3300.1 does not cover Stafford Act Employees,[61] so Reservists generally may not grieve their performance rating. Reservists may look to the Equal Employment Opportunity (EEO) process if they believe that the evaluation was the result of illegal discrimination. However, a performance review is generally not considered to be an adverse action.

---

[60] FD 010-6 Revision Number: 01 at Chapter VII.M.5.
[61] FEMA Manual 3300.1, § 1-2.b.

2. TITLE 5 Employees and COREs

a.) Non-supervisory and bargaining unit employees

Performance evaluations for non-supervisory and bargaining unit employees are currently covered under FEMA's Employee Performance System (EPS).[62]

- **Performance Appraisal Cycle** – The EPS performance appraisal cycle is a fiscal year cycle, October 1 to September 30.[63]

- **Performance Plan** - The employee Performance Plan (FEMA Form 30-60) is the first step in the appraisal process. It contains written expectations of work accomplishment and skills development. It defines the employee's performance criteria.[64] A Performance Plan should be issued within 30 days of an employee's entry on duty (EOD), and the employee acknowledges receipt of the Performance Plan by signing it. If the employee disagrees with any aspect of the Performance Plan, the reason for disagreement should be noted on the plan.[65]

- **Quarterly Performance Reviews** – Quarterly Performance Reviews are a meeting in which the employee and supervisor discuss the employee's work performance, skill levels, and individual career development. Quarterly reviews should be held four times during the performance cycle—in January, April, July, and October.[66] Each performance element is reviewed by the supervisor and judged as either On Target (OT) or 'less than expected' (LTE). Comments, including supervisor narratives explaining a judgment of LTE, are documented on FEMA Form 30-60B, and initialed and dated by the employee and supervisor.[67]

---

[62] FEMA Manual 3700.2, dated May 15, 1996. (FEMA also applies the guidance of the EPS provisions and uses the same forms for CORE employees.)
[63] FEMA Manual 3700.2 § 2.2.
[64] FEMA Manual 3700.2 § 1-8(a).
[65] FEMA Manual 3700.2 § 2-1(c). *See* "A performance plan must be in effect at least 90 days before it can be used to prepare an official Rating of Record."
[66] FEMA Manual 3700-2, §§ 1-8(f) and 2-3.
[67] FEMA Manual 3700.2, § 2-3(c).

- **Annual Appraisal** – The employee Annual Appraisal is the final step in the process and where the employee is given a final rating for each criterion.[68] The final rating will be Unacceptable, Proficient, or Superior, and "shall be given any time within 30 days following completion of the fourth quarter," specifically, by October 30.[69] Superior and unacceptable ratings require the second level supervisor's approval **prior** to any discussion with the employee, and require written comments by the first level superior.[70] The annual appraisal and final ratings are recorded on FEMA Form 30-60. Employees receive a copy of their rating of record within two weeks of final supervisory approval and acknowledge receipt of, but not necessarily agreement with, the rating by signing the rating.[71]

b.) Supervisory Employees

All TITLE 5 supervisors, except Federal Wage System (FWS) supervisors, are covered under DHS's Employee Performance Management Program (EPMP).[72]

- Supervisors hired under the FWS will continue to be covered by FEMA Manual 3700.2, EPS.

- The EPMP system aligns individual employee performance goals with departmental strategic priorities, assists each employee in the accomplishment of his or her work plan, and features a performance management appraisal cycle that includes three phases performed jointly by the employee and rating official throughout

---

[68] The rating of record is the overall and final rating for the performance cycle; represents the official evaluation of the employee's performance based on the combined final ratings for each performance criterion; and may be used as the basis for determinations, including but not limited to within grade increases, awards, and reductions in grade. FEMA Manual 3700.2, § 1-8(h).

[69] FEMA Manual 3700.2, § 2-5(a).

[70] Id. at §2-5(a) and (c).

[71] FEMA Manual 3700.2, § 2-5(b).

[72] See DHS General Instruction Guide, Performance Management Program (PMP-GIG), Issued December 1, 2008, http://dhsconnect.dhs.gov/org/comp/mgmt/dhshr/emp/Documents/Performance_Man agement_Instruction.docx

---

the appraisal cycle: 1) initial performance planning; 2) progress reviews; and 3) annual appraisal.

- Performance planning is the first step in the performance appraisal cycle, broken down into two sections: core competencies and individual performance goals.[73] During this initial phase, the employee/supervisor and first level rating official should collaborate to ensure that core competencies and performance goals are understood.

- Individual performance goals are specific, assigned goals described in the employee/supervisor's Performance Plan that describe specific desired results, impact, outcome, and critical action to be achieved during the performance cycle.[74] Each performance goal is written to be specific, measurable, achievable, realistic, and time-bound; aligned to organizational goals mission accomplishment; and weighted. The individual performance goals make up 60% of the overall rating of record.

- Core competencies are the "measurable or observable knowledge, skills, abilities, behaviors, or other characteristics required by a position;"[75] they describe how work is to be completed. DHS has vetted and validated each competency by occupational series and grade. The core competencies are communications; customer service; representing the agency; teamwork/cooperation; technical proficiency; assigning, monitoring, and evaluating work; and leadership. The core competencies are critical performance elements, equally weighted, and make up 40% of the overall rating record.[76]

- The annual appraisal and performance ratings should be completed within 30 days of the end of the performance cycle (i.e., September

---

[73] *See* http://on.fema.net/employee_tools/occhco_tools/performance_management/Pages/Supervisors-PerformancePlanning.aspx

[74] *Id.*

[75] *See* http://on.fema.net/employee_tools/occhco_tools/performance_management/Pages/Supervisors-PerformancePlanning.aspx

[76] *Id.*

---

30).[77] The rating levels are: Achieved Excellence, Exceeded Expectations, Achieved Expectations, and Unacceptable.[78]

As part of the appraisal process, Title 5 employees who disagree with an assigned rating of record may grieve the rating using the applicable grievance process. Bargaining unit employees may grieve a rating of record through the negotiated grievance procedure contained in the applicable collective bargaining agreement (CBA). Employees who are not part of a bargaining unit may grieve a rating of record using FEMA's administrative grievance system (See FEMA Manual 3300.1).[79] If Title 5 employees or Stafford Act employees believe the rating of record is based on unlawful discrimination and/or harassment, the employee may use the EEO complaint process.[80]

DHS SES employees are covered under a separate performance management system.[81]

III. The Privacy Act

As discussed in the Information Management chapter, the Privacy Act[82] regulates the collection, maintenance, use, and dissemination of personally identifiable information (PII)[83] about individuals by federal executive branch agencies. The Privacy Act strives to balance the government's need to maintain information about individuals with the

---

[77] Id.

[78] Id.

[79] Id.

[80] Id.

[81] See DHS Management Directive 3180, SES Performance Management, and SES Performance Plan Instructions, http://dhsconnect.dhs.gov/org/comp/mgmt/dhshr/emp/Documents/SES_Performance_Plan_Instructions.doc

[82] 5 U.S.C. § 552(a), as amended.

[83] Examples of PII are name, home address, home and personal cell phone numbers, disaster registration/case number, credit card number, social security number, or any identifying symbol or particular that is assigned to the individual, such as a photo or thumb print. *Department of Homeland Security Privacy Incident Handling Guidance* (DHS PIHG), Version 3.0, January 26, 2012 § 1.4.9. http://dhsconnect.dhs.gov/org/comp/priv/foia/Documents/DHS%20Privacy%20Policy%20Guidance/Privacy%20Incident%20Handling%20Guidance%20(PIHG)%2020120126.pdf

rights of individuals to be protected against unwarranted invasions of their privacy by:

- Restricting the disclosure of individually identifiable records maintained by agencies;

- Granting individuals the right to access agency records maintained on that individual;

- Granting individuals the right to seek amendment of agency records maintained on that individual, if the records are inaccurate; and

- Establishing norms for agencies to comply with in the collection, maintenance, and dissemination of records.

The Privacy Act requires federal agencies to publish in the *Federal Register* a notice of the existence and character of each system of records they maintain that contains information about individuals and from which information is retrieved by name or other personal identifier. With respect to personnel records, the following Privacy Act System of Records Notices (SORNs) cover FEMA employees and contractors:

- EEOC/GOVT-1 - Equal Employment Opportunity in the Federal Government Complaint and Appeal Records July 30, 2002 67 FR 49338 http://www.gpo.gov/fdsys/pkg/FR-2002-07-30/html/02-18895.htm

- DHS/FEMA/GOVT-001 - Federal Emergency Management Agency National Defense Executive Reserve System January 7, 2009 74 FR 722 http://www.gpo.gov/fdsys/pkg/FR-2009-01-07/html/E9-45.htm

- GSA/GOVT-3 - Travel Charge Card Program January 30, 2004 69 FR 4517 http://www.gpo.gov/fdsys/pkg/FR-2004-01-30/html/04-1946.htm

- GSA/GOVT-4 - Contracted Travel Services Program June 3, 2009 41 FR 26700 http://www.gpo.gov/fdsys/pkg/FR-2009-06-03/html/E9-12951.htm

- GSA/GOVT-6 - GSA SmartPay Purchase Charge Card Program November 3, 2006 71 FR 64707 http://www.gpo.gov/fdsys/pkg/FR-2006-11-03/html/E6-18600.htm

- GSA/GOVT-7 - Personal Identity Verification Identity Management System (PIV IDMS) September 28, 2006 71 FR 56983 http://www.gpo.gov/fdsys/pkg/FR-2006-09-28/html/E6-15901.htm

- GSA/GOVT-8 - Excluded Parties List System (EPLS) December 5, 2006 71 FR 70515 http://www.gpo.gov/fdsys/pkg/FR-2006-12-05/html/E6-20484.htm

- DOL/GOVT-1 - Office of Worker's Compensation Programs, Federal Employees' Compensation Act File January 11, 2012 77 FR 1738 http://www.gpo.gov/fdsys/pkg/FR-2012-01-11/pdf/2012-345.pdf#page=11

- DOT/ALL-8 - Employee Transportation Facilitation April 11, 2000 65 FR 19475 http://www.gpo.gov/fdsys/pkg/FR-2000-04-11/html/00-8505.htm

- MSPB/GOVT-1 - Appeals and Case Records November 21, 2002 67 FR 70254 http://www.gpo.gov/fdsys/pkg/FR-2002-11-21/html/02-29561.htm

- OGE/GOVT-1 - Executive Branch Personnel Public Financial Disclosure Reports and Other Name-Retrieved Ethics Program Records January 22, 2003 68 FR 3097 [correction published May 8, 2003, 68 FR 24722] http://www.gpo.gov/fdsys/pkg/FR-2003-01-22/html/03-1101.htm

- OGE/GOVT-2 - Executive Branch Confidential Financial Disclosure Reports January 22, 2003 68 FR 3097 [correction published May 8, 2003, 68 FR 24722] http://www.gpo.gov/fdsys/pkg/FR-2003-01-22/html/03-1101.htm

- OPM/GOVT-1 - General Personnel Records June 19, 2006 71 FR 35356 http://www.gpo.gov/fdsys/pkg/FR-2006-06-19/html/06-5459.htm

- OPM/GOVT-2 - Employee Performance File System Records April 27, 2000 65 FR 24732 http://www.gpo.gov/fdsys/pkg/FR-2000-04-27/html/00-10088.htm

- OPM/GOVT-3 - Records of Adverse Actions, Performance-Based Reduction in Grade and Removal Actions, and Termination of Probationers April 27, 2000 65 FR 24732 http://www.gpo.gov/fdsys/pkg/FR-2000-04-27/html/00-10088.htm

- OPM/GOVT-5 - Recruiting, Examining, and Placement Records June 19, 2006 71 FR 35351 http://www.gpo.gov/fdsys/pkg/FR-2006-06-19/html/06-5459.htm

- OPM/GOVT-6 - Personnel Research and Test Validation Records June 19, 2006 71 FR 35354 http://www.gpo.gov/fdsys/pkg/FR-2006-06-19/html/06-5459.htm

- OPM/GOVT-7 - Applicant Race, Sex, National Origin and Disability Status Records June 19, 2006 71 FR 35356 http://www.gpo.gov/fdsys/pkg/FR-2006-06-19/html/06-5459.htm

- OPM/GOVT-9 - File on Position Classification Appeals, Job Grading Appeals, and Retained Grade or Pay Appeals, and Fair Labor Standard Act (FLSA) Claims and Complaints June 19, 2006 71 FR 35358 http://www.gpo.gov/fdsys/pkg/FR-2006-06-19/html/06-5459.htm

- OPM/GOVT-10 - Employee Medical File System Records June 19, 2006 71 FR 35360 http://www.gpo.gov/fdsys/pkg/FR-2006-06-19/html/06-5459.htm

- DHS/ALL-014 - Department of Homeland Security Emergency Personnel Location Records System of Records October 17, 2008, 73 FR 61888 http://www.gpo.gov/fdsys/pkg/FR-2008-10-17/html/E8-24807.htm

- DHS/ALL-017 - Department of Homeland Security General Legal Records November 23, 2011, 76 FR 72428 http://www.gpo.gov/fdsys/pkg/FR-2011-11-23/html/2011-30175.htm

- DHS/ALL-023 - Department of Homeland Security Personnel Security Management February 23, 2010, 75 FR 8088 http://www.gpo.gov/fdsys/pkg/FR-2010-02-23/html/2010-3362.htm

- DHS/ALL-033 - Reasonable Accommodations Records System of Records July 13, 2011 76 FR 41274 http://www.gpo.gov/fdsys/pkg/FR-2011-07-13/html/2011-17548.htm

These SORNs cover different types of files of employee information. Thus, data elements may vary from system to system, depending on the context and purpose of the system. Also, each SORN may have different routine use recipients.

The OPM has determined that the following information about federal employees may be released to the public without the employee's consent: name, past and present positions, past and present salaries, and past and present duty stations[84]

For further information, please refer to:

- DHS Privacy Incident Handling Guidance, http://www.dhs.gov/xlibrary/assets/privacy/privacy_guide_pihg.pdf; and

- FEMA Instruction Number 1350.5, Personal Privacy and Rights of Individuals Regarding Their Personal Records (Privacy Act of 1974).

- See DOLR chapter on Information Management, Privacy Act section for a more detailed discussion of the Privacy Act.

---

[84] http://www.archives.gov/st-louis/military-personnel/foia-info.html

IV. Employment-Related Statutes

A. Equal Rights Policies

Federal discrimination laws cover all FEMA personnel, including applicants for employment. FEMA subscribes to and implements to the fullest the requirements of: Title VII of the Civil Rights Act of 1964;[85] the Rehabilitation Act of 1973;[86] the Genetic Information Nondiscrimination Act of 2008;[87] the Age Discrimination in Employment Act of 1967;[88] and Executive Order 13087 (prohibiting discrimination based on sexual orientation in the federal workforce).[89]

Employees who believe they have had their equal rights violated should report it to any level of management or the Equal Rights Office (ERO).[90] Employees must treat each other fairly and equitably regardless of role or position and, where complaints of discrimination arise, it is expected that managers and employees will work together to resolve the issues at the earliest possible stage.[91] FEMA provides annual online EEO training for each employee.

B. Equal Opportunity and Affirmative Employment

It is DHS and FEMA policy to provide equal opportunity in employment for all employees and applicants and to prohibit discrimination in every aspect of personnel policies, practices, and working conditions.[92] FEMA

---

[85] 42 U.S.C. § 2000e, *et seq.*

[86] 29 U.S.C. § 701, et seq.

[87] Pub. L. 110 – 233 (2008), 29 U.S.C. § 1182(b).

[88] 29 U.S.C. § 621, *et seq.*

[89] Title VII of the Civil Rights Act of 1964 provides protection from discrimination on the basis of race, color, national origin, sex (including sexual harassment) religion, and retaliation; § 501 of the Rehabilitation Act of 1973, 29 U.S.C. § 701, added individuals with disabilities to this list; the Genetic Information Nondiscrimination Act of 2008, Pub. L. 110-233 protects Genetic Information; the Age Discrimination in Employment Act of 1967, 29 U.S.C. § 634, prohibits age discrimination in federal employment; and Executive Order 13087.

[90] Contact must be made with the Office of Equal Rights within 45 days of occurrence of the alleged discriminatory action.

[91] Director's Policy No. 6-05, November 8, 2005.

[92] "It is the policy of the Government of the United States to provide equal opportunity in Federal employment for all persons, to prohibit discrimination in employment because of

---

fully supports and is committed to EEO and the implementation of a solid and effective affirmative employment program without regard to race, sex, religion, color, national origin, age or disability, sexual orientation, parental status, or genetic information. FEMA is committed to EEO goals that will aggressively pursue a program to recruit, retain, and advance a qualified workforce that reflects our nation and provides an environment free of all discriminatory practices.[93]

C. Reasonable Accommodation

FEMA's commitment to serving persons equally extends to providing access to applicants and employees with disabilities that is equal to the access provided to non-disabled persons under any program or activity conducted by the agency.[94] FEMA's policy is to comply with the reasonable accommodation requirements of the Rehabilitation Act and Americans with Disabilities Act (ADA).[95] These requirements have been supplemented by recent amendments to the ADA. The amendments, among other things, restate and clarify the original intent of the ADA, overturn several Supreme Court rulings that interpret the definition of "disability" too restrictively, and provide revisions to the definition that are consistent with broad coverage.[96] The amendments have been implemented by regulations promulgated by the Equal Employment Opportunity Commission (EEOC) and other federal agencies.[97]

---

race, color, religion, sex, national origin, handicap, or age, and to promote the full realization of equal employment opportunity through a continuing affirmative program in each executive department and agency. This policy of equal opportunity applies to and must be an integral part of every aspect of personnel policy and practice in the employment, development, advancement, and treatment of civilian employees of the Federal Government." Executive Order 11478, August 8, 1969; Amended by EO 13087, May 28, 1998 and EO 13152, May 2, 2000. 2011-OER-01 FEMA EEO Statement.

[93] Office of the Under Secretary, FEMA, Policy No.7-03, dated September 2, 2003. http://on.fema.net/employee_tools/forms/LegacyDirective_Heirarchy/Office%20of%20t he%20Administrator%20Policies/OER/No.%207-03%20Equal%20Opportunity%20and%20Affirmative%20Employment%209-2-03.doc

[94] 44 C.F.R. § 16.140. Rehabilitation Act, Pub. L 93-112; 29 U.S.C. § 701 et seq., 42 US.C. § 12101 et seq. 29 CFR 1614.203; Executive Order 13164 (2000).

[95] ADA, 42 U.S.C. §§ 12101 et seq.

[96] ADA Amendments Act of 2008, Pub. L. 110–325 (2008).

[97] FEMA Director's Policy No. 4-05, (2005). http://www.fema.gov/pdf/oer/state_4_05.pdf

---

FEMA is required to take all reasonable steps in making accommodations for employees with disabilities.[98] In addition, federal agencies are required to develop written procedures for providing reasonable accommodation.[99] FEMA's written procedures are outlined in FEMA's "Reasonable Accommodation for the Federal Emergency Management Agency" Manual 1430.1[100] and Director's Policy No. 4-05.[101] In general, an accommodation is any change to the rules, policies, procedures, job, work environment, or the way things are customarily done that enables a qualified individual with a disability to apply for a job, perform essential job functions, or enjoy equal access to benefits available to individuals without a disability in the workplace.[102]

The ADA does not require offer of reasonable accommodations to employees caring for others with disabilities. The Director of Equal Rights (OER) has been delegated the final authority in denying such accommodations.[103] FEMA's Disability Employment Program Manager (DPM) located in OER should be consulted on all requests for reasonable accommodation.

A variety of accommodations may be made available to employees and applicants. Specific examples of accommodations outlined in FEMA Manual 1430.1 include but are not limited to:[104]

- Computers and electronic assistive devices
- Reader or sign language interpreter
- Accessible parking
- Materials in alternative formats
- Telework
- Modified schedule

---

[98] FEMA Manual 1430.1, Ch. 1-8(a).
[99] The provisions of FEMA Manual 1430.1 are applicable to TITLE 5 and part-time employees, CORE employees, DAE employees, disaster local hires, and applicants for any of these positions at FEMA. FEMA Manual 1430.1, Ch. 1-2.
[100] FEMA Manual 1430.1, Ch. 4-3 (2002)
[101] Director's Policy 4-05.
[102] 29 CFR Part 1630; FEMA Manual 1430.1, Ch. 1-8(a).
[103] Director's Policy No. 4-05, (2005).
[104] FEMA Manual 1430.1, Ch. 3; 29 CFR 1614.203(c)(2)

Pursuant to FEMA policy, all requests for reasonable accommodation must be kept confidential.[105] Supervisors should engage FEMA's DPM to receive and review medical documents associated with reasonable accommodation requests.[106] Federal law requires that medical information obtained by FEMA in connection with the reasonable accommodation process must be kept confidential.[107] This includes medical information about functional limitations and reasonable accommodation needs. Requests for reasonable accommodation must also be kept in files separate from the individual's personnel file. Any FEMA employee who obtains or receives such information is strictly bound by these confidentiality requirements.

D. Harassment

DHS and FEMA are committed to maintaining a work environment that is free from harassment and sexual harassment, and employees are responsible for creating and maintaining that environment. FEMA has a zero-tolerance policy regarding harassment and sexual harassment that applies to all FEMA employees, as well as to all contractors, students, visitors, and guests engaging in business at any FEMA facility.[108]

- **Harassment** is any unwelcome verbal or physical conduct based on one of the bases protected under Title VII of the Civil Rights Act[109] (race, color, religion, sex, national origin, age [over 40], disability, and reprisal) that is so objectively offensive as to alter the conditions of one's employment where the conduct culminates in a tangible employment action or is sufficiently severe or pervasive so as to create a hostile work environment.[110] Examples of prohibited harassment include but are not limited to:

---

[105] FEMA Manual 1430.1, Ch. 4-3 (2002).

[106] FEMA Manual 1430.1, Ch. 4-2.2, 4-2.1, 4-3 (2002)

[107] § 701, *et seq.*

[108] FD 256-4 and 256-5.

[109] 42 U.S.C. § 2000e *et seq.*

[110] FD 256-4, 265-5; 29 C.F.R. § 1604.11; *See* Office of the Under Secretary, FEMA, Policy No. 3-03, dated September 2, 2003, http://on.fema.net/employee_tools/forms/LegacyDirective_Heirarchy/Office%20of%20t he%20Administrator%20Policies/OER/No.%203-03%20Harassment%20and%20Retaliation%209-2-03.doc

---

- o Making inappropriate comments or remarks regarding an individual because of his or her religion or national origin;

- o Continually scrutinizing, criticizing, or requiring tasks of an individual because of a protected basis while not treating a similarly situated employee in the same manner; and

- o Making derogatory or intimidating references to an individual's mental or physical impairment.

- **Sexual Harassment**[111] is unwelcome sexual advances, requests for sexual favors, and verbal or physical conduct of a sexual nature when:

- o Submission to such conduct is made a term or condition or an individual's employment;

- o Submission to or rejection of such conduct forms the basis of an employment decision affecting such individual; or

- o Such conduct has the purpose or effect of interfering with work performance or creates an intimidating, hostile, or offensive work environment.

FEMA has a duty to promptly investigate allegations of harassment.[112] Courts have found "prompt" to mean almost immediate upon learning of the harassment allegations. When allegations are raised, managers should contact OER and follow the procedures set forth in FEMA Directive 123-19 on administrative investigations.[113]

E. Retaliation and the No Fear Act[114]

It is unlawful to retaliate or engage in adverse treatment against anyone who has articulated concerns regarding unlawful harassment (sexual or nonsexual), discrimination, requested reasonable accommodation, or

---

[111] 42 U.S.C. § 2000e-3(a); FD 256-5.
[112] EEOC Enforcement Guidance: Vicarious Employer Liability for Unlawful Harassment by Supervisors, 915.002 (June 18, 1999).
[113] FD-123-19 (April 5, 2012) http://on.fema.net/employee_tools/forms/FD123-19.pdf
[114] No FEAR Act of 2002, § 101. Pub. L. 107-174; 5 U.S.C. § 2301 et seq.

religious accommodation.[115] Adverse treatment is any action or omission that would deter a reasonable person from participating in the EEOC process.[116] It is an unlawful employment practice for an employer to discriminate against any employee or applicant for employment because the employee or applicant made a charge, testified, assisted, or participated in any manner in an investigation, proceeding, or hearing.

The Notification and Federal Employee Antidiscrimination and Retaliation (No FEAR) Act of 2002[117] acknowledges Congress' recognition that federal agencies cannot be run effectively if those agencies practice or tolerate discrimination and that the United States and its citizens are best served when the federal workplace is free of discrimination and retaliation. Further, in order to maintain a productive workplace that is fully engaged with the many important missions before the government, it is essential that the rights of employees, former employees, and applicants for federal employment under discrimination, whistleblower, and retaliation laws be steadfastly protected, and that agencies that violate these rights be held accountable. The No FEAR Act increased accountability of federal departments and agencies for acts of discrimination or retaliation/reprisal against employees resulting from whistleblower complaints and complaints before the Merit Systems Protection Board (MSPB) and EEOC by:

- Requiring federal agencies to be accountable for antidiscrimination and whistleblower laws;

- Prohibiting retaliation in discrimination; and

- Ensuring adequate posting regarding rights and responsibilities.

---

[115] EEOC Compliance Manual section 8-3.
[116] *Burlington Northern and Santa Fe Railway Company v. White*, 548 U.S. 54 (2006).
[117] The Notification and Federal Employee Antidiscrimination and Retaliation (No FEAR) Act of 2002 (Pub. L. No. 107-174) was passed by both houses of Congress and was signed into law by President Bush on May 15, 2002.

F. Alcohol/Drug-Free Workplace

Pursuant to federal law, FEMA facilities provide a drug and alcohol free workplace.[118] Alcohol is prohibited in all federal facilities;[119] and the use, possession, or distribution of illegal drugs by employees, whether on or off the job, will not be tolerated. These are zero-tolerance policies.[120]

Employees may not possess or consume alcoholic beverages while at work, report to work under the influence of alcohol, perform FEMA-related work under the influence of alcohol, or operate any agency vehicle under the influence of alcohol. Law enforcement personnel on federal property may administer alcohol tests when there is an accident or reasonable cause to do so.[121]

Executive Order 12564 establishes standards and procedures for a drug-free federal workplace and mandates testing for the use of illegal drugs for all federal employees in safety and security-sensitive positions.[122]

The unlawful use, manufacture, distribution, possession, solicitation, or transfer of a controlled substance is strictly prohibited on any FEMA premises or worksite (including parking lots).

G. Smoke-Free Workplace

Pursuant to executive order, a policy was established to provide a smoke-free environment for federal employees and members of the public visiting or using federal facilities.[123] "The smoking of tobacco products is prohibited in all interior space owned, rented, or leased by the executive

---

[118] Federal Property Management Regulations, 42 C.F.R. § 102-74.405; the Drug Free Workplace Act of 1988; 41 U.S.C. § 701.
[119] Id.
[120] Id.
[121] Id.
[122] Executive Order 12564; 41 C.F.R. §§ 102-74-400.
[123] (41 C.F.R. §§ 102-74.400).

branch of the federal government and in any outdoor areas under executive branch control in front of air intake ducts."[124]

Accordingly, FEMA installations are designated as non-smoking facilities. There is no smoking inside **any** FEMA facility, including restrooms, break rooms, hallways, lobbies, elevators, tunnels, dorm rooms, or any other part of the facility, unless the area is designated for smoking.

Smoking is also prohibited in all FEMA-owned or leased vehicles.[125]

H. Weapons/Security/Safety

1. Weapons

Employees are expressly forbidden from bringing firearms or other dangerous weapons on to any FEMA facility; doing so constitutes grounds for immediate dismissal.[126]

Persons who knowingly possess or cause to be present a firearm or other dangerous weapon in a federal facility, or attempt to do so, shall be fined pursuant to federal law or imprisoned not more than one year, or both. Persons who, with intent that a firearm or other dangerous weapon be used in the commission of a crime, knowingly possess or cause to be present such firearm or dangerous weapon in a federal facility, or attempt to do so, shall be fined pursuant to federal law or imprisoned not more than five years, or both.[127]

2. Security

FEMA facilities are secured and have controlled access. All FEMA employees, contractors, and affiliates, after undergoing fingerprinting, E-Qip procedures, and the initiation and completion of a background

---

[124] Executive Order 13058 (August 9, 1997); FEMA Instructions 6900.1 (January 11, 2002).
[125] Id.
[126] 18 U.S.C. § 930, Possession of Firearms and Dangerous Weapons in Federal Facilities.
[127] Id.

investigation and suitability determination, must be badged to have unescorted access to FEMA facilities.[128]

In addition, the removal of government property from FEMA facilities must be monitored in order to avoid losses, negligence, and unauthorized use. Federal property management regulations state that "packages, briefcases and other containers in the immediate possession of visitors, employees, or other persons arriving on, working at, visiting, or departing from Federal property" are subject to inspection. Property can only be removed from a FEMA facility with an authorized property pass.

3. Safety

Federal workers have a right to a safe and secure workplace, and anyone who depends on the work of the federal government for their health, safety and security has a right to a reliable and productive federal workforce.

FEMA adheres to the provisions of regulatory statutes applicable to FEMA's goal of ensuring, to the highest degree possible, a safe and healthful workplace wherever FEMA employees are assigned or the agency's mission is executed.[129]

Under FEMA's Occupational Safety and Health Administration (OSHA) Program, goals and objectives are established for reducing and eliminating occupational accidents, injuries, and illnesses, and for appropriate corrective actions to be taken.[130] Qualified and authorized occupational safety and health inspectors inspect FEMA worksites; management and supervisory evaluations measure performance in meeting the program requirements; and all agency employees and bargaining unit representatives have an opportunity to participate in the program without restraint, coercion, interference, or reprisal.

---

[128] *See* FEMA Instruction 1210.1, FEMA Identification Cards, Credentials, and Passes, (1984); *see also* Homeland Security Presidential Directive 12 (HSPD-12), Policy for a Common Identification Standard for Federal Employees and Contractors (2004).
[129] *See* the FEMA Occupational Safety and Health Program, Policy 6900.3.
[130] *See* the Occupational Safety and Health Support Annex to the National Response Framework, (2008).

Employees are responsible for complying with OSHA standards, following all FEMA safety and health rules, reporting hazardous workplace conditions, and promptly reporting any job-related injury, illness, or accident to supervisors.

I. Workers' Compensation[131]

All federal civilian employees (including SAEs, but with the exception of non-appropriated fund employees[132]) are covered under the Federal Employees Compensation Act (FECA), more commonly referred to as workers' compensation.[133] The rules governing administration of all claims filed under the FECA are set forth at 20 C.F.R. Part 10.

The FECA provides compensation for wage loss, medical care, and vocational rehabilitation for federal employees who are injured in the performance of their duties or who develop illnesses as a result of factors of their federal employment.[134] FECA also provides monetary benefits to dependents if a job-related injury, illness, or disease causes the employee's death. Benefits cannot be paid if the injury, illness, or death is caused by the employee's willful misconduct, intent, or intoxication by alcohol or illegal drugs.[135]

The FECA is administered by the U.S. Department of Labor, Office of Workers' Compensation Program (OWCP), Division of Federal Employees' Compensation (DFEC), through district offices located

---

[131] For General Reference see – U.S. Department of Labor, Division of Federal Employees' Compensation (DFEC), Q&A Concerning Benefits of the Federal Employees' Compensation Act, http://www.dol.gov/owcp/dfec/regs/compliance/feca550q.htm

[132] Non-appropriated fund employee means a civilian employee who is paid from non-appropriated funds of Army and Air Force Exchange Service, Navy Exchange Service Command, Marine Corps exchanges, or any other instrumentality of the United States under the jurisdiction of the armed forces which is conducted for the comfort, pleasure, contentment, or physical or mental improvement of members of the armed forces. Such term includes a civilian employee of a support organization within the Department of Defense or a military department, such as the Defense Finance and Accounting Service, who is paid from non-appropriated funds on account of the nature of the employee's duties. They are typically paid from funds generated by those activities.

[133] The Federal Employees' Compensation Act, 5 USC § 8101 et seq.

[134] Damage to or destruction of medical braces, artificial limbs, and other prosthetic devices incidental to a job-related personal injury is also compensable. 5 U.S.C. § 8101(5).

[135] 5 U.S.C. § 8102(a).

---

throughout the United States. Twelve OWCP district offices adjudicate claims and pay benefits, and the costs of those benefits are charged back to the employing agency.

J. Unemployment Compensation[136]

Subject to individual state regulations, FEMA employees (including DAEs and other SAEs) may, upon completion of assignment, placement in non-pay status, or expiration of appointment, be eligible to receive unemployment insurance (UI) benefits.

UI benefits are intended to provide temporary financial assistance to unemployed workers who meet the requirements of state law. The Unemployment Compensation for Federal Employees (UCFE) program provides UI benefits for eligible former civilian federal employees who are unemployed through no fault of their own (as determined under state law) and meet other state law eligibility requirements. FEMA challenges claims by FEMA employees where the employee has quit or has been terminated for misconduct or poor performance, as a general rule. FEMA OCC represents FEMA at hearings held in state unemployment compensation offices, which take testimony and adjudicate the denial or granting of benefits in such cases.

The UI program is administered by states as agents of the federal government, within guidelines established by federal law, and operated under the same terms and conditions that apply to regular state unemployment insurance.[137] Eligibility for UI benefits, benefit amounts, and the length of time benefits are available are determined by the state law under which unemployment insurance claims are established.

In the majority of states, benefit funding is based solely on a tax imposed on employers. UI for unemployed federal workers is paid from U.S. government funds. There is no payroll deduction from a FEMA or other federal employee's wages for UI protection.

---

[136] *See generally,* U.S. Department of Labor – Find It by Topic – Unemployment Insurance (UI); http://www.dol.gov/dol/topic/unemployment-insurance/index.htm.
[137] Social Security Act, Pub. L. 74-271; 5 U.S.C. § 8501 *et seq*; 5 C.F.R. § 8501 *et seq*.

K. Fair Labor Standards Act[138]

The Fair Labor Standards Act (FLSA) prescribes standards for the basic minimum wage and overtime pay, child labor, equal pay, and portal-to-portal activities.[139] The act exempts specified employees or groups of employees from the application of certain of its provisions; requires government agencies to pay covered employees who are not otherwise exempt at least the federal minimum wage and overtime pay of one and one-half times the regular rate of pay; and prescribes penalties for the commission of specifically prohibited acts. OPM administers the provisions of the FLSA with respect to FEMA employees and other persons employed by a federal agency, except as otherwise provided.[140]

L. Family and Medical Leave Act

The Family and Medical Leave Act of 1993 (FMLA)[141] allows employees to take up to 12 workweeks of unpaid leave during any 12-month period for the following purposes:[142]

- A serious health condition of the employee that makes the employee unable to perform the essential functions of his or her position;

---

[138] The Fair Labor Standards Act is published at 29 U.S.C. §§ 201-219; OPM's FLSA regulations are published at 5 C.F.R., Part 551, §§ 551.101-551.710.

[139] "Section 3(e)(2) of the Act authorizes the application of the provisions of the Act to any person employed by the Government of the United States, as specified in that section." 5 C.F.R. § 551.102.

[140] 5 C.F.R. § 551.102(a). The U.S. Equal Employment Opportunity Commission administers the equal pay provisions contained in § 6(d) of the Act. Under the Congressional Accountability Act of 1995, as amended, 5 U.S.C. §§ 1301 et seq., the U.S. Office of Compliance administers the provisions of the FLSA for employees of the U.S. House of Representatives, U.S. Senate, Capitol Guide Service, Capitol Police, Congressional Budget Office, Office of the Architect of the Capitol, Office of the Attending Physician, and Office of Compliance. The U.S. Department of Labor, Wage and Hour Division, administers FLSA provisions for private employers, state and local governments, the Library of Congress, the United States Postal Service, the Postal Rate Commission, and the Tennessee Valley Authority. 5 C.F.R. §§ 551.102(b), (c), and (d).

[141] 29 U.S.C. § 2601, 29 C.F.R. § 825. Also See FEMA Absence and Leave Policy, Policy No. 3300.3, dated July 31, 2001, http://on.fema.net/employee_tools/forms/Directives/3300-3m-073101.pdf.

[142] 5 C.F.R. § 630.1203.

- The care of a spouse, son, daughter, or parent of the employee who has a serious health condition;

- The birth of a son or daughter of the employee and the care of such son or daughter;

- The placement of a son or daughter with the employee for adoption or foster care.

The rights and the conditions under which an employee can take leave under FMLA depend on the nature of the FEMA appointment and the schedule. Generally, permanent employees with a scheduled tour of duty and employees on temporary appointments not limited to one year or less (typically CORE employees) are covered by OPM regulations published at 5 C.F.R., Part 630, Subpart L.[143] Employees who do not have a scheduled tour of duty (i.e., those on an intermittent duty schedule) and employees on temporary appointments of one year or less are subject to Department of Labor regulations published at 29 C.F.R., Part 825.[144]

Employee rights and requirements are similar under both regulations. Both sets of regulations require 12 months of service to be eligible for FMLA leave, but the total service does not have to be recent or continuous.

- Permanent and CORE employees: The service must have been as a permanent or CORE employee. Time in temporary or intermittent service will not count toward meeting the basic eligibility requirement;

- Reservist or intermittent employees must have 12 months of service and the employee must have worked for at least 1,250 hours during the previous 12 months prior to the period for which FMLA is to be used. Further, the employee must work at a location in the United States (or one of its territories or possessions) where at least 50 persons are employed by the federal government within 75 miles.

---

[143] 29 C.F.R. § 825.109(a).
[144] 29 C.F.R. §§ 825.109(b)(3), (4).

Under certain circumstances, leave taken under the FMLA does not have to be taken all at once or continuously.[145] Employees may elect to substitute annual leave and/or sick leave, consistent with current laws and OPM regulations for using annual and sick leave, for any unpaid leave under the FMLA.[146]

V. Employee Misconduct

A. Required Notifications to the DHS Office of Inspector General

The DHS Office of Inspector General (OIG) operates independent of DHS and all DHS offices. The OIG receives and investigates complaints "concerning the possible existence of criminal or other misconduct constituting a violation of law, rules, or regulations, a cause for suspension or debarment, mismanagement, gross waste of funds, abuse of authority, or a substantial and specific danger to the public health and safety."[147] DHS MD 0810.1 <u>requires</u> that the following matters be reported to the OIG:

- All allegations of criminal misconduct against a DHS employee;

- All allegations concerning employees at the GS-15 level or higher;

- All allegations against a law enforcement officer of serious, non-criminal misconduct;

- All instances regarding discharge of a firearm that results in death or personal injury or otherwise warrants referral to the Civil Rights Criminal Division of the Department of Justice;

- All allegations of fraud by contractors, grantees, or other individuals or entities receiving DHS funds or otherwise engaged in the operation of DHS programs or operations;

---

[145] 5 C.F.R. § 630.1204.
[146] 5 C.F.R. § 630.1205.
[147] *See* DHS Management Directive (DHS-MD) 0810.1, (2004), § VI(A)(6). *Also See*, (INTERIM) FEMA Manual 123-19-1 Administrative Investigations Policy, dated 04/05/2012, http://on.fema.net/employee_tools/forms/Directives/IFM123-19-1.pdf

---

- All allegations of visa fraud by DHS employees working in the visa issuance process; and

- Allegations against individuals or entities that do not fit into the categories identified here if the allegations reflect systemic violations, such as abuse of civil rights, civil liberties, or racial and ethnic profiling; demonstrate serious management problems within the department; or otherwise represent a serious danger to public health and safety.[148]

OCC and the FEMA Office of the Chief Security Officer (OCSO) are the primary points of contact with the DHS OIG and regularly refer allegations fitting within the named parameters to the DHS OIG; however, all federal employees are required to refer the allegations shown here and may do so on their own. OCSO and OCC Personnel Law Branch should be notified of any employee conduct referred to the OIG. Until advised by the DHS OIG, investigation into the allegation should not be undertaken by the agency.[149] If substantiated, the matter will be referred to the appropriate Assistant United States Attorney or other applicable prosecution authority.[150]

All FEMA counsel must refer to the OCC Criminal Misconduct Checklist[151] to use when they become aware of any allegation of possible criminal misconduct by any FEMA employee. This checklist provides essential instructions for how to respond to, report, and investigate allegations of criminal misconduct.

---

[148] Id. at Appendix A-1.

[149] Exception to DHS OIG required notifications: Criminal activity that occurs on FEMA owned or leased facilities should be immediately reported to the Office of Federal Protective Service (FPS) with concurrent notification to FEMA's OCSO. If the FPS has no police officers or investigators in close proximity to the FEMA property, criminal activity should be reported to local law enforcement with jurisdiction (sheriff, local police, state police), generally by dialing 9-1-1, with separate notifications to FPS and FEMA's OCSO.

[150] FEMA Instruction 1200.1, ¶ 5, (2000) (emphasis added).

[151] https://esw.fema.net/esw/OCC/Field/Human%20Capital/
Criminal%20investigations/MEMO%20-
%20FEMA%20OCC%20Criminal%20Misconduct%20Checklist%20SIGNED.pdf

B. Violence in the Workplace

FEMA's policy regarding violent acts or threats of violence or other inappropriate behaviors that have the potential for causing harm to one's self or others in the performance of official duties is as follows:

FEMA strives to minimize the likelihood of violence in the workplace through early intervention and will not tolerate acts or threats of violence (explicit or implied). Employees found in violation of this policy will be subject to disciplinary action, up to and including termination of employment, and referral to appropriate law enforcement authorities. For other than FEMA employees, comparable appropriate action will be taken.[152]

It is strictly forbidden to commit any action intended or perceived to intend to threaten, intimidate, or abuse another person or to cause damage, destruction, or sabotage of property, verbally, visually, or in writing while at work. Any such behavior will be subject to immediate disciplinary action. The prohibition includes acts, remarks, or gestures that communicate a threat of harm or otherwise cause concern for the safety of any individual; or damage, destruction, or sabotage of property at a FEMA facility; or any such actions by an employee while on or because of his or her official duties. This prohibition also applies to contractors and personnel from other agencies that are performing official duties in support of FEMA's mission.[153]

All managers, supervisors, and employees should immediately contact the OCSO, OCC, or the Employee and Labor Relations Branch (ELRB) if they witness or are informed of violent, abusive or threatening behavior. In instances of imminent danger, appropriate law enforcement authorities should be immediately contacted.

---

[152] Id.
[153] Id.

C. Administrative Disciplinary Action

What happens next? If the DHS OIG or FPS decline to investigate the matter, then the matter is returned to FEMA for whatever administrative action is deemed advisable. Each agency, including DHS and its component agencies, has the right to conduct investigations into alleged employee misconduct issues.[154] The authority to investigate is derived from statutes that authorize discipline for employees.[155]

Who does the investigation? Any allegation should be elevated to one or all of the following: OCC Personnel Law Branch representative, local Human Capital ELR representative, and/or the local OCSO representative (in the Regional Office (this is usually a Security Manager). Following coordination with appropriate headquarters counterparts, a decision will be made as to who will further investigate the matter. Once complete, any substantiated allegation of misconduct may be subject to administrative disciplinary action. The Human Capital Division, ELRB, at FEMA Headquarters, has overall responsibility for ensuring equitable application of employee discipline and compliance with statutory and regulatory requirements in the proposing and effecting of actions. Management or supervisory officials desiring to take disciplinary actions beyond an official reprimand should contact their appropriate ELR point of contact, located at FEMA Headquarters. Transitional Recovery Offices (TROs) have an assigned ELR Specialist, as does Region 4 and 6.

OCC reviews any adverse employment action upon request and must review those that may result in litigation (e.g., suspensions, terminations, grievances that are going to be arbitrated). OCC represents the agency at formal hearings and appeals.[156]

---

[154] 5 U.S.C. § 7106 (a) (authorizing the agency to take disciplinary action against employees).

[155] *See*, for example, 5 U.S.C. § 7503 (authorizing suspensions for 14 days or less against employees (non-SES) for such cause as will promote the efficiency of the service); 5 U.S.C. § 7513 (authorizing suspensions in pay for more than 14 days, reductions in grade or pay, removal, and furloughs of 30 days or less against employees (non-SES) for such cause as will promote the efficiency of the service; and 5 U.S.C. § 7542 (authorizing adverse action against SES employees), *inter alia*.

[156] *See* FD 112-1

D. Administrative Discipline for Stafford Act Employees

Employees hired under the Stafford Act are hired "without regard to the provisions of Title 5, United States Code, governing appointments in competitive service".[157] SAEs do not generally have appeal rights to the MSPB.[158] Nevertheless, to ensure fairness and integrity in the disciplinary/adverse action process, appropriate steps should be taken to ensure employees are given the opportunity to demonstrate acceptable performance and conduct, prior to imposing a severe action, such as termination of employment. The types of administrative discipline that are applied to Stafford Act Employees are:

1. Counseling

The purpose of counseling is to correct behavior or performance problems soon after they occur in order to prevent the need for formal discipline.[159] This would be appropriate where the violation is minor and/or where the employee has a good record with no prior instance of misconduct or performance issues and is committed to correcting the problem. Documentation is not required; however, providing a counseling memorandum or memorandum for the record to the employee is recommended. While counseling is not disciplinary, it can be used to demonstrate that the employee was put on notice about the problem and knew of the potential for a harsh penalty if the problem continued. A memorandum documenting the counseling is not placed in the employee's official personnel folder (OPF).

2. Reprimand

A written reprimand is the lowest level of formal discipline; it is addressed to the employee and signed by the immediate supervisor (or higher level supervisor in the chain of command) for repeated lesser infractions or inadequate performance.[160] It is appropriate for a first offense of misconduct for which written formal discipline is necessary or where

---

[157] Stafford Act § 306, 42 U.S.C. § 5149
[158] 5 C.F.R. § 752.401(d)(12)
[159] FEMA Manual 3310.1.
[160] Id.

counseling and written warnings have not been effective in preventing continued problems. The reprimand should: reference previous counseling or other action that was relied on to support the action (if any); advise employee of the right to file an appeal with the next higher level supervisor within three workdays after receipt of the reprimand; advise of negative consequences for future misconduct; advise of Employee Assistance Program (EAP) services available to assist with any work-related or personal concerns that may have an impact on performance and/or behavior at work; state that a copy will be placed in the OPF for a period not to exceed three years; and identify the servicing Employee Labor Relations (ELR) Specialist to contact for advice and assistance. A copy of the final document (signed and dated by the supervisor) is forwarded to the ELR Specialist for inclusion in the OPF.

3. <u>Suspension Without Pay (COREs Only)</u>

A notice of suspension is a memorandum on FEMA letterhead, addressed to the employee and signed by the immediate supervisor (or higher level supervisor in the chain of command), that notifies the employee that he or she is being placed in a non-duty, non-pay status for a serious offense or repeated lesser infractions.[161] The notice should: identify the specific charge(s) with supporting information, regulations, or policies violated; identify the effective date of the action; advise of three workdays to appeal to the next higher level supervisor and the right to file a discrimination complaint if the person believes the action is based on a discriminatory factor; contain information on the EAP, as appropriate; and identify the servicing ELR Specialist's name and phone number to contact for advice and assistance. A copy of the notice (signed and dated by the supervisor) and the SF-52 are forwarded to the ELR Specialist. The Specialist codes the SF-52 (Request for Personnel Action) and forwards it to the HR operations staff for processing.

---

[161] Id.

4. **Termination**

A notice of termination is a memorandum on FEMA letterhead, addressed to the employee from the immediate supervisor (or higher level supervisor in the chain of command), for severe offenses and when the facts and supporting information conclude that the employee has demonstrated an unwillingness or refusal to conform to acceptable standards of performance and/or conduct,[162] This type of action is taken when the supervisor has determined that a lesser penalty would not deter future misconduct and there is little probability of rehabilitation. The notice should: identify the specific charge(s)with detailed supporting information that explains the reason for the action, and regulations or policies violated; identify the effective date of the action; advise employee to return all government property obtained during the period of employment (i.e., FEMA ID, cell phone, pager, credit card, etc.); advise of three workdays to appeal to the next higher level supervisor and of the right to file a discrimination complaint if the person believes the action is based on a discriminatory factor; contain information on the EAP, as appropriate; and identify the ELR Specialist's name and phone number to contact for advice and assistance. A copy of the notice (signed and dated by the supervisor) and the SF-52 are forwarded to the ELR Specialist. The Specialist codes the SF-52 and forwards it to the Human Resources (HR) operations staff for processing. The notice should be given to the employee at or before the effective date of the action. Request that the employee acknowledge receipt at the bottom of the last page of the notice. If the employee refuses, the supervisor should place a note on the last page to indicate that the notice was given to the employee and the employee refused to acknowledge receipt. Failure to acknowledge receipt has no impact on implementing the decision. If the notice is mailed, the date should be set so that the effective date is on or around the date of receipt of the notice. Send by overnight mail to ensure prompt delivery and for tracking purposes. The original is given to the employee. A copy of the notice is maintained in the employee relations case file and is not placed in the employee's OPF. The OPF is documented with the SF-50, Notification of Personnel Action.

---

[162] Id.

Termination of DAEs and COREs is done by the <u>supervisor of record</u> (Cadre Manager with supervisory authority or other supervisor located at HQ or Regional Office and NOT the "supervisor" or team lead in the field.) <u>Questions as to the supervisor of record should be answered through ELR</u> (National Finance Center database). That supervisor may delegate his or her authority but MUST be coordinated with prior to the action being taken. Termination of Local Hires and COREs <u>hired by the field office</u> are done by the supervisor in the field.

E. A Note about Performance-Based Actions and Stafford Act Employees

When dealing with poor performance that does not involve misconduct, the steps taken and options vary. Most performance problems can be resolved through effective communications between the supervisor and employee. The supervisor should take the following steps:

1. Counsel Employee. It is critical that supervisors counsel employees when their performance is not at an acceptable level. The counseling session provides the opportunity for the supervisor to clarify job expectations, and identify performance deficiencies and what the employee needs to do to bring performance up to an acceptable level. Document the session and provide the employee with a copy.

2. Issue a written warning if counseling has not helped to improve employee's performance. Provide employee an opportunity to improve by informing the employee in writing of the areas he or she is failing, with specific examples of problems, what is needed to bring performance up to an acceptable level, and potential for negative consequences if substantial improvement is not achieved.[163] (This is not a formal performance improvement plan such as that used for TITLE 5 employees.)

3. Monitor performance and document employee progress.

---

[163] Id.

---

4. If employee fails to improve acceptably, the supervisor can initiate action to terminate employment, reduce the employee's salary, or deny the employee's within-grade increase (CORE only).

5. The ELR Specialist will assist the supervisor with drafting any correspondence regarding performance problems. The supervisor will provide the Specialist with a signed and dated copy of the final document.

F. Status of the Stafford Act Employee During Investigation into Misconduct

Normally, employees continue to work their regular duties during the time an investigation or facts are being gathered. However, there are times where allegations or work problems are so serious that the employee's continued performance of regular duties or presence at work could be disruptive to the organization and work of other employees. In these situations, the following options are available: Assign other work to the employee, or place the employee in a non-duty, non-pay status while the investigation/fact-finding is being conducted and until other administrative decisions are made. (FEMA does not place SAEs on paid administrative leave.) The ELR Specialist will assist the supervisor with drafting a memorandum to the employee, explaining the reason and duration of the non-duty, non-pay status period. If the OIG or other external agencies are conducting a criminal investigation, that agency must be consulted with and concur in any release from duty, or release to return home from the deployment.

The fact that an employee has been arrested is not normally a basis on which to release the employee from a deployment into a non-duty, non-pay status or to terminate the employee (or, for a TITLE 5 employee, to place the person on administrative leave with pay).

G. Stafford Act Employees and Appeals from Adverse Administrative Actions

FEMA provides, as noted, a three-day internal appeal to the next higher supervisory level for suspensions and termination actions. FEMA's unions and the grievance procedures under FEMA-union negotiated agreements do not cover SAEs and, generally, SAEs have no right to appeal to the MSPB. Stafford Act Employees may, however, file an EEO complaint with FEMA's ERO if alleging that a personnel action was taken against the employee based on illegal discrimination.

H. Administrative Discipline for TITLE 5 Employees

Statutory and regulatory due process rules apply to TITLE 5 employees when taking disciplinary or performance-based actions.[164] During investigations, the same considerations apply as for Stafford Act employees in making a decision as to whether or not to assign other work or to make them leave the workplace pending the outcome of the investigation. However, in the latter case, the TITLE 5 employee will be placed on administrative leave with pay.

In general, all officially designated supervisors are authorized to issue counseling and official reprimands to subordinates.

When the agency terminates or suspends without pay for 15 days or more, TITLE 5 employees may appeal the matter to the MSPB.[165] If the employee also alleges that the matter is the result of unlawful discrimination, that claim may be added to the grounds for appeal. OCC represents FEMA in MSPB appeals.

I. Alternative Forums for Appeals

1. Negotiated Grievance Procedure

Employees who are members of a bargaining unit are covered by negotiated agreements. These negotiated agreements include grievance procedures that allow employees to challenge management actions and decisions. Employees who receive disciplinary actions may appeal that

---

[164] *See*, for example, 5 U.S.C. Chapters 43, 75; 5 C.F.R. Parts 430, 432, 735, and 752.
[165] These are not the only personnel actions that can be appealed to the MSPB by TITLE 5 employees; however, they are the most commonly appealed actions in FEMA. *See* 5 C.F.R. Part 1201.

action using the negotiate grievance procedures, which include the ability to request an arbitration hearing for some cases. The American Federation of Government Employees (AFGE) and AFL-CIO[166] local unions are the recognized exclusive representatives of the bargaining units comprised of a specified group or groups of FEMA employees whose workplace is FEMA Headquarters; Mount Weather; the National Emergency Training Center (NETC); and Regions II, III, IV, V, VII, and IX. Members of each recognized bargaining unit generally do not include part-time, temporary, or intermittent employees and consist of permanent full-time employees only.[167]

2. Administrative Grievance System

Under FEMA Manual 3300.1, the FEMA Administrative Grievance System, suspensions without pay of 14 days or less, and other personnel actions, may be grieved by TITLE 5 employees who are not covered by a negotiated agreement's grievance procedures.[168] The Administrative Grievance System does not cover SAEs;[169] is not available for grievances of reprimands or suspensions for 15 calendar days or more;[170] and, for bargaining unit employees, may be preempted by a negotiated grievance procedure

3. FEMA Equal Rights Office (ERO)

All employees may file complaints alleging that personnel actions were the result of unlawful discrimination. However, once a formal complaint has been filed, the employees may not also file the same complaint at the MSPB.[171] Employees cannot bring new complaints for matters raised in formal grievance procedures or negotiated in Alternative Dispute

---

[166] American Federation of Labor and Congress of Industrial Organizations. The AFL-CIO local, national, and international unions are autonomous; the AFL-CIO does not negotiate collective bargaining agreements and is not directly a bargaining agent of any designated group of employees.
[167] The NETC and Region II bargaining units include CORE employees.
[168] FEMA Manual 3300.1 (Sept. 1992).
[169] Id.
[170] For a list of all issues not covered by the administrative grievance system, *see* id., Ch. 2-2(b).
[171] 29 C.F.R. § 1614.107(d).

Resolution (ADR).[172] Individuals who believe they were the victim of discrimination must consult an OER counselor prior to filing a complaint in order to try to informally resolve the matter.[173] OER contact must be initiated within 45 days of the alleged discriminatory act.[174] Accepted allegations of discrimination are investigated by the agency pursuant to EEOC guidelines.[175] After an investigation is completed, employees may elect to have their claims heard by an EEOC administrative judge or request an immediate decision based on the investigative report by the DHS Division of Civil Rights and Civil Liberties (CRCL).[176]

VI. Alternative Dispute Resolution (ADR)

In an effort to significantly strengthen the mission of the Federal Government, Congress passed the Administrative Dispute Resolution Act of 1990 (reauthorized in 1996).[177] This statute requires Federal agencies to promote ADR processes. The President issued an Executive Memorandum,[178] the Attorney General issued an Order,[179] and Congress further passed the Alternative Dispute Resolution Act,[180] all advocating greater Federal use of ADR. Under these authorities, FEMA established the ADR Division within the Office of Chief Counsel in 1999 and the ADR Field Cadre in 2005.

ADR refers to a broad range of organizational, conflict management methods that eschew traditional approaches, such as litigation and formal administrative venues, in favor of less expensive and more expeditious techniques. ADR options for dispute resolution include conflict coaching, facilitated group work, and mediation. ADR also encourages conflict

---

[172] Id.

[173] Id. at § 1614.105(a).

[174] Id.

[175] 29 C.F.R. § 1614.108.

[176] Id. at § 1614.110.

[177] Administrative Dispute Resolution Act of 1996, 5 U.S.C. §§ 571-83 (2013) (enacted in 1990 and reauthorized in 1996).

[178] William J. Clinton's Memorandum on Agency Use of Alternate Means of Dispute Resolution and Negotiated Rulemaking, 1 PUB. PAPERS 663, 664 (May 1, 1998).

[179] Att'y Gen. Order OBD 1160.1, "Promoting the Broader Appropriate Use of Alternative Dispute Resolution Techniques" (Apr. 6, 1995).

[180] Alternative Dispute Resolution Act of 1998, 28 U.S.C. §§ 651–58 (2013).

prevention measures, such as team building, conflict management training, assessments, and informal listening and problem solving.

ADR can promote workplace communication, readiness, and resiliency because it can be used to:

- Build and maintain professional relationships
- Work with individual employees and/or groups to bolster engagement, trust, and motivation
- Increase the capacity of all employees to manage and reduce the sources of conflict at the lowest possible level
- Learn about, appreciate, and capitalize on different perspectives
- Advance a high-quality work environment where employees feel valued
- Multiply skill competencies and use work challenges as opportunities to excel
- Help create and develop best practices to foster success, integrity, honesty, and accountability
- Enhance the operation of FEMA and better serve the public

The prevalence of ADR is growing in all sectors of our society. The Supreme Court has ruled that an employer may offer as an affirmative defense that the employer provides ADR services to anticipate and address issues for employees.[181]

ADR is simple and effective. Participation in an ADR process generally does not prevent parties from pursuing a formal grievance or complaint process if no agreement is reached. Deadlines for initiating a formal grievance, an administrative claim (such as EEO and MSPB claims), or a lawsuit are not tolled when parties choose ADR.[182] Processes are generally confidential to encourage frank discussions. Certain information such as

---

[181] Burlington Indus. v. Ellerth, 524 U.S. 742, 765 (1998) (employer may raise as an affirmative defense, that employer provided an ADR program to prevent and correct complaints).
[182] See, e.g., Int'l Union of Elec. v. Robbins & Myers, 429 U.S. 229 (1976) (holding that use of an alternative procedure or forum other than the EEOC to resolve or pursue remedies under Title VII of the Civil Rights Act does not toll the time limit for contacting an EEO counselor); See also, Stewart v. Memphis Hous. Auth., 287 F. Supp. 2d 853 (W.D. Tenn. 2003); See also, Pearson v. Napolitano, 2012 U.S. Dist. LEXIS 30707 (E.D. La. 2012).

sexual harassment, threats of harm to self or others, fraud, or criminal acts, however, may have to be disclosed.

VII. Tax Implications of Travel Expenses Reimbursement and Per Diems

A. Overview of the Applicable Law Regarding the Reimbursement of Travel Expenses

FEMA employees, especially Reservists, are often required to deploy far from home for significant periods of time. For the purposes of Section 162(a)(2) of the Internal Revenue Code, a taxpayer's "home" is generally considered to be located at (1) the taxpayer's regular or principal (if more than one regular) place of business, or (2) if the taxpayer has no regular or principal place of business, then at the taxpayer's abode in a real and substantial sense.[183] If the taxpayer comes within neither of these categories, then the taxpayer is considered to be an itinerant whose "home" is wherever the taxpayer happens to work.[184] Generally, an employee's regular work location is a location at which the employee works or performs services on a regular basis whether or not the employee works or performs services at that location every week or on a set schedule.[185]

A taxpayer may be away from home on a temporary, as opposed to an indefinite or permanent, work assignment away from the taxpayer's regular or principal place of employment.[186] Employment is temporary

---

[183] 26 U.S.C. § 162(a); 26 C.F.R. § 1.262-1, 1.262-2. A taxpayer's abode in a "real and substantial sense" is a residence where the taxpayer maintains certain personal and business connections; Rev. Rul. 73-529, 1973-2 C.B. 37.

[184] See Rev. Rul. 73-529, 1973-1 C.B. 2; Rev. Rul. 60-189, 1960-1 C.B. 60.

[185] See Rev. Rul. 90-23, 1990-1 C.B. 28 (obsolete on other grounds by Rev. Rul. 99-7).

[186] See Rev. Rul. 54-147, 1954-1 C.B. 51; Norwood v. Commissioner, 66 T.C. 467 (1976). In Norwood, a welder was employed at a temporary job location for five months and, after that, had a number of jobs at the same site for over a period of two years. The court held that the first assignment was temporary and that the expenses related to that time period were deductible. However, once the taxpayer was retained and not let go with the rest of the crew, the job became of indefinite duration, as it was reasonable for the taxpayer to assume that he would be employed there for some time.

---

for this purpose only if its termination can be foreseen within a reasonably short period of time.

Section 162(a) (2) allows a deduction for ordinary and necessary business expenses, which include travel expenses while away from home in pursuit of a trade or business.[187] A taxpayer may be in the "trade or business" of being an employee.[188] In order to be "away from home," a taxpayer must be far enough away to require sleep or rest.[189] Section 162(a) provides that a taxpayer shall be treated as not being temporarily away from home during any period of employment that exceeds one year. Revenue Ruling 93-86 holds that, if the employment is realistically expected to last (and does in fact last) for one year or less, the employment is temporary, unless facts and circumstances indicate otherwise. If, at some point during that year, the expectation as to the duration of the employment changes to exceed one year, the employment will be treated as temporary only until the date at which the employee's realistic expectation changes, in the absence of facts and circumstances indicating otherwise. If the employment lasts for more than one year, the employment is not temporary and the taxpayer's tax home has switched to the new location.[190]

Case law regarding whether or not employment is temporary or indefinite remains relevant for purposes of determining whether employment for periods under one year is temporary. Further, case law determining whether and when the tax home of the taxpayer has shifted to what was termed the temporary location, making the original location no longer the taxpayer's tax home, and whether a series of assignments should be considered as one assignment or separate assignments remains important. A taxpayer might be said to change his tax home if there is reasonable probability known to him that he may be employed for a long period of time at his new station. What "constitutes a long period of time varies with circumstances surrounding each case. If such be the case, it is reasonable to expect the taxpayer to move his permanent abode to his new

---

[187] Id.
[188] 26 U.S.C. § 162(a)(2).
[189] See Primuth v. Commissioner, 54 T.C. 374 (1990).
[190] See United States v. Correll, 389 U.S. 299 (1967).

station, and thus avoid the double burden that the Congress intended to mitigate."[191]

The determination of whether a job location is temporary or indefinite is a question of facts and circumstances. The court looks at such factors as: length of time actually spent away from home; how long the employment is reasonably expected to last; the degree of certainty that it will come to an end in a reasonably short period; the strength of the taxpayer's business, personal, and economic ties with his original home; the extent that the living expenses are duplicated; and the foreseeable economic cost of moving one's home and family to the new location and back again.[192]

Brief interruptions of work at a particular location do not, standing alone, cause employment that would otherwise be indefinite to become temporary.[193] In *Blatnick v. Commissioner*, the taxpayer had a three-week break due to inclement weather at his remote job site. The court found that the taxpayer's employment was indefinite despite this break, and held that his travel expenses were not deductible.[194] The IRS has not published guidance regarding whether, or to what extent, a break in service at a work location will affect the determination that a taxpayer is or is not employed in a single location for one year or less.[195]

An employee's transportation expenses incurred in going between the employee's residence and a work location not involving overnight travel generally are nondeductible personal commuting expenses rather than deductible business expenses. There are, however, three exceptions to this rule.[196] One of these exceptions is that if a taxpayer has one or more

---

[191] *Harvey v. Commissioner*, 283 F. 2d 491, 495 (9th Cir. 1960), rev'g 32 T.C. 1368 (1959).
[192] *Blatnick v. Commissioner*, 56 T.C. 1344, 1348
[193] *Id.*
[194] *See Blatnick v. Commissioner*, 56 T.C. 1344, 1348 (1971) (brief interruptions of work at a particular location do not, standing alone, cause employment that would otherwise be infinite to become temporary); *see also* Chief Counsel Advice Memoranda 200026025 (May 31, 2000) ("Because of the highly individual nature of the factual inquiry involved, the IRS has not issued general guidance in this area. The determination whether a break is so significant that it warrants treating the two periods of employment as separate periods or constitutes a hiatus in one continuous period of employment is made by taking into account all facts and circumstances.").
[195] Rev. Rul. 99-7, 1997-5 I.R.B. 4
[196] *Id.*

---

regular work locations away from the taxpayer's residence, the taxpayer may deduct daily transportation expenses incurred in going between the taxpayer's residence and a temporary work location in the same trade or business, regardless of the distance.

B. FEMA's Treatment of Employees Receiving Travel Reimbursement

FEMA permanent full-time (TITLE 5) employees and COREs who are on travel away from their official station and Reservists who are on travel away from their residence routinely receive per diem and travel reimbursement for the costs of their FEMA travel. Those costs normally include such items as actual travel costs (air fare, rental car, mileage), food, lodging, and incidentals.

FEMA generally treats all of its disaster assignments to TITLE 5s, COREs, and DAEs who receive travel reimbursements as "temporary" and not "indefinite." This means that FEMA sets the baseline upon an initial assignment to a disaster that FEMA does not "realistically expect" a disaster assignment to last more than one year. Otherwise, FEMA employees would be required to report their travel reimbursements as income, and FEMA would be required to withhold appropriate amounts for income tax and FICA.

In order to ensure that FEMA employees do not trigger income tax liability for travel reimbursements by exceeding one year at a disaster assignment, FEMA has implemented the policy that FEMA employees will not be assigned to a single temporary work location away from their respective "homes" for a time period greater than 50 consecutive weeks.[197] This is known within FEMA as the "50-week rule."

FEMA has implemented two mechanisms to address situations where an employee's temporary duties are "reasonably expected" to last more than one year or actually do last more than one year. First, in those rare instances where a FEMA employee is expected to be needed for duties in a single location for period of not less than six months, but no more than

---

[197] FEMA Directive 1-05, *Duration of Temporary Duty Assignments* (2005); FEMA CFO Policy Statement No. 19, *Income Tax Reimbursement Allowance* (2008).

30 months, FEMA may authorize a temporary change of station in accordance with federal travel rules, regulations, and policies.[198] Second, FEMA may also provide an income tax reimbursement allowance when temporary duty exceeds one year.[199] The purpose of this allowance is to reimburse the employee for federal, state, and local income taxes incurred incident to the extended temporary duty assignment at one location when travel reimbursements are included in the employee's income.

---

[198] FEMA Directive 1-05, § 4.
[199] FEMA CFO Policy Statement No. 19, p. 1; 41 C.F.R. subtitle F (Federal Travel Regulation System), chap. 301 (Temporary Duty Travel Allowances), subpart F (Income Tax Reimbursement Allowance, Tax Years 1995 and Thereafter).

CHAPTER 11
Ethics
Table of Contents

Introduction

FEMA deals with individuals when they are at their most vulnerable and is entrusted with marshaling the vast resources of the federal government in support of state, tribal, and local efforts when an emergency or major disaster occurs. FEMA must maintain the public's trust in order to be successful, and its employees must be above reproach in carrying out FEMA's mission.

United States government employees have obligations to both the federal government and to the public to uphold the highest standards of ethical behavior. As such, each FEMA employee must comply with the federal ethics laws and regulations codified at Title 5 of the Code of Federal Regulations (C.F.R.) § 2635. These ethics laws apply to all FEMA employees, including and Local Hires despite their temporary nature as FEMA employees. The Office of Government Ethics (OGE) regulations state that "Status as an employee is unaffected by pay or leave status...or by the fact that the individual does not perform official duties on a given day."[1] The temporary employment status of LH Local Hires and Reservist employees, and whether they are activated or not, does not exempt them from federal ethics laws and regulations.

The ethical principles were first outlined in an executive order by President George H.W. Bush in 1989.[2] This chapter will focus on these ethical principles, the ethics rules, and their interpretation. This chapter will also provide examples of how a FEMA employee can avoid the civil and criminal penalties that may apply for violating these ethical standards. The ethics rules change regularly and sometimes quickly; accordingly, if employees have a specific ethics question, they should contact the certified Ethics Counselors named in Table 1 at the end of this chapter.

---

[1] C.F.R. § 2635.102(h).
[2] Executive Order 12674 signed by President George H.W. Bush on April 12, 1989.

In addition, all new FEMA employees must receive an initial one-hour ethics orientation within 90 days from the time they begin to work for the agency.[3] Thereafter, FEMA employees who are required to file public or confidential financial disclosure reports must receive annual one-hour ethics training as required by the regulations.[4] All other FEMA employees are required by FEMA's agency-wide plan on mandatory annual ethics training to receive one hour of ethics training every year.[5] Either the FEMA Administrator or the designated agency ethics officer issues the written directive at the start of each calendar year. For example, in 2012, FEMA required all of its employees to take the online independent study course IS-33.12 at http://training.fema.gov/is/ in lieu of other courses or trainings.

FEMA Certified Ethics Counselors

In 2011, FEMA Chief Counsel Brad J. Kieserman directed OCC staff to train and certify additional attorneys to be Adjunct Ethics Counselors with ethics advice as a collateral duty. The purpose of this action was to ensure that more Office of Chief Counsel (OCC) attorneys received specialized training and certification in ethics and to broaden significantly FEMA employee access to ethics advice. Today, all those attorneys in OCC who are certified Ethics Counselors can issue ethics opinions on behalf of FEMA. Ethics advice is now more accessible to FEMA employees, regardless of whether the employee works in FEMA headquarters, in one of the 10 regional offices, or in one of the many field offices throughout the country. Adjunct Ethics Counselors include the Regional Counsel, the Deployable Field Counsel and many of the attorneys now embedded with each of the Directorates.

II. Basic Obligations of Public Service and the 14 Ethical Principles

To ensure public confidence in the integrity of the federal government, Executive Order 12674 (as amended) forms the framework for the ethical

---

[3] 5 C.F.R. § 2638.701.
[4] 5 C.F.R. §§ 2638.704 and 2638.705, respectively.
[5] 5 C.F.R. § 2638.706, mandating that agencies have a written plan for annual ethics training.

behavior required and expected of all executive branch employees.[6] As a condition of public service, FEMA employees are expected to adhere to these fundamental principles of ethical behavior[7]:

1. Public service is public trust, requiring employees to place loyalty to the U.S. Constitution, the law, and ethical principles above private gain.

2. Employees shall not hold financial interests that conflict with the conscientious performance of duty.

3. Employees shall not engage in financial transactions using nonpublic government information or allow the improper use of such information to further any private interest.

4. An employee shall not, except pursuant to such reasonable exceptions as are provided by regulation, solicit or accept any gift or other item of monetary value from any person or entity seeking official action from, doing business with, or conducting activities regulated by the employee's agency, or whose interests may be substantially affected by the performance or nonperformance of the employee's duties.

5. Employees shall put forth honest effort in the performance of their duties.

6. Employees shall make no unauthorized commitments or promise of any kind purported to bind the government.

7. Employees shall not use public office for private gain.

8. Employees shall act impartially and not give preferential treatment to any private organization or individual.

---

[6] Executive Order 12674, signed on April 12, 1989, was amended by Executive Order 12731 (October 17, 1990), which directs the Office of Government Ethics (OGE) to issue standards of conduct for executive branch employees. Part 2635 of Title 5 of the Code of Federal Regulations implemented these standards. See 57 F.R. 35006 (August 7, 1992).
[7] The federal ethics rules are contained in Executive Orders 12674, 12731, and 13490; sections 201 to 209 of Title 18 of the United States Code; and part 2635 of Title 5 of the Code of Federal Regulations. The OGE is responsible for ensuring that executive branch employees maintain the highest ethical standards identified in these laws and regulations.
[8] As of the time of this writing, the Department of Homeland Security had not promulgated any supplemental ethics regulations.

---

9. Employees shall protect and conserve federal property and shall not use it for other than authorized activities.

10. Employees shall not engage in outside employment or activities, including seeking or negotiating for employment, that conflict with official governmental duties and responsibilities.

11. Employees shall disclose waste, fraud, abuse, and corruption to appropriate authorities.

12. Employees shall satisfy in good faith their obligations as citizens, including all just financial obligations, especially those such as federal, state, or local taxes that are imposed by law.

13. Employees shall adhere to all laws and regulations that provide equal opportunity for all Americans regardless of race, color, religion, sex, national origin, age, or disability.

14. Employees shall endeavor to avoid any actions creating the appearance that the employees are violating the law, the Standards of Ethical Conduct for Employees of the Executive Branch contained in part 2635 of Title 5 of the Code of Federal Regulations, any Department of Homeland Security (DHS) supplemental ethics regulations, or Executive Order 12674.[8]

III. Criminal Ethics Laws

While the ethical principles and standards of ethical conduct contained in 5 C.F.R. Part 2635 are applicable only to executive branch employees, the criminal ethics laws contained in title 18 of the United States Code apply to all federal employees. This subpart will discuss each of these criminal ethics laws.

A. Bribery of Public Officials Prohibited (18 U.S.C. § 201)

This statute prohibits a public official, including a federal employee, from directly or indirectly receiving or soliciting anything of value in exchange

---

[8] As of the time of this writing, the Department of Homeland Security had not promulgated any supplemental ethics regulations.

for being influenced in the performance or nonperformance of any official act, including giving testimony, or in exchange for committing fraud.

B. Restrictions on Compensated Representational Activities (18 U.S.C. § 203)

18 U.S.C. § 203 prohibits a federal employee, while in a duty or non-duty status, from seeking or accepting compensation for representational services (rendered either personally or by another) before a federal court or agency in a particular matter in which the United States is a party or has a direct and substantial interest.

There are limited exceptions, such as for representing oneself or one's immediate family or a person or estate for which the employee acts as a fiduciary, but not where the employee has participated officially or has official responsibility.

C. Restrictions on Acting as an Agent or Attorney (18 U.S.C. § 205)

18 U.S.C. § 205 prohibits a federal employee, while in a duty or non-duty status, from acting as an agent or attorney for anyone before a federal court or agency, whether compensated or not, when the United States is a party or has a direct and substantial interest.

There are some limited exceptions to this prohibition. The first exception allows an employee, when not compensated, to represent: (1) any person subject to loyalty, disciplinary, or other personnel matters; and (2) a not-for-profit organization in certain matters, when the majority of the organization's members are current federal employees, their spouses, or their dependent children. This exception does not apply when the organization is a party to the judicial or administrative proceeding or when the claim is against the United States or involves a federal grant or contract (or other agreement) in which the organization or group would receive the federal funds.

The second exception allows an employee to represent, with or without compensation, oneself or one's immediate family or a person or estate for which the employee acts as a fiduciary. This exception does not apply when the employee has participated personally and substantially as a federal employee or where the employee has official responsibility.

D. Post-Government Employment Restrictions (18 U.S.C. § 207)

This statute does not bar an individual, regardless of rank or position, from accepting employment with any private or public employer. It does impose restrictions on certain communications and appearances that employees may make as a representative of a third party (e.g., a FEMA and/or DHS contractor or grantee) back to the federal government, including any FEMA and/or DHS contract or grant they may have personally and substantially worked on as a FEMA employee.

These restrictions are covered more fully in Section XVI, Post-Government Employment Restrictions, in this chapter.

E. Conflicts of Interest (18 U.S.C. § 208)

This statute prohibits a federal employee from participating personally and substantially, on behalf of the federal government, in any particular matter in which he or she has a financial interest. Particular matters include contracts, grants, and government cooperative agreements or other transfers of agency funds to a specific person or entity.

In addition, the statute provides that the interests of certain other "persons" are the same as if they were the employee's. These include the employee's spouse, minor child, general partner, an organization in which he or she serves as an officer, trustee, partner or employee, and any person or organization with whom the employee is negotiating or has an arrangement concerning future employment.

The statute applies whether the employee is on or off duty. There are limited regulatory exemptions authorized by OGE (e.g., an exception for certain financial interests arising from holding FEMA contractor stocks up to a certain dollar limit, certain pension investments from a previous job, and a very limited waiver authority).

---

1. Financial Conflicts of Interest

The conflict of interest provisions of 5 C.F.R. 2635.401-2635.403 implement criminal conflict of interest prohibitions found in 18 U.S.C. § 208. FEMA employees are barred from participating personally and substantially in an official capacity in any particular matter (e.g., a FEMA contract or grant in which the employee or any person whose interests are imputed to him or her has a financial interest) so long as the particular matter has a direct and predictable effect on that financial interest. Certain financial interests are imputed to the employee, meaning that these interests are attributable to the employee. These financial interests imputed to the employee are the financial interests of the: (1) employee's spouse, (2) minor children, (3) general partner, (4) organization or entity which the employee serves as officer, director, trustee general partner or employee, or (5) a person with whom the employee is negotiating for or has an arrangement concerning prospective employment.[9]

The dollar amount of the financial interest is immaterial. In order to avoid such a conflict of interest, an employee should disqualify him or herself from acting on the matter that could cause a conflict of interest and so notify his or her supervisor and agency ethics officials, divest himself or herself of stock or other holdings that cause a conflict, or seek a waiver from the statute. In rare cases, an employee may request a waiver of the conflict of interest law applying to the situation, where there is some benefit to the federal government.

---

[9] 5 C.F.R. § 2635.402(b)(2).

Conflict of Interest Examples

Example 1: Negotiating with FEMA Contractor for Employment

Fred is a FEMA Disaster Reservist working as a Task Monitor for one of FEMA's Public Assistance Technical Assistance Contract (TAC) contractors. In the course of his work, Fred learns how lucrative it would be for him to work for the TAC contractor instead of FEMA. While he is overseeing this contract, he negotiates for employment with that contractor. If Fred wants to go to work for the contractor, he may do so but must first disqualify himself from any work on that contract before doing so.

Example 2: Employee Involvement with Volunteer Organizations Active in a Disaster (VOAD)

Sally, another Disaster Reservist, is on the board of directors of her local American Red Cross chapter. A flood tears through her community. Sally is deployed to work on the disaster. The community is in need of emergency supplies and shelters. Sally knows the American Red Cross has a great program and works with the board of directors to write an agreement for the Red Cross to provide supplies and shelter. Sally cannot, however, work on the Red Cross contract because the financial interests of the Red Cross are imputed to her. Sally must disqualify herself from working on this contract as part of her FEMA duties.

Example 3: Seeking Employment with Contractor While Contract Pending

Ted is a FEMA manager working on recommending sole source emergency contracts for post-disaster support. He meets with several of the proposed contractors about post-FEMA employment opportunities while still reviewing their companies for the sole source contracts. Ted must also disqualify himself from work with the contractors with whom he is discussing post-FEMA employment.

2. Impartiality and the Appearance of Conflict of Interest

The federal ethics regulations located at 5 C.F.R. 2635.501-503 prohibit a FEMA employee from participating in a particular matter involving specific parties when that employee knows that it is likely to affect that employee's financial interests, or the financial interests of someone with

...son with knowledge of the relevant facts would question the employee's impartiality in the matter. An employee has a "covered relationship" with:

- A member of one's household, including an unmarried partner, adult child, or a tenant or other relative.

- A relative with whom the employee has a close personal relationship.

- A person with whom the employee has or seeks a business or contractual relationship other than a routine consumer transaction.

- A person for whom the employee's spouse, parent, or minor child is, to the employee's knowledge, serving or is seeking to serve as an officer, director, general partner, agent, attorney, consultant, contractor, or employee.

- An organization, other than a political party, including non-profits, in which the employee is an active participant. Active participation includes serving as an organization officer or as a committee chair or spokesperson, or directing the activities of the organization, or fundraising. Just being a paying dues member does not make an employee an active participant.

This is known as the "appearance of conflict of interest" prohibition, and violation of this rule can result in disciplinary action against the offending employee, including suspension without pay and termination. An employee that may have an appearance of conflict situation that does not violate 18 U.S.C. § 208 may request that the agency designee authorize that employee to work on the matter. The agency designee may authorize the employee to work on the matter when the government's interest outweighs the concern that a reasonable person may question that employee's impartiality.[10]

---

5 C.F.R. § 2635.502(d).

Appearance of Conflict of Interest Examples

Example 1: Hiring and Supervising Relatives

Katie is a Disaster Reservist working as Public Assistance Task Force Leader. The Public Assistance Branch Director authorizes her to hire two new staff members to assist her with all of the projects that are anticipated following a massive hurricane. Katie knows that Tom, her adult son who lives with her, has the experience she's looking for, and Katie decides to hire him. Tom may submit his resume to FEMA Human Resources located at the disaster site, but he cannot work directly for Katie, and Katie cannot make the decision to hire him.

Example 2: Participating in Contracting with Relatives

Charlie works as the Individual Assistance Branch Director at a Joint Field Office (JFO) for a major disaster declaration following an outbreak of tornadoes. Charlie assists with making the determination to do a direct housing mission. Charlie advocates to the Operations Section Chief, the Federal Coordinating Officer and the Contracting Officer (CO) that the haul and install contract should be given out locally and needs to be done as a sole source contract to expedite getting disaster survivors into temporary housing. Charlie works to give this sole source contract to We Haul, a company that Charlie knows is owned by his brother, Stan. Charlie cannot participate in the determination to hire We Haul or in the justification process for a sole source contract. Charlie may, however, show Stan where the request for proposals is located so that Stan's company may submit a proposal.

Example 3: Dealings with Former Employer

Matthew is a FEMA Project Manager. Carol has been working with Matthew for several years as an employee of a FEMA contractor, Disasters R Us. Matthew decides to hire Carol and assigns her as the Contracting Officer's Technical Representative (COTR) on the contract with Disasters R Us because of her knowledge of the contract. Carol cannot work as the COTR on this contract with Disasters R Us because she was just working for that company. Carol may, however, work as a COTR but not for the contract with Disasters R Us.

Example 4: Dealing with Spouse's Employer

Martha is a local hire working in logistics. She is assigned to prepare a request for an extension of a current FEMA contract. Her husband, Mike, is an employee of the contractor. Martha cannot accept this assignment.

Example 5: Referring and Hiring In-Laws

Kyle, a FEMA senior manager, seeks to develop a pet friendly disaster policy for FEMA. His daughter Jill's fiancé, Taylor, is the vice president of the local humane society. Kyle would like to hire Taylor as a FEMA consultant to work on the policy. Kyle cannot, however, hire Taylor but may recommend that a consultant be hired. He may then show Taylor where the job is advertised so that Taylor may apply.

Example 6: Participating in Contracting with Relatives

Steve is a staging area manager for FEMA. Steve's sister Kelly is a partner in a maintenance company. The maintenance company received the FEMA contract for maintenance on the temporary housing units being used in FEMA's direct housing mission at the disaster where Steve is working. Steve does not participate in the decision to award the contract to Kelly's company. Steve recommends that the contract involving Kelly's company be modified to double the contract amount. Steve cannot participate in any decisions or make any recommendations involving FEMA's contractual relationship with Kelly's company.

F. Prohibition on Supplementation of Federal Salary (18 U.S.C. § 209)

18 U.S.C. § 209 prohibits a federal employee from receiving any salary, any contribution to or supplementation of salary, or anything of value from an outside source as compensation for services he or she is expected to perform as a federal employee.

IV. Use of Public Office

In accordance with 5 C.F.R. 2635.702, FEMA employees may not use their public office for their own private gain or for the private gain of friends, relatives, business associates, or any other entity. Except as provided by law or regulation, a FEMA employee may not use or permit the use of his or her federal position or title or any authority associated with his or her public office in a manner that could reasonably be construed to imply that FEMA or the federal government sanctions or endorses any of that employee's personal activities or the activities of another person or entity.

A FEMA employee may not use or permit the use of his or her federal position or title or any authority associated with his or her public office in a manner that is intended to coerce or induce another person, including a subordinate, to provide any benefit, financial or otherwise, to the employee or to friends, relatives, or persons with whom that employee is affiliated in a non-governmental capacity.

A. Endorsements

An executive branch employee shall not, according to 5 C.F.R. 2635.702(c), use or permit the use of his or her federal position, title or any authority associated with his or her public office to endorse any product, service, or enterprise except: (1) in furtherance of statutory authority to promote products, services, or enterprises; (2) as a result of documentation of compliance with agency requirements or standards; or (3) under an agency program in recognition for accomplishment in support of FEMA's mission.

A FEMA employee should not sign or agree to appear in FEMA contractor or vendor advertisements or sign FEMA contractor evaluation requests. Any contractor evaluations should be done through the appropriate FEMA CO and COTR.

A FEMA employee may endorse an outside program in his or her private capacity; however, the FEMA employee's endorsement may not make reference to the employee's official title or position within FEMA. The FEMA employee can mention that he or she works for FEMA in the body of the letter.

Endorsing Private Entities

Teodoro is a proud member of the Tiger's Club of America. He often participates in its fundraising activities and community parades. While Teodoro can participate in the events of Tiger's Club of America during his time away from work, he may not do so while wearing FEMA clothing or state or imply that FEMA endorses the organization's activities.

B. Letters of Recommendation

A FEMA employee may only utilize official FEMA letterhead and government title when the employee is writing a letter of recommendation or character reference based upon personal knowledge of that individual's character or ability for someone with whom the FEMA employee has dealt with in the course of federal employment or when recommending someone for federal employment.

Generally, a FEMA employee may not write letters of recommendation regarding FEMA contractors, but you (as a FEMA employee) can write a letter of recommendation for a FEMA contractor employee with whom you have actually worked and whose character and ability you observed.

V. Use of Government Property, Time, and Information

In accordance with 5 C.F.R. 2635.701-2635.705, executive branch employees have an obligation to properly use the government's property, time, and information.

A. Federal Property

Federal employees have an obligation to conserve federal property and shall not use or allow the use of such property for other than authorized purposes.[11]

1. Government Purchase Cards

A FEMA employee may not use government purchasing authority for personal acquisitions (including the employee's agency charge card), even if the employee reimburses the government.

---

[11] 5 C.F.R. § 2635.704(a).

---

2. Travel Cards

Government-issued travel cards may only be used when an employee is in official travel status and in accordance with the Federal Travel Regulations, and the policies and procedures of the DHS and FEMA.

3. Postage

A FEMA employee is prohibited from using official government envelopes (with or without applied postage) or official letterhead stationary for personal business. This includes mailing resumes and/or applications for federal or private positions. Violation of the prohibition against using franked (postage paid) envelopes may result in a fine.[12]

4. Limited Use Policy

The DHS has a limited use policy that applies only to personal use of DHS-owned or leased computers (and Internet service), telephones, fax machines, and non-color photocopiers.

This limited personal use policy does not apply to the use of government-owned or leased motor vehicles, or to the use of agency charge cards. The policy applies to government equipment used on government premises. Employees may not, without proper authorization, remove government equipment from the office for home use.

a.) Use of Computers and the Internet

Employees may use government computers and the Internet for personal use on their personal time (before and after work, during lunch and other breaks) provided there is no additional cost to the government. Employees may make personal purchases over the Internet, provided they have the purchased item sent to a non-government address. The following activities are absolutely prohibited on any government-owned or leased computer:

---

[12] 18 U.S.C. § 1719.

- Gambling
- Visiting and downloading material from pornographic websites
- Lobbying Congress or any federal agency
- Campaigning – political activity
- Online stock trading activities
- Online real estate activities
- Online activities that are connected with any type of outside work or commercial activity, including day trading
- Endorsements of any products, services, or organizations
- Fundraising for external organizations or purposes (except as required as part of your official duties under applicable statutory authority and bureau policy)
- Any type of continuous audio or video streaming from commercial, private, news, or financial organizations

b.) Use of FEMA Email

The DHS does not place any restrictions on incoming email. Under current policy, employees may send out personal email using their FEMA email address provided that:

- Personal use of email does not cause congestion, delay, or disruption of service to any government system or equipment

- Messages are not sent to more than five addresses (no mass mailings)

- The employee does not represent himself or herself as acting in an official capacity

- Messages do not contain partisan political messages

Any email on any FEMA email system may become an official record. Employees have no right to privacy for email transmissions since FEMA is often required to release employee emails pursuant to Inspector General, court, or congressional requests.

c.) Use of FEMA Telephones

FEMA employees may use FEMA landline telephones for personal calls when they are necessary, provide a benefit to FEMA, and do not result in any additional costs to the government. Such calls are deemed to be in the interest of the government to the extent they enable employees to remain at their workstations, thereby increasing government efficiency.

Personal phone calls may not adversely affect the performance of official duties or the employee's work performance, must be of reasonable duration and frequency, and could not reasonably have been made during non-duty hours. FEMA cell phones may be used for personal calls only to the extent that such calls would be authorized on a FEMA landline telephone and so long as no additional costs are imposed on the government.

B. Government Time

Each FEMA employee must use official time to put forth an honest effort in the performance of his or her duties.[13] As part of this responsibility, 5 C.F.R. 2635.705 provides that an employee may not ask a subordinate to use official time for other than the performance of his or her official duties or as is authorized by law or regulation.[14]

C. Government Information

A FEMA employee shall not engage in financial transactions using nonpublic information nor allow the improper use of nonpublic information to further his or her own private interests or the private interests of another, whether through advice, through recommendation, or by knowing unauthorized disclosure.[15]

---

[13] 5 C.F.R. §§ 2635.101, 2635.705.
[14] 5 C.F.R. § 2635.705(b).
[15] 5 C.F.R. § 2635.703.

VI. Gifts

FEMA employees may not solicit or accept any gift from a prohibited source or gifts given because of the employee's official position, unless the item is excluded from the definition of a gift or falls within one of the gift exceptions explained in the following text.[16]

A. Definition of "Gift"

A "gift" is defined in 5 C.F.R. 2635.203 as a gratuity, favor, discount, entertainment, hospitality, loan, forbearance, or other item having monetary value. It is not limited to material items; it also includes services. These services are training, transportation, local travel, lodging and meals, whether provided in-kind, by purchase of a ticket, payment in advance, or reimbursement.

Certain items, however, are expressly excluded from the definition of gift. Federal employees may accept them pursuant to certain specific regulatory exemptions.[17] These items are:

- Snacks (coffee, donuts, other modest food items not offered as part of a meal);
- Greeting cards, plaques, certificates, or trophies (items of little intrinsic value intended solely for presentation);
- Prizes in contests open to the general public (when entry to the contest is not part of official duties);
- Commercial discounts available to the general public or to all government employees, such as for rental car or hotel rooms, that aren't offered or enhanced because of official status;
- Commercial loans, pensions, and similar benefits;
- Anything for which the employee pays fair market value;
- Anything paid for by the government; and
- Anything accepted by the government pursuant to statutory gift acceptance authority.

---

[16] 5 C.F.R. § 2635.202.
[17] 5 C.F.R. § 2635.203(b).

B. Gifts from Domestic and Private Sources

As a general rule, federal employees may not, directly or indirectly, solicit or accept a gift:

(1) From a prohibited source; or

(2) If it is given because of the employee's official position.[18]

A prohibited source includes any person, company, or organization that is seeking official action by the employee's actions, has business with the employee's agency, is seeking to do business with that agency, conducts operations regulated by that agency, or has any interests that may be substantially affected by the performance or nonperformance of the employee's official duties.[19]

Examples of Prohibited Sources

- State of _____ (fill in the blank)
- _____ Tribe (fill in the blank)
- Local government receiving Public Assistance funds to repair flood-damaged buildings
- Haul and install contractor for FEMA's temporary housing units
- American Red Cross
- National Emergency Management Association (NEMA)
- Company that does business with another agency within the DHS, such as the Transportation Security Administration (TSA), Immigration and Customs Enforcement (ICE), Customs and Border Protection (CBP)

For purposes of the gift acceptance rules, "agency" refers to the entire DHS.[20] A DHS supplemental ethics regulation pending final approval

---

[18] 5 C.F.R. § 2635.202(a).

[19] 5 C.F.R. § 2635.203(d).

[20] 5 C.F.R. § 2635.203(a) defines an agency through the meaning identified in 5 C.F.R. § 2635.102(a), which makes reference to the definition in 5 U.S.C. § 105. An "Executive agency," as defined in 5 U.S.C. § 105, is an executive department, a government corporation, or independent establishment. It makes no mention of an agency that is part of an executive department.

---

would make FEMA a separate "agency" only for purposes of the OGE ethics gift acceptance, outside activities, teaching, speaking, and writing in one's personal capacity rules. It does not make FEMA a separate "agency" for job-seeking and post-employment ethics rules.[21]

"Agency" Refers to Entire DHS

During a recent disaster operation in Florida, Disney World offered all federal employees working on the disaster discounted entrance tickets to the Disney Parks. Because FEMA is a member of DHS, and one of DHS's component agencies was doing business with Disney World, FEMA employees could not accept the gift from this prohibited source.

C. Exceptions to the Gift Prohibitions

There are some limited circumstances when a FEMA employee can accept gifts because of that employee's official position or gifts from prohibited sources. Of course, an employee may never solicit such a gift or accept a gift in return for being influenced in the performance of an official act.[22] And, **it is never inappropriate and frequently prudent to decline a gift even if an exception applies**.[23] An employee should always avoid any appearance of impropriety when it comes to accepting gifts.[24]

1. Gifts Valued at $20 or Less

Employees may accept gifts offered from a prohibited source or because of an employee's official position that do not exceed $20 per occasion, provided that the total value of gifts from a single source does not exceed

---

[21] *See* Proposed Rules in the *Federal Register*, 76 FR 63208 (October 12, 2011).

[22] 18 U.S.C. § 201. 5 C.F.R. § 2635.204.

[23] 5 C.F.R. § 2635.204.

[24] Federal political appointees who signed President Barack Obama's "Ethics Pledge" contained in Executive Order 13490 may have additional gift acceptance restrictions and should consult OCC before accepting a gift pursuant to the gift exceptions. Executive Order 13490, (January 21, 2009) prohibits federal political appointees from accepting gifts from registered lobbyists or lobbying organizations and limits federal political appointees' activities after leaving federal employment. Some entities that do business with FEMA are registered lobbying organizations.

$50 in any given calendar year.[25] This exception does not apply to gifts of cash or investment interests (e.g., stocks, bonds, CDs).[26] Also, if the gift is valued over $20, an employee may not pay the difference in order to accept the gift; that employee must pay the full market value of the gift in order to accept it.[27] If an employee is presented with severable gifts that together exceed $20, the employee may accept those individual items that total $20 or less.[28] The market value of a gift may be determined from the price of comparable items, the face value of a ticket, or the retail list price.[29]

Decline Gift or Pay Fair Market Value

Brenda, a FEMA Individual Assistance Specialist working at FEMA Headquarters, received two tickets valued at $30 each to attend the symphony in Washington, D.C. from the NEMA as a thank you for her extraordinary presentation at one of its recent events. Brenda cannot accept the tickets from NEMA as they are valued at $60. She may either pay the fair market value of the tickets ($60) or politely decline them.

---

2. Gifts Based on a Personal Relationship

An employee may accept a gift given under circumstances that make it clear that the gift is motivated by a family relationship or personal friendship rather than that employee's government position. Relevant factors in making this determination include the history of the relationship and whether the family member or friend personally pays for the gift. For example, if a close friend takes you to lunch but uses the corporate card to pay, you should decline.[30]

---

[25] 5 C.F.R. § 2635.204(a).
[26] Id.
[27] 5 C.F.R. §2635.204(a).
[28] Id.
[29] Id.
[30] 5 C.F.R. § 2635.204(b).

DOLR Chapter 11: Ethics

> ### Gifts Based on Personal Relationships
>
> Jack, a FEMA Hazard Mitigation Specialist, is dating Sarah, who works in Disaster Services at the American Red Cross. The American Red Cross gave tickets to see the play *Wicked* to all of its Disaster Services employees as a thank you for their hard work after Hurricane Irene. The employees were all invited to bring a guest. Sarah invites Jack to attend. Jack may attend, as Sarah invited him because of their personal relationship and not because of his position at FEMA.

3. Discounts and Similar Benefits

This exception allows federal employees to accept favorable rates offered to all federal employees or to members of a group or class in which membership in that class is unrelated to federal employment.[31]

Additionally, FEMA employees may accept discounts given to a FEMA employee association in which membership is related to federal employee status, if similar discounts are broadly offered to other employee associations of similar size.

FEMA employees may also accept discounts from a group that is a not a prohibited source for the DHS or its components that does not discriminate by rank, rate of pay, or level of official responsibility (e.g., a discount only for senior executive service, or SES, employees).

This exception, does not, however, include benefits to which the federal government is entitled because of the expenditure of federal funds.[32]

---

[31] 5 C.F.R. § 2635.204(c).

[32] The Code of Federal Regulations specifically allow government employees to keep for their own personal use frequent flyer miles, hotel points, and other similar benefits received when using those services. 41 C.F.R. § 301-53.

> **Benefits that Belong to FEMA**
>
> A FEMA executive officer purchases 50 boxes of paper from a company that offers a free briefcase to anyone who purchases more than 30 boxes of paper. She cannot keep the briefcase for her own use since the paper was purchased with government funds, and the briefcase, if claimed and received, is government property.

4. Awards and Honorary Degrees

Awards and honorary degrees valued at more than $200 require prior departmental Ethics Office or FEMA Ethics Counselor approval.

5. Gifts based on Outside Business or Employment Relationships

A FEMA employee may accept gifts resulting from the outside business or employment activities of the employee or the employee's spouse that are not offered or enhanced based on that employee's official position.[33]

6. Gifts Permitted in Connection with Political Activities Permitted by the Hatch Act

An employee taking an active part in political activity, permitted by the Hatch Act, may accept meals, lodging, transportation, and other benefits, including free attendance at events, when provided by a political organization in connection with such active participation.[34]

7. Widely Attended Gatherings

Acceptance of free attendance at widely attended gatherings is permissible, in accordance with 5 C.F.R. 2635.204, as long as certain prior approval requirements are met. An event is widely attended if it is expected that a

---

[33] 5 C.F.R. § 2635.204(e).
[34] 5 C.F.R. § 2635.204(f). See also 5 U.S.C. §§ 7321-7326.

large number of persons will attend and that persons with a diversity of views or interests will be present.

For example, an event may be considered a widely attended gathering if it is open to members from throughout the interested industry or profession or if those in attendance represent a range of persons interested in a given matter. Employees must receive approval prior to the event using the FEMA WAG form, which is available on the FEMA homepage at: http://on.fema.net/employee_tools/forms/Documents/122-1-1-2.pdf.

If someone other than the sponsor of the event invites the employee and is paying for that employee's attendance (such as if a corporation or friends group invited the employee to sit at their table), the FEMA employee may accept free attendance only if more than 100 persons are expected to attend, the gift of that employee's attendance has a market value of $335 or less, and the employee's attendance is approved as being in the interest of DHS and/or FEMA. The allowance may be changed periodically by the OGE.

Free attendance may include waiver of all or part of a conference or other fee or the provision of food, refreshments, entertainment, instruction, and materials furnished to all attendees as an integral part of the event. It does not include travel expenses, lodging, entertainment collateral to the event, or meals taken other than in a group setting with all other attendees. (Under certain circumstances, FEMA may be able to accept travel expenses from outside sources to these events as described in the section on *Travel Expense Acceptance* in this chapter.

8. Speaking Engagements

5 C.F.R. 2635.204(g) provides that a FEMA employee assigned to participate as a speaker, panel participant, or otherwise to present information on behalf of FEMA at a conference or other event may accept free attendance at the event on the day of the presentation if it is provided by the sponsor of the event.

For speaking engagements, free attendance has the same meaning as for widely attended gatherings. As with a widely attended gathering, the FEMA employee must receive approval prior to the event.

If the event is longer than one day, and the employee is offered free attendance for any day(s) on which that employee is not assigned to present information on behalf of FEMA, waiver of the conference fee for those non-speaking days may be acceptable under the widely attended gathering exception to the gift rules, provided the employee is on a leave or an excused absence status, and the employee has prior approval.

9. Statutory Gift Acceptance Authority

If there is no exclusion or exception available for an employee to accept a gift from a third party, the DHS or FEMA may be able to accept the gift using its statutory gift acceptance authority. Employees should consult with the OCC and the FEMA Ethics Office in such cases, particularly if refusal to accept the gift would cause offense or embarrassment.

FEMA's gift acceptance procedures are outlined in the Agency Gift Acceptance and Solicitation Directive (FD 112-13) issued on July 24, 2012.[35] This directive excludes certain gifts to the agency (e.g., use of state and local government facilities) and does not apply to gifts to individual agency employees. The new directive applies to most gifts to the agency; FEMA employees should follow the gift acceptance procedures outlined in the directive and use the FEMA agency gift acceptance forms developed to help FEMA track acceptance of such gifts from third parties.

D. Gifts from Foreign Governments

In accordance with the Emoluments Clause[36] of the U.S. Constitution, an executive branch employee generally may not accept anything of value from a foreign government, unless specifically authorized by Congress.[37]

---

[35] FD 112-13, (November 20, 2012)
http://on.fema.net/employee_tools/forms/Documents/FD112-13(REV).pdf
[36] U.S. Constitution, art. I, § 6, cl. 2.
[37] U.S. Constitution, art. I, § 9, cl. 8.

This rule applies whether the employee is on or off duty. Any unit of a foreign government, whether it is national, state, local, or municipal level, is covered. It also applies to gifts from international or multinational organizations comprised of government representatives.

It also may apply to gifts of honoraria, travel, or per diem from foreign universities, which are often considered as part of the foreign government. Spouses and dependent children of federal employees are also banned from accepting gifts from foreign governments.

The following gifts from foreign governments are authorized under the Foreign Gifts and Decorations Act[38]:

- Gifts of minimal value ($335 or less, as of January 2008, but this amount is revised periodically)
- Transportation taking place entirely outside the U.S.
- Educational scholarships
- Medical treatment

In certain circumstances, particularly if refusal of a gift would cause embarrassment either to the United States or the foreign government offering the gift, the gift may be accepted on behalf of the DHS or FEMA.[39]

E. Gifts Between Employees

Gifts between employees is governed by the federal regulations contained in 5.C.F.R. 2635.301-303. Generally, a FEMA employee: (1) may not give a gift to a person above him or her in the supervisory chain of command, (2) solicit donations to buy a gift for a superior, (3) accept a gift from an employee that receives less pay than yourself, or (4) accept cash as a gift. There are, however, a few exceptions. Gifts are permissible if:

---

[38] 5 U.S.C. § 7342.
[39] 5 U.S.C. § 7342

- There is a personal relationship between the employees that would justify the gift, and there is no subordinate-official superior relationship.

- The gift is personal hospitality provided at a residence, which is of a type and value one would customarily provide to personal friends.

- The gift (bottle of wine, bouquet of flowers, etc.) is given in connection with the receipt of personal hospitality if of a type and value customarily given on such occasions.

- The gift (other than cash) has an aggregate market value of $10 or less per occasion and is given on an occasion when gifts are normally exchanged (e.g., Christmas, birthday, housewarming).

- The gift is leave transferred under an approved agency leave sharing plan (but not to the employee's immediate supervisor).

- There is a special and infrequently occurring occasion of personal significance, such as marriage, illness, the birth or adoption of a child; or an occasion that terminates a subordinate-official superior relationship, such as retirement, resignation, or transfer. On such occasions, an employee may give a suitable and appropriate gift and may request donations of nominal amounts within the office for contributions toward the gift. Donations should be entirely voluntary. Employees must be free to contribute a suggested amount, a lesser amount, or nothing at all. Remember that an employee may not solicit contractors working in the office for employee gifts, but they can voluntarily contribute to such gifts.

VII. Reimbursement of Official Business Travel Expenses

Generally, an employee's official travel must be paid for with appropriated funds. However, under certain circumstances, FEMA may be reimbursed for an employee's travel expenses by a non-federal source. The authorities that permit this are explained in this section.

A. Travel Expense Acceptance (31 U.S.C. § 1353)

This law allows executive branch agencies to accept reimbursement or in-kind donations from non-federal sources for an employee's transportation expenses (including *per diem* and registration costs) to certain functions related to the employee's official duties.

Acceptance of travel expenses from non-federal sources is only permitted when the employee's travel is for attendance at a conference, meeting, seminar, training course, speaking engagement, or similar event for the exchange of information that takes place away from the employee's official duty station. Travel under this authority may not be used for events required to carry out FEMA's statutory and regulatory functions, such as investigations, inspections, audits, or site visits.

In addition to an approved travel authorization, the employee must also have an approved ethics third party travel form [DHS Form 1560-01] and questionnaire filled out in advance of travel. Approval for accepting travel expenses is also subject to conflict of interest considerations. Acceptance of travel expenses from outside sources will not be approved if it would cause a reasonable person with knowledge of all the relevant facts to question the integrity of the programs or operations of the DHS or FEMA. It is not permissible for the employee to personally accept reimbursement for travel expenses, meals, or lodging from an outside source. All checks must be made out to the DHS and/or FEMA.

Employees may, however, accept "in-kind" items such as airline tickets, meals, or hotel accommodations. In addition to accepting travel expenses for an employee, FEMA may, in certain circumstances, accept travel for a spouse to accompany the employee to the same event where the spouse's presence is in the interest of FEMA. Prior approval by FEMA is required for spousal travel.

B. Other Authorities to Accept Travel Expenses

The preferred authority to use if reimbursement or in-kind donation of travel expenses to a meeting or similar function is offered by an outside source is 31 U.S.C. § 1353. Additional statutes authorize acceptance of employees' travel expenses for other than meetings or similar functions.

The authority under 5 U.S.C. § 4111 to accept travel expenses from non-profit organizations described by section 501(c)(3) of the Internal Revenue Code (with the approval of the designated agency ethics official or FEMA Ethics Counselor), is available when it is impractical for the agency to accept travel under 31 U.S.C. § 1353. Employees may also continue to accept travel expenses under the Intergovernmental Personnel Act when the employee is attending an event other than a conference or a meeting.[40]

Other provisions that remain in effect are (1) the authority under 5 U.S.C. § 3343 for employees to accept travel expenses in connection with details to foreign governments and public international organizations, (2) the authority under 5 U.S.C. § 5751 for employees and agencies to accept travel expenses when summoned or assigned to provide official testimony on behalf of parties other than United States, and (3) the authority under 15 U.S.C. § 3710a to carry out agreements under the Federal Technology Transfer Act.[41]

VIII. Outside Work, Activities, Fundraising, and Teaching

Outside work or activities, unless prohibited by statute or regulation or those that would require (to avoid a conflict of interest) the employee's disqualification from matters central or critical to the performance of his or her official FEMA duties, are permitted under 5 C.F.R. §§ 2635.801-2635.809,. Also, certain political appointees may be limited to the amount of outside income they can earn while a FEMA appointee.[42]

All outside work must take place outside official duty hours or while an employee is on authorized leave. Generally, FEMA Disaster Reservist employees may not work for a FEMA contractor while not activated, as it creates an appearance of conflict of interest. Also, FEMA employees

---

[40] Intergovernmental Personnel Act, 5 U.S.C. §§ 3371-76; 5 C.F.R. Part 334.
[41] Federal Technology Transfer Act, Pub. L. 99-502 (1986); 15 U.S.C. § 3701 *et seq.*
[42] *See* 5 C.F.R. Part 2636 and 5 C.F.R. § 2635.804.

generally may not work as FEMA contractor employees (e.g., Emergency Management Institute course developers and instructors) when off duty, including Disaster Reservist employees who are in a non-activated status.

A DHS supplemental agency ethics regulation pending final approval will require FEMA employees to obtain written approval of certain outside activities and employment. This pending regulation will also prohibit all FEMA employees from working for a FEMA contractor at the same time that employee works for FEMA. Employees may seek a waiver to the no working for FEMA contractor prohibition in very limited circumstances.[43]

A. Serving as an Officer or Member of a Board of Directors of an Outside Organization

Service as an officer or member of a board of directors of a non-federal entity has the potential to undermine the fairness of FEMA's acquisition and administrative processes, and otherwise call into question the integrity of the DHS and FEMA. Before entering into such a relationship, the employee must consult with the FEMA Ethics Office.

1. Service in an Official Capacity

Service as an officer or member of a board of directors in one's official capacity is generally prohibited, as it involves a great potential for preferential treatment, improper official endorsement, inappropriate use of official time, and improper disclosure of nonpublic information.

As an alternative to serving as an officer or member of a board of directors, a FEMA employee may be appointed to serve as a FEMA liaison to a non-federal entity.

Liaisons serve as part of their official duties and represent FEMA interests to the non-federal entity in an advisory capacity only. Appointment as a liaison requires a written determination by the employee's supervisor that there is a significant and continuing DHS or FEMA interest to be served by

---

[43] See Proposed Rules in the *Federal Register* vol. 76, no. 197, p. 63207 (October, 12, 2011).

such representation; it also requires the approval of the employee's servicing Ethics Counselor.

A liaison may not be involved in matters of management or control of the non-federal entity and generally may not vote on such boards.

A liaison may officially represent FEMA in discussions of matters of mutual interest with non-federal entities, provided it is made clear to the non-federal entities that the opinions expressed by the liaison do not bind DHS or FEMA to any action.

2. Service in a Personal Capacity

A FEMA employee serving as an officer or member of a board of directors or as an advisor to a non-federal entity in his or her personal capacity must also adhere to all conflict of interest statutes and standards of conduct regulations.

Personnel may not accept such a position in their personal capacity if it is offered to them because of their official FEMA position. Such service in a personal capacity also increases the risk that FEMA personnel may inadvertently violate, or appear to violate, the standards of conduct or engage in conduct that calls into question the employee's impartiality. Political appointees may only serve if they are not compensated for their work as an officer or member of the board.[44]

Serving on Board of Directors

Daniel serves on the board of directors for the local chapter of the American Red Cross, where he's been a volunteer for the past three years. Daniel gets a job working in a FEMA regional office in Individual Assistance as a Voluntary Agency Liaison. One of Daniel's principal duties is interacting with voluntary organizations, including the American Red Cross. Daniel cannot continue to serve on the American Red Cross board of directors because it would be a conflict of interest for him to be on the Board while interacting with the Red Cross as an employee of FEMA. Therefore, Daniel must discontinue his service on the Red Cross board of directors.

---

[44] 5 C.F.R. § 2636.306.

B. Fundraising

The rules governing acceptable fundraising activities by federal employees are described in 5 C.F.R. 2635.808. Fundraising in the federal workplace is only permitted when the charitable organization is approved by the Office of Personnel Management (OPM).[45] The sole charitable effort sanctioned by OPM is the Combined Federal Campaign (CFC).[46] Generally, CFC fundraising activities that can be considered "gambling" are prohibited in government-owned or leased buildings. Raffles and lotteries are prohibited in federally-owned or leased buildings and facilities except for very limited CFC activities permitted by 5 C.F.R. § 950.602(b).

An employee may generally engage in fundraising in a personal capacity provided he or she does not:

- Personally solicit funds or other support from a subordinate or from any person the employee knows is a prohibited source (see section on *Gifts from Domestic and Private Sources* in this chapter for definition of prohibited source);

- Use or permit the use of his or her official title, position, or any authority associated with his or her public office to further the fundraising effort; or

- Engage in any action that would otherwise violate the ethics laws or regulations.

Employees and other persons are generally prohibited from fundraising solicitations for non-governmental organizations within any building or on any lands occupied or used by FEMA during the duty day. Exception is granted for DHS authorized operations, including but not limited to the FEMA Employee Recreation Association or Regional Office or National Processing Service Center (NPSC) Employee Recreation Associations, and for cafeteria, newsstand, snack bar, and vending machine operations authorized by FEMA for the benefit of employees or the public.

---

[45] 5 C.F.R. § 2635.808.
[46] 5 C.F.R. Part 950 implements the rules for the Combined Federal Campaign.

Fundraising Examples

Example 1: Prohibited Solicitations on the Job

Sergio is a FEMA Disaster Reservist working as a Flood Insurance Specialist. Sergio raises money for one of the local charities in his hometown. His hometown was badly flooded, and Sergio was asked to help FEMA with the disaster recovery. Sergio wants to invite his FEMA colleagues to a pizza night that he organized at a local restaurant to benefit the local charity. Sergio cannot send out anything to his FEMA colleagues via the FEMA email system or solicit donations to the local charity. He also cannot solicit donations in the FEMA workplace, including in government-owned or leased buildings.

Example 2: OPM-Approved Fundraising

Debbie works in a regional office in external affairs. She volunteers each year as a coordinator for the CFC. Since the CFC is permitted by the OPM, all employees may participate, to the extent that they want to, in the CFC.

Example 3: Handling Charity Drives

Todd is a regional employee working at the JFO. Since winter is approaching, Todd wants to collect winter coats and other clothing to give to the local homeless shelter. With FCO approval, Todd may have a bin set up in a public area to collect clothing. Todd may not, however, directly solicit other FEMA employees to donate to the clothing drive.

C. Teaching, Speaking, and Writing

Generally, a FEMA employee may not receive compensation, other than travel expenses, for outside teaching, speaking, or writing that relates to his or her official duties.[47]

For purposes of this regulation, a teaching, speaking, or writing activity relates to the employee's official duties if:

- The activity is undertaken as part of that employee's official duties;

---

[47] 5 C.F.R. § 2635.807.

- The circumstances indicate that the invitation to engage in the activity was extended to the employee primarily because of the employee's official position rather than that employee's expertise on the particular subject matter;

- The invitation to engage in the activity or the offer of compensation for the activity was extended to the employee by a person who has interests that may be substantially affected by the performance or nonperformance of the employee's official duties;

- The information conveyed through the activity draws substantially on nonpublic information; or

- The subject of the activity deals in significant part with:

  1. A matter to which the employee is presently assigned or to which the employee has been assigned during the previous year; or

  2. Any ongoing announced policy, program, or operation of FEMA.

1. Exception for Teaching Certain Courses

Even if the subject matter deals with an employee's official duties, an employee may accept compensation for teaching a course requiring multiple presentations offered as the regularly established curriculum of an accredited institution of higher education, a secondary school, an elementary school, or a program of education sponsored and funded by the federal government or by a state or local government.[48] An employee may only receive compensation under these circumstances for outside teaching—not for teaching carried out as part of that employee's official responsibilities. If the class involves providing services to prohibited sources, prior approval is required. There are additional restrictions for non-career SES and Schedule C employees on such outside employment, teaching, speaking, and writing.

---

[48] 5 C.F.R. § 2635.807(a)(3).

2. Reference to Official Position

A FEMA employee engaged in teaching, speaking, or writing as an outside activity may not use or permit the use of his or her official title or position except:

- The employee may include his or her title or position as one of several biographical details when such information is given to identify the employee, provided that it is not given more prominence than other significant biographical details;

- The employee may use his or her title or position in connection with an article published in a scientific or professional journal, provided that it is accompanied by a disclaimer that the views expressed do not necessarily represent the views of FEMA, DHS, or the United States government; and,

- If the employee is ordinarily addressed using a general term of address such as "The Honorable," or a rank, such as a military or ambassadorial rank, the employee may use that term of address or rank.[49]

IX. Political Activity

The tension between a politically neutral, efficiently run government and the First Amendment rights of federal employees has been present since this country's infancy. The Hatch Act of 1939, with its amendments, is Congress' most recent attempt to shield the civil service from the influence of party politics by delineating those activities in which federal employees can and cannot participate.[50]

---

[49] 5 C.F.R. § 2635.807(b).

[50] United States Civil Service Comm'n v. Nat'l Ass'n of Letter Carriers, 413 U.S. 548, 565-66 (1973) (upholding constitutional challenges to the Hatch Act and noting that Congress' goal was to prevent the federal workforce from becoming a "corrupt political machine" where political views determine advancement). See also United Public Workers of America v. Mitchell, 330 U.S. 75, 98, 101 (1947).

The Hatch Act restricts federal employee involvement in partisan political activities.[51] "Political activity" means activity directed toward the success or failure of a political party, candidate for public office in a partisan election, or partisan political group.[52]

The Hatch Act's restrictions are based on three classes of employees.[53] They are:

- Most restricted: career SES employees, administrative law judges, administrative appeals judges, and those who serve on the Contract Appeals Board;

- Moderately restricted: non-career SES, Schedule C, and most other employees. This includes the majority of FEMA employees, including Reservists when deployed.[54] This group may participate in certain partisan political activity but only in a purely private capacity;

- Least restricted: presidentially-appointed, Senate-confirmed personnel, or Presidential Appointment with Senate Confirmation (PAS) employees are subject to some restrictions, but they are less constrained in terms of where and when they can engage in political activity because of their 24-hour duty status.

Violations of the Hatch Act may result in removal from federal employment or a suspension, without pay, of not less than 30 days.[55]

A. Permitted Activities

While the Hatch Act's restrictions vary based on type of federal employee, all federal employees may do the following:

- Register and vote as they please;

---

[51] 5 U.S.C. §§ 7321-7326. 5 C.F.R. Part 734. Federal employees are divided into several types for purposes of the Hatch Act.
[52] 5 C.F.R. § 734.101.
[53] As the Hatch Act relates to FEMA, a fourth category covering reservists (formerly DAEs) should be considered. Because reservists work intermittently, they are subject to the Hatch Act's provisions only when on duty. See 5 C.F.R. § 734.601.
[54] Id.
[55] 5 U.S.C. § 7326.

- Contribute money to political organizations;
- Join political clubs or parties;
- Express opinions about candidates and issues[56];
- Sign nominating petitions;
- Attend political rallies and conventions; and
- Participate in non-partisan activities.

B. Prohibited Activities

A federal employee may not:

- Solicit, accept, or receive a political contribution;
- Use official authority or influence for the purpose of interfering with or affecting the result of an election;
- Run for the nomination or as a candidate in a partisan political office;
- Engage in political activity while on duty;
- Engage in political activity in a federal building;
- Engage in political activity while wearing a uniform or official insignia identifying himself or herself as a federal employee;
- Engage in political activity while in a federally-owned or leased vehicle; or
- Solicit or discourage political activity by anyone with business before his or her agency.[57]

C. Social Media and the Hatch Act

On August 10, 2010, the Office of Special Counsel (OSC) issued guidance concerning application of the Hatch Act to social media outlets. The memorandum applies to all social media, including but not limited to

---

[56] The Hatch Act prohibits federal employees from advocating for the success or failure of a political party or partisan group. This means employees cannot wear or display items showing support, either before or after Election Day. So-called "water cooler" language is generally okay. Email and web-surfing while at work, however, is not.

[57] 5 U.S.C. §§ 7323-7324. PAS employees may engage in political activity during work hours, but the campaign must pay for all expenses.

Facebook, Twitter, MySpace and LinkedIn.[58] Any pages created for official purposes must be used solely for official business and remain politically neutral. The memorandum is in a Frequently Asked Questions format and divides its answers into two categories of employees: Less Restricted and Further Restricted employees. These categories correspond respectively to the "moderately restricted" and "most restricted" categories used previously. (The memo also discusses rules governing the "least restrictive" category of PAS employees). Further Restricted employees include employees from certain agencies (not including FEMA), SES employees, administrative law judges, Contract Appeals Board members, and administrative agency appeals judges.

1. Less Restricted Employees[59]

Regardless of what social media a less restricted employee wants to use, that employee must adhere to the same Hatch Act rules as he or she would if having a conversation or engaging in face-to-face activity. The employee cannot write a blog or engage in other partisan political activity while on duty in the federal work place, nor may the employee identify his or her official title. The employee cannot ask for contributions to a political party, partisan political candidate, or partisan political group.

2. Further Restricted Employees[60]

Further Restricted federal employees, in addition to the guidelines set forth for Less Restricted employees, are prohibited from engaging in activity that is the equivalent of distributing literature. This includes posting or linking to anything that was created by, or leads to information created by, a political party, partisan candidate, or partisan campaign.

---

[58] *See* http://www.osc.gov/haFederalfaq.htm.
[59] This would include most FEMA employees.
[60] This would include career SES FEMA employees.

Hatch Act Examples

Example 1: Displaying Support of a Candidate at the Office

Mary Sue is neither a career SES nor a PAS FEMA employee and is a lifelong friend of one of the candidates for United States Senate. She works in a regional office and wants to display campaign buttons for her friend in her office and have multiple bumper stickers on her car that she drives to work every day. Mary Sue may not display the campaign buttons in her office but may have a picture with her friend in her office. She may also have one or two political bumper stickers on her car.

Example 2: Assisting with a Campaign while Deployed

Fred is a FEMA Disaster Reservist working in a JFO located in the state where he lives, and he has always been active in politics to encourage people to vote. He especially likes one of the candidates for U.S. President and was assisting with the campaign prior to getting called to work by FEMA. Fred may still assist with the campaign but must do it on his own time away from the FEMA office. He may not solicit, accept, or receive contributions for the campaign, wear his FEMA uniform, or mention to potential voters that he works for FEMA.

Example 3: Allowed Activity on a Personal Social Media Page

Bernice works in External Affairs. She has a personal Facebook page where she notes that she works for FEMA and is "friends" with several subordinate employees. She may identify her political party on her Facebook page and post notes about her personal political views, provided they are directed toward all of her "friends" and not just the subordinate employees. If one of her friends posts a comment that links to the contribution page of a partisan candidate, she need not remove it. She cannot however "like" it or in any other way encourage people to donate to that candidate.[61]

X. Nepotism/Preferential Treatment to Relatives

Nepotism, or showing favoritism on the basis of family relationships, is prohibited.[62] FEMA employees may not appoint, employ, promote, advance, or advocate for the appointment, employment, promotion, or

---

[61] *See* http://www.osc.gov/haFederalfaq.htm.
[62] 5 U.S.C. § 3110.

advancement of a relative in or to any civilian position in the agency in which the employee serves or over which he or she exercises jurisdiction or control. The statute makes it clear that even recommending a relative for appointment or promotion is barred.[63] An individual appointed, employed, promoted, or advanced in violation of the nepotism law is not entitled to pay.[64]

Also, supervisors showing favoritism to members of their household (unmarried partner), relatives, or friends not listed in 5 U.S.C. § 3110 may also be violating appearance of conflict of interest ethics rules.[65]

1. Exceptions

When necessary to meet urgent needs resulting from an emergency posing an immediate threat to life or property, or a national emergency as defined in 5 C.F.R. § 230.402(a)(1), a public official may employ relatives to meet those needs without regard to the restrictions in 5 U.S.C. § 3110.[66] Such appointments are temporary and may not exceed 30 days, but the agency may extend such an appointment for one additional 30-day period if the emergency need still exists at the time of the extension.

---

[63] 5 U.S.C. § 3110(b).
[64] 5 U.S.C. § 3110(c).
[65] 18 U.S.C. § 208.
[66] The Office of Personnel Management prescribes regulations to authorize the temporary employment. 5 U.S.C. § 3110(d).

Nepotism Examples

Example 1: Advocating to Hire Relatives

Mario works as an Individual Assistance Branch Director. His nephew, Mike, just finished college and wants to join FEMA in Public Assistance. Mario is currently deployed to a disaster where he knows that Public Assistance is hiring a few new people. The job is posted on the USAJobs website. Mario may tell his nephew that there are Public Assistance positions on the USAJobs website and encourage him to apply. Mario may not, however, tell the Public Assistance Branch Director that his nephew is applying and advocate for him to be hired, nor may Mario give the Public Assistance Branch Director Mike's resume so that Mike will have a better chance of being hired.

Example 2: Supervising Relatives in the Chain of Command

Henry is a Community Relations (CR) Reports Writer. In a recent disaster, he was assigned to work out of the JFO collecting the reports from the lead CR staff in the field and evaluating the work they and their staff did each day. Two of the lead CR staff were relatives of Henry; one was his daughter Mayra and the other was his nephew Carlos. OCC attorneys advised Henry that the nepotism laws do not forbid family members from working in the same office; however, they could not supervise each other's work. Because Henry was evaluating the work done by his relatives Mayra and Carlos, he was reassigned to another position in the JFO that did not involve supervising his relatives directly or indirectly.

Example 3: Notifying Supervisors of Shared Household

Kelly-Marie and Larry met while working for FEMA on a disaster in the U.S. Virgin Islands. Although they are not a couple, they live together and have shared the same household for the past 10 years. They now work in the same office but do not supervise one another. They have put their supervisors on notice regarding their shared household so that they are not assigned to work supervising one another.

Example 4: Supervising Unmarried Cohabiting Employees

Francine and Abigail met while working in Public Assistance and became romantically involved. They now live together and continue to work at the same disasters all the time. They have been advised that they can continue to work in the same program and at the same disasters, but one cannot supervise the other.

XI. Gambling, Raffles, Lotteries, and Betting Pools

Unless authorized by statute or regulation, all forms of gambling activities are prohibited at all times in facilities owned or leased by the federal government.[67] Federal employees may not engage in gambling activities while on duty. Prohibited gambling activities include but are not limited to raffles, lotteries, numbers (games), and sporting pools.[68]

March Madness Pool

Dave is a Public Assistance Task Force Leader in a JFO following a major disaster declaration. He is really excited because March Madness (the big NCAA basketball tournament) is coming up, and he's always good at picking the teams that will go to the finals. He wants to set up a March Madness pool with his friends and colleagues in Public Assistance where everyone will pay $5, and whoever wins gets all the money. Dave cannot set up this pool; it is prohibited since it is a game of chance where something of value (money) is risked to win something (more money) in a federal facility on official time.

XII. Serving as an Expert Witness

Executive branch employees are restricted from serving as expert witnesses in proceedings before courts or agencies of the United States when the United States is a party or has a direct and substantial interest. This restriction applies even when an employee is serving in his or her personal capacity and regardless of whether the service is compensated or not. An employee seeking to serve or subpoenaed as an expert witness must obtain prior approval from the DHS designated agency ethics official.[69] This restriction does not apply to an employee subpoenaed to testify as a fact witness.[70]

---

[67] After Katrina, GSA helped FEMA lease office space in a hotel-casino to set up its Initial Operating Facility (IOF) in Gulfport, MS. However, the casino was closed at the time.
[68] 5 C.F.R. § 735.201; 41 C.F.R. §§ 102-74.395.
[69] 5 C.F.R. § 2635.805.
[70] 5 C.F.R. § 2635.805(d).

XIII. Procurement Integrity Act

The Procurement Integrity Act[71] restricts disclosure of contractor bid proposal or source selection information, prohibits contact between offerors and employees regarding future employment, and disallows former FEMA employees from working for contractors when the employees participated in certain procurement decisions. Violations of the Procurement Integrity Act may result in disciplinary action and/or criminal penalties.[72]

A. Prohibition on Disclosure of Contractor Information

The Procurement Integrity Act and its implementing regulations prohibit federal employees from knowingly disclosing "contractor bid or proposal information or source selection information" prior to FEMA's award of the contract unless disclosure is allowable by law.[73] "Contractor bid or proposal information" includes cost and pricing data, indirect costs, direct labor rates, and proprietary information. It also includes information that the contractor designates as contractor bid or proposal information.[74] "Source selection information" includes information prepared for the agency for purposes of evaluating the bid proposal if that information has not been previously been made available publicly.[75]

B. Contacts Regarding Employment

In addition to the non-disclosure requirements, the Procurement Integrity Act also contains prohibitions on contact between an agency official (employee) and an offeror regarding possible employment.[76] An agency official participating personally and substantially in a procurement that is in excess of the simplified acquisition threshold (now $100,000), must notify his or her supervisor and the agency ethics official of that contact. The agency official must also either reject the possibility of employment with the offeror or disqualify him or herself from working on that

---

[71] 41 U.S.C. § 423; FAR 3.104.
[72] 41 U.S.C. § 423(e).
[73] 41 U.S.C. § 423. The Procurement Integrity Act also prohibits obtaining the contract information before an agency awards the contract. 28 C.F.R. § 3.104-3.
[74] 41 U.S.C. § 423(f).
[75] 41 U.S.C. § 423(f).
[76] 41 U.S.C. § 423(c). 28 C.F.R. 3.104-3.

---

procurement and other procurements involving that particular offeror.[77] The agency official may continue working on the procurement only if that individual receives approval from a FEMA Ethics Counselor.

C. Restrictions for Former FEMA Employees

A former FEMA employee may not accept compensation from a contractor when that former employee participated in certain procurement actions or made certain procurement decisions for procurements in excess of $10,000,000.[78] This restriction on accepting compensation lasts for one year after that official participated in the procurement actions or decisions. These procurement actions include serving as the procuring CO; the source selection authority; a member of the source selection board; the chief of a technical or financial evaluation team; or the program manager, deputy program manager, or administrative CO for a contract in excess of $10,000,000.[79]

A former FEMA employee cannot accept compensation from a contractor when that employee made certain procurement decisions in contracts above $10,000,000. The procurement decisions include awarding a contract, establishing overhead rates, or approving issuance of a payment, or a decision to settle a claim with the contractor in excess of $10,000,000.[80]

Post-Employment Restrictions for Procurements

Chad worked as a CO for FEMA for several years. Chad is now on his own as a consultant. One of the contracts he awarded while working for FEMA was to Disasters, Inc. for $25,000,000 to ship goods to disaster locations on an emergency basis. The representatives from Disasters, Inc. were so impressed with Chad's skills that they asked him to do some consulting work for Disasters, Inc. Chad is prohibited from accepting compensation from Disasters, Inc. for a period of one year after he worked on the procurement involving Disasters, Inc.

---

[77] 28 C.F.R. § 3.104-3.
[78] 41 U.S.C. § 423(d).
[79] 41 U.S.C. § 423(d).
[80] Id.

XIV. Working with Contractors in the FEMA Workplace

Contractors provide a wide variety of services to FEMA during disaster response and recovery operations. The employees of these contractors are not subject to the federal ethics rules since they are not federal employees.[81] It is important, however, for contractor employees to have a familiarity with the federal ethics rules so that federal employees do not violate ethics laws and regulations.

A. Inherently Governmental Function

Federal contractors are prohibited from doing any activity that is considered to be an "inherently governmental function."[82] As a matter of policy, inherently governmental functions are those that are so intimately related to the public interest that they must be performed by government employees. Inherently governmental functions include those activities involving the interpretation and execution of United States laws to: (1) bind the government to take or not take an action; (2) advance the government's interests; (3) significantly affect the life, liberty, or property interests of private persons; (4) commission, appoint, direct, or control officers or employees of the United States; or (5) exert ultimate control over the acquisition, use, or disposition of property, whether real or personal, tangible or intangible, of the United States, including the collection, control, or disbursement of appropriated or other federal funds.[83]

Therefore, the employees of FEMA contractors may provide advice, opinions, recommendations, or ideas to federal officials but should not make policy, speak to the media, or participate in acquisition planning as they are inherently governmental in nature.[84] Additionally, a FEMA contractor's employees do not have the authority to hire, fire, evaluate, assign work, or supervise federal employees, unless specifically authorized by the contract with FEMA as "personal services."

---

[81] Federal contractors are required to have their own ethics rules and internal controls set up for accountability. Contractors are also encouraged to report government waste, fraud, and abuse. See Federal Acquisition Regulations (FAR), 48 C.F.R., Subpart 3.10, § 3.1002
[82] See Office of Management and Budget (OMB) Policy Letter 32-1 (Sept. 18, 1994).
[83] See id., section 5.
[84] A contractor's employees may only participate in acquisition meetings if that is part of the contract's scope of work.

Contractors Supervising FEMA Employees

Haley works for ABC Corporation, a company that provides Public Assistance staff to FEMA during disaster operations. Max, the Public Assistance Branch Director at the disaster operation, worked with Haley on multiple disasters in the past and values her judgment and work ethic. Max wants Haley to work as his Deputy Branch Director. As an employee of ABC Corp., one of FEMA's contractors, Haley cannot work as Max's Deputy Branch Director because she cannot supervise FEMA employees. Therefore, Max will need to choose a FEMA employee as his Deputy Branch Director.

B. Oversight of Contractor Employees

Oversight of a FEMA contractor's employees is done by the contractor itself. This includes determining work schedule, time off, and general supervision. The contractor assigns one of its employees to be a Task Monitor. The Task Monitor will work with FEMA's CO and COTR to ensure compliance with the terms of the contract and that any work done by the contractor's employees is within the scope of the contract.

C. Identifying Contractors

Employees of contractors must always identify themselves as contractors when dealing with members of the public and with FEMA employees. FEMA contractors are identified by: (1) distinctive FEMA badges that indicate contractor status; (2) business cards without the DHS or FEMA seals; (3) no use of apparel with the FEMA logo; and (4) statements in emails and on phone calls that the individual is an employee of a FEMA contractor and not a FEMA employee.

Contractor Identification

Randy works as an engineer for Disaster Specialty, Inc., a FEMA contractor. His business cards have his title of Engineer and the company name Disaster Specialty, Inc. on them but no DHS or FEMA logos. Additionally, as the Task Monitor for Disaster Specialty, Inc., he ensures that the other employees of Disaster Specialty, Inc. are complying with the work requirements of the FEMA contract and fulfilling the FEMA CO's expectations on the contract.

D. Contractors and Gifts

Under federal ethics rules, FEMA contractors and their employees are "prohibited sources" of gifts.[85] A FEMA employee may not accept a gift from a prohibited source unless it falls within one of the gift exceptions. The *de minimis* exception allows FEMA employees to accept a gift from an agency contractor with a value of up to $20 per occasion, or up to $50 in a calendar year.[86]

Contractors and Gifts Examples

Example 1: Gifts Based on Personal Relationships
Zach works as a FEMA CO in the JFO following a major disaster declaration. Zach is responsible for the procurement of the maintenance and deactivation contractor for the 1,500 temporary housing units put in after the hurricane. Multiple proposals were received; Zach awards the contract and continues to oversee the contractor's work. While overseeing the contractor's work to ensure it complies with the contract, Zach and Steve, the company's representative, discover that they have many things in common. Steve offers to take Zach with him on a fishing trip to a nearby lake that he and some friends are going on over the upcoming weekend. Zach may accept the gift of the fishing trip if it is paid for by Steve and not the contractor and if it is given because of Steve and Zach's personal friendship rather than because of Zach's official position. Zach needs to be careful in this situation, though, because going on the fishing trip could be construed as a conflict of interest.

Example 2: Soliciting Donations from Contractors
Following the retirement of the Regional Administrator, Kate collects voluntary donations for a gift from the regional staff. Greg works as a FEMA contractor in the regional office. Kate may not solicit Greg for a donation for the retirement gift for the Regional Administrator because Greg is a FEMA contractor, and the Regional Administrator is a FEMA employee.

---

[85] 5 C.F.R. § 2635.201-2635.205.
[86] 5 C.F.R. § 2635.204(a).

E. Awards to Contractors

Awards to FEMA contractors or their personnel may only be given as part of an established awards program that specifically allows for awards to contractors and/or their employees.[87] FEMA employees may not provide monetary or non-monetary awards to FEMA contractors or their personnel. Incentive awards for contractor superior performance are normally addressed in the contract between the contractor and FEMA.

XV. Seeking Other Employment

A FEMA employee considering employment outside the federal government must comply with the seeking employment rules found in 5 C.F.R. 2635.601-2635.606 and the negotiating for employment restriction included in 18 U.S.C. § 208 (see section on *Criminal Ethics Laws*, for discussion of section 208).[88] "Seeking employment" is defined as negotiating for employment, making an unsolicited communication to any person regarding possible employment, or a response to a person regarding employment other than a rejection of the offer of employment. Seeking employment does not include requesting a job application.[89] An employee who is seeking employment must disqualify himself or herself from participating personally and substantially in particular matters that have a direct and predictable effect on the financial interests of a prospective employer.[90] Disqualification requires an employee to take whatever steps are necessary to ensure that he or she no longer participates in the matter.[91]

An employee is no longer seeking employment when the employee or the prospective employer reject the possibility of employment and the discussions of prospective employment have terminated. An employee is also no longer seeking employment when two months have passed after

---

[87] 5 U.S.C. §§ 4511-4513.
[88] *See also* 18 U.S.C. § 208(a); 5 C.F.R. §§ 2635.802-2635.803 and 5 C.F.R. §§ 2635.401-2635.403.
[89] 5 C.F.R. § 2635.603(b).
[90] 5 C.F.R. § 2635.602. *See also* 18 U.S.C. § 208(a) which provides for criminal penalties for participating in a matter while negotiating for employment.
[91] 5 C.F.R. § 2635.604.

the unsolicited communication from the employee and the employee has not received a response from the prospective employer. A response deferring discussions regarding prospective employment does not terminate seeking employment.[92]

Seeking Employment Examples

Example 1: Effect of Rejecting a Job Offer
Corey is a FEMA COTR working on a contract with XYZ Corp. Corey is complimented by a representative of XYZ Corp. who tells Corey that she is impressed with his work and he should consider XYZ if he ever decides to leave federal service. He thanks her for the compliment and says he's not interested in leaving FEMA at this time, but he'll remember their conversation if he ever decides to leave federal employment. Corey has not begun seeking employment.

Example 2: Disqualification Notice Required
Helen is thinking about leaving FEMA. She works with several contractors who frequently indicate that they enjoy working with her and appreciate her strong work ethic. Helen sends one of the contractors a resume and meets with the company's representatives regarding future employment. Helen can no longer work on the contract and must provide notice disqualifying herself from working on this contract to both her supervisor and the FEMA Ethics Office.

Example 3: Need for Waiver of Disqualification
Anna works as a CO on specific Individual Assistance housing contracts. Her supervisor values her expertise on these contracts. Although she likes working for FEMA, Anna is considering leaving FEMA. One of the FEMA contractors has been trying to get Anna to come work for that company. Anna refused these offers until the last proposal, which Anna decided to consider and so notified her supervisor. Anna and her supervisor both want Anna to continue working on the contract because of her technical expertise. Anna may only continue to work on the contract with a written disqualification waiver from the FEMA Ethics Office. Otherwise, Anna must disqualify herself from work on the contract.

---

[92] 5 C.F.R. 2635.603.

a.) Additional Requirements for Public Disclosure (OGE 278) Filers:

While all FEMA employees are subject to the seeking employment restrictions found in Part 2635 subpart F of Title 5 of the Code of Federal Regulations, certain employees (SES, Schedule C, and certain IPAs) must comply with the STOCK Act.[93] The STOCK Act (or Stop Trading on Congressional Knowledge Act) was signed into law by President Obama on April 4, 2012. Under section 17 of the STOCK Act, employees filing public disclosure reports (OGE 278) may not negotiate for post-federal employment or have any agreement for future employment or compensation unless the employee files a notification statement with the agency Ethics Office **within three business days** after commencing negotiations. This notification statement may have additional implications, as it may require an employee to also recuse himself or herself from official activities and duties based on a conflict of interest or the appearance of a conflict of interest created by seeking employment with a FEMA contractor or grantee or organization of such entities, e.g., NEMA, or International Association of Emergency Managers (IAEM).

XVI. Post-Government Restrictions

While the ethics rules do not limit what entity a federal employee may work for, they may limit the type of work an employee may do for a certain period of time after that employee leaves his or her federal government position. Two statutes impose these limitations on former federal employees.[94] The first is the Procurement Integrity Act,[95] discussed in the section on *Procurement Integrity Act* in this chapter. The second is 18 U.S.C. § 207, a criminal statute that prohibits certain representational activities of former federal employees, briefly discussed in the section on *Criminal Ethics Laws, Post-Governmental Restrictions* in this chapter.

---

[93] Pub. L. 112-105 (2012).
[94] 18 U.S.C. § 207. 41 U.S.C. § 423. *See also* Executive Order 13490 (January 21, 2009), which imposes additional post-employment restrictions for political appointees.
[95] 41 U.S.C. § 423(e).

A. Representational Restrictions (18 U.S.C. § 207)

Depending on an employee's level of involvement with a particular matter, the employee may be barred for one year, two years, or permanently from working on that matter following his or her federal employment.[96]

1. Lifetime Restriction

An executive branch employee that participated personally and substantially in a particular matter involving specific parties may not represent that party before any federal department, agency, or court after leaving federal employment for the life of the particular matter.[97] Representation includes both communications and appearances on behalf of the specific party with the intent to influence the federal government regarding that particular matter.[98]

Restricted Representations

Sam served as a FEMA Public Assistance Task Force Leader at a JFO in Kentucky. Sam decided to leave FEMA and go to work for one of the public entities that he decided not to approve for Public Assistance funding, the Kentucky Housing Authority. The Kentucky Housing Authority appeals this decision and wants Sam to attend a meeting with FEMA. Sam may help the Kentucky Housing Authority behind the scenes with its FEMA Public Assistance appeal but may not have any direct contact with FEMA where he tries to influence FEMA's decision.

---

[96] 18 U.S.C. § 207. This statute also prohibits a former federal employee from aiding or advising any entity (other than the United States) in any ongoing trade or treaty negotiations that the employee participated in personally and substantially during the last year of the employee's federal service. This aiding or advising restriction lasts for one year following the termination of federal employment.
[97] 18 U.S.C. § 207(a) and 5 C.F.R. § 2641.201.
[98] 18 U.S.C. § 207(a) and 5 C.F.R. § 2641.201.

2. Two-Year Restriction

An employee is restricted, for the two years following the end of his or her federal employment, from communicating or appearing on behalf of a specific party with regard to a particular matter.[99] This two-year restriction applies to particular matters pending under the employee's official responsibility during the last year of the employee's federal service. "Official responsibility" is defined in 18 U.S.C. § 202 as the "direct or administrative authority, whether intermediate or final, and either exercisable alone or with others, and either personally or through subordinates, to approve, disapprove, or otherwise direct government action."[100]

3. One Year Restriction for Senior Employees

Certain senior employees have additional restrictions that last for one year after leaving senior service. Former senior employees[101] may not make, with the intent to influence, any communication or appearance before the department or agency in which they served in the one-year period prior to termination from senior service.[102] This restriction is regarding any contact with their old agency representing their new employer back to their old agency regarding contracts, grants, or other transfers of federal funds to an identifiable entity ("particular matter involving specific parties"); this is often referred to as the SES "one-year cooling off period." This provision does allow for such a former employee to "work behind the scenes" with a former agency contractor, but the former SES may not personally appear before or contact any employees of his or her old agency during this one-year period. [103] A former senior employee is also restricted for one year after leaving federal service, from knowingly aiding, advising, or representing a foreign entity, with the intent to influence the official actions of any employee of any U.S. agency or department.[104] The statutory annual income threshold to determine if an

---

[99] 18 U.S.C. § 207 and 5 C.F.R. § 2641.202.
[100] 18 U.S.C. § 202(b).
[101] 5 C.F.R. § 2641.104, defines "former senior employee" as an employee in a position for which the rate of pay is specified or fixed according to 5 U.S.C. §§ 5311-5318.
[102] 18 U.S.C. § 207(c) and 5 C.F.R. § 2641.204.
[103] 5 C.F.R. § 2641.201(d) (3).
[104] 18 U.S.C. § 207(f) and 5 C.F.R. § 2641. 206.

---

employee must comply with the one-year cooling off period is 86.5% of the annual rate of basic pay for Level II, Executive Schedule, which is $155,440.50 for calendar year 2012.[105]

XVII. Disclosure of Financial Interests

All FEMA employees, including special federal employees, are subject to conflict of interest restrictions and may be required to file either a public or confidential financial disclosure report. These reports are among the primary tools used by ethics personnel to determine whether employees are in compliance with the ethics and standards of conduct provisions covering a particular position. Depending on an employee's official position, grade, and employment status, he or she may be required to file either a public financial disclosure report (OGE Form 278)[106] or a confidential financial disclosure report (OGE Form 450).[107]

Generally, FEMA employees who are newly appointed to covered positions must file the required public or confidential financial disclosure reports not later than 30 days after assuming the new position or office.[108] A filer who performs the duties of his position or office for a period in excess of 60 days during the calendar year shall file, as appropriate, an OGE Form 450 on or before February 15 of the following year or an OGE Form 278 on or before May 15 of the following year[109]

An employee who files his or her public disclosure report (OGE Form 278) after the statutory deadline (and any extensions) is subject to a late filing fee required by statute and OGE regulation.[110] An employee who

---

[105] 18 U.S.C. § 207(c)(2)(ii).

[106] 5 C.F.R. § 2634.202 defines who must file a public financial disclosure form as a "public filer." Pursuant to the STOCK Act of 2012, Pub. L. 112-105 and Pub. L. 113-7 (2013), OGE 278 forms for federal elected officials and certain Senate-confirmed appointees must now be published on a federal website, and SES employees and IPAs have additional reporting requirements for periodic financial transactions involving stocks, bonds, and other financial holdings, with short reporting deadlines and website publications of this additional information.

[107] 5 C.F.R. § 2634.904 defines who must file a confidential financial disclosure form as a "confidential filer."

[108] 5 C.F.R. § 2634.201(b), "New Entrants"; 5 C.F.R. § 2634.903(b), "New Entrants."

[109] 5 C.F.R. § 2634.201(a), "Incumbents"; 5 C.F.R. § 2634.903 (a), "Incumbents."

[110] 5 C.F.R. § 2634.704, "Late filing fee."

files a confidential financial disclosure report late may be subject to administrative action.[111] An employee who falsifies his or her report may be subject to civil penalties and/or criminal prosecution by the Department of Justice.[112]

Compliance with financial disclosure requirements is a condition of employment. Employees who are required to file and fail to do so in a timely manner may be subject to disciplinary action up to and including removal from federal service.[113]

Additional Requirements for Public Disclosure Filers (OGE 278):

The STOCK Act of 2012[114] requires employees who file public disclosure reports (OGE Form 278) to also file periodic reports (OGE Form 278-T) after engaging in certain financial transactions. These transactions include any purchase, sale, or exchange of stocks, bonds, commodities, futures, or other forms of securities owed or acquired by the employee that exceed $1,000. A transaction must be reported the earlier of 30 days after receiving notification of the transaction required to be reported or not later than 45 days after such a transaction. Certain transactions are excluded from this reporting requirement. These transactions include: (1) real property; (2) mutual funds, exchange traded funds, and other "excepted investment funds;" (3) underlying holdings in an "excepted investment fund," a qualified blind or diversified trust, or an excepted trust; (4) assets owned by the employee's spouse or dependent child, if the employee does not also own the asset; (5) securities issued by the United States Treasury; (6) life insurance and annuities; (7) cash accounts, including money market mutual funds; (8) assets in a retirement system under Title 5 of the U.S. Code (including the Thrift Savings Plan); and (9) assets in any other retirement system maintained by the United States for officers or employees of the United States, and for members of the uniformed services. Public filers should note, however, that they must

---

[111] 5 C.F.R. § 2634.701(d).
[112] 18 U.S.C. §§ 1001 and 3571. Also, 5 C.F.R. § 2634.701(b) and (c).
[113] 5 C.F.R. § 2634.701(d).
[114] Pub. L. 112-105 (2012).

---

continue to report financial transactions related to these assets on Schedule B of their next annual or termination OGE 278 report. [115]

On April 15, 2013, President Obama signed into law S. 716[116], which eliminates the requirement in the STOCK Act to make available on official websites the financial disclosure forms of employees of the executive and legislative branches other than the President, the Vice President, members of and candidates for Congress, and several specified presidentially nominated and Senate-confirmed officers; and delays until January 1, 2014, the date by which systems must be developed that enable public access to financial disclosure forms of covered individuals.[117]

XVIII. Summary

This chapter focused on the laws and regulations that help FEMA employees maintain the highest ethical standards. As federal employees, FEMA employees have obligations to the citizens of the United States to act impartially and ethically in awarding contracts and grants, providing disaster assistance, and all other activities done on behalf of the agency. Failure to maintain these high ethical standards may result in civil and even criminal penalties.

Disciplinary action will not be taken against an employee who engages in conduct in good faith reliance upon the advice of an agency ethics official, provided the employee made full disclosure of all relevant circumstances.[118] Accordingly, all FEMA employees are encouraged to seek advice and counsel from the certified Ethics Counselors named in Table 1, who are ready to serve in the Field Offices, Regions, and Headquarters.

---

[115] Pub. L. 112-105 (2012).
[116] Pub.L. 113-7 (2013).
[117] Id; See also, Statement by the Press Secretary on S. 716, http://www.whitehouse.gov/the-press-office/2013/04/15/statement-press-secretary-s-716
[118] 5 C.F.R. § 2635.107(b).

TABLE 1. List of Certified Ethics Counselors

ETHICS COUNSELOR	PHONE #	ADDRESS
Administrator's Office & ORO		
Dan Hall Daniel.Hall@fema.gov	202-646-4106 BB: 202-329-0530	500 C St. SW, Room 840E Washington, DC 20472
Elizabeth Jerke Elizabeth.Jerke@fema.gov	202-646-4279 BB: 202-631-9492	500 C St. SW, Room 717A Washington, DC 20472
Ethics Training		
Paul Conrad Paul.Conrad@fema.gov	202-646-4025 BB: 202-531-6547	500 C St. SW, Room 840H Washington, DC 20472
CDP		
Kent Davis Kent.Davis@fema.gov	256-847-2122 BB: 256-591-4254	Center for Domestic Preparedness 61 Responder Dr., P.O. Box 5100 Anniston, AL 36205
Deployable Field Counsel		
Elizabeth Blair Elizabeth.Blair@fema.gov	BB:202-664-6951	400 Virginia Ave, SW, Ste 120 Washington, DC 20472
Emery Haskell Emery.Haskell@fema.gov	202-251-5243	500 C St. SW, Room 840 Washington, DC 20472
Michael Hill Michael.C.Hill@fema.gov	202-674-2242	400 Virginia Ave, SW, Ste 120 Washington, DC 20472
José Morales Jose.Morales@fema.gov	202-251-5766	500 C St. SW, Room 840 Washington, DC 20472
Rosa Rios Rosa.Rios@fema.gov	787-637-7750 BB:787-340-7894	500 C St. SW, Room 840 Washington, DC 20472
Charles Senn Charles.Senn@fema.gov	715-828-7990 BB: 202-674-1695	400 Virginia Ave, SW, Ste 120 Washington, DC 20472
Rita Sislen Rita.Sislen@fema.gov	515-224-5644 BB: 202-664-9032	400 Virginia Ave, SW, Ste 120 Washington, DC 20472
Charlotte Stewart Charlotte.Stewart@fema.gov	202-212-2064 BB:202-664-4942	400 Virginia Ave, SW, Ste 120 Washington, DC 20472
Keith Weiner Keith.Weiner@fema.gov	BB:202-812-6943	500 C St. SW, Room 840 Washington, DC 20472

ETHICS COUNSELOR	PHONE #	ADDRESS

EA, FBNP, ODIC, OPPA, NAC

Michael Delman	202-646-2447	500 C St. SW, Room 840
Michael.Delman@fema.gov	BB:202-368-8563	Washington, DC 20472

Flood Insurance & Mitigation

Alfred (Wade) Boykin	202-646-2768	1800 S. Bell Street
Alfred.W.Boykin@fema.gov	BB: 202-286-6629	Arlington, VA 20598

FOC/Finance Ctr/ MWEOC & CFR

Douglas Horton	540-542-5993	Mt. Weather Operations Cntr
Douglas.Horton2@fema.gov	BB: 202-821-7267	P.O. Box 129, Bldg. 405
		Mt. Weather, VA 22611

Louisiana Recovery Office

Janice Kazmier	504-762-2294	LA-RO 1 Seine Court
Janice.Kazmier@fema.gov	BB: 225-436-4040	New Orleans, LA 70114
John Dimos	504-762-2263	
John.Dimos@fema.gov	BB: 202-368-8542	

Response Division

Carol Ann Adamcik	202-646-7971	500 C. St., SW Room 835E
CarolAnn.Adamcik@	BB: 202-674-8488	Washington, DC 20472
fema.gov		

OCFO (Ethics Advice assigned to E. Jerke)

Michael K. Cameron	202-212-3027	Patriots Plaza,
Michael.Cameron@fema.gov		395 E St. SW, Room 218
(OCC POC)		Washington DC, 20472

Mission Support, ERO, LEA

Leigh Hoburg	202-646-7396	500 C St. SW, Room 840
Leigh.Hoburg@fema.gov	BB: 443-871-8398	Washington, DC 20472
Paula Rich	202-212-4756	1800 S. Bell Street, Rm 420
Paula.Rich@fema.gov		Arlington, VA 20598

ETHICS COUNSELOR	PHONE #	ADDRESS

PNP LD & USFA (Not MWEOC/CDP)

David Brummet David.Brummett@fema.gov	BB: 202-786-9862	800 K Street NW 9th Floor, Room 9103 Washington, DC 20001
Anthony DeFelice Anthony.DeFelice@fema.gov	BB: 202-821-5174	1800 S. Bell Street, Rm 822 Arlington, VA 20598
Michelle Mallek Michelle.Mallek@fema.gov	BB: 202-679-3678	500 C St. SW, Room 3I0-27 Washington, DC 20472
Moira O'Brien Moira.O'brien@fema.gov	202-646-3353 BB: 202-262-6139	500 C St. SW, Room 835 Washington, DC 20472

Recovery, incl ROs & NPSCs

Kim Hazel Kim.Hazel@fema.gov	202-646-4501 BB: 202-329-4186	500 C St. SW, Room 834A Washington DC, 20472
Philip Yoo Philip.Yoo@fema.gov	202-646-2823 BB: 202-412 4012	500 C St. SW Washington DC, 20472

Region 1

Scott Smith Scott.Smith@fema.gov	617-956-7609 BB: 857-205-2842	99 High Street Boston, MA 02110

Region 2 (Ethics Advice assigned to E. Jerke)

Catherine Belfi Catherine.Belfi@fema.gov (Ethics Certification Pending)	212-680-8694 BB: 646-884-3716	26 Federal Plaza, 13th Floor New York, NY 10278

Region 3

Michael Rizzo Michael.Rizzo@fema.gov	215-931-5604 BB: 215-439-1477	615 Chestnut St., 6th Floor Philadelphia, PA 19106
Twinckle Vaidya Twinckle.Vaidya@fema.gov	215-931-5957 BB: 571-481-8517	

Region 4

Stuart Baker Stuart.Baker@fema.gov	770-220-8810 BB: 404-694-0355	3003 Chamblee Tucker Rd Atlanta, GA 30341
Hope Ayers Hope.Ayers@fema.gov	770-220-5269 BB: 334-782-1361	

ETHICS COUNSELOR	PHONE #	ADDRESS

Region 5

Maureen Cunningham Maureen.Cunningham@ fema.gov	312-408-4412 BB: 312-560-5230	536 S. Clark St., Ste 600 Chicago, IL 60605

Region 6

Jill Igert Jill.Igert@fema.gov	940-898-5289 BB: 504-570-7300	800 North Loop 288 Denton, TX 76209
Alma Hernandez Alma.Hernandez@fema.gov	940-898-5300 BB: 940-235-5061	

Region 7

Leesa Morrison Leesa.Morrison@fema.gov	816-283-7595 BB:816-809-3827	9221 Ward Parkway, Ste 300 Kansas City, MO 64114
Alex Sachs Alex.Sachs@fema.gov	816-283-7688 BB: 816-398-2744	

Region 8

Jennifer Dick Jennifer.Dick@fema.gov	303-235-4903 BB: 303-563-9230	Building 710, PO Box 25267 Denver, CO 80225
Christopher Americanos Christopher.Americanos@ fema.gov	303-231-1889	

Region 9

John-Paul Henderson JohnPaul.Henderson@ fema.gov	510-627-7055 BB: 510-507-0214	1111 Broadway, Ste 1200 Oakland, CA 94607
Ann Winterman Ann.Winterman@fema.gov	510-627-7081 BB: 510-206-3728	

Region 10

David Smith David.S.Smith@fema.gov	425-487-2099 BB: 425-879-6989	130 228th St. SW Bothell, WA 98021

Advice in Crisis: Towards Best Practices for Providing Legal Advice under Disaster Conditions[1]

Eric Stern, Gregory Saathoff, Mary Ellen Martinet, and Brad Kieserman

I. Why Should You Read This Chapter?

The practice of emergency management law at FEMA, particularly during Stafford Act disaster operations, often entails involvement in highly consequential decisions and negotiations under extremely demanding conditions.[2] FEMA lawyers in the past have had mixed success in performing under these conditions and meeting the expectations of FEMA leaders and other clients.[3] This chapter provides a collection of best practices culled from a review of relevant literature and over 60 interviews with experienced emergency managers and their lawyers, both inside and outside of FEMA.[4] We have distilled the lessons learned from that effort into an organized, cohesive model called "Advice in Crisis" aimed at

---

[1] The authors wish to express their deep appreciation to Ms. Rachael Bralliar, Dr. Christopher Holstege, Ms. Elizabeth Renieris, Mr. Adrian Sevier, and Mr. Patrick Walsh, for their invaluable assistance throughout the Advice in Crisis project and the preparation of this chapter.

[2] See Keith Bea, CONG. RESEARCH SERV., RL 33053, FEDERAL STAFFORD ACT DISASTER ASSISTANCE: PRESIDENTIAL DECLARATIONS, ELIGIBLE ACTIVITIES, AND FUNDING (2010) (providing an overview of Stafford Act Disaster Assistance).

[3] In the spring of 2010, OCC conducted a web-based survey distributed to 366 FEMA clients and 130 FEMA OCC employees in the field and at headquarters. FEMA clients reported the five attributes they valued most in their law firm are (in order of importance): 1) law-related knowledge; 2) accessibility; 3) solution orientation; 4) knowledge of FEMA mission and strategy; and 5) quality of legal work. Clients reported significant misalignment with OCC on risk tolerance and solution orientation. Based on client reporting, OCC staff tended to overrate its effectiveness for the attributes of accessibility, law-related knowledge, risk tolerance, solution orientation, quality of Alternative Dispute Resolution work, and quality of legal work. Similarly, the survey indicated that OCC staff tended to underrate the importance of the following attributes when compared to the importance ratings provided by FEMA clients: providing client self-service tools; risk tolerance; solution orientation; agency coordination; understanding of non-legal risk; and knowledge of mission and strategy.

[4] See "Advice in Crisis Interviews (Phase 1)," infra pages 35-37.

---

providing you with a framework for the effective delivery of legal services during disaster operations.

II. Disasters are Different

The Advice in Crisis interviews revealed six consistent challenges for lawyers providing advice during Stafford Act major disasters and emergencies (collectively called "disasters" in this chapter):

- Crisis conditions
- Cultural clashes (for example between headquarters [HQ]/region/Joint Field Office [JFO] as well as across professions)
- The FEMA staffing (and deployment) system
- Finding the right "weight" for legal advice (in relation to other relevant aspects of the decision calculus)
- Coordinating opinions cumulatively across the organization and cases (in the absence of an effective knowledge management system)
- Promoting "heedful interrelating" across functions and professions

Disaster operations require advice and decision-making processes to function at a high level under very difficult circumstances. It is useful to conceptualize disasters like other crises in terms of three subjective criteria: threat, uncertainty, and urgency.[5] Let us consider these in turn, as they are not only helpful in distinguishing crises from other types of situations, but also provide a means for probing and preparing to act in them.

First, crises are associated with threats to (and often potential opportunities to promote) core values cherished by decision-makers and/or their constituencies. These include human life; public health and welfare; democracy; civil liberties and the rule of law; economic viability; and public confidence in leaders and institutions. Emergency managers and their lawyers must also be prepared to cope with distinct ways of

---

[5] *See* Arjen Boin, Paul 't Hart, Eric Stern, and Bengt Sundelius, THE POLITICS OF CRISIS MANAGEMENT: PUBLIC LEADERSHIP UNDER PRESSURE (2005).

thinking about, and conflicts among, such values.[6] For example, one way to approach disaster decisions "involves looking back at a disaster after it has occurred and deciding what to do about it or how to clean it up"—this perspective is called *ex post*.[7] Another approach "involves looking forward and asking what effects the decisions we make during this disaster will have in the future—on parties who are entering similar situations and [have not] yet decided what to do, and whose choices may be influenced by the consequences" of our decisions—this perspective is called *ex ante*.[8]

Second, crises exhibit high degrees of uncertainty regarding the nature of the threat, the contours of an appropriate response, and/or the possible ramifications of various courses of action. One can imagine the effects of uncertainty in the aftermath of the 2011 Japan earthquake, tsunami, and nuclear disaster as decision-makers attempted to account for aftershocks and the probability of radiological release. Another type of uncertainty has to do with media and public reactions to potential interventions or policy choices.

Third, crises are associated with a sense of urgency. Those in crisis perceive events as moving quickly, and there are fleeting windows of opportunity to influence their course. Additional time pressure stems from the relentless pace of the 24-hour news cycle. Decision-makers and their organizations must cultivate the capacity to diagnose situations and formulate responses under severe time pressure. Thus, crises force decision-makers to make some of the most consequential decisions in public life under extremely trying circumstances.

Fortunately, these criteria provide the basis for a practical diagnostic tool that can help crisis managers find their way in crisis.[9] Confronted with a threatening situation, it is useful to turn the components of this crisis definition into diagnostic questions:

---

[6] *See* Barbara R. Farnham, Roosevelt and the Munich Crisis: A Study of Political Decision-Making (1997).
[7] *See* Ward Farnsworth, The Legal Analyst: A Toolkit for Thinking about the Law (2007).
[8] Id.
[9] *See* Eric K. Stern, Crisis Navigation: *Lessons from History for the New Crisis Manager-in-Chief*, 22(2):1 Governance 89-202 (2009).

- What core values are at stake in this situation? This question helps crisis managers and their lawyers identify threats and an opportunity embedded in the contingency at hand and encourages them to design solutions that attend to them in a consciously balanced and measured way.[10] It also helps them minimize the risk of a so-called type III error—deploying the "right" solution to the wrong problem.[11]

- What are the key uncertainties associated with the situation and how can they be reduced? This question enables decision-makers and their lawyers to identify key variables and parameters and better prioritize "intelligence" and analytical resources.

- How much time is available or can be bought (through interim measures or proactive scheduling of interagency/intra-agency stakeholder, or other meetings, press conferences etc.)?

- How can the decision-making process be optimized in light of the circumstances? Effective and legitimate crisis decision-making and communication processes may look very different depending upon whether the time frame is measured in minutes, hours, days, weeks, or months. As the time frame widens, there is increasing room for consultative and coalition building processes.[12] As one moves through the phases of a disaster and as the operative and political situation evolves, conditions for making decisions and providing advice tend to change.

---

[10] See Ralph L. Keeney, VALUE-FOCUSED THINKING: A PATH TO CREATIVE DECISIONMAKING (1992).

[11] See Ian I. Mittroff and Abraham Silvers, DIRTY ROTTEN STRATEGIES: HOW WE TRICK OURSELVES AND OTHERS INTO SOLVING THE WRONG PROBLEMS PRECISELY (2010). In the discipline of statistics, a type I error occurs when one rejects the null hypothesis when it is true. For example, in criminal justice, a type I error occurs when a jury makes an error and sends an innocent person to jail. Conversely, a type II error occurs when one rejects the alternative hypothesis (that is, one fails to reject the null hypothesis) when the alternative hypothesis is true. Using a criminal justice example again, a jury commits a type two error when it sets a guilty person free. Id.

[12] See, e.g., Alexander L. George, PRESIDENTIAL DECISIONMAKING IN FOREIGN POLICY: THE EFFECTIVE USE OF INFORMATION AND ADVICE (1980).

"Normal" modes of developing, providing, communicating, and receiving advice may be inappropriate or even counterproductive under disaster conditions. Indeed, even under more "normal" conditions, many government managers and officials reported seeing "agency lawyers as essentially 'nay-sayers,' who were quick to point out the legal risks in various courses of action but less quick to array the legal risks or recommend feasible options."[13] A special task force created under the direction of Vice President Gore, known as the National Performance Review "took the view that government lawyers were insufficiently innovative and operated in a 'culture laden with red tape.'"[14] The milieu of disaster operations often further exacerbates the perception of lawyers as impediments. As one Incident Commander put it, "You lawyers never want to let us get on with things. I'm trying to save lives and protect property, and all you want to do is tie us up with legalisms. I don't have time for the law when lives and property are at stake."[15]

Taken together, the characteristics of crises (core values at stake, uncertainty, and time compression) coupled with traditional perceptions of government lawyers as obstacles, even under optimal conditions, can result in severe role conflict, within and across professions.[16] As one experienced practitioner observed:

> Emergency responders and managers attempting to save lives and protect property must be action oriented as they deal with fluid, very dangerous situations. Due to the extreme danger posed by hazardous substances that may well be weaponized, terrorism HAZMAT events in particular require prompt, correct action. In such a situation, professionals often perceive the lawyer who gets in the way of timely action as an obstacle to dealing with the event. Attorneys may find themselves literally locked out of

---

[13] See Gary J. Edles, *Assessing "Who is the Client" in the Government Context*, 31-FALL ADMIN. & REG. L. NEWS 10, 10 (2005).

[14] *Id.*

[15] See William C. Nicholson, Building Community Legal Capabilities for Post 9-11 Terrorism Preparedness, Address before the FEMA Higher Education Conference (May 30-31, 2002), available at <http://www.training.fema.gov/EMIWeb/downloads/WilliamNicholson.doc> (last visited Sept. 15, 2011).

[16] See George, *supra* note 12; *cf.* Irving L. Janis, CRUCIAL DECISIONS: LEADERSHIP IN POLICYMAKING AND CRISIS MANAGEMENT (1989).

---

emergency operations centers unless they have taken the pains to become a part of the team during the early stages of emergency management.[17]

A. What Do Clients Want and Need from Their Lawyers During Disaster Operations?

We learned from the Advice in Crisis interviews with FEMA Federal Coordinating Officers (FCOs) and other disaster managers that effective inter-professional communication—that is effective communication between emergency managers and their lawyers—is essential for crisis management but often difficult to achieve.

B. Why Is This?

First, without detailed knowledge of emergency management law—that requires thoughtful and ongoing preparation for crises across a wide range of legal disciplines—lawyers see events unfold as they labor to learn the law. Law schools provide little or no training in the law of emergency management or crisis decision-making, and most FEMA lawyers in the past have learned by doing. Many emergency managers have likewise learned by doing and are well versed in program-specific policies and practices. Unfortunately for those emergency managers, "some attorneys do not react well when their clients know more about the law than they do."[18] It can be disconcerting for attorneys, inexperienced or seasoned, to be able to recognize this and proceed authoritatively without the mantle of being the expert on the law in question in a room of laypeople.

Second is the problem of 'parachuting' into a team. FEMA emergency managers have often worked together for a long time in steady state operations or in past disasters. If the lawyer has not been part of the team before, it is possible, even likely, that he or she may be unwelcome during response and recovery. Furthermore, without a degree of shared contextual, social (see GAIN later in this appendix), and situational awareness stemming from participation in the early stages of a mission,

---

[17] *See* Nicholson, *supra* note 15.
[18] *Id.*

lawyers may be at a disadvantage in their interactions with other team members, who may well be better informed and connected. It is crucial for the attorney to understand the context of the issues and the overall situation and not just focus on the pure legal questions.

Third, traditional law practice and the emergency management profession often have diametrically different perspectives on risk. Most lawyers in most situations seek to minimize risk for the client—that is, they gravitate towards risk avoidance. What emergency managers need and want, however, is rapid advice on matters that may entail a high potential of legal liability and adverse media reactions, like evacuations, emergency contracting, and property loss that traditional lawyers in non-disaster settings would otherwise counsel against. The emergency manager often cannot "afford" to avoid risk, so what they need are knowledgeable and accessible legal advisors who can innovate, mitigate, and focus on mission accomplishment in which the traditional legal view of success may morph in order to reduce the loss of life and property. As one FCO put it in an Advice in Crisis interview: "I do not want my lawyer to keep me out of court. I want my lawyer to keep me out of jail."

Effective inter-professional communications begin with understanding what senior emergency managers want their lawyers to be and to do. During the Advice in Crisis interviews, senior FEMA emergency managers told us they wanted lawyers in the field to be prepared and competent; indeed, most said they would rather reach back to the HQ Office of Chief Counsel (OCC) than have an embedded attorney in the field who was not prepared and competent to handle the rigors of providing legal services in an emergency operations center (EOC) or JFO. FEMA emergency managers value continuity—once they have a lawyer on the team aligned with their style and expectation, they found turnover to be disruptive. Some of the characteristics valued by a majority of those interviewed include:

- Being a "team player"
- Loyalty
- Responsiveness
- Can do attitude (not bias towards "no")
- Integrity (want the emergency brake pulled if really necessary)
- The ability to keep up with the pace

- The ability to clearly distinguish between "law" and "policy" when delivering options and advice in crisis

Unfortunately, during the Advice in Crisis interviews, FEMA emergency managers reported experiencing uneven delivery of legal services. They reported large variability in:

- Attitude
- Competence
- Responsiveness
- Trust and "loyalty"
- Judgment
- Integration (in team)
- Empathy
- Influence/persuasiveness

Sometimes, faced with lawyers they perceived as "part of the problem, not part of the solution," FEMA emergency managers adopted a number of coping strategies that most lawyers would view as inimical to a climate where they could provide legal advice effectively. Eight sometimes mutually exclusive coping strategies emerged consistently during the interviews:

1. Avoidance (e.g., "better to keep the lawyers out of the response phase altogether")
2. Forgiveness (count on latitude for irregularity associated with response phase)
3. Isolation (e.g., "I put the lawyer in an office as far away from me as possible")
4. Cherry-picking (e.g., "Use favorite lawyers, avoid others")
5. Go to the top (Contact Chief Counsel personally)
6. Lay down the law (Make expectations explicit)
7. Request to be copied on all emails to HQ OCC
8. Send home "poor performers"

Finally, a key finding of the Advice in Crisis leader interviews was that FEMA decision-makers' preferences coincided with the SALT performance standard recently adopted by OCC. SALT is a set of individual performance criteria linked to OCC's Mission Statement that mandates that legal advice produced by OCC shall be:

- **Solution Oriented** – *Where others see obstacles, we focus on legally viable solutions and outcomes. We are open to ideas of others and provide options, constructive alternatives, and creative solutions to legal problems. We support continuous learning and collaborative environments that foster new ideas, understanding, and better ways to execute FEMA's mission. We help resolve conflicts and eliminate needless barriers that interfere with the Agency's efforts to achieve its mission. We assess what is valuable from current and past activity in our practice, document it, and share with those who need to know.*

- **Articulate** – *We express our positions and explain law and policy in an organized, well-reasoned, and persuasive manner, both orally and in writing. We use language that is appropriate to the client-partner, without use of undue "legalese" that might confuse or distort the message.*

- **Legally Sufficient** – *To the extent operational conditions permit, we apply the aphorism "Salt away the facts, the law will keep."*[19] *This means we aggressively develop the facts before applying the law to arrive at legal conclusions and options. When we render a legal opinion, in any form, we cite to legal authorities (using The Bluebook for all written work) to demonstrate that our opinion substantially satisfies applicable statutory, regulatory, and federal executive branch requirements so that our client-partners and those who may later review our opinions understand our reasoning. We are professionally responsible and uphold our duties to our clients, courts, and the legal profession.*

- **Timely** – *We deliver advice and counsel on demand, where and when our client-partners need it, and aggressively anticipate issues and obstacles to mission accomplishment. By being proactive, responsive, and accessible, we prevent problems. We meet the timelines required to support critical or urgent Agency operations and communicate with our clients to establish appropriately prioritized timelines for*

---

[19] *See Erickson v. Starling*, 71 S.E.2d 384, 395-96 (N.C. 1952) (Then North Carolina Supreme Court Justice Sam Ervin delivered this anecdote, wherefrom we derive the concept of "salt away the facts, the law will keep." The unfortunate turn taken by this case in the court calls to mind a bit of advice received by the writer of this opinion from his father, who was a member of the North Carolina bar for 65 years. When the writer embarked on the practice of law, his father gave him this admonition: "Always salt down the facts first; the law will keep." The trial bench and bar would do well to heed this counsel. In the very nature of things, it is impossible for a court to enter a valid judgment declaring the rights of parties to litigation until the facts on which those rights depend have been "salted down" in a manner sanctioned by law.).

routine matters. To the extent operations permit, we provide our colleagues with sufficient time in which to review, consult, and coordinate on complex issues.[20]

C. What Approach Worked for the Most Effective Disaster Operations Lawyers?

Successful FCOs and lawyers identified two distinct conditions for successful delivery of legal services during disaster operations. First is pre-mission preparation, which consists of a combination of physical (e.g., bag packed, electronic files ready, rested and mentally prepared for duty) and intellectual (e.g., extensive professional development, emergency management law expertise) readiness activities. Second is a "get in early" approach to the client relationship. Most emergency managers and lawyers were emphatic that attorney presence during the response phase is essential to both the physical and interpersonal orientation necessary to place attorneys in position of "heedful interrelating" in times of greatest pressure and tension.

What is "heedful interrelating"? "People act heedfully when they act more or less carefully, critically, consistently, purposefully, attentively, studiously, vigilantly, conscientiously, and pertinaciously."[21] Heedful performance is different from habitual performance—habitual performance is consistently replicating the last performance and usually the outcome of drill and repetition, while heedful performance involves constant learning and modification based on training and shared experience. Heedful interrelating in disaster operations involves the recognition (by lawyers and their clients) that JFO lawyers are emergency managers, too, and must structure their contributions with the understanding that they are part of a broader emergency management system consisting of connected, interdependent actions. In plain English, heedful interrelating, in this context, simply means lawyers adapting and integrating into an emergency management team in a manner that fully supports mission accomplishment.

---

[20] FEMA OCC SALT individual performance review criteria document.

[21] See Karl E. Weick and Karlene H. Roberts, *Collective Mind in Organizations: Heedful Interrelating on Flight Decks*, 38 ADMIN. SCI. Q. 357-81 (1993).

Heedful interrelationships are particularly vital for government attorneys providing advice in disaster operations. In contrast to the private bar's concept of "client," which flows from the fundamental and long-standing ethical principle that a lawyer cannot represent conflicting interests, the "relationship among agency officials, managers, and lawyers is inherently complex, and the identity of the 'client' may vary according to the nature or stage of the matter."[22] In fact, some lawyer-skeptical FCOs indicated that the lack of a definitive privilege (i.e., attorney-client) for communications between the FEMA lawyer and the FCO was a major obstacle to including lawyers in the decision-making process and expressed a desire for such protection. Another FCO felt that attorney reporting requirements 'up the line' to HQ OCC were a potential source of distrust and indicated that a standard practice in that FCO's JFO was to order the lawyer to copy the FCO on correspondence with HQ OCC on matters of significance to the FCO leadership. Successful lawyers, however, can turn what might be considered a hindrance—i.e., organizational ties to HQ—into a strength by 1) providing valuable situational awareness and intelligence on HQ's perspective or leanings on particular issues, 2) providing advice based on personal experience and knowledge on how to deal with or approach certain decision-makers in HQ, and 3) marshalling the best case and advocating for the field perspective.

A multi-jurisdictional disaster (and, by definition, every time FEMA is involved, the disaster is multi-jurisdictional) further complicates the "lawyer-client" model for government lawyers at all levels. Accordingly, government lawyers supporting disaster operations need to concentrate on management and communication structures and tools like those described in the Advice in Crisis model to overcome both the perception and reality that lawyers are obstacles to, rather than enablers of, solutions.

---

[22] See Edles, *supra* note 13, at 12.

Highly successful disaster operations attorneys reported that the following practices contributed to heedful interrelating within emergency management teams:

- "Look before you leap." When first arriving at the EOC or JFO, keep a relatively low profile, get a feel for the local environment (e.g., culture/personalities), and do not get in the way. Indeed, find ways you can help even if it does not involve the practice of law.

- "Manage risk, don't avoid it." In every encounter, focus on solutions and options for mission accomplishment, not traditional, liability-centric risk avoidance. Remember that saying "no" may answer the legal question posed but does not solve the underlying problem. Find another way to approach the problem if necessary.

- "Build trust relationships." Provide advice by walking around. Be visible and do not just sit at your desk all day—make "house calls." Make yourself useful when you are not engaged in practicing law. Build and use your network of local resources. Adapt your communication to context and personalities, including thoughtful choices about the venues for providing advice (e.g., groups, one-on-one, etc.). Be proactive—anticipate! Above all: deliver.

A precondition of heedful interrelating is understanding the demands placed on others on the team. A deeper understanding of some of the core tasks of leadership under crisis conditions promises to help lawyers support their leaders (and contribute to team leadership) more effectively.

D. Leadership Tasks

Before unpacking the Advice in Crisis model, we will review the five tasks of crisis leadership,[23] which define the responsibilities of all emergency managers and provide a consistent context for the delivery of legal services during disaster (and other crisis) operations.

---

[23] *See Boin, supra.*

Several decades of intensive empirical research on crisis has suggested that leaders face typical and recurring challenges when confronted with crises. A recent synthetic overview of the crisis studies field[24] suggested that leaders face a series of tasks that tend to emerge in facing a wide variety of crisis types. These are:

1. Sense-making;
2. Decision-making;
3. Meaning-making;
4. Terminating; and
5. Learning.

These tasks are germane not only to effective crisis leadership in a particular incident, but also to creating better preconditions for future incidents.

1. Sense-making

Sense-making in crisis refers to the challenging task of developing adequate interpretations of what are often complex, dynamic, and ambiguous situations.[25] This entails not only developing a picture of what is happening, but also understanding the implications of the situation from one's own vantage point and that of other salient stakeholders. "Sense-making is much more than sharing information and identifying patterns. It goes beyond what is happening and what may happen to what can be done about it."[26] In fact, the diagnostic questions presented previously are a useful point of departure for crisis sense-making. Note that the sense-making problem takes a somewhat different form depending upon whether the consequences of the emerging situation are latent or manifest. For example, on September 10, 2001, the sense-making problem regarding the terrorism threat to the United States was largely one of detecting relatively faint signals in a cacophonous background, a problem that had been exacerbated by political inattention

---

[24] Id.

[25] Cf. Karl E. Weick, *Enacted Sense-making in Crisis Situations*, 25 J. MGMT. STUD. 305–17 (1988); Stern forthcoming).

[26] *See* David S. Alberts and Richard E. Hayes, DoD Command and Control Research Program, POWER TO THE EDGE: COMMAND AND CONTROL IN THE INFORMATION AGE (2003), at 102.

and organizational fragmentation.[27] On September 11, 2001, suddenly the signals became very loud indeed—ushering in a completely new set of sense-making challenges associated with value, complexity, uncertainty, and acute time pressure, accompanied by paradoxical combinations of information shortage and overload.

2. Decision-making

Decision-making refers to the fact that crises tend to be experienced by leaders (and those who follow them) as a series of 'what do we do now' problems triggered by the flow of events, emerging either simultaneously or in succession. Complex crisis events may entail a considerable number of these decision-making occasions associated with different aspects of an emerging and evolving situation. Crisis decision-makers tend to (but do not always) operate on different time frames depending upon their proximity to the scene or stage upon which the crisis unfolds. During the last 20 years or so, scholars of crisis decision-making have gained important insights into the ways in which civilian and military crisis decision-makers operate at both strategic and operational levels.[28] Effective crisis decision-makers rely not only upon experience-based intuition, but also know how to get the best out of their crisis teams by facilitating functional group dynamics.

3. Meaning-making

Meaning-making refers to the fact that leaders must attend not only to the operational challenges associated with a contingency, but also to the ways in which various stakeholders and constituencies perceive and understand the event. Because of the emotional charge associated with disruptive events, followers look to leaders to help them understand the meaning of what has happened and place it in a broader context. Every crisis develops

---

[27] See Charles F. Parker and Eric K. Stern, Bolt from the Blue or Avoidable Failure: Revisiting September 11 and the Origins of Strategic Surprise, 1 FOREIGN POL'Y ANALYSIS 301-31 (2005).

[28] See Eric K. Stern, CRISIS DECISIONMAKING: A COGNITIVE-INSTITUTIONAL APPROACH (Swedish National Defense College 1999); see also Gary Klein, SOURCES OF POWER: HOW PEOPLE MAKE DECISIONS (2001); NATURALISTIC DECISION MAKING AND MACROCOGNITION (Jan Maarten Schraagen et al. eds., 2008); Boin, supra note 5.

---

its own dramaturgy in which participants are assigned roles: hero, victim, villain, fool, etc. This is not only done through words—rhetoric—but also through deeds and 'body language' that often speaks louder, and in a more compelling fashion, than words. By their words and deeds, leaders can convey images of competence, control, stability, sincerity, decisiveness, vision—or their very opposites. Through their communication, leaders may influence—i.e., raise or lower—expectations, as well as reinforce or undermine their own personal and organizational credibility. Note that different forms of protection strategies (such as evacuate or shelter in place) are associated with different advantages and disadvantages in terms of their communicative dramaturgy.

4. Terminating

Terminating refers to the non-trivial task of finding the appropriate timing and means to end the crisis and return to normalcy. For example, in anticipation of a major hurricane affecting multiple states, numerous command centers, operations centers, and emergency teams spool up to their highest levels of readiness. While that pace of operations may be necessary as the storm approaches and strikes, and in the immediate aftermath, such a tempo of operations is simply unsustainable. Hence, it is imperative to find the right time and the right way to begin the process of ratcheting down and even demobilizing. Attempting to end a crisis prematurely, however, can endanger or alienate constituencies who may still be in harm's way, traumatized, or otherwise emotionally invested in the crisis. It may also raise expectations and set the stage for disappointment. External crisis interventions or aid provision may create dependencies on that intervention and knock out or inhibit the recovery of local resources and productive systems. Finally, a crisis may be particularly difficult to terminate if the operational challenges lead to a so-called crisis after the crisis, during which recriminations against those who failed to prevent, respond effectively to, or orchestrate recovery after a negative event challenge the legitimacy and viability of affected individuals and organizations.

---

5. Learning

The final leadership task we will describe is learning. Learning entails examining the genesis of and/or the response to a crisis in order to identify lessons for the future about how to prevent, respond to, or recover from a disruptive event. Effective learning requires an active, critical process that recreates, analyzes, and evaluates key processes, tactics, techniques, and procedures in a manner designed to identify best (and lesser) practices and formulate reform suggestions in a manner conducive to enhanced performance, safety, and capability. In fact, the learning process merely begins when a "lessons learned" document is produced. In order to bring the learning process to fruition, change management/implementation must take place in a fashion that leaves the organization with improved prospects for future success.[29]

III. The Advice in Crisis Model

Figure 1. The SALT Performance Standard

---

[29] See Boin, supra note 5; see also Eric K. Stern, Crisis and Learning: A Conceptual Balance Sheet, J. CONTINGENCIES & CRISIS MGMT. (1997); Edward Deverell and Eva-Karin Olsson, Learning from Crisis: A Framework of Management, Learning and Implementation in Response to Crises, 6-1 J. HOMELAND SEC. & EMERGENCY MGMT. (ART. 85 2009).

A. Mission Preparation and Readiness (PREP)

Leaders and top lawyers at FEMA agree that a key prerequisite for success is being prepared for the rigors of practicing law in crisis or disaster environments. The pace is fast, and disaster lawyers must hit the ground running. The following section outlines four key categories of preparation that may be helpful in improving the likelihood of a successful performance. While they do not guarantee success, they clearly improve the odds. Furthermore, failure to prepare will stack the deck towards failure. Former White House Chief of Staff and Secretary of State James Baker was reportedly fond of reminding his staff of the 5 Ps: Prior Preparation Prevents Poor Performance.[30]

- Four Categories of Preparation

  1. Personal Commitment and Contact
  2. (Mission) Reconnaissance
  3. Emergency/Disaster Legal Resources
  4. Packing Lists for Field Deployments

1. Personal Commitment and Contact

The following bullet points summarize some ways to prepare oneself for deployment and pave the way for good collaborative relationships with colleagues (see the GAIN model):

- *Prepare for availability and extended absence:* Two of the factors most emphasized by FEMA leaders and top-performing lawyers interviewed by Advice in Crisis researchers are availability and commitment. Clients want lawyers to be readily available and prepared to commit to longer deployments. Though the minimum commitment for field deployments is 30 days, leaders often want and expect their lawyers to stay longer to avoid disrupting key advisory relationships in periods of intense activity.

---

[30] *See* David D. Pearce, Wary Partners: Diplomats and the Media (1995); James Baker, III, Work Hard, Study, and Keep Out of Politics (2006).

- Establish pre-departure communication by phone and/or email with:

    i. Relevant OCC/program specialists at HQ or regional offices;

    ii. JFO leadership (including the Deputy FCO and/or Chief of Staff);

    iii. The FCO (by sending at least a courtesy email);

    iv. Regional, state, county, local, or other partner organization counsel or officials/stakeholders, as appropriate; and

    v. Regional counsel – to get background information on the current state of affairs for both the Regional Office and the state, including challenges, new leadership, and other important issues.

Doing so enables lawyers to connect with their clients, other team members, and partners at an early stage by establishing relationships and providing communications links that can help improve the lawyer's situational awareness going into a situation.

- Meet and greet FCO and team broadly on arrival. Lawyers should follow up with pre-deployment contacts, and complement these contacts with additional personnel introductions, once on site. By doing so, lawyers not only signal sociability, but also approachability and willingness to be a part of the team. Find out if the FCO has any particular concerns, and determine how the FCO runs his or her office and who the gatekeeper is (e.g., the Executive Assistant or Chief of Staff). Be sure to get to know the gatekeeper.

- Know your "redlines." In engineering, "redline" refers to the maximum engine speed at which an engine or motor and its components are designed to operate without causing damage to the components themselves or other parts of the engine. For emergency management lawyers, "knowing your redlines" means having a clear understanding of your ethical duties and the limits of the law (and your personal knowledge of the law), and how each of those bounding factors might present themselves in a disaster setting before you are in the thick of providing advice in crisis. As a practical matter, you will learn and develop your own sense of redlines through professional development, exercises, and experiences, which is one reason that it is imperative for all federal emergency management lawyers to "learn the business" (that is, develop expertise in the FEMA disaster programs and operations), as well as the Stafford Act, fiscal law, emergency acquisition law, ethics, and grants law before you are confronted with challenging interdisciplinary issues in the "heat of battle."

2. (Mission) Reconnaissance

The prospects for providing successful advice improve if lawyers do not wait for field deployment or first meetings of dedicated crisis/disaster teams at HQ to begin mission reconnaissance. Once assigned, lawyers should immediately begin informing themselves about the situation, context, and role they will be assuming. There are many ways to do this kind of mission reconnaissance. Some suggestions formulated by top FEMA disaster lawyers include:

- Consult <http://www.fema.gov>

- Review the current Declaration information and the State's disaster history <http://www.fema.gov/news/disasters.fema>

- Review the FEMA Qualification System Task Book (Legal Adviser)

- Review Incident Management Assistance Team (IMAT)/situation reports

- Scan open source intelligence (local and national media/social media) including the FEMA compiled daily clips <http://www.fema.gov/news/recentnews.fema>

- Review event type (expected consequences/complications/policies) <http://www.fema.gov/hazard/index.shtm>

- Review context (historical, geographic, cultural, jurisdictional, political)

3. Emergency/Disaster Legal Resources

Gather/secure access to general and specialized legal resources in paper and/or electronic form. This is particularly relevant for field deployments but also can facilitate the development of timely and legally sufficient advice at HQ or in interagency environments.

Research and compile resources for anticipated issues such as:

- Authorities (for FEMA and collaborating agencies)
- Regulations
- Guidelines
- Policy
- Opinions
- Precedents
- New or recent initiatives or changes in policy or guidance
- Relevant local law

4. Packing Lists for Field Deployments

The following suggestions are more practically oriented and designed to make lawyers more self-sufficient, more sustainable, and more easily integrated in potentially 'austere' and often hectic field environments.

- Travel light: Be able to manage your own luggage in the field. Onc does not want to unnecessarily burden or inconvenience colleagues who may be under a great deal of stress. Think low-maintenance clothes, shoes, boots, and other personal items for fair and foul weather, including field visits.

- Develop and bring a **field kit**, including items such as:
    - o Flashlight and reserve batteries
    - o Water purification tablets (if traveling overseas)
    - o Portable radio
    - o Small amount of detergent
    - o GPS and cell phone with charger/extra batteries
    - o Computer/IPad with chargers/extra batteries
    - o Power strip

- Pack personal items, such as books, music, or DVDs.

A. Social-Behavioral Elements Required for Effective Advice in Crisis (GAIN)

From a social-behavioral perspective, the FEMA attorney faces challenges that are unusual, if not unique, within the legal profession. The first challenge is linked to the very identity of the agency. Simply put, to be effective, FEMA attorneys must embrace the fact that "emergency" is their middle name. The second challenge is that within these emergencies, whether they involve response or recovery, the FEMA attorney is like a traffic cop at a busy intersection at rush hour, facing people who must share the crisis road on their way to specific agency-specified destinations. The competition for the road reveals tensions: between field units and headquarters; FEMA and DHS (including the Inspector General); FEMA and the interagency process, state and federal government; and not least between OCC and clients. The FEMA attorney must know the law and be fair but must also expect to face myriad stakeholders coming from various directions.

One cannot read this discussion about best practices without being struck by the abrupt nature of crises in general, and disasters in particular, and the active engagement required by FEMA attorneys from the moment that they "parachute into the team." The vernacular of crisis can easily become win-lose or succeed-fail. Expressions like "team player," "responsiveness," "integration into the team," "avoidance," and "isolation" speak to just a few of the behavioral caveats specific to the very tricky business of providing advice in crisis.

In the process of interviewing crisis leaders, FCOs, and attorneys for this Advice in Crisis project, it became clear that the process of advice—how it is developed and delivered—was as important to effectiveness as the content of the advice. Although knowing the law well is necessary, it is clearly not sufficient when dealing with crisis advice during the response and recovery phases. FEMA attorneys must attend to the dynamics of communication as they stand with Regional Administrators, FCOs, or other leaders under the difficult conditions associated with disaster response and recovery.

Based upon the collective experience of crisis leaders and some of their finest attorneys, we developed the GAIN model of the social-behavioral elements of advice in crisis. The elements of GAIN include: 1) Group Dynamics; 2) Active Engagement; 3) Individual Requirements; and 4) Negotiation.

1. Group Dynamics

Because FEMA attorneys work within a crisis team, they must not only be aware of the group dynamics of the team, but also must be prepared to adapt to and try to shape them. Large-scale disaster response and recovery requires a rapid deployment of professionals from federal, state, and local arenas. These 'players' meet in group constellations within and outside of FEMA that can initially be daunting, particularly for the inexperienced crisis attorney. It is within these group settings that the attorney's ability to connect, and function effectively, with others is tested in a public arena.

The Crisis Team: To appreciate the power of group dynamics in the days and months following the onset of a disaster (or other form of crisis) it is important to be aware of the critical role of group development as a factor impacting on group performance. Often, at the outset, groups may be rapidly constituted, with many players that do not know one another well. In such situations, an effective group leader—such as an FCO—can provide form, structure, and constructive accountability to group members, minimizing individual uncertainty that might otherwise inhibit engagement and performance.[31] Leaders can clarify the rules of the game, coordinate and motivate (and support) members, and thus leverage their energy and commitment. As groups develop over time and stronger bonds emerge among the members, they may be more prone to other conformity-based group dynamics such as 'groupthink,' especially in highly stressful circumstances.[32]

An effective crisis team is greater than the sum of its parts and requires that the crisis attorney become an integral member of that group. If the

---

[31] *See* Stern, *supra* note 28; *see also* Stephen Worchel, Dawna Coutant-Sassic and Michele Grossman, *A Developmental Approach to Group Dynamics*, in GROUP PROCESS AND PRODUCTIVITY, 181 (Stephen Worchel et al. eds., 1992).

[32] *See* Janis, *supra* note 16; Paul 't Hart, BEYOND GROUPTHINK: POLITICAL GROUP DYNAMICS AND FOREIGN POLICYMAKING (Eric Stern and Bengt Sundelius eds., 1997).

---

attorney has successfully joined, real engagement and meaningful communicative interaction will occur. If not, the attorney may become irrelevant and isolated. How does an attorney become an effective member of the crisis team? First, the attorney must value the team identity and seek a role as an integral member. But that is only the first step, as one must also understand two of the most important elements of successful group integration: Time and Timing.

Time and Timing: Shared experience of dramatic, traumatic effects is a powerful connective force, and bonding within crisis groups may occur rapidly. The initial response phase can have a searing effect on a crisis team. When led by an effective FCO, the charged atmosphere of the first few days can lead to a sealing or a bonding of a group that quickly becomes not only cohesive, but also potentially exclusive. Therefore, it is advantageous for the attorney to get in early and stay for as long as possible. Hours and days matter, and once that bonding has occurred, it is more difficult for a latecomer to bond with others in the crisis team.

Group dynamics evolve over time, and this is not always to the advantage of an attorney who parachutes in and is then called away to another disaster. The group may actually feel offended if it experiences the attorney's departure as elective in nature. While timing is important, the correlate to effective crisis team integration is time itself. Any positive effect of early bonding will be lost if an attorney announces, "In two weeks I will be taking annual leave, so please get your questions to me while I am still here." Groups mature, and as time passes, the bonds become stronger. Although the initial phase is important, the attorney who arrives early and departs early has abandoned an opportunity to develop within an integrated team. If the attorney's actions suggest the calendar is more important than membership within the crisis team, then that membership will quickly lapse.

The attorney must not be perceived of as "high maintenance." This includes being overly demanding or being unreasonable about the workspace assigned to the attorney.

- One attorney was almost sent home after 9/11 for being rude and demanding on prioritizing the setup of the cubicles for the attorney staff. This was a very large operation with many top-level staff taking operational roles. Everyone had to make do.

- Another attorney complained about being in an office in the basement level of a building. The FCO had decided to place the attorneys in this office instead of in an open space on the main floor as an interim measure until the operations stabilized. It was the FCO's intention to move the attorneys closer to the FCO as part of the FCO's command staff in a large enclosed area as soon as possible.

- One attorney had to make do with a picnic table her first day on the scene because there was no space in the Emergency Operations Vehicle. She had a laptop but no Internet access, cell phone, or printing capabilities. She did have, however, a legal pad, her Stafford Act and regulations, and her computer files, and was able to set up shop and get to work.

- Another trio of attorneys had to share a data cable for email access for the first week or so after Hurricane Katrina. Each attorney had 20 minutes each hour for email and Internet access. They were seated at lunch tables with all the other FEMA staff in the cafeteria of the National Guard.

Attorneys need to be flexible on workspace issues in the field. If an enclosed office is not feasible, then is there an office or private area for consultations or phone conversations available when needed? If a dedicated fax machine cannot be arranged, can the attorney use the FCO's fax machine? Is the attorney space near the FCO and other command staff and sufficiently apart from the state staff and more open areas as a safeguard? Attorneys should adhere to the office hours of the field office and not their normal routines. If the command staff is in by 7:00 a.m., the attorney should also follow that schedule. This is particularly important for the lead attorney. Being unavailable or having a subordinate attend early morning command staff meetings will be duly noted by the command staff and will undercut the lead attorney's authority. In fact, the lead attorney may be considered the lead in name only, as folks gravitate to the attorney staff that is there for them outside of "banker's hours."

The attorney must continue to foster the relationships made as part of the crisis team after the crisis has ended and the team has disbanded until the next event. When crisis team members reach out to the attorney from their home base or from another disaster with an issue or question, the attorney needs to prioritize this inquiry whenever possible. As fellow team members, they are not just clients but colleagues who have faced adversity together.

Challenges to the Group: Not all crisis teams are created equal. Depending upon the leadership and chemistry, some groups can evolve in unhealthy and even destructive ways. A skilled crisis attorney should be aware of the dangers of the unhealthy group, which can devolve quickly into a destructive process characterized by either excessive conformity (i.e., 'groupthink') or excessive conflict.[33] Effective disaster attorneys maintain an understanding of the importance of ethics, consistency, and adherence to professional boundaries. When a group is allowed or encouraged to breach boundaries or behave in an unethical manner, or when inadequate leadership is shown, members, the agency, and other stakeholders will suffer. The attorney who maintains professional boundaries and behaves in an ethical manner not only safeguards his/her own reputation, but also serves as a model for others in the group, which can help serve as a course correction for the group. With skilled leadership from FCOs, unhealthy groups are the exception and not the rule. But even unhealthy groups can be well served by attorneys who consistently adhere to professional boundaries and ethics—this is why one of the PREP activities is "know your redlines." In fact, in crisis, as in other settings, lawyers have an opportunity—even a duty—to exercise this form of leadership.[34]

Attorney's Role within the Team: Certainly, the attorney's role within the team is to provide legal advice to clients during the response and recovery phases.

---

[33] *See* Hart, *supra* note 32.

[34] Cf. Ben W. Heineman, Jr., *Lawyers as Leaders*, 116 YALE L. J. POCKET PART 266, 266-71 (2007).

That is not as simple as it sounds and in fact requires a thoughtful situational awareness. What are the needs of the moment? What will the team require next week? Is there a legal issue that has not been addressed that will be certain to unravel unless identified by the attorney and addressed by the FCO and the team? It is not enough to bond early and integrate well into the team. Continued integration into the team requires situational awareness in order to address present legal needs while, at the same time, identifying future legal landmines.

Within the group, the crisis attorney must maintain a balance between outsider and insider status—a team player who must at times shift gears and serve as a kind of referee. This is a challenge, because the two roles must often be played more or less simultaneously. Ideally, the crisis attorney maintains the trust of individual crisis team members and relates to the group as a whole. At the same time, the crisis attorney's role is distinct from any other. Unlike the FCO, the crisis attorney does not maintain a leadership role within the group. At the same time, the attorney's distinctive skill sets are unique from any other in the group.

2. Active Engagement

In order to bond with the team, experienced crisis attorneys must also be actively engaged in the process. That activity provides opportunities to demonstrate commitment, purpose, and competence—potentially enhancing the status of the attorney in the group. In fact, many leaders would like their crisis attorneys not only to serve as technical experts on matters of the law, but also as wise counselors supporting the leader and the decision-making process in a broader sense. A leader, such as an FCO can benefit greatly from a partnership with an effective attorney. Through active listening, attorneys can acquire knowledge of the event and the concerns of the leader and other team members—thus achieving better, more productive, and seamless integration into the fabric of the team.

Active engagement is a process that requires all of the intellectual and interpersonal skills required of a fine attorney. Active engagement is antithetical to a passive or static approach. If crisis is similar to a contact sport played on a field, the attorney should be with the action on the field as a player/referee and not in the stands watching or in the press box opining. Obviously, while some discussions (and the attorney's contribution to them) in the disaster arena will be very public, other discussions with leaders and team members are best kept private (see also the discussion of **provision of advice** later in this appendix).

This pressure-filled environment demands attention and focus throughout the response and recovery phases when legal counsel is required. Active engagement is therefore a process that:

- **Begins** with accessing relevant documents even before arrival at the crisis site;

- **Continues** through phone, Internet, and face-to-face access of the attorney's collegial network both on-site and off-site; and

- **Leads** to team interactions that are sensitive to the needs of individual team members and the group as a whole.

3. Individual Requirements

The attorney's role within the crisis team represents a paradox of sorts: To be a great team member, one must remain distinct. Because most FCO-led response and recovery teams in FEMA contain only one attorney, attorneys must resist the potential to become submerged into the larger group process, if it would risk diluting the attorney's professional identity and integrity in the process. This speaks to the conundrum of being both a player on the team as well as referee. In such a scenario, the FCO may take the role of coach—not always readily embracing the calls of the referee but always appreciating the need for an experienced interpreter of the rules of the game. The one major difference is that in the game of FEMA crisis (in the JFO setting, for example), the FCO coach can ultimately overrule the attorney referee. Whether one is a player-referee or traffic cop at a busy intersection, these important roles require knowledge of the rules and sensitivity to the situation at hand. Without an appreciation for the group process, active engagement, and individual requirements, a crisis attorney is not in a position to provide the most effective counsel.

There is, therefore, a need for the attorney to absorb and deal with the natural tensions that exist within any crisis team. Even when the attorney

---

has bonded with the group and been embraced by the team, there will be conflicts among those who are dedicated to the mission. When these current or budding conflicts are legal, the crisis attorney will experience the singular brunt of the tensions that require counsel rather than judgment. How does the crisis attorney approach these situations? The best approach is through a process that attorneys are uniquely experienced and trained to deploy: negotiation.

4. Negotiation

Negotiation is a crucial challenge of providing advice in crisis. Speaking literally, various forms of negotiations take place in both intra-agency and interagency contexts associated with disasters. Lawyers may play a key role in guiding and facilitating these negotiations in order to support fulfillment of mission and other obligations within the context of the law. However, the notion of negotiation also provides insights into the lawyer's predicament in another sense. As we have already pointed out, the social, political, psychological, ethical, and legal terrain of a major disaster is complex and fraught with tensions and pitfalls that must be successfully negotiated by lawyers and leaders alike.

Our emphasis on a negotiation mindset may at first surprise new FEMA attorneys who approach advice in crisis with an FCO-led team. After all, doesn't advice in crisis involve interpretation of the Stafford Act? The Stafford Act is settled law and requires interpretation, not negotiation. So, if interpretation is the necessary skill, why is negotiation relevant?

While the Stafford Act is the critical piece of legislation that serves as the legal foundation for FEMA's response and recovery-related actions, it is written in such a way that it can be applied to disparate and often unforeseen disaster events—and the client is typically well aware of the potential for flexibility in interpretation. The crisis attorney must therefore be adept at both interpreting and translating the Stafford Act in a wide variety of situations. The attorney who wants to be persuasive and effective must also recognize that successful delivery of a legal interpretation may require a negotiation with the client who has preconceived expectations, contrary views on the scope of his or her authority, or misplaced perceptions that the legal interpretation will thwart an operational need.

Crises generate questions, and the most important sense for crisis attorneys is auditory. Hearing alone, however, is not sufficient. Listening is the real key. Crisis negotiators who deal with life and death issues are adamant about the obligation to listen prior to beginning a negotiation. In the life and death of disaster, crisis attorneys maintain that same obligation. Before rushing to an answer, one must first appreciate not only the content, but also the nature of the question. The temptation to speak too quickly, whether it is due to hubris, anxiety, or naiveté, must be resisted. This is particularly difficult since the time frame for listening and processing is severely compressed in the crisis scenario. A dearth of time however does not mean that these crucial steps are skipped but rather that they occur in rapid fashion. Before responding, the successful crisis attorney runs the issue through an almost instantaneous mental checklist of broad statutory authorities and bright line prohibitions.

In order to listen, the crisis attorney who is actively engaged realizes that the negotiation is in part a translation of the crisis into words that the client can understand. Lastly, negotiation provides a useful mind-set for the crisis attorney strategically placed in multiple agency, interagency, intergovernmental (federal, state, local, tribal) and (public, private, nonprofit) cross-sectoral processes. The delivery of a legal interpretation, even for attorneys, often requires consensus building, especially in a crisis environment.

Negotiation during crisis requires both the content of knowledge and the process of interpersonal engagement under extreme time and resource constraints and competing interests. Negotiation between the needs of the group versus individual stakeholders can fulfill a critical role in serving and supporting the FCO's leadership of the crisis team. Whether that translation process occurs between individuals or within a crisis team or an agency, the effective crisis attorney is in a position to shed light during the heat of crisis.

B. Producing Substantive Advice in Crisis (SOAP)

1. Sense-making

The first step toward effective substantive advising in a disaster is to make sense of the situation (see Leadership Tasks in previous subsection). This may seem obvious, but it is a non-trivial and ongoing task as the disaster and post-disaster contexts tend to be complex and dynamic. Just as you feel you are getting your bearings and have a good understanding of the situation and problems to be faced by you, the client, and the broader team in which you are embedded, new developments will necessitate updating and rethinking. It is an iterative process and one that may require abandoning previously held views and priorities[35] as the 'operating picture' evolves.

While sense-making is in part an intuitive activity,[36] it can be improved and facilitated by using a set of core questions to challenge the 'environment' and improve contextual and situational awareness. This is not only a way of combating the phenomenon of stress-induced tunnel vision noted previously, but also a good practice for lawyering and decision-making under more normal situations.

Asking the following questions can help lawyers (and leaders) better **make sense** of the situations facing them and improve performance in disasters and crises.

- Which **values** are at stake in this situation and for whom?[37]

- What are the key **uncertainties** in this situation (and how might information gathering, analysis, consultation, etc., reduce them.)?

- What is the **time frame** for developing and delivering advice (which is in turn related to the client's or team's time frame for

---

[35] Cf. John R. Boyd, *Destruction and Creation*, (unpublished 1976), available at <http://www.goalsys.com/books/documents/DESTRUCTION_AND_CREATION.pdf> (last visited Aug. 23, 2011).

[36] Cf. Malcolm Gladwell, BLINK: THE POWER OF THINKING WITHOUT THINKING (2005).

[37] See Ralph L. Keeney, VALUE-FOCUSED THINKING: A PATH TO CREATIVE DECISIONMAKING (1992); Ian I. Mitroff and J.R. Emshoff, *On Strategic Assumption-Making: A Dialectical Approach to Policy and Planning*, 4 ACAD. MGMT. REV. 1-12 (1979).

---

action)? Are there ways of 'buying time' without compromising the mission or public affairs messaging, or otherwise delaying the workflow in the team?

Example:
There was a critical housing shortage in Florida due to extensive hurricane damages to residences. Families were living with friends and relatives, staying in shelters, and, it is reported that in dire circumstances, living in their cars because they could not go back to their damaged/destroyed homes. It was imperative to provide housing immediately.

FEMA contracting staff had secured all available and suitable commercial pad sites for placement of FEMA temporary housing units; however, this did not meet the critical housing needs. FEMA was working feverishly on dozens of projects concurrently throughout Florida with the General Services Administration (GSA) to lease land to develop group sites and with the U.S. Army Corps of Engineers (USACE) to plan and develop the group sites. OCC staff worked with GSA and USACE on executing necessary agreements.

FEMA had an opportunity to rent a semi-developed site from a commercial developer that could cut construction time dramatically. However, the GSA leasing agent was concerned that the developer was requesting a lease payment amount that far exceeded what was fair and reasonable and would not execute a lease without a cost justification from FEMA. There was also concern about whether (a) the price could be negotiated down, (b) the commercial developer was gaining an unfair profit at the government's expense and that FEMA would be paying to complete the developer's project, and (c) the facts actually justified paying a perceived premium price for the land.

At first impression, OCC staff doubted that a cost justification could be made for the proposed action; however, it was clear that the command staff was very concerned about letting this opportunity go without an analysis of the facts: timelines, development costs, and alternatives. In one day, OCC staff obtained the relevant information from GSA, USACE, and the FEMA housing and contracting staff and then analyzed the data and prepared a cost justification memo for the FCO for the following day, which found that the lease and construction costs for the proposed action would help meet FEMA's housing mission for these disasters in a cost-effective and timely manner; that FEMA would actually realize substantial cost and time savings by utilizing the semi-developed land at the proposed lease cost amounts; and that the proposed activity was authorized under the Stafford Act.

Effective sense-making, a key part of problem solving, is facilitated by contextual awareness.[38] A very common source of failure in disaster management is building solutions around underdeveloped or inappropriate specifications of the problem.[39]

2. Options

In providing advice to leaders and other clients in disaster operations, lawyers will engage at different stages of the problem solving process. In some cases, a decision-maker will have a preferred option. For example, in one disaster in a remote Alaskan village, the FCO strongly preferred partnering with voluntary agencies to leverage assistance resources to provide replacement housing. Accordingly, FEMA attorneys developed a transactional framework allowing the Agency to provide funds for log house kits for displaced households, which were constructed under the supervision of the Mennonite Disaster Service and furnished by Samaritan's Purse.

The attorney is likely to face questions of the following nature:

- Are we authorized (or can you find me the authority) to do X?
- Are we prohibited from doing X?
- What are the legal (and possibly ethical, practical, political, or other) risks associated with doing X?
- How can we manage the legal and other risks associated with doing X?
- Is there a better (e.g., faster, cheaper, more effective, and/or less risky) way than X to achieve the goal?
- What were the lessons learned the last time we did X?

---

[38] See Mary Ellen Martinet interview.
[39] See Ian I. Mittroff and Abraham Silvers, DIRTY ROTTEN STRATEGIES: HOW WE TRICK OURSELVES AND OTHERS INTO SOLVING THE WRONG PROBLEMS PRECISELY (2010).

It is also possible that clients will identify a short list of two or more options under serious consideration and ask for a relative analysis of the costs, risks, and/or benefits associated with them. If there is a single or limited number of favored options on the table, proceed to Assessment in this section.

In other situations, and especially if the lawyer is brought into the process at an earlier stage, lawyers may be asked to be a part of the process of identifying or developing options. This may involve drawing upon historical or organizational memory or the current set of procedures to help generate options or may entail a creative process of coming up with a novel approach. Obviously, the latter is more likely to be necessary when FEMA is facing a situation that is qualitatively or quantitatively different and differs significantly from those faced in the past that have shaped the frame of reference and established action repertoire.[40] It is crucial in such circumstances for the attorney to understand the delicate interface of law and policy and the need to work in partnership with program staff in developing novel approaches. Failure to involve and integrate the subject matter program experts can lead to perfectly legal plans on paper that are not executable on the ground. Program staff must have buy-in on the suggested solution, as they will actually have to execute the plan and deal with the consequences.

Again, once an option or limited set of options has been produced, shift to assessment.

3. Assessment

The assessment process is critical to producing high quality advice in crisis. While assessment should be seen as a broad process, drawing upon multiple perspectives on the option or options under examination, many lawyers focus explicitly on only one or two of these perspectives (and perhaps treat some of them in a more intuitive or explicit fashion), but the best disaster lawyers analyze options in a systematic and comprehensive fashion, drawing upon four dimensions, and have the

---

[40] See Henry Mintzberg et. al, The Structure of 'Unstructured' Decision Processes, 21 ADMIN. SCI. Q. 246-75 (1976).

ability to weigh and integrate the results of this process in the advice they give to their clients and teams.

Dimensions of Assessment:

- Authorization
- Prohibition
- Risk
- Judgment

a.) Authorization

Does the option appear to be authorized by the Stafford Act or supplementary authority? Disaster lawyers should keep in mind that Stafford was deliberately formulated to be a broad and flexible instrument and is subject to alternative and evolving opinions. The authorities available under the Stafford Act may be interpreted broadly or narrowly, in part according to the policies and priorities set by FEMA's leadership (and the White House), as well as the zeitgeist of the times.

While the Stafford Act tends to loom large in the assortment of authorities at the disposal of FEMA, it is critical to keep in mind that other supplementary authorities may be available and provide authorization for actions that clients deem necessary or useful in addressing the needs of responding organizations, survivors, and other parties. Should these authorities not be directly available to FEMA, at times they may be 'borrowed' from other agencies through cooperative agreements.

For example, FEMA assisted the United States Agency for International Development (USAID) after the 2010 Haiti Earthquake with assets and personnel to support the response efforts. These assets included Mobile Emergency Response Support personnel and equipment, the IMAT West, and an Incident Response Vehicle to help establish communications for relief efforts on the ground and to provide subject matter expertise and technical support. These activities were undertaken pursuant to an

Interagency Agreement with USAID under the authorities of the Foreign Assistance Act of 1961.[41]

Part of being solution oriented (and getting to yes) is about being **creative** in developing (and arguing) defensible rationales for authorizing practically necessary action under extreme circumstances.

b.) Prohibition

Is there a specific legal or policy-based prohibition, and from what does it derive?

When examining prohibitions and other forms of potentially prohibitive constraints, it is critical to distinguish between prohibitions and whether they stem from the Constitution, statutes (including appropriations law), regulations, executive orders, policies, tactical guidelines (e.g., FEMA letter from the Administrator), and/or past agency policy and/or practice.

Note that lesser order prohibitions (especially those stemming from past agency policy) may well be amenable to change or dispensation in consultation with leaders within or outside of FEMA, especially if in tune with broader trends and shifts in policy and or political/operational imperatives. Situational and contextual factors will determine the viability and appropriateness of such courses of action.

When communicating to clients that certain prohibitions appear to be insurmountable obstacles to a particular course of action, be specific about the source and nature of those prohibitions! It is important to work with the clients on formulating a Plan B or C if the favored course of action appears impossible to implement. It is also important to store these non-starter options for future reference in case there are calls for post-crisis legislative proposals.

---

[41] Pub. L. 87-195, 74 Stat. 424 (1961), as amended (current version at 22 U.S.C. §§ 2151- 2431k (2011)).

---

c.) Risk

What are the legal (and other) risks associated with this option in relation to other alternative courses of action or inaction? Disaster management is fraught with risk, and disaster managers are aware and often willing to accept a degree of, and in extreme situations more than a little, risk. Many of the leaders interviewed strongly emphasized their desire "to do the right thing," despite potential legal exposure. Lawyers who seek to avoid legal risk completely will be perceived as obstacles to effective disaster management and are likely to be marginalized within their teams. Furthermore, legal risks must be weighed against other forms of risk (to life, property, FEMA reputation, political viability, ethics in the broader sense of the word, etc.), when giving advice. The old adage 'desperate times call for desperate measures' captures the balancing act that FEMA leaders are called upon to undertake when making crucial decisions during and in the aftermath of disasters.

When it is, or may be, necessary to embark upon a course of action fraught with legal risk, part of the lawyer's task is to look for ways of managing or minimizing these risks. For example, contemporaneous documentation (not only of the legal opinion, but also of the situational imperatives and deliberative process behind the measure in question) may help protect the leaders and lawyers involved. Formulating a viable exit strategy should also be part of the implementation plan. What are the metrics? Are there objective standards in place? How will this be conveyed to the state, the applicants, the public, and Congress?

d.) Judgment (Practical and Ethical)

Last, but not least, is the imperative to exercise and apply judgment to the matter in question.[42] Leaders (and other clients) told the Advice in Crisis investigators of their strong motivations to "do the right thing" during and after disasters. Leaders of good character, judgment, and intention often have an intuitive sense of what needs to be done in critical situations like disasters. Bases for such normative determinations may have to do

---

[42] See GOOD JUDGMENT IN FOREIGN POLICY (Deborah W. Larson and Stanley A. Renshon eds., 2003), at 6 ("Good . . . judgment entails integrating and balancing competing values to come up with a practical course of action.").

with meeting urgent needs of survivors, preventing disproportionate direct or collateral damage, or living up to fundamental norms of fairness. As formulated by one veteran disaster lawyer (Mary Ellen Martinet) interviewed by the Advice in Crisis team: "Is this for the greater good?"

As in other areas of the law, it is necessary to address that question in two ways:

- Is this for the greater good in this situation?
- Is this for the greater good in terms of the precedent it would set and/or the incentive structure it would create?[43]

One aspect of exercising judgment is knowing when to seek different perspectives, consult more experienced attorneys, or elevate a decision. Further complicating this exercise in judgment is the sense of urgency and attendant time compression associated with crises. As we discussed earlier, crises force decision-makers to make some of the most consequential decisions in public life under extremely trying circumstances. Hence, one important and recurring role decision-makers will ask you to play as an emergency management lawyer is helping to decide when "to ask permission" and when "to seek forgiveness." It is unlikely you will have the time and information necessary to consider thoroughly all of the potential options and consequences associated with a particular decision in crisis operations. This combination of core values, uncertainty, and time compression makes it imperative for the emergency management lawyer to come to the table with knowledge, a strong ethical compass, and a readily accessible network for technical reach back (OCC)—without these capabilities, the lawyer will not be prepared to exercise and apply judgment effectively in crises.

Another critical aspect of judgment—and this dimension emergency management lawyers share with emergency department doctors—is finding the "unmade decision." As one recent study of emergency medicine organizations reported, "Emergency physicians typically focus on finding the pathology, but the demands of surge force the [emergency

---

[43] Cf. Farnsworth, *supra* note 7.

department] to find the 'unmade' decision."[44] Pathology is the diagnosis of disease. Like our medical counterparts, emergency management lawyers often focus on the process of defining and addressing issues or problems (legal pathology, if you will). Yet, in crisis operations (as in medical surge operations), emergency management lawyers can exercise their judgment, experience, and listening skills to help leaders expose and attend to unmade decisions that may trip them up down the line. In this regard, we share here the advice of senior medical clinicians, which we think emergency management lawyers might consider applying by analogy:

Recommended Clinical Work Practices in Surge Settings[45]	Analogous Practices for Emergency Management Lawyers Providing Advice in Crisis
Do not interrupt the expression of the chief complaint.	Do not interrupt the client's expression of the issue or concern.
Chart as you listen.	Take notes as you listen.
Order laboratory investigations necessary to make a disposition, not necessarily to make a diagnosis.	Ask questions and conduct sufficient preliminary research to determine whether an issue needs to be elevated or dealt with immediately, not necessarily to solve the problem on the spot.
Limit imaging, particularly contrast imaging, as much as possible.	Don't get wrapped up in complex legal research during a crisis—delegate that work to subordinates, peers, or headquarters.
Put selected patients with a clear diagnosis and limited care needs (IV fluid, analgesia, antibiotics) under the care of a junior doctor.	Let junior attorneys, paralegals, and program specialists handle issues with simple or repetitive legal issues—the senior emergency management attorney needs to maintain the "big picture" with the senior emergency manager.
Make a disposition plan with a key family member present to optimize understanding and minimize redundant conversations.	Work directly with program clients and intergovernmental colleagues in developing and executing plans to resolve or avoid crisis-related legal issues—don't do this alone in your office.

---

[44] David A. Bradt, Peter Aitken, Gerry FitzGerald, Roger Swift, Gerard O'Reilly, and Bruce Bartley, *Emergency Department Surge Capacity: Recommendations of the Australasian Surge Strategy Working Group*, 16 ACADEMIC EMERGENCY MEDICINE, 1350, 1355 (2009).
[45] Id. at 1356.

Finally, one of the most important dimensions of judgment is determining whether a particular solution is practically viable and can be implemented. While the lawyer may not be the only one around the table who can weigh in on the practicality or mechanics of implementation, lawyers may have highly relevant input to contribute on this point because of their legal expertise, general knowledge, and experience. Ultimately, disaster management, like politics, is the art of the possible.

4. Provision of Advice

Once the previous steps have been completed, lawyers need to communicate the advice produced to clients and/or to the disaster management teams in which they are embedded. Doing so effectively requires adapting and packaging the advice in ways that are appropriate to the situation and the context in which the advice is being delivered, as noted in the discussion of the socio-behavioral (GAIN) dimension. In so doing, it is important to consider the following factors.

- *Situation*: Is the work taking place under crisis-like conditions, and what is the time frame involved? How much pressure is on the disaster management team and its leaders?

- *Organizational context*: What is the nature of the organizational context (headquarters, regional office, JFO, etc.) and the local 'culture'?

- *Venue and form*: Is it most appropriate to convey this advice to a leader or other client in a one-on-one situation, at a senior staff meeting, at an all-hands meeting (generally not!), at a meeting with state and local officials, etc.? Should one deliver an oral or a written opinion? If written, will an informal email suffice, or is a more formal written document necessary?

- *Risk picture*: Generally, it is better to package advice in terms of alternative levels of risk associated with the option or options in question, rather than binary black and white (you can or cannot go forward with a particular course of action). However, in cases characterized by unacceptably high levels of legal risk (and not least when other compensating humanitarian imperatives are not part of the picture), leaders want their lawyers to be prepared to 'pull the emergency brake' and express their objections in the strongest possible terms.

- *Leader/collaborator personalities*: Clients vary greatly in their approach to processing information, open versus closed mindedness, big picture versus detail orientation, familiarity/expertise with the relevant legal issues and modes of legal reasoning, ability to function in stressful environments, etc. The most effective disaster lawyers cultivate the ability to adapt to the personalities and (leadership) styles of their clients. Given the same problem and assessment of options, a lawyer might choose to do a three-minute nutshell brief to a 'big picture' and action-oriented leader, while presenting the same material and results in a 15-minute briefing to another more detail-oriented, reflective, and 'legally interested' leader.[46] In this sense, being articulate in a "SALTy" manner is partly in relation to the person or persons to whom the advice is being delivered.

As noted, provision of advice should be consistent with the SALT performance standard and be: **Solution Oriented**, **Articulate, Legally Sufficient**, and **Timely**. In addition, as noted previously, it is advisable to prepare to mitigate risk and defend potentially controversial measures through the production of contemporaneous documentation.

Finally, lawyers can and often should play a role in developing or reviewing communications to the public or media and/or external affairs guidance both pre- and post-decision.

For example, in response to the devastating April 2011 tornados that struck Alabama and Mississippi, FEMA OCC worked in conjunction with the White House, with FEMA leadership at HQ and in the field, and with program staff on developing a streamlined private property debris removal plan called Operation Clean Sweep. OCC also assisted the External Affairs staff and program staff on press releases and fact sheets. OCC is also engaged in gathering data for lessons learned from the project.

---

[46] *See* George, *supra* note 12; Thomas Preston, THE PRESIDENT AND HIS INNER CIRCLE (2001); Paul A. Kowert, GROUPTHINK OR DEADLOCK: WHEN DO LEADERS LEARN FROM THEIR ADVISORS? (2002).

Conclusion: Advice in Crisis

We call the interaction between lawyers and decision-makers in the context of disaster operations "Advice in Crisis." The double entendre is intentional. In the first and straightforward meaning, "advice in crisis" connotes the provision of legal advice during unstable and dangerous situations. In the second and ironic meaning, "advice in crisis" describes what happens when lawyers attempting to advise emergency managers and other crisis leaders are **not** prepared to deliver legal services in conditions where core values are threatened, uncertainty is pervasive, and time is of the essence. These lawyers, who may be very capable in steady-state transactional or litigation settings, find themselves in a crisis within a crisis as they fumble or muddle through their interactions with decision-makers. Both situations invoke the term "advice in crisis." This paper provided you with a framework to achieve the former connotation while avoiding the latter. We based that framework on data culled from specialized literature; case studies; and interviews/focus groups with FEMA veterans, and government and non-government stakeholders. Our exploration of this subject remains a work in progress, and we invite our readers to share their "advice in crisis" experiences and recommendations any time. You can send your thoughts to brad.kieserman@fema.dhs.gov.

REFERENCES

BOOKS

Alexander L. George, PRESIDENTIAL DECISIONMAKING IN FOREIGN POLICY: THE EFFECTIVE USE OF INFORMATION AND ADVICE (1980).

Arjen Boin, Paul 't Hart, Eric Stern, and Bengt Sundelius, THE POLITICS OF CRISIS MANAGEMENT: PUBLIC LEADERSHIP UNDER PRESSURE (2005).

Barbara R. Farnham, ROOSEVELT AND THE MUNICH CRISIS: A STUDY OF POLITICAL DECISION-MAKING (1997).

David S. Alberts and Richard E. Hayes, DoD Command and Control Research Program, POWER TO THE EDGE: COMMAND AND CONTROL IN THE INFORMATION AGE (2003).

David D. Pearce, WARY PARTNERS: DIPLOMATS AND THE MEDIA (1995).

Eric K. Stern, CRISIS DECISIONMAKING: A COGNITIVE-INSTITUTIONAL APPROACH (Swedish National Defense College 1999).

Gary Klein, SOURCES OF POWER: HOW PEOPLE MAKE DECISIONS (2001).

GOOD JUDGMENT IN FOREIGN POLICY (Deborah W. Larson and Stanley A. Renshon eds., 2003).

Ian I. Mittroff and Abraham Silvers, DIRTY ROTTEN STRATEGIES: HOW WE TRICK OURSELVES AND OTHERS INTO SOLVING THE WRONG PROBLEMS PRECISELY (2010).

Irving L. Janis, CRUCIAL DECISIONS: LEADERSHIP IN POLICYMAKING AND CRISIS MANAGEMENT (1989).

James Baker, III, WORK HARD, STUDY, AND KEEP OUT OF POLITICS (2006).

Malcolm Gladwell, BLINK: THE POWER OF THINKING WITHOUT THINKING (2005).

NATURALISTIC DECISION MAKING AND MACROCOGNITION (Jan Maarten Schraagen et al. eds., 2008).

Paul 't Hart, BEYOND GROUPTHINK: POLITICAL GROUP DYNAMICS AND FOREIGN POLICYMAKING (Eric Stern and Bengt Sundelius eds., 1997).

Paul A. Kowert, GROUPTHINK OR DEADLOCK: WHEN DO LEADERS LEARN FROM THEIR ADVISORS? (2002).

Ralph L. Keeney, VALUE-FOCUSED THINKING: A PATH TO CREATIVE DECISIONMAKING (1992).

Stephen Worchel, Dawna Coutant-Sassic and Michele Grossman, *A Developmental Approach to Group Dynamics, in* GROUP PROCESS AND PRODUCTIVITY, 181 (Stephen Worchel *et al.* eds., 1992).

Thomas Preston, THE PRESIDENT AND HIS INNER CIRCLE (2001).

Ward Farnsworth, THE LEGAL ANALYST: A TOOLKIT FOR THINKING ABOUT THE LAW (2007).

PERIODICALS

Keith Bea, CONG. RESEARCH SERV., RL 33053, FEDERAL STAFFORD ACT DISASTER ASSISTANCE: PRESIDENTIAL DECLARATIONS, ELIGIBLE ACTIVITIES, AND FUNDING (2010).

Ben W. Heineman, Jr., *Lawyers as Leaders*, 116 YALE L. J. POCKET PART 266, 266-71 (2007).

Charles F. Parker and Eric K. Stern, *Bolt from the Blue or Avoidable Failure: Revisiting September 11 and the Origins of Strategic Surprise*, 1 FOREIGN POL'Y ANALYSIS 301-31 (2005).

Edward Deverell and Eva-Karin Olsson, *Learning from Crisis: A Framework of Management, Learning and Implementation in Response to Crises*, 6-1 J. HOMELAND SEC. & EMERGENCY MGMT. (ART. 85 2009).

Eric K. Stern, *Crisis and Learning: A Conceptual Balance Sheet*, J. CONTINGENCIES & CRISIS MGMT. (1997).

Eric K. Stern, *Crisis Navigation: Lessons from History for the New Crisis Manager-in-Chief*, 22(2):1 GOVERNANCE 89-202 (2009).

FEMA OCC SALT individual performance review criteria document.

Gary J. Edles, *Assessing "Who is the Client" in the Government Context*, 31-FALL ADMIN. & REG. L. NEWS 10, 10-13 (2005).

Henry Mintzberg et. al, *The Structure of 'Unstructured' Decision Processes*, 21 ADMIN. SCI. Q. 246-75 (1976).

Ian I. Mitroff and J.R. Emshoff, *On Strategic Assumption-Making: A Dialectical Approach to Policy and Planning*, 4 ACAD. MGMT. REV. 1-12 (1979).

John R. Boyd, *Destruction and Creation*, (unpublished 1976), available at <http://www.goalsys.com/books/documents/DESTRUCTION_AND_CREATION.pdf> (last visited Aug. 23, 2011).

Karl E. Weick, *Enacted Sense-making in Crisis Situations*, 25 J. MGMT. STUD. 305–17 (1988).

Karl E. Weick and Karlene H. Roberts, *Collective Mind in Organizations: Heedful Interrelating on Flight Decks*, 38 ADMIN. SCI. Q. 357-81 (1993).

William C. Nicholson, Building Community Legal Capabilities for Post 9-11 Terrorism Preparedness, Address before the FEMA Higher Education Conference (May 30-31, 2002), available at <http://www.training.fema.gov/EMIWeb/downloads/WilliamNicholson.doc> (last visited Sept. 15, 2011).

Advice in Crisis Interviews (Phase 1)

Thad Allen – Former Commandant, U.S. Coast Guard

Josie Arcurio – Director, Southern California Area Field Office, FEMA

Karen Armes – Deputy Regional Administrator, Region IX, FEMA

Marty Bahamonde – External Affairs Senior Policy Advisor, FEMA

Tom Balint – Associate Chief Counsel, Protection and National Preparedness, FEMA

Sally Brice-O'Hara – Vice Commandant, U.S. Coast Guard

Pauline Campbell – Director, Office of Equal Rights, FEMA

Nancy Casper – Federal Coordinating Officer, FEMA

Luletha Cheatham – Director, Hazard Mitigation, FEMA

Sandy Coachman – Federal Coordinating Officer, FEMA

Linda Davis – Director, Professional Development, Office of Chief Counsel, FEMA

Steve DeBlasio – Federal Coordinating Officer, FEMA

Justin Dombrowski – Director, Disaster Operations Division, Region IX, FEMA

Diane Donley – Deputy Chief of Staff, Office of Chief Counsel, FEMA

Greg Eaton – Federal Coordinating Officer, FEMA

David Garratt – Associate Administrator, Mission Support, FEMA

Lee Hamilton – Co-Chairman, Iraq Study Group (2006); U.S. Congressman (1965-1999)

Brad Harris – Federal Coordinating Officer, FEMA

Bob Haywood – Long-Term Community Recovery Officer, FEMA

Mike Haralambakis – Deputy Director, Disaster Assistance Division, Region IX, FEMA

J. P. Henderson – Regional Counsel, Region IX, FEMA

Mike Hill – Legal Counsel, FEMA

Matt Jadacki – Deputy Inspector General, Office of Emergency Management Oversight, Office of Inspector General, DHS

Mike Karl – Federal Coordinating Officer, FEMA

Lisa Katchka – Chief of Staff for Legal Policy, Office of Chief Counsel, FEMA

Don Keldsen – Federal Coordinating Officer, FEMA

Brad Kieserman – Chief Counsel, FEMA

Cal Lederer – Deputy Judge Advocate General, U.S. Coast Guard

Albie Lewis – Federal Coordinating Officer, FEMA

Lynda Lowe – Branch Director, Individual Assistance, FEMA

Ron Mackert – Equal Rights Officer, FEMA

Mary Ellen Martinet – Associate Chief Counsel, Response and Recovery, FEMA

Phil May – Regional Administrator, Region IX, FEMA

Doug Mayne – Federal Coordinating Officer, FEMA

Cindy Mazur – Director, Alternative Dispute Resolution, FEMA

Bryan McCreary – Branch Chief, Acquisition Operations, FEMA

Dennis McKeown – Planning Branch Chief, Disaster Operations Division, Region IX, FEMA

Jason McNamara – Chief of Staff, FEMA

Edwin Meese – Chairman, Center for Legal and Judicial Studies, Heritage Foundation; U.S. Attorney General (1985-1988)

Ted Monette – Director, Office of Federal Coordinating Officer Operations, FEMA

Mark Neveau – Federal Coordinating Officer, FEMA

Mike Parker – Federal Coordinating Officer, FEMA

Phil Parr – Federal Coordinating Officer, FEMA

Mike Rizzo – Regional Counsel, Region III, FEMA

Charles Robb – U.S. Senator (1989-2001); Governor of Virginia (1982-1986)

Bill Roche – Infrastructure Branch Chief, Disaster Assistance Division, Region IX, FEMA

Rich Serino – Deputy Administrator, FEMA

Adrian Sevier – Deputy Chief Counsel, FEMA

Marty Shoffner – Deputy Branch Director, Public Assistance, FEMA

Gerard Stoler – Federal Coordinating Officer, FEMA

Tom Stufano – Federal Coordinating Officer, FEMA

Joel Sullivan – Regional CEO, Nashville Area Chapter, American National Red Cross

Gracia Szczech – Federal Coordinating Officer, FEMA

Terry Tanner – Public Assistance Officer, Tennessee EMA

Nancy Ward – Regional Adminstrator, Region IX, FEMA

Ann Winterman – Deputy Regional Counsel, Region IX, FEMA

David Zocchetti – Chief Counsel, California EMA

Terrie Zuiderhoek – Director, Disaster Assistance Division, Region IX, FEMA

Disaster Operations Legal Analysis Checklist

I. FACT GATHERING AND ISSUE DEFINITION

A. What?

What do we want to do or are we being asked to do?

B. So What?

What makes this important?

What makes this difficult or controversial?

C. Why?

Why are we doing this? (Purpose of the assistance/activity)

To provide:

1. **Logistics support**: equipment, transportation, commodities, base camps, personnel

2. **Subject matter Expertise**: technical assistance, federal agency expertise

3. **Operations Assistance**:

   a. Response: short term, immediate assistance that is life saving/sustaining; protects property, health, and safety; and is for the general public welfare.

   b. Recovery: longer-term, focused (individualized) assistance to recover from the incident and to mitigate damages in the future.

D. Why Not?

Are there limiting factors or special considerations that need to be addressed?

1. Scope of applicable authority
2. Political
3. Fiscal
4. Liability concerns
5. Special needs
6. Public interest
7. Time constraints
8. Policy concerns
9. Long-term effects
10. Environmental
11. Contracting
12. Insular
13. Tribal
14. Other federal law limitations

II. CONTEXT

A. When: (Is this before or after a declaration has been issued?)

Is there a declaration or likely to be a declaration?

1. **No Declaration-none likely (foreign assistance, non–Stafford Act domestic event, Other Federal Authority triggered, readiness/steady state)**

   a. Stafford Act Title II: Disaster Preparedness and Mitigation
   b. Stafford Act Title VI Emergency Preparedness
   c. Flood Insurance Program Authority
   d. Homeland Security Act (HSA) Authorities

6 U.S.C., Chapter 1—Homeland Security Organization
Subchapter V—National Emergency Management, §§311-321n

§ 313 Federal Emergency Management Agency.
Administrator - Principal advisor on emergency management

§ 314 Authority and responsibilities
- Federal leadership
- All-hazards approach

§ 317 Regional offices

§ 318 National Advisory Council
Applicability of Federal Advisory Committee Act (FACA)

§ 319 National Integration Center
National Response Framework (NRF) (successor to the National Response Plan)
National Incident Management System (NIMS)
Incident Management

§ 320 Credentialing and typing

§ 321b Disability Coordinator

§ 321f Nuclear incident response

§ 321e Chief Medical Officer

§ 321h Use of national private   sector networks in emergency response

§ 321n Acceptance of gifts

Chapter 2—National Emergency Management, 6 U.S.C. §§ 701-811

§ 701 Definitions

Subchapter I—Personnel Provisions, §§ 711-728

§ 711 Surge Capacity Force

§ 721 Evacuation preparedness technical assistance

§ 722 Urban Search and Rescue Response System

§ 723 Metropolitan Medical Response Grant Program

§ 724 Logistics

§ 725 Pre-positioned equipment program

§ 728 Disclosure of certain information to law enforcement agencies

Subchapter II—Comprehensive Preparedness System, §§ 741-811

Part A—National Preparedness System, §§ 741-760
Part B—Additional Preparedness, §§ 761-764
Part C—Miscellaneous Authorities, §§ 771-777

§ 771 National Disaster Recovery Strategy
§ 772 National Disaster Housing Strategy
§ 773 Individuals with disabilities guidelines
§ 774 Reunification
§ 775 National Emergency Family Registry and Locator System

Part D—Prevention of Fraud, Waste, and Abuse, §§ 778-797

§ 791 Advance contracting
§ 792 Limitations on tiering of subcontractors
§ 793 Oversight and accountability of Federal disaster expenditures
§ 794 Limitation on length of certain noncompetitive contracts
§ 795 Fraud, waste, and abuse controls
§ 796 Registry of disaster response contractors
§ 797 Fraud prevention training program

Part E—Authorization of Appropriations, §811

a. National Response Framework

b. Other Federal Agency (OFA) Authority and Responsibility
1) No FEMA action
2) Coordination with OFAs
3) Servicing agency under an Interagency Agreement (IAA)

c. Readiness type activities
1) Establishment and training of teams and cadres
2) Federal agency authority to loan/sell commodities
3) Memorandums of Understanding (MOUs) with OFAs and Voluntary Agencies: coordination of activities

2. Pre-Declaration: declaration likely/imminent

a. Stafford Act Title II: Disaster Preparedness and Mitigation

b. Stafford Act Title VI Emergency Preparedness

c. Flood Insurance Program Authority

d. Homeland Security Act (see HSA shown previously)

e. Readiness type activities
1) Federal agency authority to loan/sell commodities

    2) Necessary Expense pre-positioning of equipment, commodities and personnel

  f. OFA Authority and Responsibility

    1) No FEMA action

    2) Coordination with OFA

3. Declaration Issued

  a. Emergency Declaration Assistance Authorities

Stafford Act Emergency Declaration Assistance Authorities

§502 Includes General Federal Assistance and Public Assistance (PA) Emergency Work

§407 Debris removal per §502(a)(5)

§408 Individuals and Households Program per §502(a)(6)

§418 Emergency Communications (Direct Federal Assistance only)

§425 Transportation for Individuals and Households

Additional Stafford Act Emergency Declaration Assistance Authorities (provided by/in coordination with another agency/organization

§ 413 Food Commodities- U.S. Department of Agriculture (USDA)

Stafford Act Process Authorities

§§401/501 Procedure for Declaration (401-Disasters, 501-Emergencies)

§422 Simplified Procedures (for PA Small Projects)

§305 Non-liability of Federal Government

§318 Audits and Investigations

§321 Rules and Regulations

§325 Public Notice, Comment, and Consultation Requirements (for PA projects)

§326 Designation of Small State/Rural Advocate

<u>Other Stafford Act and Homeland Security Act Operational Authorities</u>

§302 Coordinating Officers

§303 Emergency Support and Response Teams

§306 Performance of Services-(Use of State/Local Facilities and Disaster Assistance Employee (DAE)/ Cadre of On-Call Response Employees (CORE) hiring)

§309 Use and Coordination of Relief Organizations (Voluntary Agency coordination coupled with Title V for logistical support)

§323 Minimum Standards for Public and Private Structures

Stafford Act Title VI Emergency Preparedness

§701(b) Gift Authority

See HSA authorities previously shown

<u>Limiting Stafford Act and Related Authorities</u>

§503 Amount of Assistance

§102 Definitions

§307 Use of Local Firms and Individuals

§308 Nondiscrimination in Disaster Assistance

42 U.S.C. §5154a Prohibited Flood Disaster Assistance (non-Stafford Act)

§312 Duplication of Benefits

§316 NEPA Statutory Exclusion

§320 Sliding Scale

§324 Management Costs

§427 Utility Company Access

§705 Grant Closeout

§706 Firearms

Executive Order (E.O.) 11988 Flood Plain Management

E.O. 11990 Wetland Protection

Coastal Barriers Resources Act, (16 U.S.C. §3501, et seq.)

National Flood Insurance Act, (42 U.S.C. § 4001, et seq.)

See HSA authorities previously shown

Other Stafford Act Authorities

§ 101 Congressional Findings and Declarations

Title II Disaster Preparedness and Mitigation Authorities

§ 304 Reimbursement of Federal Agencies

§ 314 Penalties (Fraud actions)

§ 317 Recovery of Assistance

b. Major Disaster Declaration (DR) Assistance Authorities

Stafford Act DR Assistance Authorities

§ 402 General Federal Assistance

§ 403 Essential Assistance (Public Assistance (PA) Emergency Work)

§ 404 Hazard Mitigation

§ 406 Repair, Restoration, and Replacement of Damaged Facilities (PA Permanent Repair)

§ 407 Debris removal

§ 408 Federal Assistance to Individuals and Households (IHP)

§ 417 Community Disaster Loans

§ 418 Emergency Communications (Direct Federal Assistance only)

§ 419 Emergency Public Transportation (Direct Federal Assistance only)

§ 425 Transportation Assistance to Individuals and Households

Additional Stafford Act DR Assistance Authorities (provided by/in coordination w/ another agency/organization)

§ 410 Disaster Unemployment Assistance- (U.S. Department of Labor)

42 U.S.C. §5177a: Grants to Assist Low-Income Migrant and Seasonal Farmworkers- (USDA (non-Stafford Act))

§ 412 Food Benefits and Distribution-(USDA)

§ 413 Food Commodities-(USDA)

§ 415 Legal Services-(American Bar Association (ABA) MOU)

§ 416 Crisis Counseling assistance and Training (U.S. Department of Health and Human Services (HHS) tech support for state grant)

§ 421 Timber Sales-USDA

---

§ 426 Case Management-Services (HHS Direct Federal Assistance
       and/state grant)

Process Related Stafford Act Authorities

§401 Procedure for Declaration
§422 Simplified Procedure (for small PA projects)
§423 Appeals of Assistance Decisions
§305 Non-liability
§310 Priority to Certain Applications for Public Facility and Public
      Housing Assistance (non-Stafford Act programs)
§318 Audits and Investigations
§321 Rules and Regulations
§325 Public Notice Requirements
§326 Small State/Rural advocate

Eligibility Related Stafford Act DR Authorities

§424 Date of Eligibility; Expenses Incurred Before Date of Disaster

Other Stafford Act and HSA Operational Authorities

§301 Waiver of Administrative Conditions
§302 Coordinating Officers
§303 Emergency Support and Response Teams
§306 Performance of Services-(Use of State Facilities and DAE/CORE
      hiring)
§309 Use and Coordination of Relief Organizations (coupled with
      Title IV for logistical support).
§315 Availability of Materials (survey/allocation)
§319 Advance of Non-Federal Share
§323 Minimum Standards for Public and Private Structures
Title VI Emergency Preparedness
§701 Gift authority
See HSA authorities previously shown

Limiting Stafford Act and Related Authorities

§102 Definitions
§307 Local Firms
§308 Nondiscrimination in Disaster Assistance

---

§311   Insurance

42 U.S.C. §5154a Prohibited flood disaster assistance (non-Stafford Act)

§312   Duplication of Benefits

§316   Protection of Environment (NEPA Statutory Exclusion)

§320   Limitation on Sliding Scales

§322   Mitigation Planning (cross ref §404 re funding)

§324   Management Costs

§427   Essential Service Providers (Utility Company access)

§705   Disaster Grant Closeout Procedures

§706   Firearms Policies

E.O. 11988: Flood Plain Management

E.O. 11990: Wetland Protection

Coastal Barriers Resources Act, (16 U.S.C. §3501, *et seq.*)

National Flood Insurance Act, (42 U.S.C. §4001, *et seq.*)

See HSA authorities previously shown

Other Stafford Act Authorities

§101   Congressional Findings and Declarations Title II Disaster Preparedness and Mitigation Authorities

§304   Federal agency reimbursement

§314   Fraud actions

§317   Recovery actions

§405   Federal facility repair

§414   Relocation eligibility

c. Fire Management Assistance Grant (FMAG) Authorities

FMAG Assistance Authorities

§420   Fire Management Assistance (which also authorizes 403 assistance as warranted)

Process Related Stafford Act Authorities

§422   Appeals of Assistance Decisions

§305   Non-liability of Federal Government

§321   Rules and Regulations

<u>Other Operational Authorities</u>

§306 Performance of Services −(Use of State Facilities and DAE/CORE hiring)

§318 Audits and Investigations

Title VI Emergency Preparedness

§701(b) Gift Authority

See HSA Authorities previously shown

<u>Limiting Stafford Act and HSA Authorities</u>

§102 Definitions

§307 Use of Local Firms and Individuals

§308 Non-Discrimination in Disaster Assistance

§312 Duplication of benefits

§316 Protection of Environment ((NEPA) Statutory Exclusion

§705 Disaster Grant Closeout Procedures

§706 Firearms Policies

See HSA authorities previously shown

<u>Other Stafford Act Authorities</u>

§101 Findings

Title II Disaster Preparedness and Mitigation

§304 Reimbursement of Federal Agencies

§314 Penalties (Fraud actions)

§317 Recovery of Assistance

B. WHO: (Requester/Recipient/Responsible Party/Interested Party)

1. Who is asking for this?
2. Who is this for?
3. Who is responsible for this?
4. Who needs to be consulted on this?
   a. States
   b. Tribe
   c. Local government
   d. PNP
   e. Individuals

  f. Voluntary agency

  g. OFA

  h. Private sector

  i. FEMA

   1) Headquarters (HQ)

   2) Region

   3) Joint Field Office (JFO)

  j. Department of Homeland Security (DHS)

III. Proposed Action

How:

A. How do we provide the assistance?

1. Financial Assistance:

  a. Stafford Act Authority

   1) Disaster Declaration(DR)/Emergency (EM) Authority

    a) Individual Assistance (IA) (DR/EM rare)

    b) PA

     i. Emergency Work (DR/EM)

     ii. Permanent Work (DR)

    c) Hazard Mitigation Grants Program (HMGP) (DR)

    d) FMAG

   2) Other Stafford Act Authority

    a) Title II

    b) Title VI

   3) Flood Insurance Program Authority

   4) Homeland Security Authority

2. Direct Assistance:

  a. Determine who is going to do it and pay for it.

   1) Authority − May I?

   2) Capability − Knowledge/skills (mental) − Can I?

   3) Capacity − Time/staff/resources (physical and fiscal) − Can I?

---

b. Determine what the underlying authority is for the action. Is there FEMA/OFA Authority? (Review relevant MOUs and OFA authorities as part of analysis.

  1) If no federal authority: decline/refer as appropriate

  2) If both have authority, determine which is more specific

  3) If OFA has sole or more specific authority, refer to OFA for action

    a) However, if FEMA has capability/capacity, an IAA with FEMA as servicing agency may be appropriate

  4) If FEMA has sole or more specific authority for the proposed action:

    a) Then determine if appropriate for internal action first if we have the Capacity and Capability. (Logistics)

    b) If we do not have the Capability and Capacity, then we:

      i. Contract with the private sector (Acquisitions)

      ii. Task OFA via Mission Assignment (MA)/ Interagency Agreement (IAA)

        (a.) MA (Response)

          (i.)   Direct Federal Assistance (DFA)

          (ii.)   Technical Assistance (TA)

          (iii.) Federal Operations Support (FOS)

        (b.) IAA: including MA transition (Response/Recovery and Acquisitions)

          (i.)   DR authority

          (ii.)   Other Stafford Act authority

          (iii.) Economy Act

      iii. Voluntary Agency: Capability/Capacity? Contract or partner with a Voluntary Agency

        (a.) MOU (Recovery)

        (b.) Contract (Acquisitions)

        (c.) Logistics Support (Recovery and Logistics)

          (i.)   Transportation of personnel/goods

          (ii.)   Space

          (iii.) Equipment

        (d.) Invitational Travel (Recovery and Office of Chief Financial Officer (OCFO)

B. How do we pay for it?

1. Disaster Relief Fund
2. Other FEMA appropriations
3. OFA funds
4. Cost shared

C. How do we determine when we are done and how to end it?

1. Deadlines
2. Objective factors
3. Messaging
4. Exit strategy/termination
5. Enforcement

Key to Significant Stafford Act and Regulatory Provisions

Title of Stafford Act	Statute Citation 42 U.S.C. §	C.F.R. * Citation 44 C.F.R. §	Summary of Areas Covered in Each Title and Stafford Act Section Number
Title I	42 U.S.C. §§ 5121 – 5122	206.1 – 206.3	• Purpose of statute: supplemental assistance to state and local governments • Discretionary statute – eligible, but not entitled to assistance • Lists program authorities – preparedness; insurance; hazard mitigation; federal assistance programs • Definitions
Title II	42 U.S.C. §§ 5131 – 5134	300.1 – 300.3	• In the absence of a major disaster or an emergency • Preparedness includes being ready for initial response and mitigation, which ensures a long-term reduction of damage • Pre-disaster mitigation – § 203

* C.F.R. is the abbreviation for the Code of Federal Regulations

Title of Stafford Act	Statute Citation 42 U.S.C. §	C.F.R. * Citation 44 C.F.R. §	Summary of Areas Covered in Each Title and Stafford Act Section Number
Title III	42 U.S.C. §§ 5141 – 5165		• Applies to implementation of Title IV and V declarations
		206.41 – 206.43 208.1 – 208.66	• FCO/SCO/EST authorities – §§ 302, 303 • Urban Search and Rescue
		206.41 – 206.43 208.1 – 208.66	• FCO/SCO/EST authorities – §§ 302, 303 • Urban Search and Rescue
		206.8 206.9 206.10	• Reimbursing federal agencies – § 304 • Non-liability of federal government – § 305 • Authority to hire temporary personnel without regard to competitive service requirements – § 306 • Use of local firms and individuals – § 307
		206.11	• Nondiscrimination in Disaster Assistance – § 308
		206.12	• Use and Coordination of Relief Organizations – § 309
		206.191	• Duplication of Benefits – § 312
		10.8	• Limited NEPA exception – § 316
		206.430 – 439	• Hazard Mitigation Planning – § 322 (state/local plans and HMGP 20%)
		206.400 – 402	• Standards and codes for reconstruction or repair – § 323
		206.207	• Management Costs – § 324 • Public notice requirements for public assistance changes – § 325

Title of Stafford Act	Statute Citation 42 U.S.C. §	C.F.R. * Citation 44 C.F.R. §	Summary of Areas Covered in Each Title and Stafford Act Section Number
Title IV – Major Disaster Assist. Programs	42 U.S.C. §§ 5170 – 5189b	Generally, 206.31 – 206.48	• Declaration for major disasters – § 401 (note parallel to § 501)
		206.36, 206.37	• Process – Governor requests
		206.44	• FEMA-State Agreement
		206.40	• Designating counties • Response General Authorities - § 402 (note parallel to § 502) (mission assignment authority)
		206.200 – 206.228	• Public Assistance – §§ 403, 407
		206.224 – .225	• Essential "emergency" assistance (immediate needs)/debris removal – §§ 403, 407 • Primary preparedness grant: EMPG – multi-hazard, consolidated (warning systems, training responders, equipment, shelters, evacuation, etc.)
		206.430 – 206.440	• HMGP - § 404
		206.203(b) , .47, .65, .432(c)	• Proportion of assistance under PA and IA; cost-effective, reduce or avoid damage • Federal facility – § 405
		206.226	• Permanent repair and construction of public and certain non-profit entities – § 406
		206.224	• Debris Removal – § 407
		206.110 – 206.118	• Individual and Households Assistance - § 408

Title of Stafford Act	Statute Citation 42 U.S.C. §	C.F.R. * Citation 44 C.F.R. §	Summary of Areas Covered in Each Title and Stafford Act Section Number
Title IV (Continued)		206.119 – 206 .120	• Other Needs Assistance – § 408(e)
		206.141	• Unemployment Assistance – § 410 • Food Coupons – § 412
		206.151	• Food Commodities – § 413
		206.161	• Relocation Assistance – § 414
		206.164	• Legal Services – § 415
		206.171	• Crisis Counseling – § 416
		206.225	• Emergency Communications – § 418
		206.225	• Emergency Public Transportation – § 419 • Transportation Assistance – § 425 • Case management – § 426
		206.46, 206.115, 206.206	• Appeals – § 423 • Meaning of Essential Service Provider – § 427
Title V – Emergency Assistance Programs	42 U.S.C. §§ 5191 – 5193	206.61 – 206.67	• Declaration based on a state request in § 501(a) or as a result of federal jurisdiction in § 501(b) • Assistance § 502 (similar to § 403 immediate needs – main difference is *major disaster* declaration can provide assistance for physical damage, see § 406) • Amount of Assistance – § 503

Title of Stafford Act	Statute Citation 42 U.S.C. §	C.F.R. * Citation 44 C.F.R. §	Summary of Areas Covered in Each Title and Stafford Act Section Number
Title VI – Emergency Preparedness	42 USC 5195 – 5197g		• Declaration of policy – vests in federal and states and localities • Definitions – applicable only to this Title VI • Authority to deal with immediate emergency conditions – in preparation for hazards; during a hazard; following a hazard • Detailed functions of Administrator Title VI
	42 USC 5195 – 5197g		• Preparedness compacts • Financial contribution to states and for personnel and administration expenses
Title VII – Miscellaneous	42 U.S.C. 5201 – 5206	206.181	• Donations and gifts – §701(b) • Grant Close Out Procedures – § 705 • Firearms – § 706

Electric Power Restoration Primer

What Is "The Grid?"

The North American electric system "the Grid" is comprised of a complex interconnected network of generating plants, transmission lines, and distribution facilities. There are three regional grids: one in the east that connects the eastern seaboard and the plains states and Canadian provinces; another in the west that connects the Pacific coast and the mountain states and Canadian provinces; and another that operates in most of Texas. There are very limited connections between the three grids to help minimize the impact of disruptions to the system.

How Does the Grid work?

The process begins with production facilities (power plants) which generate electricity through a variety of means; coal, hydro, nuclear, etc. When electricity leaves a power plant, its voltage is increased or "stepped-up" at a substation near the plant to make it readily transmittable. Next, Transmitters send the high-voltage energy along electrical transmission lines (those tall ones), to substations near where it is needed. At the substation the voltage is decreased or "stepped-down" where it is readily distributable commercially. Finally, a distributor transfers the electricity to a power line which carries the electricity until it reaches a home or business. Electricity travels at nearly the speed of light, arriving at a destination at almost the same moment it is produced.

The process is extremely complex because electricity cannot be easily or economically stored, and demand constantly fluctuates. To coordinate power flow, and ensure the right amount of power is sent where it is needed, control areas have been formed. Control areas consisting of one or several transmission operators ensure that there is always a balance between electricity generation and the amount of electricity needed at any given moment to meet demand. A margin of capacity beyond the actual load is needed to ensure reliability at times of peak demand and to provide for maintenance down times. Independent system operator or regional transmission organizations (ISOs and RTOs) use computerized systems to exercise minute-by-minute control over the network and to ensure that power transfers occur during specified times in pre-arranged amounts. They monitor system loads and voltage profiles; operate transmission facilities and direct generation; define operating limits and develop contingency plans; and implement emergency procedures.

Electric companies have interconnected their transmission systems so that they may buy and sell power from each other and from other power suppliers, and to ensure reliability of service. Redundancy is built into the transmission system to provide electric companies with alternative power paths in emergencies.

Key Terms

Transmission lines. Transmission lines serve two primary purposes: They move electricity from generation sites to customers and they interconnect systems. Voltages in the transmission system are high, which makes it possible to carry electric power efficiently over long distances and deliver it to substations near customers.

Transmission and distribution substations. Substations are located at the ends of transmission lines. A transmission substation located near a power plant uses large transformers to increase the voltage. At the other end of a transmission line, a substation uses transformers to step transmission voltages back down so the electricity can be distributed to customers.

Control centers. Control centers have sophisticated monitoring and control systems and are staffed by operators 24 hours per day, 365 days per year. These operators are responsible for several key functions, including balancing power generation and demand, monitoring flows over transmission lines to avoid overloading, planning and configuring systems to operate reliably, maintaining system stability, preparing for emergencies, and placing equipment is and out of service for maintenance and during emergencies.

Distribution lines. Distribution lines carry electricity from substations to end users.

Control systems. Supervisory Control and Data Acquisition Systems (SCADA) and Distributed Control Systems (DCS) monitor the flow of electricity from generators through transmission and distribution lines. These electronic systems enable efficient operation and management of electric systems through the use of automated data collection and equipment control.

Smart Grid Technologies. Under the American Recovery and Reinvestment Act (ARRA) of 2009 funds have been made available to utilities to incorporate "smart technologies" into electricity distribution systems.

Who Owns the Grid?

The primary types of electric power suppliers include:

Private, shareholder-owned electric companies, which serve nearly 70 percent of all customers, are tax-paying businesses that are highly regulated at the federal, state, and local levels.

Electric cooperatives are private companies owned by their customer members; they are eligible for subsidized financing from the Rural Utilities Service (part of the U.S. Department of Agriculture), and are generally unregulated. Significant energy infrastructure is owned by cooperatives, especially in the electric distribution sector. These assets can include generation, transmission, and distribution.

State and municipal-owned electric utilities include municipal systems, public power districts, state projects. Municipal utilities are owned by the municipality in which they operate and are financed through municipal bonds. Government-owned utilities generally are unregulated.

Federal government-owned utilities. The Federal Government is a major owner of energy assets and critical infrastructure throughout the United States and its Territories. Examples include Tennessee Valley

Authority (TVA), a major owner of hydroelectric dams, nuclear and fossil power generation stations, and high-voltage transmission; Bureau of Reclamation (BOR), a major dam owner; The Department of Energy (DOE), which oversees the Strategic Petroleum Reserve (SPR) and the Northeast Home Heating Oil Reserve; and power administrations such as the Western Area Power Administration and the Bonneville Power Administration. Federally owned utilities are involved in the generation and/or transmission of electricity, most of which is sold at wholesale prices to local government-owned utilities and electric cooperatives.

How is the Grid Regulated?

Federal Energy Regulatory Commission (FERC)

The Federal Power Act (FPA), 16 U.S.C. §§ 791a-825r, enacted in 1935, is the primary federal law that regulates the shareholder-owned segment of the electric power industry. The FPA created the Federal Power Commission (FPC), which ensured that electricity rates were "reasonable, nondiscriminatory, and just to the consumer." In 1970, the FPC's functions were transferred to FERC and the newly created Department of Energy.

Today, FERC regulates the transmission and sale of electricity in interstate wholesale electricity markets; utility sales of assets; mergers and acquisitions; and interconnections of certain facilities. FERC also provides oversight of grid reliability. Additionally, FERC regulates interstate transmission and interstate wholesale power transactions, which involve shareholder-owned electric companies buying or selling electricity from one another or from other power suppliers for resale to the ultimate customer. FERC has the authority to regulate the prices, terms, and conditions of these wholesale power sales and transmission services.

FERC helps to protect the reliability of the high-voltage interstate transmission system with oversight authority for mandatory electric reliability standards, which include cyber security. In 2006, FERC certified the North American Electric Reliability Corporation (NERC) as the Electric Reliability Organization—an independent, self-regulating entity created by Congress that enforces reliability standards

In 2008, FERC conditionally approved the industry's first mandatory cyber security standards. The standards require users, owners, and operators of the nation's electricity grid to implement training, physical security, and asset recovery plans to protect against the threat of cyber attack. Today, utilities are working to ensure that forthcoming cyber security regulations will promote reliable and cost-effective service.

FERC also has encouraged the formation of regional transmission organizations (RTOs) and Independent System Operators (ISOs) to oversee electricity markets. These organizations help to run the transmission grid on a regional basis. There are currently seven RTO/ISO regions across the United States.

The FERC does NOT regulate the activities of State or municipal power systems, federal power marketing agencies like the TVA, and most rural electric cooperatives. (State governments, through their public utility commissions or equivalent, regulate retail electric service as well as facility planning and siting.) The FERC Does NOT address reliability problems related to failures of local distribution facilities.

North American Electric Reliability Corporation (NERC):

This private entity has been certified by the FERC to enforce and develop reliability standards for the bulk power industry for the US, and engages in some coordination with Canada. The reliability standards are planning and operating rules that apply electric utilities. The NERC also has infrastructure security responsibilities, for both cyber and physical threats. The NERC Operates the Electricity Sector Information Sharing and Analysis Center (ESISAC) under DHS and Public Safety Canada, to enhance communications among Federal agencies. DOE has also designated NERC as the electricity coordinator for critical infrastructure protection. The critical infrastructure protection committee (CIPC) provides technical and subject matter expertise. The CIPC executive committee, along with the president and CEO of NERC serve as the Electricity Sector coordinating council to collaborate with DHS and DOE on critical infrastructure and security matters.

Additional Federal Regulators

The electric power industry must comply with literally hundreds of environmental regulations, including dozens of rules created under the federal Clean Air Act and Clean Water Act. The U.S. Environmental Protection Agency (EPA) has primary responsibility for developing and enforcing most federal environmental regulations. Other federal agencies have broad authority over electric company facilities crossing federal lands or affecting unique interests, such as historical sites or endangered species.

Electric companies also are regulated by the Federal Communications Commission. Electric companies are required to allow telecommunications companies to use electric poles for wires and other facilities supporting wireless, fiber, broadband, and other communications systems. The structural integrity, safety, security, and reliability of utility poles are fundamental components of the nation's critical energy infrastructure—and the cost to companies for maintaining these poles is considerable.

State Regulators

Shareholder-owned electric companies are also regulated by state agencies, typically known as Public Utility Commissions or Public Service Commissions. All states regulate rates for the delivery of electricity to end users (customers) through distribution wires and related systems. How the price for electricity is set, however, varies by state. Also, electric companies also are subject to environmental regulations issued by individual states. And, states have the primary role in approving the siting of company facilities, including transmission facilities that may serve many different states.

How does the Federal Government Protect the Grid?

National Infrastructure Protection Plan (NIPP)

On June 30, 2006, the U.S. Department of Homeland Security (DHS) announced completion of the National Infrastructure Protection Plan (NIPP), a comprehensive risk management framework that defines critical infrastructure protection (CIP) roles and responsibilities for all levels of government, private industry, and other sector partners. The NIPP builds on the principles of the President's National Strategy for Homeland Security, and strategies for the protection of critical infrastructure and key resources (CIKR). The NIPP was reissued in January 2009.

The NIPP fulfills the requirements of the Homeland Security Act of 2002, which assigns DHS the responsibility to develop a comprehensive national plan for securing CIKR, as well as Homeland Security Presidential Directive 7 (HSPD-7), which provides overall guidance for developing and implementing the national CIP program. In accordance with HSPD-7, the national infrastructure is divided into 18 distinct CIKR sectors, and CIKR protection responsibilities are assigned to select Federal agencies called Sector-Specific Agencies (SSAs).

2010 Energy Sector-Specific Plan (SSP)

DOE is the Sector Specific Agency (SAA) responsible for energy security. In its role as the Sector-Specific Agency for the Energy Sector, the DOE has worked closely with dozens of government and industry partners to prepare the 2010 Energy Sector-Specific Plan (SSP) which is an annex to the NIPP. Much of that work was conducted through the two Energy Sector Coordinating Councils (SCCs) and the Energy Government Coordinating Council (GCC). The Electricity SCC and the Oil and Natural Gas SCC comprise the Energy SCC and represent the interests of their respective industries. The Energy GCC represents all levels of government – Federal, State, local, territorial, and tribal – that are concerned with the Energy Sector. The SSP, in relevant part, addresses the following areas.

CIKR Assessment and Prioritization

As the sector is characterized by very diverse assets and systems, prioritization of sector assets and systems is highly dependent upon changing threats and consequences. The significance of many individual components in the network is highly variable, depending on location, time of day, day of the week, and season of the year. Owners and operators of sector assets, whether oil and natural gas or electricity, have well-developed protocols in place to identify priorities and ensure business continuity and operational reliability.

Therefore, prioritization of assets and systems in the sector needs to be flexible according to circumstances. Further dialogue among DOE, DHS, and other public and private stakeholders is necessary to examine cross-sector needs and approaches to support national infrastructure protection programs.

Information Collection and Sharing

The Energy Sector has considerable data available to support a wide range of consequence, risk, and vulnerability assessments. The data is collected and used by owners, operators, trade associations, and a variety of industry organizations such as NERC, the American Gas Association (AGA), and American Petroleum Institute (API). In addition, the Government collects a wide variety of Energy Sector information, principally through the authorities of various Federal agencies and—at the State and local levels—through authorities of public utility commissions, State energy offices, and State and local homeland security initiatives. Established communication links also exist between Federal, State, and local government representatives and industry. However, the amount of Energy Sector cyber data is limited.

During times of increased security posture or emergency situations, the best information sources are the trusted relationships between government and industry. Such relationships ensure that necessary information is provided when and where it is needed and can be directly applied to protect and recover key energy infrastructure and resources. Established relationships between industry and all levels of government and other key stakeholders will continue to facilitate information flow, when necessary, through Homeland Security Information network (HSIN) and other information-sharing mechanisms. Further, working with the Department of Energy, sector partners will continue to communicate with DHS regarding additional needs, information resources, and database approaches required to support DHS programs. State energy emergency preparedness and response plans highlight the identification of assets and the role of State government officials, in conjunction with their private sector counterparts, in addressing various levels of an energy emergency.

The Energy Sector owners and operators have a long history of mutual aid and support that can be relied on in emergency situations. This aid is largely focused on emergency response and recovery to support restoration of service to customers. Regional planning groups in the natural gas and electricity industries plan for regional reliability and often conduct exercises to prepare for energy emergencies. States also conduct regional energy emergency exercises involving the private sector to assure coordinated responses across State borders and with the private sector.

Screening Infrastructure

Electric grid operators utilize their energy management systems to run sophisticated contingency analysis programs every 5 to 10 seconds to identify the most critical components of the electric grid. The operators are always aware of the critical components, as well as the consequences if a key component is removed from service, and operate the system to mitigate the loss of any key components.

Assessing Consequences

The potential physical and cyber consequences of any incident, including terrorist attacks and natural or manmade disasters, are the primary consideration in risk assessment. In the context of the NIPP, consequence is measured as the range of loss or damage that can be expected.

The consequences that are considered for the national-level comparative risk assessment are based on the criteria set forth in HSPD-7. These criteria can be divided into four main categories:

- Human Impact: Effect on human life and physical well-being (e.g., fatalities, injuries).

- Economic Impact: Direct and indirect effects on the economy (e.g., costs resulting from disruption of products or services, costs to respond to and recover from the disruption, costs to rebuild the asset, and long-term costs due to environmental damage).

- Impact on Public Confidence: Effect on public morale and confidence in national economic and political institutions.

- Impact on Government Capability: Effect on the government's ability to maintain order, deliver minimum essential public services, ensure public health and safety, and carry out national security-related missions.

An assessment of all categories of consequence may be beyond the capabilities available for a given risk analysis. Most Energy Sector assets are not associated with the possibility of mass casualties, but may have economic and long-term health and safety implications if disrupted. However, the redundancy of system-critical facilities and overall system resilience minimize the potential for such consequences.

Assessing Threats

The Energy Sector takes a broad view of threat analysis, one that encompasses natural events, criminal acts, insider threats, and foreign and domestic terrorism. Natural events are typically addressed as part of emergency response and business continuity planning. In the context of risk assessment, the threat component is calculated based on the likelihood that an asset will be disrupted or attacked. Such information is essential for conducting meaningful vulnerability and risk assessments. Therefore, relevant and timely threat information must be disseminated whenever possible. A number of sector representatives hold national security clearances that facilitate the sharing of classified threat information. In addition, the ES-ISAC facilitates communications between Electricity subsector participants, the Federal Government, and other critical infrastructures, and is a conduit for disseminating sensitive threat and incident information. A number of State and local authorities, with DHS support, have created fusion centers that combine relevant law enforcement and intelligence information analysis and coordinate security measures to reduce threats in their respective communities.

Asset owners and operators must rely on threat information from DHS and Federal, State, and local law enforcement organizations in order to assess the relative risk associated with a given asset. The DHS Homeland Infrastructure Threat and Risk Analysis Center (HITRAC), which conducts integrated threat analysis for all CIKR sectors, works in partnership with owners and operators and other Federal, State, and local government agencies to ensure that suitable threat information is made available. Furthermore, the same level of partnership must exist within all levels of Federal, State, and local law enforcement.

Assessing Vulnerabilities

Vulnerabilities are the characteristics of an asset, system, or network's design, location, security posture, process, or operation that render it susceptible to destruction, incapacitation, or exploitation by mechanical failures, natural hazards, terrorist attacks, or other malicious acts. Vulnerability assessments identify areas of weakness that could result in consequences of concern, taking into account intrinsic structural weaknesses, protective measures, resilience, and redundancies.

Energy Sector owners and operators have well-developed protocols, organizations, and systems for ensuring the reliability of energy networks. The importance of sector assets, both physical and cyber, is affected by changing threats and continually changing consequences. Prioritization of assets and systems in the Energy Sector is dynamic—it changes constantly and goes on continuously. Static prioritization of assets could lead to critical decision making based on outdated or erroneous asset information in efforts to direct scarce resources to those assets, systems, and networks that may be the most critical at any point in time. The public and private partners in the Energy Sector will continue its dialogue with DHS/DOE and other stakeholders to examine cross-sector needs and approaches to support DHS programs. DOE works with DHS to identify gaps in existing energy information and to identify publicly available databases or sources that could provide data to support DHS efforts to prioritize assets.

How Are Electric Power Assets Restored When They are Damaged?

Emergency Support Function (ESF) #12 - Energy

The National Response Framework (NRF) established ESF #12 to facilitate the restoration of damaged energy systems and components when activated by the Secretary of Homeland Security for incidents requiring a coordinated Federal response. Under DOE leadership, ESF #12 is an integral part of the larger DOE responsibility of maintaining continuous and reliable energy supplies for the United States through preventive measures and restoration and recovery actions.

The other primary and support agencies that comprise ESF #12 are:

Department of Agriculture
Department of Commerce
Department of Defense
Department of Homeland Security
Department of the Interior
Department of Labor
Department of State
Department of Transportation
Environmental Protection Agency
Nuclear Regulatory Commission
Tennessee Valley Authority

As the Coordinator of ESF #12, DOE:

- Serves as the focal point within the Federal Government for receipt of information on actual or projected damage to energy supply and distribution systems and requirements for system design and operations, and on procedures for preparedness, restoration, recovery, and mitigation.

- Is the primary Federal point of contact with the energy industry for information sharing and requests for assistance from private- and public-sector owners and operators.

- Maintains lists of energy-centric critical assets and infrastructures, and continuously monitors those resources to identify and mitigate vulnerabilities to energy facilities.

- Establishes policies and procedures regarding preparedness for attacks to U.S. energy sources and response and recovery due to shortages and disruptions in the supply and delivery of electricity, oil, natural gas, coal, and other forms of energy and fuels that impact or threaten to impact large populations in the United States.

- Undertakes all preparedness, response, recovery, and mitigation activities for those parts of the Nation's energy infrastructure owned and/or controlled by DOE. Restoration of normal operations at energy facilities for non-federal entities is the responsibility of the facility owners.

- Assists Federal departments and agencies by locating fuel for transportation, communications, emergency operations, and national defense.

- Provides assistance to Federal, State, tribal, and local authorities utilizing Department of Homeland Security (DHS)/Federal Emergency Management Agency (FEMA)-established communications systems.

When Activated by DHS/FEMA, ESF #12:

- Provides representatives to the DHS National Operations Center, Domestic Readiness Group, and National Response Coordination Center (NRCC).

- Assigns Regional Coordinators to each of the 10 DHS/FEMA regions. These coordinators attend meetings, participate in exercises, and develop expertise on regional issues and infrastructure.

- Deploys personnel to the Regional Response Coordination Center (RRCC) and Joint Field Offices (JFO). Within the JFO, ESF #12 serves as the primary source for reporting of CIKR damage and operating status for the energy systems within the impacted area. The Infrastructure Liaison, if assigned, proactively coordinates with ESF #12 on matters relating to security, protection, and/or restoration that involve sector-specific, cross-sector, or cascading effects impacting ESF #12.

- Deploys personnel as members of Incident Management Teams and as members of the Rapid Needs Assessment Teams State emergency operations centers.

- Provides incident-related reports and information to ESF #5 – Emergency Management.

- Assesses the energy impacts of the incident, provides analysis of the extent and duration of energy shortfalls, and identifies requirements to repair energy systems. ESF #12 coordinates preliminary damage assessments in the energy sector to determine the extent of the damage to the infrastructure and the effects of the damage on the regional and national energy system.

- In coordination with DHS and State, tribal, and local governments, prioritizes plans and actions for the restoration of energy during response and recovery operations. State, tribal, and local governments have primary responsibility for prioritizing the restoration of energy facilities. State, tribal, and local governments are fully and consistently integrated into ESF #12 operations.

- Coordinates with the private sector. DOE provides subject-matter experts to the private sector to assist in the restoration efforts. This support includes assessments of energy systems, latest technological developments in advanced energy systems, and best practices from past disruptions. The private sector normally takes the lead in the rapid restoration of infrastructure-related services after an incident occurs. Appropriate entities of the private sector are integrated into ESF #12 planning and decision-making processes. ESF #12 coordinates information and requests for assistance with the following private-sector entities: the electricity and the oil and natural gas sector coordinating councils, the Electric Reliability Organization, and various associations that represent portions of the energy sector.

- Facilitates the restoration of energy systems through legal authorities and waivers

Practical Aspects of Incident Response

Before a power restoration effort can begin, conditions must be safe for restoration operations. High winds, darkness and flooded conditions, for example, may prohibit restoration work when lines are down. Also, debris must be cleared so the first crews in are debris removal crews, followed by line repair crews. The crews belong to the utilities as employees, contractors, or are provided under mutual aid pacts. The crews will not move into place until they are requested by the state, due to cost considerations. DOE does not play a large role in this process, as plans and priorities are worked out in advance in coordination with DOE, and little oversight of the process is usually necessary. However, DOE has the authority inject itself into the process and require a company complete a repair as a priority. For example, if a water treatment plant is down, and the nearby utility would not repair it because it was not their customer, DOE can require them to make the repair if the functioning of the plant is critical and the servicing utility is unable to make the repair in a timely fashion. This extraordinary authority is rarely exercised.

DOE can also override regulations, and request waivers of regulations. For example, if there were a critical need to buy gas from Canada, but the Canadian gas was not within U.S. specifications, DOE could waive those specifications.

DOE tracks power outages, reporting numbers and percentages of customers without power. "Customers" are accounts, rather than individuals, so a "customer" could be one household, or business, therefore many more people may be without power than reported. It is also important to note that the percentage of customers without power in a given area may be more important than the raw number of customers without power, because it is more likely that a large segment of support services will be without power as well as residential customers when the percentages are high.

Although restoration requirements are prioritized to reach the greatest needs first, that is often not possible because fixing local lines to places like hospitals can only take place after damaged plants, substations or major transmission lines have been repaired.

What is USACE's Role in Providing Emergency Power?

USACE is an integral part of ESF #7- Logistics. USACE has the capability to provide local and State officials broad support for their unmet emergency power needs (emergency power restoration). This support ranges from technical expertise and assistance to determine what generator(s) are needed at a critical public facility through complete management of an emergency power mission including the procurement, installation and operation of generators.

USACE assets utilized to fulfill emergency power mission requirements include elements of the U.S. Army 249th Engineering Battalion "Prime Power," Emergency Power Planning & Response Teams (PRTs) from across USACE, USACE-contracted forces, and USACE Deployable Tactical Operations System (DTOS) for communications. USACE also coordinates with other federal partners such as the Federal Emergency Management Agency (FEMA) and the Department of Energy (DOE). These assets can provide technical assistance which include, but is not limited to, the following:

- Assessing emergency power requirements needed at a facility.

- Assessing conditions & capabilities of existing emergency generation equipment

- Troubleshooting, repair, & operation of emergency generation/distribution equipment

- Installation, operations, fueling and maintaining emergency power generation equipment

- Safety inspections of electrical distribution systems and equipment

- Assessing damaged electrical distribution systems and equipment

- All hazards emergency power planning

The execution of a power mission involves the combined efforts of the 249th, the Power PRT, DTOS, Pre-established contracts, and state and federal partners. During these missions, the technical assistance items discussed above are brought to bear along with the following:

- Provide assistance to State and local officials in determining priorities for assessing and installing generators at critical public facilities.

- Preparation, hauling, and installation of generators.

- Operation, fueling, service, and maintenance of installed generators.

- De-installation and return of generators. This can also include remediation of the generator installation site to its pre-installation site condition.

- Service, maintenance, and repair of generators prior to their return to long-term storage to ensure they are Fully Mission Capable (FMC). This may also include load testing.

- Replenishing any Bill of Materials (BOM) used during execution of the mission Generator procurement and/or lease, if required, can be performed by USACE through a collaborate team comprised of the supporting Districts technical and contract staff.

Operational maintenance of FEMA generators can be performed by a combination of 249th, PRT, and contractual support. The 249th may also be requested to complete power needs assessments of critical public facilities in support of training exercises and/or Catastrophic Disaster Planning efforts, or other pre-disaster response planning activities.

What is FEMA's role in Providing Emergency Power?

Assessment:

FEMA Logistics and the U.S. Army Corps of Engineers (USACE) work with states and territories to conduct power assessments for pre-identified critical facilities. Assessments record the location, power requirements, and contact POC for each facility, and determine if the facility needs to install a generator connection for emergency use. USACE and FEMA jointly built the Emergency Power Facility Assessment Tool (EPFAT), where facility data can be uploaded by the owners, reducing the need for on-site assessment teams.

Generator Support.

FEMA maintains a fleet of approximately 850 generators in its Distribution Centers (DCs) throughout the country and three OCONUS locations. The generators are maintained FEMA as a set of pre-configured generator packages called "54 Packs" composed of generators of varying power, and are designed to support a variety of power requirements. These generators are deployed by FEMA to disaster locations and either provided directly to states to install, or provided to USACE for installation and other services.

FEMA also routinely provides mission assignments to USACE to provide generators, and associated services. A tertiary source of generators is GSA, and FEMA can also lease additional generators if required to meet emergency needs. FEMA procures fuel to support generator missions primarily through an Interagency Agreement with the Defense Logistics Agency, or mission assignment to USACE.

FEMA often mission assigns USACE to provide:

- Technical Assistance.

- Generator assets.

- Preparation, transportation, installation, fuel and maintenance of generators at deployed locations, including FEMA generators.

- De-installation, service, maintenance, and repair of FEMA generators prior to their return to long-term storage to ensure they are Fully Mission Capable (FMC). This may also include load testing and remediation of the generator installation site to its pre-installation site condition.

- Replenishing any Bill of Materials (BOM) used during execution of the mission.

Conclusion

Numerous characteristics of the Nation's energy infrastructure, including the wide diversity of owners and operators and the variety of energy supply alternatives and delivery mechanisms, make protecting it a challenge. Energy infrastructure assets and systems are geographically dispersed. Millions of miles of electricity lines and oil and natural gas pipelines and many other types of assets exist in all 50 States and Territories. In many cases these assets and systems are interdependent subject to regulation in various forms. Although the private sector has the lead in power restoration activities, the Federal government has played a large role in shaping those activities, and close coordination between industry and government at all levels is necessary to maintain the Grid, and restore it when it is compromised by natural disaster or other hazards.

Appendix A

Authorities Affecting Multiple Segments of the Energy Sector

American Recovery and Reinvestment Act of 2009, Public Law 111-5

The ARRA granted supplemental appropriations for Fiscal Year 2009 to DOE for, among other things, programs for energy efficiency and renewable energy, electricity delivery and energy reliability, and fossil energy research and development. Section 405 specifically provides financial support for Smart Grid demonstration projects in urban, suburban, tribal, and rural areas, as well as to electric utilities that invest in advanced grid technology. This section also requires the Secretary of Energy to establish and maintain a Smart Grid information clearinghouse which will make data from Smart Grid demonstration projects and other sources available to the public. The ARRA provides a number of additional financial incentives for renewable energy, energy efficiency, and biomass projects on the State, local, and individual level.

Homeland Security Presidential Directive 5 (HSPD-5)

This directive enhances the ability of the United States to manage domestic incidents by establishing a single, comprehensive National Incident Management System. It requires all Federal departments and agencies to cooperate with the Secretary of Homeland Security by providing their full and prompt cooperation, resources, and support, as appropriate and consistent with their own responsibilities for protecting the Nation's security. The directive provides for Federal assistance to State and local authorities when their resources are overwhelmed, or when Federal interests are involved.

Homeland Security Presidential Directive 7 (HSPD-7)

This directive establishes a national policy for Federal departments and agencies to identify and prioritize U.S. CIKR and protect them from terrorist attacks. Federal departments and agencies are required to: (1)

identify, prioritize, and coordinate CIKR protection to prevent, deter, and mitigate the effects of deliberate efforts to destroy, incapacitate, or exploit them; and (2) work with State and local governments and the private sector to accomplish this objective. Federal departments and agencies are directed to protect information associated with carrying out this directive. Voluntarily provided information and information that would facilitate terrorist targeting of CIKR must be handled in a manner consistent with the Homeland Security Act of 2002 and other applicable legal authorities.

Federal Information Security Management Act of 2002 (FISMA); E-Authentication Guidance for Federal Agencies, Office of Management and Budget (OMB) (December 16, 2003); FIPS Publication 199, Standards for Security Categorization of Federal Information and Information Systems (February 10, 2004); National Information Assurance Acquisition Policy for National Security Systems (NSTISSP 11); Federal Preparedness Circular 65, Federal Executive Branch Continuity of Operations (June 2004)

DOE, like other Federal agencies, is responsible for complying with FISMA as well as guidelines and practices developed by OMB that implement the law. While FISMA applies strictly to Federal Government agencies, DOE has carefully implemented requirements that support protection of the energy infrastructure. These include, for example, OMB's e-authentication guidance for remote authentication, National Institute of Standards and Technology guidelines for securing and procuring national security systems, and other related guidance.

Protected Critical Infrastructure Information (PCII) Program of the Critical Infrastructure Information Act of 2002, 6 U.S.C. §§ 131-134

The PCII Program, established pursuant to the CII Act, creates a framework that enables members of the private sector to voluntarily submit sensitive information regarding the Nation's critical infrastructure to DHS with assurance that the information, if it satisfies the requirements of the CII Act, will be protected from public disclosure. To implement and manage the program, DHS has created the PCII Program Office within DHS' Office of Infrastructure Protection. The PCII Program Office or other Federal agencies designated by the PCII program manager can receive critical infrastructure information to be validated as PCII if such information qualifies for protection under the CII Act. On September 1, 2006, DHS issued the Final Rule on Procedures for Handling Critical Infrastructure Information.

Chemical Facility Anti-Terrorism Standards (CFATS), 6 C.F.R. Part 27

In section 550 of the Department of Homeland Security Appropriations Act of 2007, Public Law 109-295, Congress gave DHS the authority to require high-risk chemical facilities to complete vulnerability assessments, develop site security plans, and implement protective measures necessary to meet DHS-defined performance standards. In accordance with this authority, on April 2, 2007, DHS released CFATS as an interim final rule.

Through CFATS, DHS established risk-based performance standards for the security of the Nation's chemical facilities. CFATS requires covered chemical facilities to prepare Security Vulnerability Assessments (SVAs), which identify facility security vulnerabilities, and to develop and implement Site Security Plans, which include measures that satisfy the identified risk-based performance standards. It also allows certain covered chemical facilities, in specified circumstances, to submit Alternate Security Programs (ASPs) in lieu of SVAs, Site Security Plans, or both.

CFATS also contains associated provisions addressing inspections and audits, recordkeeping, and protection of information that constitutes Chemical-terrorism Vulnerability Information (CVI). Finally, the rule provides DHS with authority to seek compliance through the issuance of Orders, including Orders Assessing Civil Penalty and Orders for the Cessation of Operations.

Bonneville Project Act of 1937, 16 U.S.C. § 832 et seq.; Reclamation Act of 1939, as amended, 43 U.S.C. § 485 et seq.; Flood Control Act of 1944, 16 U.S.C. § 825s; Colorado River Storage Act of 1956, 43 U.S.C. § 620 et seq.; Pacific Northwest Preferences Act of 1964, 16 U.S.C. § 837; Federal Columbia River Transmission System Act of 1974, 16 U.S.C. § 838; Department of Energy Organization Act, Section 302, 42 U.S.C. § 7152; Pacific Northwest Electric Planning and Conservation Act of 1980, 16

U.S.C. § 839 et seq.; and Energy and Water Development Appropriation Act of 1985, 16 U.S.C. § 837g

Under enabling legislation, DOE's PMAs have general powers to manage multiple areas of CIP. These range from protection to response and restoration, and cover generation, transmission, and related facilities. Congress provides similar authority to the Tennessee Valley Authority (TVA) to protect and reconstitute TVA generation, transmission, and related facilities.

Federal Power Act (FPA), 16 U.S.C. §§ 791a-825r; **Public Utility Regulatory Policies Act** (PURPA) of 1978, 16 U.S.C. § 2601 et seq.; **Energy Policy Act of 1992**, 42 U.S.C. § 13201

Congress provides a statutory foundation for FERC's oversight of power markets. While generation siting, intrastate transportation, and retail sales are generally regulated by State or local entities, wholesale sales and interstate transportation generally fall under Federal regulation, primarily by FERC.

One of FERC's strategic goals is to protect customers and market participants through vigilant and fair oversight of energy markets in transition. To pursue this goal, the Commission promotes a competitive market structure by fostering an understanding of energy market operations and using objective benchmarks to assess market conditions. FERC's Office of Market Oversight and Investigations is charged with assessing the competitive performance and efficiency of U.S. wholesale natural gas and electricity markets.

Federal Power Act, as amended, Section 202(a), 16 U.S.C. § 824a; and the Public Utility Regulatory Policies Act, Section 209(b), 16 U.S.C. §§ 824a-2

The Secretary of Energy has authority with regard to reliability of the interstate electric power transmission system. FERC has authority to define reliability regions and encourage interconnection and coordination within and between regions. DOE also has authority to gather information regarding reliability issues and make recommendations regarding industry security and reliability standards.

Defense Production Act (DPA) of 1950, as amended, Sections 101(a), 101(c), and 708, 50 U.S.C. §§ 2071 (a), (c), 2158

The Secretaries of Energy and Commerce have been delegated the President's authorities under sections 101(a) and 101(c) of DPA to require the priority performance of contracts or orders relating to materials (including energy sources), equipment, or services, including transportation, or to issue allocation orders, as necessary or appropriate for the national defense or to maximize domestic energy supplies. DPA section 101(a) permits the priority performance of contracts or orders necessary or appropriate to promote the national defense. "National defense" is defined in DPA section 702(13) to include "emergency preparedness activities conducted pursuant to title VI of the Robert T. Stafford Disaster Relief and Emergency Act and critical infrastructure protection and assurance." The Secretary of Energy has been delegated (Executive Orders 12919 and 11790) DPA section 101(a) authority with respect to all forms of energy. The Secretary of Commerce has been delegated (Executive Order 12919) the section 101(a) authority with respect to most materials, equipment, and services relevant to repair of damaged energy facilities. Section 101(c) of DPA authorizes contract priority ratings relating to contracts for materials (including energy sources), equipment, or services to maximize domestic energy supplies, if the Secretaries of Commerce and Energy, exercising their authorities delegated by Executive Order 12919, make certain findings with respect to the need for the material, equipment, or services for the exploration, production, refining, transportation, or conservation of energy supplies.

The DPA priority contracting and allocation authorities could be used to expedite repairs to damaged energy facilities, and for other purposes, including directing the supply or transportation of petroleum products, to maximize domestic energy supplies, meet defense energy needs, or support emergency preparedness activities. In the case of both the section 101(a) and 101(c) authorities, if there are contracts in place between the entity requiring priority contracting assistance and one or more suppliers of the needed good or service, DOE (with respect to the section 101(c) authority) or DOC (with respect to the section 101(a) authority) would issue an order requiring suppliers to perform under the contract on a priority basis before performing other non-rated commercial contracts. If no contracts are in place, DOE or DOC would issue a directive authorizing an entity requiring the priority contracting assistance to place a rated order with a supplier able to provide the needed materials, equipment, or services. That contractor would be required to accept the order and place it ahead of other nonrated commercial orders.

DPA section 708 provides a limited antitrust defense for industry participating in voluntary agreements "to help provide for the defense of the United States through the development of preparedness programs and the expansion of productive capacity and supply beyond levels needed to meet essential civilian demand in the United States." In the event of widespread damage to energy production or delivery systems, this authority, for example, could be used to establish a voluntary agreement of service companies to coordinate the planning of the restoration of the facilities.

Robert T. Stafford Disaster Relief and Emergency Assistance Act, as amended, 42 U.S.C. 5121 et seq.

FEMA, following a presidential declaration of emergency or major disaster, provides assistance and may require other Federal agencies to provide resources and personnel to support State and local emergency and disaster assistance efforts. Requests for a presidential declaration of emergency or major disaster must be made by the Governor of the affected State based on a finding by the Governor that the situation is of such severity and magnitude that effective response is beyond the capabilities of the State. DOE supports DHS/FEMA relief efforts by assisting Federal, State, and local governments as well as industry with their efforts to restore energy systems in disaster areas. When necessary, DOE also may deploy response staff to disaster sites. DOE is the lead agency directing ESF-12 (Energy), which assists the restoration of energy systems and provides an initial point-of-contact for the activation and deployment of DOE resources. These activities are performed pursuant to the Stafford Act, HSPD-5 (Management of Domestic Incidents) and NRF.

Chapter 24 of the **Merchant Marine Act** of 1920, as amended ("Jones Act"), 46 U.S.C. App. § 883
Chapter 24 of the **Jones Act**

This directs the Secretary of Homeland Security to waive the provisions requiring the use of U.S.-flag, U.S.-built, and U.S.-crewed vessels in coastwise trade, upon the request of the Secretary of Defense to the extent the Secretary of Defense deems necessary in the interest of the national defense. The act authorizes the Secretary of Homeland Security to waive compliance with the act either upon his own initiative or upon the written recommendation of the head of another agency whenever the Secretary determines that waiver is necessary in the interest of the national defense. In the case of a SPR drawdown, the President may direct the Secretary of Homeland Security to waive the Jones Act, if the volume of crude oil to be moved is significantly greater than the capacity of the existing, available U.S.-flag "Jones Act" crude oil tanker fleet. Interagency procedures have been established to expedite actions on Jones Act waiver requests during a petroleum supply disruption.

Ports and Waterways Safety Act, 33 U.S.C. § 1221 et seq., Natural Gas Pipeline Safety Act and Hazardous Liquids Pipeline Safety Act, as amended, 49 U.S.C. § 60109 et seq.

The Ports and Waterways Safety Act authorizes the Secretary of Transportation to establish vessel traffic systems for ports, harbors, and other navigable waters and control vessel traffic in areas determined to be hazardous (e.g., because of reduced visibility, adverse weather, vessel congestion, etc.) (33 U.S.C. § 1223).

Two statutes provide the framework for the Federal pipeline safety program. The Natural Gas Pipeline Safety Act of 1968 as amended authorizes DOT to regulate pipeline transportation of natural (flammable, toxic, or corrosive) gas and other gases as well as the transportation and storage of LNG. Similarly, the Hazardous Liquid Pipeline Safety Act of 1979 as amended authorizes DOT to regulate pipeline transportation of hazardous liquids (crude oil, petroleum products, anhydrous ammonia, and carbon dioxide). Both acts have been recodified as 49 U.S.C. Chapter 601. The Federal pipeline safety regulations (1) ensure safety in design, construction, inspection, testing, operation, and maintenance of pipeline facilities in the siting, construction, operation, and maintenance of LNG facilities; (2) set parameters for administering the pipeline safety program; and (3) delineate requirements for onshore oil pipeline response plans. The regulations are written as minimum performance standards.

The Magnuson Act (50 U.S.C. 191 et seq.) directs the Secretary of Transportation to issue regulations governing the movement of any vessel within U.S. territorial waters, upon a presidential declaration of a national emergency by reasons of actual or threatened war, insurrection or invasion, or disturbance or threatened disturbance of the international relations of the United States.

Maritime Transportation Security Act (MTSA), Public Law 107-295, 46 U.S.C. § 2101 et seq.

MTSA, which amended the Merchant Marine Act of 1936, requires implementation of regulations for improving the security of ports, waterfront facilities, and vessels, including those involved with the oil and gas sectors. Most energy sites with waterfront facilities are affected by MTSA and must conduct vulnerability assessments and develop security plans to be approved by the USCG.

Communications Act of 1934, as amended, 47 U.S.C. § 151 et seq., and Executive Order 12472, as amended

The National Security Emergency Preparedness Telecommunications Service Priority System, created by the National Communications System (NCS), an interagency body established by Executive Order 12472, authorizes priority treatment for restoration and provisioning (installation of new service) of certain domestic telecommunication services during several categories of emergency. Under this program, DOE is authorized to sponsor energy industry requests for priority restoration of existing telecommunications or requests for priority installation of new telecommunications as well as priority access to the Public Switch

Network. Authority to order priority restoration of electric service resides in the States rather than the Federal Government. DOE, in its role supporting FEMA and DHS under the NRF as ESF-12, has been successful in requesting and obtaining priority restoration of electric service for specific important electric loads and areas.

Aviation and Transportation Security Act (ATSA), Public Law 107-71, 115 Stat. 597, November 19, 2001

As established by ATSA, TSA is responsible for security in all modes of transportation. The six modes of transportation include mass transit, aviation, maritime, highway, rail, and pipeline systems. As further noted in the NIPP, TSA is the SSA for all modes of transportation except maritime, for which the USCG is the SSA.

Critical Energy Infrastructure Information, FERC Orders 630 and 630A

FERC issued a final rule restricting access to Critical Energy Infrastructure Information and establishing new procedures for requesting access to it.

Authorities Affecting Electric Power

Energy Policy Act of 2005, Public Law 109-58, Title XII: Electricity, Subtitle A: Reliability Standards, Section 1211: Electric Reliability Standards; Electricity Modernization Act of 2005, August 8, 2005, 42 U.S.C. § 15801; 16 U.S.C. § 824o

This subtitle provides for Federal jurisdiction over certain activities that are required to support reliability of the U.S. bulk power system. Title XII authorizes FERC to certify a national Electric Reliability Organization (ERO) to enforce mandatory reliability standards for the bulk-power system. FERC will oversee the ERO in the United States and all ERO standards must be approved by FERC. The ERO can impose penalties on a user, owner, or operator of the bulk-power system for violations of any

FERC-approved reliability standard, but such penalties are subject to FERC review and potential change.

FERC Order Issued in Docket No. RR06-1-000, Certifying NERC as the Electric Reliability Organization, July 20, 2006

Pursuant to EPA Act of 2005, FERC conditionally certified NERC as the Nation's ERO. NERC must make specified changes and file them with FERC in order to continue as the ERO. As the ERO, NERC will be responsible for developing and enforcing mandatory electric reliability standards under FERC's oversight. The standards will apply to all users, owners, and operators of the bulk-power system.

FERC Order 706 Issued in Docket No. RM06-22-000, Mandatory Reliability Standards for Critical Infrastructure Protection, January 18, 2008

Pursuant to section 215 of FPA, FERC approved eight CIP Reliability Standards submitted to FERC for approval by NERC. The standards require certain users, owners, and operators of the bulk power system to comply with specific requirements to safeguard critical cyber assets.

FERC Order Issued in Docket No. RD09-7-000, Approving Revised Reliability Standards for Critical Infrastructure Protection and Requiring Compliance Filing, September 30, 2009

Pursuant to section 215(d)(5) of the FPA, FERC in Order 706 directed NERC to develop modifications to the eight CIP Reliability Standards using its Reliability Standards Development Process. On May 22, 2009, NERC filed revised Reliability Standards for Critical Infrastructure Protection. In its filing, NERC indicated it is developing responsive modifications in multiple phases, and the instant filing represents the results of the first phase of the initiative. The revised CIP Reliability Standards will become effective April 1, 2010.

Federal Power Act, 16 U.S.C. §§ 791a-825r; Public Utility Regulatory Policies Act, 16 U.S.C. § 2705; DOE Organization Act, 42 U.S.C. §§ 7101-7352; 18 C.F.R. Parts 4, 12, and 16; MOU between FERC, Army Corps of Engineers and Bureau of Reclamation

Congress authorizes FERC to oversee the Nation's non-Federal hydropower infrastructure. Congressional and other legal delegations also define hydropower responsibilities among FERC and other agencies, such as USACE and BOR.

With regard to FERC authorities, delegations in the FPA include a range of activities, such as issuing licenses for non-Federal hydropower projects; requiring safety and operating conditions; investigating and taking over facilities (or levying fines) for administrative violations, such as safety and security; defining construction, maintenance, and operation requirements by licensees; and other acts to carry out the purposes of the FPA. In addition, section 405(d) of PURPA, 16 U.S.C. § 2705, authorizes a hydropower project's exemption from licensing under certain conditions. Finally, the Department of Energy Organization Act, 42 U.S.C. §§ 7101-7352: Title IV establishes FERC (as the successor agency to the Federal Power Commission) and enumerates its authority regarding hydropower facilities.

In addition to congressional delegations, regulations further define FERC authorities over hydropower facilities. These rules address such issues as project safety and security, procedures for relicensing or Federal takeover of licensed hydropower projects, and investigations.

FERC has several MOUs with regard to hydropower facilities:

> **USACE•** , which has responsibility for ownership and operation of Federal dams for electric power production and other purposes. This MOU describes procedures for agency cooperation during the processing of hydropower applications to facilitate the investigation, construction, operation, and maintenance of FERC-licensed hydro projects at USACE dams.

BOR• , which has responsibility for ownership and operation of dams for electric power production and other purposes. This MOU describes procedures for agency cooperation during the processing of hydropower applications to facilitate the investigation, construction, operation, and maintenance of FERC-licensed hydro projects at BOR dams.

Executive Order 10485, Providing for the Performance of Certain Functions Heretofore Performed by the President with Respect to Electric Power and Natural Gas Facilities Located on the Borders of the United States, September 3, 1953, as amended by Executive Order 12038, Relating to Certain Functions Transferred to the Secretary of Energy by the Department of Energy Organization Act, February 3, 1978

DOE is authorized to issue presidential permits for the construction, operation, maintenance, and connection of electric transmission facilities at U.S. international borders if it determines that the issuance of such a permit is in the public interest. In determining whether issuance of the permit is consistent with the public interest, DOE considers the impact the proposed project would have on the operating reliability of the U.S. electric power supply and the environmental impacts of the proposed project pursuant to the National Environmental Policy Act (NEPA) of 1969, and any other factors that DOE may also consider relevant to the public interest. DOE must also obtain favorable recommendations from the Secretary of State and Secretary of Defense before issuing a permit.

Federal Power Act, as amended, Section 202(c), 16 U.S.C. § 824a(c)

The Secretary of Energy has authority in time of war or other emergency to order temporary interconnections of facilities and generation, delivery, interchange, or transmission of electric energy that the Secretary deems necessary to meet an emergency. This authority may be used upon receipt of a petition from a party requesting the emergency action or it may be initiated by DOE on its own initiative.

Federal Power Act, as amended, § 202(e), 16 U.S.C. § 824a(e)

Exports of electricity from the United States to a foreign country are regulated by FERC pursuant to sections 301(b) and 402(f) of the Department of Energy Organization Act (42 U.S.C. 7151(b), 7172(f)) and require authorization under section 202(e) of FPA (16 U.S.C. § 824a(e)).

Department of Energy Organization Act and FPA, 10 CFR Parts 205.350-205.353

DOE has authority to obtain current information regarding emergency situations in the electric supply systems in the United States. DOE has established mandatory reporting requirements for electric power system incidents or possible incidents. This reporting is required to meet DOE's national security requirements and other responsibilities contained in NRF.

Power Plant and Industrial Fuel Use Act (FUA), § 404(a), 42 U.S.C. § 8374(a)

Under section 404(a), the President has authority to allocate coal (and require the transportation of coal) for use by any power plant or major fuel-burning installation during a declared severe energy supply interruption as defined by section 3(8) of EPCA, 42 U.S.C. § 6202(8). The President may also exercise such allocation authority upon a published finding that a national or regional fuel supply shortage exists or may exist that the President determines is, or is likely to be, of significant scope and duration, and of an emergency nature; causes, or may cause, major adverse impact on public health, safety, welfare or on the economy; and results, or is likely to result, from an interruption in the supply of coal or from sabotage, or from an act of God. Section 404(e) stipulates that the President may not delegate his authority to issue orders under this authority. It does not, however, prevent the President from directing any Federal agency to issue rules or regulations, or take other action consistent with section 404, in the implementation of such an order.

The FUA section 404(a) authority could be used to help provide coal as an alternative fuel source to electric power plants and other major fuel-burning installations that have received orders prohibiting the burning of natural gas or petroleum as a primary energy source, assuming these facilities actually have the capability to burn coal. Many likely do not, so the authority may be of limited utility. This authority also could be used during a coal supply shortage to ensure that coal-burning electric power plants or major fuel-burning installations have adequate supplies of coal.

As an alternative to the use of FUA section 404(a), the President, or the President's delegate(s), could allocate coal supplies under the authority of section 101(a) of DPA, 50 U.S.C. App. § 2071(a) and Executive Order 12919 (1994).

Clean Air Act, 42 U.S.C. § 7401 et seq.

Section 110(f) of the Clean Air Act permits a State Governor to issue an emergency temporary suspension of any part of a State Implementation Plan (SIP) (as well as a temporary waiver of penalties for excess SOx or NOx emissions) in accordance with the following: (1) the owner/operator of a fuel-burning source petitions the State for relief; (2) the Governor gives notice and opportunity for public hearing on the petition; (3) the Governor finds that an emergency exists in the vicinity of the source involving high levels of unemployment or loss of necessary energy supplies for residential dwellings, and that the unemployment or loss can be totally or partially alleviated by an emergency suspension of SIP requirements applicable to the petitioning source; (4) the President, in response to the Governor's request, declares a national or regional emergency exists of such severity that a temporary SIP suspension may be necessary and other means of responding to the energy emergency may be inadequate; and (5) the Governor issues an emergency suspension to the source. DOE may be asked to advise the President of fuel supply situations regarding requests for presidential emergency declarations for SIP relief.

[62] **EPA Act of 2005** mandated that FERC establish an ERO with powers to enforce rules affecting the reliability of the Nation's electric grid. NERC has been designated by FERC as the ERO. All users of the Nation's high-voltage electric grid will be subject to these mandatory reliability rules, even if they are not otherwise regulated by FERC for rates or tariff.

Acknowledgements

The Disaster Operations Legal Reference (DOLR) (pronounced "dollar") owes its publication to the many FEMA staff who contribute their knowledge and expertise. Many emails, phone calls, and person-to-person discussions take place in an effort to accurately gather, understand, and explain the most up-to-date information available. Not only does the DOLR team tap into the expertise of lawyers from FEMA's Office of Chief Counsel, but information is sought and received from subject matter experts in FEMA, who range from members of the FCO cadre, to personnel at the Department of Homeland Security Office of Inspector General, to Public and Individual Assistance Branch leadership, and to numerous other personnel who work daily with FEMA's emergency and disaster relief programs.

The DOLR team thanks:

Brad Kieserman, Chief Counsel, for the concept of the book.

Adrian Sevier and Mary Ellen Martinet as primary editors of the book.

FEMA Office of Chief Counsel staff for their many contributions to DOLR 2.0, including but not limited to:

Jotham Allen	Emery Haskell	Sean O' Hara
Michelle Anderson	Daniel Hall	Bob Parker
Katie A. Barnes	Kim Hazel	Dan Piccaluga
Richard Bernstein	Leigh Hoburg	Paula Rich
Elizabeth Blair	Elizabeth Jerke	Michael Saltalamachea
Chad Clifford	Lisa Katchka	Robert Scott
Paul Conrad	Audrey Liebross	Charles Senn
Keyonna Davis	Quinn Lucie	Kristen Shedd
Michael Delman	Munira Mack	Joshua Stanton
Ashley Darbo	Deirdre Macneil	Kyle Symanowitz
Kim Farley	Jose Morales	Smitha Vemuri
Stephanie Fell	Deirdre MacNeil	Phillip Yoo
Erin Greten	Jeff Neurauter	Kevin Yusman

Thanks also to the members of the FEMA staff who contributed issues to the DOLR Team and who provided issues in the DOLR Drop Box.

Sincerely, the **DOLR Team**

Courtney Dow, Managing Editor, and
Carol Ann Adamcik, Gayle Hoopes, and Rosa Ríos

Disaster recovery assistance is available without regard to race, color, national origin, sex, age, religion, disability, English proficiency, or economic status. Anyone who believes he or she has been discriminated against should contact the FEMA Helpline at 1-800-621-3362 or (TTY) 1-800-462-7585.

Report fraud, waste, and abuse to DHS Office of Inspector General on the Hotline at 1-800-323-8603.